EVIDENCE BASED SOFTWARE ENGINEERING

EVIDENCE BASED SOFTWARE ENGINEERING

Babatunde Alabi
Kiprop cheruiyot

Kruger Brentt
Publishers

2026

Kruger Brentt Publishers UK. LTD.
Company Number 9728962

Regd. Office: 68 St Margarets Road, Edgware, Middlesex HA8 9UU

ISBN: 978-1-78715-639-5

For information on all our publications visit our website at http://krugerbrentt.com/

PREFACE

The discipline of software engineering has evolved rapidly, driven by increasing system complexity, diverse user needs, and the demand for reliable, maintainable, and high-quality software. In this dynamic landscape, decision-making based on assumptions or anecdotal experience is no longer sufficient. Evidence-based practices, grounded in empirical research, data analysis, and systematic evaluation, offer a robust foundation for improving software processes, tools, and outcomes.

This book, *Evidence Based Software Engineering*, presents a structured approach to integrating empirical evidence into every stage of software development and management. It is designed for students, researchers, practitioners, and policymakers seeking to apply scientific rigor to software engineering decisions. The text emphasizes the importance of systematic studies, reproducible experiments, and critical evaluation of data to guide best practices in design, implementation, testing, maintenance, and project management.

The chapters introduce the fundamental principles of evidence-based methodologies, including systematic literature reviews, meta-analysis, experimental design, and observational studies. Readers are guided through the process of generating, evaluating, and synthesizing empirical evidence to support engineering judgments. Real-world case studies illustrate how evidence-based thinking enhances productivity, reduces risk, improves code quality, and strengthens decision-making in modern software development environments.

By bridging empirical research and practical application, *Evidence Based Software Engineering* encourages a culture of critical inquiry and scientific thinking within the software community. It equips readers with the tools and mindset needed to assess claims, validate results, and build software systems grounded in proven, data-driven practices.

Babatunde Alabi

Kiprop cheruiyot

CONTENTS

Chapter 1

Introduction

Software is a product of human cognitive labor, applying the skills and know-how acquired through personal practical experience; it is a craft activity. The expensive and error prone process of learning through personal experience needs to be replaced by an engineering approached derived from the successes and mistakes of others; evidence is the basis for creating an engineering approach to building and maintaining software systems.

The craft approach has survived because building software systems has been a sellers market, customers have paid what it takes because the potential benefits have been so much greater than the costs. In a competitive market for development work and staff, paying people to learn from mistakes that have already been made by many others is an unaffordable luxury.

This book discusses all the publicly available software engineering data, with software engineering treated as an economically motivated cognitive activity occurring within one or more ecosystems. Cognition, economics and ecosystems underpin the analysis of software engineering activities:

- the labour of the cognitariate is the means of production of intangible goods. Maximising the return on investment from this labor requires an understanding of human cognition,
- cognitive capitalism, the economics of intangible goods, is fundamentally different from the economics of tangible goods, e.g., the zero cost of replicating software means that the entire cost of production is borne by the cost of creating the first item, [i]
- software systems are created and operated within ecosystems of intangibles. The needs and desires of members of these ecosystems supply the energy that drives evolutionary change, and these changes can reduce the functionality provided by existing software systems, i.e., they wear out and break.

The intended audience of this book are those involved in building software systems. Software ecosystems have been continually disrupted by improvements to their host, the electronic computer, which began [316,610,649,1788] infiltrating the human ecosystem 70+ years ago. [ii] During this period the price of computer equipment continually declined, averaging 17.5% per year, [1844] an economic firestorm that devoured existing practices; software systems are apex predators. Figure 1.1 shows the continual fall in the cost of compute operations. However, without cheap mass storage, computing would be a niche market; the continual reduction in the cost of storage generated increasing economic incentives for employing the processing power; see figure 1.2. The pattern of hardware performance improvements, and shortage of trained personnel, were appreciated almost from the beginning.

A shift in perception, from computers as calculating machines, to computing platforms responding in real-time, to multiple independent users, created new problem-solving opportunities, e.g., responding in real-time to multiple users. Figure 1.3 shows the growth of US based systems capable of sharing cpu time between multiple users.

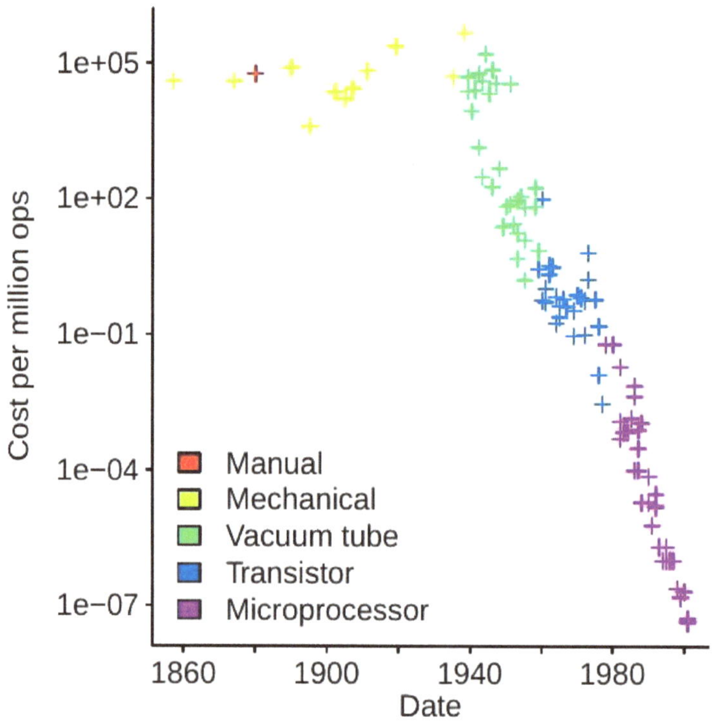

Figure 1.1: Total cost of one million computing operations over time. Data from Nordhaus. [1388] Github-Local

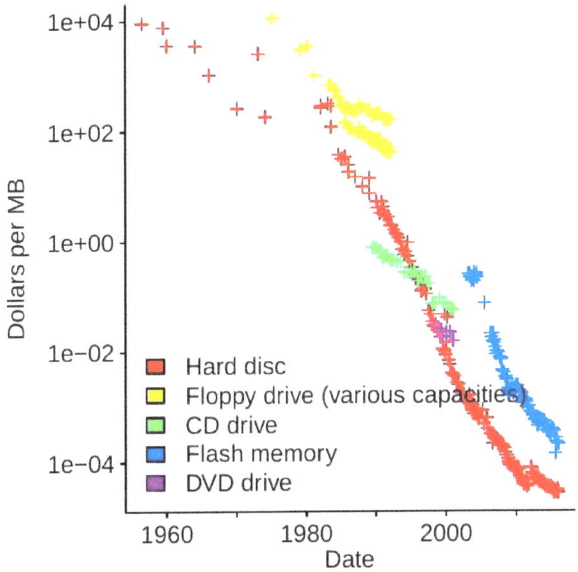

Figure 1.2: Storage cost, in US dollars per Mbyte, of mass market technologies over time. Data from McCallum, floppy and CD-ROM data kindly provided by Davis. Github-Local

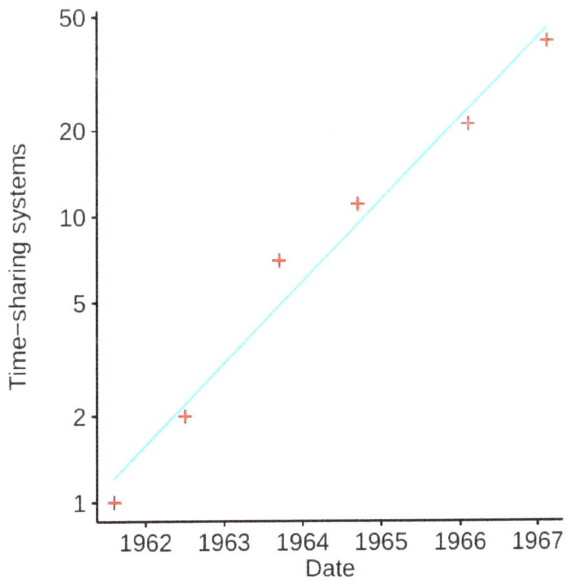

Figure 1.3: Growth of time-sharing systems available in the US, with fitted regression line. Data extracted from Glauthier. Github-Local

The continued displacement of existing systems and practices has kept the focus of practice on development (of new systems and major enhancements to existing systems). A change in the focus of practice to infrastructure has to await longer term stability.

The demand for people with the cognitive firepower needed to implement complex software systems has drawn talent away from research. Consequently, little progress has been made towards creating practical theories capable of supporting an engineering/scientific approach to software development. However, many vanity theories have been proposed (i.e., based on the personal beliefs of researchers, rather than evidence obtained from experiments and measurements). Academic software engineering research has been a backwater primarily staffed by those interested in theory, with a tenuous connection to practical software development.

Research into software engineering is poorly funded compared to projects where, for instance, hundreds of millions are spent on sending spacecraft to take snaps of other planets, and telescopes [1355] to photograph faint far-away objects.

In a sellers market, vendors don't need to lobby government to fund research into reducing their costs. The benefits of an engineering/scientific approach to development, are primarily reaped by customers, e.g., lower costs, more timely delivery, and fewer fault experiences. Those who develop software systems are not motivated to invest in change when customers are willing to continue paying for systems developed using craft practices (unless they are also the customer).

The focus of this book's analysis is on understanding, not prediction. Those involved in building software systems want to control the process. Control requires understanding; an understanding of the many processes involved in building software systems is the goal of software engineering research. Theories are a source of free information, i.e., they provide a basis for understanding the workings of a system, and for making good enough predictions.

Fitting a model to data without some understanding of the processes involved is clueless button pushing. For instance, ancient astronomers noticed that some stars (i.e., planets) moved in regular patterns across the night sky. Figure 1.4 shows one component of Tycho Brahe's 1641 published observations of Mars in the night sky, i.e., the declination of Mars at the meridian on given a night; the line is a simple fitted regression model, based on a sine wave and a few harmonics (and explains 79% of the variance in the data).

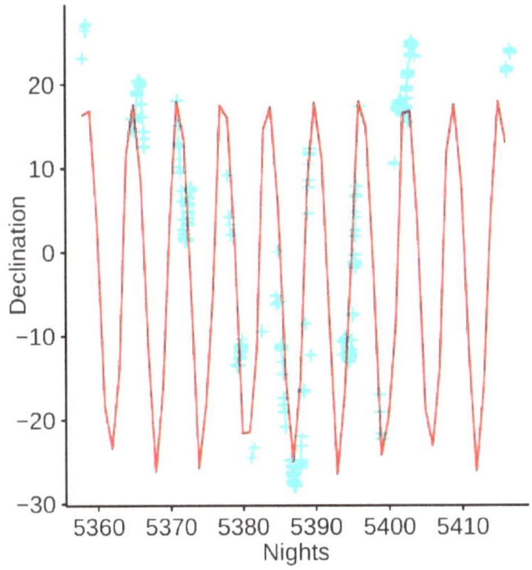

Figure 1.4: Tycho Brahe's observations of Mars and a fitted regression model. Data from Brahe via Wayne Pafko. Github-Local

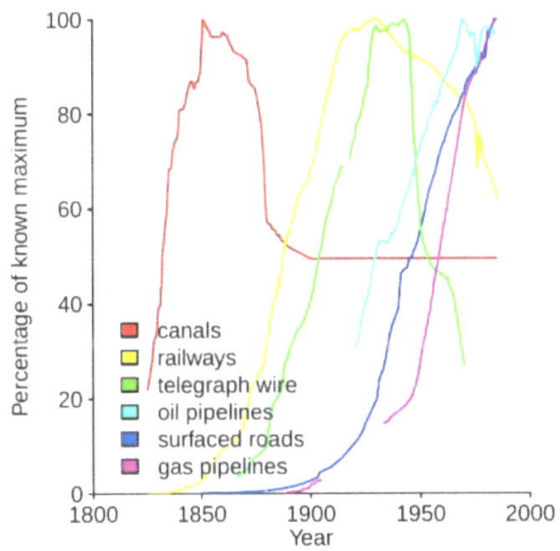

Figure 1.5: Growth of transport and product distribution infrastructure in the USA (underlying data is measured in miles). Data from Grübler et al. Github-Local

The hypothesis that planets orbit the Sun not only enables a much more accurate model to built, but provides an understanding that explains occasional changes of behavior, e.g., Mars sometimes reversing its direction of travel across the night sky.

Evidence (i.e., experimental and measurement data) is analysed using statistics, with statistical techniques being wielded as weaponised pattern recognition. Those seeking discussions written in the style of a stimulant for mathematical orgasms, will not find satisfaction here.

Statistics does not assign a meaning to the patterns it uncovers; interpreting the patterns thrown up by statistical analysis, to give them meaning, is your job dear reader (based on your knowledge and experience of the problem domain).

Software is written by people having their own unique and changeable behavior patterns. Measurements of the products and processes involved in this work are intrinsically noisy, and variables of influence may not be included in the measurements. This situation does not mean that analysis of the available measurements is a futile activity, what it means is that the uncertainty and variability is likely to be much larger than typically found in other engineering disciplines.

The tool used for statistical analysis is the R system. R was chosen because of its extensive ecosystem; there are many books, covering a wide range of subject areas, using *R* and active online forums discussing R usage (answers to problems can often be found by searching the Internet, and if none are found a question can be posted with a reasonable likelihood of receiving an answer).

The data and *R* code used in this book are freely available for download from the book's website. [939]

Like software development, data analysis contains a craft component, and the way to improve craft skills is to practice.

In January 2018 the U.S. Congress passed the Foundations for Evidence-Based Policymaking Act of 2018, whose requirements include: "(1) A list of policy-relevant questions for which the agency intends to develop evidence to support policymaking. (2) A list of data the agency intends to collect, use, or acquire to facilitate the use of evidence in policymaking."

1.1 What has been learned?

What useful information can be learned from the 600 + [iii] datasets analyzed in this book?

There are a few high-level take-aways from the recurring patterns seen in the analysis; these include:

- there is little or no evidence for many existing theories of software engineering,
- most software has a relatively short lifetime, e.g., source code is deleted, packages are withdrawn or replaced, and software systems cease to be supported. A cost/benefit analysis of an investment intended to reduce future development costs needs to include the possibility that there is no future development; see fig 4.24, fig 5.7, fig 5.52, fig 5.69, fig 6.9, fig 3.31.

Changes within the ecosystems in which software is built also has an impact on the viability of existing code; see fig 4.13, fig 4.22, fig 4.59, fig 4.61, fig 11.76,

- software developers should not be expected to behave according to this or that mathematical ideal. People come bundled with the collection of cognitive abilities and predilections that enabled their ancestors, nearly all of whom lived in stone-age communities, to reproduce; see chapter 2.

The patterns found in the analysed data have various uses, including:

- helping to rule out behaviors that are thought likely to occur. In situations where the outcome is uncertain, being able to exclude a range of possibilities reduces costs by removing the need to investment in events that are unlikely to be encountered,
- provide ideas about ranges of behaviors that have been encountered. Nothing more specific can be inferred because most of the data applies to one experiment, collection of measurements of projects at one point in time, or a few projects over an extended period.
- Many plots include one or more lines showing fitted regression models. The purpose of fitting these models is to highlight patterns that are present. Most of these models were created by your author after seeing the data, what is sometimes known as HARKing (Hypothesizing After the Results are Known), or less technically they are just-so stories created from a fishing expedition. This is not how rigorous science is done.

Software development involves a complicated mix of interactions across many activities, and creating general theories requires data on a wide variety of specific topics. Building reasonably accurate models of these processes will require weaving together results from many replicated studies. The available data does cover many topics, but the coverage is sparse and does not include enough data on topics of specific interest to enable reliable models to be built (at least an order of magnitude more data is required).

Much of the existing data is based on Open Source projects, which are readily available in quantity. To what extent are findings from the analysis of Open Source projects applicable to non-Open Source software development (researchers sometimes use a popularity metric, such as Github stars, to filter out projects that have not attracted enough attention from others)? The definitive answer can only come from comparing findings from software systems developed in both environments (enterprise-driven open source is available [1750]).

There are threats to the validity of applying findings from Open Source projects to other Open Source projects, these include:

- the choice of Open Source packages to analyse is a convenience sample:
- a variety of tools have been created for extracting data, with many tools targeting a particular language; mostly Java, with C the second most popular, at the time of writing,
- native speakers of English are served by many repositories, and have to put effort into finding and using repositories targeting non-English speakers, e.g., the Android App stores supporting Chinese users, [37]
- using an easily accessible corpus of packages. Creating a corpus is a popular activity because it currently provides a low-cost route to a published paper for anyone with programming skills, and can potentially acquire many citations, via the researchers who use it,
- characteristics of Open Source development that generate large measurement biases are still being discovered. Some of the major sources of measurement bias, that have been found, include:
- the timing of commits and identity of the committer may not be those of the developer who wrote the code. For instance, updates to the Linux kernel are submitted by developers to the person responsible for the appropriate subsystem, who forwards those that are accepted to Linus Torvalds, who integrates those that he accepts into mainline Linux; a lot of work is needed to extract an accurate timeline from the hundreds of separate developer repositories,
- a large percentage of fault reports have been found to be requests for enhancement.

In many cases the analysis performed on a particular set of measurements, and the techniques used are different from those of the researchers who made the original measurements. Reasons for this include: wanting to highlight a different issue, making use of more powerful techniques to extract more information, and in the data analysis section wanting to illustrate a particular technique.

1.1.1 Replication

The results from one experiment provide a positive indication that something might be true, but it is possible that random events aligned to produce the results seem. Replication is necessary, [178] i.e., the results claimed by one researcher need to be reproducible by other people, if they are to be become generally accepted. Without replication researchers are amassing a graveyard of undead theories. [595] One study [1521] of medical practices, based on papers published between 2001 and 2010 addressing a medical practice, found that 40% of follow-up studies reversed the existing practice and 48% confirmed it.

Discovering an interesting pattern in experimental data is the start, not the end of experimentation involving that pattern (the likelihood of obtaining a positive result is as much to do with the subject studied as the question being asked). The more often behavior is experimentally observed the greater the belief that the effect seen actually exists. Replication is the process of duplicating the experiment(s) described in a report or paper to confirm the findings previously obtained. For replication to be practical, researchers need to be willing to share their code and data, something that a growing numbers of software engineering researchers are starting to do; those attempting replication are meeting with mixed success.

The gold standard of the scientific method is the controlled randomised experiment, followed by replication of the results by others (findings from earlier studies failing to replicate is common). In this kind of experiment, all the factors that could influence the outcome of an experiment are either controlled or randomly divided up such that any unknown effects add noise to the signal rather than spurious ghost patterns.

Replication is not a high status activity, with high impact journals interested in publishing research that reports new experimental findings, and not wanting to dilute their high impact status by publishing replications (which, when they are performed and fail to replicate previous results considered to be important discoveries, can often only find a home for publication in a low impact journal). A study replicating 100 psychology experiments found that while 97% of the original papers reported p -values less than 0.05 , only 36% of the replicated experiments obtained p-values this low; a replication study of 67 economics papers was able to replicate 22(33%) without assistance from the authors, 29 with assistance.

1.2 Software markets

The last 60 years, or so, has been a sellers market; the benefits provided by software systems has been so large that companies that failed to use them risked being eclipsed by competitors; the status quo was not a viable option. [462] Whole industries have been engulfed, and companies saddled with a Red Queen, [133] loosing their current position if they failed to keep running.

Provided software development projects looked like they would deliver something that was good enough, those involved knew that the customer would wait and pay; complaints received a token response. Software vendors learned that one way to survive in a rapidly evolving market was to get products to market quickly, before things moved on.

Experience gained from the introduction of earlier high-tech industries suggests that it takes many decades for major new technologies to settle down and reach market saturation. For instance, the transition from wood to steel for building battleships, [1435] started in 1858 and reached it zenith during the second world war. There is a long history of growth and decline of various forms of infrastructure; see figure 1.5. Various models of the evolution of technological innovations have been proposed.

Over the last 70 years a succession of companies have dominated the computing industry. The continual reduction in the cost of computing platforms created new markets, and occasionally one of these grew to become the largest market, financially, for computing products. A company dominates the computer industry when it dominates the market that dominates the industry. Once dominant companies often continue to grow within their market after their market ceases to be the largest market for computers.

Figure 1.6 shows market capitalization as a percentage of the top 100 listed US tech companies, as of the first quarter of 2015, and illustrates the impact of the growth of new markets on the relative market capitalization of three companies; IBM dominated when mainframes dominated the computer industry, the desktop market grew to dominate the computer industry and Microsoft dominated, smartphones removed the need for computers sitting on desks, and these have grown to dominate the computer market with Apple being the largest company in this market (Google's Android investment was a defensive move to ensure they are not locked out of advertising on mobile, i.e., it is not as intended to be a direct source of revenue, making it extremely difficult to estimate its contribution to Google's market capitalization).

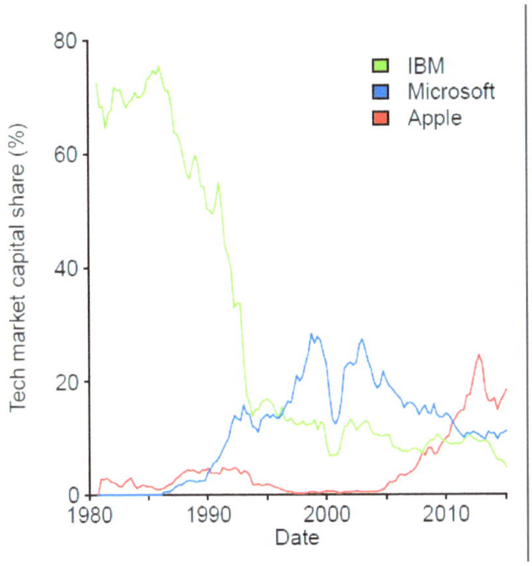

Figure 1.6: Market capitalization of IBM, Microsoft and Apple (upper), and expressed as a percentage of the top 100 listed US tech companies (lower). Data extracted

from the Economist website.528

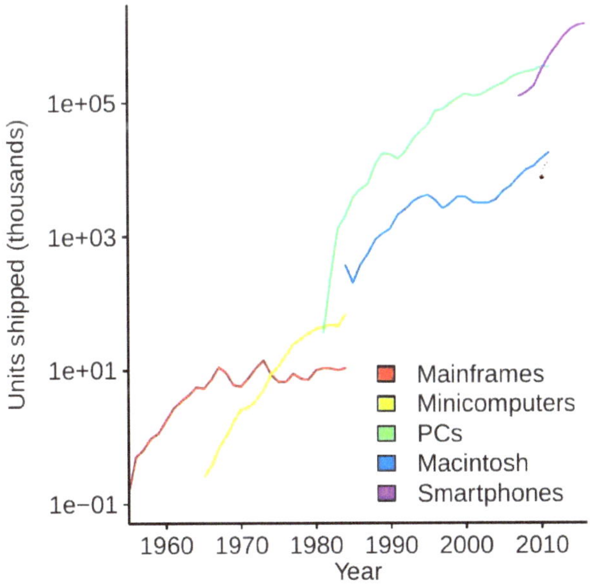

Figure 1.7: Total annual sales of some of the major species of computers over the last 60 years. Data from Gordon (mainframes and minicomputers), Reimer (PCs) and Gartner (smartphones). Github-Local

The three major eras, each with its own particular product and customer characteristics, have been (figure 1.7 shows sales of major computing platforms):

- the IBM era (sometimes known as the mainframe era, after the dominant computer hardware, rather than the dominant vendor): The focus was on business customers, with high-priced computers sold, or rented, to large organizations who either rented software from the hardware vendor or paid for software to be developed specifically for their own needs. Large companies were already spending huge sums employing the (tens of) thousands of clerks needed to process the paperwork used in the running of their businesses; these companies could make large savings, in time and money, by investing in bespoke software systems, paying for any subsequent maintenance, and the cost of any faults experienced.
- When the actual cost of software faults experienced by one organization is very high (with potential for even greater costs if things go wrong), and the same organization is paying all, or most of the cost of create the software, that organization can see a problem that it thinks it should have control over. Very large organizations are in a position to influence research agendas to target the problems they want solved.

Large organizations tend to move slowly. The rate of change was slow enough for experience and knowledge of software engineering to be considered essential to do the job (this is not to say that anybody had to show that their skill was above some a minimum level before they would be employed as a software developer).

- the Wintel era: The Personal Computer running Microsoft Windows, using Intel's x86 processor family, was the dominant computing platform. The dramatic reduction in the cost of owning a computer significantly increased the size of the market, and it became commercially profitable for companies to create and sell software packages. The direct cost of software maintenance is not visible to these customers, but they pay the costs of the consequences of faults they experience when using the software.

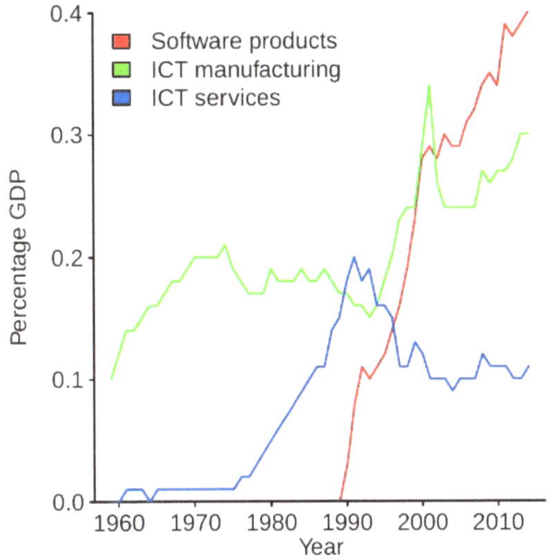

Figure 1.8: Percentage of US GDP for Software products, ICT Manufacturing (which includes semiconductors+computers+communications equipment), and ICT services (which includes software publishing+computer systems design+telecom+data processing). Data kindly provided by Corrado. Github-Local

Microsoft's mantra of a PC on every desk required that people write software to cover niche markets. The idea that anyone could create an application was promoted as a means of spreading Windows, by encouraging people with application domain knowledge to create software running under MS-DOS and later Windows.

Figure 1.8 shows the impact of a computer on every desk; software product sales, as a percentage of US GDP, took off.

Programming languages, libraries and user interface experienced high rates of change, which meant that developers found themselves on a relearning treadmill. An investment in learning had short payback periods; becoming an expert was often not cost effective.

- the Internet era: No single vendor dominates the Internet, but some large niches have dominant vendors, e.g., mobile phones, It is not known whether the rate of change has been faster than in previous eras, or the volume of discussion about the changes has been higher because the changes have been visible to more people, or whether niche dominant vendors continue to drive change to suit their needs, or some other reason,
- Mobile communications is not the first technology to set in motion widespread structural changes to industrial ecosystems. For instance, prior to electrical power

> becoming available, mechanical power was supplied by water and then steam. Mechanical power is transmitted in straight lines using potentially dangerous moving parts; factories had to be organized around the requirements of mechanical power transmission. Electrical power transmission does not suffer from the straight line restrictions of mechanical power transmission. It took some time for the benefits of electrical power (e.g., machinery did not have to be close to the generator) to diffuse through industry.

The ongoing history of new software systems, and computing platforms, has created an environment where people are willing to invest their time and energy creating what they believe will be the next big thing. Those with the time and energy to do this are often the young and inexperienced outsiders, in the sense that they don't have any implementation experience with existing systems. If one of these new systems take off, the developers involved are likely to have made, or will make, many of the same mistakes made by the developers involved in earlier systems. The rate of decline of existing major software platforms is slow enough that employees with significant accumulated experience and expertise can continue to enjoy their seniority in well-paid jobs, they have no incentive to jump ship to apply their expertise to a still emerging system.

Mobile computing is only commercially feasible when the cost of computation, measured in Watts of electrical power, can be supplied by user-friendly portable batteries. Figure 1.9 shows the decline in electrical power consumed by a computation between 1946 and 2009; historically, it has been halving every 1.6 years.

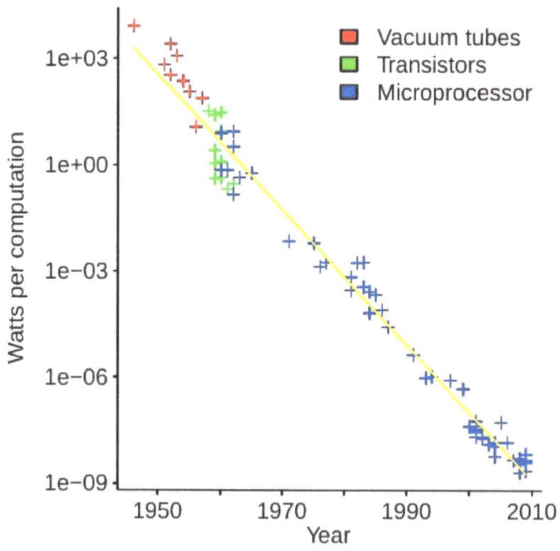

Figure 1.9: Power consumed, in Watts, executing an instruction on a computer available in a given year. Data from Koomey et al. [1035] Github-Local

Software systems have yet to reach a stable market equilibrium in many of the ecosystems they have colonised. Many software systems are still new enough that they are expected to adapt when the ecosystem in which they operate evolves. The operational procedures of these systems have not yet been sufficiently absorbed into the fabric of life that they enjoy the influence derived from users understanding that the easiest and cheapest option is to change the world to operates around them.

Economic activity is shifting towards being based around intangible goods; [782] cognitive capitalism is becoming mainstream.

A study by Goodridge, Haskel and Wallis estimated the UK investment in intangible assets, as listed in the audited accounts that UK companies are required to file every year. Figure 1.10 shows the total tangible (e.g., buildings, machinery and computer hardware) and intangible assets between 1990 and 2012. Economic competencies are items such as training and branding, Innovative property includes scientific R&D, design and artistic originals (e.g., films, music and books); accounting issues associated with software development are discussed in chapter 3.

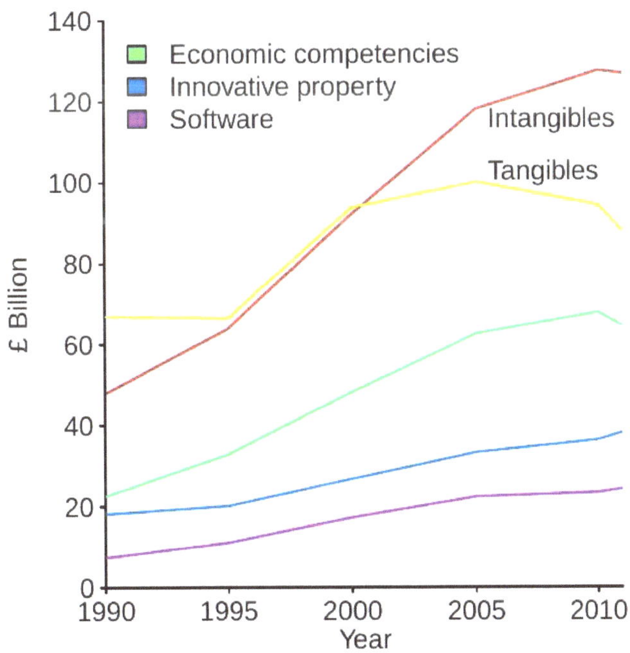

Figure 1.10: Total investment in tangible and intangible assets by UK companies, based on their audited accounts. Data from Goodridge et al. [707] Github-Local

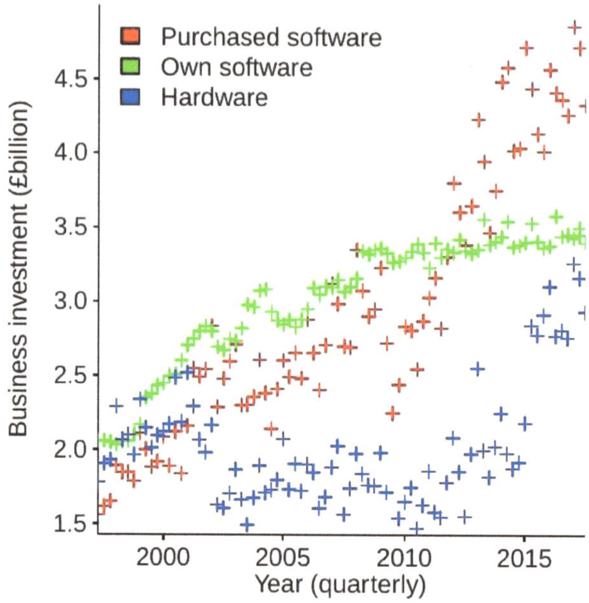

Figure 1.11: Quarterly value of newly purchased and own software, and purchased hardware, reported by UK companies as fixed-assets. Data from UK Office for National Statistics. Github-Local

Some companies treat some software as fixed-assets. Figure 1.11 shows quarterly totals for newly purchased and own software, and computer hardware, reported by UK companies as new fixed-assets.

A study by Wang found that while firms associated with the current IT fashion have a higher reputation and pay their executives more, they do not have higher performance. As companies selling hardware have discovered, designing products to become technologically obsolete (perceived or otherwise), or wear out and cease to work after a few years, creates a steady stream of sales. Given that software does not wear out, the desire to not be seen as out of fashion provides a means for incentivizing users to update to the latest version.

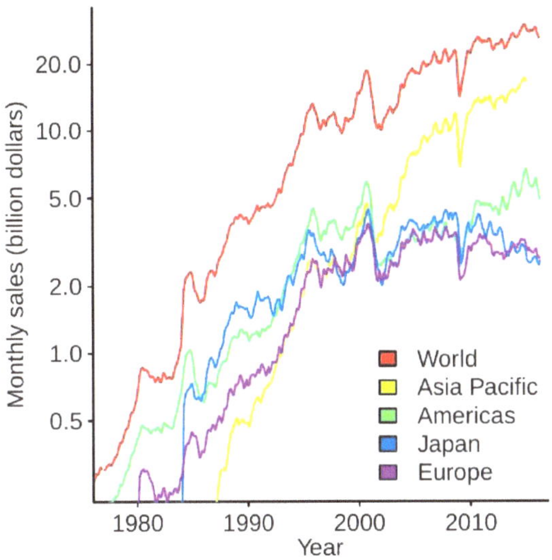

Figure 1.12: Billions of dollars of worldwide semiconductor sales per month. Data from World Semiconductor Trade Statistics. [1979] Github-Local

Based on volume of semiconductor sales (see figure 1.12), large new computer-based ecosystems are being created in Asia; the rest of the world appears to have reached the end of their growth phase.

The economics of chip fabrication, from which Moore's law derived, [iv] was what made the computing firestorm possible. The ability to create more products (by shrinking the size of components; see figure 1.13) for roughly the same production cost (i.e., going through the chip fabrication process); faster processors and increased storage capacity were fortuitous, customer visible, side effects. The upward ramp of the logistic equation has now levelled off, and today Moore's law is part of a history that will soon be a distant memory. Fret not, new methods of measuring progress in fabrication technology are available.

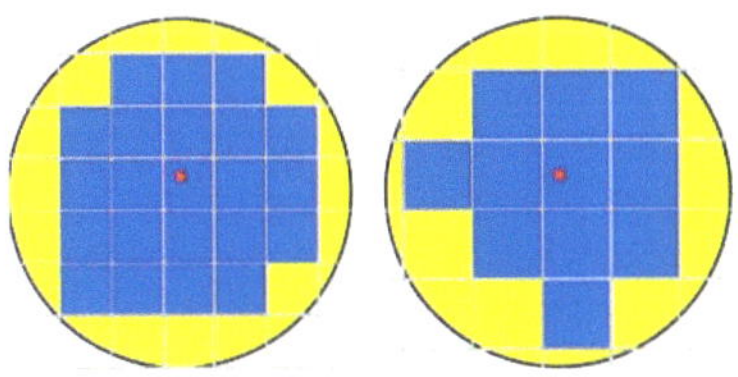

Figure 1.13: Smaller component size allows more devices to be fabricated on the same slice of silicon, plus material defects impact a smaller percentage of devices (increasing product yield). Github-Local

Software systems are part of a world-wide economic system that has been rapidly evolving for several hundred years; the factors driving economic growth are slowly starting to be understood. Analysis of changes in World GDP have found cycles, or waves, of economic activity; Kondratieff waves are the longest, with a period of around 50 years (data from more centuries may uncover a longer cycle), a variety of shorter cycles are also seen, such as the Kuznets swing of around 20 years. Five Kondratieff waves have been identified with major world economic cycles, e.g., from the industrial revolution to information technology. Figure 1.14 shows a spectral analysis of estimated World GDP between 1870 and 2008; adjusting for the two World-wars produces a smoother result.

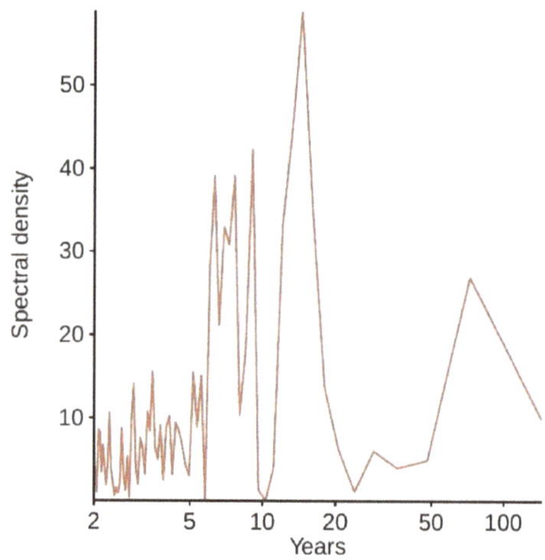

Figure 1.14: Spectral analysis of World GDP between 1870-2008; peaks around 17 and 70 years. Data from Maddison. [1189] Github-Local

While the rate at which new technologies have spread to different countries has been increasing over time, there has still been some lag in the diffusion of software systems around the world.

Computers were the enablers of the latest wave, from the electronic century.

1.2.1 The primary activities of software engineering

Software engineering is the collection of activities performed by those directly involved in the production and maintenance of software.

Traditionally, software development activities have included: obtaining requirements, creating specifications, design at all levels, writing and maintaining code, writing manuals fixing problems and providing user support. Large organizations compartmentalise activities and the tasks assigned to software developers tend to be primarily software related.

In small companies there is greater opportunity, and sometimes a need, for employees to become involved in tasks that would not be considered part of the job of a software developer in a larger company. For instance, being involved in any or all of a company's activities from the initial sales inquiry through to customer support of the delivered system; the financial aspect of running a business is likely to be much more visible in a small company.

Some software development activities share many of the basic principles of activities that predate computers. For instance, user interface design shares many of the characteristics of stage magic.

Software is created and used within a variety of ecosystems, and software engineering activities can only be understood in the context of the ecosystem in which it operates.

While the definition of software engineering given here is an overly broad one, let's be ambitious and run with it, allowing the constraints of data availability and completing a book to provide the filtering.

These activities are subject to path dependency: once the know-how and infrastructure for performing some activity becomes widely used, this existing practice is likely to continue to be used.

Perhaps the most entrenched path dependency in software development is the use of twovalued logic, i.e., binary. The most efficient radix, in terms of representation space (i.e., number of digits times number of possible values of each digit), is: 2.718 ..., [793] whose closest integral value is 3 . The use of binary, rather than ternary, has been driven by the characteristics of available electronic switching devices. [V] Given the vast quantity of software making an implicit, and in some cases explicit, assumption that binary representation is used, a future switching technology supporting the use of a ternary representation might not be adopted, or be limited to resource constrained environments. [1929] The debate over the identity of computing as an academic discipline is ongoing. [1818]

1.3 History of software engineering research

The fact that software often contained many faults, and took much longer than expected to produce, was a surprise to those working at the start of electronic computing, after World War II. Established practices for measuring and documenting the performance of electronics were in place and ready to be used for computer hardware, but it was not until the end of the 1960s that a summary of major software related issues appeared in print.

Until the early 1980s most software systems were developed for large organizations, with over 50% of US government research funding for mathematics and computer science coming from the Department of Defense, an organization that built large systems, with time-frames of many years. As customers of software systems, these organizations promoted a customer orientated research agenda, e.g., focusing on minimizing customer costs and risks, with no interest in vendor profitability and risk factors. Also, the customer was implicitly assumed to be a large organization.

Very large organizations, such as the DOD, spend so much on software it is cost effective for them to invest in research aimed at reducing costs, and learning how to better control the development process. During the 1970s project data, funding and management by the Rome Air Development Center, [vi] RADC, came together to produce the first collection of wide-ranging, evidence-based, reports analysing the factors involved in the development of large software systems.

For whatever reason the data available at RADC was not widely distributed or generally known about; the only people making use of this data in the 1980s and 1990s appear to be Air Force officers writing Master's theses.

The legacy of this first 30 years was a research agenda oriented towards building large software systems.

Since around 1980, very little published software engineering research has been evidencebased (during this period, not including a theoretical contribution in empirical research was considered grounds for rejecting a paper submitted for publication [13]). In the early 1990s, a review [1170] of published papers, relating to software engineering, found an almost total lack of evidence-based analysis of its engineering characteristics; a systematic review of 5,453 papers published between 1993 and 2002[775] found 2% reporting experiments. When experiments were performed, they suffered from small sample sizes (a review using papers from 2005 found that little had changed), had statistical power falling well below norms used in other disciplines [523] or simply failed to report an effect size (of the 92 controlled experiments published between 1993 and 2002 only 29% reported an effect size).

Why have academics working in an engineering discipline not followed an evidencebased approach in their research? The difficulty of obtaining realistic data is sometimes cited as the reason; however, researchers in business schools have been able to obtain production data from commercial companies, perhaps the real reason is those in computing departments are more interested in algorithms and mathematics, rather than the human factors and economic issues that dominate commercial software development.

The publication and research culture within computing departments may have discouraged those wanting to do evidence-based work (a few intrepid souls did run experiments using professional developers). Researchers with a talent for software engineering either moving on to other research areas or to working in industry, leaving the field to those with talents in the less employable areas of mathematical theory, literary criticism (of source code) or folklore.

Prior to around 1980 the analysis of software engineering data tended to make use of the best statistical techniques available. After around 1980, the quality of statistical analysis dropped significantly (when any was used), with the techniques applied often being a hold-over from pre-computer times, when calculations had to be done by hand, i.e., techniques that could be performed manually, sometimes of low power and requiring the data to have specific characteristics. Also, the methods used to sample populations have been not been rigorous.

Human psychology and sociology continue to be completely ignored as major topics of software research, a fact pointed out over 40 years ago. The irrelevance of most existing software engineering research to industry is itself the subject of academic papers.

A lack of evidence has not prevented researchers expounding plausible sounding theories that, in some cases, have become widely regarded as true. For instance, it was once claimed, without any evidence, that the use of source code clones (i.e., copying code from another part of the project) is bad practice (e.g., clones are likely to be a source of faults, perhaps because only one of the copies was updated). [628] In practice, research has shown that the opposite is true, clones are less likely to contain faults than 'uncloned' source.

Many beliefs relating to software engineering processes, commonly encountered in academic publications, are based on ideas formulated many years ago by researchers who were able to gain access to a relevant (often tiny) dataset. For instance, one study divided software interface faults into 15 categories using a data set of 85 modification requests to draw conclusions; this work is still being cited in papers 25 years later. These fossil theories have continued to exist because of the sparsity of experiments needed to refute or improve on them.

It is inevitable that some published papers contain claims about software engineering that turn out to be roughly correct; coincidences happen. Software engineering papers can be searched for wording which can be interpreted as foreseeing a recent discovery, in the same way it is possible to search the prophecies of Nostradamus to find one that can be interpreted as predicting the same discovery.

The quantity of published papers on a topic should not be confused with progress towards effective models of behavior. For instance, one study of research into software process improvement, over the last 25 years, found 635 papers, with experience reports and proposed solutions making up two-thirds of publications. However, proposed solutions were barely evaluated, there were no studies evaluating advantages and disadvantages of proposals, and the few testable theories are waiting to be tested.

Over the last 15 years or so, there has been an explosion of evidence-based research, driven by the availability of large amounts of data extracted from Open source software. However, existing theories and ideas will not die out overnight. Simply ignoring all research published before 2005 (roughly when the public data deluge began) does not help, earlier research has seeded old wives tales that have become embedded in the folklore of software engineering, creating a legacy that is likely to be with us for sometime to come.

A study by Rousseau, Di Cosmo and Zacchiroli tracked the provenance of source code in the Software Heritage archive. Figure 1.15 shows the number of unique blobs (i.e., raw files) and commits that first appeared in a given month, based on date reported by file system or version control (the doubling time for files is around 32 months, and for commits around 46 months). Occurrences at future dates put a lower bound on measurement noise.

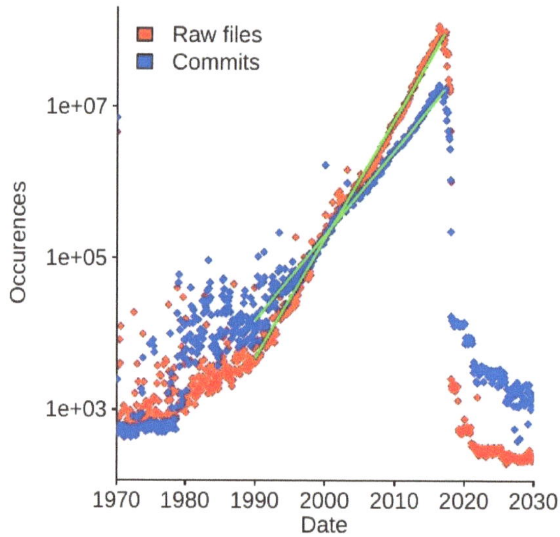

Figure 1.15: Number of unique files and commits first appearing in a given month; lines are fitted regression models of the form: Files $\propto e^{0.03\ \text{months}}$ and Commits $\propto e^{0.022\ \text{months}}$. Data kindly provided by Rousseau. Github-Local

This book takes the approach that, at the time of writing, evidence-based software engineering is essentially a blank slate. Knowing that certain patterns of behavior regularly occur is an empirical observation; a theory would make verifiable predictions that include the observed patterns. Existing old wives tales are discussed when it is felt that their use in an engineering environment would be seriously counter-productive; spending too much effort debunking theories can be counter-productive.

1.3.1 Folklore

The dearth of experimental evidence has left a vacuum that has been filled by folklore and old-wives' tales. Examples of software folklore include claims of a 28 -to- 1 productivity difference between best/worst developers, and the Halstead and McCabe complexity metrics; folklore metrics are discussed in section 7.1.4.

The productivity claim, sometimes known as the Grant-Sackman study, is based on a casual reading of an easily misinterpreted table appearing in a 1968 paper [1624] by these two authors. The paper summarised a study that set out to measure the extent to which the then new time-sharing approach to computer use was more productive for software development than existing batch processing systems (where jobs were typically submitted via punched cards, with programs executing (sometimes) hours later, followed by their output printed on paper). A table listed the ratio between the best subject performance using the fastest system, and the worst subject performance on the slowest system (the 28:1 ratio included programmer and systems performance differences, and if batch/timesharing differences are separated out the maximum difference ratio is 14: 1, the minimum 6:1). The actual measurement data was published in a low circulation journal, and was immediately followed by a strongly worded critique; see fig 8.22. A 1981 study by Dickey separated out subject performance from other factors, adjusted for individual subject differences, and found a performance difference ratio of 1: 5. However, by this time the 28:1 ratio had appeared in widely read magazine articles and books, and had become established as fact. In 1999, a study by Prechelt [1522] explained what had happened, for a new audience.

1.3.2 Research ecosystems

Interactions between people who build software systems and those involved in researching software has often suffered from a misunderstanding of each other's motivations and career pressures.

Until the 1980s a significant amount of the R&D behind high-tech products was done in commercial research labs (at least in the US). For instance, the development of Unix and many of its support tools (later academic derived versions were reimplementations of the commercial research ideas). Since then many commercial research labs have been shut or spun-off, making universities the major employer of researchers in some areas.

Few people in today's commercial world have much interaction with those working within the ecosystems that are claimed to be researching their field. The quaint image of researchers toiling away for years before publishing a carefully crafted manuscript is long gone. [532] Although academics continue to work in a feudal based system of patronage and reputation, they are incentivised by the motto "publish or perish", with science perhaps advancing one funeral at a time. Hopefully the migration to evidence-based software engineering research will progress faster than fashions in men's facial hair (most academics researching software engineering are men); see figure 1.16.

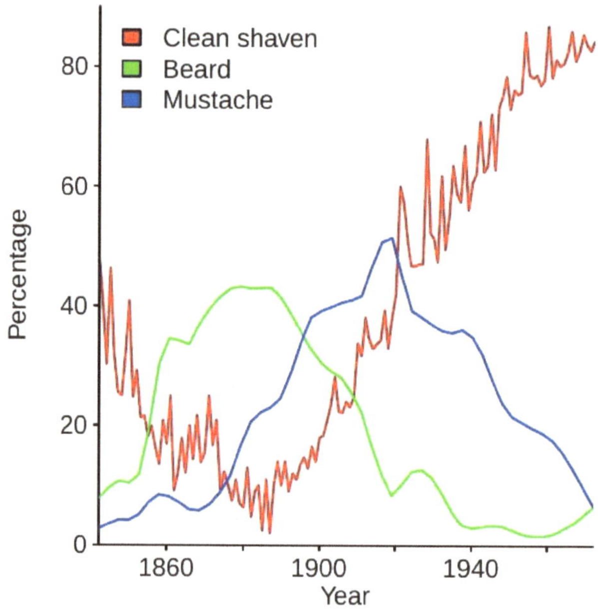

Figure 1.16: Changing habits in men's facial hair. Data from Robinson. [1593] Github-Local

Academic research projects share many of the characteristics of commercial start-ups. They involve a few people attempting to solve a sometimes fuzzily defined problem, trying to make an improvement in one area of an existing product, and they often fail, with the few that succeed producing spectacular returns. Researchers are serial entrepreneurs in that they tend to only work on funded projects, moving onto other projects when funding runs out (and often having little interest in previous projects). Like commercial product development, the choice of research topics may be fashion driven; see figure 1.17.

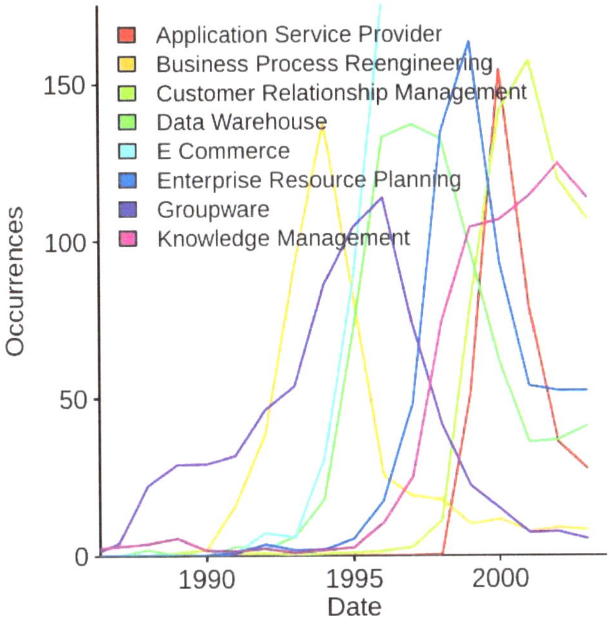

Figure 1.17: Number of papers, in each year between 1987 and 2003, associated with a particular IT topic. The Ecommerce paper count peaks at 1,775 in 2000 and in 2003 is still off the scale compared to other topics. Data kindly provided by Wang. Github-Local

The visible output from academic research are papers published in journals and conference proceedings. It is important to remember that: " . . . an article about computational science in a scientific publication is not the scholarship itself, it is merely advertising of the scholarship. The actual scholarship is the complete software development environment, and the complete set of instructions, which generated the figures."

Many journals and conferences use a process known as peer review to decide which submitted papers to accept. The peer review process involves sending submitted papers to a few referees (whose identity is unknown to the authors, and the identity of the authors may be unknown to the reviewers), ideally chosen for their expertise of the topic covered, who make suggestions on how to improve the paper and provide a yes/no/maybe acceptance decision. The peer review process first appeared in 1665, however, it only became widely used in the 1970s in response to concerns over public accountability of government funded research. [125] It now looks to be in need of a major overhaul [1524] to improve turn-around time, and handle the work load generated by a proliferation of journals and conferences, as well as addressing corruption; [1981] some journals and conferences have become known for the low quality of their peer reviews, even accepting fake papers. The status attached to the peer review process has resulted in it being adopted by journals covering a variety of subjects, e.g., psychic research.

In the past most researchers have made little, if any, effort to archive the data they gather for future use. One study requested the datasets relating to 516 biology related studies, with ages from 2 to 22 years; they found that the probability of the dataset being available fell by 17% per year. Your author's experience of requesting data from researchers is that it often fails to survive beyond the lifetime of the computer on which it was originally held.

Researchers may have reasons, other than carelessness, for not making their data generally available. For instance, a study of 49 papers in major psychology journals found that the weaker the evidence for the researcher's hypothesis the less likely they were to be willing to share their data.

The importance of making code and data available is becoming widely acknowledged, with a growing number of individual researchers making code/data available for download, and journals having explicit policies about authors making code/data available. [1783] In the UK researchers who receive any funding from a government research body are now required to archive their data, and make it generally available. [1577]

For some time now, academic performance has often been measured by number of papers published, and the impact factor of the journal in which they were published [1058] (scientific journals publish a percentage of the papers submitted to them, with prestigious high impact journals publishing a lower percentage than those have lower impact factors; journals and clubs share a common economic model). Organizations that award grants to researchers often consider the number of published papers and impact factor of the publication journal, when deciding whether to fund a grant application; the effect is to generate an evolutionary pressure that selects for bad science (as well as predatory journals [882] that accept any submitted paper, provided the appropriate fee is paid).

One consequence of the important role of published paper count in an academic's career, is an increase in scientific fraud, most of which goes undetected; one study found that most retracted papers (67.4%) were attributable to misconduct, around a 10 -fold increase since 1975. More highly ranked journals have been found to publish a higher percentage of retracted papers, it is not known whether this represents an increased in flawed articles, or an increase in detection. [1770] Only a handful of software engineering papers have been retracted, perhaps a lack of data makes it very difficult to verify the claims made by the authors. The website retractionwatch.com reports on possible and actual paper retractions.

Figure 1.18 shows the number of citations, in this book, to research published in a given year, plus the number of associated datasets; lines are fitted regression models.

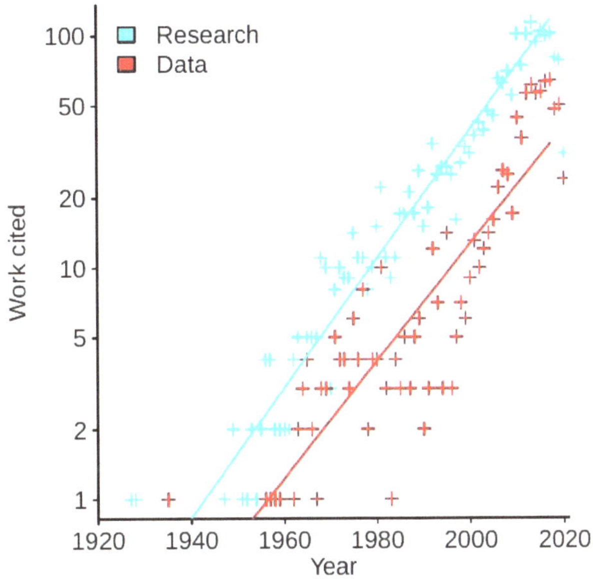

Figure 1.18: Number of articles appearing in a given year, cited in this book, plus number of corresponding datasets per year; both fitted regression lines have the form: Citations $\propto e^{0.06\ \text{Year}}$. Github-Local

Pointing out that academics are often more interested in career development than scientific development, and engage in questionable research practices is not new; Babbage complained about this behavior in 1830.

Commercial research labs Many large companies have research groups. While the researchers working in these groups often attend the same conferences as academics and publish papers in the same journals; their performance is often measured by the number of patents granted.

Citation practices This book attempts to provide citations to any factual statements, so readers can perform background checks. To be cited papers have to be freely available for public download, unless published before 2000 (or so), and when data is analysed it has to be free for public distribution. Programs, packages and libraries are not cited; others do sometimes cite software.

When academics claim their papers can be freely downloaded, what they may mean is that the university that employs them has paid for a site-wide subscription that enables university employees to download copies of papers published by various commercial publishers. Taxpayers pay for the research and university subscriptions, and most of these taxpayers do not have free access to it. Things are slowly changing. In the UK researchers in receipt of government funding are now incentivized to publish in journals that will make papers produced by this research freely available after 6-12 months from publication date. Your author's attitude is that academics are funded by taxpayers, and if they are unwilling to provide a freely downloadable copy on their web page, they should not receive any credit for the work.

Software developers are accustomed to treating documents that are more than a few years old, as being out-of-date; a consequence of the fast changing environment in which they often operate. Some fields, such as cognitive psychology, are more established, and people do not feel the need to keep repeating work that was first performed decades ago (although it may be replicated as part of the process of testing new hypothesis). In more established fields, it is counter-productive to treat date of publication as a worthiness indicator.

Researchers being disconnected from the practical realities of their field is not unique to software engineering; other examples include medicine and high-energy physics.

Your author sent email requests for the data associated with over 574 papers or reports. For papers more than 5-10 years old, an email was only sent if the data looked particularly interesting. If no reply was received within 6 -months, a follow-up email was sent (sometimes multiple times). An initial positive reply classifies the email as pending, although many of these now ought to be moved to the no-reply outcome (i.e., no longer replying to email). Data was not requested when it appeared obvious that the data was confidential. Table 1.1 shows the main outcomes of these requests.

Table 1.1: Outcome of author's email requests for data associated with 574 published papers.

Outcome	Total	Percent
No reply	201	35%
Received data	151	26%
Pending	95	16%
Confidential	65	11%
No longer have data	39	7%
Best known address bounces	23	4%

1.4 Overview of contents

The contents are driven by the publicly available data, and contains two distinct halves:

- the first half organizes the data within seven chapters: an introduction, three chapters covering the forces driving software development (i.e., human cognition, economics and the ecosystem within which they operate), and three chapters covering desired outcomes (i.e., projects, reliability and source code).
- Each chapter contains a patchwork issues, with each section containing related issues. The small amount of available data does not permit joined up discussions, rather a few paragraphs cluster around each dataset. Many topics usually covered in software engineering textbooks not discussed, because public data relating to them could not be located.
- the second half discusses data analysis techniques applicable to the kinds of measurement data, and problems, expected to be encountered by software developers. The intended readership is software developers wanting to apply techniques, who don't want to learn about the mathematics that underlies their implementation.

The results of the analysis are intended to help managers and developers understand the processes that generated the data.

Human cognition: Human brains supply the cognitive effort that directs and performs the activities involved in software production. An understanding of the operating characteristics of the human brain is needed to make the best use of the cognitive resources available. Characteristics such as cognitive capacity, memory storage/recall performance, learning, processing of visual information, reasoning, and decision-making are discussed.

Software developers come preloaded with overlearned behaviors, derived from the native culture of their formative years, and at least one human language which they have used for many hours when speaking and reading.

Cognitive capitalism: A knowledge of basic economic issues is needed to understand the software business, and the chapter starts with a basic tutorial on analyzing the economic issues involved in possible investments; there is also an outline of company economics (current economic theories and practices are predominantly based around the use of labor as the means of production; the economics of the products of intellectual effort has become a major issue).

Software is often written by teams and group dynamics is an important factor in any project.

The approach to software economics is from the perspective of the software engineer or software company, rather than the perspective of the customer or user of software (which differs from much existing work, which adopts the customer or user perspective).

Ecosystems: Software is created in a development ecosystem, and is used in a customer ecosystem. Customer demand motivates the supply of energy that drives software ecosystems. Software does not wear out, and the motivation for change comes from the evolution of these ecosystems.

Ecosystem evolution puts an upper limit on the productive lifetime of software (internal development factors have their own impact on lifetime). Lifetime is a key component of return on investment calculations.

Various developer ecosystems (e.g., careers), and development (e.g., APIs) ecosystems are discussed, along with non-software issues having an impact on developers.

Estimating population size is a common problem in ecology (e.g., potential employees, customers, and fault experiences); population dynamics are discussed.

Projects: Incentive structures are a key component to understanding the creation of software systems, from bidding to delivery, and ongoing maintenance: risks and returns, client/vendor interaction, and what's in it for developers and managers.

Resource estimation is a common problem, various models are discussed, along with patterns found in the few available details datasets.

Reliability: Software systems have a minimum viable reliability, i.e., what the market will tolerate. The little that is known about mistakes and fault experiences is discussed (i.e, the interaction between input values and a coding mistakes); where mistakes are made, their lifetime, and the cost-effectiveness of reducing or removing mistakes.

The cost-effectiveness of some techniques for checking software for intended behavior is discussed.

Source code: What are desirable source code characteristics, and what can be learned from existing patterns of use, i.e., where are the opportunities for investment in the production of source code?

What patterns appear in existing code and what can be learned from them?

Some folklore metrics that continue to haunt are debunked.

Stories told by data: There is no point analysing data unless the results can be effectively communicated to the intended audience. This chapter contains a compendium of examples of techniques that might be used to communicate a story found in data, along with issues to look out for in the stories told by others.

Data analysis: Developers are casual users of data analysis who don't want to spend time learning lots of mathematics; they want to make use of techniques, not implement them. The approach taken in the second half of the book is similar to that of a Doctor examining a patient for symptoms that might suggest underlying processes.

It is assumed that developer time is expensive and computer time is cheap. Every attempt is made to consistently use a single, general, statistical technique; this minimal, but general approach focuses on what developers need to know, and the price paid is that sometimes cpu resources are wasted.

It is assumed that readers have basic algebra skills, and can interpret graphs; no other statistical knowledge is assumed.

In many practical situations, the most useful expertise to have is knowledge of the application domain that generated the data, along with how any findings might be applied. It is better to calculate an approximate answer to the correct problem, than an exact answer to the wrong problem.

Because evidence-based software engineering has only recently started to be applied, there is uncertainty about which statistical techniques are most likely to be generally applicable. Therefore, an all encompassing approach is taken, and a broad spectrum of topics is covered, including:

- probability: making inferences about individual events based on the characteristics of the population (statistics makes inferences about the population based on the characteristics of a sample of the population). Concepts discussed include: probability distributions, mean and variance, Markov chains, and rules of thumb,
- statistics: statistics could be defined as the study of algorithms for data analysis; algorithms covered include: sampling, describing data, p-value, confidence intervals, effect size, statistical power, bootstrapping, model building, comparing two or more groups,
- regression modeling: the hammer used to analyse much of the data in this book. The kind of equation fitted to data can provide information about the underlying

processes that generated the data, and which variables have the most power to explain the behavior measured.

Software engineering measurements come in a wide variety of forms, and while ordinary least-squares might be widely used in the social sciences, it is not always suitable for modeling software datasets; more powerful techniques such as generalized leastsquares, nonlinear models, mixed models, additive models, structural equation models and others are discussed,

- time series: analysis of data where measurements at time *t* are correlated with measurements made earlier is the domain of time series analysis (regression modeling assumes that successive measurements are independent of each other),
- survival analysis: measurements of time to an event occurring (e.g., death) are the domain of survival analysis,
- circular and compositional statistics: software is developed over days and weeks; time recording is circular in that the distance between 12, 24 and 1 may be small. Circular statistics deals with such data. Software may be composed of multiple subcomponents. When dealing with percentage measurements of components, an increase in one subcomponent can cause the percentage of another to decrease; compositional statistic deals with such data.
- miscellaneous: various techniques for finding patterns in data, such as clustering and ordering of items. Machine learning can be useful when the person doing the analysis has little or no knowledge of the data, or the application domain that produced it. Sometimes we are clueless button pushers, and machine learning can be a useful guide.

Experiments: Probably the most common experiment performed by developers is benchmarking of hardware and software. The difficulties and complications involved in performing reliable benchmarks are discussed.

General issues involving the design of experiments are discussed. Data cleaning: Garbage in garbage out. Data cleaning is the penultimate chapter (it goes unmentioned in some books), and is often the most time-consuming data analysis activity, it is a very necessary activity for obtaining reliable results.

Common data cleaning tasks, along with possible techniques for detecting potential problems, and solving them using R, are discussed.

Overview of R: An overview aimed at developers who are fluent in at least one other computer language, i.e., it assumes that readers know how to program. The discussion concentrates on those language features likely to be commonly used.

Obtaining and installing : If you cannot figure out how to obtain and install *R*, this book is not for you.

Your author's goto book for R use in "The R Book" by Crawley. RStudio is a widely used R IDE that is also sometimes used by your author.

1.4.1 Why use R?

The main reasons for selecting *R* as the language+support library in which to perform the statistical analysis used in this book are:

- it is possible to quickly write a short program that solves the kind of problems that often occur when analysing software engineering data. The process often follows the sequence: read data from one of a wide variety of sources, operate on it using functions selected from an extensive library of existing packages, and finally, graphically display the results or print values,
- lots of data analysis people are using it. There is an active ecosystem with many *R* books, active discussion forums where examples can be found, answers to common questions found and new questions posted,
- accuracy and reliability: a comparison of the reliability of 10 statistical software packages found that GAUSS, LIMDEP, Mathematica, MATLAB, R, SAS, and Stata provided consistent reliable estimation results, and a comparison of the statistical functions in Octave, Python, and R[41] found that R yielded the best results. A study of the precision of five spreadsheets (Calc, Excel, Gnumeric, NeoOffice and Oleo), running under Windows Vista, Ubuntu, and macOS, found that no one spreadsheet provided consistently good results (it was recommended that none of these spreadsheets be used for nonlinear regression and/or Monte Carlo simulation); another study [1237] found significant errors in the accuracy of the statistical procedures in various versions of Microsoft Excel.
- an extensive library of add-on packages (over 15,000 at the time of writing): CRAN, the Comprehensive R Archive Network is the official package library, although some packages are only available on R-Forge and Github.

A freely available open source implementation is always nice to have.

1.5 Terminology, concepts and notation

Much of the basic terminology used in probability and statistics in common use today derives from gambling and experimental research in medicine and agriculture, because these were the domains in which researchers were employed during the early days of statistical analysis.

- group: each sample is sometimes referred to as a group,
- treatment: the operation or process performed on subjects is sometimes referred to as a treatment,
- explanatory variables (also known as independent, stimulus, predictor variables is used when the variables are used to make predictions, control variables is sometimes used in an experimental setting), are used to explain, predict or stimulate the value of response variables; they are independent of the response variable,
- response variable also known as a dependent variable, responds/depends to/on changes of values of explanatory variables; their behavior depends on the explanatory variables (or rather, it is believed by the researchers to depend on them),
- data is truncated when values below, or above some threshold are unobserved (or removed from the dataset).
- data is censored when values below, or above some threshold are set equal to the threshold,
- between subjects: comparing two or more samples, when samples are obtained from different groups of subjects, often with the different groups performing a task under different experimental conditions,
- within subjects: comparing two or more samples, when samples are obtained from the same group of subjects, often with the subjects performing a task under two or more different experimental conditions,
- a parametric test is a statistical technique that assumes the sample has some known probability distribution,
- a nonparametric test is a statistical technique that does not make any assumptions about the sample distribution (the term distribution free test is sometimes used).

The following are some commonly encountered symbols and notation:

- $n!$ (n factorial), denotes the expression $n(n-1)(n-2)\cdots 1$; calculated by R's factor ial function,
- $\binom{n}{r} = \frac{n!}{r!(n-r)!}$, is a commonly occurring quantity in the analysis of probability problems; calculated by R's choose function,
- a hat above a variable, $\hat{y}$, denotes an estimate; in this case an estimate of y 's value,
- μ(mu), commonly denotes the mean value; calculated by R's mean function,
- σ (sigma), commonly denotes the standard deviation; calculated by R's sd function. The terms 1 -sigma, 2 -sigma, etc. are sometimes used to refer to the probability of an event occurring. Figure 1.19 shows the sigma multiplier for various probabilities,

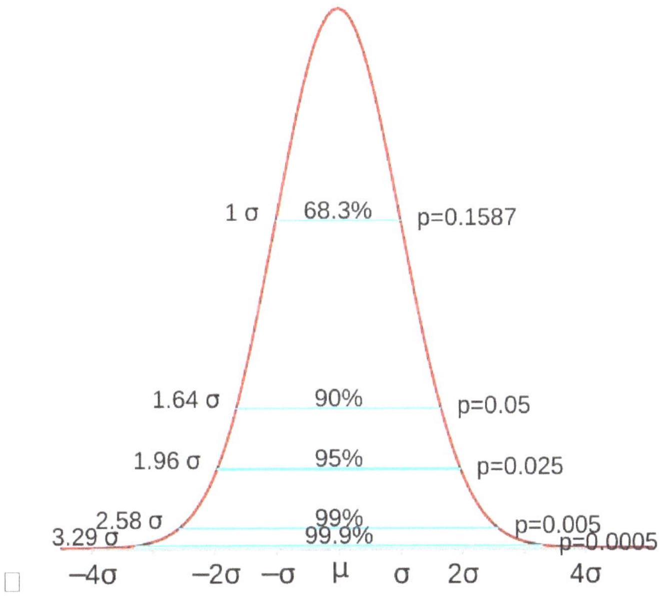

Figure 1.19: Normal distribution with total percentage of values enclosed within a given number of standard deviations. Github-Local

- $n \to \infty$, as n goes to infinity, i.e., becomes very very large,
- $n \to 0$, as n goes to zero, i.e., becomes very very small,

- $P(x)$, the probability of x occurring, and sometimes used to denote the Poisson distribution with parameter x (however, this case is usually written using λ (lambda), e.g., $P(\lambda)$),

- $P(a < X)$, the probability that $a < X$. The functions pnorm, pbinom and ppois can be used to obtain the probability of encountering a value less than or equal to x for the respective distribution (e.g., Normal, Binomial and Poisson, as suggested by the naming convention),

- $P(|a - X|)$, the probability of the absolute value of the difference between a and X,

- $\prod_{i=1}^{6} a_i$, the product: $a_1 \times a_2 \times \cdots \times a_6$,

- $\sum_{i=1}^{6} P(a_i)$, the sum: $P(a_1) + P(a_2) + \cdots + P(a_6)$,

The sum of the probabilities of all the mutually exclusive things that could happen, when an action occurs, is always one. For instance, when a die is rolled, the six probabilities of a particular number occurring sum to one, irrespective of whether the die is fair, or has been tampered with in some way.

- $P(D \mid S)$, the probability of D occurring, given that S is true; known as the conditional probability. For instance, S might be the event that two dice have been rolled, and their face-up numbers sum to five, and D the event that the value of the first die is four.

- The value can be calculated as follows:

$P(D \mid S) = \frac{P(DS)}{P(S)}$ where $P(DS)$ is the probability of both D and S occurring together. If D and S are independent of each other, then we have: $P(DS) = P(D)P(S)$, and the above equation simplifies to: $P(D \mid S) = P(DS)$A lot of existing theory in statistics assumes that variables are independent. For instance, characteristics unique to each dice means that using a different dice for each roll will produce values having more independence than using the same dice for both rolls.

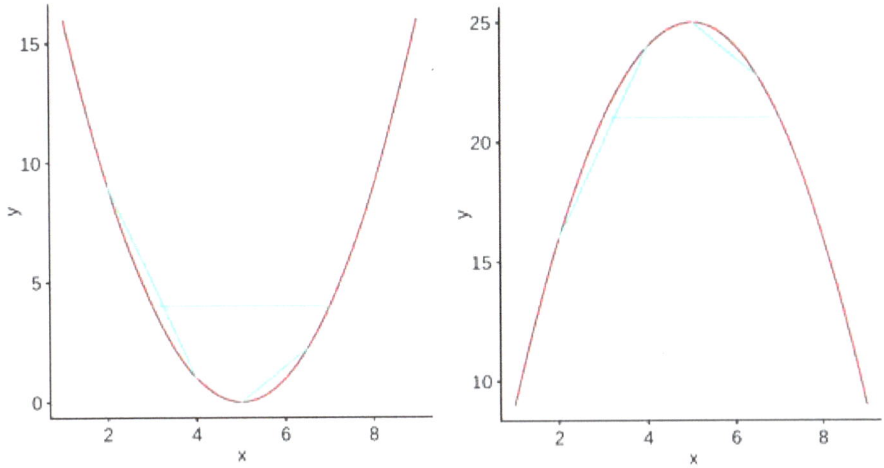

Figure 1.20: Example convex, upper, and concave, lower, functions; lines are three chords of the function. Github-Local

- Convex/concave functions: a function $f(x)$ is convex, between a and b, if every chord of the function is above the function. If the chord is always below the function, it is concave; see figure 1.20. The word convex tends to be spoken with a smiley face, while concave induces more of a frown (and in the example plot looks like the entrance to a cave).

1.6 Further reading

Readers wanting a more expansive discussion of the major topics covered in this book might like to look at the following:

Human cognition: "Cognitive Psychology: A Student's Handbook" by Eysenck and Keane, and "Cognitive Psychology and its Implications" by Anderson.

A readable collection of papers on how people make use categories to solve problems quickly without a lot of effort: "Simple Heuristics That Make Us Smart" by Gerd Gigerenzer, Peter M. Todd and The ABC Research Group. An upper graduate level book dealing with some of the more higher-level aspects of how people create and use categories "The Big Book of Concepts" by Gregory L. Murphy.

"Metaphors We Live By" by Lakoff and Johnson is a very readable introduction to metaphors.

"Human Error" by James Reason is still the best discussion on this topic.

Economics: "Return on Software" by Steve Tockey, and "Principles of Corporate Finance" by Brealey and Myers.

Culture: "The Origin and Evolution of Cultures" by Robert Boyd and Peter J. Richerson, for those interested in modeling of the evolution of culture.

Probability: "Grinstead and Snell's Introduction to Probability" by Grinstead and Snell is available as a free download.

More advanced books include: "Introduction to Probability Models" by Ross, and "An Introduction to Probability Theory and its Applications" by Feller is a classic that is full of interesting examples.

Statistics: "Applied Robust Statistics" by Olive and "Introduction to Probability and Statistics Using R" by G. Jay Kerns, are available as a free download.

Regression modeling: "Applied Predictive Modeling" by Kuhn and Johnson covers a wide variety of regression modeling techniques where a predictive model is required.

"Introductory Time Series with R" by Paul S.P. Cowpertwait and Andrew V. Metcalfe, and "Displaying Time Series, Spatial, and Space-Time Data with R" by Oscar Perpiñán Lamigueiro.

"Analyzing Compositional Data with R" by van den Boogaart and Tolosana-Deldago. Experiments: "Statistics for experimenters" by Box, Hunter and Hunter, and "Design and Analysis of Experiments" by Douglas C. Montgomery.

R: "The R Book" by Michael Crawley, and "R In a Nutshell" by Joseph Adler.

"An Introduction to R" by Venables and Smith, "R for programmers" by Norman Matloff, and "icebreakR" by Andrew Robinson, are both available as a free download.

Chapter 2

Human Cognition

2.1 Introduction

Software systems are built and maintained by the creative output of human brains, which supply the cognitive effort that directs and performs the activities required. The creation and maintenance of software systems are limited by the cognitive effort available; maximizing the effort delivered requires an understanding of the operating characteristics of the computing platform that produces it.

Modern humans evolved from earlier humanoids, who in turned evolved from earlier members of the ape family, who in turn evolved from etc., etc. The collection of cognitive characteristics present in the Homo sapien brain is the end-result of a particular sequence of survival pressures that occurred over millions of years of evolutionary history; with the last common ancestor of the great apes, and the line leading to modern humans, living 5 to 7 million years ago, [621] the last few hundred thousand years spent as hunter-gatherers roaming the African savannah, followed by 10,000 years or so having a lifestyle that involved farming crops and raising domesticated animals.

Our skull houses a computing system that evolved to provide responses to problems that occurred in stone-age ecosystems. However, this system is adaptable; neural circuits established for one purpose may be redeployed, during normal development, for different uses, often without losing their original functions, e.g., in many people, learning to read and write involves repurposing the neurons in the ventral visual occipito-temporal cortex (an area of the brain involved in face processing and mirror-invariant visual recognition). [476] Reuse of neural circuitry is a central organizational principle of the brain. [60]

Figure 2.1: Unless cognition and the environment in which it operates closely mesh together, problems may be difficult or impossible to solve; the blades of a pair of scissors need to closely mesh for cutting to occur. Github-Local

The collection of cognitive characteristics supported by an animal's brain only makes sense in the context of the problems the species had to solve within the environment in which it evolved. Cognition and the environment are like the two blades of a pair of scissors both blades have to mesh together to achieve the desired result; see figure 2.1:

- the structure of the natural environment places constraints on optimal performance (an approach to analyzing human behavior known as rational analysis),
- cognitive, perception, and motor operations have their own sets of constraints (an approach known as bounded cognition, which targets good-enough performance).

Degraded, or incorrect, performance occurs when cognitive systems have to operate in a situation that violates the design assumptions of the environment they evolved to operate within; the assumptions are beneficial because they simplify the processing of ecologically common inputs. For instance, the human visual system assumes light shines from above, because it has evolved in an environment where this is generally true. A consequence of this assumption of light shining from above is the optical illusion in figure 2.2, i.e., the top row appears as mounds while the lower row appears as depressions.

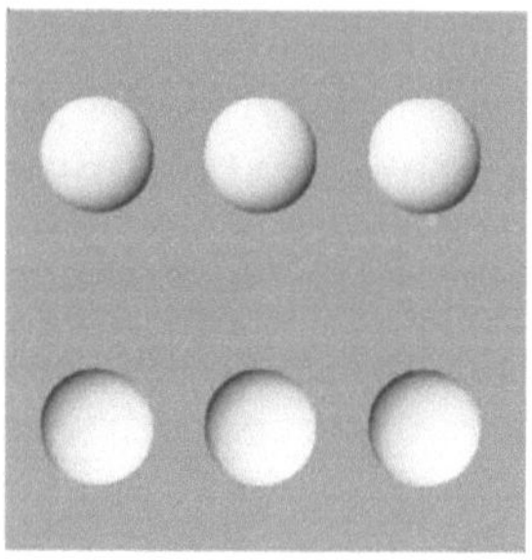

Figure 2.2: The assumption of light shining from above creates the appearance of bumps and pits. Github-Local

Optical illusions are accepted as curious anomalies of the visual system; there is no rush to conclude that human eyesight is faulty. Failures of the cognitive system to produce answers in agreement with mathematical principles, chosen because they appeal to those making the selection, indicates that the cognitive system has not been tuned by the environment in which it has been successful to produce answers compatible with the selected mathematical principles.

This book is written from the viewpoint that the techniques used by people to produce software systems should be fitted around the characteristics of the computing platform in our head (the view that developers should aspire to be omnipotent logicians is driven by human self-image, a counter-productive mindset). [i] Builders of bridges do not bemoan the lack of unbreakable materials available to them, they learned how to work within the limitations of the materials available.

Evolutionary psychology is an approach to psychology that uses knowledge and principles from evolutionary biology to help understand the operation of the human mind. Physical implementation details, the biology of the brain, [962] also have an impact on psychological performance.

Figure 2.3: Overlearning enables readers to effortlessly switch between interpretations of curved lines. Github-Local

The fact that particular cognitive abilities have benefits in some environments, that outweigh their costs, means they are to be found in a variety of creatures, e.g., numerical competence across the animal kingdom, [1379] and in particular the use of numbers by monkeys and syntax by birds. [1801] A study by Mechner rewarded rats with food, if they pressed a lever N times (with N taking one of the values 4, 8, 12 or 16), followed by pressing a second lever.

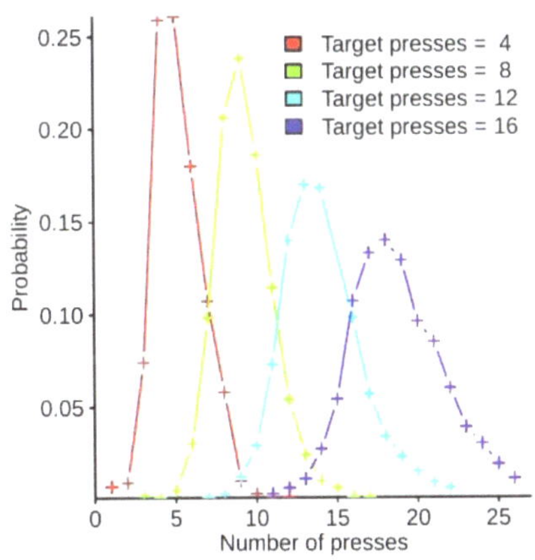

Figure 2.4: Probability that rat N 1 will press a lever a given number of times before pressing a second lever to obtain food, when the target count is 4, 8, 12 and 16 . Data extracted from Mechner. Github-Local

Figure 2.4 suggests that rat N 1 is making use of an approximate number system. Other examples of non-human cognition are briefly discussed elsewhere, the intent is to show how deep-seated some of our cognitive abilities are, i.e., they may not depend on high-level functionality that is human specific.

Table 2.1 shows a division of human time scales by the kind of action that fits within each interval.

Does the brain contain a collection of modules (each handling particular functionality) or a general purpose processor? This question is the nature vs. nurture debate, rephrased using implementation details, i.e., a collection of modules pre-specified by nature or a general purpose processor that is configured by nurture. The term modularity of mind refers to a model of the brain containing a general purpose processor attached to special purpose modules that handle perceptual processes (e.g., hearing and sight); the term massive modularity hypothesis refers to a model that only contains modules.

Table 2.1: Time scales of human action. Based on Newell. [1369]

Scale (sec)	Time Units	System	World (theory)
10000000	months		
1000000	weeks		Social Band
100000	days		
10000	hours	Task	Rational Band
1000	10 min	Task	
100	minutes	Task	
10	10 sec	Unit task	Cognitive Band
1	1 sec	Operations	
0.1	100 msec	Deliberate act	
0.01	10 msec	Neural circuit	Biological Band
0.001	1 msec	Neuron	
0.0001	100μsec	Organelle	

Consciousness is the tip of the iceberg, most of what goes on in the mind is handled by the unconscious. Problems that are experienced as easy to solve may actually involve very complex neural circuitry, and be very difficult to program computers to solve.

The only software engineering activities that could be said to be natural, in that they use prewired biological structures in the brain, involve social activities. The exactitude needed for coding is at odds with the fast and frugal approach of our unconscious mind, whose decisions our conscious mind later does its best to justify. Reading and writing are not natural in the sense that specialist brain structures have evolved to perform these activities; it is the brain's generic ability to learn that enables this skill to be acquired through many years of deliberate practice.

What are the likely differences in cognitive performance between human males and females? A study by Strand, Deary and Smith [1790] analyzed Cognitive Abilities Test (CAT) scores from over 320,000 school pupils in the UK. Figure 2.5 provides a possible explanation for the prevalence of males at the very competent/incompetent ends of the scale, and shows that women outnumber men in the middle competency band (over time differences have remained, but male/female performance ratios have changed). A model where one sex engages in relatively selective mate choice produces greater variability in the opposite sex.

A study by Jørgensen and Grimstad asked subjects from three Asian and three east European countries to estimate the number of lines of code they wrote per hour, and the effort needed to implement a specified project (both as part of a project investigating cognitive biases). Both country and gender were significant predictors of the estimates made; see Github-developers/estimation-biases.R.

While much has been written on how society exploits women, relatively little has been written on how society exploits men. There are far fewer women than men directly involved in software engineering. [ii]

2.1.1 Modeling human cognition

Models of human cognitive performance are based on the results of experiments performed using subjects drawn almost entirely from Western, Educated, Industrialized, Rich and Democratic (WEIRD) societies. While this is a problem for those seeking to uncover the cognitive characteristics of humans in general, it is not a problem for software engineering; because those involved have usually had a WEIRD society education.

Characteristics of WEIRD people that appear to differ from the populations of other cultures include:

- WEIRD people are willing to think about, and make inferences about, abstract situations, without the need for having had direct experience; studies [1174] of non-WEIRD people have found they are unwilling to discuss situations where they don't have direct experience,

- when mapping numbers onto space, WEIRD people have been found to use a linear scale for mapping values between one and ten; studies of non-WEIRD people have found they often use a logarithmic scale, [480]

- WEIRD people have been found to have complex, but naive, models of the mechanisms that generate the everyday random events they observe. [1424]

Much of the research carried out in cognitive psychology draws its samples from people between the ages of 18 and 21, studying some kind of psychology degree. There has been discussion on the extent to which these results can be extended to the general WEIRD populace, however, results obtained by sampling from this subpopulation may well be good enough for dealing with software engineering issues.

The reasons why students are not appropriate subjects to use in software engineering experiments, whose results are intended to be applied to professional software developers, are discussed in chapter 13.

Several executable models of the operation of human cognitive processes have been created. The ACT-R model has been applied to a wide range of problems, including learning, the visual interface, perception and action, cognitive arithmetic, and various deduction tasks.

Studies have found a poor correlation between an individual's estimate of their own cognitive ability and measurements of their ability.

Studies of personnel selection have found that general mental ability is the best predictor of job performance.

Bayesian models of human cognition have been criticised for assuming that performance on a range of tasks is at, or near, optimal. Everyday human performance needs to be good enough, and an investment in finding a (near) optimal solution may not be cost effective.

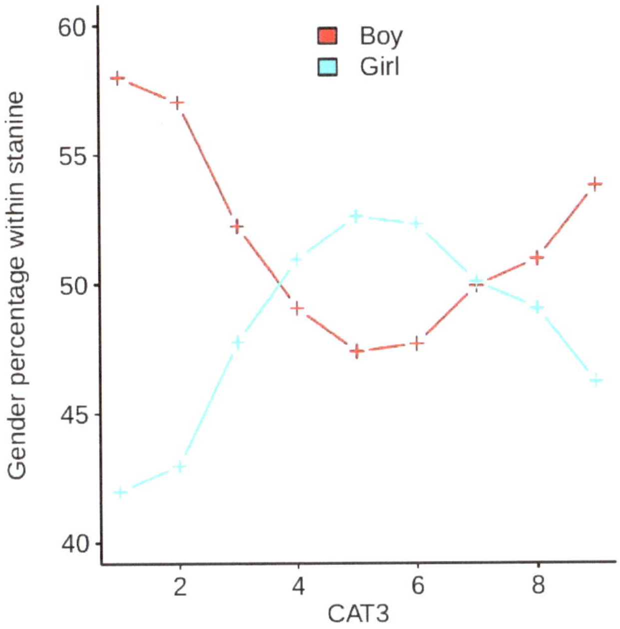

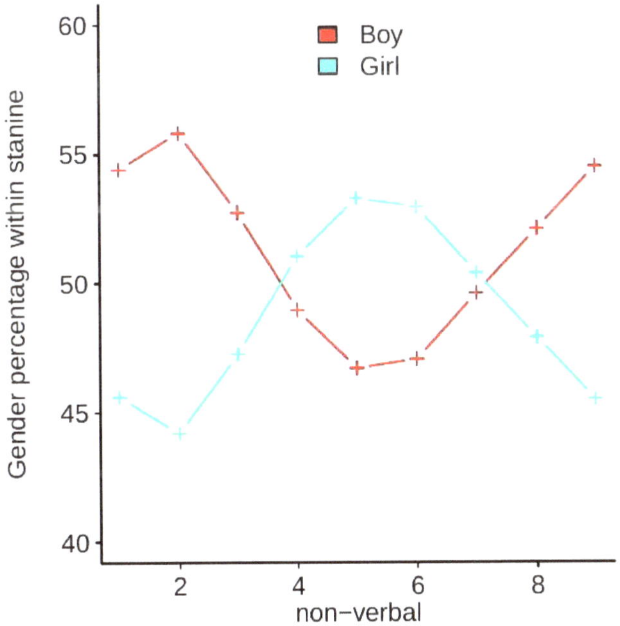

Figure 2.5: Boy/girl (aged 11-12 years) verbal reasoning, quantitative reasoning, non-verbal reasoning and mean CAT score over the three tests; each stanine band is 0.5 standard deviations wide. Data from Strand et al. Github-Local

The evidence-accumulation model is used in the cognitive analysis of decision-making. As its name suggests, the model operates by accumulating evidence until the quantity of evidence for one of the options exceeds the threshold needed to trigger its selection. The diffusion model, and the Linear Ballistic Accumulator (LBA) are currently two leading forms of this model.

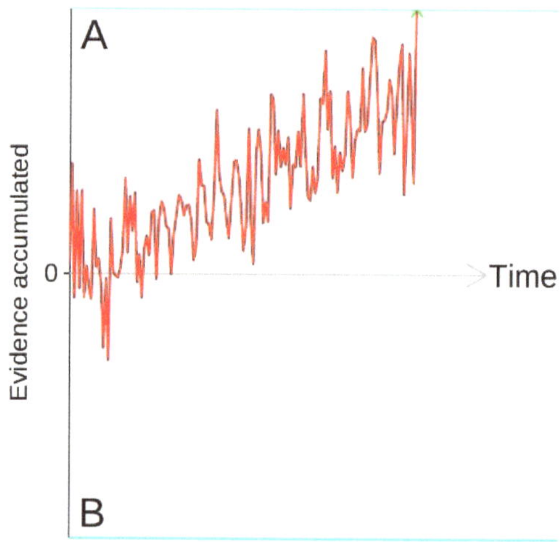

Figure 2.6: Example of the evolution of the accumulation of evidence for option "A", in a diffusion model. Github-Local

Figure 2.6 shows the basic components of evidence-accumulation models; this particular example is of a diffusion model, for a 2 -choice decision, i.e., "A" or "B".

The drift rate is the average rate at which evidence accumulates in the direction of the correct response; noise in the process creates variability in the response time and the possibility of making an incorrect response. Evidence accumulation may start from a non-zero value.

The distance between the options' decision thresholds, on the evidence axis, impacts response time (increasing distance, increases response time), and error rate (decreasing distance, increases the likelihood that noise can cause sufficient evidence to accumulate to cross the threshold of the incorrect option).

The Linear Ballistic Accumulator model differs from the diffusion model, in that each option has its own register holding the evidence accumulated for that option. The first option whose accumulated evidence reaches threshold, is selected (the diffusion model accumulates evidence in a single register, until reaching the threshold of one option).

The measured response time includes what is known as nondecision time, e.g., tasks such as information encoding and time taken to execute a response.

Fitting data from experiments on a lexical decision task, to a diffusion model, shows that drift rate increases with word frequency, and that some characteristics of non-words (e.g., whether they were similar to words or were random characters) had an impact on the model parameters.

2.1.2 Embodied cognition

Embodied cognition is the theory that many, if not all, aspects of a person's cognitive processing are dependent on, or shaped by, sensory, motor, and emotional processes that are grounded in the features of their physical body. [686]

A study by Presson and Montello [1529] asked two groups of subjects to memorize the locations of objects in a room. Both groups were then blindfolded, and then asked to point to various objects; their performance was found to be reasonably fast and accurate. Subjects in one group were then asked to imagine rotating themselves 90°, they were then asked to point to various objects. Their performance was found to be much slower and less accurate. Subjects in the other group were asked to actually rotate 90°; while still blindfolded, they were then asked to point to various objects. The performance of these subjects was found to be as good as before they rotated. These results suggest that mentally keeping track of the locations of objects, a task that might be thought to be cognitive and divorced from the body, is in fact strongly affected by body position.

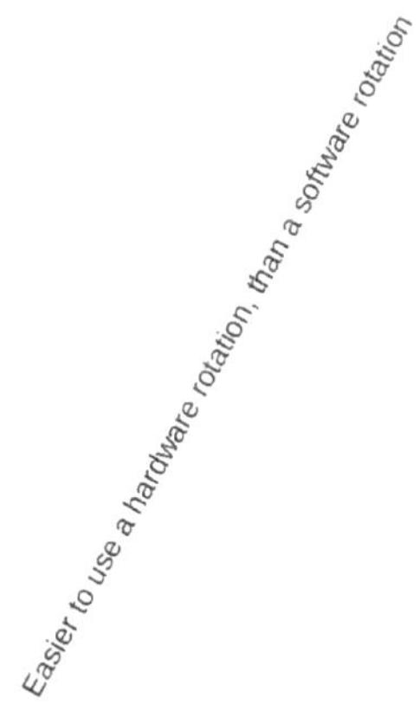

Figure 2.7: Rotating text in the real world; is it most easily read by tilting the head, or rotating the image in the mind? Github-Local

Tetris players have been found to prefer rotating an item on screen, as it descends, rather than mentally perform the rotation. [1010]

A study by Shepard and Metzler showed subjects pairs of figures and asked if they were the same. Some pairs were different, while others were the same, but had been rotated relative to each other. The results showed a linear relationship between the angle of rotation (needed to verify that two objects were the same), and the time taken to make a matching comparison. Readers might like to try rotating, in their mind, the pair of images in each row of figure 2.8, to find out if they are the same.

Figure 2.8: Two objects paired with another object that may be a rotated version. Based on Shepard et al. [1691] Github-Local

A related experiment by Kosslyn showed subjects various pictures and asked questions about them. One picture was of a boat, and subjects were asked a question about the front of the boat and then asked a question about the rear of the boat. The response time, when the question shifted from the front to the rear of the boat, was longer than when the question shifted from one about portholes to one about the rear. It was as-if subjects had to scan their image of the boat from one place to another to answer the questions.

Many WEIRD people use a mental left-to-right spatial orientation for the number line. This mental orientation has an embodiment in the SNARC effect (spatial numerical association of response codes). Studies have shown subjects single digit values, and asked them to make an odd/even decision by pressing the left/right response button with the left-/right-hand. When using the right-hand response time decreases as the value increases (i.e., the value moves from left-to-right along the number line), and when using the left-hand response time decreases as the value decreases. The effect persists when arms are crossed, such that opposite hands are used for button pressing.

Figure 2.9 shows the left/right-hand error rate found in a study by Nuerk, Wood and Willmes [1393] of the SNARC effect.

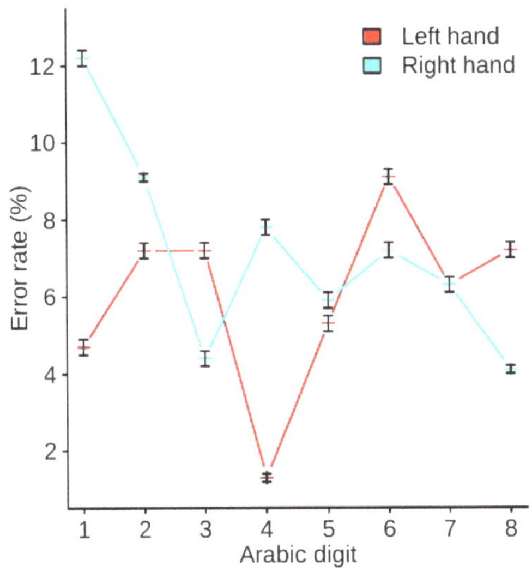

Figure 2.9: Error rate, with standard error, for the left/right-hand from a study of the SNARC effect. Data from Nuerk et al. Github-Local

2.1.3 Perfection is not cost-effective

Evolution is driven by survival of the fittest, i.e., it is based on relative performance. A consistent flawless performance is not only unnecessary, but a waste of precious resources.

Socially, making mistakes is an accepted fact of life and people are given opportunities to correct mistakes, if that is considered necessary.

For a given task, obtaining information on the kinds of mistakes that are likely to be made (e.g., entering numeric codes on a keyboard), and modeling behavior (e.g., subtraction mistakes made by children learning arithmetic) is very time-consuming, even for simple tasks. Researchers are still working to build good models [1740] for the apparently simple task of text entry.

One technique for increasing the number of errors made by subjects, in an experiment, is to introduce factors that will increase the likelihood of mistakes being made. For instance, under normal circumstances the letters/digits viewed by developers are clearly visible, and the viewing time is not constrained. In experiments run under these conditions subjects make very few errors. To obtain enough data to calculate letter similarity/confusability, studies have to show subjects images of single letters/digits that have been visually degraded, or to limit the amount of time available to make a decision, or both, until a specified error rate is achieved. [1839] While such experiments may provide the only available information, on the topic of interest, their ecological validity has to be addressed (compared to say asking subjects to rate pairs of letters for similarity).

How often do people make mistakes?

A lower bound on human error rate, when performing over an extended period, is probably that of astronauts in space; making an error during a space mission can have very serious consequences, and there is a huge investment in astronaut training. NASA maintains several databases of errors made by operators during simulation training and actual missions; human error rates, for different missions, of between $1.9 \cdot 10^{-3}$ and $1.05 \cdot 10^{-4}$ have been recorded.

Studies of the error rate for touch typists, performing purely data entry have found: with no error correction 4% (per keystroke), typing nonsense words (per word) 7.5%.

A number of human reliability analysis methods [319] for tasks in safety critical environments are available. The Cognitive Reliability Error Analysis Model (CREAM) is widely used; Calhoun et al work through a calculation of the probability of an error during the International Space Station ingress procedure, using CREAM. The HEART method [1964] is another method.

How do people respond when their mistakes are discovered?

A study by Jørgensen and Moløkken [955] interviewed employees, from one company, with estimation responsibilities. Analysis of the answers showed a strong tendency for people to perceive factors outside their control as important contributing factors for inaccurate estimates, while factors within their control were typically cited as reasons for accurate estimates.

2.2 Motivation

Motivation is a powerful influence on an individuals' priorities. The desire to complete an immediate task can cause a person to alter their priorities in a way they might not choose in more relaxed circumstances. A study by Darley and Batson asked subjects (theological seminary students) to walk across campus to deliver a sermon. Some subjects were told that they were late, and the audience was waiting, the remainder were not told this. Their journey took them past a victim moaning for help in a doorway. Only 10% of

subjects who thought they were late stopped to help the victim, while 63% of the other subjects stopped to help. These results do not match the generally perceived behavior pattern of theological seminary students.

What motivations do developers have while working on software systems? Possible motivations include those that generally apply to people (e.g., minimizing cognitive effort; discussed in section 2.2.2), apply to company employees (e.g., seeking promotion, or doing a job because it pays well), and apply to those involved in creative activities (e.g., organizing activities to maximize the pleasure obtained from work). Motivating members team is discussed in section 3.4.2.

Hedonism is an approach to life that aims to maximise personal pleasure and happiness (section 11.3.5 discusses a study investigating the importance of fun as a motivation for software development). Many theories of motivation take as their basis that people intrinsically seek pleasure and avoid pain, i.e., they are driven by hedonic motivation.

People involved in work that requires creativity can choose to include personal preferences and desires in their decision-making process, i.e., they are subject to hedonic motivation. Todate, most research on hedonic motivation has involved studies of consumer behavior.

The theory of regulatory focus theory is based around the idea that people's different approaches to pleasure and pain influences the approach they take towards achieving an end-state (or, end-goal). The theory contains two end states, one concerned with aspirations and accomplishments (a promotion focus), and the other concerned with attainment of responsibilities and safety (a prevention focus).

A promotion focus is sensitive to presence and positive outcomes, seeks to insure hits and insure against errors of omission. A prevention focus is sensitive to absence and negative outcomes, and seeks to insure against correct rejections and insure against errors of commission.

People are able to exercise some degree of executive control over the priorities given to cognitive processes, e.g., deciding on speed/accuracy trade-offs. Studies [626] have found that subjects with a promotion focus will prefer to trade-off accuracy for speed of performance, and those with a prevention focus will trade-off speed for improved accuracy.

The concept of Regulatory fit has been used to explain why people engage more strongly with some activities and "feel right" about it (because the activity sustains, rather than disrupts, their current motivational orientation or interests).

2.2.1 Built-in behaviors

Early researchers, investigating human behavior, found that people often fail to respond in ways that are consistent with the mathematically optimal models of behavior that they had created. The term cognitive bias has become the umbrella term used to describe such behavior.

Evolution selects for traits that provide an organism with advantages within its ecosystem. The failure of the mathematical models created by researchers to predict human responses, is a failure of researchers to understand the problems that human behavior is intended to solve within their environment. Researchers are starting to create models [1140] where, what were once thought to be cognitive biases, are actually ecologically rational uses of cognitive resources.

Evidence-based software engineering has to take into account whatever predispositions come included, as standard, with every human brain. The fact that many existing models of human behavior poorly describe real-life behaviors means that extreme caution is needed when attempting to model developer behaviors.

Anchoring bias and confirmation bias are two commonly discussed cognitive biases.

Anchoring: Behavior where people assign too much weight to the first piece of information they obtain, relating to the topic at hand.

A study by Jørgensen and Sjøberg asked professionals and students to estimate the development effort for a project, with one group of subjects being given a low estimate from the `customer', a second group a low estimate (and no rationale), and the third group no 'customer' estimate. The results found that estimates from subjects given a high/low customer estimate were much higher/lower than subjects who did not receive any customer estimate; see Github-developer/anchor-estimate.R.

A study by Jørgensen and Grimstad asked subjects to estimate the number of lines of code they wrote per hour, with subjects randomly split into two groups; one anchored with the question: "Did you on average write more or less than 1 Line of Code per work-hours in your last project?", and the other with: "Did you on average write more or less than 200 Lines of Code per work-hours in your last project?" Fitting a regression model to the results showed that the form of the question changed the value estimated by around 72 lines (sd 10). Github-developers/estimation-biases.R

Confirmation bias: Occurs when ambiguous evidence is interpreted as (incorrectly) confirming a person's current beliefs about the world. For instance, developers interpreting program behavior as supporting their theory of how it operates, or using the faults exhibited by a program to conform their view that it was poorly written.

When shown data from a set of observations, a person may propose a set of rules about the processes that generated the data. Given the opportunity to test proposed rules, what strategy are people likely to use?

A study by Wason, which became known as the 2-4-6 Task, asked subjects to discover a rule known to the experimenter; subjects' guessed a rule, told it to the experimenter, who then told them whether the answer was correct. For instance, on being informed that the sequence 2 – 4 – 6 was an instance of the experimenter's rule, possible subject rules might be "two added each time" or "even numbers in order of magnitude", when perhaps the actual rule was "three numbers in increasing order of magnitude".

An analysis of the rules created by subjects found that most were test cases designed to confirm a hypothesis about the rule (known as a positive test strategy), with few test cases attempting to disconfirm a hypothesis. Some subjects declared rules that were mathematically equivalent variations of rules they had already declared.

The use of a positive test strategy has been claimed to be a deficiency, because of the work of Popper who proposed that scientists should perform experiments designed to disprove their hypothesis. Studies of the hypothesis testing strategies used by scientists found that positive testing is the dominant approach.

A study by Klayman and Ha investigated the structure of the problems subjects were asked to solve in rule discovery studies. The problem is a search problem, find the experiment's rule, and in some environments a positive test strategy is more effective for solving search problems, compared to a negative test strategy.

Figure 2.10 shows the five possible ways in which the experimenter's rule and subject's hypothesis can overlap.

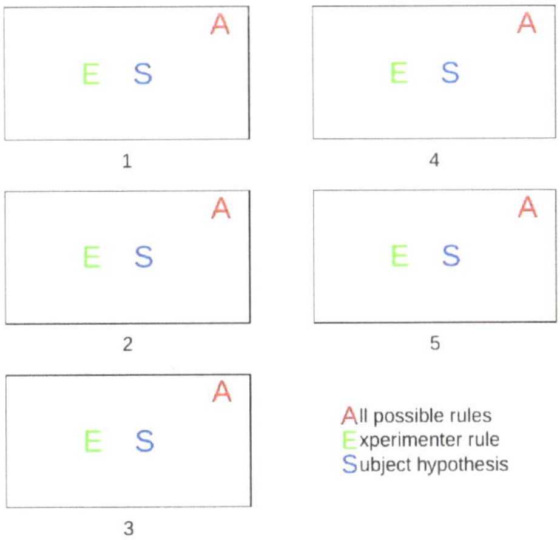

Figure 2.10: The five possible ways in which experimenter's rule and subject's rule hypothesis can overlap, in the space of all possible rules; based on Klayman et al. Github-Local

A positive test strategy is more effective when the sought after rule describes a minority case, i.e., there are more cases not covered by the rule, or when the hypothesized rule includes roughly as many cases as the actual rule, that is, the hypothesized rule is about the right size. Klayman and Ha claimed these conditions hold for many real-world rule search problems, and a positive test strategy is therefore an adaptive strategy; the realworldness claim continues to be debated.

The implementation of positive and negative test cases is discussed in section 6.6.2.3.

2.2.2 Cognitive effort

When attempting to solve a problem, a person's cognitive system (consciously and unconsciously) makes cost/accuracy trade-offs. The details of how it forms an estimate of the value, cost and risk associated with an action, and carries out the trade-off analysis is not known (various models have been proposed). An example of the effects of these trade-offs is provided by a study by Fu and Gray, where subjects had to copy a pattern of colored blocks (on a computer-generated display). Remembering the color of the block to be copied, and its position in the target pattern, created a memory effort. A perceptual-motor effort was introduced by graying out the various areas of the display, where the colored blocks were visible; these grayed out areas could be made temporarily visible using various combinations of keystrokes and mouse movements. Subjects had the choice of investing memory effort (learning the locations of different colored blocks) or perceptual-motor effort (using keystrokes and mouse movements to uncover different areas of the display). A subject's total effort is the sum of perceptual motor effort and memory storage and recall effort.

The subjects were split into three groups; one group had to expend a low effort to uncover the grayed out areas, the second acted as a control, and the third had to expend a high effort to uncover the grayed out areas. The results showed that the subjects who had to expend a high perceptual-motor effort uncovered grayed out area fewer times than the other two groups. These subjects also spent longer looking at the areas uncovered, and moved more colored blocks between uncoverings. The subjects faced with a high investment in perceptual-motor effort reduced their total effort by investing in memory effort. Another consequence of this switch of effort investment, to use of memory, was an increase in errors made.

What are the physical processes that generate the feeling of mental effort? The processes involved remain poorly understood, and proposals include: metabolic constraints (the brain accounts for around 20% of heart output, and between 20% to 25% of oxygen and glucose requirements), a feeling of mental effort is the body's reaction to concentrated thinking and is intended to create a sense of effort that induces a reduction in mental workload, to conserve energy [1060] (the energy consumption of the visual areas of the brain while watching television are higher than the consumption levels of those parts of the brain associated with difficult thinking)

2.2.3 Attention

Most sensory information received by the brain does not require conscious attention, it is handled by the unconscious. Conscious attention is like a spotlight shining cognitive resources on a selected area. In today's world, there is often significantly more information available to a person than they have available attention resources, WEIRD people live in an attention economy.

People can direct attention to their internal thought processes and memories. For instance, read the bold text in the following paragraph:

Somewhere Among hidden the in most the spectacular Rocky Mountains cognitive near abilities Central City is Colorado the an ability old to miner select hid one a message box from of another. gold. We Although do several this hundred by people focusing have our looked attention for on it, certain they cues have such not as found type it style.

What do you remember from the non-bold text? Being able to make a decision to direct conscious attention to inputs matching a given pattern is a technique for making efficient use of limited cognitive resources.

Much of the psychology research on attention has investigated how inputs from our various senses are handled. It is known that they operate in parallel, and at some point there is a serial bottleneck, beyond which point it is not possible to continue processing input stimuli in parallel. The point at which this bottleneck occurs is a continuing subject of debate; there are early selection theories, late selection theories, and theories that combine the two.

A study by Rogers and Monsell investigated the impact of task switching on subject performance. Subjects were split into three groups; one group was given a letter classification task (is a letter a consonant or vowel), the second group a digit classification task (is the digit odd or even), and the third group had to alternate tasks (various combinations were used) between letter, and digit classification. The results found that having to alternate tasks slowed response times by 200 to 250 ms , and the error rates went up from between $2 - 3\%$, to between $6.0 - 7.6\%$. A study by Altmann [47] found that when the new task had many features in common with the previous task (e.g., switching from classifying numbers as odd or even, to classifying them as less than or greater than five) the memories for the related tasks interfered, causing a reduction in subject reaction time, and an increase in error rate.

2.3 Visual processing

Visual processing is of interest to software development because it consumes cognitive resources, and is a source of human error. The 2-D image falling on the retina does not contain enough information to build the 3-D model we see; the mind creates this model by making assumptions about how objects in our environment move and interact. [839]

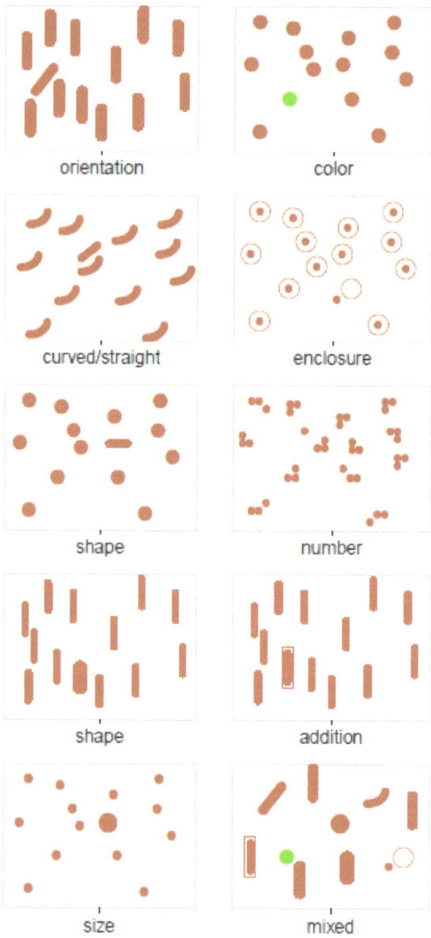

Figure 2.11: Examples of features that may be preattentively processed; when items having distinct features are mixed together, individual items no longer jump out.

The perceptual systems of organisms have evolved to detect information in the environment that is relevant to survival, and ignore the rest. The relevant information is about opportunities afforded by the world.

The human visual system contains various hardware systems dedicated to processing visual information; low level details are preprocessed to build structures having a higher level of abstraction, e.g., lines. Preattentive processing, so-called because it occurs before conscious attention, is automatic and apparently effortless. This preprocessing causes items to appear to pop-out from their surroundings. Figure 2.11 shows examples of items that pop-out at the reader.

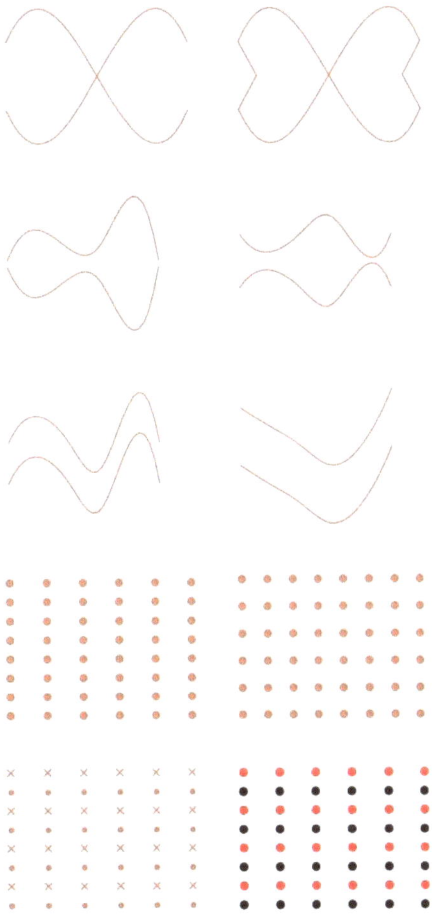

Figure 2.12: Continuity-upper left plot is perceived as two curved lines; Closure-when the two perceived lines are joined at their end (upper right), the perception changes to one of two cone-shaped objects; Symmetry and parallelism-where the direction taken by one line follows the same pattern of behavior as another line;

Proxim-ity-the horizontal distance between the dots in the lower left plot is less than the vertical distance, causing them to be perceptually grouped into lines (the relative distances are reversed in the right plot); Similarity-a variety of dimensions along which visual items can differ sufficiently to cause them to be perceived as being distinct; rotating two line segments by 180° does not create as big a perceived difference as rotating them by 45°. Github-Local

Preattentive processing is independent of the number of distractors; a search for the feature takes the same amount of time whether it occurs with one, five, ten, or more other distractors. However, it is only effective when the features being searched for are relatively rare. When a display contains many, distinct features (the mixed category in figure 2.11), the pop-out effect does not occur.

The Gestalt laws of perception ("gestalt" means "pattern" in German, also known as the laws of perceptual organization) are based on the underlying idea that the whole is different from the sum of its parts. These so-called laws do not have the rigour expected of a scientific law, and some other term ought to be used, e.g., principle. The Gestalt principles are preprogrammed (i.e., there is no conscious cognitive cost). The following are some commonly occurring principles:

- continuity, also known as good continuation: Lines and edges that can be seen as smooth and continuous are perceptually grouped together; figure 2.12 upper left,
- closure: elements that form a closed figure are perceptually grouped together; figure 2.12 upper right,
- symmetry: treating two, mirror image lines as though they form the outline of an object; figure 2.12 second row down. This effect can also occur for parallel lines,
- proximity: elements that are close together are perceptually grouped together; figure 2.12 second row up,
- similarity: elements that share a common attribute can be perceptually grouped together; figure 2.12 lower row,
- other: principles include grouping by connectedness, grouping by common region, and synchrony. [1441]

Visually grouping the elements in a display, using these principles, is a common human trait. However, different people can make different choices, when perceptually grouping of the same collection of items. Figure 2.13 shows items on a horizontal line, which readers may group by shape, color, or relative proximity. A study by Kubovy and van den Berg [1050] created a model that calculated the probability of a particular perceptual grouping (i.e., shape, color, or proximity in two dimensions) being selected for a given set of items.

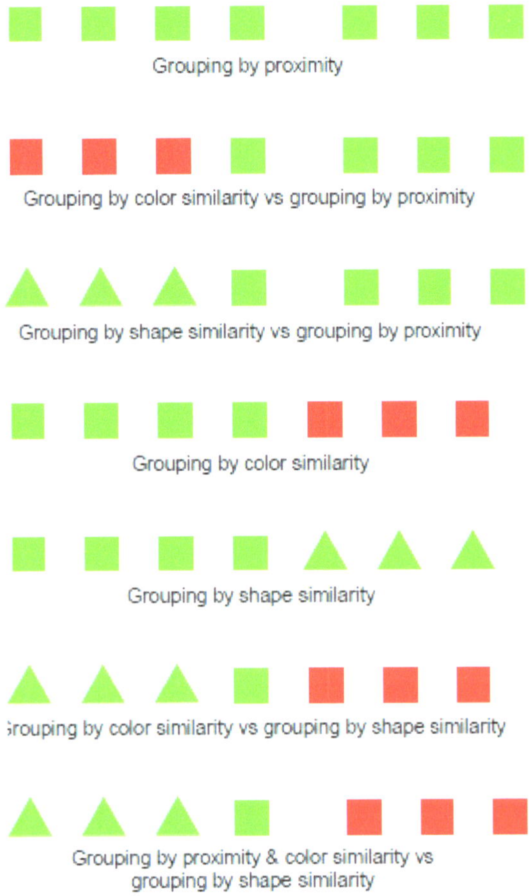

Figure 2.13: Perceived grouping of items on a line may be by shape, color or proximity. Based on Kubovy et al. Github-Local

Studies have found that when mapping the prose specification of a mathematical relationship to a formula, the visual proximity of applicable names has an impact on the error rate.

A study by Palmer, Horowitz, Torralba and Wolfe [1440] investigated the distribution of subject response times when searching for targets having varying degrees of distinctiveness from the surrounding items, and with varying numbers of surrounding items. Subjects each completed 400 trials locating a target among items sharing some visual characteristics with the target; in 50% of trials the target was not present. Figure

2.14 shows examples of the three tasks used, each containing a target that had various levels of distinctiveness from the other surrounding items.

Figure 2.14: Examples of the three tasks subjects were asked to solve. Left (RV GV): solid red rectangle having same alignment with outline green rectangle, middle (RV RHGV): solid vertical rectangle among solid horizontal rectangles and outlined vertical green rectangles, and right (2 5): digital 2 among digital 5s. Adapted from Palmer et al. Github-Local

Figure 2.15 shows the mean response time for each subject, when target was present (+ character) or absent (o character) from the display, along with fitted regression lines (solid when target present, dashed when absent).

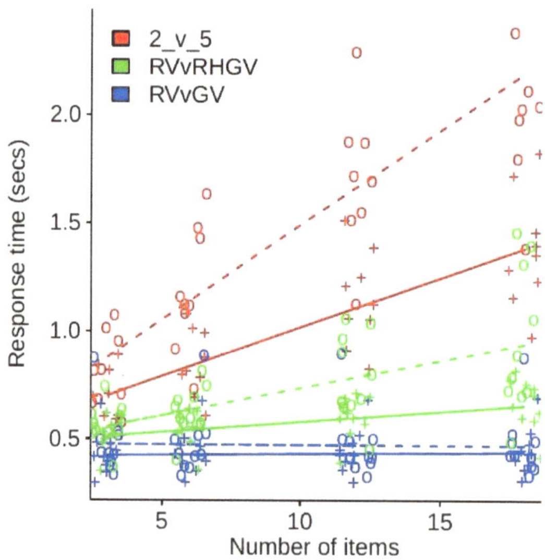

Figure 2.15: Average subject response time to find a target in an image containing a given number of items (x -axis), when target present (+ and solid line) and absent (o and dashed line); lines are fitted regression models. Data from Palmer et al.[1440] Github-Local

Depending on the visual characteristic, the search for an item may be sequential (e.g., shape, when many items share the same shapes), or have some degree of parallelism (e.g., color, when items have one of a few distinct colors); for an example, see figure 8.35.

Grouping by proximity & color similarity vs grouping by shape similarity

2.3.1 Reading

Building software systems involves a significant amount of reading. Research on the cognitive processes involved in reading prose, written in human languages, has uncovered the processes involved and various models have been built. [1564]

When reading prose, a person's eyes make short rapid movements, known as saccades, taking 20 ms to 50 ms to complete; a saccade typically moves the eyes forward 6 to 9 characters. No visual information is extracted during a saccade, and readers are not consciously aware of them. Between saccades the eyes are stationary, typically for 200 ms to 250 ms , these stationary periods are known as fixations. A study [1486] of consumer eye movements, while comparing multiple brands, found a fixation duration of 354 ms when subjects were under high time pressure and 431 ms when under low time pressure.

Individual readers can exhibit considerable variations in performance, a saccade might move the eyes by one character, or 15 to 20 characters; fixations can be shorter than 100 ms or longer than 400 ms (there is also variation between languages [1423]). The content of fixated text has a strong effect on performance.

The eyes do not always move forward during reading- 10% to 15% of saccades move the eyes back to previous parts of the text. These backward movements, called regressions, are caused by problems with linguistic processing (e.g., incorrect syntactic analysis of a sentence), and oculomotor error (e.g., the eyes overshooting their intended target).

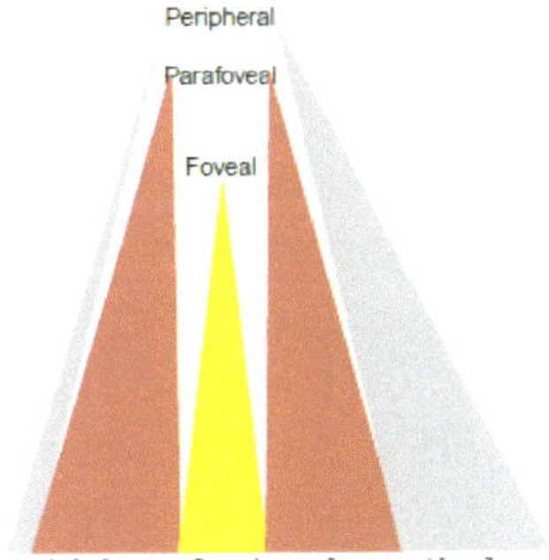

Figure 2.16: The foveal, parafoveal and peripheral vision regions when three characters visually subtend 3°. Based on Schotter et al. Github-Local

Saccades are necessary because the eyes' field of view is limited. Light entering an eye hits light-sensitive cells in the retina, where cells are not uniformly distributed. The visual field (on the retina) can be divided into three regions: foveal (the central 2°, measured from the front of the eye looking toward the retina), parafoveal (extending out to 5°), and peripheral (everything else); see figure 2.16. Letters become increasingly difficult to identify as their angular distance from the center of the fovea increases.

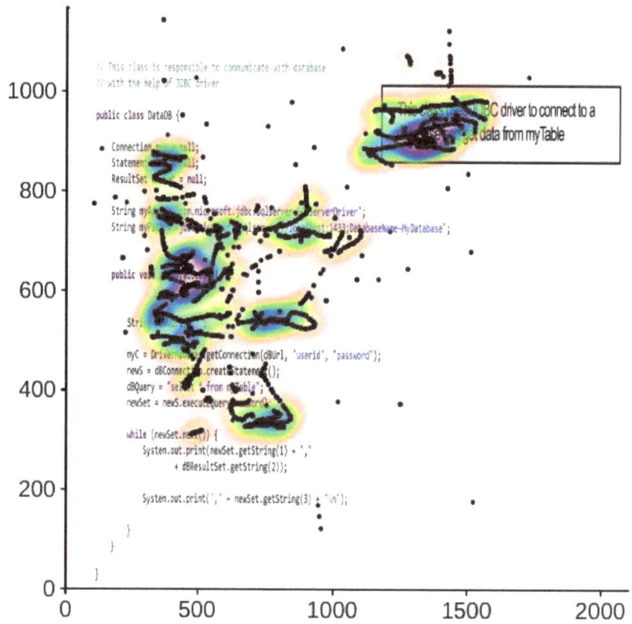

Figure 2.17: Heat map of one subject's cumulative fixations (black dots) on a screen image. Data kindly provided by Ali. Github-Local

During the fixation period, two processes are active: identifying the word (or sequence of letters forming a partial word), and planning the next saccade (when to make it and where to move the eyes). Reading performance is speed limited by the need to plan and perform saccades (removing the need to saccade, by presenting words at the same place on a display, results in a threefold speed increase in reading aloud, and a two-fold speed increase in silent reading). The time needed to plan and perform a saccade is approximately 180 ms – 200 ms (known as the saccade latency), which means the decision to make a saccade occurs within the first 100 ms of a fixation.

The contents of the parafoveal region are partially processed during reading, and this increases a reader's perceptual span. When reading words written using alphabetic characters, the perceptual span extends from 3 to 4 characters on the left of fixation, to 14 to 15 letters to the right of fixation. This asymmetry in the perceptual span is a result of the direction of reading, attending to letters likely to occur next is a cost effective use of resources. Readers of Hebrew (which is read right-to-left) have a perceptual span that has opposite asymmetry (in bilingual Hebrew/English readers the direction of the asymmetry depends on the language being read, showing the importance of attention during reading). [1563]

Characteristics used by the writing system affect the asymmetry of the perceptual span and its width, e.g., the span can be smaller for Hebrew than English (Hebrew words can be written without the vowels, requiring greater effort to decode and plan the next saccade). It is also much smaller for writing systems that use ideographs, such as Japanese (approximately 6 characters to the right) and Chinese.

The perceptual span is not hardwired, but is attention-based. The span can become smaller when the fixated words become difficult to process. Also, readers extract more information in the direction of reading when the upcoming word is highly predictable (based on the preceding text).

Models of reading that have achieved some level of success include: Mr. Chips [1109] is an ideal-observer model of reading (it is not intended to model how humans read, but to establish the pattern of performance, when optimal use is made of available information), which attempts to calculate the distance, in characters, of the next saccade. It combines information from visual data obtained by sampling the text through a retina, lexical knowledge of words and their relative frequencies, and motor knowledge of the statistical accuracy of saccades, and uses the optimization principle of entropy minimization. The SWIFT model [544] attempts to provide a realistic model of saccade generation, while E-Z Reader [1503] attempts to account for how cognitive and lexical processes influence the eye movements of skilled readers (it can handle the complexities of garden path sentences [1571iv]).

English text is read left to right, on lines that go down the page. The order in which the components of a formula are read depends on its contents, with the visual processing of subexpressions by experienced users driven by the mathematical syntax, with the extraction of syntax happening in parallel. Studies have started to investigate the functional areas of the brain involved in processing expressions.

A study by Pelli, Burns, Farell, and Moore [1463] found that 2,000 to 4,000 trials were all that was needed for novice readers to reach the same level of efficiency as fluent readers in the letter-detection task (efficiency was measured by comparing human performance compared to an ideal observer). They tested subjects aged 3 to 68 with a range of different (and invented) alphabets (including Hebrew, Devanagari, Arabic and English). Even fifty years of reading experience, over a billion letters, did not improve the efficiency of letter detection. They also found this measure of efficiency was inversely proportional to letter perimetric complexity (defined as: inside and outside perimeter squared, divided by ink area).

The choice of display font is a complex issue. The use of Roman, rather than Helvetica (or serif vs. sans serif), is often claimed to increase reading speed and comprehension. The issues involved in selecting fonts are covered in a report detailing "Font Requirements for Next Generation Air Traffic Management Systems". Vision provides information about what people are thinking about; gaze follows shifts of visual attention. Tracking a subject's eye movements and fixations, when viewing images or real-life scenes, is an established technique in fields such as marketing and reading research. This technique is now starting to be used in research of developer code reading; see figure 2.17.

2.4 Memory systems

Memory evolved to supply useful, timely information to an organism's decision-making systems, [1021] subject to evolutionary constraints. Memory subsystems are scattered about the brain, with each subsystem/location believed to process and store distinct kinds of information. Figure 2.18 shows a current model of known long-term memory subsystems, along with the region of the brain where they are believed to operate.

Declarative memory has two components, each processing specific instances of information, one handles facts about the world, while the other, episodic memory, deals with events (i.e., the capacity to experience an event in the context in which it occurred; it is not known if non-human brains support episodic memory). We are consciously aware of declarative memory, facts and events can be consciously recalled; it is the kind of memory that is referred to in everyday usage as memory. Declarative memory is representational, it contains information that can be true or false.

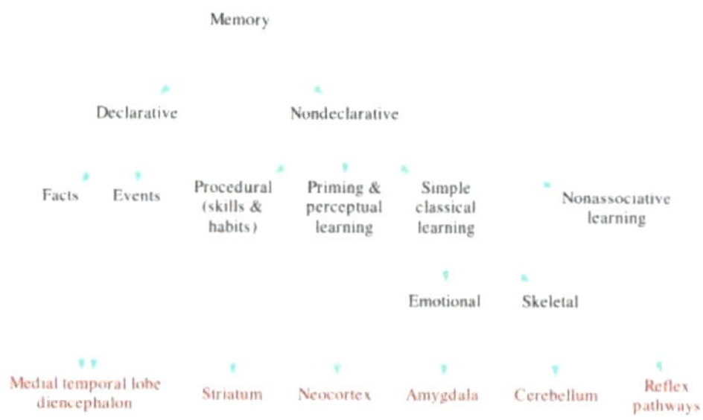

Figure 2.18: Structure of mammalian long-term memory subsystems; brain areas in red. Based on Squire et al.

Nondeclarative memory (also known as implicit memory) extracts information from recurring instances of an experience, to form skills (e.g., speaking a language) and habits, simple forms of conditioning, priming (i.e., response to a stimulus is modified by a preceding stimulus; an advantage in a slowly changing environment, where similar events are likely to occur on a regular basis), and perceptual learning (i.e., gradual improvement in the detection or discrimination of visual stimuli with practice).

Information in nondeclarative memory is extracted through unconscious performance, e.g., riding a bike. It is an unconscious memory and is not available for conscious recall; information use requires reactivation of the subsystem where the learning originally occurred.

These subsystems operate independently and in parallel, the parallelism creates the possibility of conflicting signals being fed as inputs to higher level systems. For instance, a sentence containing the word blue may be misinterpreted because information about the word, and the color in which it appears, green, is returned by different memory subsystems (known as the Stroop effect).

A Stroop-like effect has also been found to occur with lists of numbers. Readers might like to try counting the number of characters occurring in each row in the outside margin. The effort of counting the digit sequences is likely to be greater, and more error prone, than for the letter sequences.

Studies have found that when subjects are asked to enumerate visually presented digits, the amount of Stroop-like interference depends on the arithmetic difference between the magnitude of the digits used, and the quantity of those digits displayed. Thus, a short, for instance, list of large numbers is read more quickly, and with fewer errors, than a short list of small numbers. Alternatively a long list of small numbers (much smaller than the list length) is read more quickly, and with fewer errors, than a long list of numbers where the number has a similar magnitude than the length of the list.

Making use of patterns that can be seen in the environment is one technique for reducing memory load.

Studies have found that people organize their memory for objects within their visual field according to the relative positions of the objects. A study by McNamara, Hardy, and Hirtle [1247] gave subjects two minutes to memorize the location of objects on the floor of a room; see figure 2.19, upper plot. The objects were then placed in a box, and subjects were asked to replace the objects in their original position; the memorize/recall cycle was repeated, using the same layout, until the subject could place all objects in their correct position.

The order in which each subject recalled the location of objects was mapped to a hierarchical tree (one for each subject). The resulting trees (see figure 2.19, lower plot) showed how subjects' spatial memory of the objects had an organization based on spatial distance between items.

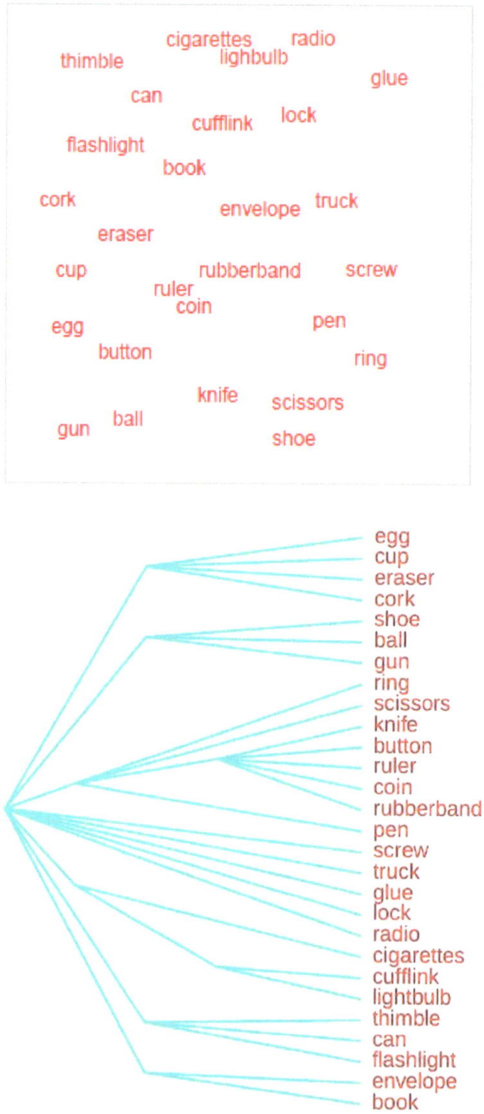

Figure 2.19: Example object layout, and the corresponding ordered tree produced from the answers given by one subject. Data extracted from McNamara et al. [1247] Github-Local

Other research on the interaction between human memory and software development includes: a study [46] which built a computational process model, based on SOAR, and fitted it to 10.5 minutes of programmer activity (debugging within an emacs window); the simulation was used to study the memories built up while trying to solve a problem.

2.4.1 Short term memory

As its name implies, short term memory (STM) is a memory system that can hold information for short periods of time. Short term memory is the popular term for what cognitive psychologists call working memory, named after its function, rather than the relative duration holds information. Early researchers explored its capacity, and a paper by Miller became the citation source for the now-famous 7 ± 2 rule (Miller did not propose 7 ± 2 as the capacity of STM, but simply drew attention to the fact that this range of values fitted the results of several experiments). Things have moved on in the 65+ years since the publication of his paper, [928] with benchmarks now available for evaluating models of STM. [1400]

Readers might like to try measuring their STM capacity, using the list of numbers in the outside margin. Any Chinese-speaking readers can try this exercise twice, using the English and Chinese words for the digits (use of Chinese should enable readers to apparently increase the capacity of their STM). Slowly and steadily read the digits in a row, out loud. At the end of each row, close your eyes and try to repeat the sequence of digits in the same order. If you make a mistake, go on to the next row. The point at which you cannot correctly remember the digits in any two rows, of a given length, indicates your capacity limit, i.e., the number of digits in the previous two rows.

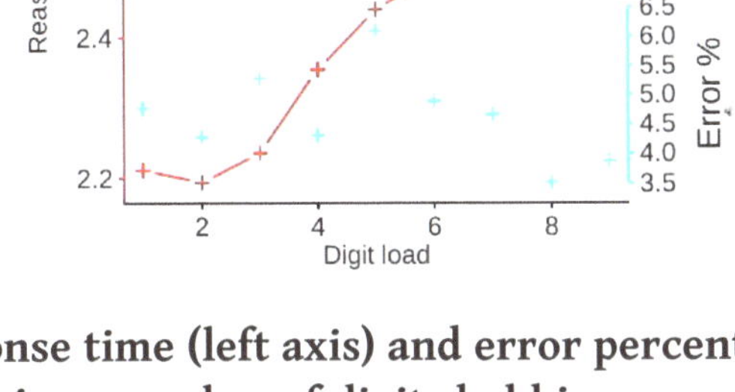

Figure 2.20: Response time (left axis) and error percentage (right axis) on reasoning task with a given number of digits held in memory. Data extracted from Baddeley. [111] Github-Local

The performance impact of reduced working memory capacity can be shown by having people perform two tasks simultaneously. A study by Baddeley [111] measured the time taken to solve a simple reasoning task (e.g., $B \rightarrow A$, question: "A follows B" True or False?), while remembering a sequence of digits (the number of digits is known as the digit load). Figure 2.20 shows response time (left axis) and percentage of incorrect answers (right axis) for various digit loads.

Measuring memory capacity using lists of digits relies on a variety of assumptions, such as assuming all items consume the same amount of memory resources (e.g., digits and letters are interchangeable), that relative item ordering is implicitly included in the measurement and that individual concepts are the unit of storage. Subsequent studies have completely reworked models of STM. What the preceding exercise measured was the amount of sound that could be held in STM. The spoken sound used to represent digits in Chinese is shorter than in English, and using Chinese should enable readers to maintain information on more digits (average 9.9 [852]) using the same amount of sound storage. A reader using a language in which the spoken sound of digits is longer, can maintain information on fewer digits, e.g., average 5.8 in Welsh, [542] and the average for English is 6.6.

Observations of a 7 ± 2 capacity limit derive from the number of English digits spoken in two seconds of sound (people speak at different speeds, which is one source of variation included in the ± 2; an advantage for fast talkers). The two seconds estimate is based on the requirement to remember items, and their relative order; the contents of STM do not get erased after two seconds, this limit is the point at which degradation of its contents start to become noticeable. [1321] If recall of item order is not relevant, then the limit increases because loss of this information is not relevant.

Studies [1401] involving multiple tasks have been used to distinguish the roles played by various components of working memory (e.g., storage, processing, supervision and coordination). Figure 2.21 shows the components believed to make up working memory, each with its own independent temporary storage areas, each holding and using information in different ways.

The central executive is assumed to be the system that handles attention, controlling the phonological loop, the visuo-spatial sketch pad, and the interface to long-term memory. The central executive needs to remember information while performing tasks, such as text comprehension and problem-solving. It has been suggested that the focus of attention is capacity-limited, but that the other temporary storage areas are time-limited (without attention to rehearse them, they fade away).

26
12

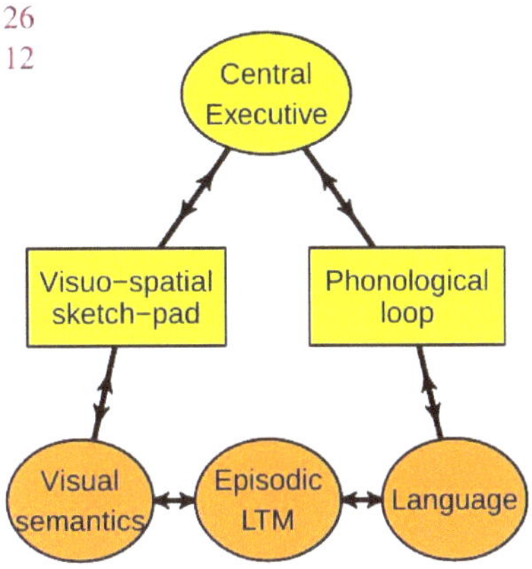

Figure 2.21: Major components of working memory: working memory in yellow, long-term memory in orange. Based on Baddeley. [112] Github-Local

Visual information held in the visuo-spatial sketch pad decays very rapidly. Experiments have shown that people can recall four or five items immediately after they are presented with visual information, but that this recall rate drops very quickly after a few seconds.

Mental arithmetic provides an example of how different components of working memory can be combined to solve a problem that is difficult to achieve using just one component; for example, multiply 23 by 15 without looking at this page. Information about the two numbers, and the intermediate results, has to be held in short term memory and the central executive. Now perform another multiplication, but this time look at the two numbers being multiplied (see outer margin for values), while performing the multiplication. Looking at the numbers reduces the load on working memory by removing the need to remember them.

Table 2.2 contains lists of words; those at the top of the table contain a single syllable, those at the bottom multiple syllables. Readers should have no problems remembering a sequence of five single-syllable words, a sequence of five multi-syllable words is likely to be more difficult. As before, read each word, going down a list, slowly out loud.

Making an analogy between phonological loop and a loop of tape in a tape recorder, suggests that it might only be possible to extract information as it goes past a read-out point. A study by Sternberg asked subjects to hold a sequence of digits in memory, e.g., 4185, and measured the time taken to respond yes/no, about whether a particular digit was in the sequence. Figure 2.22 shows that as the number of digits increases, the time taken for subjects to respond increases; another result was that response time was not affected by whether the answer was yes or no. It might be expected that a yes answer would enable searching to terminate, but the behavior found suggests that all digits were always being compared. Different kinds of information has different search response times. [309]

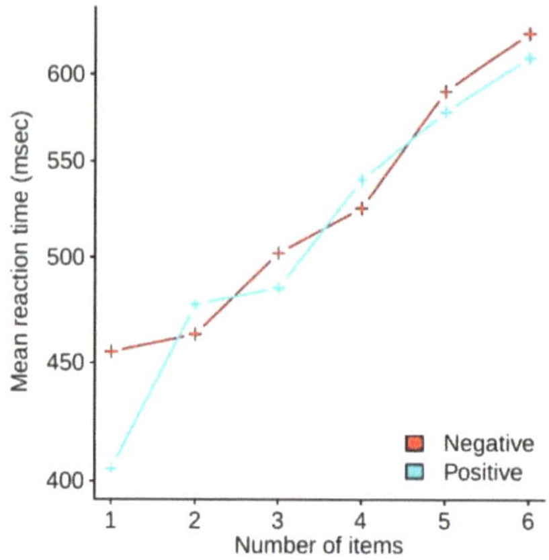

Figure 2.22: Yes/no response time (in milliseconds) as a function of number of digits held in memory. Data extracted from Sternberg. Github-Local

Table 2.2: Words with either one or more than one syllable (and thus varying in the length of time taken to speak).

List 1	List 2	List 3	List 4	List 5
one	cat	card	harm	add
bank	lift	list	bank	mark
sit	able	inch	view	bar
kind	held	act	fact	few
look	mean	what	time	sum
ability	basically	encountered	laboratory	commitment
particular	yesterday	government	acceptable	minority
mathematical	department	financial	university	battery
categorize	satisfied	absolutely	meaningful	opportunity
inadequate	beautiful	together	carefully	accidental

Extrapolating the results from studies based on the use of natural language, to the use of computer languages, needs to take into account that reader performance has been found to differ between words (character sequences having a recognized use in the reader's native human language) and non-words, e.g., naming latency is lower for words, [1939] and more words can be held in short term memory, i.e., $\text{word\_span} = 2.4 + 2.05 \times \text{speech\_rate}$, and $\text{nonword\_span} = 0.7 + 2.27 \times \text{speech\_rate}$.

The ability to comprehend syntactically complex sentences is correlated with working memory capacity. A study by Miller and Isard investigated subjects' ability to memorize sentences that varied in their degree of embedding. The following sentences have increasing amounts of embedding (figure 2.23 shows the parse-tree of two of them):

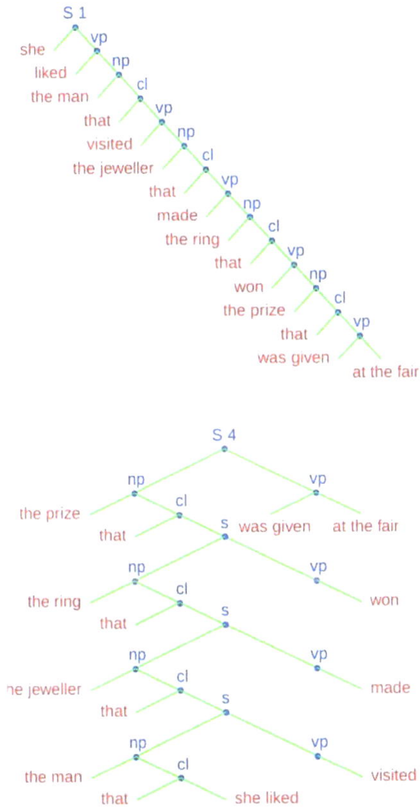

Figure 2.23: Parse tree of a sentence with no embedding, upper "S 1", and a sentence with four degrees of embedding, lower "S 4". Based on Miller et al. [1285]
Github-Local

She liked the man that visited the jeweller that made the ring that won the prize that was given at the fair.

The man that she liked visited the jeweller that made the ring that won the prize that was given at the fair.

The jeweller that the man that she liked visited made the ring that won the prize that was given at the fair.

The ring that the jeweller that the man that she liked visited made won the prize that was given at the fair.

The prize that the ring that the jeweller that the man that she liked visited made won was given at the fair.

Subjects' ability to correctly recall wording decreased as the amount of embedding increased, although performance did improve with practice. People have significant comprehension difficulties when the degree of embedding in a sentence exceeds two. [210]

Human language has a grammatical structure that enables it to be parsed serially, e.g., as it is spoken. [1482] One consequence of this expected characteristic of sentences is that so called garden path sentences (where one or more words at the end of a sentence changes the parsing of words read earlier) generate confusion that requires conscious effort to reason about what has been said. Examples of garden path sentences include:

The old train their dogs. The patient persuaded the doctor that he was having trouble with to leave. While Ron was sewing the sock fell on the floor. Joe put the candy in the jar into my mouth. The horse raced past the barn fell.

A study by Mathy, Chekaf and Cowan [1221] investigated the impact, on subject performance, of various patterns in a list of items to be remembered. Figure 2.24, upper plot, shows an example of how items on a list might share one or more of the attributes: color, shape or size. A list was said to be "chunkable", if its items shared attributes in a way that enabled subjects to reduce the amount of item specific information they needed to remember (e.g., all purple, small/large, triangle then circle). The items on a "non-chunkable" list did not share attributes in a way that reduced the amount of information that needed to be remembered. A chunkability value was calculated for each list.

In the simple span task subjects saw a list of items, and after a brief delay had to recall the items on the list. In the complex span task, subjects saw a list of items, and had to judge the correctness of a simple arithmetic expression, before recalling the list.

An item span score was calculated for each subject, based on the number of items correctly recalled from each list they saw (the chunkability of the list was included in the calculation). Figure 2.24, lower plot, shows the mean span over all subjects, with corresponding standard deviation.

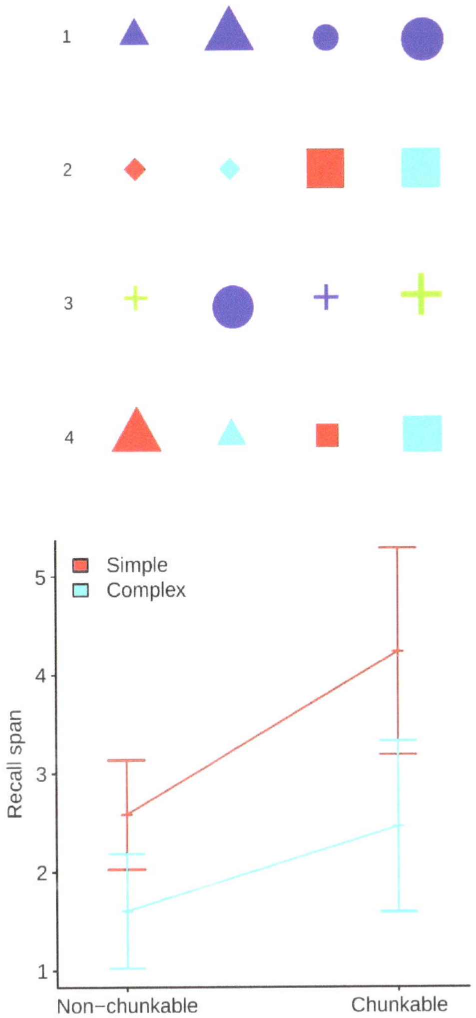

Figure 2.24: Examples of the kind of pattern of symbol sequence stimuli seen by subjects (upper); mean span over all subjects, with standard deviation (lower). Data from Mathy

The two competing models for loss of information in working memory are: [580] passive decay (information fades away unless a person consciously spends time rehearsing or refreshing it), and interference with new incoming information (a person has to consciously focus attention on particular information to prevent interference with new information).

2.4.2 Episodic memory

Episodic memory is memory for personally experienced events that are remembered as such, i.e., the ability to recollect specific events or episodes in our lives. When the remembered events occurred sometime ago, the term autobiographical memory is sometimes used.

What impact does the passage of time have on episodic memories?

A study by Altmann, Trafton and Hambrick [48] investigated the effects of interruption on a task involving seven steps. Subjects performed the same task 37 times, and were interrupted at random intervals during the 30 – 50 minutes it took to complete the session. Interruptions required subjects to perform a simple typing task that took, on average, 2.8, 13,22 or 32 seconds (i.e., a very short to long interruption).

Figure 2.25 shows the percentage of sequencing errors made immediately after an interruption, and under normal working conditions (in red; sequence error rate without interruptions in green). A sequence error occurs when an incorrect step is performed, e.g., step 5 is performed again, having already performed step 5, when step 6 should have been performed; the offset on the x -axis is the difference between the step performed, and the one that should have been performed.

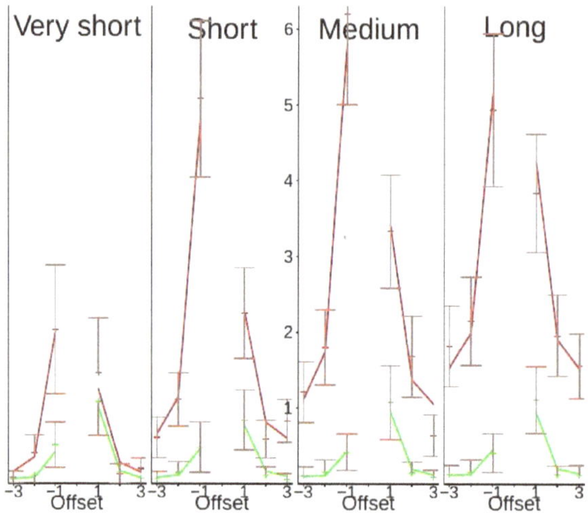

Figure 2.25: Sequencing errors (as percentage), after interruptions of various length (red), including 95% confidence intervals, sequence error rate without interruptions in green; lines are fitted model predictions. Data from Altmann et al. Github-Local

The sequence error rate, as a percentage of total number of tasks performed at each interruption interval, was 2.4,3.6,4.6 and 5.1%. The lines are predictions made by a model fitted to the data.

2.4.3 Recognition and recall

Recognition memory is the ability to recognise previously encountered items, events or information. Studies [1036] have found that people can often make a reasonably accurate judgement about whether they know a piece of information or not, even if they are unable to recall that information at a particular instant; the so-called feeling of knowing is a good predictor of subsequent recall of information,

Recall memory is the ability to retrieve previously encountered items, events or information. Studies have investigated factors that influence recall performance [267] (e.g., the structure of the information to be remembered, associations between new and previously learned information, and the interval between learning and recall), techniques for improving recall performance, and how information might be organized in memory.

The environment in which information was learned can have an impact on recall performance. A study by Godden and Baddeley [688] investigated subjects' recall of words memorized in two different environments. Subjects were divers, who learned a list of spoken words, either while submerged underwater wearing scuba apparatus, or while sitting at a table on dry land. The results found that subject recall performance was significantly better, when performed in the environment in which the word list was learned.

When asked to retrieve members of a category, people tend to produce a list of semantically related items, before switching to list another cluster of semantically related items and so on. This pattern of retrieval is similar to that seen in strategies of optimal food foraging, [830] however the same behavior can also emerge from a random walk on a semantic network built from human word-association data. [2]

Figure 2.26: Semantic memory representation of alphabetic letters (the numbers listed along the top are place markers and are not stored in subject memory).

Readers may recognize the structure of a nursery rhyme in the letter sequences. Derived from Klahr. Github-Local

Chunking is a technique commonly used by people to help them remember information. A chunk is a small set of items (4 ± 1 is seen in many studies) having a common, strong, association with each other (and a much weaker one to items in other chunks). For instance, Wickelgren [1953] found that people's recall of telephone numbers is optimal, if numbers are grouped into chunks of three digits. An example, using random-letter sequences is: fbicbsibmirs. The trigrams (fbi, cbs, ibm, irs), within this sequence of 12 letters, are well-known acronyms in the U.S.A. A person who notices this association can use it to aid recall. Several theoretical analyses of memory organizations have shown that chunking of items improves search efficiency (optimal chunk size $3-4$, [502] number items at which chunking becomes more efficient than a single list, $5-7$[1183]).

A study by Klahr, Chase, and Lovelace [1017] investigated how subjects stored letters of the alphabet in memory. Through a series of time-to-respond measurements, where subjects were asked to name the letter that appeared immediately before or after the presented probe letter, they proposed the alphabet-storage structure shown in figure 2.26.

2.4.3.1 Serial order information

Information about the world is processed serially. Studies [879] have consistently found a variety of patterns in recall of serial information (studies often involve recalling items from a recently remembered list), patterns regularly found include:

- higher probability of recall for items at the start (the primacy effect) and end (the recency effect) of a list (known as the serial position effect; [1331] see figure 2.27). The probability that an item will be remembered as occupying position i, at time $t+1$, is approximately given by, [1349] for interior positions: $P_{i,t+1} = (1-\theta)P_{i,t} + \frac{\theta}{2}P_{i-1,t} + \frac{\theta}{2}P_{i+1,t}$, and for the first item: $P_{1,t+1} = \left(1-\frac{\theta}{2}\right)P_{1,t} + \frac{\theta}{2}P_{2,t}$, and similarly for the last time. One study, [1349] involving lists of five words, found that using $\theta = 0.12$, for each 2 -hour retention interval, produced predictions in reasonable agreement with the experimental data (more accurate models have been created [267]),

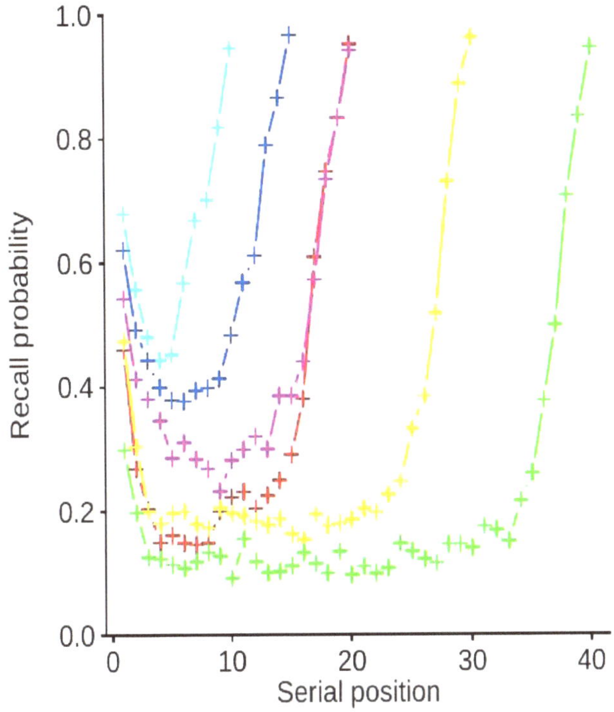

Figure 2.27: Probability of correct recall of words, by serial presentation order; for lists of length 10, 15 and 20 each word visible for 1 , for lists of length 20,30 and 40 each word visible for 2 seconds. Data from Murdoch, via Brown. Github-Local

- recall of a short list tends to start with the first item, and progress in order through the list, while for a long list people are more likely to start with one of the last four items. [1926] When prompted by an entry on the list people are most likely to recall the item following it; [862] see Github-developers/misc/HKJEP99.R,

- when recalling items from an ordered list, people tend to make anticipation errors (i.e., recall a later item early), shifting displaced items further along the list. [579]

A method's parameters have a serial order, and the same type may appear multiple times within the parameter list.

A study by Chekaf, Gauvrit, Guida, and Mathy [341] investigated subjects' recall performance of a sequence of similar items. Subjects saw a sequence of colored dots, each dot visible for less than a second, and had to recall the presented sequence of colors. The number of colors present in a sequence varied from two to four, and the sequence length varied from two to ten.

Figure 2.28 shows the proportion of correctly recalled dot sequences of a given length, containing a given number of colors; lines are fitted Beta regression models.

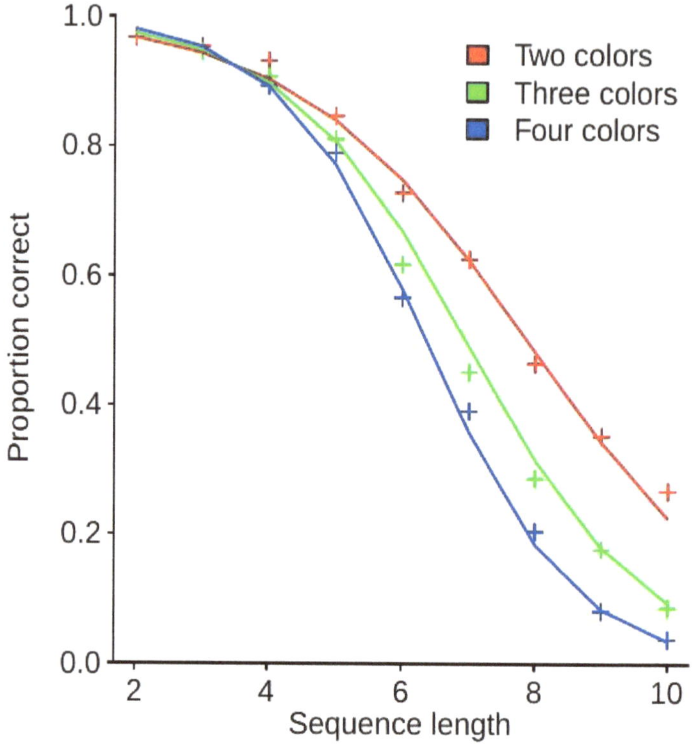

Figure 2.28: Proportion of correctly recalled colored dot sequences of a given length, containing a given number of colors; lines are fitted regression models. Data kindly provided by Chekaf. Github-Local

A study by Adelson [9] investigated the organization present in subject's recall order of previously remembered lines of code. Subjects saw a total of 16 lines of code, one line at a time, and were asked to memorise each line for later recall. The lines were taken from three simple programs (two containing five lines each and one containing six lines), the program order being randomised for each subject. Five subjects were students who had recently taken a course involving the language used, and five subjects had recently taught a course using the language.

Subjects were free to recall the previously seen lines in any order. An analysis of recall order showed that students grouped lines by syntactic construct (e.g., loop, function header), while the course teachers recalled the lines in the order in which they appeared in the three programs (i.e., they reconstructed three programs from the 16 randomly ordered lines); see figure 2.29.

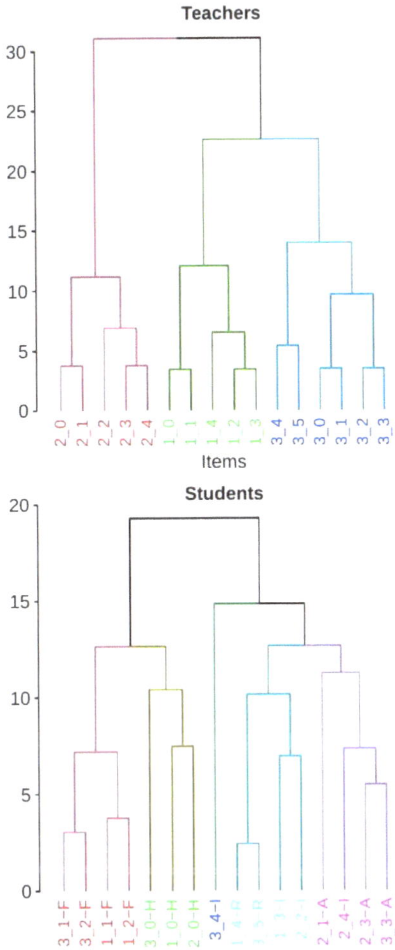

Figure 2.29: Hierarchical clustering of statement recall order, averaged over teachers and students; label names are: program_list-statementkind, where statementkind might be a function header, loop, etc. Data extracted from Adelson. Github-Local

A study by Pennington found that developers responded slightly faster to questions about a source code statement when its immediately preceding statement made use of closely related variables.

2.4.4 Forgetting

People are unhappy when they forget things; however, not forgetting may be a source of unhappiness. The Russian mnemonist Shereshevskii found that his ability to remember everything cluttered up his mind. [1175] Having many similar, not recently used, pieces of information matching during a memory search can be counterproductive; forgetting is a useful adaptation. For instance, a driver returning to a car wants to know where it was last parked, not the location of all previous parking locations. It has been proposed that human memory is optimized for information retrieval based on the statistical properties of the likely need for the information, in peoples' everyday lives (which, these days, includes the pattern of book borrowings from libraries). The rate at which the mind forgets seems to mirror the way that information tends to lose its utility, over time, in the world in which we live. Organizational forgetting is discussed in section 3.4.5.

Some studies of forgetting have found that a power law is a good fit to the reduction, over time, in subjects' ability to correctly recall information, while results from other studies are better fitted by an exponential equation (over the measurement range of many experiments, the difference between the two fitted models is usually small). [v] As more experimental data has become available, more complicated models have been proposed. [1257]

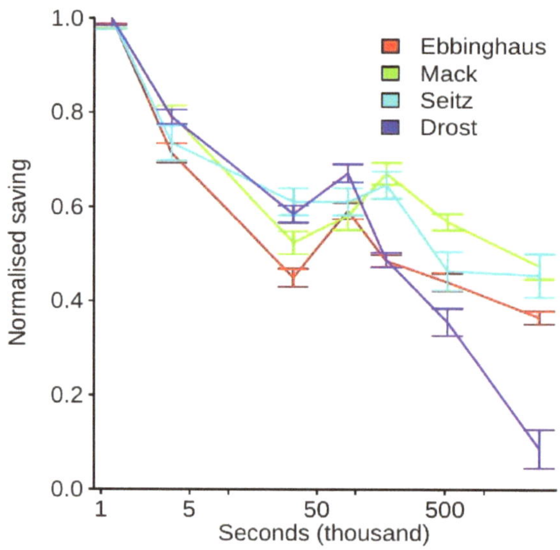

Figure 2.30: Fraction of relearning time saved (normalised) after given interval since original learning; original Ebbinghaus study and three replications (with standard errors). Data from Murre et al. Github-Local

A study by Ebbinghaus, [526] using himself as a subject, performed what has become a classic experiment in forgetting. The measure of learning and forgetting used was based on the relative time saved, when relearning previously learned information, compared to the time taken to first learn the information. Ebbinghaus learned lists of 104 nonsense syllables, with intervals between relearning of 20 minutes, 1 hour, 9 hours, 1 day, 2 days, 6 days and 31 days. Figure 2.30 shows the fraction of time saved, after a given duration, when relearning list contents to the original learned standard (with standard errors).

Another measure of information retention was used in a study by Rubin, Hinton and Wenzel. [1616] Subjects saw a pair of words on a screen, which they had to remember; later, when the first word appeared on the screen, they had to type the second word of the pair. Subjects saw a sequence of different word pairs; lag is defined as the number of words seen between first seeing a word pair and being asked to give the second word in response to the appearance of the first word of the pair.

Figure 2.31 shows the fraction of correct second words at various lag intervals. The red line is a fitted bi-exponential regression model, with blue and green lines showing its two exponential components.

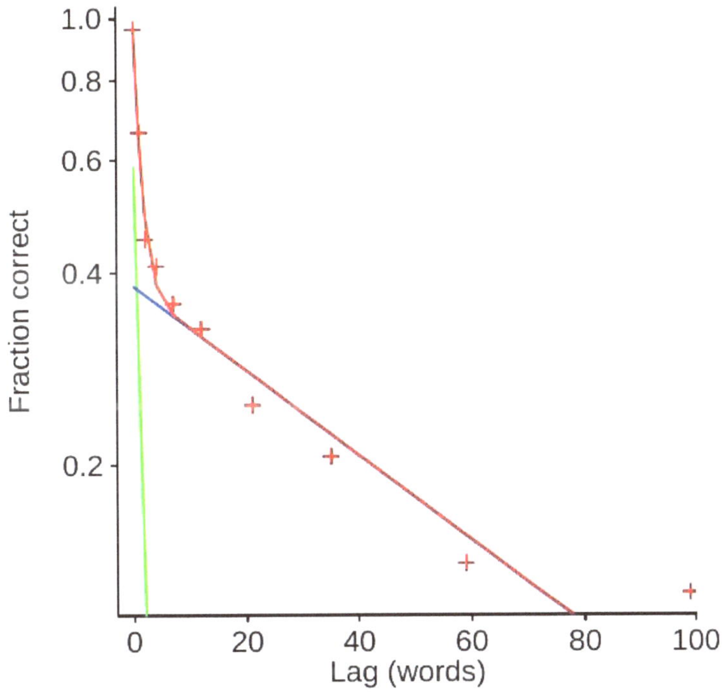

Figure 2.31: Fraction of correct subject responses, with fitted bi-exponential model in red (blue and green lines are its two exponential components). Data from Rubin et al. Github-Local

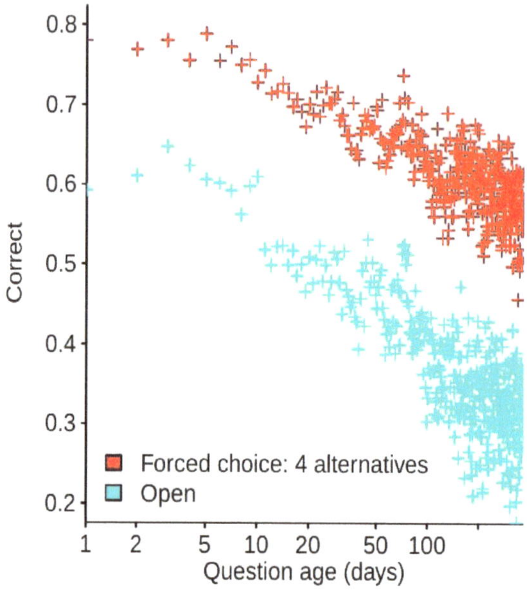

Figure 2.32: Fraction of news items correctly recalled each day, after a given number of days since the event; Forced choice of one alternative from four, and Open requiring an answer with no suggestions provided. Data from Meeter et al. Github-Local

A study by Meeter, Murre and Janssen investigated the likelihood of prominent of news stories being correctly recalled over a period of 16 months. The questions subjects were asked had two possible forms: forced choice, where four possible answers were listed and one had to be selected, and: open, where an answer had to be provided with no suggestions listed. Data was collected from 14,000 people, via an internet news test. Figure 2.32 shows the fraction of correct answers each day, against time elapsed since the event in the question was reported.

2.5 Learning and experience

Humans are characterized by an extreme dependence on culturally transmitted information.

People have the ability to learn, and on many tasks human performance improves with practice, e.g., time taken to deciding whether a character sequence is an English word. [991] Many studies have fitted a power law to measurements of practice performance (the term power law of learning is often used). If chunking is assumed to play a role in learning, a power law is a natural consequence; [1370] the equation has the form: [vi]

$RT = a + bN^{-c}$, where: RT is the response time, N the number of times the task has been performed, and a, b, and c are constants obtained by model fitting.

There are also theoretical reasons for expecting the measurements to be fitted by an exponential equation, and this form of model has been fitted to many learning data sets; [797] the equation has the form: [vii]

$RT = a + be^{-cN}$ Both equations often provide good enough fits to the available data, and without more measurements than is usually available, it is not possible to show one is obviously better than the other.

Implicit learning occurs when people perform a task containing information that is not explicitly obvious to those performing it. A study by Reber and Kassin [1567] compared implicit and explicit pattern detection. Subjects were asked to memorize sets of words, with the words in some sets containing letter sequences generated using a finite state grammar. One group of subjects thought they were just taking part in a purely memorybased experiment, while the second group were told of the existence of a letter sequence pattern in some words, and that it would help their performance if they could deduce this pattern. The performance of the two groups, on the different sets of words (i.e., pattern words only, pattern plus non-pattern words, non-pattern words only), matched each other. Without being told to do so, subjects had used patterns in the words to help perform the memorization task.

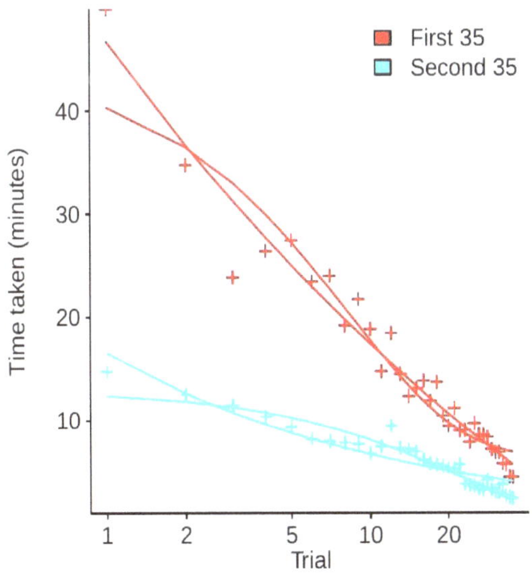

Figure 2.33: Time taken to solve the same jig-saw puzzle 35 times, followed by a two-week interval and then another 35 times, with power law and exponential fits. Data extracted from Alteneder. Github-Local

Explicit learning occurs when the task contains patterns that are apparent, and can be remembered and used on subsequent performances. A study by Alteneder [45] recorded the time taken, by the author, to solve the same jig-saw puzzle 35 times (over a four-day period). After two weeks, the same puzzle was again solved 35 times. Figure 2.33 shows both a fitted power law and exponential; the exponent of the fitted power law, for the first series, is -0.5

Social learning, learning from others, is discussed in section 3.4.4, and organizational learning is discussed in section 3.4.5.

For simple problems, learning can result in the solution being committed to memory; performance is then driven by reaction-time, i.e., the time needed to recall and give the response. Logan [1156] provides an analysis of subject performance on these kinds of problems.

The amount of practice needed to learn any patterns present in a task (to be able to perform it), depends on the complexity of the patterns. A study by Kruschke [1047] asked subjects to learn the association between a stimulus and a category; they were told that the category was based on height and/or position, During the experiment subjects were told whether they had selected the correct category for the stimulus. When the category involved a single attribute (i.e., one of height or location), learning was predicted to be faster, compared to when it involved two attributes, i.e., learning difficulty depends on the number of variables and states.

Figure 2.34 shows the probability of a correct answer, for a particular kind of stimulus (only height or position, and some combination of height and position), for eight successive blocks of eight stimulus/answer responses.

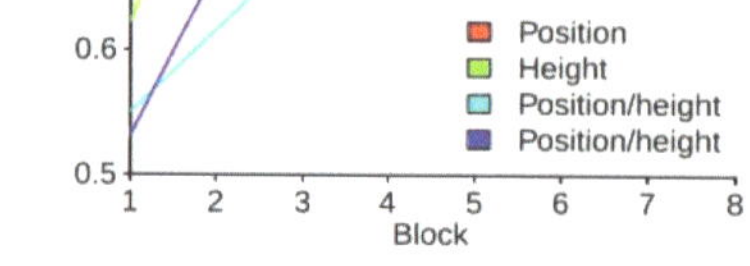

Figure 2.34: Probability of assigning a stimulus to the correct category, where the category involved: height, position, and a combination of both height and position. Data from Kruschke. Github-Local

The patterns present in a task may change. What impact do changes in task characteristics have on performance? A study by Kruschke [1048] asked subjects to learn the association between a stimulus and a category described by three characteristics (which might be visualized in a 3-D space; see fig 2.46). Once their performance was established at close to zero errors, the characteristics of the category were changed. The change pattern was drawn from four possibilities: reversing the value of each characteristic (considered to be a zero-dimension change), changes to one characteristic, two characteristics and three characteristics (not reversal).

Figure 2.35 shows average subject performance improving to near perfect (over 22 successive blocks of eight stimulus/answer responses), a large performance drop when the category changes, followed by improving performance, over successive blocks, as subjects learn the new category. The change made to the pattern for the learned category has a noticeable impact on the rate at which the new category is learned.

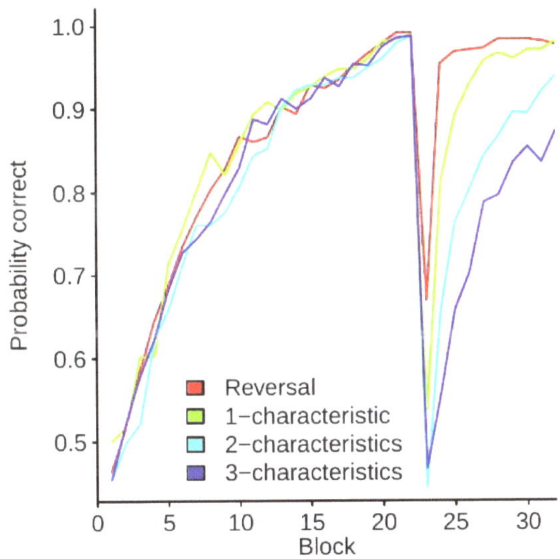

Figure 2.35: Probability of assigning a stimulus to the correct category; learning the category, followed in block 23 by a change in the characteristics of the learned category. Data from Kruschke. Github-Local

The source code for an application does not have to be rewritten every time somebody wants a new copy of the program; it is rare for a developer to be asked to reimplement exactly the same application again. However, having the same developer reimplement the same application, multiple times, provides information about the reduced implementation time that occurs with practice.

A study by Lui and Chan [1168] asked 24 developers to implement the same application four times; 16 developers worked in pairs (i.e., eight pair programming teams) and eight worked solo. Before starting to code, the subjects took a test involving 50 questions from a computer aptitude test; subjects were ranked by number of correct answers, and pairs selected such that both members were adjacent in the ranking.

Learning occurs every-time the application is implemented, and forgetting occurs during the period between implementations (each implementation occurred on a separate weekend, with subjects doing other work during the week) . Each subject had existing knowledge and skill, which means everybody started the experiment at a different point on the learning curve. In the following analysis the test score is used as a proxy for each subject's initial point on the learning curve.

Figure 2.36 shows the completion times, for each round of implementation, for solo and pairs. The equation: $\text{Completion\_time} = a \times (b \times \text{Test\_score} + \text{Round})^c$, provides a good fit, where: Completion_time is time to complete an implementation of the application, Test_score the test score and Round the number of times the application has been implemented, with a, b and c constants chosen by the model fitting process. However, its predictions are in poor agreement with actual values, suggesting that other factors are making a significant contribution to performance.

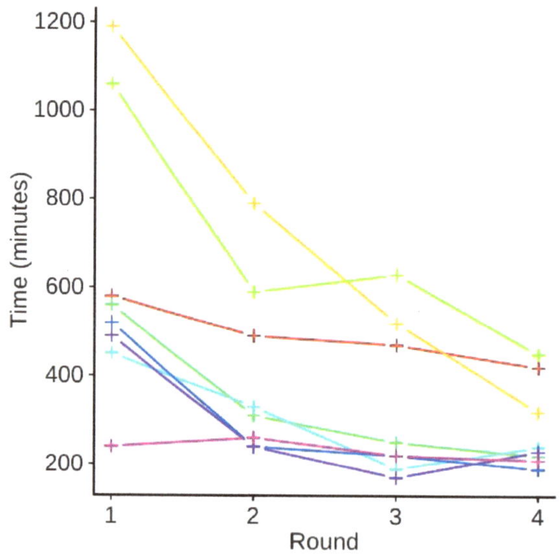

Figure 2.36: Completion times of eight solo developers for each implementation round. Data kindly provided by Lui. Github-Local

After starting work in a new environment, performance can noticeable improve as a person gains experience working in that environment. A study by Brooks [265] measured the performance of an experienced developer, writing and debugging 23 short programs (mean length 24 lines). The time taken to debug each program improved as more programs were implemented; see Github-developers/a013582.R.

Developers sometimes work in several programming languages on a regular basis. The extent to which learning applies across languages is likely to be dependent on the ease with which patterns of usage are applicable across the languages used.

A study by Zislis [2031] measured the time taken (in minutes) by himself, to implement 12 algorithms, with the implementation performed three times using three different languages (APL, PL/1, Fortran), and on the fourth repetition using the same language as on the first implementation. Figure 2.37 shows total implementation time for each algorithm, over the four implementations; fitting a mixed-effects model finds some performance difference between the languages used (see figure code for details).

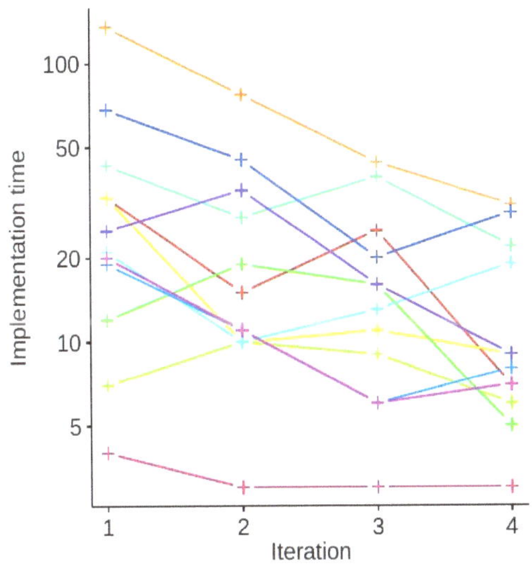

Figure 2.37: Time taken, by the same person, to implement 12 algorithms from the Communications of the ACM (each colored line), with four iteration of the implementation process. Data from Zislis. Github-Local

A study by Jones [931] investigated developer beliefs about binary operator precedence. Subjects saw an expression containing two binary operators, and had to specify the relative precedence of these operators by adding parenthesis to the expression, e.g., $a + b \mid c$. In a coding environment, the more frequently a pair of binary operators appear together, the more often developers have to make a decision about their relative precedence; the hypothesis was that the more often developers have to make a particular precedence decision, when reading code, the more likely they are to know the correct answer. Binary operator usage in code was used as a proxy for developer experience of making binary operator decisions (C source code was measured). Figure 2.38 shows the fraction of correct answers to the relative operator precedence question, against the corresponding percentage occurrence of that pair of binary operators.

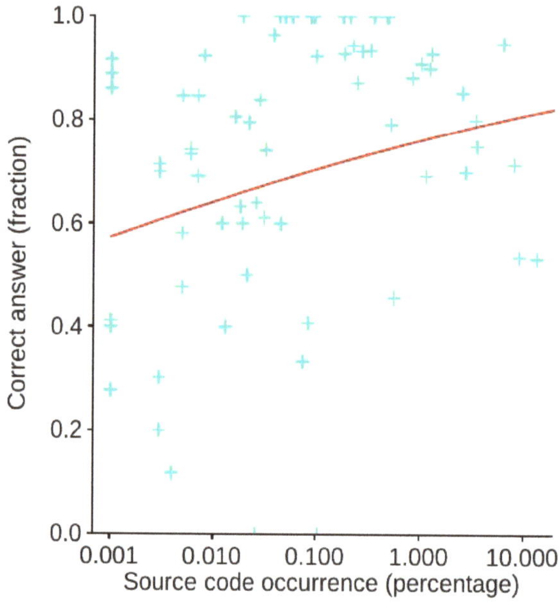

Figure 2.38: Percentage occurrence of binary operator pairs (as a percentage of all such pairs) against the fraction of correct answers to questions about their precedence, red line is beta regression model. Data from Jones. Github-Local

A study by Mockus and Weiss [1303] found that the probability of a developer introducing a fault into an application, when modifying software, decreased as the log of the total number of changes made by the developer, i.e., their experience or expertise.

Job advertisements often specify that a minimum number of years of experience is required. Number of years may not be a reliable measure of expertise, but it does provide a degree of comfort that a person has had to deal with the major issues that might occur within a given domain.

A study by Latorre [1092] investigated the effect of developer experience on applying unit-test-driven development. The 24 subjects, classified as junior (one-to-two-years professional experience), intermediate (three-to-five-years experience) or senior (more than sixyears experience), were taught unit-test-driven development, and the time taken for them to implement eight groups of requirements was measured. The implementations of the first two groups was included as part of the training and familiarization process; the time taken, by each subject, on these two groups was used to normalise the reported results.

Figure 2.39 shows the normalised time taken, by each subject, on successive groups of requirements; color is used to denote subject experience. While there is a lot of variation between subjects, average performance improves with years of experience, i.e., implementation time decreases (a fitted mixed-effects model is included in the plot's code).

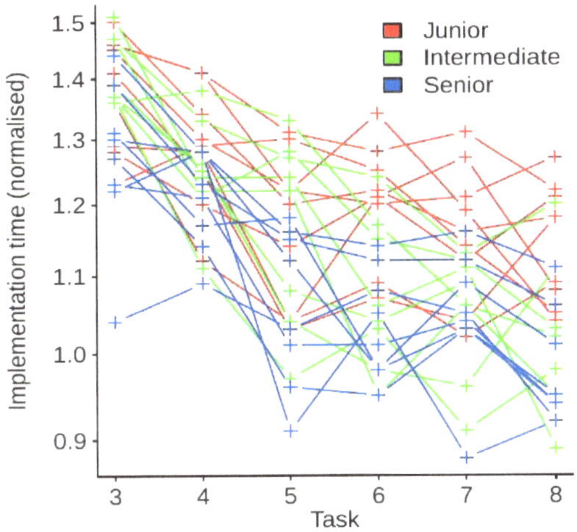

Figure 2.39: Time taken by 24 subjects, classified by years of professional experience, to complete successive tasks. Data from Latorre. Github-Local

What is the long term impact of learning on closely related cognitive activities? Isaac Asimov was a prolific author who maintained a consistent writing schedule. Figure 2.40 shows the number of published books against elapsed months. The lines are the fitted models $books \approx 27\ months^{0.48}$, and $books \approx -0.6\ months + 40\sqrt{months}$ (a better fit).

To quote Herbert Simon: [1711] "Intuition and judgement-at least good judgement-are simply analyses frozen into habit and into the capacity for rapid response through recognition. . . . Every manager needs also to be able to respond to situations rapidly, a skill that requires the cultivation of intuition and judgement over many years of experience and training."

2.5.1 Belief

People hold beliefs derived from the information they have received, and the analysis of information accumulated over time.

How are existing beliefs modified by the introduction of new evidence?

In the belief-adjustment model [843] the current degree of belief has the form of a moving average of updates produced by the history of prior encounters with items of evidence:

$S_k = S_{k-1} + w_k[s(x_k) - R]$, where: $0 < S_k < 1$ is the degree of belief in some hypothesis after evaluating k items of evidence, S_{k-1} is the prior belief (S_0 denotes the initial belief), $s(x_k)$ is the subjective evaluation of the k th item of evidence (different people may assign different values for the same evidence, x_k), R is the reference point or background, against which the impact of the k th item of evidence is evaluated, and $0 < w_k < 1$ is the adjustment weight for the k th item of evidence.

When presented with an item of evidence, a person can use an evaluation process or an estimation process.

- an evaluation process encodes new evidence relative to a fixed point, i.e., the hypothesis addressed by a belief. If the new evidence supports the hypothesis, a person's belief increases, and decreases if it does not support the hypothesis. This change occurs irrespective of the current state of a person's belief; for this case $R = 0$, and $-1 \leq s(x_k) \leq 1$.

  An example of an evaluation process might be the belief that the object X always holds a value that is numerically greater than Y ,

- an estimation process encodes new evidence relative to the current state of a person's beliefs; for this case $R = S_{k-1}$, and $0 \leq s(x_k) \leq 1$.

If multiple items of evidence are presented, a response may be required after each item (known as Step-by-Step), or a response may only need to be given after all the evidence is presented (known as End-of-Sequence). The response mode is handled by the model.

A study by Hogarth and Einhorn [843] investigated order, and response mode effects in belief updating. Subjects were presented with a variety of scenarios (e.g., a defective stereo speaker thought to have a bad connection, or a baseball player whose hitting improved dramatically after a new coaching program), followed by two or more additional items of evidence. The additional evidence was either positive (e.g., "The other players on Sandy's team did not show an unusual increase in their batting average over the last five weeks"), or negative (e.g., "The games in which Sandy showed his improvement were played against the last-place team in the league"). The positive and negative evidence was worded to create either strong or weak forms.

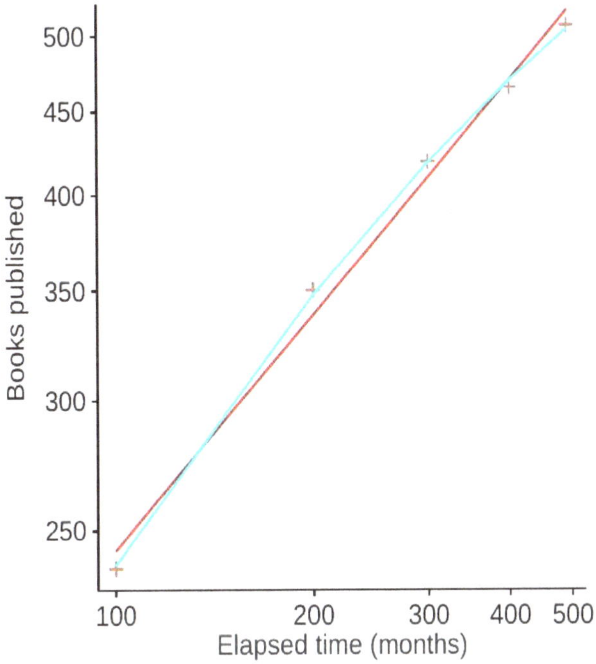

Figure 2.40: Elapsed months during which Asimov published a given number of books, with lines for two fitted regression models. Data from Ohlsson. Github-Local

The evidence was presented in three combinations: strong positive and then weak positive, upper plot in figure 2.41; strong negative and then weak negative, middle plot of figure 2.41; positive negative and then negative positive, lower plot of figure 2.41. Subjects were then asked, "Now, how likely do you think X caused Y on a scale of 0 to 100 ?" For some presentations, subjects had to respond after seeing each item of evidence (the step-by-step procedure), in the other presentations subjects did not respond until seeing all the evidence (the end-of-sequence procedure).

Figure 2.41 shows the impact of presentation orders and response modes on subjects' degree of belief.

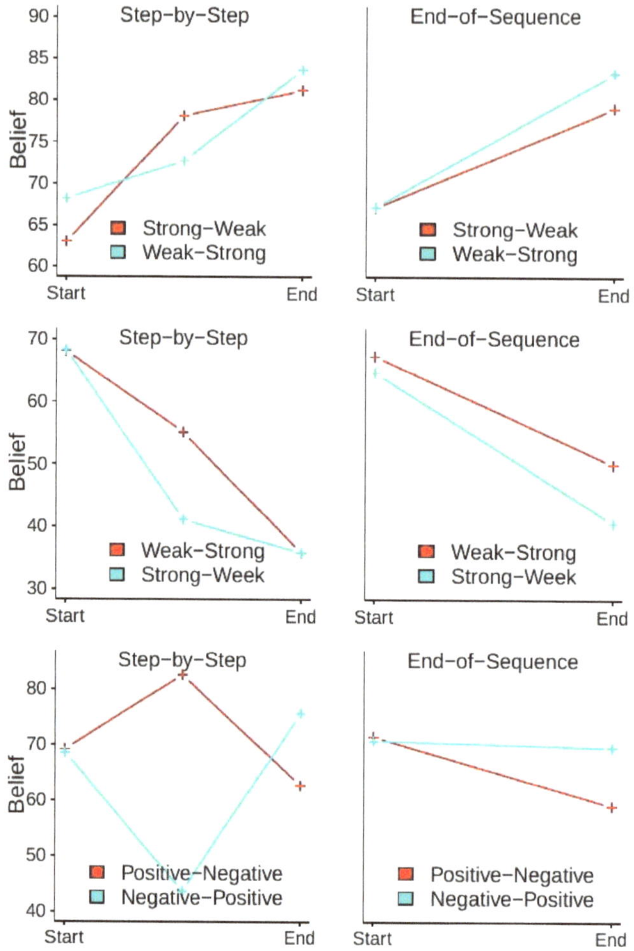

Figure 2.41: Subjects' belief response curves when presented with evidence in the sequences: (upper) positive weak, then positive strong, (middle) negative weak then negative strong, (lower) positive then negative. Based on Hogarth et al. Github-Local

Other studies have replicated these results, for instance, professional auditors have been shown to display recency effects in their evaluation of the veracity of company accounts. 1451

One study found that when combining information from multiple sources, to form beliefs, subjects failed to adjust for correlation between the information provided by different sources (e.g., news websites telling slightly different versions of the same events). Failing to adjust for correlation results in the creation of biased beliefs.

Studies [1606] have found that people exhibit a belief preservation effect; they continue to hold beliefs after the original basis for those beliefs no longer holds.

The mathematical approach used to model quantum mechanics is started being used to model some cognitive processes, such as order effects and holding conflicting beliefs at the same time. [1847]

2.5.2 Expertise

The term expert might be applied to a person because of what other people think (i.e., be socially based), such as professional standing within an organization, and selfproclaimed experts willing to accept money from clients who are not willing to take responsibility for proposing what needs to be done [72] (e.g., the role of court jester who has permission to say what others cannot); or, be applied to a person because of what they can do (i.e., performance based), such as knowing a great deal about a particular subject, or being able to perform at a qualitatively higher level than the average person, or some chosen top percentage, or be applied to a person having a combination of social and performance skills. [687]

This section discusses expertise as a high-performance skill; something that requires many years of training, and where many individuals fail to develop proficiency.

How might people become performance experts?

Chess players were the subject of the first major study of expertise, by de Groot, [450] and techniques used to study Chess, along with the results obtained, continue to dominate the study of expertise. In a classic study, de Groot briefly showed subjects the position of an unknown game and asked them to reconstruct it. The accuracy and speed of experts (e.g., Grand Masters) was significantly greater than non-experts when the pieces appeared on the board in positions corresponding to a game, but was not much greater when the pieces were placed at random. The explanation given for the significant performance difference, is that experts are faster to recognise relationships between the positions of pieces, and make use of their large knowledge of positional patterns to reduce the amount of working memory needed to remember what they were briefly shown.

A study by McKeithen, Reitman, Rueter and Hirtle [1244] gave subjects two minutes to study the source code of a program, and then gave them three minutes to recall the program's 31 lines. Subjects were then given another two minutes to study the same source code, and asked to recall the code; this process was repeated for a total of five trials.

Figure 2.42 shows the number of lines recalled by experts (over 2,000 hours of general programming experience), intermediates (just completed a programming course), and beginners (about to start a programming course) over the five trials. The upper plot are the results for the 31 line program, and the lower plot a scrambled version of the program.

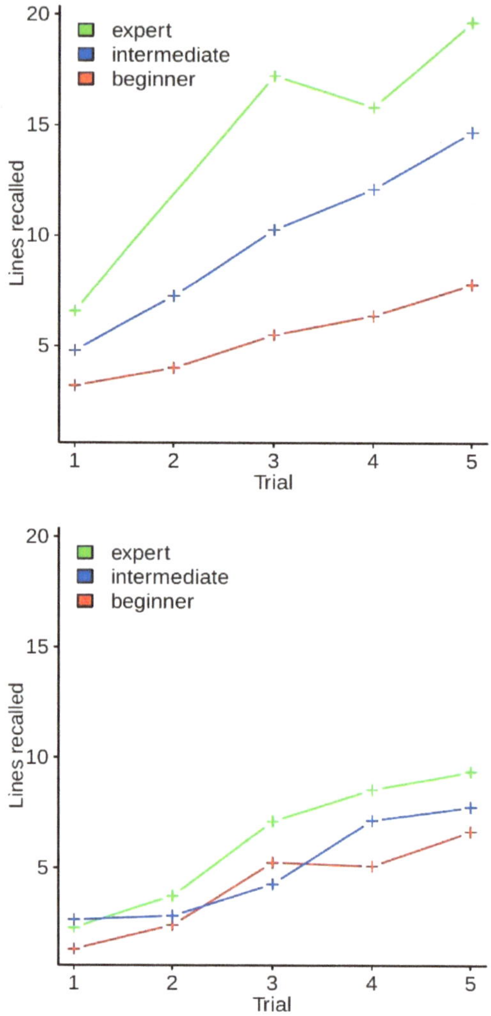

Figure 2.42: Lines of code correctly recalled after a given number of 2-minute memorization sessions; actual program in upper plot, scrambled line order in lower plot. Data extracted from McKeithen et al. Github-Local

Some believe that experts have an innate ability, or capacity, that enables them to do what they do so well. Research has shown that while innate ability can be a factor in performance (there do appear to be genetic factors associated with some athletic performances), the main factor in developing expert performance is time spent in deliberate practice [551] (deliberate practice does not explain everything [772]).

Deliberate practice differs from simply performing the task, [552] in that it requires people to monitor their practice with full concentration, and to receive feedback [844] on what they are doing (often from a professional teacher). The goal of deliberate practice being to improve performance, not to produce a finished product, and may involve studying components of the skill in isolation attempting to improve on particular aspects. The goal of this practice being to improve performance, not to produce a finished product.

A study by Lorko, Servátka and Zhang [1160] investigated the effect of lack of feedback, and anchoring, on the accuracy of duration estimates of a repeatedly performed task. One round of the task involved making an estimate of time to complete the task, followed by giving 400 correct true/false answers to questions involving an inequality between two numbers (whose value was between 10 and 99); there were three rounds of estimating and correctly answering 400 questions. The amount of money paid to subjects, for taking part, was calculated using: earnings $= 4.5 - 0.05($ abs (actual - estimate)), and a performance formula involving number of correct and incorrect answers given; the intent was to motivate subjects to provide an accurate estimate, and to work as quickly as possible without making mistakes. Subjects did not receive any feedback on the accuracy of their estimates, i.e., they were not told how much time they took to complete the task.

The task was expected to take around 10 to 12.5 minutes. Approximately one third of subjects were given a low anchor (i.e., 3 -minutes), one third high a high anchor (i.e., 20 - minutes), and the other third no anchor.

The results show that the estimates of low-anchor subjects increased with each round, while high-anchor subject estimates decreased, and no anchor subject estimates showed no pattern; see Github-developers/Lorko-Servatka-Zhang.R.

In many fields expertise is acquired by memorizing a huge amount of domain-specific information, organizing it for rapid retrieval based on patterns that occur when problemsolving within the domain, and refining the problem-solving process. [554]

Studies of the backgrounds of recognized experts, in many fields, found that the elapsed time between them starting out and carrying out their best work was at least 10 years, often with several hours of deliberate practice every day of the year. For instance, a study of violinists [553] (a perceptual-motor task) found that by age 20 those at the top-level had practiced for 10,000 hours, those at the next level down 7,500 hours, and those at the lowest level of expertise had practiced for 5,000 hours; similar quantities of practice were found in those attaining expert performance levels in purely mental activities (e.g., chess).

Expertise within one domain does not confer any additional skills within another domain, [57] e.g., statistics (unless the problem explicitly involves statistical thinking within the applicable domain), and logic. [346] A study [338] in which subjects learned to remember long sequences of digits (after 50-100 hours of practice they could commit to memory, and later recall, sequences containing more than 20 digits) found that this expertise did not transfer to learning sequences of other items.

There are domains in which those acknowledged as experts do not perform significantly better than those considered to be non-experts, [293] in some cases non-experts have been found to outperform experts within their domain. [1959] An expert's domain knowledge can act as a mental set that limits the search for a solution, with the expert becoming fixated within the domain. In cases where a new task does not fit the pattern of highly proceduralized behaviors of an expert, a novice has an opportunity to do better.

What of individual aptitudes? In the cases studied, the effects of aptitude, if there was any, were found to be completely overshadowed by differences in experience, and deliberate practice times. Willingness to spend many hours, every day, studying to achieve expert performance is certainly a necessary requirement. Does an initial aptitude, or interest, in a subject lead to praise from others (the path to musical and chess expert performance often starts in childhood), which creates the atmosphere for learning, or are other issues involved? IQ scores do correlate to performance during, and immediately after training, but the correlation reduces over the years. The IQ scores of experts has been found to be higher than the average population, at about the level of college students.

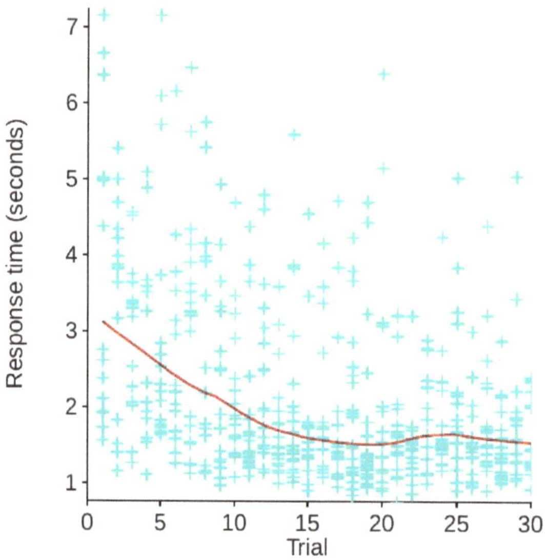

Figure 2.43: One subject's response time over successive blocks of command line trials and fitted loess (in green). Data kindly provided by Remington. Github-Local

Education can be thought of as trying to do two things (of interest to us here)-teach students skills (procedural knowledge), and providing them with information, considered important in the relevant field, to memorize (declarative knowledge).

Does attending a course on a particular subject have any measurable effect on students' capabilities, other than being able to answer questions in an exam? That is, having developed some skill in using a particular system of reasoning, do students apply it outside the domain in which they learnt it?

A study by Lehman, Lempert, and Nisbett [1111] measured changes in students' statistical, methodological and conditional reasoning abilities (about everyday-life events) between their first and third years. They found that both psychology and medical training produced large effects on statistical and methodological reasoning, while psychology, medical and law training produced effects on the ability to perform conditional reasoning; training in chemistry had no effect on the types of reasoning studied. An examination of the skills taught to students studying in these fields showed that they correlated with improvements in the specific types of reasoning abilities measured.

A study by Remington, Yuen and Pashler [1576] compared subject performance between using a GUI and a command line (with practice, there was little improvement in GUI performance, but command line performance continued to improve and eventually overtook GUI performance). Figure 2.43 shows the command line response time for one subject over successive blocks of trials, and a fitted loess line.

2.5.3 Category knowledge

Children as young as four have been found to use categorization to direct the inferences they make, [666] and many studies have shown that people have an innate desire to create and use categories (they have also been found to be sensitive to the costs and benefits of using categories; [1190] Capuchin monkeys have learned to classify nine items concurrently [1242]). By dividing items into categories, people reduce the amount of information they need to learn, [1514] and can generalize based on prior experience. [1385] Information about the likely characteristics of a newly encountered item can be obtained by matching it to one or more known categories, and then extracting characteristics common to previously encountered items in these categories. For instance, a flying object with feathers, and a beak might be assigned to the category bird, which suggests the characteristics of laying eggs and potentially being migratory.

Categorization is used to perform inductive reasoning (i.e., the derivation of generalized knowledge from specific instances), and also acts as a memory aid (about the members of a category). Categories provide a framework from which small amounts of information can be used to infer, seemingly unconnected (to an outsider), useful conclusions.

Studies have found that people use roughly three levels of abstraction in creating hierarchical relationships. The highest level of abstraction has been called [1601] the superordinatelevel (e.g., the general category furniture), the next level down the basic-level (this is the level at which most categorization is carried out, e.g., car, truck, chair or table), the lowest level is the subordinate-level (which denotes specific types of objects, e.g., a family car, a removal truck, my favourite armchair, a kitchen table). Studies [1601] have found that basic-level categories have properties not shared by the other two categories, e.g., adults spontaneously name objects at this level, it is the abstract level that children acquire first, and category members tend to have similar overall shapes.

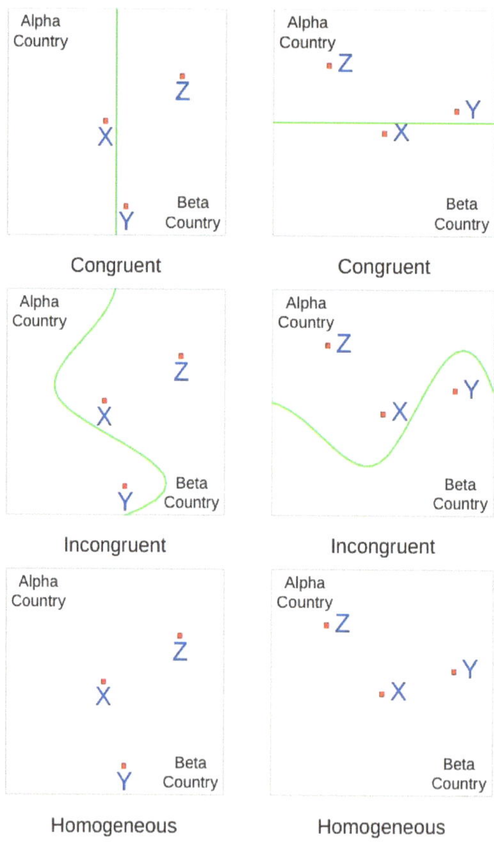

Figure 2.44: Country boundaries (green line) and town locations (red dots). Congruent: straight boundary aligned with question asked, incongruent: meandering boundary and locations sometimes inconsistent with question asked. Based on Stevens et al. Github-Local

When categories have a hierarchical structure, it is possible for an attribute of a higherlevel category to affect the perceived attributes of subordinate categories. A study by Stevens and Coupe [1779] asked subjects to remember the information contained in a series of maps (see figure 2.44). They were asked questions such as: "Is X east or west of Y ?", and "Is X north or south of Y?" Subjects gave incorrect answers 18% of the time for the congruent maps (i.e., country boundary aligned along axis of question asked), but 45% of the time for the incongruent maps (i.e, country boundary meanders, and locations sometimes inconsistent with question asked); 15% for homogeneous (i.e., no country boundaries). These results were interpreted as subjects using information about the relative locations of countries to answer questions about the city locations.

Studies [1724] have found that people do not consistently treat subordinate categories as inheriting the properties of their superordinates, i.e., category inheritance is not always a tree.

How categories should be defined and structured is a long-standing debate within the sciences. Some commonly used category formation techniques, their membership rules and attributes include:

- defining-attribute theory: members of a category are characterized by a set of defining attributes. Attributes divide objects up into different concepts whose boundaries are well-defined, with all members of the concept being equally representative. Concepts that are a basic-level of a superordinate-level concept will have all the attributes of that superordinate level; for instance, a sparrow (small, brown) and its superordinate: bird (two legs, feathered, lays eggs),
- prototype theory: categories have a central description, the prototype, that represents the set of attributes of the category. This set of attributes need not be necessary, or sufficient, to determine category membership. The members of a category can be arranged in a typicality gradient, representing the degree to which they represent a typical member of that category. It is possible for objects to be members of more than one category, e.g., tomatoes as a fruit, or a vegetable,
- exemplar-based theory: specific instances, or exemplars, act as the prototypes against which other members are compared. Objects are grouped, relative to one another, based on some similarity metric. The exemplar-based theory differs from the prototype theory in that specific instances are the norm against which membership is decided. When asked to name particular members of a category, the attributes of the exemplars are used as cues to retrieve other objects having similar attributes,

- explanation-based theory: there is an explanation for why categories have the members they do. For instance, the biblical classification of food into clean and unclean is roughly explained by the correlation between type of habitat, biological structure, and form of locomotion; creatures of the sea should have fins, scales and swim (sharks and eels don't), and creatures of the land should have four legs (ostriches don't).

  From a predictive point of view, explanation-based categories suffer from the problem that they may heavily depend on the knowledge and beliefs of the person who formed the category; for instance, the set of objects a person would remove from their home, if it suddenly caught fire.

Figure 2.45 shows the eight possible combinations of three, two-valued attributes, color/size/shape. It is possible to create six unique categories by selecting four items from these eight possibilities (see figure 2.46; there are 70 different ways of taking four things from a choice of eight, 8!/(4! 4!), and taking symmetry into account reduces the number to unique categories to six).

A study by Shepard, Hovland, and Jenkins [1690] measured subject performance in assigning objects to these six categories. Subject error rate decreased with practice.

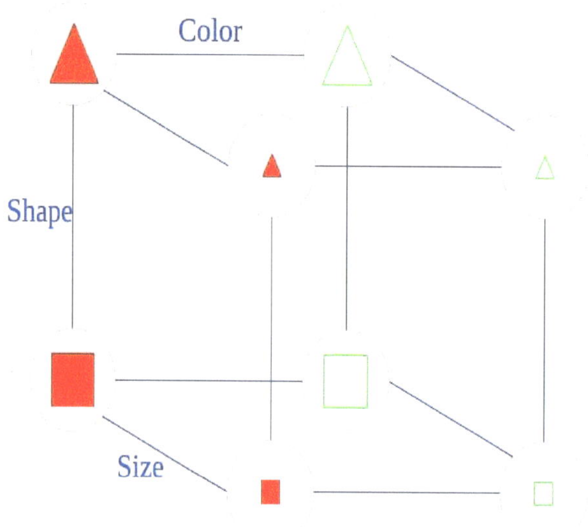

Figure 2.45: Orthogonal representation of shape, color and size stimuli. Based on Shepard.

Estes [561] proposed the following method for calculating the similarity of two objects. Matching attributes have the same similarity coefficient, $0 \leq t \leq \infty$, and nonmatching attributes have similarity coefficient, $0 \leq s_i \leq 1$ (which is potentially different for each nonmatch). When comparing objects within the same category, the convention is to use $t = 1$, and to give the attributes that differ the same similarity coefficient, s.

Table 2.3: Similarity of a stimulus object to: category A: red triangle and red square; category B: green triangle and green square.

Stimulus	Similarity to A	Similarity to B
Red triangle	$1 + s$	$s + s^2$
Red square	$1 + s$	$s + s^2$
Green triangle	$s + s^2$	$1 + s$
Green square	$s + s^2$	$1 + s$

As an example, consider just two attributes shape/color in figure 2.45, giving the four combinations red/green-triangles/squares; assign red-triangle and red-square to category A, assign green-triangle and green-square to category B, i.e., category membership is decided by color. Table 2.3 lists the similarity of each of the four possible object combinations to category A and B. Looking at the top row: red-triangle is compared for similarity to all members of category A ($1 + s$, because it does not differ from itself and differs in one attribute from the other member of category A), and all members of category B($s + s^2$, because it differs in one attribute from one member of category B and in two attributes from the other member).

If a subject is shown a stimulus that belongs in category A , the expected probability of them assigning it to this category is: $\frac{1+s}{(1+s)+(s+s^2)} \rightarrow \frac{1}{1+s}$. When s is 1 , the expected probability is no better than a random choice; when s is 0 , the probability is a certainty.

A study by Feldman investigated categories containing objects having either three or four attributes. During an initial training period subjects learned to distinguish between a creature having a given set of attributes, and other creatures that did not. Subjects then saw a sequence of example creatures, and had to decide whether they were a member of the learned category.

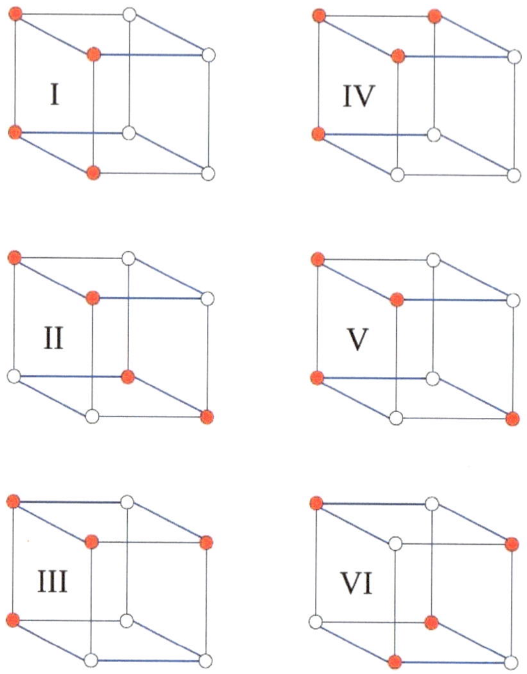

Figure 2.46: The six unique configurations of selecting four times from eight possibilities, i.e., it is not possible to rotate one configuration into another within these six configurations. Based on Shepard.

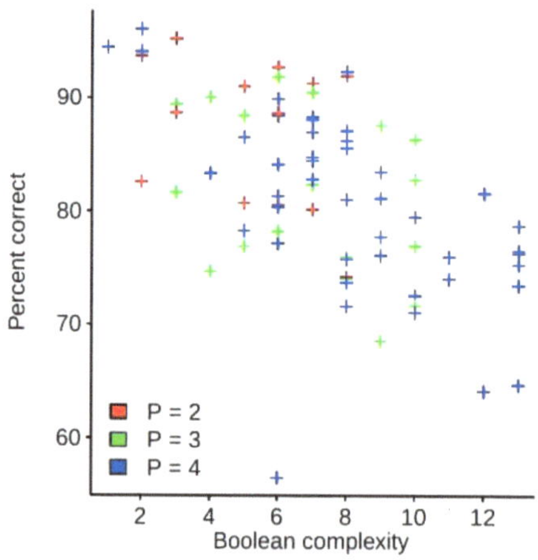

Figure 2.47: Percentage of correct category answers produced by one subject against boolean-complexity, broken down by number of positive cases needed to define the category used in the question (three colors). Data kindly provided by Feldman. Github-Local

A later study specified category membership algebraically, e.g., membership of category IV in the top right of figure 2.46 is specified by the expression: $S\bar{H}\bar{C} + SH\bar{C} + \bar{S}H\bar{C} + \overline{SHC}$, where: S is size, H is shape, C is color, and an overline indicates negation. The number of terms in the minimal boolean formula specifying the category (a measure of category complexity, which Feldman terms boolean complexity) was found to predict the trend in subject error rate. Figure 2.47 shows, for one subject, the percentage of correct answers against boolean complexity; the number of positive cases needed to completely define the category of the animals in the question is broken down by color.

A few human generated semantic classification datasets are publicly available. [449]

2.5.4 Categorization consistency

Obtaining benefits from using categories requires some degree of consistency in assigning items to categories. In the case of an individual's internal categories, the ability to consistently assign items to the appropriate category is required; within cultural groups there has to be some level of agreement between members over the characteristics of items in each category.

Cross-language research has found that there are very few concepts that might be claimed to be universal (they mostly relate to the human condition).

Culture, and the use of items, can play an important role in the creation and use of categories.

A study by Bailenson, Shum, Atran, Medin and Coley compared the categories created for two sets (US and Maya) of 104 bird species, by three groups; subjects were US bird experts (average of 22.4 years bird watching), US undergraduates, and ordinary Itzaj (Maya Amerindians people from Guatemala). The categorization choices made by the three groups of subjects were found to be internally consistent within each group. The US experts' categories correlated highly with the scientific taxonomy for both sets of birds, the Itzaj categories only correlated highly for Maya birds (they used ecological justifications; the bird's relationship with its environment), and the nonexperts had a low correlation for both set of birds. Cultural differences were found in that, for instance, US subjects were more likely to generalise from songbirds, while the Itzaj were more likely to generalize from perceptually striking birds.

A study by Labov [1065] showed subjects pictures of items that could be classified as either cups or bowls (see upper plot in figure 2.48; colors not in the original). These items were presented in one of two contexts-a neutral context in which the pictures were simply presented, and a food context (they were asked to think of the items as being filled with mashed potatoes).

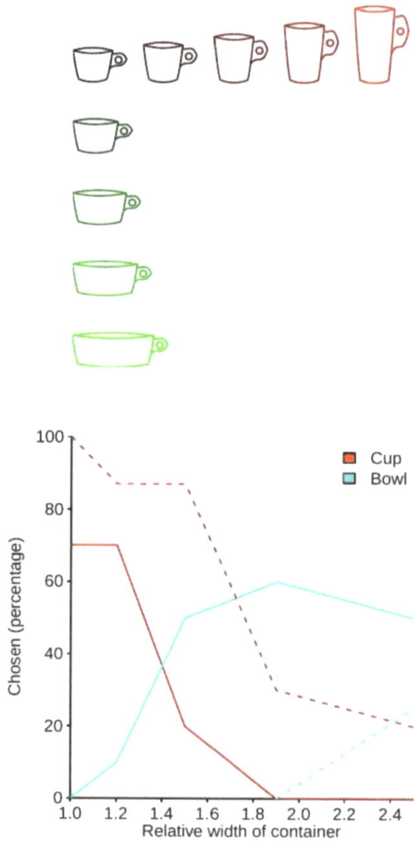

Figure 2.48: Cup- and bowl-like objects of various widths (ratios 1.2, 1.5, 1.9, and 2.5), and heights (ratios 1.2, 1.5, 1.9, and 2.4), with dashed lines showing neutral context and solid lines food context. The percentage of subjects who selected the term cup or bowl to describe the object they were shown (the paper did not explain why the figures do not sum to 100%, and color was not used in the original). Based on Labov. Github-Local

The lower plot of figure 2.48 shows that as the width of the item seen was increased, an increasing number of subjects classified it as a bowl (dash lines). Introducing a food context, shifted subjects' responses towards classifying the item as a bowl at narrower widths (solid lines).

The same set of items may be viewed from a variety of different points of view (the term frame is sometimes used); for instance, commercial events include: buying, selling, paying, charging, pricing, costing, spending, and so on. Figure 2.49 shows four ways (i.e., buying, selling, paying, and charging) of classifying the same commercial event.

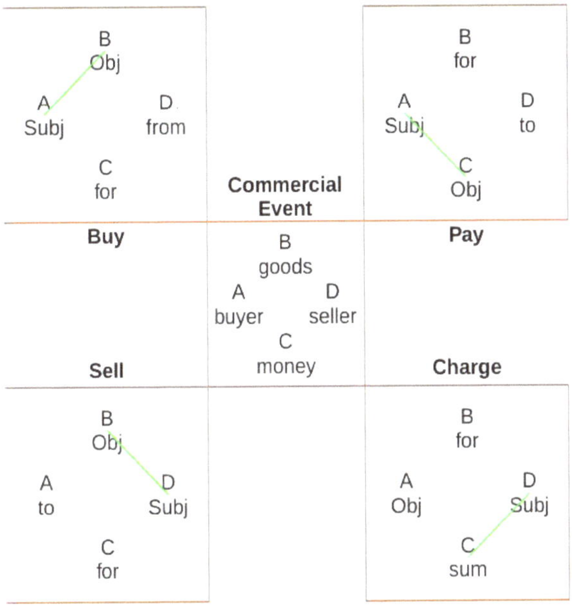

Figure 2.49: A commercial event involving a buyer, seller, money and goods; as seen from the buy, sell, pay, or charge perspective. Based on Fillmore. Github-Local

A study by Jones [934] investigated the extent to which different developers make similar decisions when creating data structures to represent the same information; see fig 12.5.

2.6 Reasoning

Reasoning enhances cognition. The knowledge-based use-case for the benefits of being able to reason, is the ability it provides to extract information from available data; adding constraints on the data (e.g., known behaviors) can increase the quantity of information that may be extracted. Dual process theories [1723,1760,1761] treat people as having two systems: unconscious reasoning and conscious reasoning. What survival advantages does an ability to consciously reason provide, or is it primarily an activity WEIRD people need to learn to pass school tests?

Outside of classroom problems, a real world context in which people explicitly reason is decision-making, and here "fast and frugal algorithms" [677,680] provide answers quickly, within the limited constraints of time and energy. Context and semantics are crucial inputs to the reasoning process. [1773]

Alfred North Whitehead: "It is a profoundly erroneous truism . . . that we should cultivate the habit of thinking of what we are doing. The precise opposite is the case. Civilization advances by extending the number of important operations which we can perform without thinking about them."

Understanding spoken language requires reasoning about what is being discussed, [1264] and in a friendly shared environment it is possible to fill in the gaps by assuming that what is said is relevant, [1747] with no intent to trick. In an adversarial context sceptical reasoning, of the mathematical logic kind, is useful for enumerating possible interpretations of what has been said. [1265]

The kinds of questions asked in studies of reasoning appear to be uncontentious. However, studies [1174,1664] of reasoning using illiterate subjects, from remote parts of the world, received answers to verbal reasoning problems that were based on personal experience and social norms, rather than the western ideal of logic. The answers given by subjects, in the same location, who had received several years of schooling were much more likely to match those demanded by mathematical logic; the subjects had learned how to act WEIRD and play the game. The difficulties experienced by those learning formal logic suggests that there is no innate capacity for this task (innate capacity enables the corresponding skill to be learned quickly and easily). The human mind is a story processor, not a logic processor. [763]

Reasoning and decision-making appear to be closely related. However, reasoning researchers tied themselves to using the norm of mathematical logic for many decades, and created something of research ghetto, [1775] while decision-making researchers have been involved in explaining real-world problems.

The Wason selection task [1931] is to studies of reasoning like the fruit fly is to studies of genetics. Wason's study was first published in 1968, and considered mathematical logic to be the norm against which human reasoning performance should be judged. The reader might like to try this selection task:

Figure 2.50 depicts a set of four cards, of which you can see only the exposed face but not the hidden back. On each card, there is a number on one side and a letter on the other.

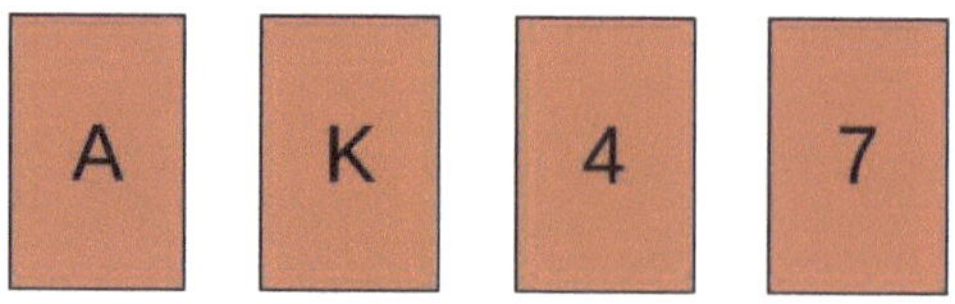

Figure 2.50: The four cards used in the Wason selection task. Based on Wason. [1931] Github-Local

- Below there is a rule, which applies only to these four cards. Your task is to decide, which, if any, of these four cards you must turn in order to decide whether the rule is true.
- Don't turn unnecessary cards. Specify the cards you would turn over.

Rule: If there is a vowel on one side, then there is an even number on the other side.

Answer: ?

The failure of many subjects to give the expected answer [ix] (i.e., the one derived using mathematical logic) surprised many researchers, and over the years a wide variety of explanations, experiments, thesis, and books have attempted to explain the answers given. Explanations for subject behavior include: human reasoning is tuned for detecting people who cheat within a group where mutual altruism is the norm, interpreting the wording of questions pragmatically based on how natural language is used rather than as logical formula (i.e., assuming a social context; people are pragmatic virtuosos rather than logical defectives), and adjusting norms to take into account cognitive resource limitations (i.e., computational and working memory), or a rational analysis approach.

Some Wason task related studies used a dialogue protocol (i.e., subjects' discuss their thoughts about the problem with the experimenter), and transcriptions of these studies read like people new to programming having trouble understanding what it is that they have to do to solve a problem by writing code.

People have different aptitudes, and this can result in them using different strategies to solve the same problem, e.g., an interaction between a subject's verbal and spatial ability, and the strategy used to solve linear reasoning problems. However, a person having high spatial ability, for instance, does not necessarily use a spatial strategy. A study by Roberts, Gilmore and Wood [1591] asked subjects to solve what appeared to be a spatial problem (requiring the use of a very inefficient spatial strategy to solve). Subjects with high spatial ability used non-spatial strategies, while those with low spatial ability used a spatial strategy. The conclusion drawn was that those with high spatial ability were able to see the inefficiency of the spatial strategy, and selected an alternative strategy, while those with less spatial ability were unable to make this evaluation.

A study by Bell and Johnson-Laird investigated the effect of kind of questions asked on reasoning performance. Subjects had to give a yes/no response to two kinds of questions, asking about what is possible or what is necessary. The hypothesis was that subjects would find it easier to infer a yes answer to a question about what is possible, compared to one about what is necessary; because only one instance needs to be found for the possible question, whereas all instances need to be checked, to answer yes to a question about necessity. For instance, in a game in which only two can play, and the following information:

```
If Allan is in then Betsy is in.
If Carla is in then David is out.
```

answering yes to the question: "Can Betsy be in the game?" (a possibility), is easier than giving the same answer: to "Must Betsy be in the game?" (a necessity); see table 2.4.

Table 2.4: Percentage of correct answers to possible/necessary questions, and the two kinds of response. Data from Bell et al.

Question	Correct yes	Correct no
is possible	91%	65%
is necessary	71%	81%

However, subjects would be expected to find it easier to infer a no answer to a question about what is necessary, compared to one about what is possible; because only one instance needs to be found to answer a necessary question, whereas all instances need to be checked to answer no to a question about possibility. For instance, in another two-person game, and the following information:

```
If Allan is out then Betsy is out.
If Carla is out then David is in.
```

answering no to the question: "Must Betsy be in the game?" (a necessity), is easier than giving the same answer to: "Can Betsy be in the game?" (a possibility); see table 2.4.

Conditionals in English: In human languages the conditional clause generally precedes the conclusion, in a conditional statement. An example where the conditional follows the conclusion is: "I will leave, if you pay me", given as the answer to the question: "Under what circumstances will you leave?". In one study of English, [624] the conditional preceded the conclusion in 77% of written material, and 82% of spoken material. There is a lot of variation in the form of the conditional. [192,304]

2.6.1 Deductive reasoning

Deductive reasoning is the process of reasoning about one or more statements (technically known as premises) to reach one or more logical conclusions.

Studies [110] have found that the reasoning strategies used by people involve building either a verbal or spatial model, from the premises. Factors found to affect peoples performance in solving deductive reasoning problems include the following:

- Belief bias: people are more willing to accept a conclusion, derived from given premises, that they believe to be true than one they believe to be false. A study by Evans, Barston, and Pollard [564] gave subjects two premises and a conclusion, and asked them to state whether the conclusion was true or false (based on the premises given; the conclusions were rated as either believable or unbelievable by a separate group of subjects); see the results in table 2.5,
- Studies have modeled the response behavior using multinomial processing trees [1018] and system detection theory; [1845] see Github-developers/Trippas-2018.R.
- Form of premise: a study by Dickstein [495] measured subject performance on the 64 possible two premise syllogisms (a premise being one of the propositions: All S are P, No S are P, Some S are P, and Some S are not P). For instance, the following syllogisms show the four possible permutations of three terms (the use of S and P is interchangeable):

All M are S	All S are M	All M are S	All S are M
No P are M	No P are M	No M are P	No M are P

The results found that performance was affected by the order in which the terms occurred in the two premises of the syllogism. The order in which the premises are processed may affect the amount of working memory needed to reason about the syllogism, which in turn can affect human performance. [683]

Table 2.5: Percentage of subjects accepting that the stated conclusion could be logically deduced from the given premises. Based on Evans et al. [564]

Status-context	Example	Accepted
Valid-believable	No Police dogs are vicious	
	Some highly trained dogs are vicious	

	Therefore, some highly trained dogs are not police dogs	88%
Valid-unbelievable		
	No nutritional things are inexpensive	
	Some vitamin tablets are inexpensive	
	Therefore, some vitamin tablets are not nutritional things	56%
Invalid-believable		
	No addictive things are inexpensive	
	Therefore, some addictive things are not cigarettes	72%
Invalid-unbelievable	No millionaires are hard workers	
	Some rich people are hard workers	
	Therefore, some millionaires are not rich people	13%

2.6.2 Linear reasoning

Being able to make relational decisions is a useful skill for animals living in hierarchical social groups, where aggression is sometimes used to decide status. Aggression is best avoided, as it can lead to death or injury; the ability to make use of relative dominance information (obtained by watching interactions between other members of the group) may remove the need for aggressive behavior during an encounter between two group members who have not recently contested dominance (i.e., there is nothing to be gained in aggression towards a group member who has recently been seen to dominate a member who is dominant to yourself).

Another benefit of being ability to make relational comparisons is being able to select which of two areas contains the largest amount of food. Some animals, including humans, have a biologically determined representation of numbers, including elementary arithmetic operations, what one researcher has called the number sense. 477

The use of relational operators have an interpretation in terms of linear syllogisms. A study by De Soto, London, and Handel [457] investigated a task they called social reasoning, using the relations better and worse. Subjects were shown two relationship statements involving three people, and a possible conclusion (e.g., "Is Mantle worse than

Moskowitz?"), and were given 10 seconds to answer "yes", "no", or "don't know". The British National Corpus [1106] lists better as appearing 143 times per million words, while worse appears under 10 times per million words, and is not listed in the top 124,000 most used words.

Table 2.6: Eight sets of premises describing the same relative ordering between A, B, and C (peoples names were used in the study) in different ways, followed by the percentage of subjects giving the correct answer. Based on De Soto et al. [457]

1.	Relationships	Correct %		Relationships	Correct %
	A is better than B		5.	A is better than B	
	B is better than C	60.5		C is worse than B	61.8
2.	B is better than C		6.	C is worse than B	
	A is better than B	52.8		A is better than B	57.0
3.	B is worse than A		7.	B is worse than A	
	C is worse than B	50.0		B is better than C	41.5
4.	C is worse than B		8.	B is better than C	
	B is worse than A	42.5		B is worse than A	38.3

Table 2.6 shows the percentage of correct answers: a higher percentage of correct answers were given when the direction was better-to-worse (case 1), than mixed direction (cases 2 and 3); the consistent direction worse-to-better performed poorly (case 4); a higher percentage of correct answers were given when the premises stated an end term (better or worse; cases 1 and 5) followed by the middle term, than a middle term followed by an end term.

A second experiment, in the same study, gave subjects printed statements about people. For instance, "Tom is better than Bill". The relations used were better, worse, has lighter hair, and has darker hair. The subjects had to write the peoples names in two of four possible boxes; two arranged horizontally and two arranged vertically.

The results found 84% of subjects selecting a vertical direction for better/worse, with better at the top (which is consistent with the up is good usage found in English metaphors

[1070]). In the case of lighter/darker, 66% of subjects used a horizontal direction, with no significant preference for left-to-right or right-to left.

A third experiment in the same study used the relations to-the-left and to-the-right, and above and below. The above/below results were very similar to those for better/worse. The left-right results found that subjects learned a left-to-right ordering better than a right-to-left ordering.

Subject performance on linear reasoning improves, the greater the distance between the items being compared; the distance effect is discussed in section 2.7.

Source code constructs relating to linear reasoning are discussed in section 7.1.2.

2.6.3 Causal reasoning

A question asked by developers, while reading source, is "what causes this /situation/event to occur?" Causal questions, such as this, also occur in everyday life. However, there has been relatively little mathematical research on causality (statistics deals with correlation; Pearl [1459] covers some mathematical aspects of causality), and little psychological research on causal reasoning. [1726]

It is sometimes possible to express a problem in either a causal or conditional form. A study by Sloman, and Lagnado [1727] gave subjects one of the following two reasoning problems, and associated questions:

- Causal argument form:

```
A causes B
A causes C
B causes D
C causes D
D definitely occurred
```

with the questions: "If B had not occurred, would D still have occurred?", or "If B had not occurred, would A have occurred?"

- Conditional argument form:

```
If A then B
If A then C
If B then D
If C then D
```

```
D is true
```

with the questions: "If B were false, would D still be true?", or "If B were false, would A be true?".

Table 2.7 shows that subject performance depended on the form in which the problem was expressed.

Table 2.7: Percentage "yes" responses to various forms of questions (based on 238 responses). Based on Sloman et al.

Question	Causal	Conditional
D holds?	80%	57%
A holds?	79%	36%

A study by Bramley investigated causal learning. Subjects saw three nodes (e.g., grey filled circles, such as those at the center of figure 2.51), and were told that one or more causal links existed between the nodes. Clicking on a node activated it, and clicking the test icon resulted in zero or more of the other two nodes being activated (depending on the causal relationship that existing between nodes; nodes had to be activated to propagate an activation); subjects were told that the (unknown to them) causal links worked 80% of the time, and in 1% of cases a node would independently activate. Subjects, on Mechanical Turk, were asked to deduce the causal links that existed between the three nodes, by performing 12 tests for each of the 15 problems presented.

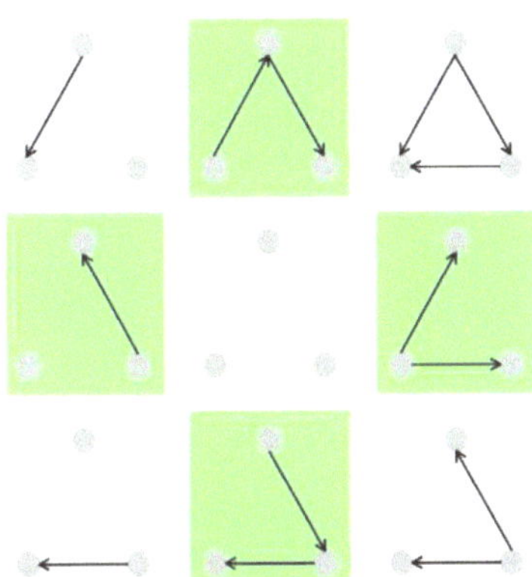

Figure 2.51: Example causal chains used Bramley. Github-Local

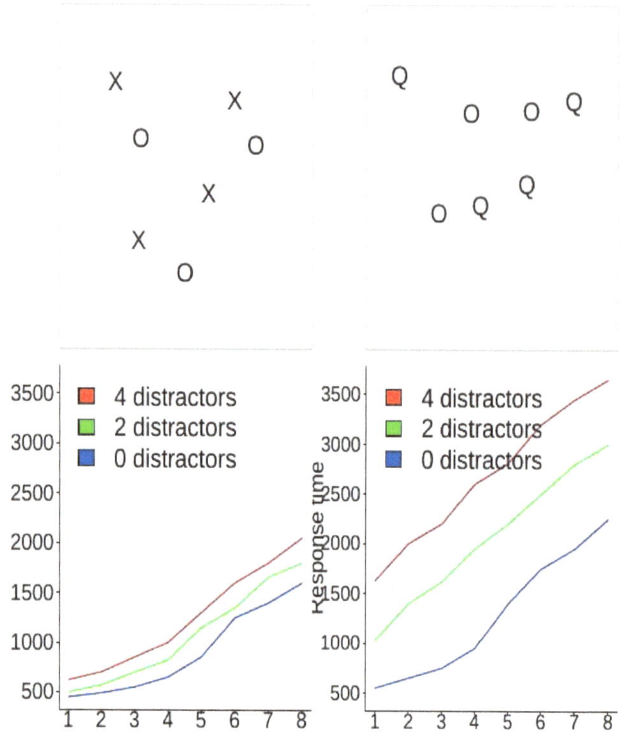

Figure 2.52: Average time (in milliseconds) taken for subjects to enumerate O's in a background of X or Q distractors. Based on Trick and Pylyshyn. Github-Local

Figure 2.51 shows some possible causal links, e.g., for the three nodes in the top left, clicking the test icon when the top node was activated would result in the left/below node becoming activated (80% of the time).

On average, subjects correctly identified 9(sd = 4.1) out of 15 causal links, with 34% getting 15 out of 15. A second experiment included on-screen reminder information and a summary of previous test results; the average score increased to 11.1(sd = 3.5), and 12.1 (sd = 2.9) when previous test results were on-screen.

Common mistakes included: a chain $[X_1 \rightarrow X_2 \rightarrow X_3]$ being mistakenly judged to be fully connected $[\ X_1 \rightarrow X_2 \rightarrow X_3, X_1 \rightarrow X_3\ ]$, or a fork $[\ X_2 \leftarrow X_1 \rightarrow X_3\ ]$; the opposite also occurred, with fully connected judged to be a chain.

2.7 Number processing

Having a sense of quantity, and being able to judge the relative size of two quantities, provides a number of survival benefits, including deciding which of two clusters of food is the largest, and being able to repeat a task an approximate number times (e.g., pressing a bar is a common laboratory task, see fig 2.4).

Being able to quickly enumerate small quantities is sufficiently useful for the brain to support preattentive processing of up to four, or so, items. [1843] When asked to enumerate how many dots are visible in a well-defined area, subjects' response time depends on the number of dots; with between one and four dots, performance varies between 40 ms to 100 ms per dot, but with five or more dots, performance varies between 250 ms to 350 ms per dot. The faster process is known as subitizing (people effortlessly see the number of dots), while the slower process is called counting.

Studies have found that a variety of animals make use of an approximate mental number system (sometimes known as the number line); see fig 2.4. The extent to which brains have a built-in number line, or existing neurons are repurposed through learning, is an active area of research. [475,1395] Humans are the only creatures known to have a second system, one that can be used to represent numbers exactly: language.

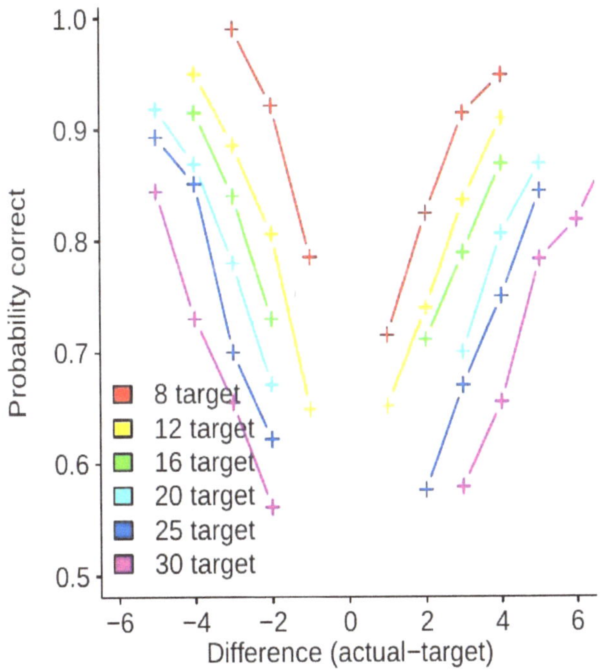

Figure 2.53: Probability a subject will successfully distinguish a difference between the number of dots displayed, and a specified target number (x -axis is the difference between these two values). Data extracted from van Oeffelen et al. [1878] Github-Local

A study by van Oeffelen and Vos [1878] investigated subjects' ability to estimate the number of dots in a briefly displayed image (100 ms, i.e., not enough time to be able to count the dots). Subjects were given a target number, and had to answer yes/no on whether they thought the image they saw contained the target number of dots. Figure 2.53 shows the probability of a correct answer for various target numbers, and a given difference between target number and number of dots displayed.

What are the operating characteristics of the approximate number system? The characteristics that have most occupied researchers are the scale used (e.g., linear or logarithmic), the impact of number magnitude on cognitive performance, and when dealing with two numbers the effect of their relative difference in value on cognitive performance. [477]

Studies of the mental representation of single digit numbers [480] have found a linear scale used by subjects from western societies, and a logarithmic scale used by subjects from indigenous cultures that have not had formal schooling.

Engineering and science sometimes deal with values spanning many orders of magnitude, a range that people are unlikely to encounter in everyday life. How do people mentally represent large value ranges?

A theoretical analysis [1485] found that a logarithmic scale minimized representation error, assuming the probability of a value occurring follows a power law distribution, assuming relative change is the psychologically-relevant measure, and that noise is present in the signal.

A study by Landy, Charlesworth and Ottmar asked subjects to click the position on a line (labeled at the left end with one thousand and at the right end with one billion) corresponding to what they thought was the appropriate location for each of the 182 values they saw (selected from 20 evenly spaced values between one thousand and one million, and 23 evenly spaced values between one million and one billion).

Figure 2.54 shows some of the patterns that occurred in subject responses; the one in the top left was one of the most common. Most subjects placed one million at the halfway point (as-if using a logarithmic scale), placing values below/above a million on separate linear scales. Landy et al developed a model based on the Category Adjustment model, [512] where subjects selected a category boundary (e.g., one million, creating the categories: the thousands and the millions), a location for the category boundary along the line, and a linear(ish) [x] mapping of values to relative position within their respective category.

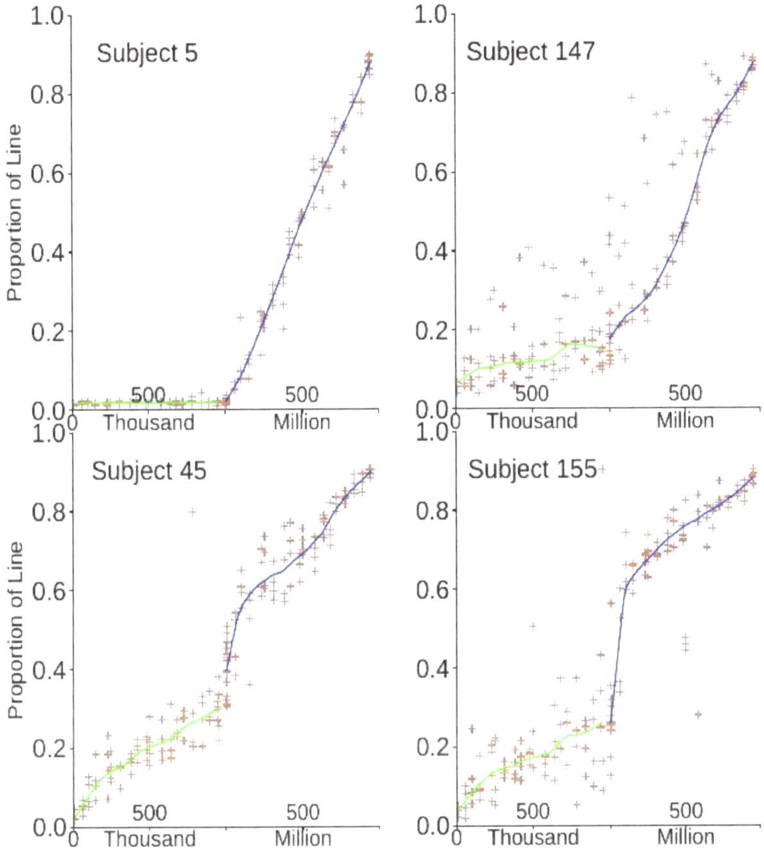

Figure 2.54: Line locations chosen for the numeric values seen by each of four subjects; color of fitted loess line changes at one million boundary. Data kindly provided by Landy. Github-Local

Studying the learning and performance of simple arithmetic operations has proven complicated; [616,1881] models of simple arithmetic performance [1100] have been built. Working memory capacity has an impact on the time taken to perform mental arithmetic operations, and the likely error rate, e.g., remembering carry or borrow quantities during subtraction; [889] the human language used to think about the problem also has an impact. [888]

How do people compare multi-digit integer constants? For instance, do they compare them digit by digit (i.e., a serial comparison), or do they form two complete values before comparing their magnitudes (the so-called holistic model)? Studies show that the answer depends on how the comparisons are made, with results consistent with the digit by digit [2007] and holistic [479] approaches being found.

Other performance related behaviors include:

- split effect: taking longer to reject false answers that are close to the correct answer (e.g., $4 \times 7 = 29$), than those that are further away (e.g., $4 \times 7 = 33$),
- associative confusion effect: answering a different question from the one asked (e.g., giving 12 as the answer to $4 \times 8 = ?$, which would be true had the operation been addition),
- plausibility judgments: using a rule, rather than retrieving a fact from memory, to verify the answer to a question; for instance, adding an odd number to an even number always produces an odd result,

Trial judges have been found [1550] to be influenced by the unit of measurement in sentencing (i.e., months or years), and to exhibit anchoring effects when deciding award damages.

2.7.1 Numeric preferences

Measurements of number usage, in general spoken and written form, show that people prefer to use certain values, either singly (sometimes known as round numbers) or as number pairs.

Number pairs (e.g., "10 to 15 hours ago") have been found to follow a small set of rules, [555] including: the second number is larger than the first, the difference between the values is a divisor of the second value, and the difference is at least 5% of the second value.

A round number is any number commonly used to communicate an approximation of nearby values; round numbers are often powers of ten, divisible by two or five, and other pragmatic factors. [914] Round numbers can act as goals [1505] and as clustering points. [1738].

A usage analysis [145] shows that selecting a rounded interpretation yields the greater benefit when there is a small chance that a rounded, rather than or non-rounded, use occurred. If a speaker uses a round number, round_value, the probability that the speaker rounded a nearby value to obtain it is given by:

$P(\text{ Speaker\_rounded} \mid \text{round\_value}) = \frac{k}{k+\frac{1}{x}-1}$, where: k is the number of values likely to be rounded to round_value, and x the probability that the speaker chooses to round. Figure 2.55 shows how the likelihood of rounding being used increases rapidly as the number of possible rounded values increases.

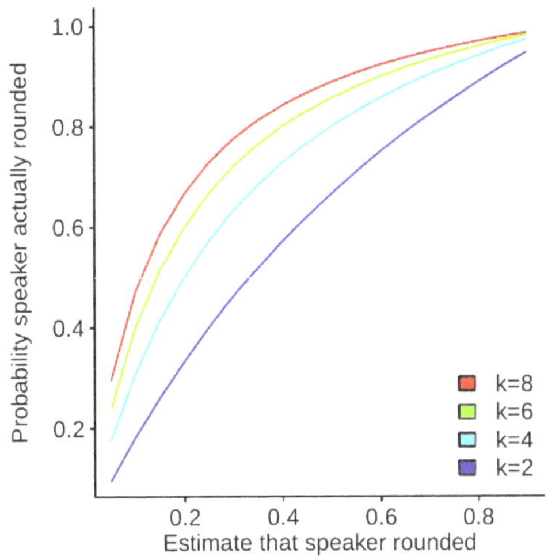

Figure 2.55: Probability the rounded value given has actually been rounded, given an estimate of the likelihood of rounding, and the number of values likely to have been rounded; grey line shows 50% probability of rounding. Github-Local

A study by Basili, Panlilio-Yap, Ramsey, Shih and Katz [141] investigated the redesign and implementation of a software system. Figure 2.56 shows the number of change requests taking a given amount of time to decide whether the change was needed, and the time to design+implement the change. There are peaks at the round-numbers 1, 2 and 5, with 4 hours perhaps being the Parkinson's law target of a half day.

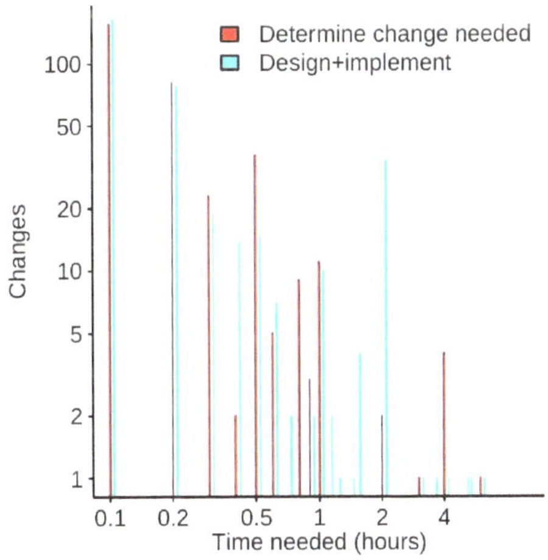

Figure 2.56: Number of change requests having a given recorded time to decide whether change was needed, and time to implement. Data from Basili et al. Github-Local

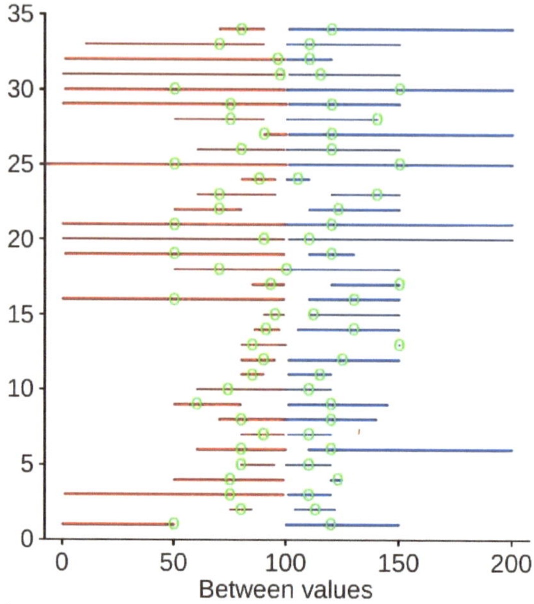

Figure 2.57: Min/max range of values (red/blue lines), and best value estimate (green circles), given by subjects interpreting the value likely expressed by statements containing "less than 100" and "more than 100". Data kindly provided by Cummins. Github-Local

A study by King and Janiszewski showed integer values between 1 and 100 , in random order, to 360 subjects, asking them to specify whether they liked the number, disliked it, or were neutral. Numbers ending in zero had a much higher chance of being liked, compared to numbers ending in other digits; see Github-developers/like-n-dis.R for a regression model fitted to the like and dislike probability, based on the first/last digits of the number.

A study by van der Henst, Carles and Sperber [1873] approached people on the street, and asked them for the time; there was a 20% probability that the minutes were a multiple of five. When subjects were wearing an analogue watch, 98% of replies were multiples of five-minutes, when subjects were wearing digital watches the figure was 66%. Many subjects invested effort in order to communicate using a round number.

People sometimes denote approximate values using numerical expressions containing comparative and superlative qualifiers, such as "more than n " and "at least n ".

A study by Cummins [421] investigated the impact of number granularity on the range of values assigned by subjects to various kinds of numerical expressions. Subjects saw statements of the form "So far, we've sold fewer than 60 tickets." (in other statements fewer was replaced by more), and subjects were asked: "How many tickets have been sold? From ?? to ??, most likely ??.". Three numeric granularities were used: coarse, e.g., a multiple of 100 , medium e.g., multiple of 10 and non-multiple of 100 , and fine e.g., non-round such as 77 .

The results found that the most likely value, given by subjects, was closest to the value appearing in the statement when it had a fine granularity and furthest away when it was coarse; see Github-reliability/CumminsModifiedNumeral.R. Figure 2.57 shows the "From to" range given by each subject, along with their best estimate (in green) for statements specifying "less than 100 " and "more than 100 ".

When specifying a numeric value, people may also include information that expresses their uncertainty, using a so-called hedge word, e.g., "about", "around", "almost", "almost exactly", "at least", "below" and "nearly".

A study by Ferson, O'Rawe, Antonenko, Siegrist, Mickley, Luhmann, Sentz and Finkel [598] investigated interpretations of numerical uncertainty. Subjects were asked to specify minimal and maximal possible values, for their interpretation of the quantity expressed in various statements, such as: "No more than 100 people."

Figure 2.58 shows the cumulative probability of relative uncertainty of numeric phrases (calculated as: $\frac{\text{minimal} - \text{actual}}{\text{minimal}}$ and $\frac{\text{maximal} - \text{actual}}{\text{maximal}}$), for the hedge words listed in the legends.

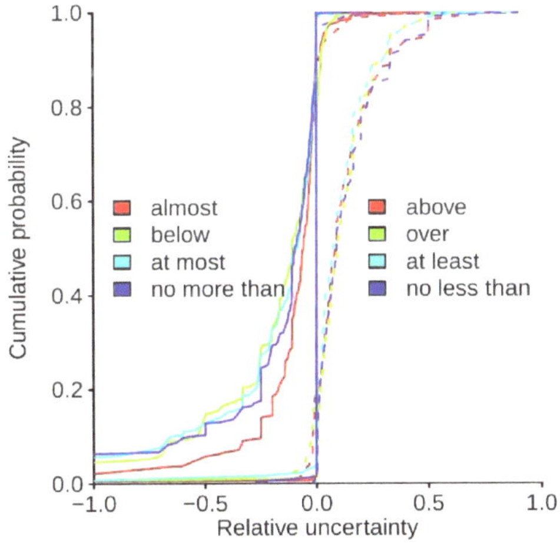

Figure 2.58: The cumulative probability of subjects expressing a given relative uncertainty, for numeric phrases using given hedge words. Data kindly provided by Ferson. Github-Local

The relative size of objects being quantified has been found to have an effect on the interpretation given to quantifiers. [1371]

2.7.2 Symbolic distance and problem size effect

When people compare two items sharing a distance-like characteristic, the larger the distance between two items, the faster people are likely to respond to a comparison question involving this characteristic (e.g., comparisons of social status and geographical distance; [834] also see fig 2.19); this is known as the symbolic distance effect. Inconsistencies between a symbolic distance characteristic and actual distance for the question asked, can increase the error rate, [805] e.g., is the following relation true? $3 > 5$.

A study by Tzelgov, Yehene, Kotler and Alon [1860] investigated the impact of implicit learning on the symbolic distance effect. Subjects trained one-hour per day on six different days (over ten days) learning the relative order of pairs of nine graphical symbols. During the first three training sessions all subjects only saw pairs of symbols that were adjacent in the overall relative ordering, i.e., pairs: (1,2), (2,3), (3,4), (4,5), (5,6), (6,7), (7,8) and (8,9). During the next three sessions one group of subjects continued to train on the same pairs, while another group trained on 14 non-adjacent pairs (i.e., a subset of possible non-adjacent pairs).

On completion of the training sessions, subjects answered questions about pairs of symbols having various relative ordering distances. A symbolic distance effect was seen in answer response times; subjects who had trained on non-adjacent pairs consistently responded faster than subjects who had only trained on adjacent pairs.

Studies have found that the time taken to solve a simple arithmetic problem, and the error rate, increase as the value of both operands increases (e.g., subjects are slower to solve $9 + 7$, than $2 + 3$, [294] see Github-developers/campbell1997.R); this is known as the problem size effect. As in many experiments, the characteristics of student performance can vary widely.

A study by LeFevre and Liu investigated the performance of Canadian and Chinese university students on simple multiplication problems (e.g., 7×4). Figure 2.59 shows the percentage error rate for problems containing values from a given operand family (e.g., 2×6 contains values from the 2 and 6 operand family, and an incorrect answer to this problem counts towards both operand families). The hypothesis for the difference in error rate was student experience; during their education Canadian students were asked to solve more multiplication problems containing small values, compared to large values; an analysis of the work-books of Chinese students found the opposite distribution of operand values, i.e., Chinese students were asked to solve more problems involving large operands, compared to small operands.

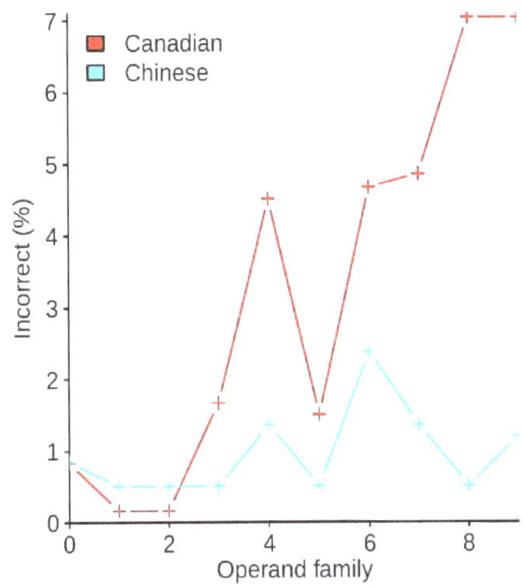

Figure 2.59: Percentage of incorrect answers to arithmetic problems, given by Canadian and Chinese students, for each operand family value. Data kindly provided by LeFevre. Github-Local

The magnitude of a measurement value depends on the unit of measurement used, e.g., inches, feet, yards, and meters are units of length, or distance.

A study Jørgensen asked commercial developers to estimate the time needed to implement a project. Some were asked to estimate in work-hours and others in work days. The results found that those answering in work-hours gave lower estimates, for the same project, than those working in workdays; see Github-developers/time-unit-effect.R.

2.7.3 Estimating event likelihood

The ability to detect regularities in the environment, and to take advantage of them is a defining characteristic of intelligent behavior.

In some environments, the cost of failing to correctly detect an object or event may be significantly higher than the cost of acting as-if an event occurred, when none occurred. People appear to be hardwired to detect some patterns, e.g., seeing faces in a random jumble of items.

People sometimes have expectations of behavior for event sequences. For instance, an expectation that sequences of random numbers have certain attributes, [570, 1424] e.g., frequent alternation between different values (which from a mathematical perspective, are a form of regularity).

Figure 2.60 shows data from various surveys of public perception of demographic questions involving the percentage of a population containing various kinds of people, along with a fitted log-odds proportional model (grey line shows estimated equal actual).

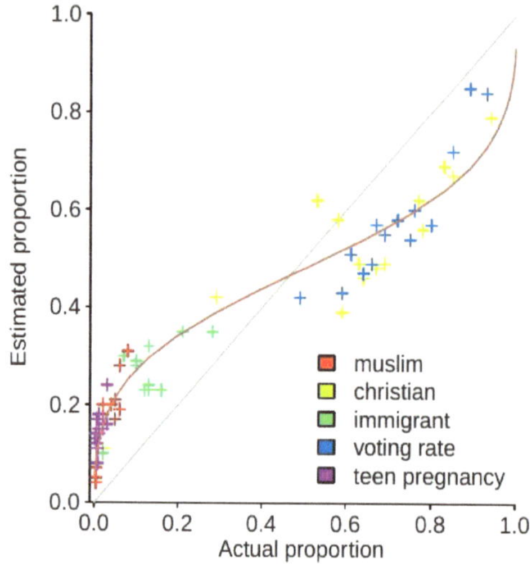

Figure 2.60: Estimated proportion (from survey results), and actual proportion of people in a population matching various demographics; line is a fitted regression having the form: $lo_{\text{Estimated}} \propto \gamma \times lo_{\text{Actual}} + (1-\gamma) \times \delta$, where γ and δ are fitted constants; grey line shows estimated equals actual. Data from Landy et al. [1081] Github-Local

People tend to overestimate the likelihood of uncommon events and underestimate the likelihood of very common events. A variety of probability weighting functions have been proposed to explain the experimental evidence. [703] The log-odds of the proportion estimated, $\log \frac{p_e}{1-p_e} \Rightarrow l_{pe}$ (where p_e is the proportion estimated), is given by:

$lo_{pe} = \gamma lo_{pa} + (1-\gamma)\delta$, where: γ is a constant (interpreted as a relative weight on the perception of lo_{pa}, the log-odds of the actual proportion), and δ is a constant (interpreted as a prior expectation). [xi]

The probability of a particular event occurring may not be fixed, the world is constantly changing, and the likelihood of an event may change. Studies have found that people are responsive to changes in the frequency with which an event occurs, [647] and to changes in the available information. [1105]

A study by Khaw, Stevens and Woodford [994] investigated changes in decision-maker answers when operating in a changing environment. Subjects were asked to estimate the likelihood of drawing a green ring from a box containing an unknown (to them) percentage of red and green rings; the percentage of color rings remained fixed for some number of draws, and then changed. During a session each subject made 999 draws and estimates of probability of drawing a green ring. Subjects were paid an amount based on how accurately they estimated, over time, the percentage of green rings, with eleven subjects each performing ten sessions.

The results found discrete jumps in subject estimates (rather than a continual updating of probability as each draw revealed more information, as a Bayesian decision-maker would behave), and a preference for round numbers.

Figure 2.61 shows two subjects' estimates (blue/green lines) of the probability of drawing a green ring, for a given actual probability (red line), as they drew successive rings.

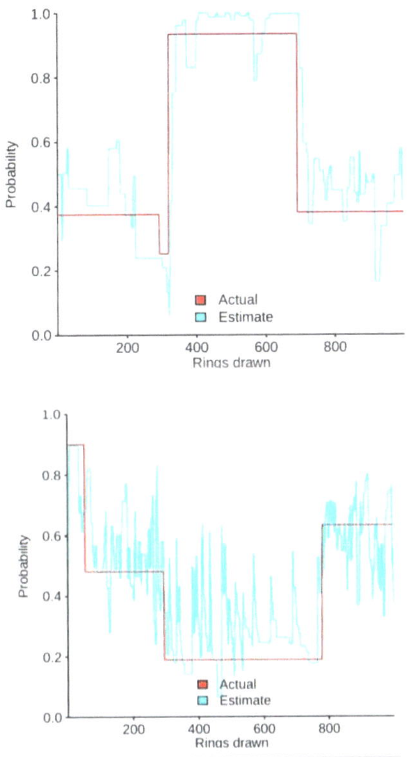

Figure 2.61: Estimated probability (blue/green lines) of drawing a green ring by two subjects (upper: subject 10, session 8 , lower: subject 7 , session 8), with actual probability in red. Data from Khaw et al. Github-Local

A change in the occurrence of an event can result in a change to what is considered to be an occurrence of the event. A study by Levari, Gilbert, Wilson, Sievers, Amodio and Wheatley [1118] showed subjects a series of randomly colored dots, one at a time (the colors varied on a continuous scale, between purple and blue); subjects were asked to judge whether each dot they saw was blue (each subject saw 1,000 dots). Subjects were divided into two groups: for one group the percentage of blue dots did not change over time, while for the second group the percentage of blue dots was decreased after a subject had seen 200 dots.

Figure 2.62 is based on data from the first and last series of 200 dots seen by each subject; the x-axis is an objective measure of the color of each dot, the y-axis is the percentage of dots identified as blue (averaged over all subjects). Lines are fitted logistic regression models. The responses for subjects in the constant blue group did not change between the first/last 200 dots (red and green lines). For the decreased blue group, after subjects experienced a decline in the likelihood of encountering a blue dot, the color of what they considered to be a blue dot shifted towards purple (blue and purple lines).

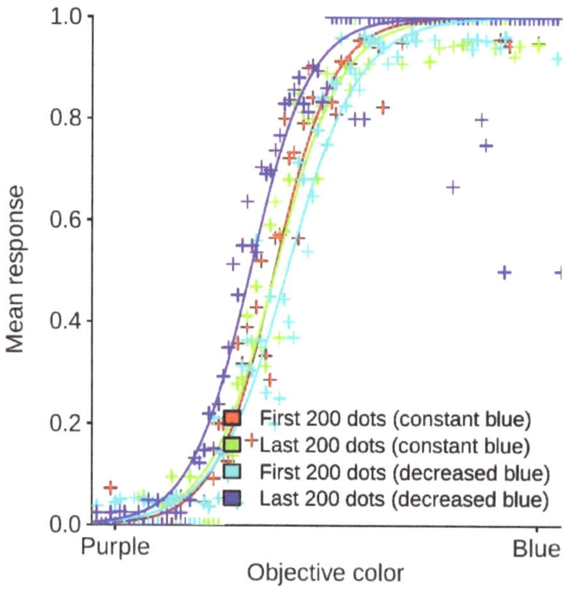

Figure 2.62: Mean likelihood that a subject considered a dot of a given color to be blue, for the first/last 200 dots seen by two groups of subjects; lines are fitted logistic regression models. Data from Levari et al. Github-Local

In later experiments subjects were told that the prevalence of blue dots "might change", and would "definitely decrease"; the results were unchanged.

2.8 High-level functionality

This section discusses high-level cognitive functionality that has an impact on software development, but for which there is insufficient material for a distinct section.

2.8.1 Personality & intelligence

Perhaps the most well-known personality test is the Meyer-Briggs type indicator, or MBTI (both registered trademarks of Consulting Psychologists Press). The reliability and validity of this test has been questioned, [1235,1492] with commercial considerations, and a changing set of questions making research difficult. The International Personality Item Pool (IPIP) [697] is a public domain measure, which now has available samples containing hundreds of thousands of responses. [920]

The Five-Factor model [696] structures personality around five basic traits: neuroticism, extroversion, openness, agreeableness, and conscientiousness; it has its critics, [1675] and appears to be WEIRD person specific. [1169] Studies that have attempted to identify personality types, based on these five traits have suffered from small sample size (e.g., 1,000 people); studies based on IPIP data, using samples containing 100,000 to 500,000 responses, claim to have isolated four personality types. [669]

Tests measuring something called IQ have existed for over 100 years. The results are traditionally encapsulated in a single number, but tests claiming to measure the various components of intelligence are available. [463] The model is that people possess a general intelligence g, plus various domain specific intelligences, e.g., in tests involving maths the results would depend on g and maths specific intelligence, and in tests involving use of language the results would depend on g and language specific intelligence.

The cultural intelligence hypothesis is that humans have a specific set of social skills for exchanging knowledge in social groups; children and chimpanzees have been found to have similar cognitive skills for dealing with the physical world, but children have more sophisticated skills for dealing with the social world. [818]

Without reliable techniques for measuring personality traits, it is not possible to isolate characteristics likely to be beneficial or detrimental to software development. For instance, how important is the ability to concentrate for large amounts of time on particular activities?

2.8.2 Risk taking

Making a decision based on incomplete or uncertain information involves an element of risk. How do people integrate risk into their decision-making process?

The term risk asymmetry refers to the fact that people have been found to be risk averse when deciding between alternatives that have a positive outcome, but are risk seeking when deciding between alternatives that have a negative outcome. [xii]

While there is a widespread perception that women are more risk averse than men, existing studies are either not conclusive or show a small effect [600] (many suffer from small sample sizes, and dependencies on the features of the task subjects are given). For the case of financial risks. the evidence [337] that men are more willing to take financial risks than women is more clear-cut. The evidence from attempts to improve road safety is that "protecting motorists from the consequences of bad driving encourages bad driving". [8]

A study by Jones [936] investigated the possibility that some subjects, in an experiment involving recalling information about previously seen assignment statements, were less willing to risk giving an answer when they had opportunity to specify that in real-life they would refer back to previously read code. Previous studies [931,932] had found that a small percentage of subjects consistently gave much higher rates of "would refer back" answers. One explanation is that these subjects had a smaller short term memory capacity than other subjects (STM capacity varies between people), another is that these subjects are much more risk averse than the other subjects.

The Domain-Specific Risk-Taking (DOSPERT) questionnaire [208,1937] was used to measure subject's risk attitude. The results found no correlation between risk attitude (as measured by DOSPERT), and number of "would refer back" responses.

2.8.3 Decision-making

A distinction is commonly made between decisions made under risk, and decisions made under uncertainty. Decisions are made under risk when all the information about the probability of outcomes is available, and one of the available options has to be selected. Many studies investigating human decision-making provide subjects with all the information about the probability of the outcomes, and ask them to select an option, i.e., they involve decision under risk.

Decisions are made under uncertainty when the available information is incomplete and possibly inaccurate. Human decision-making often takes place in an environment of incomplete information and limited decision-making resources (e.g., working memory capacity and thinking time); people have been found to adopt various strategies to handle this situation, [1205] balancing the predicted cognitive effort required to use a particular decision-making strategy against the likely accuracy achieved by that strategy.

The term bounded rationality is used to describe an approach to problem-solving that makes limited use of cognitive resources. A growing number of studies [680] have found that the methods used by people to make decisions, and solve problems, are often close enough to optimal [xiii], given the resources available to them; even when dealing with financial matters. [1240] If people handle money matters in this fashion, their approach to software development decisions is unlikely to fare any better.

A so-called irregular choice occurs when, a person who chooses B from the set of items {A, B, C} does not choose B from the set {A, B}; irregular decision makers have been found [1822] to be more common among younger (18-25) subjects, and are less common with older (60-75) subjects.

Consumer research into understanding how shoppers decide among competing products uncovered a set of mechanisms that are applicable to decision-making in general, e.g., decision-making around the question of which soap will wash the whitest is no different from the question of whether an if statement, or a switch statement should be used. Before a decision can be made, a decision-making strategy has to be selected, and people have been found to use a number of different decision-making strategies. [1456]

Decision strategies differ in several ways, for instance, some make trade-offs among the attributes of the alternatives (making it possible for an alternative with several good attributes to be selected, instead of the alternative whose only worthwhile attribute is excellent); they also differ in the amount of information that needs to be obtained, and the amount of cognitive processing needed to make a decision. Named decision-making strategies include: the weighted additive rule, the equal weight heuristic, the frequency of good and bad features heuristic, the majority of confirming dimensions heuristic, the satisficing heuristic the lexicographic heuristic, the habitual heuristic and in recent years decision by sampling. [1780]

There is a hierarchy of responses for how people deal with time pressure: [1456] they work faster; if that fails, they may focus on a subset of the issues; if that fails, they may change strategies (e.g., from alternative based to attribute based).

Studies have found that having to justify a decision can affect the choice of decisionmaking strategy used. [1824] One strategy for handling accountability is to select the alternative that the perspective audience is thought most likely to select. [1823] People who have difficulty determining which alternative has the greatest utility tend to select the alternative that supports the best overall reasons (for choosing it). [1712]

Requiring developers to justify why they have not followed existing practice can be a double-edged sword. Developers can respond by deciding to blindly follow everybody else (a path of least resistance), or they can invest effort in evaluating alternatives (not necessarily cost effective behavior, since the invested effort may not be warranted by the expected benefits). The extent to which some people will blindly obey authority was chillingly demonstrated in a number of studies by Milgram. [1278]

Making decisions can be difficult, and copying what others do can be a cost effective strategy. Who should be copied? Strategies include: copy the majority, copy successful individuals, copy kin, copy "friends", copy older individuals. Social learning is discussed in section 3.4.4.

A study by Morgan, Rendell, Ehn, Hoppitt and Laland [1312] investigated the impact of the opinions expressed by others on the answers given by subjects. One experiment asked subjects to decide whether one object was a rotated version of a second object (i.e., the task shown in figure 2.8), and to rate their confidence in their answer (on a scale of 0 to 6 , with 6 being the most confident). After giving an answer, subjects saw the number of yes/no answers given by up to twelve other people (these answers may or may not have been correct); subjects were then asked to give a final answer. The 51 subjects each completed 24 trials, and after seeing other responses changed their answer, on average, in 2.8 trials.

Figure 2.63 shows the behavior of a fitted regression model for the probability that a subject (y-axis), who makes three switches in 24 trials, does switch their answer, when told that a given fraction of other responses were the opposite of the subject's initial guess (x-axis); lines show the percentage for subject's expressing a given confidence in their answer (colored lines).

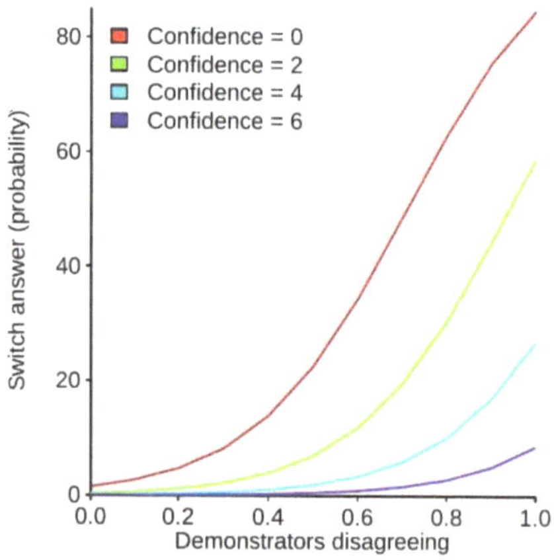

Figure 2.63: Fitted regression model for probability that a subject, who switched answer three times, switches their initial answer when told a given fraction of opposite responses were made by others (x-axis), broken down by confidence

expressed in their answer (colored lines). Data kindly provided by Morgan. [1312] Github-Local

Social pressure can cause people to go along with decisions voiced by others involved in the decision process (i.e., social conformity as a signal of belonging, [197] such as corporate IT fashion: see fig 1.17). A study by Asch [81] asked groups of seven to nine subjects to individually state, which of three black strips they considered to be the longest (see figure 2.64). The group sat together in front of the stripes, and subjects could interact with each other; all the subjects, except one, were part of the experiment, and in 12 of 18 questions selected a stripe that was clearly not the longest (i.e., the majority gave an answer clearly at odds with visible reality). It was arranged that the actual subject did not have to give an answer until hearing the answers of most other subjects.

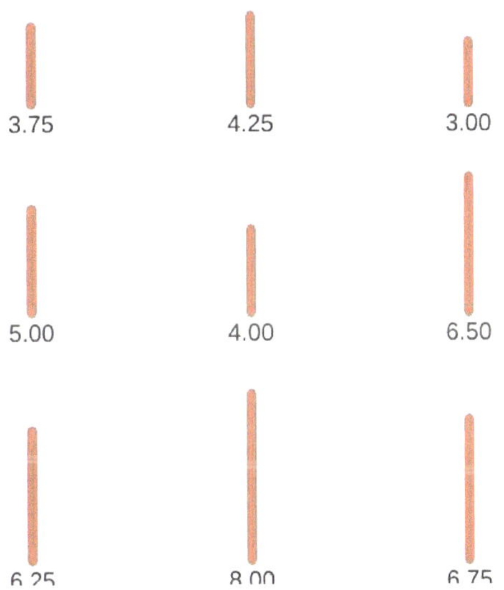

Figure 2.64: Each row shows a scaled version of the three stripes, along with actual lengths in inches, from which subjects were asked to select the longest. Based on Asch. Github-Local

The actual subject, in 24% of groups, always gave the correct answer; in 27% of groups the subject agreed with the incorrect majority answer between eight and twelve times, and just under half varied in the extent to which they followed the majority decision. When the majority selected the most extreme incorrect answer (i.e., the shortest stripe), subjects giving an incorrect answer selected the less extreme incorrect answer in 20% of cases.

Later studies [219] have found that the extent to which subjects conform to group responses varies across cultures, with the least conformity in individualist societies and the greatest in collectivist societies. [1432]

How a problem is posed can have a large impact on the decision made. A study by Regnell, Höst, och Dag, Beremark and Hjelm [1569] asked 10 subjects to assign a relative priority to two lists of requirements (subjects' had a total budget of 100,000 units and had to assign units to requirements). One list specified that subjects should prioritize the 17 high level requirements, and the other list specified that a more detailed response, in the form of prioritizing every feature contained within each high level requirement, be given.

Comparing the totals for the 17 high level requirements list (summing the responses for the detailed list) with the more detailed response, showed that the subject correlation between the two lists was not very strong (the mean across 10 subjects was 0.46); see Github-projects/prioritization.R.

2.8.4 Expected utility and Prospect theory

The outcome of events is often uncertain. If events are known to occur with probability p_i, with each producing a value of X_i, then the expected outcome value is given by:

$$[x] = p_1X_1 + p_2X_2 + p_3X_3 + \cdots + p_nX_n$$

For instance, given a 60% chance of winning £10 and a 40% chance of winning £20, the expected winnings are: $0.6 \times 10 + 0.4 \times 20 = 14$

When comparing the costs and benefits of an action, decision makers often take into account information on their current wealth, e.g., a bet offering a 50% chance of winning £1 million, and a 50% chance of losing £0.9 million has an expected utility of £0.05 million; would you take this bet, unless you were very wealthy? Do you consider £20 to be worth twice as much as £ 10 ?

The mapping of a decision's costs and benefits, to a decision maker's particular circumstances, is made by what is known as a utility function, u; the above equation becomes (where W is the decision maker's current wealth):

$$E[x] = p_1u(W + X_1) + p_2u(W + X_2) + p_3u(W + X_3) + \cdots + p_nu(W + X_n)$$

In some situations a decision maker's current wealth might be effectively zero, e.g., they have forgotten their wallet, or because they have no authority to spend company money on work related decisions (personal wealth of employees is unlikely to factor into many of their work decisions).

Figure 2.65 shows possible perceived utilities of an increase in wealth. A risk neutral decision maker perceives the utility of an increase in wealth as being proportional to the increase (green, $(w) = w$), a risk loving decision maker perceives the utility of an increase in wealth as being proportionally greater than the actual increase (e.g., red, $u(w) = w^2$), while a risk averse decision maker perceives the utility of an increase having proportionally less utility (e.g., blue, $u(w) = \sqrt{w}$).

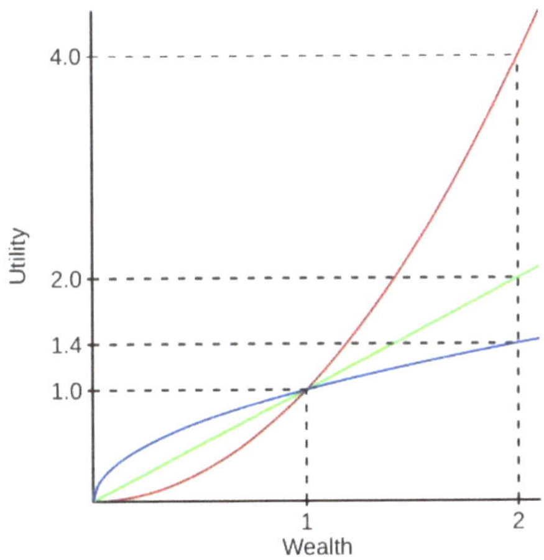

Figure 2.65: Risk neutral (green, $(w) = w$), and example of risk loving (red, quadratic) and risk averse (blue, square-root) utility functions. Github-Local

A study by Kina, Tsunoda, Hata, Tamada and Igaki [1002] investigated the decisions made by subjects (20 Open source developers) when given a choice between two tools, each having various probabilities of providing various benefits, e.g., Tool $_1$ which always saves 2 hours of work, or Tool_2 which saves 5 hours of work with 50% probability, and has no effect on work time with 50% probability.

Given a linear utility function, Tool_1 has an expected utility of 2 hours, while Tool_2 has an expected utility of 2.5 hours. The results showed 65% of developers choosing Tool_1, and 35% choosing Tool $_2$: those 65% were not using a linear utility function; use of a squareroot utility function would produce the result seen, i.e., $1 \times \sqrt{2} > 0.5 \times \sqrt{5} + 0.5 \times \sqrt{0}$.

2.8.5 Overconfidence

While overconfidence can create unrealistic expectations, and lead to hazardous decisions being made (e.g., allocating insufficient resources to complete a job), simulation studies [919] have found that overconfidence has benefits in come situations, averaged over a population; see Github-developers/overconfidence/0909.R. A study [83] of commercialization of new inventions, found that while inventors are significantly more confident and optimistic than the general population, the likely return on their investment of time and money in their invention is negative; a few receive a huge pay-off.

A study by Lichtenstein and Fishhoff [1133] asked subjects general knowledge questions, with the questions divided into two groups, hard and easy. Figure 2.66 shows that subjects' overestimated their ability (x -axis) to correctly answer hard questions, but underestimated their ability to answer easy questions; green line denotes perfect self-knowledge.

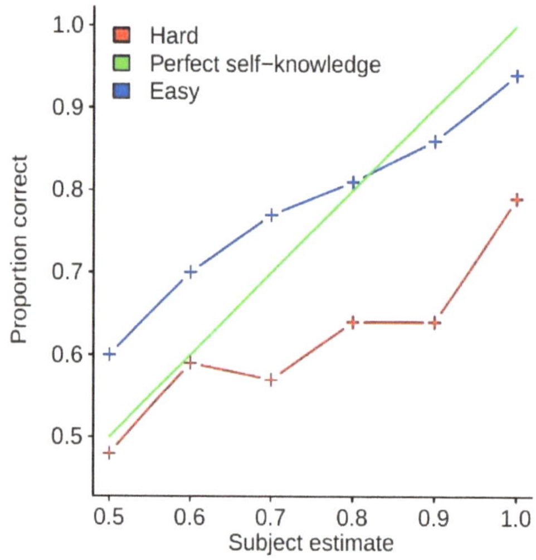

Figure 2.66: Subjects' estimate of their ability (x -axis) to correctly answer a question and actual performance in answering on the left scale. The responses of a person with perfect self-knowledge is given by the green line. Data extracted from Lichtenstein et al. Github-Local

These, and subsequent results, show that the skills and knowledge that constitute competence in a particular domain are the same skills needed to evaluate one's (and other people's) competence in that domain. Metacognition is the term used to denote the ability of a person to accurately judge how well they are performing.

Peoples' belief in their own approach to getting things done can result in them ignoring higher performing alternatives; [70] this behavior has become known as the illusion of control. [1082]

Studies [1337] have found cultural and context dependent factors influencing overconfidence; see Github-developers/journal-pone-0202288.R.

It might be thought that people, who have previously performed some operation, would be in a position to make accurate predictions about future performance on these operations. However, studies have found [1613] that, while people do use their memories of the duration of past events to make predictions of future event duration, their memories are systematic underestimates of past duration. People appear to underestimate future event duration because they underestimate past event duration.

2.8.6 Time discounting

People seek to consume pleasurable experiences sooner, and to delay their appointment with painful experiences, i.e., people tend to accept less satisfaction in the short-term, than could be obtained by pursuing a longer-term course of action; a variety of models have been proposed. [509] Studies have found that animals, including humans, appear to use a hyperbolic discount function for time variable preferences. [483] The hyperbolic delay discount function is:

$v_d = \frac{V}{1+kd}$, where: v_d is the delayed discount, V the undiscounted value, d the delay and k some constant.

A property of this hyperbolic function is that curves with different values of V and d can cross. Figure 2.67 shows an example where the perceived present value of two future rewards (red and blue lines) starts with red have a perceived value greater than blue, as time passes (i.e., the present time moves right, and the delay before receiving the rewards decreases) the perceived reward denoted by the blue line out-grows the red line, until there is a reversal in perceived present value. When both rewards are far in the future, the larger amount has the greater perceived value; studies have found [1009] that subjects switch to giving a higher value to the lesser amount as the time of receiving the reward gets closer.

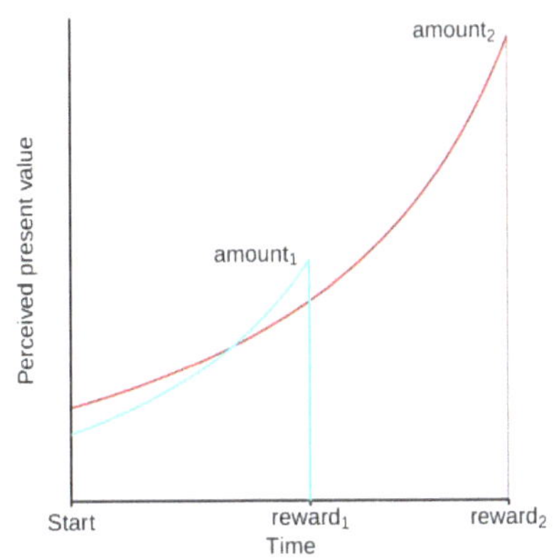

Figure 2.67: Perceived present value (moving through time to the right) of two future rewards. Github-Local

A study by Becker, Fagerholm, Mohanani and Chatzigeorgiou [158] asked professional developers how many days of effort would need to be saved, over the lifetime of a project, to make it worthwhile investing time integrating a new library, compared to spending that time implementing a feature in the project backlog. The developers worked at companies who developed and supported products over many years, and were asked to specify saving for various project lifetimes.

Figure 2.68 shows the normalised savings specified by developers from one company, for given project lifetimes. Many of the lines are concave, showing that these developers are applying an interest rate that decreases, for the time invested, as project lifetime increases (if a fixed interest rate, or hyperbolic rate, was applied, the lines would be convex, i.e., curve up).

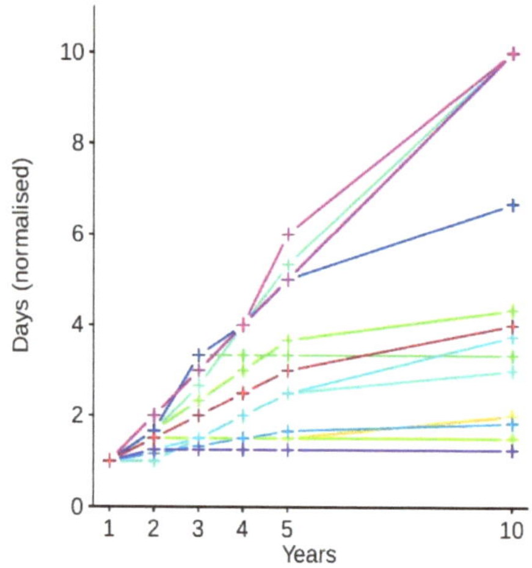

Figure 2.68: Saving required (normalised), over a project having a given duration, before subjects would make a long term investment. Data from Becker et al. Github-Local

2.8.7 Developer performance

Companies seek to hire those people who will give the best software development performance. Currently, the only reliable method of evaluating developer performance is by measuring developer outputs (this is a good enough model of the workings of human mental operations remains in the future). Conscientiousness has consistently been found to be an effective predictor of occupational performance. [1969]

One operational characteristic of the brain that can be estimated is the number of operations that could potentially be performed per second (a commonly used method of estimating the performance of silicon-based processors).

The brain might simply be a very large neural net, so there may be no instructions to count as such; Merkle [1266] used the following approaches to estimate the number of synaptic operations per second (the supply of energy needed to fire neurons limits the number that can be simultaneously active, in a local region, to between 1% and 4% of the neurons in that region [1114]):

- multiplying the number of synapses (10^{15}), by their speed of operation (about 10 im pulses/second), gives 10^{16} synapse operations per second (if the necessary energy could be delivered to all of them at the same time),
- the retina of the eye performs an estimated 10^{10} analog add operations per second. The brain contains 10^2 to 10^4 times as many nerve cells as the retina, suggesting that it can perform 10^{12} to 10^{14} operations per second,
- the brain's total power dissipation of 25 watts (an estimated 10 watts of useful work), and an estimated energy consumption of $5 \cdot 10^{-15}$ joules for the switching of a nerve cell membrane, provides an upper limit of $2 \cdot 10^{15}$ operations per second.

A synapse switching on and off is the same as a transistor switching on and off, in that they both need to be connected to other switches to create a larger functional unit. It is not known how many synapses are used to create functional units, or even what those functional units might be. The distance between synapses is approximately 1 mm , and sending a signal from one part of the brain to another part requires many synaptic operations, for instance, to travel from the front to the rear of the brain requires at least 100 synaptic operations to propagate the signal. So the number of synaptic operations per high-level, functional operation, is likely to be high. Silicon-based processors can contain millions of transistors; the potential number of transistor-switching operations per second might be greater than 10^{14}, but the number of instructions executed is significantly smaller.

Although there have been studies of the information-processing capacity of the brain (e.g., visual attention, [1890] and storage rate into long-term memory [238,1075]), we are a long way from being able to deduce the likely work rates of the components of the brain while performing higher level cognitive functions.

Processing units need a continuous supply of energy to function. The brain does not contain any tissue that stores energy, and obtains all its energy needs through the breakdown of blood-borne glucose. Consuming a glucose drink has been found to increase blood glucose levels, and enhance performance on various cognitive tasks. [987] Fluctuations in glucose levels have an impact on an individual's ability to exert self-control, [642] with some glucose intolerant individuals not always acting in socially acceptable ways. [xiv]

How do developers differ in their measurable output performance?

Although much talked about, there has been little research on individual developer productivity (a few studies [1638] have used project level data to estimate productivity). One review [878] of studies of employee output variability, found that standard deviation, about the mean, increased from 19% to 48%, as job complexity increased (not software related). Claims of a 28 -to- 1 productivity difference between developers, is sometimes still bandied about. The, so-called Grant-Sackman study [727] is based on an incorrect interpretation of a summary of their experimental data. [1522] The data shows a performance difference of around 6-to-1 between developers using batch vs. online, for creating software; see Github-group-compare/GS-perm-diff.R and fig 8.22.

Lines of working code produced per unit-time is sometimes used; figures in the hundreds of instructions per man-month can sometimes be traced back to measurements made in the 1960s. [800]

A study by Nichols [1377] investigated the performance of those attending the Personal Software Process (PSP) training given at CMU (average professional experience 3.7 years, sd 6.5). The training involves writing programs to solve 10 problems, with each expected to take a few hours; participants also have to estimate how long various components of the task will take and record actual times.

Figure 2.69 shows violin plots for the actual time taken by the 593 participants, programming in C , to solve the problems (sorted by the mean solution time; white line shows mean time, colors intended to help visualise individual plots). There is almost an order of magnitude difference between developers, and between individual performance on different problems.

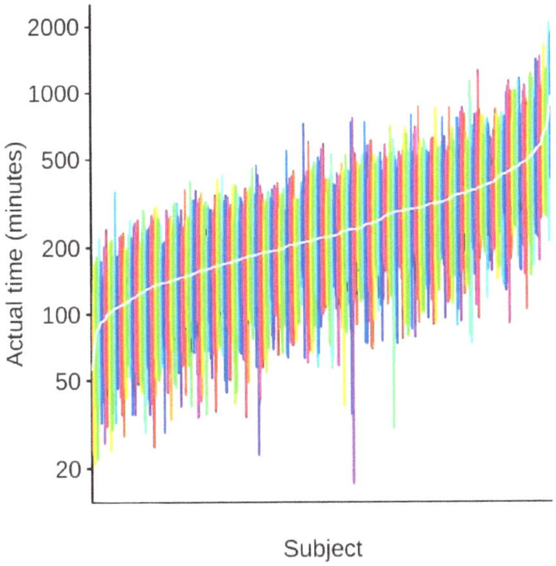

Figure 2.69: Violin plots for actual time to complete problems for each of the 593 participants, sorted by mean solution time; colors to help break up the plots, and white line shows subject mean. Data from Nichols. Github-Local

Most organizations do not attempt to measure the mental performance of job applicants for developer roles; unlike many other jobs where individual performance is an important consideration. Whether this is because of existing non-measurement culture, lack of reliable measuring procedures, or fear of frightening off prospective employees is not known.

One study [2001] of development and maintenance costs of programs written in C and Ada found no correlation between salary grade (or employee rating), and rate of bug fix or feature implementation rate.

One study [2023] investigating tasks completed per month by developers, over a three year period, found that completion rate increased with developer tenure.

One metric used in software testing is number of fault experiences encountered. In practice non-failing tests, written by software testers, are useful because they provide evidence that particular functionality behaves as expected.

A study by Iivonen [885] analysed the defect detection performance of those involved in testing software at several companies. Table 2.8 shows the number of defects detected by six testers (all but the first column, show percentages), along with self-classification of seriousness, followed by the default status assigned by others.

Table 2.8: Defects detected by six testers (left two columns; some part-time and one who left the company during the study period), the percentage assigned a given status (next three columns), and percentage outcomes assigned by others. Data from Iivonen. [885]

Tester	Defects	Extra Hot	Hot	Normal	Open	Fixed	No fix	Duplicate	Cannot reproduce
A	74	4	1	95	12	62	26	12	0
B	73	0	56	44	15	87	6	2	5
C	70	0	29	71	36	71	24	0	4
D	51	0	27	73	33	85	6	0	9
E	50	2	16	82	30	89	9	0	3
F	18	0	22	78	22	64	14	0	21

A tester performance comparison, based on defects reported, requires combining these figures (and perhaps others, e.g., likelihood of fault being experienced by a customer) into a value that can be reliably compared across testers. Defects differ in their commercial importance, and a relative weight for each classification has to be decided, e.g., should the weight of "No fix" be larger than that given to "Cannot reproduce" or "Duplicate"?

To what extent would a tester's performance, based on measurements involving one software system in one company, be transferable to another system in the same company or another company? Iivonen interviewed those involved in testing, to find out what characteristics were thought important in a tester. Knowledge of customer processes and use cases, was a common answer; this customer usage knowledge enables testers to concentrate on those parts of the software that customers are most likely to use and be impacted by incorrect operation, it also provides the information needed to narrow down the space of possible input values.

Knowledge of the customer ecosystem and software development skills are the two blades, in figure 2.1, that have to mesh together to create useful software systems.

2.8.8 Miscellaneous

Research in human-computer interaction has uncovered a variety of human performance characteristics, including: physical movement (e.g., hand or eye movement) and mental operations. The equations fitted to experimental performance data for some of these characteristics often contain logarithms, and attention has been drawn to the similarity of form to the equations used in information theory. [1187] The use of a logarithmic scale, to quantify the perception of stimuli, minimizes relative error. [1510] Some commonly encountered performance characteristics include:

- Fitts' law: time taken, RT, to move a distance D, to an object having width W, is: $RT = a + b\log\left[\frac{2D}{W}\right]$, where a and b are constants. In deriving this relationship, Fitts drew on ideas from information theory, and used a simplified version of Shannon's law; the unsimplified version implies: $RT = c + d\log\left[\frac{D+W}{W}\right]$, [1187]
- Hick's law: time taken, RT, to choose an item from a list of K items, is: $RT = a + b\log(K)$, where a and b are constants; a is smaller for humans than pigeons. [1898]

A study by Hawkins, Brown, Steyvers and Wagenmakers [790] displayed a number of squares on a screen, and asked subjects to select the square whose contents had a particular characteristic. Figure 2.70 shows how subject response time increased (and accuracy decreased), as the log of number of choices. A different color is used for each of the 36 subjects, with colors sorted by performance on the two-choice case; data has been jittered to help show the density of points. This study found that problem context could cause subjects to make different time/accuracy performance trade-offs,

- Ageing effects: the Seattle Longitudinal Study [1642] has been following the intellectual development of over six thousand people since 1956 (surveys of individuals in the study are carried out every seven years). Findings include: ". . . there is no uniform pattern of age-related changes across all intellectual abilities, . . . ", and ". . . reliable replicable average age decrements in psychometric abilities do not occur prior to age 60, but that such reliable decrements can be found for all abilities by age 74 . . " An analysis [225] of the workers on the production line at a Mercedes-Benz assembly plant found that productivity did not decline until at least up to age 60 .
- Studies of professional developers that have included age related information, [931,934] have not found an interaction with subject experimental performance. See figure 8.13 for an example of developer age distribution, the sunk cost effect is the tendency to persist in an endeavour, once an investment of time, or money, has been made. [205] This effect is observed in other animals, [1358] and so presumably this behavior provides survival benefits.

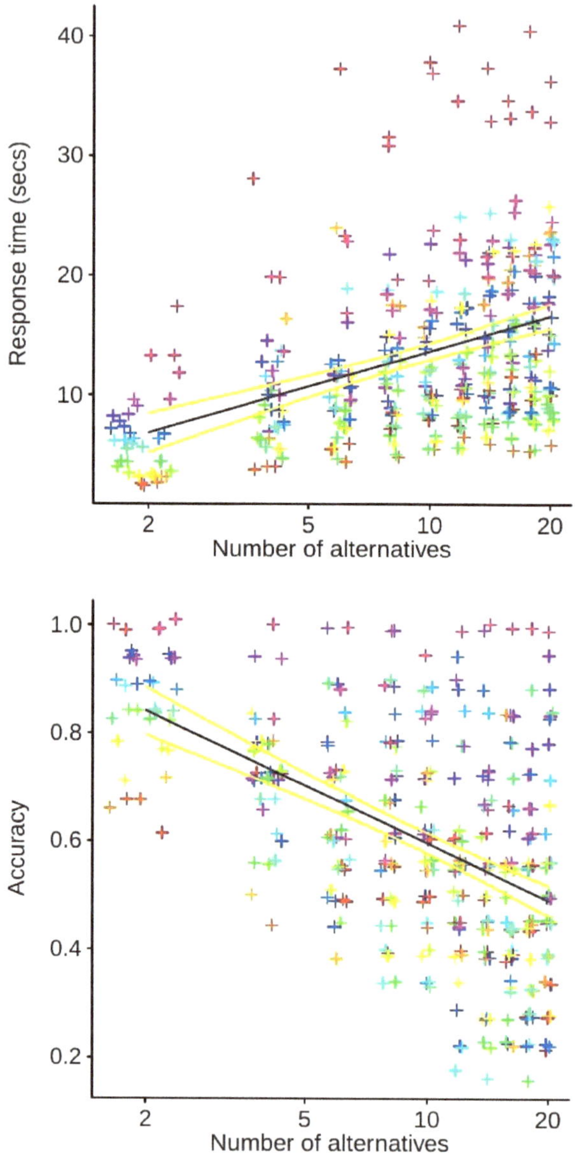

Figure 2.70: Mean time for each of 36 subjects to choose between a given number of alternatives (upper), and accuracy rate for a given number of alternatives (lower), data has been jittered; lines are regression fits (yellow shows 95% confidence intervals), and color used for each subject sorted by performance on the two-choice case. Data from Hawkins et al. Github-Local

Chapter 3

Cognitive Capitalism

3.1 Introduction

Software systems are intangible goods that are products of cognitive capitalism; human cognition is the means of production.

Major motivations for individuals to be involved in the production of software include money and hedonism. People might be motivated to write software by the salary they are paid, by the owners of an organization that employs them, or they might be motivated by non-salary income (of an individual's choosing), e.g., enjoyment from working on software systems, scratching an itch, being involved in a social activity, etc.

Motivation can be affected by the work environment in which software is produced. To make the cognitariate feel happy and fulfilled, spending their cognitive capital striving to achieve management goals, organizations have industrialised Bohemia.

Intangible goods incur intangible production costs, including the emotional distress experienced by cognitariate when their ideas or work goes unused or unnoticed. The importance and value of an individuals' contribution is propagandized, while organizations strive to minimise their reliance on individuals. [249]

While salary based production is likely to be distributed under a commercial license, and hedonism based production under some form of Open source [i] license, this is not always the case.

This chapter discusses cognitive capitalism using the tools of economic production, which deals with tradeable quantities, such as money, time and pleasure. Many of the existing capitalist structures are oriented towards the production of tangible goods, [ii] and are slowly being adapted to deal with the growing market share of intangible goods. [174,782].

This book is oriented towards the producers of software, rather than its consumers, e.g., it focuses on maximizing the return on investment for producers of software.

Human characteristics that affect cognitive performance are the subject of chapter 2. Almost 200 years ago Babbage analysed [100] the economics of calculating mathematical tables (along with the economics of the manufacture of tangible goods), and later proposed a machine capable of performing these calculations.

The sector economic model groups human commercial activities into at least three sectors: [986] the primary sector produces or extracts raw materials, e.g., agriculture, fishing and mining, the secondary sector processes raw materials, e.g., manufacturing and construction, and the tertiary sector provides services. The production of intellectual capital is sometimes referred to as the quarternary sector. Figure 3.1 shows the percentage of the US workforce employed in the three sectors over the last 160 years (plus government employment).

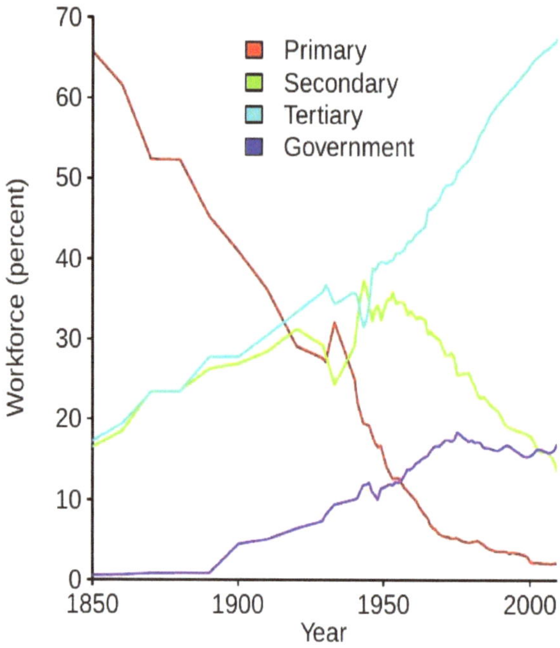

Figure 3.1: Percentage of employment by US industry sector 1850-2009. Data kindly provided by Kossik. Github-Local

How much money is spent on software production? A study by Parker and Grimm [1445] investigated business and government expenditure on software in the U.S.A. They divided software expenditure into two categories: custom software, as software tailored to the specifications of an organization, and own-account software which consists of in-house expenditures for new or significantly-enhanced software created by organizations for their own use. Figure 3.2 shows annual expenditure from 1959 to 1998, by US businesses (plus lines), and the US federal and state governments (smooth lines).

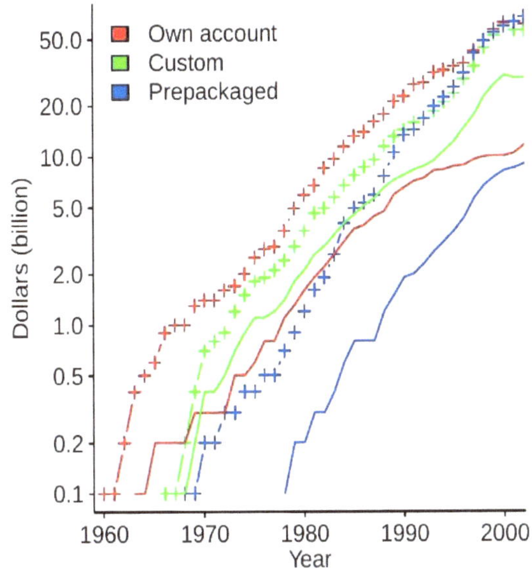

Figure 3.2: Annual expenditure on custom, own account and prepackaged software by US business (plus lines) and the US federal and state governments (smooth lines). Data from Parker et al. Github-Local

Figure 3.3 shows the growth in the number of people employed by some major software companies.

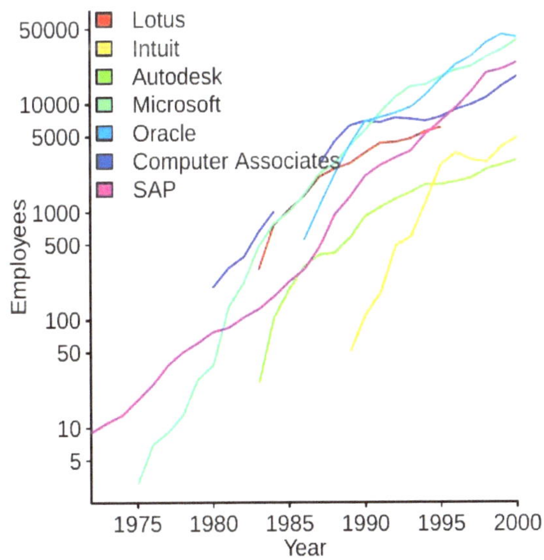

Figure 3.3: Number of people employed by major software companies. Data from Campbell-Kelly. Github-Local

Some governments have recognized the importance of national software ecosystems, [1404] both in economic terms (e.g., industry investment in software systems [347] that keep them competitive), and as a means of self-determination (i.e., not having important infrastructure dependent on companies based in other countries); there is no shortage of recommendations [1792] for how to nurture IT-based businesses, and government funded reviews of their national software business. [1194,1600] Several emerging economies have created sizeable software industries. [77]

The software export figures given for a country can be skewed by a range of factors, and the headline figures may not include associated costs. [798]

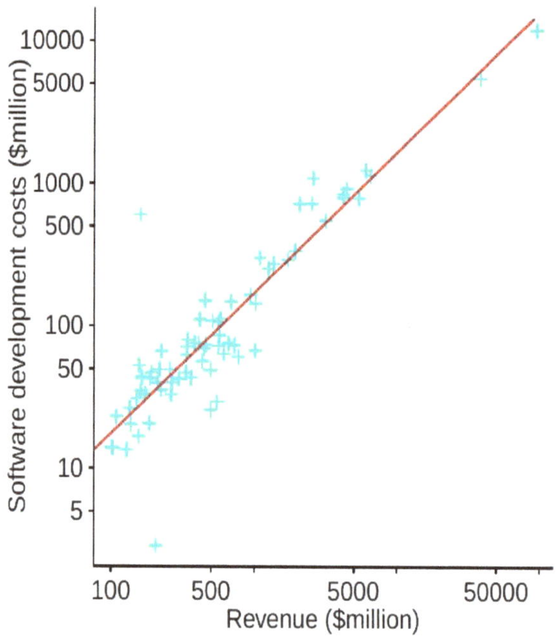

Figure 3.4: Company revenue ($millions) against total software development costs; line is a fitted regression model of the form: developmentCosts ∝ 0.19 Revenue. Data from Mulford et al. Github-Local

What percentage of their income do software companies spend on developing software? A study by Mulford and Misra [1324] of 100 companies in Standard Industry Classifications (SIC) 7371 and 7372[iii], with revenues exceeding $100 million during 2014-2015, found that total software development costs were around 19% of revenue; see figure 3.4 ; sales and marketing varies from 22% to 40%, [335] general and administrative (e.g., salaries, rent, etc) varies from 11% to 22%, [335] with the any remainder assigned to profit and associated taxes.

3.2 Investment decisions

Creating software is an irreversible investment, i.e., incomplete software has little or no resale value, and even completed software may not have any resale value.

The investment decisions involved in building software systems share some of the characteristics of other kinds of investments; for instance, making sequential investments, with a maximum construction rate, are characteristics that occur in factory construction. [1193]

Is it worthwhile investing resources, to implement software that provides some desired functionality? In the case of a personal project, an individual may decide on the spur of the moment to spend time implementing or modifying a program; for commercial projects a significant early stage investment may be made analyzing the potential market, performing a detailed cost/benefit analysis, and weighing the various risk factors.

This sections outlines the major factors involved in making investment decisions, and some of the analysis techniques that may be used. While a variety of sophisticated techniques are available, managers may choose to use the simpler ones. [1809]

The term cost/benefit applies when making a decision about whether to invest or not; the term cost-effectiveness applies when a resource is available, and has to be used wisely, or when an objective has to be achieved as cheaply as possible.

Basic considerations for all investment decisions include:

- the value of money over time. A pound/dollar in the hand today is worth more than a pound/dollar in the hand tomorrow,
- risks. Investors require a greater return from a high risk investment, than from a low risk investment,
- uncertainty. The future is uncertain, and information about the present contains uncertainty,
- opportunity cost. Investing resources in project *A* today, removes the opportunity to invest them project *B* tomorrow. When investment opportunities are abundant, it is worth searching for one of the better ones, while when opportunities are scarce searching for alternatives may be counter-productive.
- For instance, when deciding between paying for Amazon spot instances [15] at a rate similar to everybody else, or investing time trying to figure out an algorithm that makes

- it possible to successfully bid at much lower prices, the time spent figuring out the algorithm is an opportunity cost (i.e., the time spent is a lost opportunity for doing something else, which may have been more profitable). [iv]

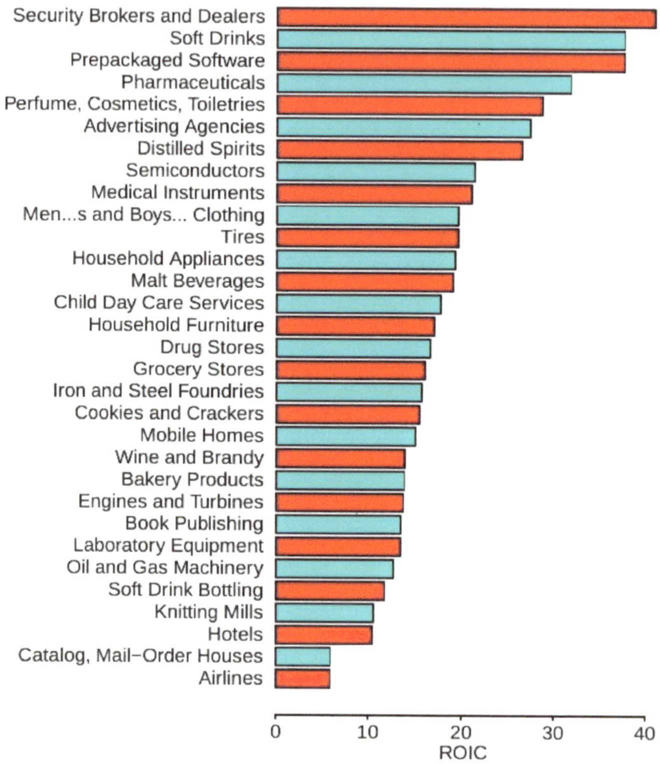

Figure 3.5: Average Return On Invested Capital of various U.S. industries between 1992-2006. Data from Porter. [1509] Github-Local

Return on investment (ROI) is defined as:

$R_{est} = \frac{B_{est} - C_{est}}{C_{est}}$, where: B_{est} is the estimated benefit, and C_{est} the estimated cost.

Both the cost, and the benefit estimates are likely to contain some amount of uncertainty, and the minimum and maximum ROI are given by:

$$R_{\text{est}} - \delta R = \frac{B_{\text{est}} - \delta B}{C_{\text{est}} + \delta C} - 1 \text{ and } R_{\text{est}} + \delta R = \frac{B_{\text{est}} + \delta B}{C_{\text{est}} - \delta C} - 1$$

where: δ is the uncertainty in the corresponding variable.

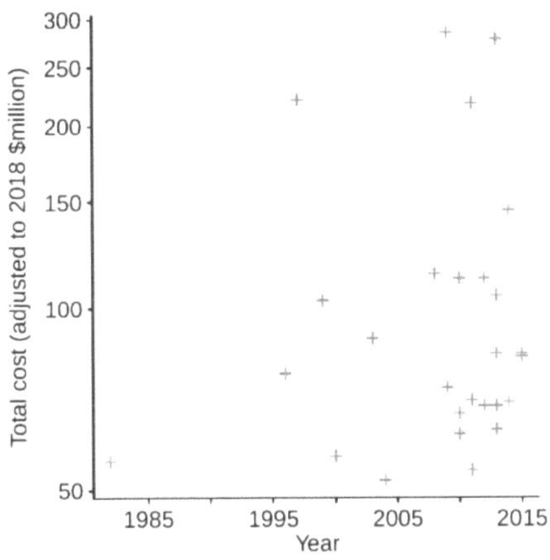

Figure 3.6: Development cost (adjusted to 2018 dollars) of computer video games, whose cost was more than $50 million. Data from Wikipedia. Github-Local

In practice, ROI uncertainty is unlikely to take an extreme value, and its expected value is given by: [228]

$$E[\delta R] \approx \frac{B_{\text{est}}}{C_{\text{est}}}\sqrt{\left(\frac{\delta B}{B_{\text{est}}}\right)^2 + \left(\frac{\delta C}{C_{\text{est}}}\right)^2}$$

Figure 3.6 shows the development cost of video games (where the cost was more than $50 million). The high risk of a market that requires a large upfront investment, to create a new product for an uncertain return, is offset by the possibility of a high return.

3.2.1 Discounting for time

A dollar today is worth more than a dollar tomorrow, because today's dollar can be invested and earn interest; by tomorrow, the amount could have increased in value (or at least not lost value, through inflation). The present value (PV) of a future payoff, C, might be calculated as:

$$PV = \text{discount\_factor} \times C, \text{ where: discount\_factor} < 1.$$

discount_factor is usually calculated as: $(1 + r)^{-1}$, where: r is the known as the rate of return (also known as the discount rate, or the opportunity cost of capital), and represents the size of the reward demanded by investors for accepting a delayed payment (it is often quoted for a period of one year).

The PV over n years (or whatever period r is expressed in) is given by:

$$PV = \frac{C}{(1+r)^n}$$

When comparing multiple options, expressing each of their costs in terms of present value enables them to be compared on an equal footing.

For example, consider the choice between spending $250,000 purchasing a test tool, or the same amount on hiring testers; assuming the tool will make an immediate cost saving of $500,000 (by automating various test procedures), while hiring testers will result in a saving of $750,000 in two years time. Which is the more cost-effective investment (assuming a 10% discount rate)?

$$PV_{\text{tool}} = \frac{\$500{,}000}{(1+0.10)^0} = \$500{,}000 \text{ and } PV_{\text{testers}} = \frac{\$750{,}000}{(1+0.10)^2} = \$619{,}835$$

Based on these calculations, hiring the testers is more cost-effective, i.e., it has the greater present value.

3.2.2 Taking risk into account

The calculation in the previous section assumed there was no risk of unplanned events. What if the tool did not perform as expected, what if some testers were not as productive as hoped? A more realistic calculation of present value would take into account the possibility that future payoffs are smaller than expected.

A risky future payoff is worth less than a certain future payoff, for the same amount invested and payoff. Risk can be factored into the discount rate, to create an effective

discount rate: $k = r + \theta$, where: r is the risk-free rate, and θ a premium that depends on the amount of risk. The formulae for present value becomes:

$$PV = \frac{C}{(1+k)^n}$$

When r and θ can vary over time, we get:

$$PV = \sum_{i=1}^{t} \frac{\text{return}_i}{(1+k_i)^i}, \text{ where: return}_i \text{ is the return during period } i.$$

Repeating the preceding example, assuming a 15% risk premium for the testers option, we get:

$$PV_{\text{tool}} = \frac{\$500{,}000}{(1+0.10)^0} = \$500{,}000 \text{ and } PV_{\text{testers}} = \frac{\$750{,}000}{(1+0.10+0.15)^2} = \$480{,}000$$

Taking an estimated risk into account, suggests that buying the tool is the most costeffective of the two options.

The previous analysis compares the two benefits, but not the cost of the investment that needs to be made to achieve the respective benefit. Comparing investment costs requires taking into account when the money is spent, to calculate the total cost terms of a present cost.

Purchasing the tool is a one time, up front, payment:

$$\text{investment\_cost}_{\text{tool}} = \$250{,}000$$

The cost of the testers approach is more complicated; let's assume it is dominated by monthly salary costs. If the testing cost is $10,416.67 per month for 24 months, the total cost after two years, in today's terms, is (a 10% annual interest rate is approximately 0.8% per month):

$$\text{investment\_cost}_{\text{testers}} = \sum_{m=0}^{23} \frac{\$10{,}416.67}{(1+0.008)^m} = \$10{,}416.67 \left[\frac{1-(1+0.008)^{-22}}{1-(1+0.008)^{-1}}\right] = \$211{,}042.90$$

Spending $250,000 over two years is equivalent to spending $211,042.90 today. Investing $211,042.90 today, at 10%, would provide a fund that supports spending $10,416.67 per month for 24 months.

Net Present Value (NPV) is defined as: NPV = PV - investment_cost

Plugging in the calculated values gives:

$$NPV_{\text{tool}} = \$500{,}000 - \$250{,}000 = \$250{,}000$$

$$NPV_{\text{testers}} = \$480{,}000 - \$211{,}042.90 = \$268{,}957.10$$

Based on NPV, hiring testers is the more cost-effective option.

Alternatives to NPV, their advantages and disadvantages, are discussed by Brealey [250] and Raffo. [1553] One commonly encountered rule, in rapidly changing environments, is the payback rule, which requires that the investment costs of a project be recovered within a specified period; the payback period is the amount of time needed to recover investment costs (a shorter payback period being preferred to a longer one).

Accurate estimates for the NPV of different options requires accurate estimates for the discount rate, and the impact of risk. The discount rate represents the risk-free element, and the closest thing to a risk-free investment is government bonds and securities (information on these rates is freely available). Governments face something of a circularity problem in how they calculate the discount rate for their own investments. The US government discusses these issues in its "Guidelines and Discount Rates for Benefit-

Cost Analysis of Federal Programs", [1948] and at the time of writing the revised Appendix C specified rates, varied between 0.9% over a three-year period and 2.7% over 30 years. Commercial companies invariably have to pay higher rates of interest than the US Government.

3.2.3 Incremental investments and returns

Investments and returns are sometimes incremental, occurring at multiple points in time, over an extended period.

The following example is based on the idea that it is possible to make an investment, when writing or maintaining code, that reduces subsequent maintenance costs, i.e., produces a return on the investment. At a minimum, any investment made to reduce later maintenance costs must be recouped; this minimum case has an ROI of 0%.

Let d be the original development cost, m the base maintenance cost during time period t, and r the interest rate; to keep things simple assume that m is the same for every period of maintenance; the NPV for the payments over t periods is: $\text{Total\_cost} = d + \sum_{k=1}^{t} \frac{m}{(1+r)^k} = d + m\left[\frac{1-(1+r)^{-(t+1)}}{1-(1+r)^{-1}} - 1\right] \approx d + m \times t[1 - 0.5 \times (t+1)r]$ with the approximation applying when $r \times t$ is small.

If an investment is made for all implementation work (i.e., development cost is: $(1+i)d$), in expectation of achieving a reduction in maintenance costs during each period of $(1 - b)$, then: $\text{Total\_cost}_{\text{invest}} = (1+i)d + m \times (1+i)(1-b) \times t[1 - 0.5 \times (t+1)r]$

For this investment to be worthwhile: $\text{Total\_cost}_{\text{invest}} \leq \text{Total\_cost}$, giving: $(1+i)d + m \times (1+i)(1-b) \times T < d + m \times T$, where: $T = t[1 - 0.5 \times (t+1)r]$, which simplifies to give the following lower bound for the benefit/investment ratio, $\frac{b}{i}$:

$$1 + \frac{d}{mT} < \frac{b}{i} + b$$

In practice many systems have a short lifetime. What value must the ratio $\frac{b}{i}$ have, for an investment to break even, after taking into account system survival rate (i.e., the possibility that there is no future system to maintain)?

If s is the probability the system survives a maintenance period, the total system cost is:

$\text{Total\_cost} = d + \sum_{k=1}^{t} \frac{m \times s^k}{(1+r)^k} = d + m\frac{S(1-S^t)}{1-S}$, where: $S = \frac{s}{1+r}$.

The minimal requirement is now:

$$1 + \frac{d}{m}\frac{1-S}{S(1-S^t)} < \frac{b}{i} + b$$

The development/maintenance break-even ratio depends on the regular maintenance cost, multiplied by a factor that depends on the system survival rate (not the approximate total maintenance cost).

Fitting regression models to system lifespan data, in section 4.5.2, finds (for an annual maintenance period): $s_{\text{mainframe}} = 0.87$ and $s_{\text{Google}} = 0.79$. Information on possible development/maintenance ratios is only available for mainframe software (see fig 4.47), and the annual mean value is: $\frac{d}{m} = 4.9$.

Figure 3.7 shows the multiple of any additional investment (y -axis), made during development, that needs to be recouped during subsequent maintenance work, to break even for a range of payback periods (when application survival rate is that experienced by Google applications, or 1990s Japanese mainframe software; the initial development/annual maintenance ratios are 5, 10 and 20); the interest rate used is 5%.

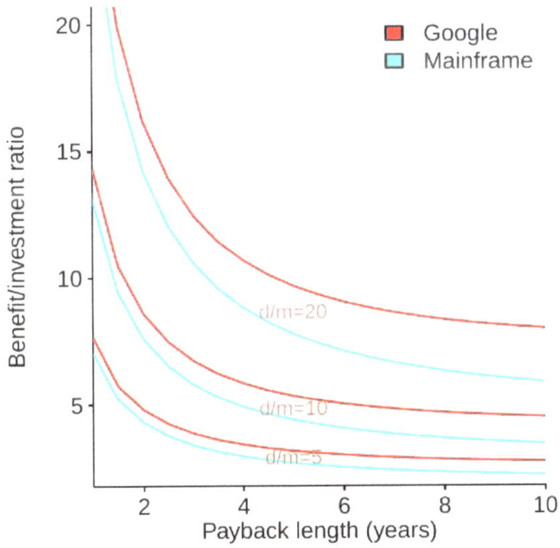

Figure 3.7: Return/investment ratio needed to break-even, for Google and Mainframe application survival rate, having development/annual maintenance ratios of 5, 10 and 20; against payback period in years. Data from: mainframe Tamai, [1811] Google SaaS Ogden. Github-Local

This analysis only considers systems that have been delivered and deployed. Projects are sometimes cancelled before reaching this stage, and including these in the analysis would increase the benefit/investment break-even ratio.

While some percentage of a program's features may not be used, [530] those features that will go unused is unknown at the time of implementation. Incremental implementation, driven by customer feedback, helps reduce the likelihood of investing in program features that are not used by customers.

Figure 7.18 shows that most files are only ever edited by one person. The probability that source will be maintained by developers other than the original author may need to be factored into the model.

3.2.4 Investment under uncertainty

The future is uncertain, and the analysis in the previous sections assumed fixed values for future rates of interest and risk. A more realistic analysis would take into account future

An investment might be split into random and non-random components, e.g., Brownian motion with drift. The following equation is used extensively to model the uncertainty involved in investment decisions [503] (it is a stochastic differential equation for the change in the quantity of interest,):

$$dx = a(x, t)dt + b(x, t)dz$$

This equation contains a drift term (given by the function a, which involves x and time) over an increment of time, dt, plus an increment of a Wiener process, [v]dz (the random component; also known as a Brownian process), and the function, b, involves x and time.

The simplest form of this equation is: $dx = \alpha dt + \sigma dz$, i.e., a constant drift rate, α, plus a random component having variance σ. Figure 3.8 illustrates this drift-diffusion process; with the grey line showing the slope of the drift component, and green lines showing possible paths followed when random increments are added to the drift (red lines bound possible paths, for the value of σ used).

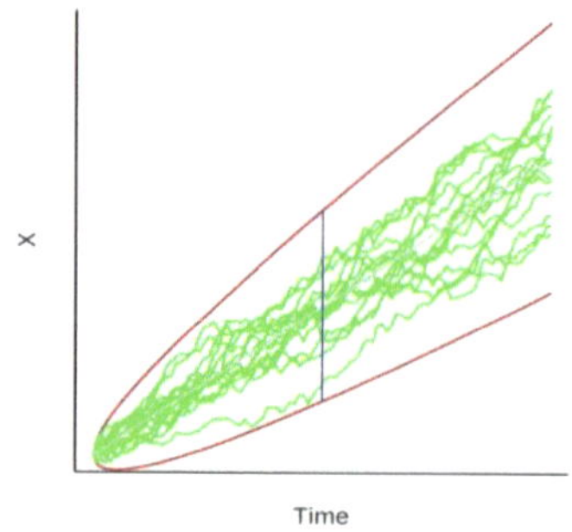

Figure 3.8: Illustration of a drift diffusion process. Green lines show possible paths, red lines show bounds of diffusion and grey line shows drift with no diffusion component. Github-Local

This equation can be solved to find the standard deviation in the value of : it is $\sigma\sqrt{T}$, where T is elapsed time.

The analysis of the cost/benefit of the maintenance investment, in the previous section, assumed a fixed amount of maintenance in each interval. In practice, the amount of maintenance is likely to grow to a maximum commercially supportable value, and then fluctuate about this value over time, i.e., it becomes a mean-reverting process. The OrnsteinUhlenbeck process (also known as the Vasicek process) is the simplest mean-reverting process, and its corresponding equation is:

$$dx = \eta(\hat{x} - x)dt + \sigma dz \qquad (3.1)$$

where: η is the speed of reversion, and $\hat{x}$ is the mean value.

This equation can be solved to give the expected value of x at future time t, given its current value x_0, which is: $E[x_t] = \hat{x} + (x_0 - \hat{x})e^{-\eta t}$; its variance is: $\frac{\sigma^2}{2\eta}(1 - e^{-2\eta t})$; section 11.10.7 discusses techniques for obtaining values for σ and η.

Figure 3.9 shows ten example paths (in green) of an Ornstein-Uhlenbeck process, each starting at zero, and growing to fluctuate around the process mean; red line is the expected value, blue lines are at one standard deviation.

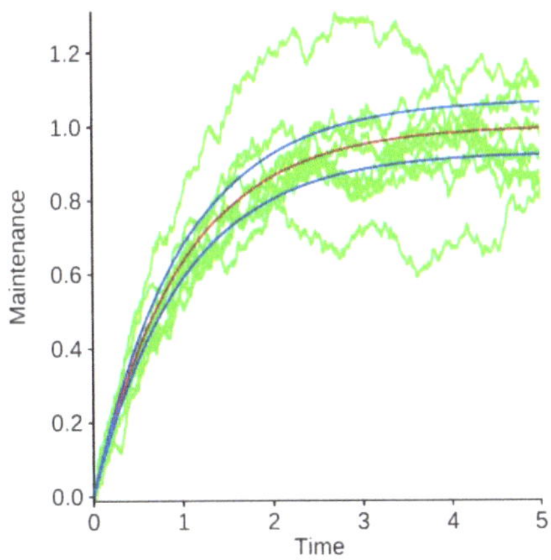

Figure 3.9: Illustration of an Ornstein-Uhlenbeck process starting from zero and growing to its mean; green lines show various possible paths, red line is expected value, and blue lines one standard deviation. Github-Local

Uncertainty in the investment cost and/or the likely benefit returned from a project, means that even under relatively mild conditions, a return of twice as much as the investment is considered to be the break-even condition. [503,1488]

Obtaining insight about a possible investment, by setting up and solving a stochastic differential equation [1659] can be very difficult, or impractical. A variety of numerical methods are available for analyzing investment problems based on a stochastic approach, see section 11.10.7.

Current market conditions also need to be taken into account. For instance: how likely is it that other companies will bring out competing products, and will demand for the application still be there once development is complete?

3.2.5 Real options

It may be possible to delay making an investment until circumstances are more favorable. [399,503] For instance, when new functionality has to be implemented as soon as possible, it may be decided to delay investing the resources needed to ensure the new code conforms to project guidelines; there is always the option to invest the necessary resources later. By using Net Present Value, management is taking a passive approach to their investment strategy; a fixed calculation is made, and subsequent decisions are based on this result; real options offer a more flexible approach.

In financial markets, a call option is a contract between two parties (a buyer and a seller), where the buyer pays the seller for the right (but not the obligation) to buy (from the seller) an asset, at an agreed price on an agreed date (the initial amount paid is known as the premium, the agreed price the strike price, and the date the expiry or maturity date). When the option can only be exercised on the agreed date, the contract is known as a European option, when the option can be exercised at any time up to the agreed date, it is known as a American option.

A put option is a contract involving the right (but not the obligation) to sell. The term real options (or real options valuation ROV, or real options analysis) is applied to the analysis of decisions made by managers in industry that have option-like characteristics. In this environment many items are not traded like conventional financial options; another notable difference, is that those involved in the management of the asset, may have an influence on the value of the option (e.g., they have a say in the execution of a project).

In financial markets, volatility information can be obtained from an assets past history. In industry, managers may have information on previous projects carried out within the company, but otherwise have to rely on their own judgment to estimate uncertainty. Call and put options are established practice in financial markets. In industry, managers have to create or discover possible options; they need an entrepreneurial frame of mind.

ROV requires active management, continuously ready to respond to changing circumstances. It is an approach that is most applicable when uncertainty is high, and managers have the flexibility needed to make the required changes.

The Binomial model [399] can be used to estimate the percentage change in starting costs S, at time t_i, given the probability p, of costs going up by $U\%$, and the probability $1 - p$, of costs going down by $D\%$, at each time step.

Figure 3.10 illustrates how after three time-steps, there is one path where costs can increase by $U^3\%$, and one where they can decrease by increase by $D^3\%$; there are three paths where the cost can increase by $3U^2D\%$, and three where they can decrease by $3D^2U\%$. All paths leading to a given U/D point occur with the same probability, which can be calculated from p.

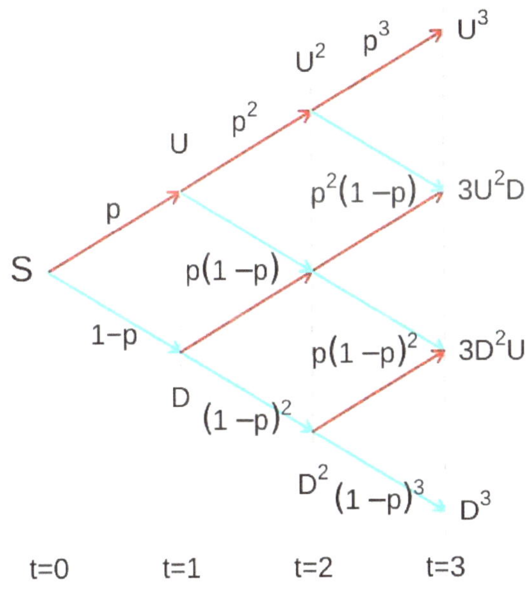

Figure 3.10: Example of a binomial model with three time-steps, given the probability p, of costs going up by $U\%$, and the probability $1 - p$, of costs going down by $D\%$, at each time step, starting at S. Github-Local

Implementing functionality using the minimum of investment, with the intent of investing more later, has the form of an American call option. [vi] The call option might not be exercised, e.g., if the implemented functionality becomes unnecessary.

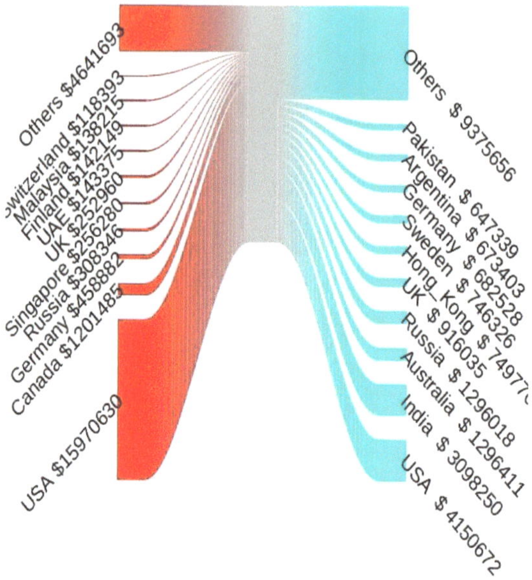

Figure 3.11: Bug bounty payer (left) and payee (right) countries (total value $23,632,408$). Data from hackerone. Github-Local

The Black-Scholes equation provides a solution to the optimal pricing of European options (e.g., the value of the premium, strike price, and maturity date). Some researchers have applied this equation to the options associated with developing software; this is a mistake. [596] The derivation of the Black-Scholes equation involves several preconditions, which often apply to financial risks, but don't apply to software development, including:

- liquidity is required, to enable the composition of a portfolio of assets to be changed, at will, by investing or divesting, i.e., buying or selling. Software production does not create liquid assets, the production is a sunk cost. Once an investment has been made in writing code, it is rarely possible to immediately divest a percentage of the investment in this code (a further investment in writing new code may make little business sense),
- detailed historical information on the performance of the item being traded is an essential input to portfolio risk calculations. Historical data is rarely available on one, let alone all, of the major performance factors involved in software development; chapter 5 discusses the distribution of development activities over the lifetime of a project.

Some of the issues involved in a cost/benefit analysis of finding and fixing coding mistakes is discussed in section 3.6.

3.3 Capturing cognitive output

Organizations whose income is predominantly derived from the output of cognitariate are social factories. [312] To increase the fraction of cognitive output they capture, organizations involve themselves in employees' lives to reduce external friction points; free meals and laundry service are not perks, they are a means of bringing employees together to learn and share ideas, by reducing opportunities to mix in non-employee social circles (and create employee life-norms that limit possible alternative employers, i.e., a means of reducing knowledge loss and spillover).

Organizations that continue to be based around work-life separation also use software systems, and offer software related jobs. In these organizations the primary focus may be on the cognitive efforts of people working on non-software activities, with those working on software related activities having to fit in with the existing workplace norms of the host industry.

Some developers are more strongly motivated by the enjoyment from doing what they do, than the money they receive for doing it. [1328] This lifestyle choice relies on the willingness of organizations to tolerate workers who are less willing to do work they don't enjoy, or alternating between high paying work that is not enjoyed, and working for pleasure. Freelancing in tasks such as trying to earn bug bounties is only profitable for a few people (see fig 4.43).

3.3.1 Intellectual property

Governments have created two legal structures that might be used by individuals, or organizations, to claim property rights over particular source code, or ways of doing things (e.g., business processes): patents and copyright.

A patent gives its owner rights to exclude others from making or selling an item that makes use of the claims made in the patent (for a term of 20 years from the date of filing; variations apply). In the U.S. software was not patentable until 1995, and since then the number of software patents has continued to grow, with 109,281 granted in 2014 [1504] (36% of all utility patents). Figure 3.12 shows the number of US patents granted in various software related domains (the dip in the last few years is due to patents applications not yet granted).

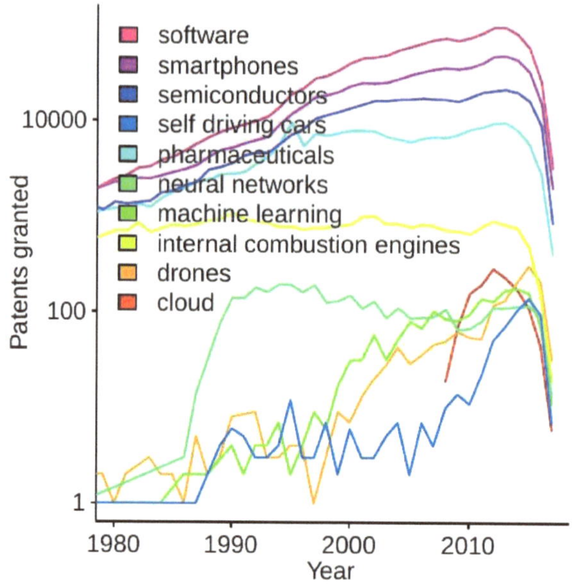

Figure 3.12: Number of US patents granted in various areas. Data from Webb et al. Github-Local

Patents grant their holder exclusive use of the claimed invention in the jurisdiction that granted the patent. In a fast moving market the value of a patent may be in the strategic power [777] it gives to deny market access to competitive products. An analysis [768] of the stock-price of ICT companies in the US found that those with software patents had a slightly higher value than those without software patents.

A license is a legal document, chosen or created by the copyright owner of software, whose intended purpose is to control the use, distribution, and creation of derivative works of the software. Licensing is an integral component of the customer relationship.

Licensing is a source of ecological pressure (e.g., applications available under one kind of license may find it difficult to remain viable in ecosystems containing similar applications available under less restrictive licenses). The ideology associated with some kinds of licenses may be strong enough for people to create license-based ecosystems, e.g., Debian distributions only contain software whose source is licensed under a Free Software license. The restrictions imposed by a license, on the use of a software system, may be sufficiently at odds with the ideology of some developers that they decide to invest their time in creating a new implementation of the functionality under a different license.

Code distributed under an Open source license is often created using a non-contract form of production. [174]

People have been making source code available at no cost, for others to use, since software was first created; [71] however, the formal licensing of such software is relatively new. [1602] Open source licenses have evolved in response to user needs, court decisions, and the growth of new product ecosystems; there has been a proliferation of different, and sometimes incompatible, open source licenses. [1293] Factors driving the evolution of licensing conditions, and combinations of conditions, include: evolution of the legal landscape (e.g., issues around what constitutes distribution and derivative works [752]), commercial needs for a less restrictive license (e.g., the 3-clauses and 2-clauses variants of the original, more restrictive BSD license, now known as 4-clauses BSD), ideological demands for a more restrictive license (e.g., GPL [1052] version 3 added wording to address issues such as hardware locks and digital rights management, that were not addressed in GPL version 2), the desire to interoperate with software made available under an incompatible, but widely used, license (often the GPL), [671] or the desire to operate a business supporting a particular open source software system (e.g., dual licensing [1869]).

License selection, by commercial vendors, is driven by the desire to maximise the return on investment. Vendor licensing choice can vary from a license that ties software to a designated computer (with the expectation that the customer will later buy licenses for other computers), to a very permissive open source license [vii] (whose intent is to nullify a market entry-point for potential competitors). [298]

A study by Zhang, Yang, Lopes and Kim [2010] investigated Java code fragments, containing at least 50 tokens, appearing in answers to questions on Stack Overflow, that later appeared within the source code of projects on Github. They found 629 instances of code on Github that acknowledged being derived from an answer on Stack Overflow, and 14,124 instances on Github of code that was similar to code in appearing Stack Overflow answers (a clone detection tool was used). The most common differences between the Stack Overflow answer and Github source were: use of a different method, and renaming of identifiers and types.

Figure 3.13 shows the normalised frequency of occurrences of matched code fragments containing a given number of lines, for the attributed use and unattributed close clone instances.

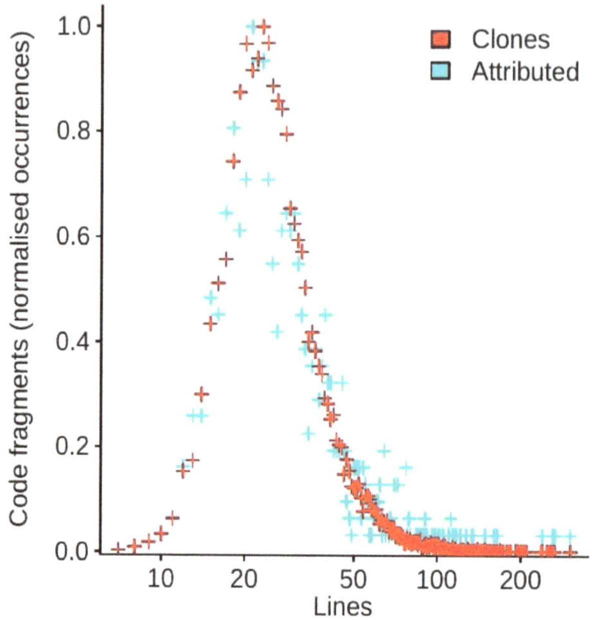

Figure 3.13: Normalised frequency of occurrences of code fragments containing a given number of lines; attributed to Stack Overflow answers, and unattributed close clones (a lognormal distribution is not sufficiently spikey to fit the data well). Data from Zhang et al. Github-Local

The majority of source code files do not contain an explicit license. [1889] Developers who do specify a license, may be driven by ideology, or the desire to fit in with the license choices made by others in their social network. [1715] One study [40] found that developers were able to correctly answer questions involving individual licenses (as-in, the answer agreed with a legal expert), but struggled with questions that required integrating conditions contained in multiple licenses.

Commercial vendors may invest in creating a new implementation of the functionality provided by software licensed under an Open source license, because, for instance, they want the licensing fee income, or the existing software has a license that does not suit their needs. For instance, Apple have been a longtime major funder of the LLVM compiler project, an alternative to GCC (one is licensed under the GPL, the other under the University of Illinois/NCSA open source license; the latter is a more permissive license).

Details of any applicable license(s) may appear within individual files, and/or in a license file within the top-level directory of the source code. In the same way that software can be changed, the license under which software is made available can change. [1905] Any changes to the licensing of a software system become visible to users when a new release is made.

When the files used to build a software system contain a license, different files may contain different licenses, and the different licenses may specify conditions that are incompatible, with each other. For instance, Open source licenses might be classified as restrictive (i.e., if a modified version of the software is distributed, the derived version must be licensed under the same terms), or permissive (i.e., derived works may incorporate software licensed under different terms).

A study by Vendome, Linares-Vásquez, Bavota, Di Penta, German and Poshyvanyk [1889] investigated license use in the files of 16,221 Java projects (a later study also included projects written in other languages). Nearly all files did not include a license, and when a license was present it was rarely changed (the most common change, by an order of magnitude, was to/from a license being present).

Figure 3.14 shows the cumulative percentage of licenses present in files, over time, in the 10% of projects having the most commits. The lines show 16 of the 80 different licenses appearing in files, with the other 64 licenses appearing in less than 1,000 files. The downward trend, for some licenses, is caused by the increasing project growth rate, with most files not including any license (upper line in plot).

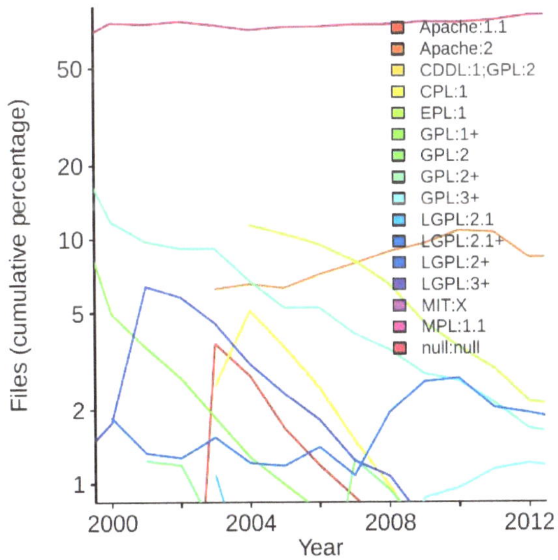

Figure 3.14: Cumulative percentage of files, from the top 10% largest Java projects, containing a given license (upper line is no license). Data from Vendome et al. Github-Local

A study by German, Manabe and Inoue [672] investigated the use of licenses in the source code of programs in the Debian distribution (version 5.0.2). They found that 68.5% of files contained some form of license statement (the median size of the license was 1,005 bytes). The median size of all files was 4,633 bytes; the median size of files without a license was 2,137 bytes, and the files with a license 5,488 .

Programs and libraries may have dependencies on packages made available under licenses that specify conditions which are incompatible with each other, e.g., mobile apps having licenses that are incompatible with one or more of the licenses in the source files from which they were created. [1301].

A study by Meloca, Pinto, Baiser, Mattos, Polato, Wiese, and German [1260] investigated licensing files appearing in all packages from the npm (510,964 packages), RubyGems (135,481 packages), and CRAN (11,366 packages) networks (from the launch of the package site to October 2017).

Figure 3.15 shows the number of package releases containing a given number of licenses (some packages were updated, and an updated version released: there were 4,367,440 releases; a package must contain a license to appear on CRAN).

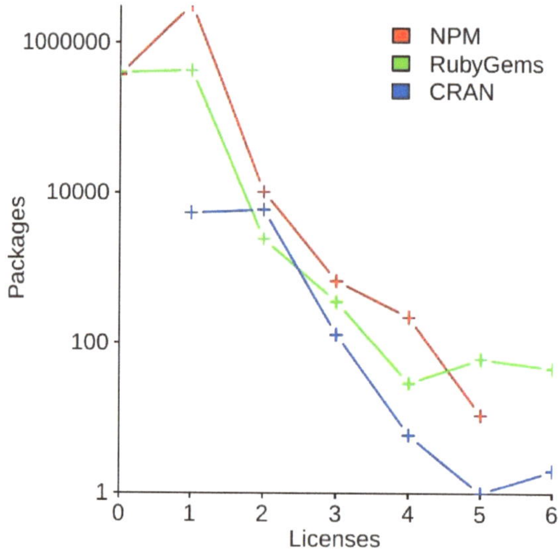

Figure 3.15: Number of releases of packages containing a given number of licenses (a package has to contain a license to appear on CRAN). Data from Meloca et al. Github-Local

Table 3.1 shows the percentage of all npm package releases using a given license, or lack thereof (column names), that migrated (or not) to another license (row names), from the launch of the npm network in 2009, until October 2017. During this period 85% of all package releases contained an OSI license; see Github-economics/msr2018b_evol.R.

Table 3.1: Percentage migration of licenses used by all npm package releases (between 2009 and 2017), from license listed in column names, to license in row names. Data from Meloca et al. [1260]

To/From	OSI	Incomplete	non-OSI	Missing	Other	Copyright
OSI	99.7	6.8	7.7	2.6	4.8	2.8
Incomplete	0.12	92.0	0.1	0.09	3.3	3.0
non-OSI	0.08	0.07	91.1	0.07	0.95	0.81
Missing	0.08	0.22	0.65	97.2	0.49	0.26
Other	0.02	0.54	0.28	0.02	88.1	3.7
Copyright	0.00	0.31	0.2	0.01	2.3	90.0

When licensing conditions are not followed, what action, if any, might the copyright holders of the software take?

The licensee has the option of instigating legal proceedings to protect their property. Those seeking to build market share may not take any action against some license violations (many people do not read end-user license agreements (EULAs) [1209]).

Some companies and individuals have sought to obtain licensing fees from users of some software systems made available under an Open source license. If the licensing fee sought is small enough, it may be cheaper for larger companies to pay, rather than legally contest the claims. [1944]

A license is interpreted within the framework of the laws of the country in which it is being used. For instance, the Uniform Commercial Code (UCC) is a series of laws, intended to harmonise commercial transactions across the US; conflicts between requirements specified in the UCC and a software license may have be resolved by existing case law, or by a new court case. [1243] Competing against free is very difficult. The Free Software Foundation were the (successful) defendants in a case where the plaintiff argued that the GPL violated the Sherman Act, e.g., "the restraint of trade by way of a licensing scheme to fix the prices of computer software products". [1835]

A country's courts have the final say in how the wording contained in software licenses is interpreted. The uncertainty over the enforceability [701,1056] of conditions contained in

Open source licenses is slowly being clarified, as more cases are being litigated, in various jurisdictions. [1148,1850]

In litigation involving commercial licenses, the discovery that one party is making use of Open source software without complying with the terms of its Open source license, provides a bargaining chip for the other party, [1719] i.e., if the non-compliance became public, the cost of compliance, with the open source license, may be greater than the cost of the commercial licensing disagreement.

The Open Source Initiative (OSI) is a non-profit organization, that has defined what constitutes Open source, and maintains a list of licenses that meet this definition. OSI has become the major brand, and the largest organization operating in this area; licenses submitted, to become OSI-approved, have to pass a legal and community wide review.

Figure 3.16 shows the survival curve for the 107 OSI licenses that have been listed on the OSI website since August 2000; at the start of 2019, 81 licenses were listed on the OSI website.

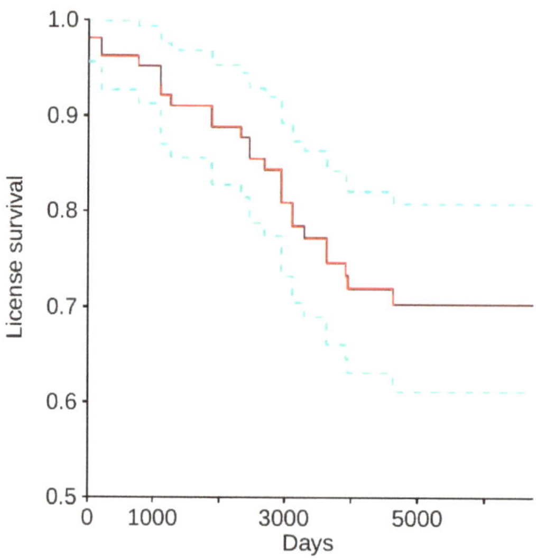

Figure 3.16: Survival curve of OSI licenses that have been listed on the approved license webpage, in days since 15 August 2000, with 95% confidence intervals. Data from opensource.org, via The Wayback Machine, web.archive.org. Github-Local

A software system may be dependent on particular data, for correct or optimal operation. The licensing of data associated with software, or otherwise, can be an important issue itself. [796]

Open source licensing ideology is being applied to other goods, in particular the hardware on which software runs. [221]

3.3.2 Bumbling through life

The expectation of career progression comes from an era when many industries were stable for long enough for career paths to become established. In rapidly changing work ecosystems, the concept of career progression is less likely to apply. Some software companies have established career progression ladders for their employees, [1751] and one study [1180] found that staff turnover was reduced when promotions were likely to be frequent and small, rather than infrequent and large; Gruber [751] discusses the issues of IT careers, in detail.

Companies have an interest in offering employees a variety of career options: it is a means of retaining the knowledge acquired by employees based on their experience of the business. Employees may decide that they prefer to continue focusing on technical issues, rather than people-issues, or may embrace a move to management. Simulations [1495] have found some truth to the Peter principle: "Every new member in a hierarchical organization climbs the hierarchy until they reach their level of maximum incompetence."

In fast changing knowledge-based industries, an individuals' existing skills can quickly become obsolete (this issue predates the computer industry [1906]). Options available to those with skills thought likely to become obsolete include, include having a job that looks like it will continue to require the learned skills for a many years, and investing in learning appropriate new skills.

Filtering out potential cognitariate who are not passionate about their work is a component of the hiring process at some companies. Passion is a double-edged sword; passionate employees are more easily exploited, [1000] but they may exploit the company in pursuit of their personal ideals (e.g., spending time reworking code that they consider to be ugly, despite knowing the code has no future use).

Job satisfaction is an important consideration for all workers. [1328] In areas where demand for staff outstrips supply, the risk of loosing staff is a motivation for employers to provide job satisfaction.

Human capital theory suggests there is a strong connection between a person's salary and time spent on the job at a company, i.e., the training and experience gained over time increases the likelihood that a person could get a higher paying job elsewhere; it is in a company's interest to increase employee pay over time [159] (one study [1722] of 2,251 IT professionals, in Singapore, found a linear increase in salary over time). Regional employment (see Github-ecosystems/MSA_M2016_CM.R) and pay differences [391] reflect differences in regional cost of living, historical practices (which include gender pay differences [1372]) and peoples' willingness to move.

A study by Couger and Colter [412] investigated approaches to motivating developers working on maintenance activities, the factors included: the motivating potential of the job (based on skill variety required, the degree to which the job requires completion as a whole, the impact of the job on others, i.e., task significance, degree of freedom in scheduling and performing the job, and feedback from the job), and a person's need for personal accomplishment, to be stimulated and challenged.

In some US states, government employee salaries are considered to be public information, e.g., California (see Github-ecosystems/transparentcalifornia.R). A few companies publish employee salaries, so-called Open salaries; the information may be available to company employees only, or it may be public, e.g., Buffer. [657]

If the male/female cognitive ability distribution seen in figure 2.5 carries over to software competencies, then those seeking to attract more women into software engineering, and engineering in general, should be targeting the more populous middle competence band, and not the high-fliers. The mass market for those seeking to promote female equality is incompetence; a company cannot be considered to be gender-neutral until incompetent women are equally likely to be offered a job as incompetent men.

3.3.3 Expertise

To become a performance expert, a person needs motivation, time, economic resources, an established body of knowledge to learn from, and teachers to guide; while learning, performance feedback is required.

An established body of knowledge to learn from requires that the problem domain has existed in a stable state for long enough for a proven body of knowledge to become established. The availability of teachers requires that the domain be sufficiently stable that most of what potential teachers have learned is still applicable to students; if the people with the knowledge and skills are to be motivated to teach, they need to be paid enough to make a living.

The practice of software development is a few generations old, and the ecosystems within which developers work have experienced a steady stream of substantial changes; substantial change is written about as-if it is the norm. Anybody who invests in many years of deliberate practice on a specific technology may find there are few customers for the knowledge and skill acquired, i.e., are willing to pay a higher rate to do the job, than that paid to somebody with a lot less expertise. Paying people based on their performance requires a method of reliably measuring performance, or at least differences in performance.

Software developers are not professional programmers any more than they are professional typists; reading and writing source code is one of the skills required to build a software system. Effort also has to be invested in acquiring application domain knowledge and skills, for the markets targeted by the software system.

What level of software development related expertise is worth acquiring in a changing ecosystem? The level of skill required to obtain a job involving software development is judged relative to those who apply for the job, employers may have to make do with whoever demonstrates the basic competence needed. In an expanding market those deemed to have high skill levels may have the luxury of being able chose the work that interests them.

Once a good enough level of programming proficiency is reached, if the application domain changes more slowly than the software environment, learning more about the application domain may provide a greater ROI (for an individual), compared to improving programming proficiency (because the acquired application knowledge/skills have a longer usable lifetime).

People often learn a skill for some purpose (e.g., chess as a social activity, programming because it provides pleasure or is required to get a job done), without aiming to achieve expert performance. Once a certain level of proficiency is achieved, such people stop trying to learn, and concentrate on using what they have learned; in work, and sport, a distinction is made between training for, and performing the activity. During everyday work, the goal is to produce a product, or provide a service. In these situations people need to use well-established methods, to be certain of success, not try new ideas (which potentially lead to failure, or a dead-end). Time spent on non-deliberate practice does not lead to any significant improvement in expertise, although it may increase the fluency of performing a particular subset of skills; computer users have been found to have distinct command usage habits. [1651]

Higher education once served as a signalling system, [1746] used by employers looking to recruit people at the start of their professional careers (i.e., high cognitive firepower was once required to gain a university degree). However, some governments' policy of encouraging a significant percentage of their citizens to study for a higher education degree led to the dilution of university qualifications to being an indication of not below average IQ. By taking an active interest in the employability of graduates with a degree in a STEM related subject, [1673] governments are suffering from cargo-cult syndrome.

Knowledgebased businesses want employees who can walk-the-talk, not drones who can hum a few tunes.

3.4 Group dynamics

People may cooperate with others to complete a task that is beyond the capacity of an individual, for the benefit of all those involved. The effectiveness of a group is dependent on cooperation between its members, which makes trust [448] and the enforcement of group norms [193] an essential component of group activity.

In a commercial environment people are paid to work. The economics of personnel selection [1099] are a component of an employer's member selection process; the extent to which employees can select who to work with, will vary.

Groups may offer non-task specific benefits for individuals working within the group, e.g., social status and the opportunity for social learning; discussed in section 3.4.3 and section 3.4.4.

Conflicts of interest can arise between the aims of the group and those of individual members, and those outside the group who pay for its services. Individuals may behave different when working on their own, compared to when working as a member of a group (e.g., social loafing [975]); cultural issues (e.g., individualism vs. collectivism) are also a factor. [525]

When a group of people work together, a shared collection of views, beliefs and rituals (ways of doing things) is evolved, [842] i.e., a culture. Culture improves adaptability. Culture is common in animals, but cultural evolution [1269] is rare; perhaps limited to humans, song birds and chimpanzees. [236]

While overconfidence at the individual level decreases the fitness of the entrepreneur (who does not follow the herd, but tries something new), the presence of entrepreneurs in a group increases group level fitness (by providing information about the performance of new ideas). [186]

People may be active members of multiple groups, with each group involved with different software development projects. Figure 3.17 shows the cumulative number of hours, in weeks since the start of the project, worked by the 47 people involved in the development of an avionics software system. Dashed grey lines are straight lines fitted to three people, and show these people working an average of 3.5,9 and 13.8 hours per week on this one project.

3.4.1 Maximizing generated surplus

Given the opportunity, workers will organise their tasks to suit themselves. [1816] The so called scientific management approach seeks to find a way of organizing tasks that maximises the surplus value produced by a group (i.e., value produced minus the cost of production), [viii] subject to the constraint that management maintains control of the process. The surplus going to the owners of the means of production. [249]

A study by Taylor [1816] investigated the performance of workers in various industries. He found that workers were capable of producing significantly more than they routinely produced, and documented the problems he encountered in getting them to change their existing practices. Workers have been repeatedly found to set informal quotas amongst themselves, [1951] e.g., setting a maximum on the amount they will produce during a shift.

The scientific management approach was first widely applied to hardware production where most of the tasks could be reduced to purely manual activities (i.e., requiring little thinking by those who performed them), such as: iron smelting and automobile production. Over the years its use has been extended to all major forms of commercial work, e.g., clerical activities. [1314]

The essence of the scientific management approach is to break down tasks into a small number of component parts, to simplify the component parts so they can be performed by less skilled workers, and then rearrange tasks in a way that gives management control over the production process (because workers don't have knowledge of all the steps involved). Deskilling jobs increases the size of the pool of potential workers, decreasing labor costs and increasing the interchangeability of workers.

Given the almost universal use of this management technique, it is to be expected that managers will attempt to apply it to the production of software, [425,1042] e.g., chief programmer teams. [122]

The production of software is different from hardware manufacture, in that once the first copy has been created, the cost of reproduction is virtually zero. The human effort invested in creating software systems is primarily cognitive. The division between management and workers is along the lines of what they think about, not between thinking and physical effort.

When the same task is repeatedly performed by different people, it is possible to obtain some measure of average/minimum/maximum individual performance. Task performance improves with practice, and an individual's initial task performance will depend on their prior experience (see section 2.5). Measuring performance based on a single performance of a task provides some indication of minimum performance (see fig 5.27). To obtain information on an individual's maximum performance they have to be measured over multiple performances of the same task (see fig 2.36).

It may be possible to quantify developer productivity in terms of their contribution to the creation and maintenance of a software system. However, until the effort consumed by the many kinds of activities involved in the creation of a software system is quantified, it is not possible to estimate developer productivity.

Performance need not be correlated with productivity, e.g., a developer may deliver a high performance when writing unproductive code.

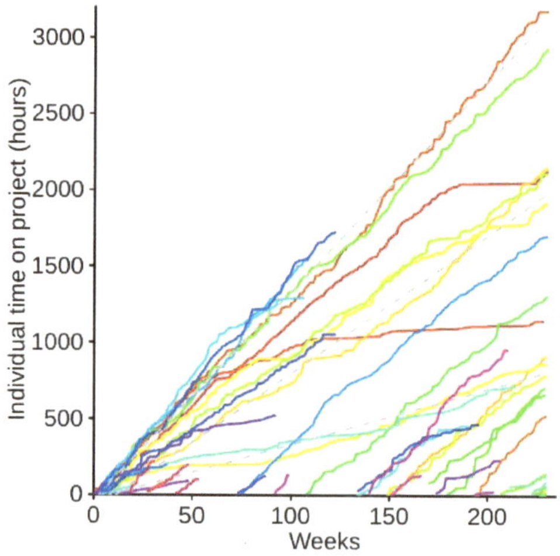

Figure 3.17: The cumulative number of hours worked per week by the 47 individuals involved with one avionics development project; dashed grey lines are straight lines fitted to three individuals. Data from Nichols et al. Github-Local

3.4.2 Motivating members

To maintain or improve their position in a changing world, organizations have to motivate employees and third parties who have become comfortable in their established practices to risk trying something new. [462]

As inhabitants of the intangible the cognitariate are consumers of intangible motivations. Organizations can enlist the human need to believe and be part of something larger to motivate and retain members; Apple is perhaps the most well known example. [1499] Quasireligious narratives are used to enlist developers as participants in a shared mission, e.g., foundation myths and utopian visions. Developer evangelists [979] are employed to seek out third party developers, to convert them to believers in a company and its products; providing technical aid opens the door to engagement. Employer branding [1398] is a way of attracting and retaining staff.

Technological progress continues to be written about as a form of religious transcendence.

Employee motivation will depend on the relationship they have with their work, which has been categorized as one of: job, career or calling. [1983] Those who treat work as a job see it as providing material benefits (e.g., money), and don't seek other kinds of reward; money as an incentive to motivate employees is a complex issue incentives. [1951] Having a career involves personal investment in the work, with achievements marked with advancement within an organizational structure (advancement may be considered to bring higher social standing, increased authority, and greater self-esteem). People with callings see their work as inseparable from their life, working for the fulfilment that doing the work brings (the work may be seen as socially valuable).

A study by Chandlera and Kapelner [320] investigated the impact of what subjects believed to be meaningfulness of a task on their performance. Workers on Mechanical Turk were paid to complete a task that was framed using one of three descriptions: 1) labelling tumour cells to assist medical researchers (meaningful), 2) the purpose of the task was not given (a control group), and 3) the purpose of the task was not given and subjects were told that their work would be discarded. Subjects in the meaningful group labeled more images and were more accurate; see Github-economics/1210-0962.R.

Some brands acquire a cult following, e.g., Macintosh [163] (and even failed products such as Apple's Newton [1329]). A base of loyal third-party developers who have invested in learning a technology can make it difficult for companies to introduce new, incompatible technologies. The Carbon API was thoroughly entrenched with established with developers creating apps for the Macintosh. Apple's transition from Carbon to a new API (i.e., Cocoa) was significantly helped by the success of the iPhone, whose SDK supported Cocoa (effectively killed continuing interest in Carbon). [865]

Meetings can play a role as rituals of confirmation, reenchantment and celebration.

3.4.3 Social status

The evidence [55] points to a desire for social status as being a fundamental human motive. Higher status (or reputation) provides greater access to desirable things, e.g., interesting projects and jobs. [1311] To be an effective signalling system, social status has to be costly to obtain. [807]

Social animals pay more attention to group members having a higher social status (however that might be measured). People may seek out and pay deference to a highly skilled individual in exchange for learning access. When attention resources are constrained, people may choose to preferentially invest attention on high-status individuals.

Social status and/or recognition is a currency that a group can bestow on members whose activities are thought to benefit the group. The failure of an academic community to treat the production of research related software as worthy of the appropriate academic recognition [1330] may slow the rate of progress in that community; although academic recognition is not always the primary motive for the creation of research software. [863]

A study by Simcoe and Waguespack [1708] investigated the impact of status on the volume of email discussion on proposals submitted to the Internet Engineering Task Force (IETF). A proposal submitted by an IETF working group had a much higher chance of becoming a published RFC, compared to one submitted by a group of individuals (i.e., 43%vs. 7%). The IETF list server distributed proposals with the authors names, except during periods of peak load, when the author list was shortened (by substituting one generic author, "et al"). The, essentially random, shortening of the proposal author list created a natural experiment, i.e., the identity of the authors was available for some proposals, but not others. Proposals unlikely to become a published RFC (i.e., those submitted by individuals), would be expected to receive less attention, unless the list of authors included a high status individual (a working group chairman was assumed to be a high status individual).

An analysis of the number of email posts involving the 3,129 proposals submitted by individuals (mean 3.4 proposals, sd 7.1), found: 1) when a working group chair appeared on the author list, the weighted number of responses increased by 0.8 , and 2) when a working group chair name was one of the authors but had been replaced by "et al", the weighted number of responses fell by 1.7 ; see Github-economics/EtAlData.R.

Figure 3.18 shows the number of proposals receiving a given number of mentions in IETF email discussions, with lines showing fitted regression models; colors denote whether the author list included a working group chairman and whether this information was visible to those receiving the email.

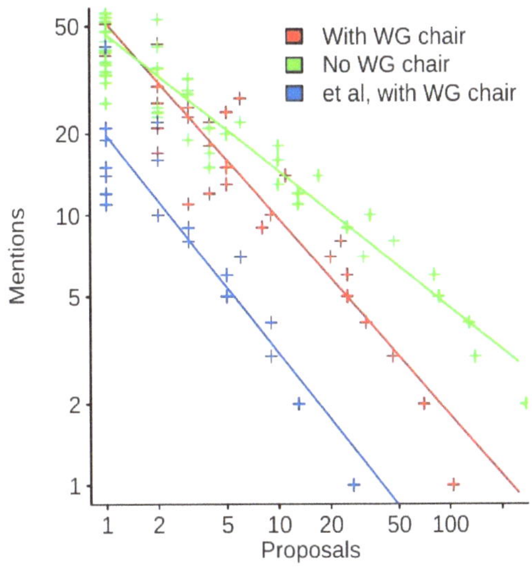

Figure 3.18: Number of proposals receiving a given number of mentions in emails; lines are a fitted regression models of the form: Mentions $\propto$ Proposals $^{-a}$, where a is $0.51, 0.71$, and 0.81 . Data from Simcoe et al. Github-Local

3.4.4 Social learning

Learning by observing others, social learning, enables animals to avoid the potentially high cost of individual learning. [67,854] A population's average fitness increases when its members are capable of deciding which of two learning strategies, social learning or individual learning, is likely to be the most cost effective [235] (i.e., the cost of individual learning can be invested where its benefit is likely to be maximized). Incremental learning can occur without those involved understanding the processes that underlie the activities they have learned. [485]

Prestige-biased transmission occurs when people select the person with the highest prestige as being the most likely to possess adaptive information [810] for a learner to imitate.

Duplicating the behavior of others is not learning, it is a form of social transmission. Following leaders generates a pressure to conform, as does the desire to fit in with a group, known as conformist transmission.

In England, milk was once left in open bottles on customer doorsteps; various species of birds were known to drink some of this milk. When bottles were sealed (these days with aluminium foil), some birds learned to peck open milk bottle tops, with the blue tit being the primary scavenger. [606ix] The evidence suggests those bird species that forage in flocks, have the ability to learn both socially and individually, while species that are territorial (i.e., chase away other members of their species), primarily use individual learning. [1107]

Social learning is a major human skill, where 2.5 -year-old children significantly outperform adult chimpanzees and orangutans, our closest primate relatives [818] (performance on other cognitive tasks is broadly comparable).

Just using social learning is only a viable strategy in an environment that is stable between generations of learners. If the environment is likely to change between generations, copying runs the risk of learning skills that are no longer effective. Analysis using a basic model [1239] shows that for a purely social learning strategy to spread in a population of individual learners, the following relation must hold: $u < \frac{c}{b}$, where: u is the probability of environmental change in any generation, b is the benefit of social learning of behavior in the current environment, and c is the cost of learning.

A study by Milgram, Bickman and Berkowitz [1279] investigated the behavior of 1,424 pedestrians walking past a group of people looking up at the 6th-floor window of the building on the opposite side of the street. Figure 3.19 shows the percentage of passersby lookup up or stopping in response to a crowd of a given size.

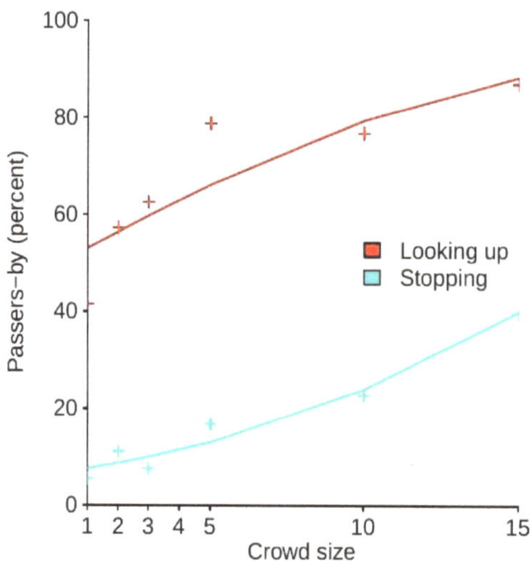

Figure 3.19: Percentage of passers-by looking up or stopping, as a function of group size; lines are fitted linear beta regression models. Data extracted from Milgram et al. Github-Local

A study by Centola, Becker, Brackbill and Baronchelli [315] investigated the relative size of subgroups acting within a group, needed to change a social convention previously established by group members. Groups containing between 18 and 30 people worked in pairs, with pairs changing after every interaction, performing a naming task; once consistent naming conventions had become established within the group, a subgroup was instructed to use an alternative naming convention. The results found that a committed subgroup containing at least 25% of the group were able to cause the group to switch, to using the subgroup's naming conventions. The rate of change depended on group size and relative size of the subgroup; see Github-economics/Centola-Becker.R.

Discoveries and inventions are often made by individuals, and it might be expected that larger populations will contain more tools and artefacts, and have a more complex cultural repertoire than smaller populations. [1112] The evidence is mixed, with population size having a positive correlation with tool complexity in some cases. [385]

Useful new knowledge is not always uniformly diffused out into the world, to be used by others; a constantly changing environment introduces uncertainty [1527] (i.e., noise is added to the knowledge signal), and influential figures may suppress use of the ideas (e.g., some physicists suppressed the use of Feynman diagrams [190]).

Conformist transmission is the hypothesis that individuals possess a propensity to preferentially adopt the cultural traits that are most frequent in the population. Under conformist transmission, the frequency of a trait among the individuals within the population provides information about the trait's adaptiveness. This psychological bias makes individuals more likely to adopt the more common traits than they would under unbiased cultural transmission. Unbiased transmission may be conceptualized in several ways: for example, if an individual copies a randomly selected individual from the population, then the transmission is unbiased; if individuals copy their parents or just their mother, then transmission is unbiased.

The rate of change in the popularity list of baby names, dog breeds and pop music can be fitted [176] by a model where most of the population, N, randomly copy an item on the list, containing L items, and a fraction, μ, select an item not currently on the list. Empirically, the turnover of items on the list has been found to be proportional to: $L\sqrt{\mu}$; a theoretical analysis [556] finds that population size does have some impact, i.e., $L\sqrt{\mu \log \frac{N}{L}}$.

Studies have found that subjects are able to socially learn agreed conventions when communicating within networks having various topologies (containing up to 48 members; the maximum experimental condition). One advantage of agreed conventions is a reduction in communications effort when performing a joint task, e.g., a reduction in the number of words used. [370]

The impact of the transmission of information about new products is discussed in section 3.6.3.

3.4.5 Group learning and forgetting

The performance of groups, like that of individuals (see fig 2.33), improves with practice; groups also forget (in the sense that performance on a previously learned task degrades with time). [905] Industrial studies have focused on learning by doing, [1833] that is the passive learning that occurs when the same, or very similar, product is produced over time.

The impact of organizational learning during the production of multiple, identical units (e.g., a missile or airplane) can be modeled to provide a means of estimating the likely cost and timescale of producing more of the same units. Various models of organizational production [868,1248] based on connected components, where people are able to find connections between nodes that they can change to improve production, produce the power laws of organizational learning encountered in practice.

There are trade-offs to be made in investment in team learning; there can be improvements in performance and team performance can be compromised. [279]

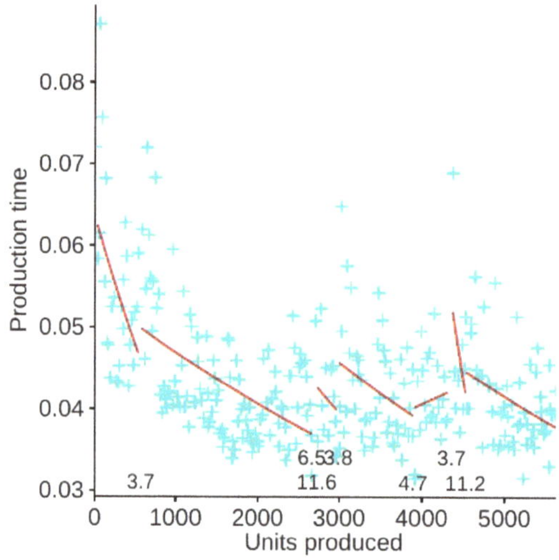

Figure 3.20: Hours required to build a car radio after the production of a given number of radios, with break periods (shown in days above x -axis); lines are regression models fitted to each production period. Data extracted from Nembhard et al. Github-Local

A study by Nembhard and Osothsilp [1365] investigated the impact of learning and forgetting on the production time of car radios; various combined learning-forgetting models have been proposed, and the quality of fit of these models to the data was compared. Figure 3.20 shows the time taken to build a car radio against cumulative production, with an exponential curve fitted to each period of production (break duration in days appears above the x -axis). Note, build time increases after a break, and both a power law and exponential have been proposed as models of the forgetting process.

Writing source code differs from building hardware in that software is easily duplicated, continual reimplementation only occurs in experiments (see fig 2.36). Repetitive activities do occur when writing code, but the repetition is drawn from a wide range of activities sequenced together to create distinct functionality (patterns of code use are discussed in section 7.3).

Figure 3.21 shows the man-hours needed to build three kinds of ships, 188 in total, at the Delta Shipbuilding yard, between January 1942 and September 1945. As experience is gained building Liberty ships the man-hours required, per ship, decreases. [1833] Between May 1943 and February the yard had a contract to build Tankers, followed by a new contract to build Liberty ships, and then Colliers. When work resumes on Liberty ships, the man-hours per ship is higher than at the end of the first contract, presumably some organizational knowledge about how to build this kind of ship had been lost.

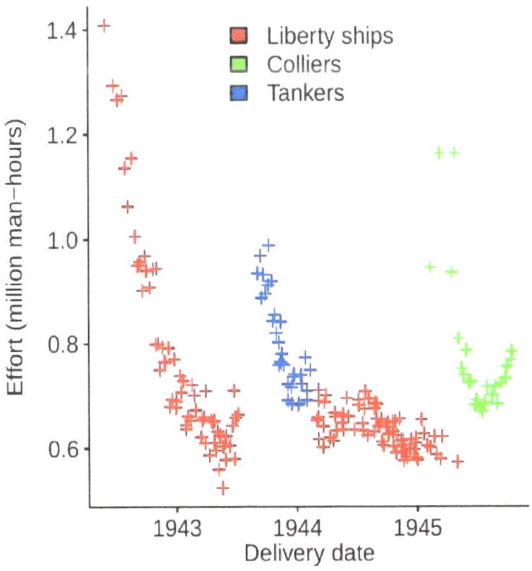

Figure 3.21: Man-hours required to build a particular kind of ship, at the Delta Shipbuilding yard, delivered on a given date (x -axis). Data from Thompson. Github-Local

When an organization loses staff having applicable experience, there is some loss of performance. [69] It has been proposed [806] that the indigenous peoples' of Tasmania lost valuable skills and technologies because their effective population size shrunk below the level needed to maintain a reliable store of group knowledge (when the sea level rose the islander's were cut off from contact with mainland Australia).

An organization's knowledge and specialist skills are passed on to new employees by existing employees and established practices.

A study by Muthukrishna, Shulman, Vasilescu and Henrich investigated the transmission of knowledge and skills, between successive generations of teams performing a novel (to team members) task. In one experiment, each of ten generations was a new team of five people (i.e., 50 different people), with every team having to recreate a target image using GIMP. After completing the task, a generation's team members were given 15 -minutes to write-up two pages of information, whose purpose was to assist the team members of the next generation. Successive teams in one sequence of ten generations, were given the write-up from one team member of the previous generation, while successive teams in another sequence of ten generations, were given the write-ups from the five members of the previous generation team (i.e., the experiment involved 100 people).

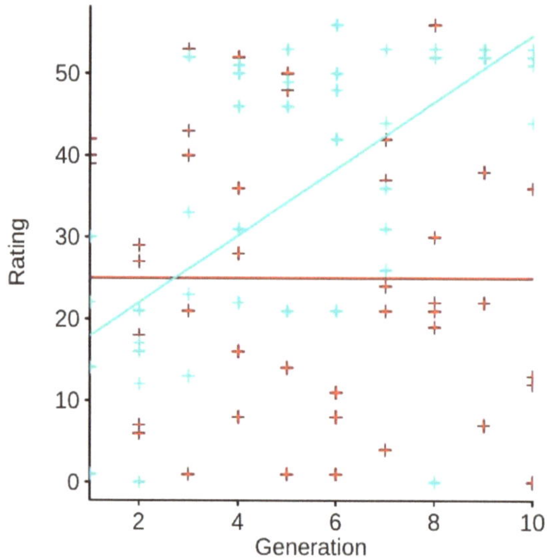

Figure 3.22: Task rating given to members of successive generations of teams; lines are a regression model fitted to the one (red) and five (blue-green) write-up generation sequences. Data from Muthukrishna et al. Github-Local

Figure 3.22 shows the rating given to the image produced by each team member, from each of successive generation; lines show fitted regression models. The results suggest that more information was present in five write-ups (blue-green) than one write-up (red), enabling successive generations to improve (or not).

Outsourcing of development work, offshore or otherwise, removes the learning-by-doing opportunities afforded by in-house development; in some cases management may learn from the outsource vendor. [317]

3.4.6 Information asymmetry

The term information asymmetry describes the situation where one party in a negotiation has access to important, applicable, information that is not available to the other parties. The information is important in the sense that it can be used to make more accurate decisions. In markets where no information about product quality is available, low quality drives out higher quality. [26]

Building a substantial software system involves a huge amount of project specific information; a large investment of cognitive resources is needed to acquire and understand this information. The kinds of specific information involve factors such as: application domain, software development skills and know-how, and existing user work practices.

Vendors bidding to win the contract to implement a new system can claim knowledge on similar systems, but cannot claim any knowledge of a system that does not yet exist. In any subsequent requests to bid to enhance the now-existing system, one vendor can claim intimate familiarity with the workings of the software they implemented. This information asymmetry may deter other vendors from bidding, and places the customer at a disadvantage in any negotiation with the established vendor.

Figure 3.23 shows the ratio of actual to estimated effort for 25 releases of one application, over six years (release 1.1 to 9.1, figures for release 1 are not available). [870] Possible reasons for the estimated effort being so much higher than the actual effort include: cautiousness on the part of the supplier, and willingness to postpone implementation of features planned for the current release to a future release (one of the benefits of trust built up between supplier and customer, in an ongoing relationship, is flexibility of scheduling).

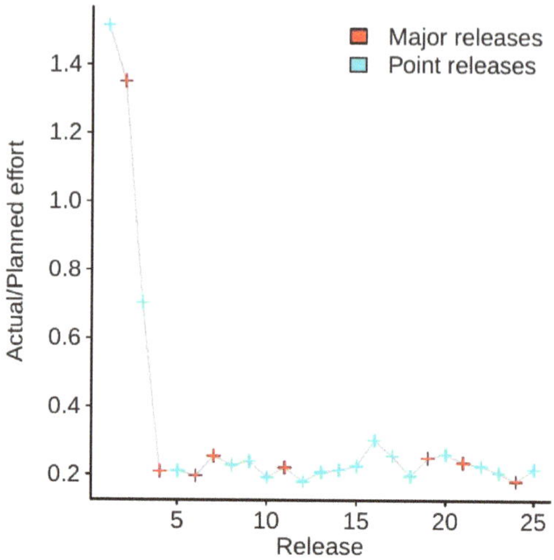

Figure 3.23: Ratio of actual to estimated hours of effort to enhance an existing product, for 25 versions of one application. Data from Huijgens et al. Github-Local

The term vaporware is used to describe the practice of announcing software products with a shipment date well in the future. [1528] These announcements are a signalling mechanism underpinned by asymmetrical information, because there may or may not be a real product under development; uses include: keeping existing customer happy that an existing product has a future and deterring potential competitors. [482]

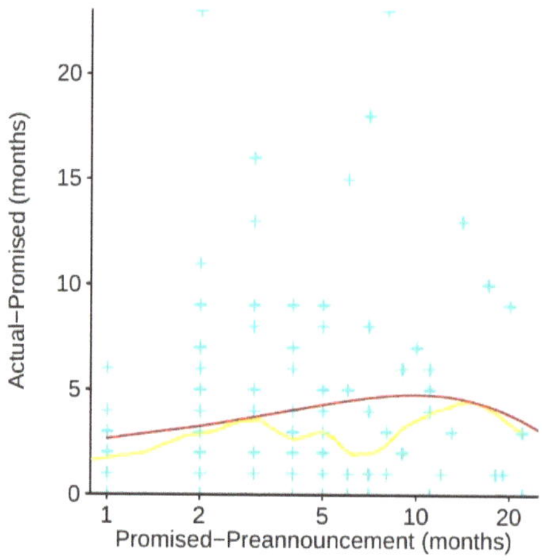

Figure 3.24: Interval between product announcement date and its promised availability date, against interval between promised date and actual date the product became available; lines are a fitted regression model of the form: $A\_P \propto e^{0.3-0.1P\_P+0.8\sqrt{P\_P}}$, and a loess fit. Data from Bayus et al. Github-Local

A study by Bayus, Jain and Rao [155] investigated the delay between promised availability, and actual availability, of 123 software products. Figure 3.24 shows that the interval, in months, between the announcement date and promised product availability date has little correlation with the interval between promised and actual delivery date. The fitted regression line shows that announcements promising product delivery in a month or two are slightly more accurate than those promising delivery further in the future.

3.4.7 Moral hazard

A moral hazard occurs when information asymmetry exists, and the more informed party has some control over the unobserved attributes. The traditional example is a manager running a business for those who own the company (the manager has opportunities to enrich himself, at the expense of the owners, who lack the information needed to detect what has happened), but it can also apply to software developers making implementation decisions, e.g., basing their choice on the enjoyment they expect to experience, rather than the likely best technical solution.

Agency theory deals with the conflict of interests of those paying for work to be done, and those being paid to do it.

With so many benefits on offer to the cognitariate, employers need a mechanism for detecting free-riders: employees have to signal hedonic involvement, e.g., by working long hours. [1076]

The reliability of a product may only become visible after extensive use, e.g., the number of faults experienced. Clients may not be able to distinguish the rhetoric and reality of vendor quality management. [2000]

3.4.8 Group survival

Groups face a variety of threats to their survival, including: more productive members wanting to move on (i.e., brain drain), the desire of less productive people to join (i.e., adverse selection), and the tendency of members to shirk (e.g., social loafing).

Groups function through the mutual cooperation between members. Reciprocity: actions towards another involving an expectation of a corresponding cooperative response from the other party is a fundamental component of group cohesion.

Simulations [732] have found that the presence of reciprocity (e.g., x helps/harms y, who in term helps/harms x), and transitivity (e.g., if x and y help each other, and y helps z , then x is likely to help z) in a uniform population, are sufficient for distinct subgroups to form; see Github-economics/2014+Gray+Rand.R.

Cooperation via direct reciprocity is only stable when the probability of interacting with a previously encountered member P_i, meets the condition: [1410] $\frac{c}{b} < P_i$, where: c is the cost of cooperation, and b is the benefit received (by one party if they defect, and by both parties if they both cooperate; if an altruist member does not start by cooperating, both parties receive zero benefit); cooperation via indirect reciprocity, where decisions are based on reputation (rather than direct experience), is only stable when the probability of knowing a members' reputation, P_k, meets the condition: [1391] $\frac{c}{b} < P_k$.

Members may be tempted to take advantage of the benefits of group membership, [1882] without making appropriate contributions to the group, or failing to follow group norms. [193] If a group is to survive, its members need to be able to handle so-called free-riders. Reputation is a means of signalling the likelihood of a person reciprocating a good deed; some combinations of conditions [1411] linking reputation dynamics and reciprocity have been found to lead to stable patterns of group cooperation.

In an encounter between two people, either may choose to cooperate, or not, with the other. A problem known as the prisoner's dilemma has dominated the theoretical analysis of interactions between two people. Encounters involving the same person may be a recurring event (known as the iterated prisoner's dilemma); in a noise free environment (i.e., those involved correctly recall the previous action of their partner), Tit-for-Tat (TfT, start by cooperating, and then reciprocate the partner's behavior) is currently the best known solution. In practice TfT is easily disrupted by noise, e.g., response based on imperfect recall of the previous interaction; [1907] one alternative strategy is generous TfT (follow TfT, except cooperate with some probability when a partner defects).

While the analysis of prisoner's dilemma style problems can produce insights, it may not be possible to obtain sufficiently accurate values for the variables used in the model. The following analysis [91] illustrates some of the issues.

In a commercial environment, developers may be vying with each other for promotion, or a pay rise. Developers who deliver projects on schedule are likely to be seen by management as worthy of promotion or a pay rise.

Consider the case of two software developers who are regularly assigned projects to complete, by a management specified date: with probability p, the project schedules are unachievable. If the specified schedule is unachievable, performing Low quality work will enable the project to be delivered on schedule, alternatively the developer can tell management that slipping the schedule will enable High quality work to be performed.

Performing Low quality work is perceived as likely to incur a penalty of Q_1 (because of its possible downstream impact on project completion) if one developer chooses Low, and Q_2

if both developers choose Low. It is assumed that: $Q_1 < Q_2 < C$. A High quality decision incurs a penalty that developers perceive to be C (telling management that they cannot meet the specified schedule makes a developer feel less likely to obtain a promotion/payrise).

Let's assume that both developers are given a project, and the corresponding schedule. If either developer faces an unachievable deadline, they have to immediately decide whether to produce High or Low quality work. When making the decision, information about the other developer's decision is not available.

An analysis [91] shows that, both developers choosing High quality is a pure strategy (i.e., always the best) when: $1 - \frac{Q_1}{C} \leq p$, and High-High is Pareto superior to both developers choosing Low quality when: $1 - \frac{Q_2}{C - Q_1 + Q_2} < p < 1 - \frac{Q_1}{C}$.

Obtaining a reasonable estimate for p, C, and Q_1 is likely to be problematic. Inferences drawn from the forms of the equations intended to encourage a High-High decision (e.g., be generous when schedule implementation time, and don't penalise developers when they ask for more time), could have been inferred without using a Prisoner's dilemma model.

Social pressure may not be sufficient to prevent free-riding. Group members have been found to be willing to punish, at a cost to themselves, members who fail to follow group norms (in real-life [1406] and experimental situations [1426]).

A study by Li, Molleman and van Dolder [1129] investigated the impact of prevailing group social norms on the severity with which members punish free-riders. Pairs of subjects played a two-stage game. In the first stage either individual could choose to cooperate (if both cooperate, they each earn 18 points), or defect (i.e., a single defector earns 25 points and the attempted cooperator earns 9; mutual defection earns 16 points). In the second stage, subjects had the opportunity to punish their defecting partner (if the partner had defected) by specifying the number of points to deduct from their partner's earnings; the cost of deduction was a 1 -point deduction from the cooperator for every 3-points they wanted to deduct from their defecting partner. Every subject played eleven times, each time with a randomly selected partner.

Prevailing group norms were set by giving subjects information on the behaviour of subjects in an earlier experiment (labeled as the reference group). One group (318 subjects; the CC treatment) read information about the percentage of cooperators in a reference group, the other group (275 subjects; the CP treatment) read information about the number of points deducted by the cooperators in a reference group.

Figure 3.25 shows the mean number of deduction points specified by CC treatment subjects, when told that a given percentage of subjects in a reference group cooperated. Lines show subjects broken out by four response patterns.

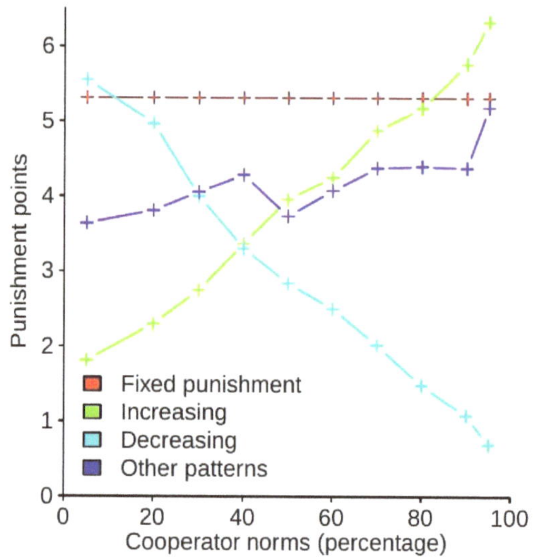

Figure 3.25: Mean number of deduction points specified by subjects told that a given percentage of subjects in a reference group cooperated; broken down by four subject response patterns. Data from Li et al. Github-Local

For the roughly 60% of subjects who punished their partner in at least one game: in both CC and CP treatments, approximately 30% of subjects always specified the same number of points to deduct. For the CC treatment, just over 33% of subjects deducted more points as the percent of cooperators in the reference group increased, and around 20% deducted fewer points, with 17% following other patterns. For the CP treatment, approximately 45% of subjects deducted fewer points as the mean number of deducted points in the reference group increased, and around 2% deducted fewer points, with 20% following other patterns.

3.4.9 Group problem solving

Group problem solving performance [1093] can be strongly affected by the characteristics of the problem; problem characteristics include:

- unitary/divisible: is there one activity that all members have to perform at the same time (e.g., rope pulling), or can the problem be divided into distinct subcomponents and assigned to individual members to perform?

- maximizing/optimizing: is quantity of output the goal, or quality of output (e.g., a correct solution)?
- interdependency: the method of combining member outputs to produce a group output; for instance: every member completes a task, individual member outputs are added together or averaged, or one member's output is chosen as the group output.

When solving Eureka-type problems (i.e., a particular insight is required), the probability that a group containing k individuals will solve the problem is: $P_g = 1 - (1 - P_i)^k$, where: P_i is the probability of one individual solving the problem. When the solution involves s subproblems, the probability of group success is (i.e., a combination-of-individuals model): $P_g = \left[1 - \left(1 - P_i^{1/s}\right)^k\right]^s$. Some studies [1159] have found group performance to have this characteristic.

Studies [1791] have consistently found that for brainstorming problems (i.e., producing as many creative ideas as possible), individuals consistently outperform groups (measured by quantity and quality of ideas generated, per person). Despite overwhelming experimental evidence, the belief that groups outperform individuals has existed for decades. [x]

A study by Bowden and Jung-Beeman [232] investigated the time taken, by individuals, to solve word association problems. Subjects saw three words, and were asked to generate a fourth word that could be combined with each of word to produce a compound word or phrase; for instance, the words SAME/TENNIS/HEAD can all be combined with MATCH. [xi] The 289 subjects were divided into four groups, each with a specified time limit on generating a problem solution (2, 7, 15 and 30 seconds).

Figure 3.26 shows the percentage of subjects who correctly answered a problem against the mean time taken. Each plus corresponds to one of the 144 problems, with colors denoting the time limit (solution time was not collected for the group having a 2 -second time limit). Lines link a sample of time/percent performance for answers to the same problem, in each time-limit group.

The results show that the problems have Eureka-type characteristics, with some problems solved quickly by nearly all subjects, and other problems solved more slowly by a smaller percentage of subjects.

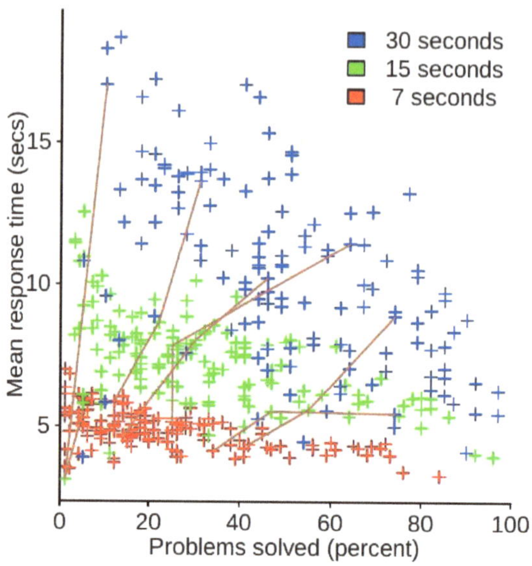

Figure 3.26: Percentage of individuals (x -axis) who correctly generated a solution, against mean response time, for 144 problems; colors denote time limits, and a sample of lines connecting performance pairs for the same program. Data from Bowden et al. Github-Local

The presence of others (e.g., spectators or bystanders) has been found to have a small effect on an individual's performance (i.e., plus/minus 0.5% to 3%). [220]

The information-sampling model [1767] suggests that the likelihood of a group focusing on particular information increases with the number of members who are already aware of it, i.e., information known by one, or a few members, is less likely to be discussed because there are fewer people able to initiate the discussion. The term hidden profile has been used to denote the situation where necessary task information is not widely known, and distributed over many group members.

Studies have found that as group size increases, the effort exerted by individuals decreases; [975] the terms social loafing and Ringelmann effect (after the researcher who first studied [1588] group effort, with subjects pulling on a rope), are used to describe this behavior. Social loafing has been found to occur in tasks that do not involve any interaction between group members, e.g., when asked to generate sound by clapping and cheering in a group, the sound pressure generated by individuals decreases as group size increases. [1091] An extreme form of social loafing is bystander apathy, such as when a person is attacked and onlookers do nothing because they assume somebody else will do something. [1090]

A study by Akdemir and Ahmad Kirmani [25] analyzed student performance when working in teams and individually, based on marks given for undergraduate projects. Students completed two projects working in a team and one project working alone, with all team members given the same mark for a project. Figure 3.27 shows a density plot of the difference between mean team mark and individual mark, for the 386 subjects, broken down by team size.

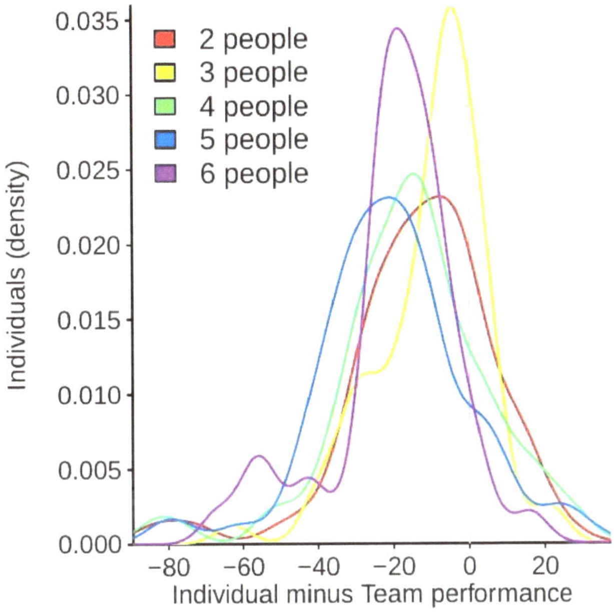

Figure 3.27: Density plot of the difference between mean team mark and individual mark, broken down by team size. Data from Akdemir et al. Github-Local

A study by Lewis [1121] investigated the number of ideas generated by people working in groups or individually. Subjects were given a task description and asked to propose as many methods as possible for handling the various components of the task. Experiment 1 involved groups of 1,2,4 and 6 people, who were given 50 minutes to produce ideas (every 5 -minutes groups recorded the total number of ideas created).

Figure 3.28 shows the average number of ideas produced by each group size. The solid lines show actual groups, the dashed lines show nominal groups, e.g., treating two subjects working individually as a group of two and averaging all their unique ideas.

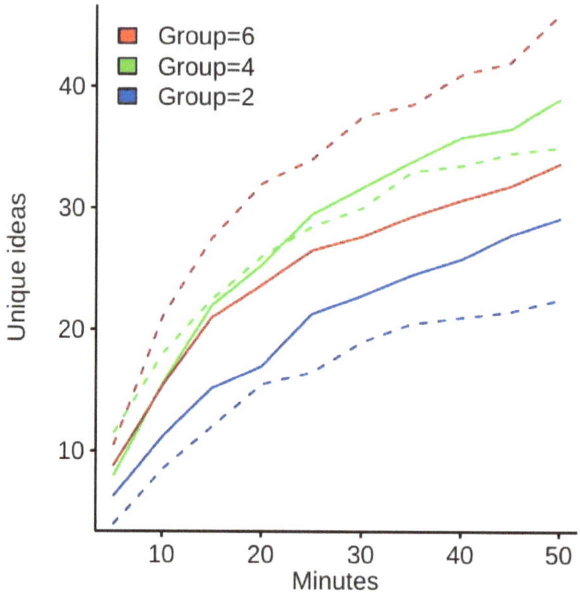

Figure 3.28: Average number of ideas produced by groups of a given size, at 5-minute interval elapsed time; dashed lines are nominal groups created by aggregating individual ideas. Data from Lewis. Github-Local

3.4.10 Cooperative competition

Within ecosystems driven by strong network effects, there can be substantial benefits in cooperating with competitors, e.g., the cost of not being on the winning side of the war, to set a new product standard, can be very high, [1678] and sharing in a winner take-all market is an acceptable outcome.

Software systems need to be able to communicate with each other, agreed communication protocols are required. The communication protocols may be decided by the dominant vendor (e.g., Microsoft with its Server protocol specifications [1277]), by the evolution of basic communication between a few systems to something more complicated involving many systems, or by interested parties meeting together to produce an agreed specification. The components of hardware devices also need to interoperate, and several hundred interoperability standards are estimated to be involved in a laptop. [194]

Various standards' bodies, organizations, consortia, and groups have been formed to document agreed-upon specifications. Committee members are often required to notify other members of any patents they have, that impinge on the specification being agreed to. Organizations that failed to reveal patents they hold, if they subsequently attempt to extract royalties from companies implementing the agreed specification, may receive large fines and licensing their patents under reasonable terms may be government enforced. [584]

A study by Simcoe [1706] investigated the production of communication specifications (i.e., RFCs) by the Internet Engineering Task Force (IETF) between 1993 and 2003 (the formative years of the Internet). Figure 3.29 shows that the time taken to produce an RFC having the status of a Standard, increased as the percentage of commercial membership of the respective committee increased, but there was no such increase for RFCs not having the status of a standard.

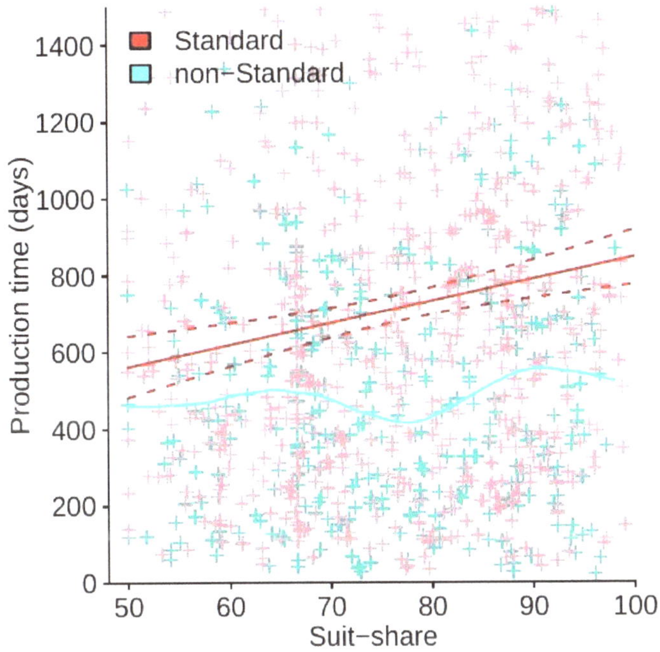

Figure 3.29: Time taken to publish an RFC having Standard or non-Standard status, for IETF committees having a given percentage of commercial membership (i.e., people wearing suits); lines are a fitted regression model with 95% confidence intervals (red), and a loess fit (blue/green). Data from Simcoe. Github-Local

If several companies have to build a large software system that they don't intend to sell as a product (i.e., it's for in-house use), a group of companies may agree to cooperate in building the required system. The projects to build these systems involve teams containing developers from multiple companies.

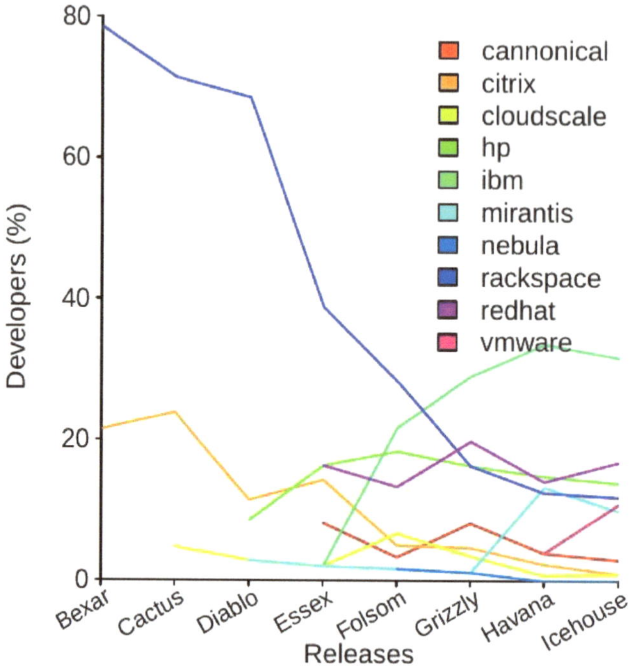

Figure 3.30: Percentage of developers, employed by given companies, working on OpenStack at the time of a release (x-axis). Data from Teixeira et al. Github-Local

A study by Teixeira, Robles and González-Barahona [1820] investigated the evolution of company employees working on the releases of the OpenStack project, between 2010 and 2014. Figure 3.30 shows the involvement of top ten companies, out of over 200 organizations involved, as a percentage of employed developers working on OpenStack.

3.4.11 Software reuse

Reuse of existing code has the potential to save time and money, and reused code may contain fewer mistakes than newly written code (i.e., if the reused code has been executed, there has been an opportunity for faults to be experienced and mistakes fixed). Many equations detailing the costs and benefits of software reuse have been published, [1280] and what they all have in common is not being validated against any evidence.

Reuse of preexisting material is not limited to software, e.g., preferential trade agreements. [32]

Multiple copies of lexically, semantically, or functionally similar source code may be referred to as reused code, duplicate code or as a clone. [xii] Investigating whether cloned code is more fault prone than non-cloned code [855] is something of a cottage industry, but these studies often fail to fully control for mistakes in non-cloned versions of the code. There are specific mistake patterns that are the result of copy-and-paste errors. [169]

Creating reusable software can require more investment than that needed to create a nonreusable version of the software. Without an expectation of benefiting from the extra investment, there is no incentive to make it. In a large organization, reuse may be worthwhile at the corporate level, however the costs and benefits may be dispersed over many groups who have no incentive for investing their resources for the greater good. [599]

Reasons for not reusing code include: the cost of performing due diligence to ensure that intellectual property rights are respected (clones of code appearing on Stack Overflow [xiii] have been found in Android Apps [53] having incompatible licenses, and Github projects [127]), ego (e.g., being recognized as the author of the functionality), and hedonism (enjoyment from inventing a personal wheel, creates an incentive to argue against using somebody else's code). Reusing significant amounts of code complicates cost and schedule estimation; [392] see fig 5.31.

Reuse first requires locating code capable of being cost effectively reused to implement a given requirement. Developers are likely to be familiar with their own code, and the code they regularly encounter. The economics of reusable software are more likely to be cost effective at a personal consumption level, and members of a group may feel obligated to make an investment in the group well-being.

A study by Li, Lu, Myagmar and Zhou [1131] investigated copy-and-pasted source within and between the subsystems of Linux and FreeBSD. Table 3.2 shows that Linux subsystems contain a significant percentage of replicated sequences of their own source; replication between subsystems is less common (the same pattern was seen in FreeBSD 5.2.1).

Table 3.2: Percentage of a subsystem's source code cloned within and across subsystems of Linux 2.6.6. Data from Li et al. [1131]

subsystem	arch	fs	kernel	mm	net	sound	drivers	crypto	others	LOC
arch	25.1	1.4	0.5	0.3	1.1	1.3	3.2	0.1	0.8	724,858
fs	1.4	16.5	0.6	0.5	1.7	1.2	2.2	0.0	0.7	475,946
kernel	3.0	1.8	7.9	0.6	2.3	1.6	2.8	0.1	0.8	30,629
mm	2.6	2.2	0.8	6.2	1.7	1.1	2.0	0.0	0.7	23,490

net	1.8	2.5	1.1	0.7	20.7	2.1	3.7	0.1	1.0	334,325
sound	2.3	2.0	1.0	0.6	2.2	27.4	4.6	0.2	1.1	373,109
drivers	2.3	1.7	0.6	0.4	1.8	2.0	21.4	0.1	0.6	2,344,594
crypto	2.3	2.2	0.3	0.1	1.1	1.5	2.5	26.1	2.2	9,157
others	3.8	1.9	0.8	0.4	1.7	1.5	2.6	0.3	15.2	49,016

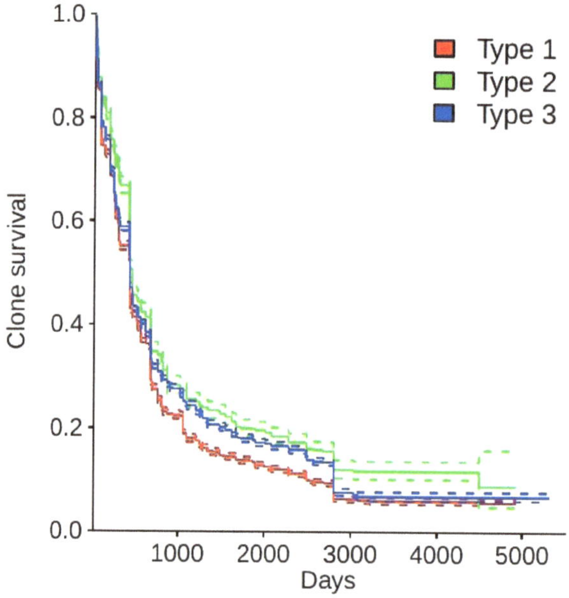

Figure 3.31: Survival curves of type I, II and III clones in the Linux high/medium/low level SCSI subsystems; dashed lines are 95% confidence intervals. Data from Wang. Github-Local

A study by Wang investigated the survival of clones (a duplicate sequence of 50 or more tokens; Type 1 clones are identical, ignoring whitespace and comments, while Type 2 clones allow identifiers and literal values to be different, and Type 3 clones allow nonmatching gaps) in the Linux high/medium/low level SCSI subsystems (the architecture of this system has three levels). Figure 3.31 shows the clone survival curves, which all have an initial half-life of around 18 months, followed by much longer survival lifetimes.

3.5 Company economics

The value of a company is derived from two sources: tangible goods such as buildings it owns, equipment and working capital, and intangible assets which are a product of knowledge (e.g., employee know-how, intellectual property [21] and customer switching costs); see fig 1.10.

Governments have been relatively slow to include intangible investments in the calculation of GDP (starting in 1999 in the US and 2001 in the UK), and different approaches to valuing software [20] has led to increased uncertainty when comparing country GDP (McGee [1241] discusses accounting practices, for software, in the UK and US during the 1970s early 1980s). The accounting treatment of intangibles depends on whether it is purchased from outside the company, requiring it to be treated as an asset, or generated internally where is often treated as an expense. [1324] A company's accounts may only make sense when its intangible assets are included in the analysis. [873]

The financial structure of even relatively small multinational companies, is likely to be complicated. [1041]

3.5.1 Cost accounting

The purpose of cost accounting is to help management make effective cost control decisions. In traditional industries the primary inputs are the cost of raw materials (e.g., the money needed to buy the materials needed to build a widget), and labor costs (e.g., the money paid to the people involved in converting the raw materials into a widget); other costs might include renting space where people can work, and the cost of consumables such as electricity.

The production of software systems is people driven, and people are the primary cost source.

The total cost of a software developer can be calculated from the money they are paid, plus any taxes levied by the government, on an employer, for employing somebody (e.g., national insurance contributions in the UK [xiv]); the term fully loaded cost is sometimes used.

3.5.2 The shape of money

Money is divided up, and categorized, in various ways for a variety of different reasons. Figure 3.32 illustrates the way in which UK and US tax authorities require registered companies to apportion their income to various cost centers.

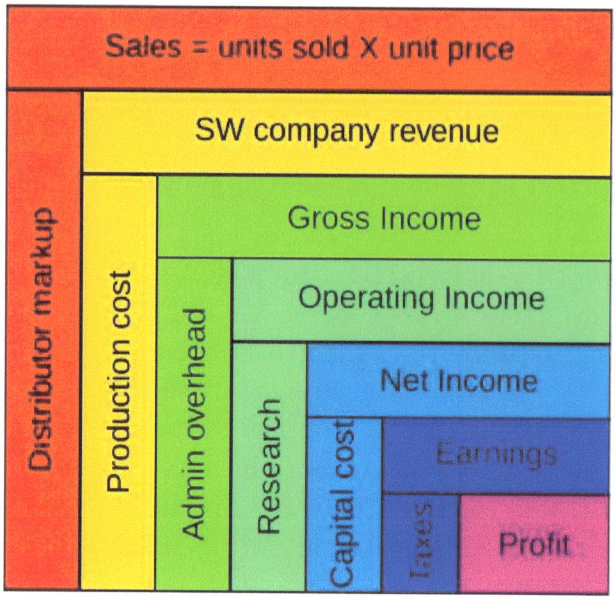

Figure 3.32: Accounting practice for breaking down income from sales, and costs associated with major business activities. Github-Local

Within a company, the most senior executives allocate a budget for each of the organizational groups within the company. These groups, in turn, divide up their available budget between their own organizational groups, and so on. This discrete allocation of funds can have an impact on how software development costs are calculated.

Take the example of a development project, where testing is broken down into two phases, i.e., integrating testing and acceptance testing, each having its own budget, say B_i and B_a.

One technique sometimes used for measuring the cost of faults is to divide the cost of finding them (i.e., the allocated budget), by the number of faults found. For instance, if 100 unique fault experiences occur during integration testing, the cost per fault in this phase is $\frac{B_i}{100}$, and if five unique fault experiences occur during acceptance testing, the cost per fault in this phase is $\frac{B_a}{5}$.

One way of reducing the cost per fault experienced during acceptance testing would be to reduce the effectiveness of integration testing. Because, for a fixed budget, the cost per fault decreases as the number of faults experienced increases.

This accountancy-based approach to measuring the cost of faults, creates the impression that it is more costly to find faults later in the process, compared to finding them earlier.

226 This conclusion is created through the artefact of a fixed budget, along with the typical case that fewer unique fault experiences occur later in the development process.

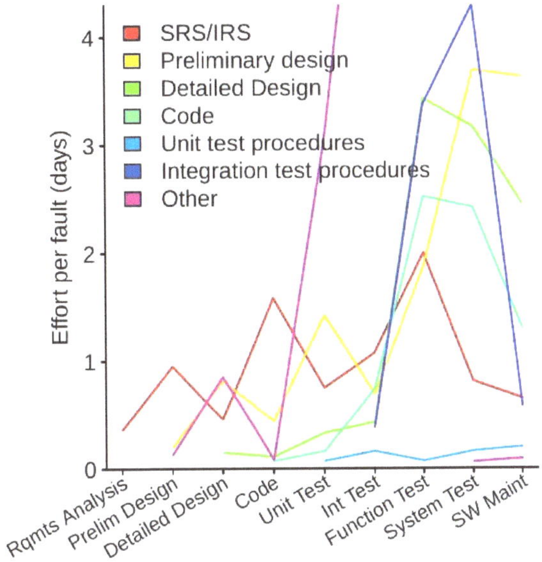

Figure 3.33: Average effort (in days) used to fix a fault experienced in a given phase (x-axis) caused by a mistake that had been introduced in an earlier phrase (colored lines), introduced in an earlier phase (total of 38,120 defects in projects at Hughes Aircraft). Data extracted from Willis et al. Github-Local

Time taken to fix faults may less susceptible to accounting artefacts, provided the actual time is used (i.e., not the total allocated time). Figure 3.33 shows the average number of days used to fix a reported fault in a given phase (x -axis), caused by a mistake that had been introduced in an earlier phase (colored lines), based on 38,120 faults in projects at Hughs Aircraft; [1966] also see fig 6.42.

3.5.3 Valuing software

Like any other item, if no one is willing to pay money for the software, it has zero sales value. The opportunity cost of writing software from scratch, along with the uncertainty of being able to complete the task, and the undocumented business rules it implements, is what makes it possible for existing software to be worth significantly more than the original cost of creating it (along with any installed based). However, for accounting purposes, software may be valued in terms of the cost of producing it.

Various approaches to valuing software, and any associated intellectual property are available. [1954]

An organization seeking to acquire a software system has the option of paying for its implementation, and the cost of creating a software system is one approach to valuing it. However, this approach to valuing an existing system assumes that others seeking to reimplement it have access to the application domain expertise needed to do the job (along with successfully hiring developers with the necessary skills). A reimplementation has a risk premium attached, along with a lead time (which may be the crucial factor in a rapidly changing market).

A study by Gayek, Long, Bell, Hsu and Larson [661] obtained general effort/size information on 452 military/space projects. Figure 3.34 shows executable statements and the developer effort (in months) used to create them (the range of developer salaries is known). Lines are quantile regression fits at 10 and 90% for the one of the application domains, and show a factor of five variation in developer effort (i.e., costs) for the same ESLOC.

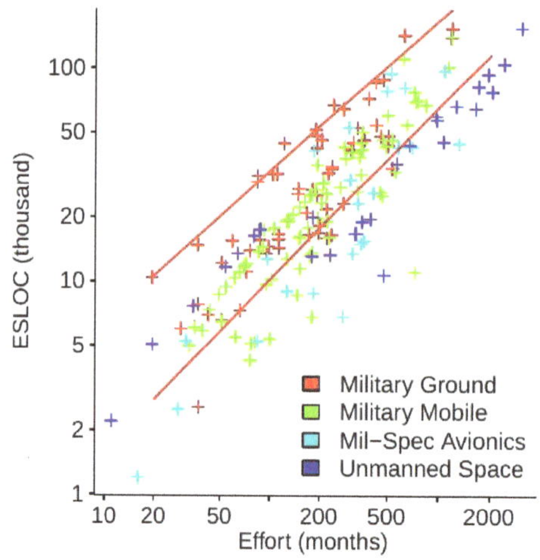

Figure 3.34: Months of developer effort needed to produce systems containing a given number of lines of code, for various application domains; lines are quantile regression fits at 10 and 90%, for one application domain. Data from Gayek et al. Github-Local

Commercial companies are required to keep accurate financial accounts, whose purpose is to provide essential information for those with a financial interest in the company, including governments seeking to tax profits. Official accounting organizations have created extensive, and ever-changing, rules for producing company accounts, including methods for valuing software and other products of intellectual effort. [801] In the US, the Financial Accounting Standards Board has issued an accounting standard "FASB Codification 98520" (FAS 80[602] was used until 2009) covering the "Accounting for the Costs of Computer Software to Be Sold, Leased, or Otherwise Marketed". This allows software development costs to be treated either as an expense or capitalized (i.e., treated like the purchase of an item of hardware). An expense is tax-deductible in the financial year in which it occurs, but the software does not appear in the company accounts as having any value; the value of a capitalized item is written down over time (i.e., a percentage of the value is tax-deductible over a period of years), but has a value in the company accounts. [1001]

The decision on how software development costs appear in the company accounts can be driven by the desire to project a certain image to interested outsiders (e.g., the company is worth a lot because it owns valuable assets [4]), or to minimise tax liabilities. A study by Mulford and Roberts [1325] of 207 companies (primarily industry classification SIC 7372) in 2006, found that 30% capitalized some portion of their software development, while a study by Mulford and Misra [1324] of 100 companies in 2015, found 18% capitalizing their development.

Software made available under an Open Source license may be available at no cost, but value can be expressed in terms of replacement cost, or the cost of alternatives. For accounting purposes, the cost of hardware is depreciated over a number of years. While software does not wear out, it could be treated as having a useful lifespan (see section 4.2.2).

3.6 Maximizing ROI

Paying people to write software is an investment, and investors want to maximise the return on their investments.

To be viable, a commercial product requires a large enough market capable of paying what it takes. One study [992] of Android Apps found that 80% of reviews were made by people owning a subset of the available devices (approximately 33%). Given the cost of testing an App in the diverse Android ecosystem, the ROI can be increased by ignoring those devices that are owned by a small percentage of the customer base.

Some people write software to acquire non-monetary income, but unless this is the only income sought (e.g., income derived purely from the creation process, or the pride in releasing an App), maximising returns will be of interest.

A study by Li, Bissyandé and Klein [1125] investigated the release history of 3,271,646 Apps in Google Play (the App market does not make available a release history, and the data collection process may have missed some releases). Figure 3.35 shows the number of Apps in Google Play having a given number of releases, along with a regression line fitted to the first 20 releases.

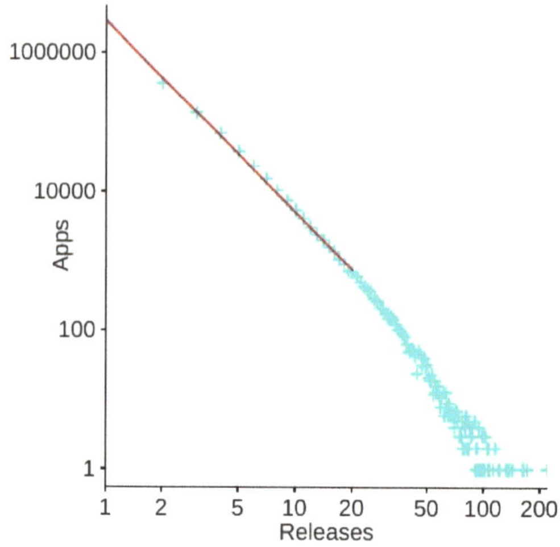

Figure 3.35: Number of Apps in the Google playstore having a given number of releases; line is a fitted regression model of the form: Apps ∝ Releases $^{-2.8}$. Data kindly provided by Li. Github-Local

Accounting issues around choices such as purchase vs. leasing, contractors vs. employees, and making efficient use of income held offshore, [195] are outside the scope of this book.

3.6.1 Value creation

A business model specifies an organization's value creation strategy. [1644]

Many businesses structure their value creation processes around the concept of a value chain; in some software businesses value creation is structured around the concept of a value network. [1757]

A value chain is the collection of activities that transform inputs into products. "A firm's value chain and the way it performs individual activities are a reflection of its history, its strategy, its approach to implementing its strategy, and the underlying economics of the activities themselves.". [1508] Governments tend to view [460] creative value chains as applying to artistic output, and in the digital age artistic output shares many of the characteristics of software development.

A value chain for bespoke software development might be derived from the development methodology used to produce a software system, e.g., the phases of the waterfall model. [216]

The business model for companies selling software products would include a value chain that included marketing, [334] customer support and product maintenance.

A company whose business is solving customer problems (e.g., professional services) might be called a value shop. [1757]

In a two-sided market, value flows from one side to the other. Companies create value by facilitating a network relationship between their customers, e.g., Microsoft encourage companies to create applications running under Microsoft Windows, and make money because customers who want to run the application need a copy of Windows; applications and platforms are discussed in section 4.5.

3.6.2 Product/service pricing

Vendors can set whatever price they like for their product or service. The ideal is to set a price that maximises profit, but there is no guarantee that income from sales will cover the investment made in development and marketing. Even given extensive knowledge of potential customers and competitors, setting prices is very difficult. [1348,1701]

Like everything else, software products are worth what customers are willing to pay. When prices quoted by vendors are calculated on an individual customer basis, inputs considered include how much the customer might be able to pay. [1647] Shareware, software that is made freely available in the hope that users will decide it is worth paying for, [1807] is one of the purest forms of customer payment decision-making.

Customer expectation, based on related products, acts as a ballpark from which to start the estimation process; figure 3.36 shows the relative price/performance used by Intel for one range of processors. It may be possible to charge more for a product that provides more benefits, or perhaps the price has to match that of the established market leader, and the additional benefits are used to convince existing customers to switch.

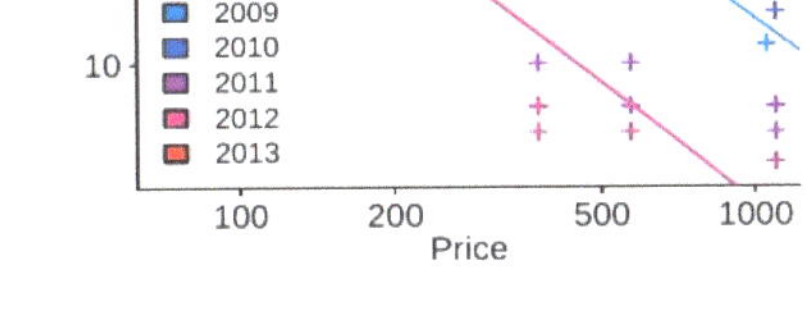

Figure 3.36: Introductory price and performance (measured using wPrime32 benchmark; lower is better) of various Intel processors between 2003-2013. Data from Sun. Github-Local

Figure 3.37 shows the prices charged by several established C/C + compiler vendors. In 1986[xv] Zorland entered the market with a £29.95C compiler, an order of magnitude less than what most other vendors were charging at the time. This price was low enough for many developers to purchase a copy out of company petty cash, and Zorland C quickly gained a large customer base. Once the product established a quality reputation, Zorland were able to increase prices to the same level as those charged by other major vendors (Zorland sounds very similar to the name of another major software vendor of the period, Borland. Letters from company lawyers are hard evidence that a major competitor thinks your impact on their market is worthy of their attention; Zorland became Zortech). [xvi]

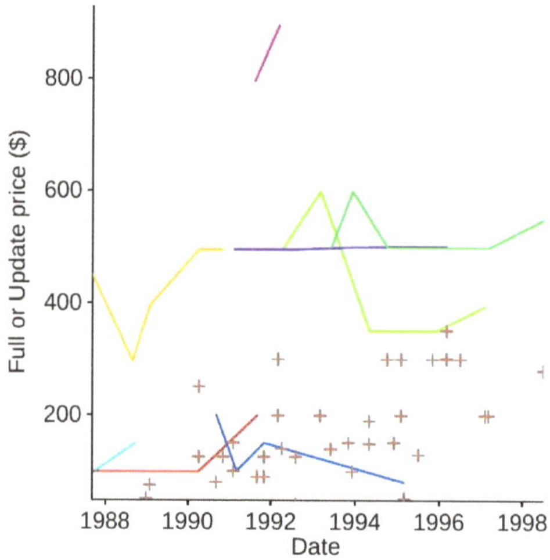

Figure 3.37: Vendor C and C + + compiler retail price (different line for each product), and upgrade prices (pluses) for products available under MS-DOS and Microsoft Windows between 1987 and 1998. Data kindly provided by Viard. Github-Local

A study by Viard [1897] investigated software retail and upgrade pricing, in particular C and C+ compilers available under Microsoft DOS and Windows, between 1987 and 1998. Figure 3.37 shows that the retail price of C/C++ compilers, running under Microsoft DOS and Windows, had two bands that remained relatively constant. Microsoft had a policy of encouraging developers to create software for Windows, [1494] on the basis that sales of applications would encourage sales of Windows, and significantly greater profits would be made from the increased volume of Windows' sales, compared to sales of compilers. Microsoft's developer friendly policy kept the price of C/C++ compilers under Windows down, compared to other platforms. [xvii]

Many companies give managers the authority to purchase low cost items, with the numeric value of low price increasing with seniority. The upper bound on the maximum price that can be charged for a product or service, that can be sold relatively quickly to businesses, is the purchasing authority of the target decision maker. Once the cost of an item reaches some internally specified value (perhaps a few thousand pounds or dollars), companies require that a more bureaucratic purchase process be followed, perhaps involving a purchasing committee, or even the company board. Navigating a company's bureaucratic processes requires a sales rep, and a relatively large investment of time, increasing the cost of sales, and requiring a significant increase in selling price; a price dead-zone exists between the maximum amount managers can independently sign-off, and the minimum amount it is worth selling via sales reps.

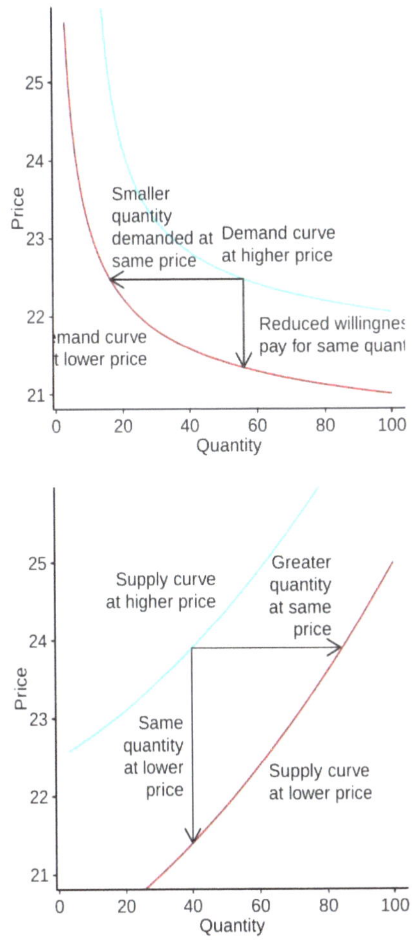

Figure 3.38: Examples of supply (lower) and demand (upper) curves. Github-Local

Supply and demand is a commonly cited economic pricing model. The supply curve is the quantity of an item that a supplier is willing, and able, to supply (i.e., sell) to customers at a given price, and the demand curve is the quantity of a product that will be in demand (i.e., bought by customers) at a given price. If these two curves intersect, the intersection point gives the price/quantity at which suppliers and customers are willing to do business; see figure 3.38.

Events can occur that cause either curve to shift. For instance, the cost of manufacturing an item may increase/decrease, shifting the supply curve up/down on the price axis (for software, the cost of manufacturing is the cost of creating the software system); or customers may find a cheaper alternative, shifting the demand curve down on the price axis.

In some established markets, sufficient historic information has accumulated for reasonably accurate supply/demand curves to be drawn. Predicting the impact of changing circumstances on supply-demand curves remains a black art for many products and services. Software is a relatively new market, and one that continues to change relatively quickly. This changeability makes estimating supply/demand curves for software products little more than wishful thinking.

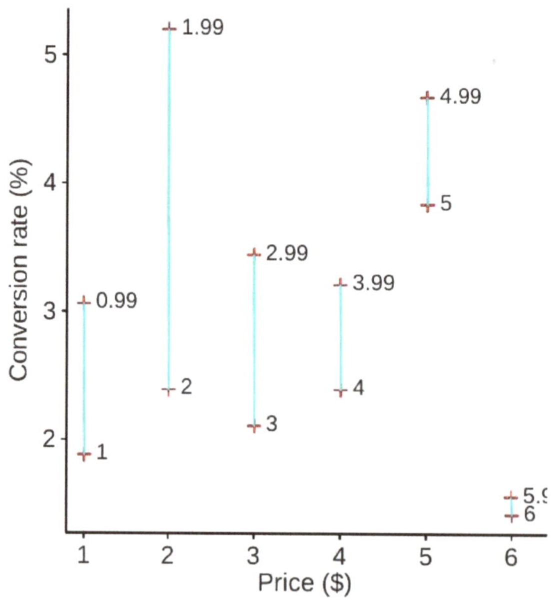

Figure 3.39: Rates at which product sales are made on Gumroad at various prices; lines join prices that differ in 1¢, e.g., \$1.99 and \$2. Data from Nichols. [1376] **Github-Local**

Listed prices are often slightly below a round value, e.g., £3.99 or £3.95 rather than £4.00. People have been found to perceive this kind of price difference to be greater than the actual numerical difference [1830] (the value of the left digit, and the numeric distance effect have been used to explain this behavior). Figure 3.39 shows the impact that visually distinct, small price differences, have on the rate of sale of items listed on Gumroad (a direct to consumer sales website). Other consumer price perception effects include precise prices vs. round prices.

Other pricing issues include site licensing, discounting and selling through third-parties. [1684] The lack of data prevents these issues being discussed here.

The price of a basket of common products, over time, is used to calculate the consumer price index, and changes in product prices over time can be used to check the accuracy of official figures. [1446] Products may evolve over time, with new features being added, and existing features updated; techniques for calculating quality adjusted prices have been developed; [1794] see figure 3.36.

3.6.3 Predicting sales volume

The likely volume of sales is a critical question for any software system intended to be sold to multiple customers.

When one product substitutes another, new for old, market share of the new product is well fitted by a logistic equation, [607] whose maximum is the size of the existing market.

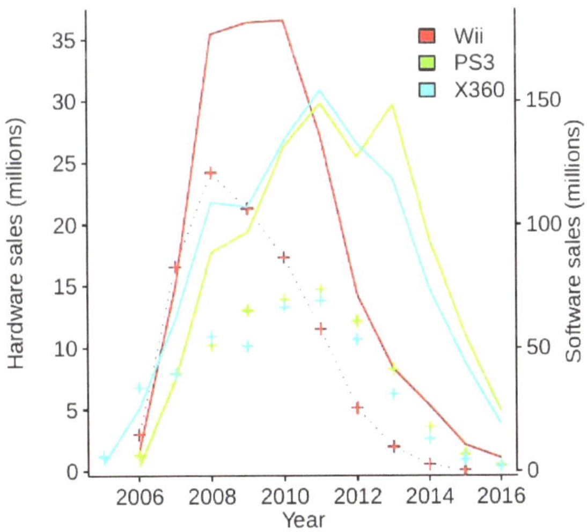

Figure 3.40: Sales of game software (solid lines) for the corresponding three major seventh generation hardware consoles (dotted lines). Data from VGChartz. Github-Local

Software may be dependent on the functionality provided by the underlying hardware, which may be rapidly evolving. [1016] Figure 3.40 shows how software sales volume lags behind sales of the hardware needed to run it. An installed hardware base can be an attractive market for software. [1203]

Estimating the likely sales volume for a product intended to fill a previously unmet customer need, or one that is not a pure substitution, is extremely difficult (if not impossible). [1788]

The Bass model [143,1461] has been found to fit data on customer adoption of a new product and successive releases, and has been used to make short term sales predictions [1984] (the following analysis deals with the case where customers are likely to make a single purchase; the model can be extended to handle repeat sales [144]). The model divides customers into innovators, people who are willing to try something new, and imitators, people who buy products they have seen others using (this is a diffusion model). The interaction between innovators, imitators and product adoption, at time t, is given by the following relationship:

$\frac{f(t)}{1-F(t)} = p + qF(t)$, where: $F(t)$ is the fraction of those who will eventually adopt (i.e., have purchased) by time t, $f(t)$ is the probability of purchase at time t (i.e., the derivative of $F(t), f(t) = dF(t)/dt$), p the probability of a purchase by an innovator, and q the probability of a purchase by an imitator.

This non-linear differential equation [xviii] has the following exact solution, for the cumulative number of adopters (up to time), and the instantaneous number of adopters (at time t):

$$F(t) = \frac{1-e^{-(p+q)t}}{1+\frac{q}{p}e^{-(p+q)t}} \text{ and } f(t) = \frac{(p+q)^2}{p}\frac{e^{-(p+q)t}}{\left[1+\frac{q}{p}e^{-(p+q)t}\right]^2}$$

Actual sales, up to, or at, time t, are calculated by multiplying by m, the total number of product adopters.

When innovators dominate (i.e., $\leq p$), sales decline from an initial high-point; when imitators dominate (i.e., $q > p$), peak sales of $m\left(\frac{1}{2} - \frac{p}{2q}\right)$ occurs at time $\frac{m}{p+q}\log\frac{q}{p}$, before declining; the expected time to adoption is: $E(T) = \frac{m}{q}\log\frac{p+q}{p}$.

The exact solution applies to a continuous equation, but in practice sales data is discrete (e.g., monthly, quarterly, yearly). In the original formulation the model was reworked in terms of a discrete equation, and solved using linear regression (to obtain estimates for p, q); however, this approach produces biased results. Benchmarking various techniques [1461] finds that fitting the above non-linear equation to the discrete data produces the least biased results.

Vendors want reliable estimates of likely sales volume as early in the sales process as possible, but building accurate models requires data covering a non-trivial range of the explanatory variable (time in this case). Figure 3.41 shows the number of Github users during its first 58 months, and Bass models fitted to the first 24,36,48 and 58 months of data. [xix].

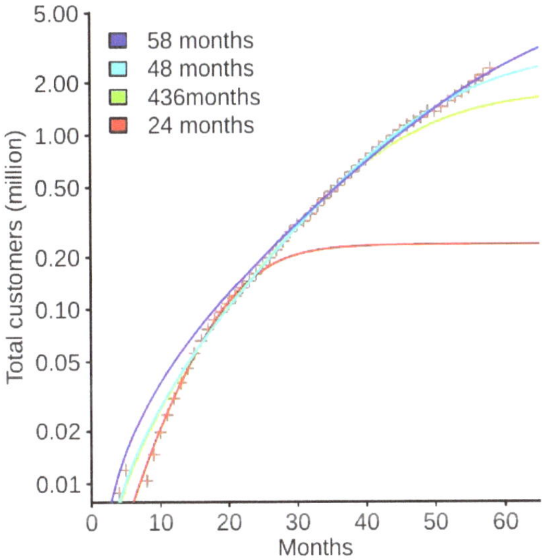

Figure 3.41: Growth of Github users during its first 58 months, with Bass models fitted to data up to a given number of months. Data from Irving. Github-Local

The Bass model includes just two out of the many possible variables that could affect sales volume, and models that include more variables have been developed. [1290] Intel have used an extended Bass Model to improve forecasting of design wins. [1984]

The Bass model can be extended to handle successive, overlapping generations of a product; the following example is for two generations: [1389]

$$S_1(t) = F_1(t)m_1 - F_2(t-\tau_2)F_1(t)m_1 = F_1(t)m_1\big(1 - F_2(t-\tau_2)\big)$$
$$S_2(t) = F_2(t-\tau_2)(m_2 + F_1(t)m_1)$$

where: $S_i(t)$ are all sales up to time t for product generation i, m_i the total number who adopt generation i, and τ_2 the time when the second generation can be bought; p_i and q_i are the corresponding purchase probabilities for each generation.

The Bass model uses two of the factors driving product sales, other factors that can play a significant role include advertising spend, and variability in market size caused by price changes. Monte Carlo simulation can be used to model the interaction of these various factors. [1875]

How much value, as perceived by the customer, does each major component add to a system? A technique for obtaining one answer to this question, is Hedonic regression (this approach is used to calculate the consumer price index): this fits a regression model to data on product price and product configuration data. A study by Stengos and Zacharias [1772] performed a hedonic analysis of the Personal Computer market, based on data such as price, date, CPU frequency, hard disc size, amount of RAM, screen width and presence of a CD; see Github-economics/0211_Computers.R.

The ease with which software can be copied makes piracy an important commercial issue. Studies [684,1932] have extended the Bass model to include the influence of users of pirated software, on other people's purchasing decisions (e.g., Word processors and Spreadsheet programs between 1987 and 1992). The results, based on the assumptions made by the models, and the data used, suggest that around 85% of users run pirated copies; see Github-economics/MPRA/. The Business Software Alliance calculates piracy rates by comparing the volume of software sales against an estimate of the number of computers in use, a method that has a high degree of uncertainty because of the many assumptions involved; [1498] see Github-economics/piracy $_H$ ICSS - 2010.R.

In some ecosystems (e.g., mobile) many applications are only used for a short period, after they have been installed; see fig 4.44.

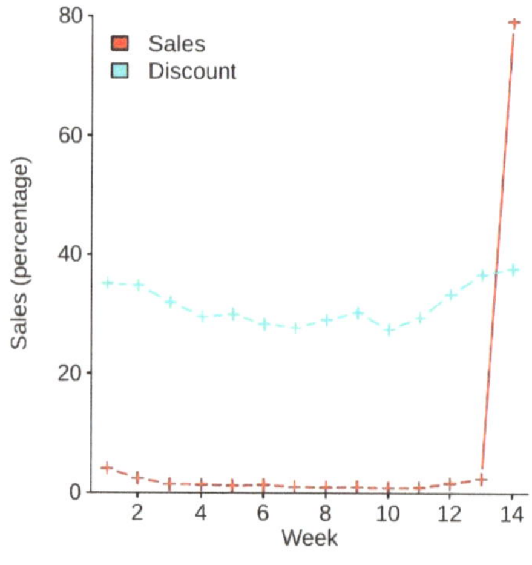

Figure 3.42: Percentage of sales closed in a given week of a quarter, with average discount given. Data from Larkin. Github-Local

In some markets most sales are closed just before the end of each yearly sales quarter, e.g., enterprise software. A study by Larkin [1086] investigated the impact of non-linear incentive schemes [xx] on the timing of deals closed by salespeople, whose primary income came from commission on the sales they closed. Accelerated commission schemes create an incentive for salespeople to book all sales in a single quarter.

Figure 3.42 shows the number of deals closed by week of the quarter, and the average agreed discount. Reasons for the significant peak in the number of deals closed at the end of the quarter include salespeople gaming the system to maximise commission and customers holding out for a better deal.

3.6.4 Managing customers as investments

Acquiring new customers can be very expensive, and it is important to maximise the revenue from those that are acquired.

What is the total value of a customer to a company?

If a customer makes regular payments of m, the customer lifetime value (CLV) is given by (assuming the payment is made at the end of the period; simply add m if payment occurs at the start of the period):

$$CLV = \frac{mr}{(1+i)} + \frac{mr^2}{(1+i)^2} + \frac{mr^3}{(1+i)^3} + \cdots = m\frac{r}{1-r+i}\left[1 - \left(\frac{r}{1+i}\right)^n\right]$$

where: r is the customer retention rate for the period, i the interest rate for the period, and n is the number of payment periods. As $n \to \infty$, this simplifies to: $CLV = m\frac{r}{1-r+i}$.

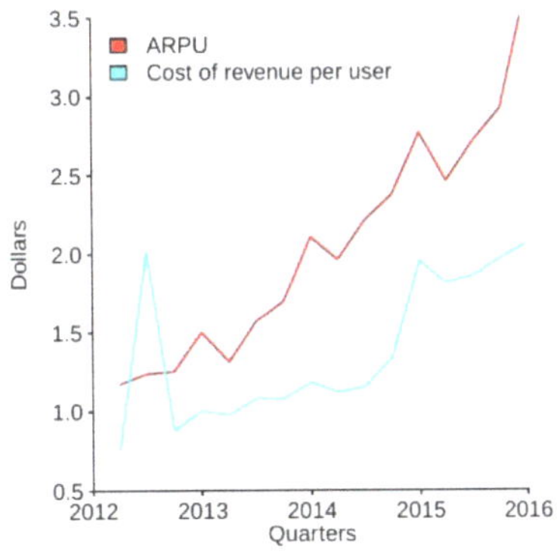

Figure 3.43: Facebook's ARPU and cost of revenue per user. Data from Facebook's 10-K filings. Github-Local

A person who uses a software system without paying for it may be valued as a product. Facebook values its users (whose eyeballs are the product that Facebook sells to its customers: advertisers) using ARPU, [xxi] defined as "... total revenue in a given geography during a given quarter, divided by the average of the number of MAUs in the geography at the beginning and end of the quarter." Figure 3.43 shows ARPU, and cost of revenue per user (the difference is one definition of profit, or loss).

In the business world, annual maintenance agreements are a common form of regular payment, another is the sale of new versions of the product to existing customers (often at a discount).

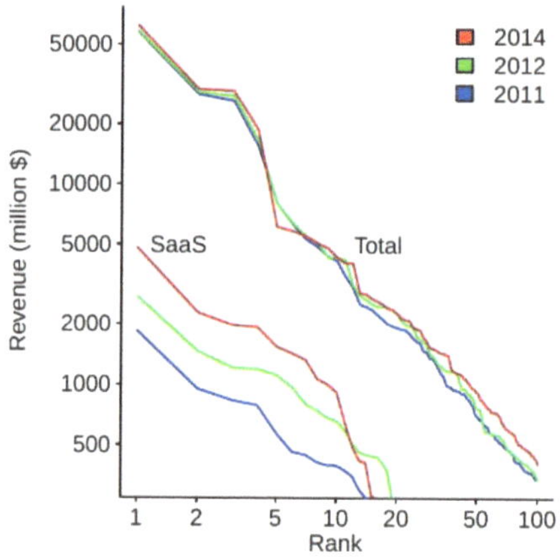

Figure 3.44: Top 100 software companies ranked by total revenue (in millions of dollars) and ranked by Software-as-a-Service revenue. Data from PwC. Github-Local

Before renewing their maintenance agreement, customers expect to see a worthwhile return on this investment. Possible benefits include new product features (or at least promises of these), and support with helping to fix issues encountered by the customer. Vendor's need to be able to regularly offer product improvements means it is not in their interest to include too many new features, or fix too many open issues, in each release; something always needs to be left for the next release.

3.6.5 Commons-based peer-production

The visibility of widely used open source applications, created by small groups of individuals, continues to inspire others to freely invest their energies creating or evolving software systems.

The quantity of open source software that is good enough for many commercial uses has made the support and maintenance of some applications a viable business model. [1644]

Some commercial companies relicense software they have developed internally under an Open source license, and may spend significant amounts of money paying employees to work on open source software. The possible returns from making investments include:

- driving down the cost of complementary products (i.e., products used in association with the vendor's product, that are not substitutes that compete), this reduces the total cost to the customer, increasing demand, and making it more difficult for potential competitors to thrive. [247] Methods for driving down costs include supporting the development of free software that helps ensure there is a competitive market for the complementary product,
- giving software away to make money from the sale of the hardware that uses it,
- control of important functionality. For instance, Apple is the primary financial supporter of the LLVM compiler chain, which is licensed under the University of Illinois/NCSA Open source license; this license does not require contributors to supply the source code of any changes they make (unlike the GNU licensed GCC compilers). Over time LLVM has become an industrial strength compiler, making it the compiler of choice for vendors who don't want to release any code they develop.

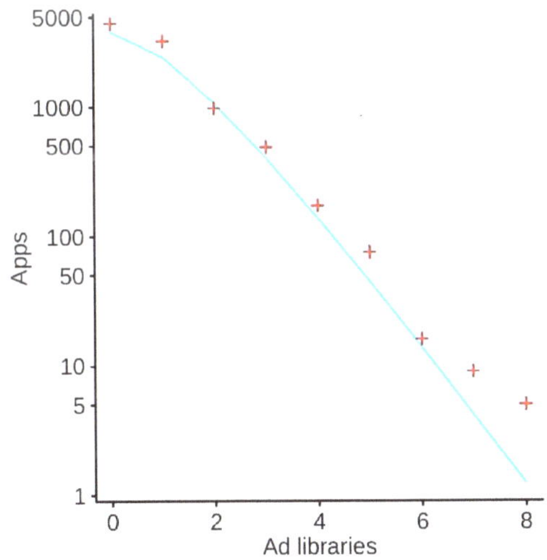

Figure 3.45: Number of applications in the Android market and Amazon App Store, during 2012, containing a given number of advertising libraries (line is a fitted Negative Binomial distribution). Data from Shekhar et al. Github-Local

The income stream for some applications comes from advertising, that runs during program execution. A study by Shekhar, Dietz and Wallach investigated advertising libraries used by 10,000 applications in the Android market, and the Amazon App Store, during 2012. Figure 3.45 shows the number of apps containing a given number of advertising libraries; line is fitted a Negative Binomial distribution.

Chapter 4

Ecosystems

4.1 Introduction

Customer demand motivates the supply of energy that drives software ecosystems.

Computer hardware is the terrain on which software systems have to survive, and the history of the capacity limits of this terrain has shaped the culture of those that live off it.

Figure 4.1: Connections between the 164 companies that have Apps included in the Microsoft Office365 Marketplace (Microsoft not included); vertex size is an indicator of the number of Apps a company has in the Marketplace. Data kindly provided by van Angeren. Github-Local

People and existing code are the carriers of software culture within an ecosystem; continual evolution of the terrain has imbued many software cultures with a frontier mentality spirit.

The amount of memory available on customer computers limits the size and complexity of commercially viable applications. A team of one or two developers can build a commercially viable application for computers limited to 64 K of memory. When customers acquire computers supporting larger capacity memory, the commercial development environment changes. Being able to create ever larger software systems makes it possible to sell applications containing an ever-increasing number of features; a many person team is now needed to implement and support the increasing size and complexity of software systems (which increases the cost of market entry).

Figure 4.2 shows the amount of memory installed on systems running a SPEC benchmark on a given date, along with two fitted quantile regression models. The lower line divides systems such that 95% are above it (i.e., contain more memory than systems below the line), the upper lines divides systems such that 50% are above it. For the 95% line, the amount of installed memory doubles every 845 days (it doubles every 825 days for the 50% line).

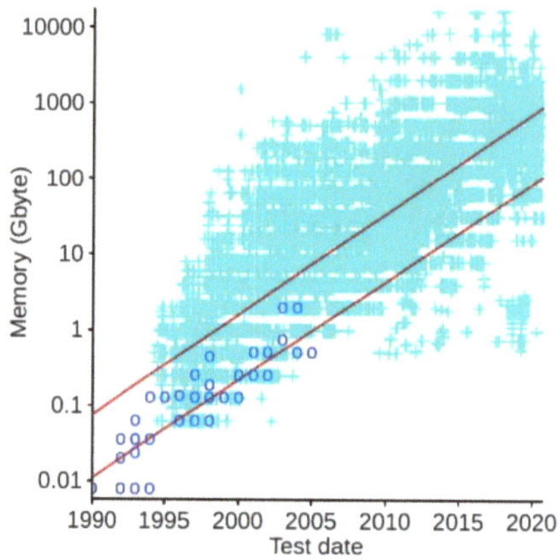

Figure 4.2: Amount of memory installed on systems running a SPEC benchmark on a given date; lines are fitted quantile regression models dividing systems into 50% above/below, and 95% above with 5% below.. Data from SPEC [1742] Github-Local

Software vendors have an interest in understanding the ecosystems in which they operate, want to estimate the expected lifetime of their products, estimate of the size of the potential market for their products and services, and to understand the community dynamics driving the exchange of resources. Governments have an interest in consumer well-being, which gives them an interest in the functioning of ecosystems with regard to the cooperation and competition between vendors operating within an ecosystem.

While software ecosystems share some of the characteristics of biological ecosystems, there are some significant differences, including:

- software ecosystem evolution is often Lamarkian [i], rather than Darwinian, [ii]
- software can be perfectly replicated with effectively zero cost, any evolutionary pressure comes from changes in the world in which the software is operated,
- like human genes, software needs people in order to replicate, but unlike genes software is not self-replicating; people replicate software when it provides something they want, and they are willing to invest in its replication, and perhaps even its ongoing maintenance,

- software has an unlimited lifetime, in theory, in practice many systems have dependencies on the ecosystem in which they run, e.g., third-party libraries and hardware functionality,
- resource interactions are based on agreement, while in biological ecosystems creatures go to great lengths to avoid common resource interactions, e.g., being eaten.

Customer demand for software systems takes many forms, including: a means of reducing costs, creating new products to be sold for profit, tools that people can use to enhance their daily life, coercive pressure from regulators mandating certain practices, [1067] and experiencing the pleasure of creating something, e.g., writing open source, where the developer is the customer. Customer demand cannot always be supplied at a profit, and the demand for new products is often insufficient for them to be profitable. [iii] New products will diffuse into existing commercial ecosystems [1788] when they can be seen to provide worthwhile benefits.

The initial customer demand for computer systems followed patterns seen during the industrial revolution, [35] with established industries seeking to reduce their labor costs by investing in new technologies; the creation of new industries based around the use of computers came later. The first computers were built from components manufactured for other purposes (e.g., radio equipment), as the market for computers grew, it became profitable to manufacture bespoke devices.

The data processing and numerical calculation ecosystems [741,845] existed prior to the introduction of electronic computers; mechanical computers were used. Figure 4.3 shows UK government annual expenditure on punched cards, and mechanical data processing devices.

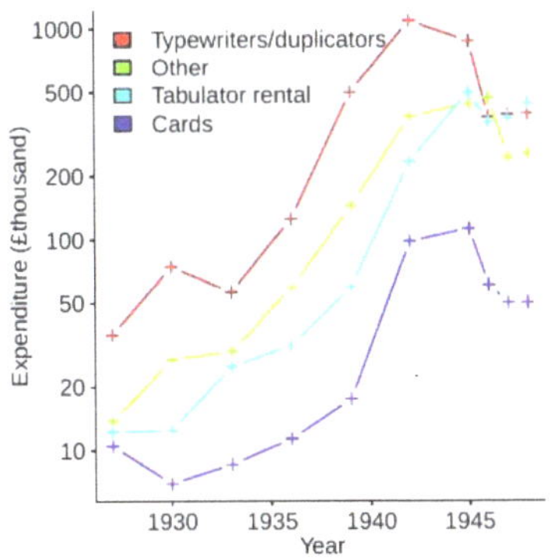

Figure 4.3: Yearly expenditure on punched cards, and tabulating equipment by the UK government. Data from Agar. Github-Local

Customer demand for solutions to the problems now solved using software may have always existed; the availability of software solutions had to wait for the necessary hardware to become available at a price that could be supplied profitably; [282] see fig 1.1. Significant improvements in hardware performance meant that many customers found it cost effective to regularly replace existing computer systems. With many applications constrained by memory capacity, there was customer demand for greater memory capacity, incremental improvements in technology made it possible to manufacture greater capacity devices, and the expected sales volume made it attractive to invest in making the next incremental improvements happen; figure 4.4 shows the growth in world-wide DRAM shipments, by memory capacity shipped.

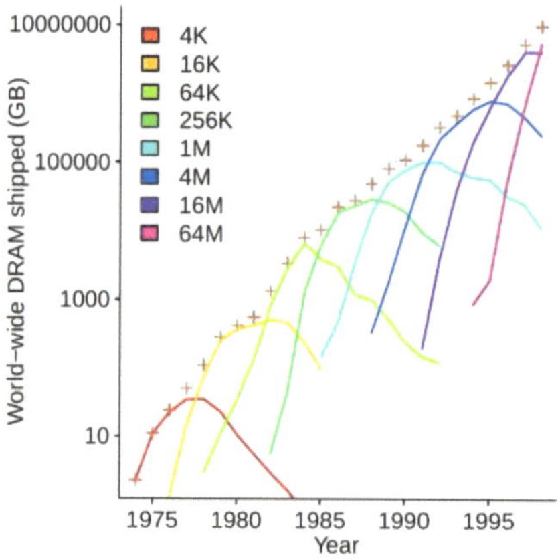

Figure 4.4: Total gigabytes of DRAM shipped world-wide in a given year, stratified by device capacity (in bits). Data from Victor et al. Github-Local

Who is the customer, and, which of their demands can be most profitably supplied? These tough questions are entrepreneurial and marketing problems, [334] and not the concern of this book.

The analysis in this book is oriented towards those involved in software development, rather than their customers, however it is difficult to completely ignore the dominant supplier of the energy (i.e., money) driving software ecosystems. The three ecosystems discussed in this chapter are oriented towards customers, vendors (i.e., companies engaged in economic activities, such as selling applications), and developers, i.e., people having careers in software development.

The firestorm of continual displacement of existing systems has kept the focus of practice on development of new systems, and major enhancements to existing systems. Postfirestorm, the focus of practice in software engineering is as an infrastructure discipline. [1858]

Software ecosystems have been rapidly evolving for many decades, and change is talked about as-if it were a defining characteristic, rather than a phase that ecosystems go through on the path to relative stasis. Change is so common that it has become blasé, the mantra has now become that existing ways of doing things must be disrupted. The real purpose of disruption is redirection of profits, from incumbents to those financing the development of systems intended to cause disruption. The fear of being disrupted by others is an incentive for incumbents to disrupt their own activities; only the paranoid survive [748] is a mantra for those striving to get ahead in a rapidly changing ecosystem.

The first release of a commercial software project implements the clients' view of the world, from an earlier time. In a changing world, unimportant software systems have to adapted, if they are to continue to be used; important software systems force the world to adapt to be in a position to make use of them.

A study by van Angeren, Alves and Jansen investigated company and developer connections in several commercial application ecosystems. Figure 4.1 shows the connections between the 164 companies in the Microsoft Office365 Apps Marketplace (to be included, Apps have to meet platform added-value requirements).

Figure 4.5 illustrates how one company, IBM, dominated the first 30 + years of the computer industry. Figure 4.6 illustrates how, in new markets (mobile phones in this case) the introduction of a new platform can result in new market entrants replacing the existing dominant product ecosystems.

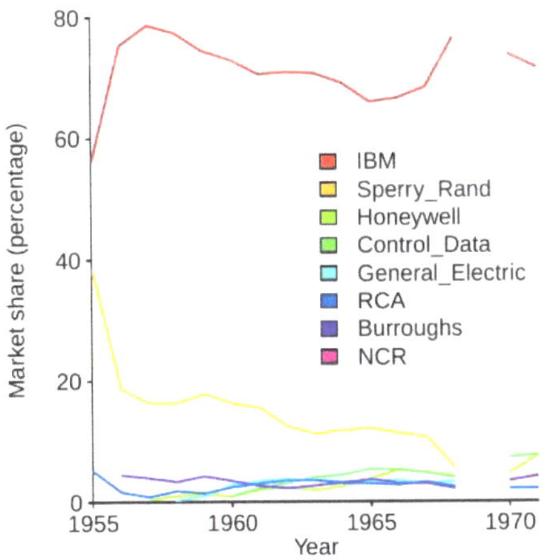

Figure 4.5: Computer installation market share of IBM, and its top seven competitors (known at the time as the seven dwarfs; no data is available for 1969). Data from Brock. Github-Local

Major geopolitical regions have distinct customer ecosystems, providing opportunities for region specific software systems to become established, e.g., Brazillian developer response to the imposition of strong trade barriers.

The analysis of ecosystems can be approached from various perspectives: the populationcommunity view of ecosystems is based on networks of interacting populations, while a process-functional view is based on the processing of resources across functional components. The choice of perspective used for ecosystem analysis may be driven by what data is available, e.g., it may be easier to measure populations than the resources used by a population.

4.1.1 Funding

The continued viability of a software ecosystem is dependent on funding (which may take the form of money or volunteer effort).

In a commercial environment the funding for development work usually comes from the products and services the organization provides. In a few cases investors fund startups with the intent of making a profit from the sale of the company (Martínez [1212] discusses working in a VC funded company).

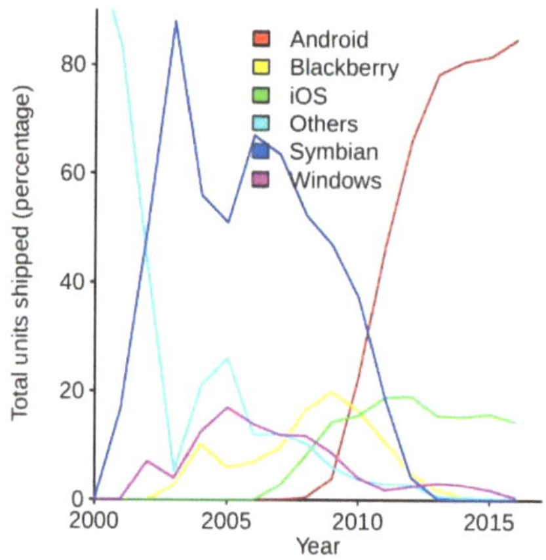

Figure 4.6: Mobile phone operating system shipments, as percentage of total per year. Data from Reimer (before 2007), and Gartner (after 2006). Github-Local

Venture capital is a hits business, with a high failure rate, and most of the profit coming from a few huge successes. Exit strategies (extracting the profit from investments made in a company) used by VCs include: selling startups to a listed company (large companies may buy startups to acquire people with specific skills, [415] to remove potential future competitors, or because the acquired company has the potential to become a profit center; see figure 4.7), and an IPO (i.e., having the company's shares publicly traded on a stock exchange; between 2011 and 2015 the number of software company IPOs was in the teens, and for IT services and consulting companies the number was in single digits [1542]). Venture capitalists are typically paid a 2% management fee on committed capital, and a 20% profit-sharing structure; [1375] the VCs are making money, while those who invested in VCs over the last 20-years would have received greater returns by investing in a basket of stocks in the public exchanges. [1323]

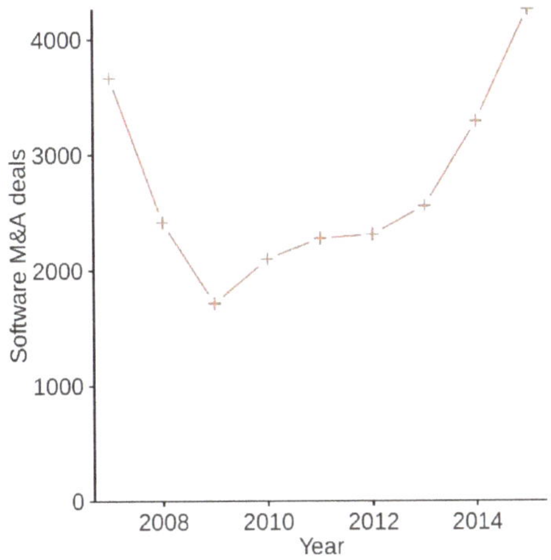

Figure 4.7: Reported number of worldwide software industry mergers and acquisitions (M&A), per year. Data from Solganick. Github-Local

Individuals who invest their own money in the early stage startups are sometimes called Angel investors. One study [1970] found that 30% of Angel investors lost their money, another 20% had a ROI of less than one, while 14% had a ROI greater than five; see Github-economics/SSRN-id1028592.R

Many Open source projects are funded by the private income of the individuals involved.

A study by Overney, Meinicke, Kästner and Vasilescu [1430] investigated donations to Open Source projects. They found 25,885 projects on Github asking for donations, out of 78 million projects (as of 23 May 2019). Paypal was the most popular choice of donation platform, but does not reveal any information about donations received. Both Patreon and OpenCollective do reveal donation amounts, and 58% of the projects using these platforms received donations. Figure 4.8 shows the average monthly dollar amount received by Github projects having a Patreon or OpenCollective donate button in their README.md.

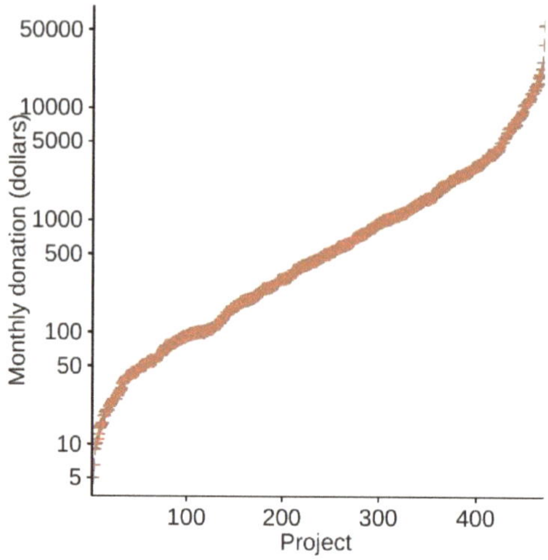

Figure 4.8: Average monthly donations received by 470 Github repositories using Patreon and OpenCollective. Data from Overney et al. Github-Local

Advertising revenue as the primary income stream for software products is a relatively new phenomena, and vendor Ad libraries have been rapidly evolving. [19]

In the last 15 years over 100 non-profit software foundations have been created [904] to provide financial, legal and governance support for major open systems projects.

4.1.2 Hardware

The market for software systems is constrained by the number of customers with access to the necessary computer hardware, with the number of potential customers increasing as

the cost of the necessary computing hardware decreases. The functionality supported by software systems is constrained by the performance and capacity constraints of customer computing platforms; see fig 1.1 and fig 13.14 for illustrations of the cost of operations, and fig 1.2 for the cost of storage.

The general classification of computer systems into mainframes, minicomputers [165] and microcomputers was primarily marketing driven, with each platform class occupying successively lower price points, targeting different kinds of customers (e.g., mainframes for large businesses, [V] minicomputers for technical and engineering companies, and micros for small companies and individuals). Supercomputing [167] (i.e., the fastest computers of the day, often used for scientific and engineering applications) is an example of a significant niche hardware ecosystem that has always existed. Embedded systems (where the computing aspect may be invisible to users) support several major ecosystems, with their own associations, conferences and trade press, but have not attracted as much attention from the software engineering research community as desktop systems. Figure 4.9 and Figure 4.11 show that in terms of microprocessor sales volume, the embedded systems market is significantly larger than what might be called the desktop computer market.

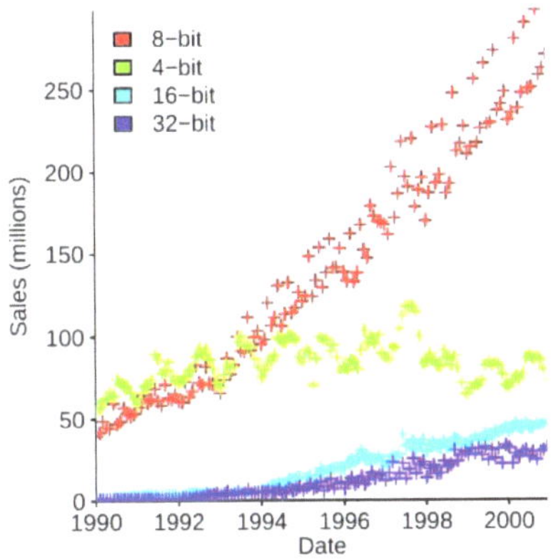

Figure 4.9: Monthly unit sales (in millions) of microprocessors having a given bus width. Data kindly provided by Turley. Github-Local

Figure 4.10 shows performance (in MIPS) against price for 106 computers, from different markets, in 1981. Microprocessors eventually achieved processor performance, and memory capacity, comparable to the more expensive classes of computers, at a lower cost; the lower cost hardware increased sales, which motivated companies to write applications for a wider customer base, which motivated the sale of more computers. [1083]

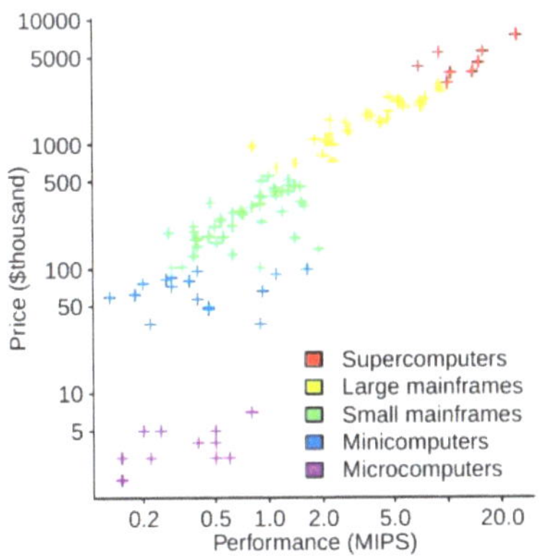

Figure 4.10: Performance, in MIPS, against price of 106 computer systems available in 1981. Data from EinDor. Github-Local

Manufacturers of computing systems once regularly introduce new product ranges containing cpus [151] that were incompatible with their existing product ranges. Even IBM, known for the compatibility of its 360/370 family of computers (first delivered in 1965, the IBM 360[1736] was the first backward compatible computer family: that is successive generations could run software that ran on earlier machines), continued to regularly introduced new systems based on cpus that were incompatible with existing systems.

What was the impact on software engineering ecosystems, of businesses having to regularly provide functionality on new computing platforms? At the individual level, a benefit for developers was an expanding job market, where they were always in demand. At the professional level the ever present threat of change makes codifying a substantial body of working practices a risky investment.

For its x86 family of processors, Intel made backwards compatibility a requirement [vi]. 1315 An apparently insatiable market demand for faster processors, and large sales volume, created the incentive to continually make significant investments in building faster processors; see figure 4.11. The x86 family steadily increased market share, [1771] to eventually become dominant in the non-embedded computing market; one-by-one manufacturers of other processors ceased trading, and their computers have become museum pieces.

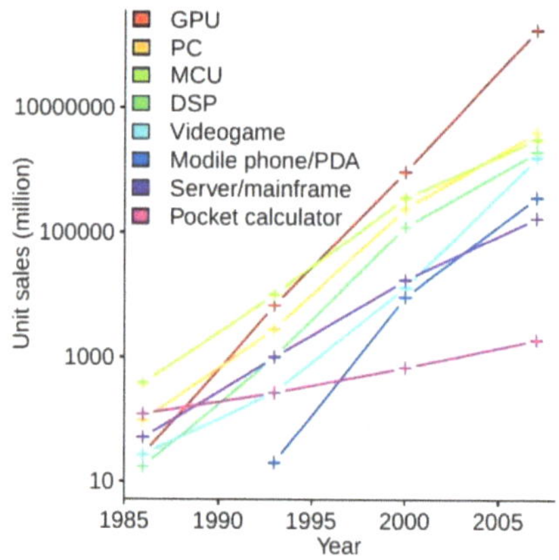

Figure 4.11: Total sales of various kinds of processors. Data from Hilbert et al. Github-Local

The market dominance of IBM hardware and associated software (50 to 70% of this market during 1969-1985; [510] see fig 1.6) is something that developers now learn through reading about the history of computing. However, the antitrust cases against IBM continue to influence how regulators think about how to deal with monopolies in the computer industry, and on how very large companies structure their businesses. [1452]

While the practices and techniques used during one hardware era (e.g., mainframes, minicomputers, microcomputers, the internet) might not carry over into later eras, they leave their mark on software culture, e.g., language standards written to handle more diverse hardware than exists today. [930] Also, each major new platform tends to be initially been populated with developers who are relatively inexperienced, and unfamiliar with what already exists, leading to many reinventions (under different names).

Changes in the relative performance of hardware components impact the characteristics of systems designed for maximum performance, which in turn impacts software design choices, which may take many years to catch up. For instance, the analysis of sorting algorithms once focused on the cost of comparing two items, [1028] but as this cost shrank in comparison to the time taken to load the values being compared, from memory, the analysis switched to focusing on cpu cache size. [1071]

The greater the functional capacity of a computing system, the more power it consumes; see Github-benchmark/brl/brl.R. The energy consumed by computing devices is an important factor in some markets, from laptop and mobile phone battery usage, [129] compute infrastructure within a building [981] to the design of Warehouse-scale systems [138] (there are large energy efficiency gains to be had running software in the Cloud [1215]). The variation in power consumption between supposedly identical components can have a performance impact, i.e., devices reducing their clock rate to keep temperature within limits; see section 13.3.2.1.

The division between hardware and software can be very fuzzy; for instance, the hardware for Intel's Software Guard Extensions (SGX) instructions consists of software micro operations performed by lower level hardware. [409]

4.2 Evolution

Left untouched, software remains unchanged from the day it starts life; use does not cause it to wear out or break. However, the world in which software operates changes, and it is this changing world that reduces the utility of unchanged software. Software systems that have had minimal adaptation, to a substantially changed world, [198] are sometimes known as legacy systems.

The driving forces shaping software ecosystems have been rapidly evolving since digital computing began, e.g., hardware capability, customer demand, vendor dominance and software development fashion.

Competition between semiconductor vendors has resulted in a regular cycle of product updates; this update cycle has been choreographed by a roadmap published by the

Semiconductor Industry Association. [1643] Cheaper/faster semiconductors drives cheaper/faster computers, generating the potential for businesses to update and compete more aggressively (than those selling or using slower computers, supporting less capacity). The hardware update cycle drives a Red Queen [133] treadmill, where businesses have to work to maintain their position, from fear that competitors will entice away their customers.

Figure 4.12 shows how wafer production revenue at the world's largest independent semiconductor foundry (TSMC) has migrated to smaller process technologies over time (upper), and how demand has shifted across major market segments (lower).

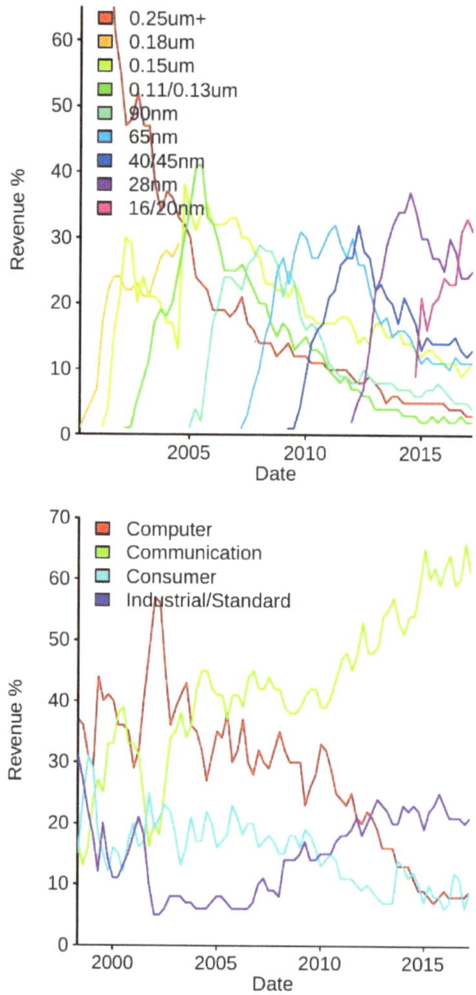

Figure 4.12: TSMC revenue from wafer production, as a percentage of total revenue, at various line widths. Data from TSMC. Github-Local

Companies introduce new products, such as new processors, and over time stop supplying them as they become unprofitable. Compiler vendors respond by adding support for new processors, and later reducing support costs by terminating support for those processors that have ceased to be actively targeted by developers. Figure 4.13 shows the survival curve for processor support in GCC, since 1999, and non-processor specific options.

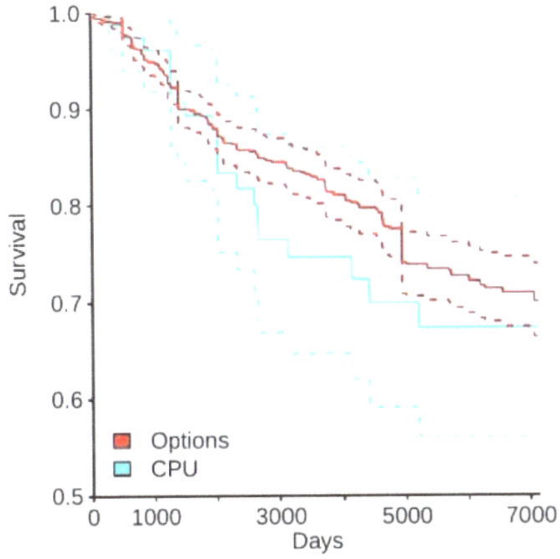

Figure 4.13: Survival curve for GCC's support for distinct cpus and non-processor specific compile-time options; with 95% confidence intervals. Data extracted from gcc website. Github-Local

Software evolves when existing source code is modified, or has new code added to it. Evolution requires people with the capacity to drive the changes, e.g., ability to make the changes, and/or fund others to do the work. Incentives for investing to adapt software, to a changed world, include:

- continuing to make money, from existing customers, through updates of an existing product. Updates may not fill any significant new customer need, but some markets have been trained, over decades of marketing, to believe that the latest version is always better than previous versions,
- needing to be competitive with other products,
- a potential new market opens up, and modifying an existing product is a cost effective way of entering this market, e.g., the creation of a new processor creates an opportunity for a compiler vendor to add support for a new cpu instruction set,
- the cost of adapting existing bespoke software is less than the cost of not changing it, i.e., the job the software did, before the world changed, still has to be done,

- software developers having a desire, and the time, to change existing code (the pleasure obtained from doing something interesting is a significant motivation for some of those involved in the production of software systems).

A product ecosystem sometimes experiences a period of rapid change; exponential improvement in product performance is not computer specific. Figure 4.14 shows the increase in the maximum speed of human vehicles on the surface of the Earth, and in the air, over time.

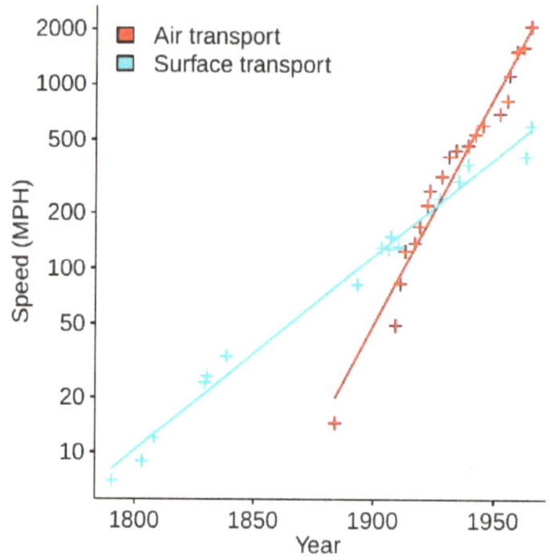

Figure 4.14: Maximum speed achieved by vehicles over the surface of the Earth, and in the air, over time. Data from Lienhard. Github-Local

The evolution of a product may even stop, and restart sometime later. For instance, Microsoft stopped working on their web browser, Internet Explorer, reassigned and laid off the development staff; once this product started to lose significant market share, product development was restarted.

Ecosystem evolution is path dependent. [1765] Things are the way they are today because past decisions caused particular paths to be followed, driven by particular requirements, e.g., the QWERTY keyboard layout was designed to reduce jamming in the early mechanical typewriters, [438] not optimise typist performance (which requires a different layout [361]). The evolutionary paths followed in different locations can be different, e.g., evolution of religious [vii] beliefs. [1982]

Some evolutionary paths eventually reach a dead-end. For instance, NEC's PC-98 series of computers, first launched in 1979, achieved sufficient market share in Japan to compete with IBM compatible PCs, until the late 1990s (despite not being compatible with the effective standard computing platform outside of Japan). [1945]

Rapid semiconductor evolution appears to be coming to an end: an 18 -month cycle for processor performance increases is now part of history. Figure 4.15 shows that while the number of transistors in a device has continued to increase, clock frequency has plateaued (the thermal energy generated by running at a higher frequency cannot be extracted fast enough to prevent devices destroying themselves).

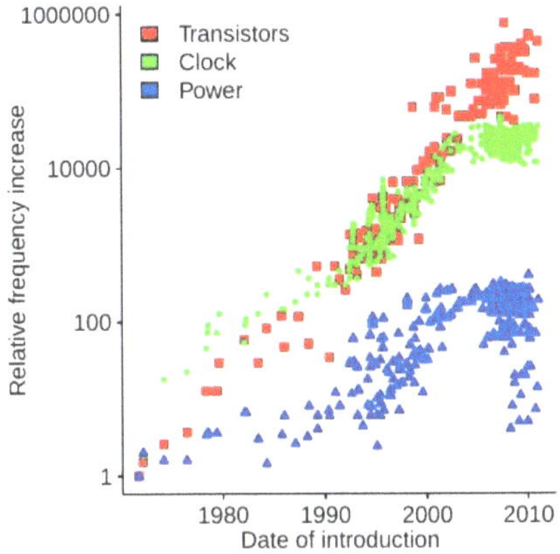

Figure 4.15: Number of transistors, frequency and SPEC performance of cpus when first launched. Data from Danowitz et al. Github-Local

When an ecosystem is evolving, rather than being in a steady state, analysis of measurements made at a particular point in time can produce a misleading picture. For instance, a snapshot of software systems currently being maintained may find that the majority have a maintenance/development cost ratio greater than five; however, the data suffers from survivorship bias, the actual ratio is closer to 0.8 ; see Github-ecosystems/maint-dev-ratio.R and fig 4.47. With many software ecosystems still in their growth phase, the rate of evolution may cause the patterns found in measurement data to change equally quickly.

4.2.1 Diversity

Diversity [viii] is important in biological ecology [327] because members of a habitat feed off each other (directly by eating, or indirectly by extracting nutrients from waste products). Software is not its own self-sustaining food web, its energy comes from the people willing to invest in it, and it nourishes those who choose to use it. The extent to which diversity metrics used in ecology are applicable to software, if at all, is unknown.

Studies [1786] have found that it was possible for organizations to make large savings by reducing software system diversity.

If software diversity is defined as variations on a theme, then what drives these variations and what are the themes?

Themes include: the software included as part of operating system distributions (e.g., a Linux distribution), the functionality supported by applications providing the same basic need (e.g., text editing), the functionality supported by successive releases of an application, by customised versions of the same release of an application, and the source code used to implement an algorithm; see fig 9.14.

A software system is forked when the applicable files are duplicated, and work progresses on this duplicate as a separate project from the original. The intent may be to later merge any changes into the original, to continue development independently of the original, some combination of these, or other possibilities, e.g., a company buying a license to adapt software for its internal use.

The Fork button on the main page of every project on GitHub is intended as a mechanism for developers, who need not be known to those involved in a project, to easily copy a project from which to learn, and perhaps make changes; possibly submitting any changes back to the original project, a process known as fork and pull. As of October 2013, there were 2,090,423 forks of the 2,253,893 non-forked repositories on GitHub. [917]

A study by Robles and González-Barahona, [1594] in 2011, attempted to identify all known significant forks; they identified 220 forked projects, based on a search of Wikipedia articles, followed by manual checking. Figure 4.16 suggests that after an initial spurt, the number of forks has not been growing at the same rate as the growth of open source projects.

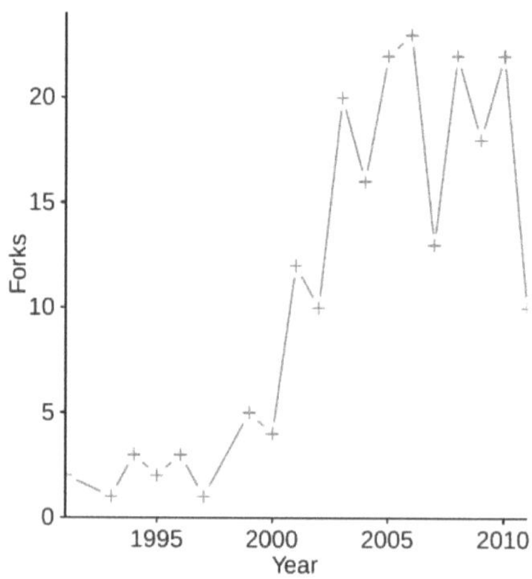

Figure 4.16: Number of major forks of projects per year, identified using Wikipedia during August 2011. Data from Robles et al. Github-Local

Software is created by people, and variations between people will produce variations in the software they write; other sources of variation include funding, customer requirements, and path dependencies present in the local ecosystem.

Reduced diversity is beneficial for some software vendors. The desktop market growth to dominance of Wintel [ix] reduced desktop computing platform diversity (i.e., the alternatives went out of business), which reduced support costs for software vendors, i.e., those still in business did not have to invest in supporting a wide diversity of platforms.

A study by Keil, Bennett, Bourgeois, Garcá-Peña, MacDonald, Meyer, Ramirez and Yguel [984] investigated the packages included in Debian distributions. Figure 4.17 shows a phylogenetic tree of 56 Debian derived distributions, based on the presence/absence of 50,708 packages in each distribution.

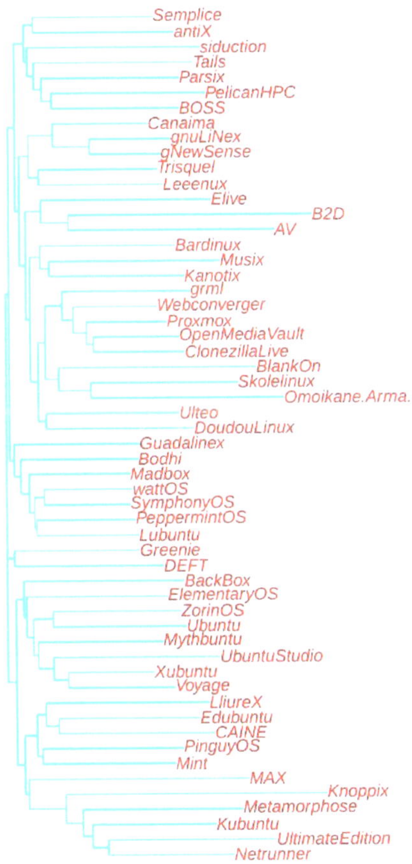

Figure 4.17: Phylogenetic tree of Debian derived distributions, based on which of 50,708 packages are included in each distribution. Data from Keil et al. [984] Github-Local

The BSD family of operating systems arose from forking during the early years of their development, and each fork has evolved as separate but closely related projects since the early-mid 1990s. Figure 9.22 illustrates how a few developers working on multiple BSD forks communicate bug fixes among themselves.

A study by Ray [1561] investigated the extent to which code created in one of NetBSD, OpenBSD or FreeBSD was ported to either of the other two versions, over a period of 18 years. Ported code not only originated in the most recently written code, but was taken from versions released many years earlier. Figure 4.18 shows the contribution made by 14 versions of NetBSD (versions are denoted by stepping through the colors of the rainbow) to 31 versions of OpenBSD; the contribution is measured as percentage of lines contained in all the lines changed in a given version.

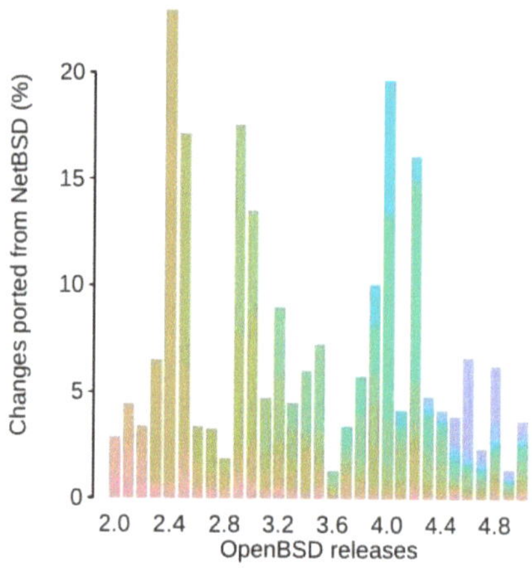

Figure 4.18: Percentage of code ported from NetBSD to various versions of OpenBSD, broken down by version of NetBSD in which it first occurred (denoted by incrementally changing color). Data kindly provided by Ray. Github-Local

Products are sometimes customised for specific market segments. Customization might be used to simplify product support, adapt to hardware resource constraints, and segmentation of markets as a sales tool.

Customization might occur during program start-up, with configuration information being read and used to control access to optional functionality, or at system build time, e.g., optional functionality is selected at compile time, creating a customised program.

Each customized version of a product can experience its own evolutionary pressures, [1450] and customization is a potential source of mistakes.

A study by Rothberg, Dintzner, Ziegler and Lohmann [1609] investigated the number of optional Linux features shared (i.e., supported) by a given number of processor architectures (for versions released between May 2011 and September 2013, during which the number of supported architectures grew from 24 to 30). Table 4.1 shows that the number of features only supported in one, two, three architectures, plus all supported architectures (and all but one, two and three).

Table 4.1: Number of distinct features, in Linux, shared across (i.e., supported) a given number of architectures (header row), for versions 2.6.39 to 3.11; All denotes all supported architectures (All-1 is one less than All, etc), which is 24 in release 2.6.39, growing to 30 by release 3.9. Data from Rothberg et al.

Version	1	2	3	All-3	All-2	All-1	All
2.6.39	3,989	182	50	2,293	944	1,189	2,617
3.0	3,990	183	53	2,345	968	1,211	2,637
3.1	4,026	184	52	2,440	968	1,155	2,667
3.2	4,028	181	57	1	2,788	512	4,054
3.3	4,077	180	51	1	2,837	512	4,133
3.4	4,087	183	51	1	2,907	520	4,184
3.5	4,129	179	50	2	3,001	520	4,265
3.6	4,158	184	51	2	3,098	527	4,298
3.7	4,139	183	50	1	3,173	539	4,384
3.8	4,148	178	35	3	3,269	548	4,399
3.9	4,269	177	36	3	3,403	581	4,413
3.10	4,280	173	35	3	3,447	577	4,460
3.11	4,270	178	33	2	0	0	8,654

The official Linux kernel distribution does not include all variants that exist in shipped products; [803] while manufacturers may make the source code of their changes publicly available, either they do not submit these changes to become part of the mainline distribution, or their submissions are not accepted into the official distribution (it would be a heavy burden for the official Linux kernel distribution to include every modification made by a vendor shipping a modified kernel).

In general the number of optional features increases as the size of a program increases; see fig 7.36.

When a new version of a software system becomes available, there may be little, or no incentive for users to upgrade. As part of customer support, vendors may continue to provide support for previous versions, for some period after the release of a new version.

Widely used software systems may support their own ecosystem of third-party add-ons. For instance, Wordpress is written in PHP, and third-party add-ons are executed by the version of PHP installed on the server running Wordpress. The authors of these add-ons have to take into account the likely diversity in both the version of Wordpress and version of PHP used on any website.

A study by Ruohonen and Leppänen [1620] investigated the version of PHP available on more than 200 K websites (using data from the httparchive [866]). Figure 4.19 shows the number of websites running a given version of PHP on the first day of February 2016 and February 2017; the x-axis is ordered by version number of the release (there is some intermingling of dates).

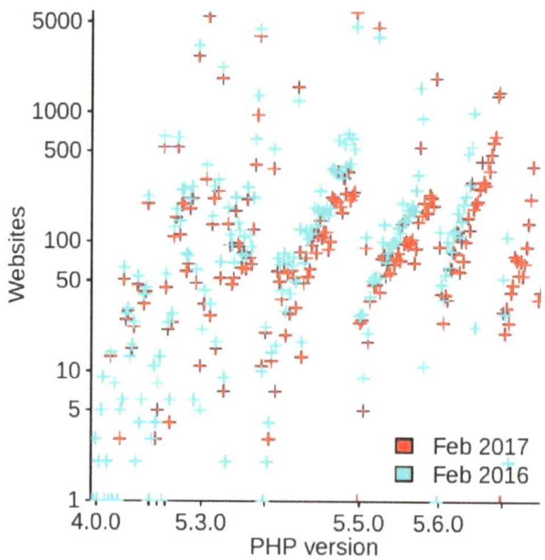

Figure 4.19: Number of websites running a given version of PHP on the first day of February, 2016 and 2017, ordered by PHP version number. Data kindly provided by Ruohonen. Github-Local

Hardware diversity (i.e., computer manufacturers offering a variety incompatible cpus and proprietary operating systems; with vendors seeking to create product moats) was once a major driver of software diversity; hardware issues are discussed in section 4.1.2.

4.2.2 Lifespan

The expected lifespan of a software system is of interest to those looking to invest in its creation or ongoing development. The investment may be vendor related (e.g., designing with an eye to future product sales) or customer related, e.g., integrating use of the software into business workflow. The analysis of data where the variable of interest is measured in terms of time-to-event is known as survival analysis; section 11.11 discusses the analysis of time-to-event data.

Governments may publicly express a preference for longer product lifetimes, [1308] because they are answerable to voters (the customers of products), not companies answerable to shareholders. In theory, a software system can only said to be dead when one or more of the files needed to run it ceases to exist. In practice, the lifespan of interest to those involved is the expected period of their involvement with the software system.

Factors affecting product lifetime include:

- in a volatile ecosystem there may be little or no incentive to maintain and support existing products. It may be more profitable to create new products without concern for compatibility with existing products,
- a product may not have sold well enough to make further investment worthwhile, or the market itself may shrink to the point where it is not economically viable to continue operating in it,
- while software does not wear out, it is intertwined with components of an ecosystem, and changes to third-party components that are depended upon can cause programs to malfunction, or even fail to execute. Changes in the outside world can cause unchanged software to stop working as intended,
- software depends on hardware for its interface to the world. Hardware wears out and breaks, which creates a post-sales revenue stream for vendors, from replacement sales. Manufacturing hardware requires an infrastructure, and specific components will have their own manufacturing requirements. The expected profit from future sales of a device may not make it worthwhile continuing to manufacture it, e.g., the sales volume of hard disks is decreasing, as NAND memory capacity performance, and cost per-bit improves, [623]

- users may decide not to upgrade because the software they are currently using is good enough. In some cases software lifespan may exceed the interval implied by the vendors official end-of-life support date.

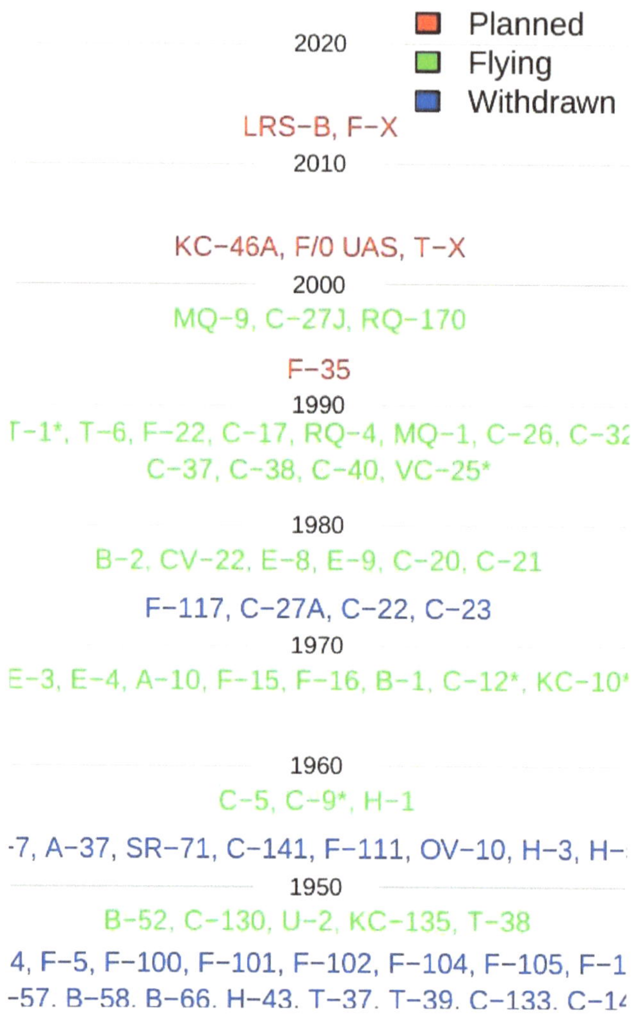

Figure 4.20: Decade in which newly designed US Air Force aircraft first flew, with colors indicating current operational status. Data from Echbeth el at. Github-Local

The rate of product improvements can slow down for reasons that include: technology maturity, or a single vendor dominating the market (i.e., enjoys monopoly-like power). Figure 4.20 illustrates how the working life of jet-engined aircraft (invented in the same decade as computers) has increased over time. Figure 4.21 shows the mean age of installed mainframes at a time when the market was dominated by a single vendor (IBM), who decided product pricing and lifespan; the vendor could influence product lifespan to maximise their revenue.

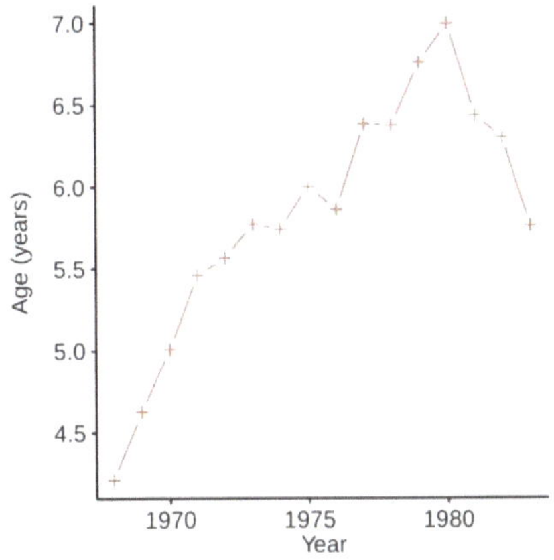

Figure 4.21: Mean age of installed mainframe computers, 1968-1983. Data from Greenstein. Github-Local

Organizations and individuals create and support their own Linux distribution, often derived from one of the major distributions, e.g., Ubuntu was originally derived from Debian. Lundqvist and Rodic [1171] recorded the life and death of these distributions. Figure 4.22 shows the survival curve, stratified by the parent distribution.

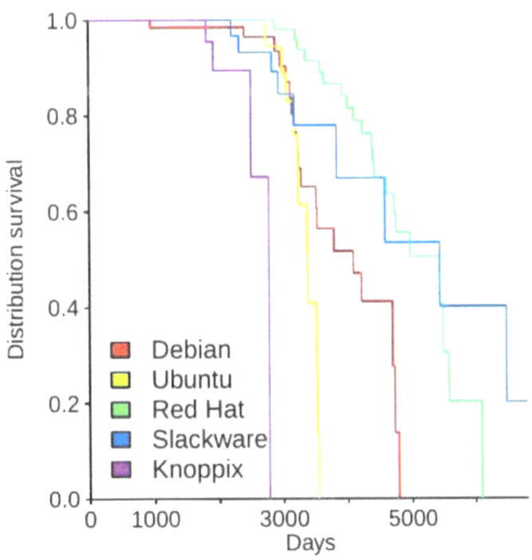

Figure 4.22: Survival curve of Linux distributions derived from five widely-used parent distributions (identified in legend). Data from Lundqvist et al. [1171] Github-Local

The market share of the latest version of a software system typically grows to a peak, before declining as newer versions are released. Villard tracked the Android version usage over time. Figure 4.23 shows the percentage share of the Android market held by various releases, based on days since launch of each release.

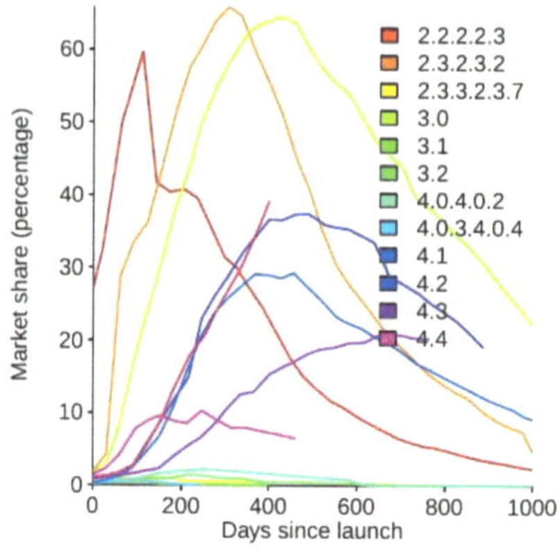

Figure 4.23: Percentage share of Android market, of a given release, by days since its launch. Data from Villard. Github-Local

A study by Tamai and Torimitsu [1811] investigated the lifespan of 95 software systems (which appear to be mostly in-house systems). Figure 4.24 shows (in red) the number of systems terminated after a given number of days, along with a fitted regression model of the form: systems $= ae^{b\times \text{years}}$ (with $b = -0.14$ for the mainframe software and $b = -0.24$ for Google's SaaS).

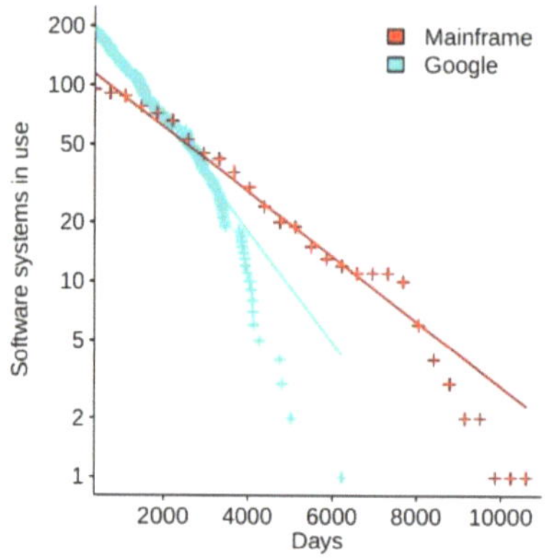

Figure 4.24: Number of software systems surviving for a given number of days and fitted regression models: Japanese mainframe software (red), Google software-as-a-service (blue; 202 systems as of October 2020). Data from: mainframe Tamai, [1811] Google's SaaS Ogden. Github-Local

A website setup and maintained by Ogden [1405] records Google applications, services and hardware that have been terminated. Figure 4.24 shows (in blue/green) the number that have been terminated after a given number of days, along with a fitted regression model.

System half-life for the 1991 Japanese corporate mainframe data is almost 5-years; for the Google SaaS it is almost 2.9-years. Does the Japanese data represent a conservative upper bound, and the Google data a lower bound for a relatively new, large company finding out which of its acquired and in-house developed products are worth continuing to support?

Products with a short lifespan are not unique to software system. Between 1927 and 1960 at least 62 aircraft types were built and certified for commercial passenger transport [1481] (i.e., with seating capacity of at least four), and failed to be adopted by commercial airlines.

Communities of people have a lifespan. When the energy for the community comes directly from commercially activity, the community will continue to exist for as long as there are people willing to work for the money available, or they are not out competed by another community. [1406] When the energy comes directly from those active in the community, community existence is dependent on the continuing motivation and beliefs of its members. [838]

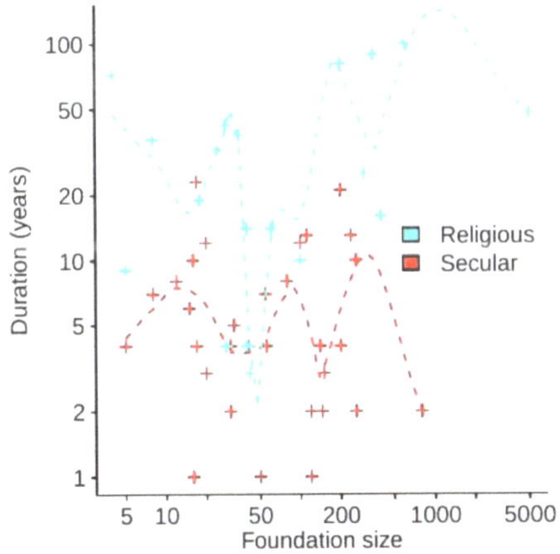

Figure 4.25: Size at foundation and lifetime of 32 secular and 19 religious 19th century American utopian communities; lines are fitted loess regression. Data from Dunbar et al. Github-Local

A study by Dunbar and Sosis [514] investigated human community sizes and lifetime. Figure 4.25 shows the number of founding members of 53, 19th century secular and religious utopian communities, along with the number of years they continued to exist, with loess regression lines.

4.2.3 Entering a market

Markets for particular classes of products (e.g., electric shavers, jet engines and video cassette recorders) and services evolve, with firms entering and existing. [774] Manufacturing markets have been found to broadly go through five stages, from birth to maturity. [12]

The invention of the Personal Computer triggered the creation of new markets, including people starting manufacturing companies to seek their fortune selling lower cost computers. Figure 4.26 shows how the growth and consolidation of PC manufacturers followed a similar trend to the companies started to manufacture automobiles, i.e., hundreds of companies started, but only a few survived.

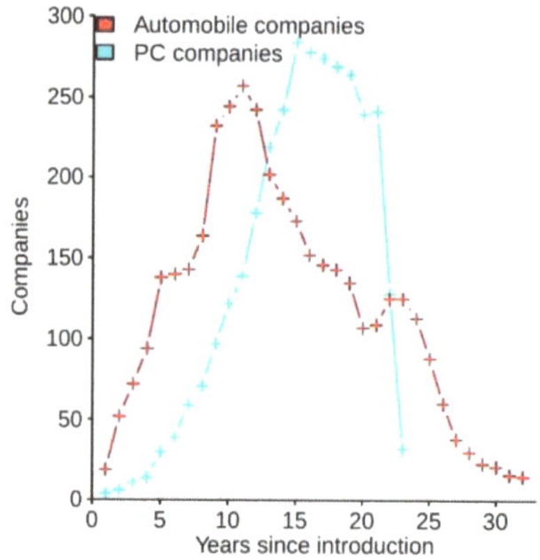

Figure 4.26: Number of US companies manufacturing automobiles and PCs, over the first 30-years of each industry. Data extracted from Mazzucato. Github-Local

Vendors want to control customer evolution, to the extent it involves product purchasing decisions. Evolution might be controlled by erecting barriers (the term moat is sometimes used) to either make it unprofitably for other companies to enter the market, or to increase the cost for customers seeking to switch suppliers.

- economies of scale (a supply side effect, a traditional barrier employed by hardware manufacturers): producing in large volumes allows firms to spread their fixed costs over more units, improving efficiency (requires that production be scalable in a way that allows existing facilities to produce more). Competing against a firm producing in volume requires a large capital investment to enter the market, otherwise the new entrant is at a cost disadvantage.

With effectively zero replication costs, once created software systems do not require a large capital investment. A large percentage of the cost of software production is spent on people, who provide few opportunities for economies of scale (there may even be diseconomies of scale, e.g., communication overhead increases with head count),

- network effects [80] (a demand-side effect): are created when customers' willingness to buy from a supplier increases with the number of existing customers. A company entering a market that experiences large network effects, where they are competing against an established firm, has to make a large capital investment to offer incentives, so that a significant percentage of customers switch suppliers. Companies selling products that rely on network effects employ developer evangelists, [979] whose job includes creating a positive buzz around use of the product and providing feedback from third-party developers to in-house developers,
- switching costs: 577 a switching cost is an investment specific to the current supplier that must be duplicated to change to a new supplier, e.g., retraining staff and changes to procedures. The UK government paid £37.6 million transition costs to the winning bidder of the ASPIRE contract, with £5.7 million paid to the previous contract holder to facilitate changeover. [1534] Information asymmetry can create switching costs by deterring competition. To encourage competition in bidding on the replacement ASPIRE contract (the incumbent had inside knowledge and was perceived to be strong) the UK government contributed £8.6 million towards bidders' costs. [1534]

Figure 4.27 shows the retail price of Model T Fords and the number sold, during the first nine years of the product.

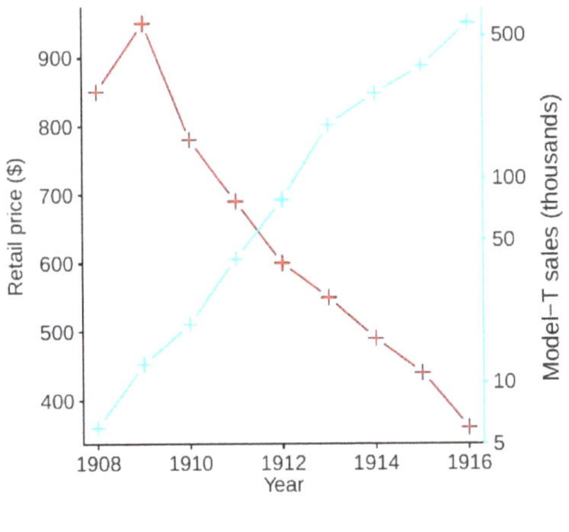

Figure 4.27: Retail prices of Model T Fords and sales volume. Data from Hounshell. Github-Local

A vendor with a profitable customer base, protected by products with high switching costs, is incentivised to prioritise the requirements of customers inside their walled garden. Income from existing customers sometimes causes vendors to ignore new developments that eventually lead to major market shifts, [578] that leave the vendor supporting a marooned customer based.

The competitive forces faced by companies include: [1509] rivalry between existing competitors, bargaining power of suppliers, bargaining power of buyers, possibility of new entrants, and possibility product being substituted by alternative products or services.

4.3 Population dynamics

Population dynamics [1239,1390] is a fundamental component of ecosystems. When the connections between members of an ecosystem are driven by some non-random processes, surprising properties can emerge, e.g., the friends paradox, where your friends have more friends, on average, than you do, [587] and the majority illusion, where views about a complete network are inferred from the views of local connections. [1116] In general, if there is a positive correlation, for some characteristic, between connected nodes in a network, a node's characteristic will be less than the average of the characteristic for the nodes connected to it. [549]

The choices made by individual members of an ecosystem can have a significant impact on population dynamics, which in turn can influence subsequent individual choices. Two techniques used to model population dynamics are: mathematics and simulation (covered in section 12.5).

The mathematical approach is often based on the use of differential equations: the behavior of the important variables are specified in one or more equations, which may be solved analytically or numerically.

One example is the evolution of the population of two distinct entities within a selfcontained ecosystem. If, say, entities A and B have fitness a and b respectively, both have growth rate c, and an average fitness of ϕ, then the differential equations describing the evolution of their population size, x and y, over time are given by: [1390]

$$\dot{x} = ax^c - \phi x$$
$$\dot{y} = by^c - \phi y$$

Solving these equations shows that, when $c < 1$, both A and B can coexist, when $c = 1$, the entity with the higher fitness can invade and dominate an ecosystem (i.e., lower fitness eventually dies out), but when $c > 1$, an entity with high fitness cannot successfully invade an occupied ecosystem, i.e., greater fitness is not enough to displace an incumbent.

The mathematics approach has the advantage that, if the equations can be solved, the behavior of a system can be read from the equations that describe it (while simulations provide a collection of answers to specific initial conditions). The big disadvantage of the mathematical approach is that it may not be possible to solve the equations describing a real world problem.

The advantage of simulations is that they can handle most real world problems. The disadvantages of simulations include: difficulty of exploring the sensitivity of the results to changes in model parameters, difficulty of communicating the results to others, and computational cost; for instance, if 10^4 combinations of different model parameter values are needed to cover the possible behaviors in sufficient detail, with 10^3 simulations for each combination (needed to reliably estimate the mean outcome), then 10^7 simulation runs are needed, which at 1 second each is 116 cpu days.

When a product ecosystem experiences network effects, it is in vendors' interest to create what is known as a virtuous circle; encouraging third-party developers to sell their products within the ecosystem attracts more customers, which in turn attracts more developers, and so on.

Given two new technologies, say A and B , competing for customers in an existing market, what are the conditions under which one technology comes to dominate the market [79] ?

Assume that at some random time, a customer has to make a decision to replace their existing technology, and there are two kinds of customer: R -agents perceive a greater benefit in using technology A (i.e., $a_R > b_R$), and S -agents perceive a greater benefit in using technology B (i.e., $a_S < b_S$); both technologies are subject to network effects, i.e., having other people using the same technology provides a benefit to everybody else using it.

Figure 4.28 illustrates the impact of the difference in customer adoption of two products (y -axis), with time along the x -axis; red-line is an example difference in the number of customers using products A and B . Between the blue/green lines, R and S -agents perceive a difference in product benefits; once the difference in the number of customers of each product crosses some threshold, both agents perceive the same product to have the greater benefit.

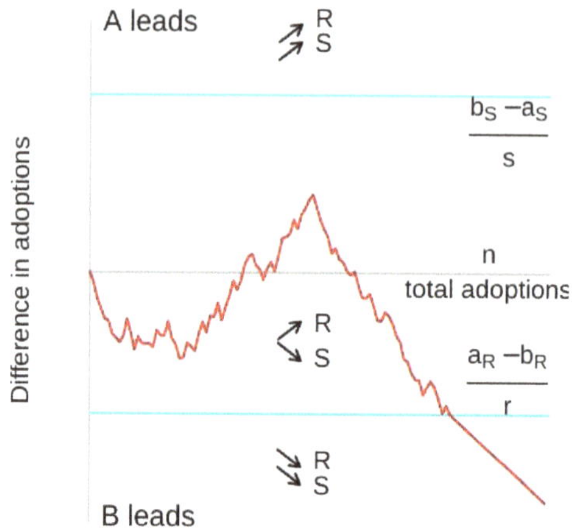

Figure 4.28: Example showing difference in number of customers using two products. Github-Local

Table 4.2 shows the total benefit available to each kind of customer, from adopting one of the technologies; n_A and n_B are the number of users of A and B at the time a customer makes a decision, r and s are the benefits acrued to the respective agents from existing users (there are increasing returns when: $r > 0$ and $s > 0$, decreasing returns when: $r < 0$ and $s < 0$, and no existing user effect when: $r = 0$ and $s = 0$).

Table 4.2: Returns from choosing A or B, given previous technology adoptions by others. From Arthur.

	Technology	Technology
A	B	
R-agent	$a_R + rn_A$	$b_R + rn_B$
S-agent	$a_S + sn_A$	$b_S + sn_B$

For increasing returns, lock-in of technology A occurs [80] (i.e., it provides the greater benefit for all future customers) when: $n_A(t) - n_B(t) > \frac{b_S - a_S}{s}$, where: $n_A(t)$ and $n_B(t)$ are the time dependent values of n.

The condition for lock-in of technology B is: $n_B(t) - n_A(t) > \frac{a_R - b_R}{r}$

Starting from a market with both technologies having the same number of customers, the probability that technology A eventually dominates is:

$$\frac{s(a_R - b_R)}{s(a_R - b_R) + r(b_S - a_S)}$$

and technology B dominates with probability:

$$\frac{r(b_S - a_S)}{s(a_R - b_R) + r(b_S - a_S)}$$

With decreasing returns, both technologies can coexist.

Governments have passed laws intended to ensure that the competitive process works as intended within commercially important ecosystems (in the US this is known as antitrust law, while elsewhere the term competition law is often used). In the US antitrust legal thinking [993] in the 1960s had a market structure-based understanding of competition, i.e., courts blocked company mergers that they thought would lead to anticompetitive market structures. This shifted in the 1980s, with competition assessment based on the short-term interests of consumers (i.e., low consumer prices), not based on producers, or the health of the market as a whole.

The legal decisions and rules around ensuring that the competitive process operates in the commercial market for information are new and evolving. [1452]

In the UK and US it is not illegal for a company to have monopoly power within a market. It is abuse of a dominant market position that gets the attention of authorities; governments sometimes ask the courts to block a merger because they believe it would significantly reduce competition. [1661]

4.3.1 Growth processes

Population dynamics are sometimes modeled using a one-step at a time growth algorithm; one common example is preferential attachment, which is discussed in section 8.3.1.

The percentage of subpopulations present in a population can be path dependent. Consider the population of an urn containing one red and one black ball. The growth process iterates the following sequence (known as the Polya urn process): a ball is randomly drawn from the urn, this ball, along with another ball of the same color is placed back in the urn. After a many iterations, what is the percentage of red and black balls in the urn?

Polya proved that the percentage of red and black balls always converges to some, uniformly distributed, random value. Each converged value is the outcome of the particular sequence of (random) draws that occurred early in the iteration process; any converged percentage between zero and 100 can occur. Convergence also occurs when the process starts with an urn containing more than two balls, with each ball having a different color; see Github-ecosystems/Polya-urn.R.

The Polya urn process has been extended to include a variety of starting conditions (e.g., an urn containing multiple balls of the same color), and replacement rules, e.g., adding multiple balls of the same color, or balls having the other color. General techniques for calculating exact solutions to problems involving balls of two colors are available. [608]

The spread of software use may involve competition between vendors offering compatible systems (e.g., documents and spreadsheets created using Microsoft Office or OpenOffice [1607]), a system competing with an earlier version of itself (the Bass model is discussed in section 3.6.3), or the diffusion of software systems into new markets. [404]

Over time various techniques have been developed to make it more difficult for viruses to hijack programs; it takes time for effective techniques to be discovered, implemented and then used by developers. Figure 4.29 shows the growth in the number of programs in the Ubuntu AMD64 distribution that are hardened with a given security technique (Total ELF is the total number of programs).

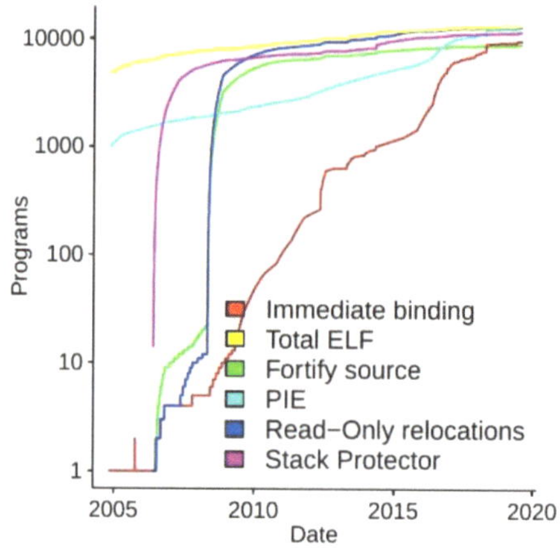

Figure 4.29: Number of programs in the Ubuntu AMD64 distribution shipped using a given security hardening technique (Total ELF is the number of ELF executables). Data from Cook. Github-Local

Software change is driven by a mixture of business and technical factors. A study by Branco, Xiong, Czarnecki, Küster and Völzer [243] analysed over 1,000 change requests in 70 business process models of the Bank of Northeast of Brazil. Figure 4.30 shows the distribution of the 388 maintenance requests made during the first three years of the Customer Registration project. Over longer time-scales the rate of evolution of some systems exhibits a cyclic pattern. [2011]

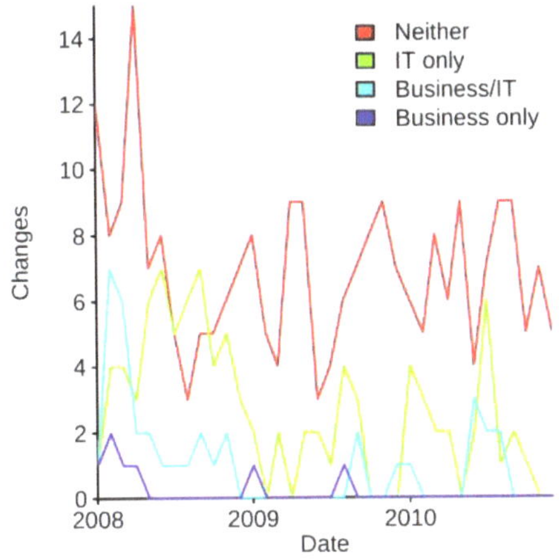

Figure 4.30: Number of process model change requests made in three years of a banking Customer registration project. Data kindly provided by Branco. Github-Local

Some very large systems grow through the integration of independently developed projects.

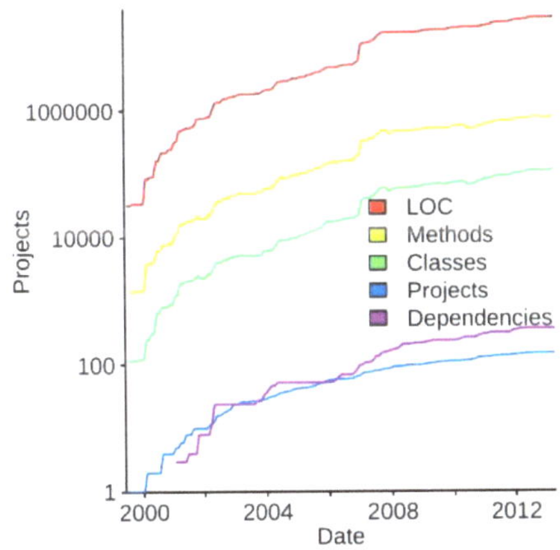

Figure 4.31: Growth in the number of projects within the Apache ecosystem, along with the amount of contained code. Data from Bavota et al. [152] Github-Local

A study by Bavota, Canfora, Di Penta, Oliveto and Panichella [152] investigated the growth of projects in the Apache ecosystem. Figure 4.31 shows the growth in the number of projects, and coding constructs they contain. The number of dependencies between projects increases as the number of projects increases, along with the number of methods and/or classes; see Github-ecosystems/icsm2013_apache.R.

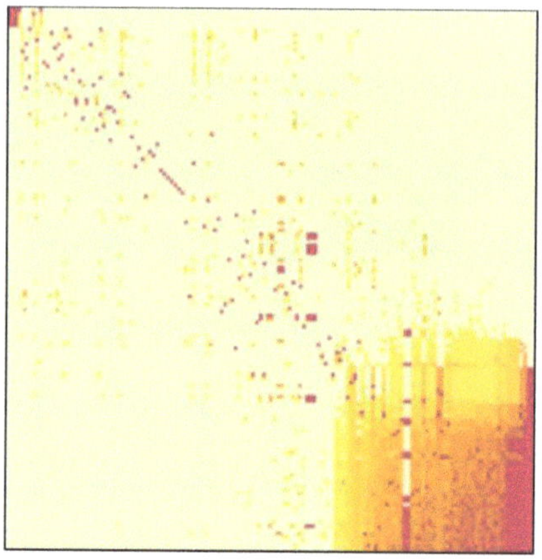

Figure 4.32: Percentage overlap of developers contributing, during 2013, to both of each pair of 147 Apache projects. Data kindly provided by Panichella. Github-Local

A later study by the same group [153] analyzed the 147 Java projects in the Apache ecosystem. Figure 4.32 shows, for each pair of projects, the percentage overlap of developers contributing to both projects (during 2013; white 0%, red 100%); the rows/columns have been reordered to show project pair clusters sharing a higher percentage of developers; see section 12.4.1.

4.3.2 Estimating population size

It may be impossible, or too costly, to observe all members of a population. Depending on the characteristics of the members of the population, it may be possible to estimate the number of members based on a sample; population estimates might also be derived from a theoretical analysis of the interaction between members. [1112]

In some cases it is possible to repurpose existing data. For instance, the U.S. Bureau of Labor Statistics (BLS) publishes national census information, [280] which includes information on citizens' primary occupation. The census occupation codes starting with 100 , 101, 102, 104, and 106 have job titles that suggest a direct involvement in software development, with other codes suggesting some involvement. This information provides one means of estimating the number of software developers in the U.S. (one analysis [1493] of the 2016 data estimated between 3.4 million and 4.2 million).

When sampling from a population whose members have been categorized in some way (e.g., by species), two common kinds of sampling data are: abundance data which contains the number of individuals within each species in the sample, and incidence data giving a yes/no for the presence/absence of each species in the sample.

It is not possible to use incidence data to distinguish between different exponential order growth models, [1283] e.g., models based on a nonhomogeneous Poisson process. Modeling using incidence data requires samples from multiple sites, e.g., faults experienced within different companies, who use the software, tagged with location-id for each fault experience.

4.3.2.1 Closed populations

In a closed population no members are added or removed, and the characteristics of the input distribution remain unchanged.

One technique for estimating (say) the number of fish in a lake, is to capture fish for a fixed amount of time, count and tag them, before returning the fish to the lake. After allowing the captured fish to disperse (but not so long that many fish are likely to have died or new fish born), the process is repeated, this time counting the number of tagged fish, and those captured for the first time, i.e., untagged.

The Chapman estimator is an unbiased, and more accurate estimate, [1626] than the simpler formula usually derived, i.e., $N = \frac{C_1 C_2}{C_{12}}$. Assuming that all fish have the same probability of being caught, and the probability of catching a fish is independent of catching any other fish:

$$N = \frac{(C_1+1)(C_2+1)}{C_{12}+1} - 1,$$

where: N is the number of fish in the lake, C_1 the number of fish caught on the first attempt, C_2 the number caught on the second attempt, and C_{12} the number caught on both attempts.

Using the Chapman estimator to estimate (say) the number of issues not found during a code review assumes that those involved are equally skilled, invest the same amount of effort in the review process, and all issues are equally likely to be found. When reviewers have varying skills, invest varying amounts of effort, or the likelihood of detecting issues varies, the analysis is much more complicated. The Rcapture package supports the analysis of capture-recapture measurements where capture probability varies across items of interest, and those doing the capturing; also see the VGAM package.

The Chaol estimator [326] gives a lower bound on the number of members in a population, based on a count of each member captured; it assumes that each member of the population has its own probability of capture, that this probability is constant over all captures, and the population is sampled with replacement:

$$S_{\text{est}} \geq S_{\text{obs}} + \frac{n-1}{n}\frac{f_1^2}{2f_2}$$

where: S_{est} is the estimated number of unique members, S_{obs} the observed number of unique members, n the number of members in the sample, f_1 the number of items captured once, and f_2 the number of members captured twice.

If a population, containing N members, is sampled without replacement, the unseen member estimate added to S_{obs} becomes: $\frac{f_1^2}{\frac{n}{n-1}2f_2+\frac{q}{1-q}f_1}$, [330] where: $q = \frac{n}{N}$.

Taking into account members occurring three and four times gives an improved lower bound. [355]

The ChaoSpecies function in the SpadeR package calculates species richness using a variety of models. The SpadeR and iNEXT packages contain functions for estimating and plotting species abundance data.

The number of additional members, m_g, that need to be sampled to be likely to encounter a given fraction, g, of all expected unique members in the population is: [328]

$$m_g \approx \frac{nf_1}{2f_2}\log\left[\frac{f_0}{(1-g)S_{\text{est}}}\right]$$

where: n is the number of members in the current sample and $f_0 = \frac{f_1^2}{2f_2}$. For $g = 1$, the following relationship needs to be solved for m : $2f_1\left(1+\frac{m}{n}\right) < e^{\frac{m}{n}\frac{2f_2}{f_1}}$

If m additional members are sampled, the expected number of unique members encountered is, [1687] assuming $m < n$ (when $n \leq m \leq n\log n$, more complicated analytic estimates are available [1422]):

$$S(n+m) = S_{\text{obs}} + f_0\left[1-\left(1-\frac{f_1}{nf_0+f_1}\right)^m\right]$$

If m is much less than n, this equation approximates to: $S(n+m) \approx S_{obs} + m\frac{f_1}{n}$.

The formula to calculate the number of unique members shared by two populations is based on the same ideas, and is somewhat involved. [1442]

When capture probabilities vary by time and individual item, the analysis is more difficult. [329]

Section 6.3.3 discusses the estimation of previously unseen fault experiences in a closed population.

4.3.2.2 Open populations

Evolving ecosystems contain open populations; in an open population existing members leave and new ones join, e.g., companies are started or enter a new market, and companies are acquired or go bankrupt. Estimates of the size of an open population that fail to take into account the impact of the time varying membership will not produce reliable results.

Most open population capture-recapture models are derived from the Cormack-JollySeber (CJS) and Jolly-Seber (JS) models. CJS models estimate survival rate based on using an initial population of captured individuals and modeling subsequent recapture probabilities; CJS models do not estimate abundance. JS models estimate abundance and recruitment (new individuals entering the population). The openCR and Rcapture packages support the analysis of measurements of open populations.

Section 6.3.4 discusses the estimation of previously unseen fault experiences in an open population.

4.4 Organizations

Organizations contain ecosystems of people who pay for, use and create software systems.

4.4.1 Customers

Given that customers supply the energy that drives software ecosystems, the customers supplying the greatest amount of energy are likely to have the greatest influence on software engineering culture and practices (if somewhat indirectly). Culture is built up over time, and is path dependent, i.e., practices established in response to events early in the history of a software ecosystem may continue to be followed long after they have ceased to provide any benefits.

The military were the first customers for computers, and financed the production of oneoff systems. [609] The first commercial computer, the Univac I, was introduced in 1951, and 46 were sold; the IBM 1401, [654] introduced in 1960, was the first computer to exceed one thousand installations, with an estimate 8,300 systems in use by July 1965.[1182] During the 1950s and 1960s the rapid rate of introduction of new computers created uncertainty, with many customers initially preferring to rent/lease equipment (management feared equipment obsolescence in a rapidly changing market, [1098] and had little desire to be responsible for maintenance [1064]), and vendors nearly always preferring to rent/lease rather than sell (a license agreement can restrict customers' ability to connect cheaper peripherals to equipment they do not own [482]). Figure 4.33 shows the shift from rental to purchase of computers by the US Federal Government.

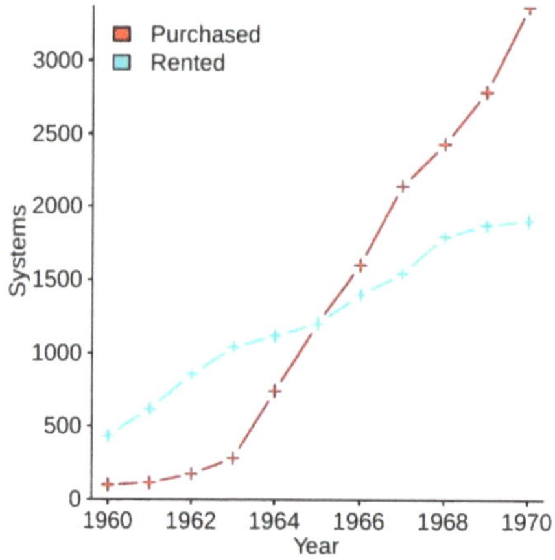

Figure 4.33: Total computer systems purchased and rented by the US Federal Government in the respective fiscal years ending June 30. Data from US Government General Accounting Office. [389] Github-Local

The U.S. Government was the largest customer for computing equipment during the 1950s and 1960s, and enacted laws to require vendors to supply equipment that conformed to various specified standards, e.g., the Brooks Act [1840] in 1965. The intent of these standards was to reduce costs, to the government, by limiting vendors ability to make use of proprietary interfaces that restricted competition.

The customers for these very expensive early computers operated within industries where large scale numeric calculations were the norm (e.g., banks, life insurance companies, [1992] and government departments [368]), and specific applications such as payroll in organizations employing thousands of people, each requiring a unique weekly or monthly payroll calculation. [736] Scientific and engineering calculations were a less profitable business.

Large organizations had problems that were large enough to warrant the high cost of buying and operating a computer. [1680] A computer services industry [1994] quickly sprang up (in the US during 1957, 32 of the 71 systems offered were from IBM [1181]), providing access to computers in central locations (often accessed via dial-in phone lines), with processing time rented by the hour. [87] Computing as a utility service for general use, like electricity, looked likely to become a viable business model. [1671] Figure 4.34 shows, for the US, service business revenue in comparison to revenue from system sales.

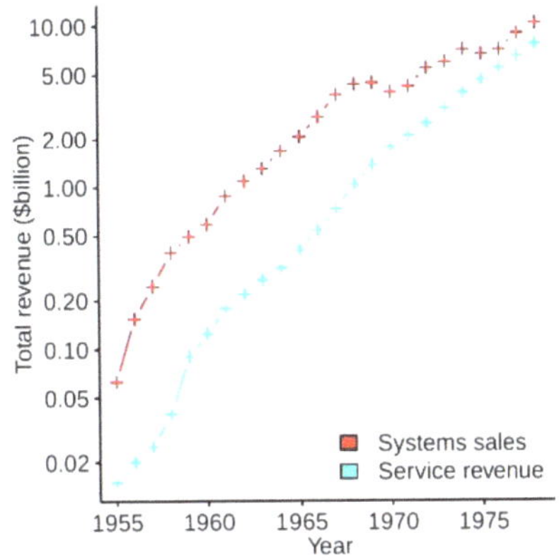

Figure 4.34: Total U.S. revenue from sale of computer systems and data processing service industry revenue. Data from Phister table II.1.20 and II.1.26. Github-Local

The introduction of microcomputers decimated the computer services business; [297] the cost of buying a microcomputer could be less than the monthly rental paid to a service bureau.

How much do customer ecosystems spend on software?

Figure 4.35 shows the total yearly amount spent by the UK's 21 industry sectors on their own software (which was reported by companies as fixed-assets; note: money may have been spent on software development, which for accounting purposed was not treated as a fixed-asset).

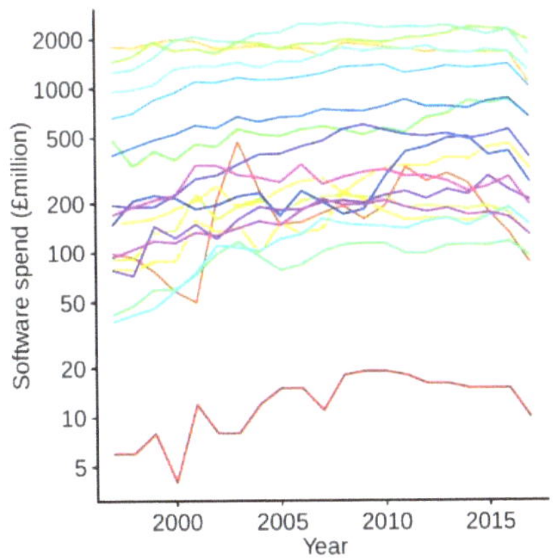

Figure 4.35: Total yearly spend on their own software by the 21 industry sectors in the UK, reported by companies as fixed-assets. Data from UK Office for National Statistics. [1356] Github-Local

Customer influence over the trade-offs associated with software development ranges from total (at least in theory, when the software is being funded by a single customer [x]), to almost none (when the finished product is to be sold in volume to many customers). One trade-off is the reliability of software vs. its development cost; this issue is discussed in chapter 6. If the customer is operating in a rapidly changing environment, being first to market may have top priority. In a global market, variation in customer demand between countries [1144] has to be addressed.

Companies sometimes work together to create a product or service related ecosystem that services their needs. Competing to best address customer need results in product evolution; new requirements are created, existing requirements are modified or may become unnecessary.

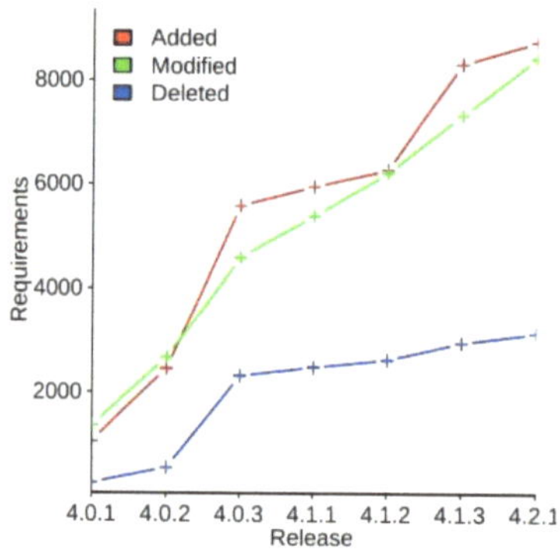

Figure 4.36: Cumulative number of software requirements added, modified and deleted, over successive releases, to the $11,000+$ requirements present in release 4.0.0. Data kindly provided by Motta. Github-Local

A group of automotive businesses created AUTOSAR (Automotive Open System Architecture) with the aim of standardizing communication between the ECUs (Electronic Control Unit) supplied by different companies. A study by Motta [1318] investigated the evolution of the roughly 21,000 AUTOSAR requirements, over seven releases of the specification between 2009 and 2015. Figure 4.36 shows the cumulative addition, modification and deletion of software requirements during this period.

4.4.2 Culture

Cultures occur at multiple organizational levels. Countries and regions have cultures, communities and families have cultures, companies and departments have cultures, application domains and products have cultures, software development and programming languages have cultures. Cultural differences are a source of confusion and misunderstanding, in dealings with other people. [1972]

Organizational routines are sometimes encapsulated as grammars of action, e.g., the procedures followed by a support group to solve customer issues. [1468]

The culture (e.g., learned behaviours, knowledge, beliefs and skills) embodied in each developer will influence their cognitive output. Shared culture provides benefits, such as, existing practices are understood and followed (e.g., the set of assumptions and expectations about how things are done), and using categorization to make generalizations from relatively small data sets; see section 2.5.4. Social learning is discussed in section 3.4.4.

Figure 4.37 shows what were considered to be typical memory capacities and costs, for 167 computer systems available from the major vendors, between 1970 and 1978; lines are fitted regression models for 1971, 1974 and 1977; see Github-ecosystems/CompWorld85.R. The performance and storage capacity limitations of early computers encouraged a software culture that eulogized the use of clever tricks, whose purpose was to minimise the amount of code and/or storage required to solve a problem.

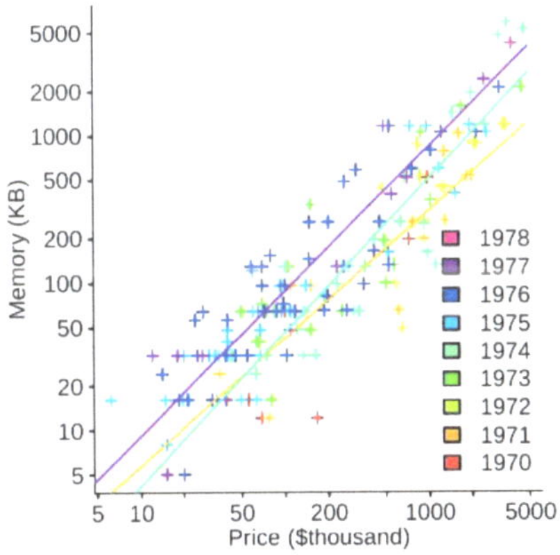

Figure 4.37: Typical memory capacity against cost of 167 different computer systems from 1970 to 1978; fitted regression lines are for 1971, 1974 and 1977. Data from Cale. Github-Local

A shared culture provides an aid for understanding others, but does not eliminate variability. When asked to name an object or action, people have been found to give a wide range of different names. A study by Furnas, Landauer, Gomez, and Dumais [638,639] described operations to subjects who were not domain experts (e.g., hypothetical text editing commands, categories in Swap `n Sale classified ads, keywords for recipes), and asked them to suggest a name for each operation. The results showed that the name selected by one subject was, on average, different from the name selected by 80% to 90% of the other subjects (one experiment included subjects who were domain experts, and the results for those subjects were consistent with this performance). The frequency of occurrence of the names chosen tended to follow a power law.

Metaphors [1070] are a figure of speech, which apply the features associated with one concept to another concept. For instance, concepts involving time are often expressed by native English speakers using a spatial metaphor. These metaphors take one of two forms- one in which time is stationary, and we move through it (e.g., "we're approaching the end of the year"); in the other, we are stationary and time moves toward us, e.g., "the time for action has arrived".

A study by Boroditsky [224] investigated subjects' selection of either the ego-moving, or the time-moving, frame of reference. Subjects first answered a questionnaire dealing with symmetrical objects moving to the left or to the right; the questions were intended to prime either an ego-moving or object-moving perspective. Subjects then read an ambiguous temporal sentence (e.g., "Next Wednesday's meeting has been moved forward two days") and were asked to give the new meeting day. The results found that 71% of subjects responded in a prime-consistent manner: of the subjects primed with the ego-moving frame, 73% thought the meeting was on Friday and 27% thought it was on Monday, and subjects primed with the object-moving frame showed the reverse bias, i.e., 31% and 69%.

Native Chinese speakers also use spatial metaphors to express time related concepts, but use the vertical axis rather than the horizontal axis used by native English speakers.

Cultural conventions can be domain specific. For instance, in the US politicians run for office, while in Spain and France they walk, and in Britain they stand for office. These metaphors may crop up as supposedly meaningful identifier names, e.g., run_for, is_standing.

Have the ecosystems inhabited by software changed so rapidly that cultural behaviors have not had time to spread and become widely adopted, before others take their place? Distinct development practices did evolve at the three early computer development sites in the UK. [295] Character encodings have been evolving since the 1870 s , [604] with the introduction of the telegraph. Early computer capacity restrictions drove further evolution, [1185] and the erosion of technical restrictions has allowed a single encoding for all the World's characters [1864] to slowly spread; cultural factors and competing interests work to slow the pace of change. [881]

Is English the lingua-franca of software development?

There has been a world-wide diffusion of software systems such as Unix, MS-DOS, and Microsoft Windows, along with the pre-internet era publicly available source code, such as X11, gcc, and Unix variants such as BSD; books and manuals have been written to teach software developers about this software. English is the language associated with these software systems and associated books, which has created incentives for developers in non-English speaking countries to attain good enough English proficiency.

When the interval between product updates is short, an investment in adapting products to non-English speaking markets is less likely to be economically worthwhile.

The world-wide spread of popular American culture is another vector for the use of English. In countries with relatively small populations it may not be economically viable to dub American/British films and TV programs, subtitles are a cheaper option (and these provide the opportunity for a population to learn English; see Github-ecosystems/Test_Vocab.txt).

The office suite LibreOffice was originally written by a German company, and many comments were written in German. A decision was made that all comments should be written in English. Figure 4.38 shows the decline in the number of comments written in German, contained in the LibreOffice source code.

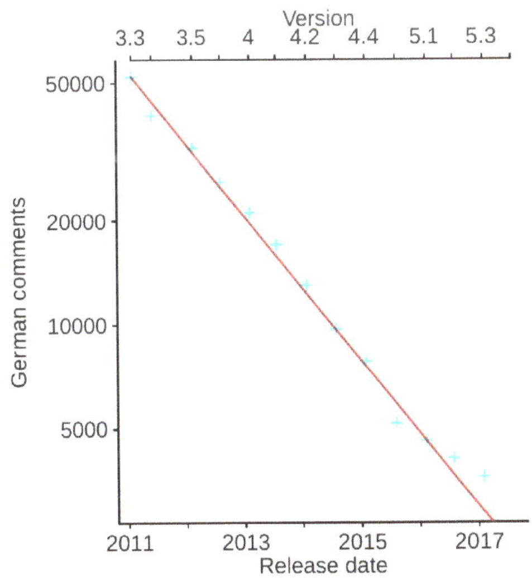

Figure 4.38: Estimated number of comments written in German, in the LibreOffice source code. Data from Meeks. Github-Local

Some companies, in non-English speaking countries, may require their staff to speak English at work.

In ALGEC, [847] a language invented in the Soviet Union, keywords can be written in a form that denotes their gender and number. For instance, Boolean can be written: логическое (neuter), логический (masculine), логическая (feminine) or логические (plural). The keyword for the "go to" token is to; something about Russian makes use of the word "go" unnecessary.

A fixation on a particular way of doing things is not limited to language conventions, examples can be found in mathematics. For instance, WEIRD people have been drilled in the use of a particular algorithm for dividing two numbers, which leads many to believe that the number representation used by the Romans caused them serious difficulties with division. Division of Roman numerals is straight-forward, if the appropriate algorithm is used. [360]

Ethnographic studies of engineering culture have investigated a large high-tech company in the mid-1980s, [1057] and an internet startup that had just IPO'ed. [1604]

Hacker culture are communities of practice, and encompass a variety of belief systems. [384]

4.4.3 Software vendors

A company is a legal entity that limits the liability of its owners. The duty of the directors of a company is to maximise the return on investment to shareholders. Commercial pressure is often to deliver results in the short term rather than taking a longer term view. [765]

The first software company, selling software consulting services, was founded in March 1955. [1049] Commercial software products, from third-parties, had to wait until computer usage became sufficiently widespread that a profitable market for them was considered likely to exist. One of the first third-party software products ran on the RCA 501, in 1964, and created program flowcharts. [921]

The birth, growth, and death of companies [1024] is of economic interest to governments seeking to promote the economic well-being of their country. Company size, across countries and industries, roughly follows a Pareto distribution, [461] while company age has an exponential distribution; [375] most companies are small, and die young.

Figure 4.39 shows the number of UK companies registered each month having the word software (45,422 entries) or computer (18,001 entries) in their SIC description.

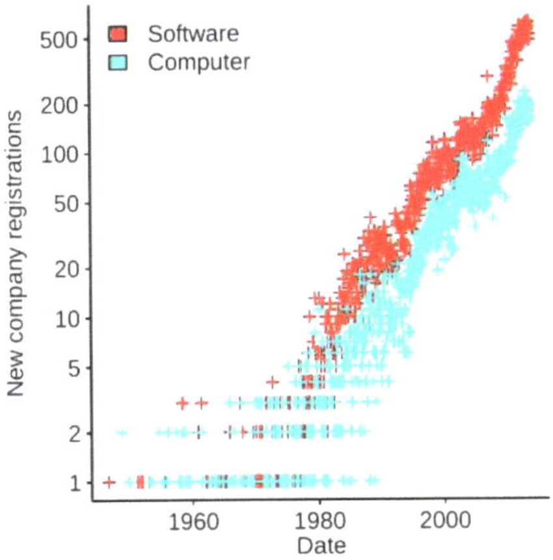

Figure 4.39: Number of new UK companies registered each month, whose SIC description includes the word software (45,422 entries) or computer (18,001 entries). Data extracted from OpenCorporates. Github-Local

The development of a software system can involve a whole ecosystem of supply companies. For instance, the winner of a contract to develop a large military system often subcontracts-out work for many of the subsystems to different suppliers; each supplier using different computing platforms, languages and development tools (Baily et al [117] describes one such collection of subsystems). Subcontractors in turn might hire consultants, and specialist companies for training and recruitment. [376]

Companies may operate in specific customer industries (which themselves may be business ecosystems, e.g., the travel business), or a software ecosystem might be defined by the platform on which the software runs, e.g., software running on Microsoft Windows.

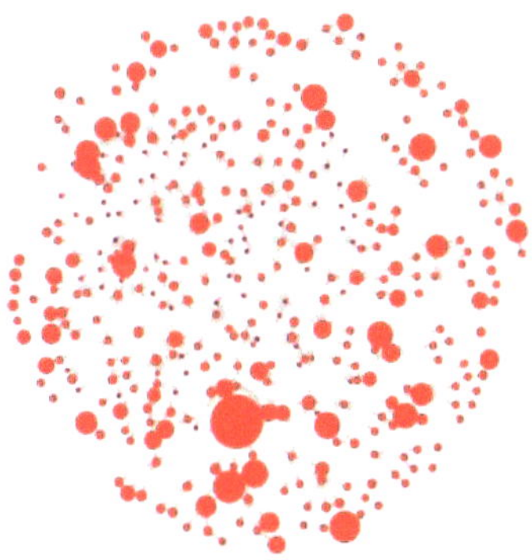

Figure 4.40: Connections between companies in a Dutch software business network. Data kindly provided by Crooymans. Github-Local

A study by Crooymans, Pradhan and Jansen [417] investigated the relationship connections between companies in a local software business network. Figure 4.40 shows the relationship links between these companies, with a few large companies and many smaller ones. [xi]

4.4.4 Career paths

The availability of computing power has resulted in many new industries being created, [1261] but the stability needed to establish widely recognised software industry specific career paths has not yet occurred. A common engineering career path involves various levels of engineering seniority, taking on increasing management responsibilities, potentially followed by various levels of purely management activities; [36] the Peter principle may play a role in career progression. [175]

Coding was originally classified as a clerical activity (a significant under-appreciation of the cognitive abilities required), and the gender-based division of working roles prevalent during the invention of electronic computing assigned women to coding jobs; mens' role in the creation of software, during this period, included non-coding activities such as specifying the formulas to be used. [1142]

What are the skills and knowledge that employers seek in employees involved in software development, and what are the personal characteristics of people involved in such occupations? [xii]

The U.S., the Occupational Information Network (O*NET) [1416] maintains a database of information on almost 1,000 occupations, based on data collected from people currently doing the job. [xiii] The freely available data is aimed at people such as job seekers and HR staff, and includes information on the skills and knowledge needed to do the job, along with personal characteristics and experience of people doing the job.

Software companies employ people to perform a variety of jobs, including management, [1099] sales, marketing, engineering, Q/A, customer support, and internal support staff, e.g., secretarial. A study [911] of academic research units found that the ratio of support staff to academic staff was fitted by a power law having an exponent of around 1.30 (a hierarchical management model of one administrator per three sub-units produces an exponent of 1.26). Figure 3.4 shows that even in a software intensive organization around 87% of revenue is spent on non-software development activities.

Employment opportunities are the stepping stones of a career path, and personal preferences will result in some opportunities being considered more attractive than others. The popularity of particular software development activities [301] will have an impact on the caliber of potential employees available for selection by employers, e.g., maintenance activities are perceived as low status, an entry-level job for inexperienced staff to learn. [1803]

What roles might people having a career in software development fill, what are the common role transitions, how many people are involved, and how long do people inhabit any role?

Census information, and government employment statistics, are sources of data covering people who might be considered to be software developers; however, this data may include jobs that are not associated with software development. A study by Gilchrist and Weber [681] investigated the number of employed computer personnel in the US in 1970. The data for what was then known as automatic data processing included keypunching and computer operations personnel; approximately 30% of the 810,330[xiv] people appear to have a claim to be software developers; see Github-ecosystems/50790641-II.R. This data does not include software development classified under R&D.

Figure 4.41 shows the number of people, stratified by age, employed in the 12 computer related U.S. Census Bureau occupation codes during 2014 (largest peak is the total).

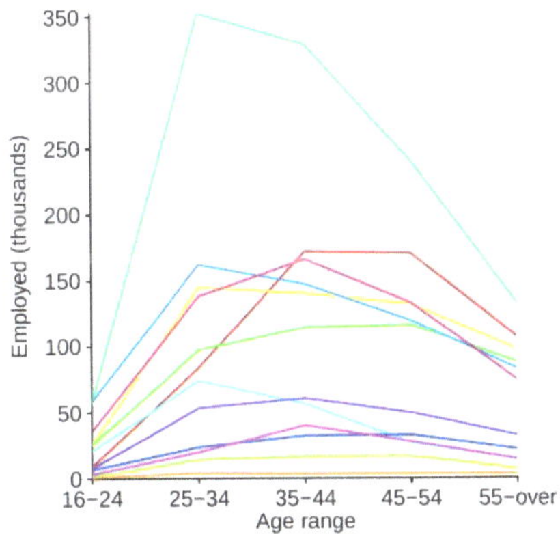

Figure 4.41: Number of people employed in the 12 computer occupation codes assigned by the U.S. Census Bureau during 2014, stratified by ages bands (main peak is the total, "Software developers, applications and system software" is the largest single percentage; see code for the identity of other occupation codes). Data from Beckhusen. Github-Local

People change, the companies they work for change, and software ecosystems evolve, which creates many of opportunities for people to change jobs. [445]

When companies experience difficulties recruiting people with the required skills, salaries for the corresponding jobs are likely to increase. A growing number of companies ask employees to sign non-compete and no-poach agreements. [1764] An antitrust action was successfully prosecuted [583] against Adobe, Apple, Google, Intel, Intuit, and Pixar for mutually agreeing not to cold-call each other's employees (with a view to hiring them).

Startups have become a form of staff recruitment, with large companies buying startup companies to obtain a team with specific skills [1669] (known as acqhiring or acqui-hiring). One study [999] found that acqui-hired staff had higher turn-over compared to regular hires.

A study [212] of manufacturing industry found that family-friendly workplaces were associated with a higher-skilled workforce and female managers; based on the available data, there was no correlation with firm productivity.

One technique for motivating employees, when an organization is unable to increase their pay, is to give them an impressive job title. UK universities have created the job title research software engineer. [978]

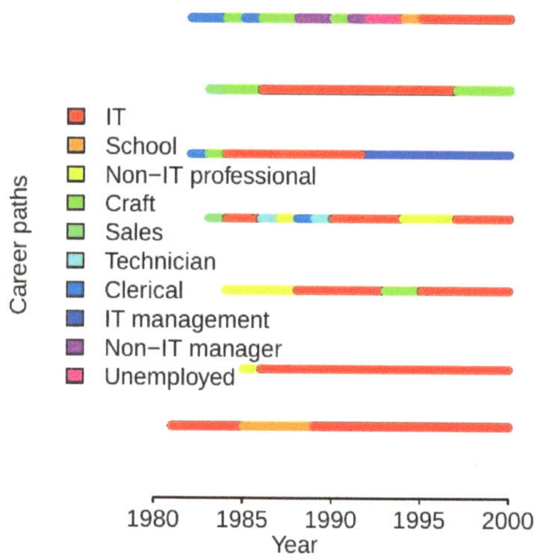

Figure 4.42: The job categories contained within the seven career paths in which people spent at least five years working in technical IT role. Data from Joseph et al. Github-Local

A study by Joseph, Boh, Ang and Slaughter [959] investigated the job categories within the career paths of 500 people who had spent at least a year working in a technical IT role, based on data drawn from the National Longitudinal Survey of Youth. Figure 4.42 shows the seven career paths that (out of 13) included at least five years working in a technical IT role.

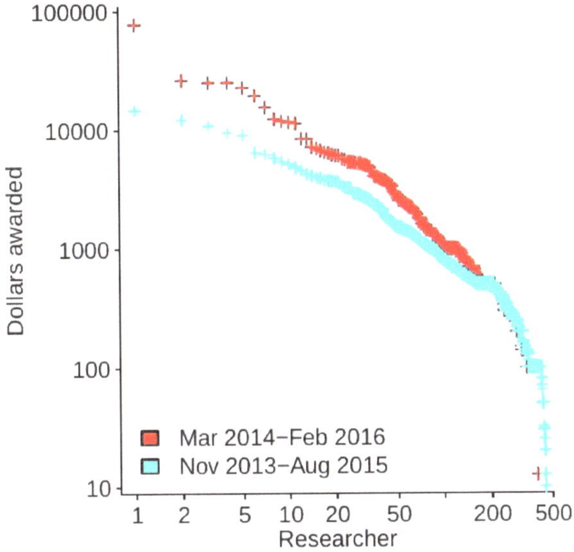

Figure 4.43: Sorted list of total amount awarded by bug bounties to individual researchers, based on two datasets downloaded from HackerOne. Data from Zhao et al [2014] and Maillart et al. Github-Local

There are opportunities for developers to make money outside formal employment. Figure 4.43 shows a sorted list of the total amount earned by individuals through bug bounty programs. Both studies downloaded data available on the HackerOne website; the study by Zhao, Grossklags and Liu [2014] used data from November 2013 to August 2015, and the study by Maillart, Zhao, Grossklags and Chuang [1192] used data from March 2014 to February 2016.

4.5 Applications and Platforms

A successful software system attracts its own ecosystem of users and third-party developers. The accumulation of an ecosystem may be welcomed and encouraged by the successful owner, or it may be tolerated as a consequence of being successful.

Operating in a market where third-parties are tolerated by the apex vendor is a precarious business. Small companies may be able to eek out a living filling small niches that are not worth the time and effort for the apex vendor, or by having the agility to take advantage of short-term opportunities.

In a few product ecosystems the first release is everything, there is little ongoing market. Figure 4.44 shows the daily minutes spent using an App, installed from Apple's AppStore, against days since first used. This behavior was the case when people paid for games software to play on their phones; a shift to in-game purchases created an ongoing relationship.

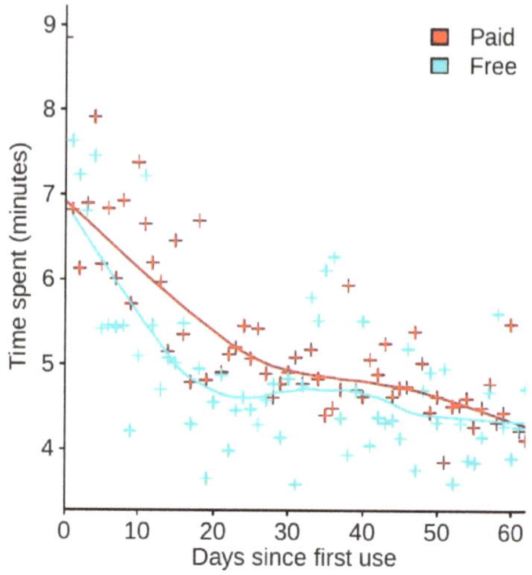

Figure 4.44: Daily minutes spent using an App, from Apple's AppStore (data from 2009); lines are a loess fit. Data extracted from Ansar. Github-Local

In a rapidly evolving market, an ecosystem may effectively provide small companies within it, resources that exceed those available to much larger companies seeking to do everything themselves.

The rise of Open source has made it viable for substantial language ecosystems to flower, or rather substantial package ecosystems, with each based around a particular language. For practical purposes, a significant factor in language choice has become the quality and quantity of their ecosystem.

4.5.1 Platforms

Platform businesses [427] bring together producers and consumers, e.g., shopping malls link consumers and merchants, and newspapers connect readers (assumed to be potential customers) and advertisers; it is a two-sided market. Microsoft Windows is the poster child of a software platform.

Platforms create value by facilitating interactions between third-party producers and consumers; which differs from the value-chain model, which creates value by controlling a sequence of activities. An organization may act as an aggregator, collecting and making available items such as packages, source code, or job vacancies.

What has been called the Bill Gates line, [1832] provides one method of distinguishing between an aggregator and a platform: "A platform is when the economic value of everybody that uses it, exceeds the value of the company that creates it."

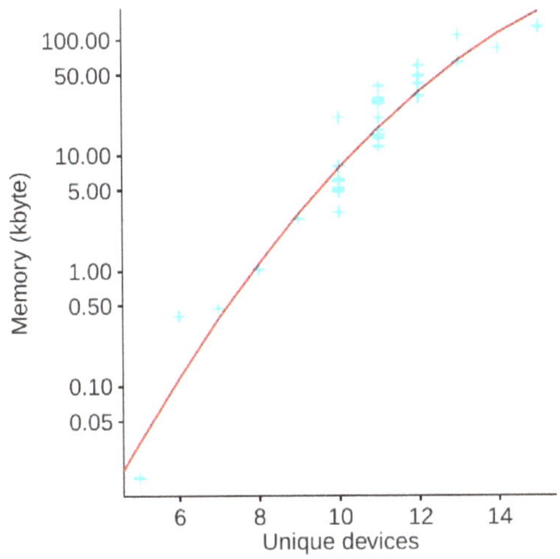

Figure 4.45: Size of 40 operating systems (Kbytes, measured in 1975) capable of controlling a given number of unique devices; line is a quadratic regression fit. Data from Elci. Github-Local

Platform owners aim to maximize the total value extracted from their ecosystem. In some cases this means subsidizing one kind of member to attract another kind (from which a greater value can be extracted). For instance, Microsoft once made development tools (e.g., compilers) freely available to attract developers, who wrote the applications that attracted end-users (there are significantly fewer developers than end-users, and any profit from selling compilers is correspondingly smaller).

Value-chains focus on customer value, and seek to maximize the lifetime value of individual customers, for products and services.

Organizations gain an advantage by controlling valuable assets that are difficult imitate. In the platform business the community, and the resources its members own and contribute is a valuable, hard to copy, asset. In a value-chain model these assets might be raw materials or intellectual property.

Building a platform requires convincing third-parties that it is worth joining, ecosystem governance is an important skill.

An organization that can create and own a de facto industry standard does not need to coordinate investments in creating the many enhancements and add-ons; an ecosystem of fragmented third-parties can work independently, they simply need to adhere to an established interface (what provides the coordination). The owner of a platform benefits from the competition between third-parties, who are striving to attract customers by creating desirable add-ons (which enhance the ecosystem, and fills the niches that are not worth the time and effort of the apex vendor).

Platform owners want customers to have a favorable perception of the third-party applications available on their platform. One way that platform owners can influence customer experience is to operate and police an App store that only allows approved Apps to be listed. A study [1919] of Google Play found that of the 1.5 million Apps listed in 2015, 0.79 million had been removed by 2017 (by which time 2.1 million Apps were listed).

Operating systems were the first software ecosystem, and OS vendors offered unique functionality to third-party developers in the hope they would use it extensively in the code they wrote (effectively increasing their own switching costs).

Vendors wanting to sell products on multiple operating systems have to decide whether to offer the same functionality across all versions of their product (i.e., not using functionality unique to one operating system to support functionality available to users of that OS), or to provide some functionality that varies between operating systems.

The term middleware is applied to software designed to make it easier to port applications across different operating systems; the Java language, and its associated virtual-machine, is perhaps the most well-known example of middleware.

Operating system vendors dislike middleware because it reduces switching costs. Microsoft, with successive versions of Microsoft Windows, was a dominant OS vendor during the 1990s and 2000s, and had an ecosystem control mechanism that others dubbed embrace and extend. Microsoft licensed Java, and added Windows specific functionality to its implementation, which then failed to pass the Java conformance test suite. Sun Microsystems (who owned Java at the time) took Microsoft to court and won; [1950] Microsoft then refused to ship a non-extended version of Java as part of Windows, Sun filed an antitrust case and won. [1319]

Small organizations seeking to create a platform might start out by building a base within an existing ecosystem. For instance, Zynga started as a games producer on the Facebook ecosystem, but then sought to migrate players onto its own platform (where it controlled the monetisation process).

4.5.2 Pounding the treadmill

Once a product ecosystem is established, investment by the apex vendor is focused on maintaining their position, and growing the ecosystem. A recurring trend is for software ecosystems to lose their business relevance, with the apex vendor remaining unchanged; see section 1.2.

Once up and running, some bespoke software systems become crucial assets for operating a business, and so companies have no choice but to pay whatever it takes to keep them running. From the vendors' perspective, maintenance is the least glamorous, but often the most profitable aspect of software systems; companies sometimes underbid to win a contract, and make their profit on maintenance activities; see chapter 5.

Over time, customers' work-flow molds itself around the workings of software products; an organization's established way of doing things evolves to take account of the behavior of the software it uses; staff training is a sunk cost. The cost of changing established practices, real or imaginary, is a moat that reduces the likelihood of customers switching to competing products; it is also a ball-and-chain for the vendor, in that it can limit product updates to those that do not generate costly changes for existing customers. At some point the profit potential of new customers may outweigh that of existing customers, resulting in a product update that requires existing customers to make a costly investment before they can adopt the new release.

Pressure to innovate comes from the economic benefits of having the installed base upgrade. Continual innovation avoids the saturation of demand, and makes it difficult for potential competitors to create viable alternatives.

Commercial products evolve when vendors believe that investing in updates is economically worthwhile. Updated versions of a product provide justification for asking customers to pay maintenance or upgrade fees, and in a competitive market work to maintain, or improve, market position, and address changing customer demand; product updates also signal to potential customers that the vendor has not abandoned the product (unfavourable publicity about failings in an existing product can deter potential new customers).

Product version numbers can be used to signal different kinds of information, such as which upgrades are available under a licensing agreement (e.g., updates with changes to the minor version number are included), and as a form of marketing to potential customers (who might view higher numbers as a sign of maturity). The release schedule and version of some systems is sufficiently stable that a reasonably accurate regression model can be fitted; [1883] see Github-regression/release_info/cocoon_mod.R.

The regular significant improvement in Intel cpu performance (see fig 4.15), starting in the last 1980s, became something that was factored into software system development, e.g., future performance improvements could be used as a reason for not investing much effort in tuning the performance of the next product release.

Files created by users of a product are a source of customer switching costs (e.g., cost of conversion), and vendor ball-and-chain, e.g., the cost of continuing to support files created by earlier versions. File written using a given format can have very long lifetime; a common vendor strategy is to continue supporting the ability to read older formats, but only support the writing of more recent formats. A study by Jackson [906] investigated pdf files created using a given version of the pdf specification. Figure 4.46 shows the total number of pdf files created using a given version of the pdf specification, available on websites having a .uk web domain between 1996 and 2010 (different pdf viewers do not always consistently generate the same visual display from the same pdf file [1051]).

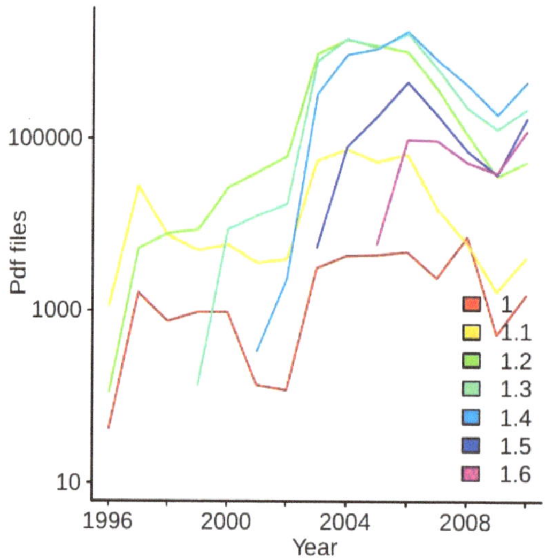

Figure 4.46: Number of pdf files created using a given version of the portable document format appearing on sites having a .uk web address between 1996 and 2010. Data from Jackson. [906] Github-Local

A few software systems have existed for many decades, and are expected to last many more decades, e.g., simulation of nuclear weapon performance (the nuclear test-ban treaty prohibits complete device testing).

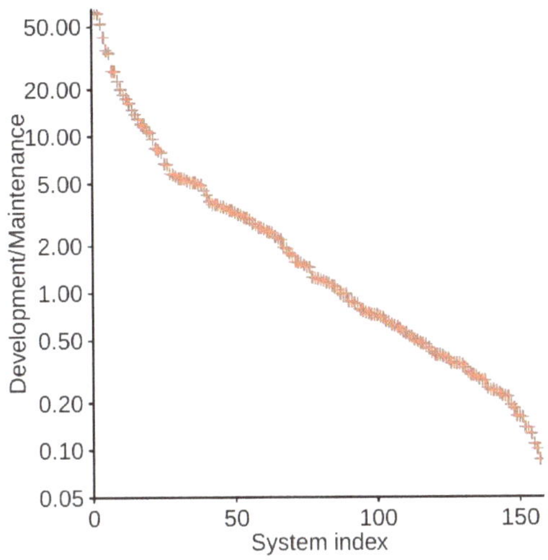

Figure 4.47: Ratio of development costs to average annual maintenance costs (over 5 -years) for 158 IBM software systems sorted by size; curve is a beta distribution fitted to the data (in red). Data from Dunn. Github-Local

What are the costs associated with maintaining a software system?

A study by Dunn [517] investigated the development and maintenance costs of 158 software systems developed by IBM (total costs over the first five years); some of these contained a significant percentage of COTS components. The systems varied in size from 34 to 44,070 man-hours of development effort, and involved from 21 to 78,121 man-hours of maintenance. Figure 4.47 shows the ratio of development to average annual maintenance cost. The data is for systems at a single point in time, i.e., 5 -years. Modeling, using expected system lifetime, finds that the mean total maintenance to development cost ratio is less than one; see Github-ecosystems/maint-dev-ratio.R. The correlation between development and maintenance man-hours is 0.5 ($0.38 - 0.63$ is the 95% confidence interval); see Github-economics/maint-dev-cost-cor.R.

Hedonism funded software systems continue to change for as long as those involved continue to enjoy the experience.

The issues around fixing reported faults during maintenance are discussed in chapter 6. In safety critical applications the impact of changes during maintenance has to be thought through; [451] this issue is discussed in chapter 6.

4.5.3 Users' computers

A software system has to be usable within the constraints of the users' hardware, and the particular libraries installed on their computer.

The days when customers bought their first computer to run an application are long gone. Except for specialist applications [1089] and general hardware updates, it is not usually cost effective for customers to invest in new computing hardware specifically to run an application. Information on the characteristics of existing customer hardware is crucial because software that cannot be executed with a reasonable performance in the customer environment will not succeed (figure 8.27 shows the variation in basic hardware capacity of desktop systems).

The distribution of process execution times often has the form of either power law or an exponential. [585] In large computer installations, workload analysis, analyzing computer usage and balancing competing requirements to maximise throughput, may employ teams in each time zone. Figure 4.48 shows the distribution of the execution time of 184,612 processes running on a 1995 era Unix computer.

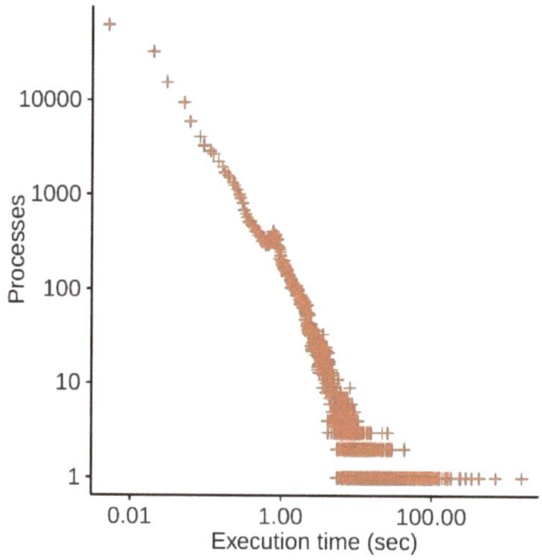

Figure 4.48: Number of Unix processes executing for a given number of seconds, on a 1995 era computer. Data from Harchol-Balter et al. Github-Local

Obtaining solutions to a few problems is sufficiently important that specialist computers are built to run the applications, e.g., super computers (see Github-Rlang/Top500.R), and bespoke hardware to solve one problem. [1682]

4.6 Software development

Most computer hardware is brought because it is needed to run application software, [xv] i.e., software development is a niche activity.

Computers were originally delivered to customers as bare-metal (many early computers were designed and built by established electronics companies [649]); every customer wrote their own software, sometimes obtaining code from other users. [xvi] As experience and customers accumulated, [108] vendors learned about the kinds of functionality that was useful across their customer base. [277] Supplying basic software functionality needed by customers decreased computer ownership costs, and increased the number of potential customers.

Figure 4.49 shows how the amount of code shipped with IBM computers increased over time. Applications need to receive input from the outside world, and produce output in a form acceptable to their users; interfacing to many different peripherals is a major driver of OS growth, see figure 4.45.

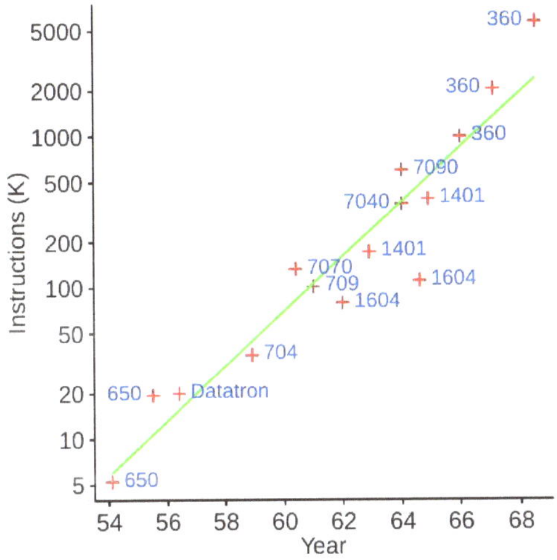

Figure 4.49: Total instructions contained in the software shipped with various models of IBM computer, plus Datatron from Burroughs; line is a fitted regression of the form: Instructions $\propto e^{0.4 \text{ Year}}$. Data extracted from Naur et al. Github-Local

All software for the early computers was written using machine code, which made it specific to one particular kind of computer. New computers were constantly being introduced, each having different characteristics (in particular machine instructions). [206,1252,1941,1942]

Machine independent programming languages (e.g., Fortran in 1954[107] and Cobol in 1961[171]) were created with the aim of reducing costs. The cost reduction came through reducing the dependency of program source code on the particular characteristics of the hardware on which it executed, and reuse of programming skills learned on one kind of computer to different computers, e.g., removing the need to learn the assembly language for each new machine.

4.6.1 Programming languages

Organizations with an inventory of source code have an interest in the current and future use of programming languages: more widely used languages are likely to have more developers capable of using it (reducing hiring costs), likely to have more extensive tool support (than less widely used languages), and are likely to be available on a wider range of platforms.

Some people enjoy creating new language, writers of science fiction sometimes go to great length to create elaborate, and linguistically viable, languages for aliens to speak. [1603] Factors found to influence the number of human languages actively used, within a geographic region, include population size, country size, and the length of the growing season; [1367] see Github-ecosystems/009_.R.

The specification of Plankalkül, the first high-level programming language, was published in 1949; [147,2034] the specification of a still widely used language (Fortran) was published in 1954. [883] A list of compilers [xvii] for around 25 languages appears in a book [722] published in 1959 (see Github-ecosystems/Grabbe_59.txt), and in 1963 it was noted [788] that creating a programming language had become a fashionable activity. A 1976 report [605] estimated that at least 450 general-purpose languages and dialects were currently in use within the US DoD.

Many thousands of programming languages have been created, but only a handful have become widely used. Figure 4.50 shows the number of new programming languages, per year, that have been described in a published paper.

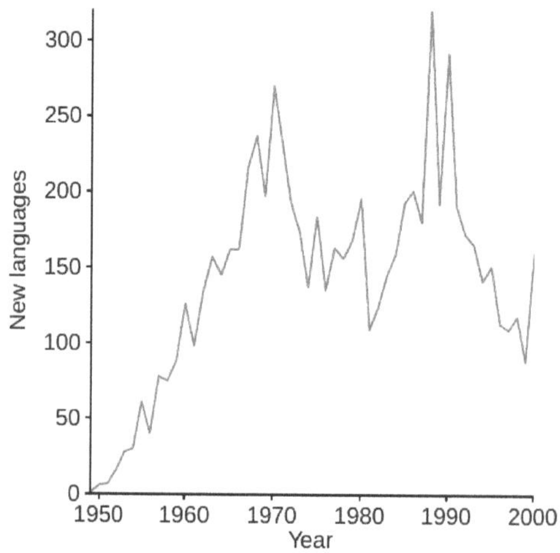

Figure 4.50: Number of new programming languages, per year, described in a published paper. Data from Pigott et al. Github-Local

Despite their advantages, [1583] high-level languages did not immediately displace machine code for the implementation of many software systems. A 1977 survey [1756] of programmers in the US Federal Government, found 45% with extensive work experience, and 35% with moderate work experience, of machine code. Developing software using early compilers could be time-consuming and labor-intensive; memory limits required compiling to be split into a sequence of passes over various representations of the source (often half-a-dozen or more [256]), with the intermediate representations being output on papertape, which was read back in as the input to the next pass (after reading the next compiler pass from the next paper-tape in the sequence), eventually generating assembler. Some compilers required that the computer have an attached drum-unit [109] (an early form of hard-disk), which was used to store the intermediate forms (and increase sale of peripherals). Developer belief in their own ability to produce more efficient code than a compiler was also a factor. [108]

The creation of a major new customer facing ecosystem provides an opportunity for new languages and tools to become widely used within the development community working in that ecosystem. For instance, a new language might provide functionality often required by applications targeting users of particular ecosystem, that is more convenient to use (compared to preexisting languages), alternatively there may only be one language initially available for use, e.g., Solidity for writing Ethereum contracts.

Within geographical, or linguistic, separated regions the popularity of existing languages has sometimes evolved along different paths, e.g., Pascal remained popular in Russia [1194] longer than elsewhere, and in Japan Cobol remains widely used. [27]

Existing languages and their implementations evolve. Those responsible for maintaining the language specification add new constructs (which are claimed to be needed by developers), and compiler vendors need to add new features to have something new to sell to existing customers. One consequence of language evolution is that some implementations may not support all the constructs contained in the source code used to build a program. [177]

A history of the evolution [1769] of Lisp lists the forces driving its evolution: "Overall, the evolution of Lisp has been guided more by institutional rivalry, one-upsmanship, and the glee born of technical cleverness that is characteristic of the "hacker culture" than by sober assessments of technical requirements."

There are incentives for vendors to invest in a language they control, when they also control a platform supporting an ecosystem of applications written by third-parties, e.g., C♯ on Microsoft Windows, Objective-C on iOS, and Kotlin on Android. Writing an application in the vendor's ecosystem language is a signal of commitment (because it entails a high switching cost).

The legal case between Oracle and Google, over Java copyright issues, [44] motivated the need for a Java compatible language that was not Java; Kotlin became available in 2017. Developers have started to use Kotlin specific features in their existing Java source. [1220]

The term language popularity suggests that the users of the language have some influence on the selection process, and like the language in some way. In practice developers may

not have any say in the choice of language, and may have no positive (or negative) feelings towards the language. However, this term is in common use, and there is nothing to be gained by using something technically correct.

Figure 4.51 shows the number of lines contained in the source code of the 32 major releases of Debian, broken down by programming language (the legend lists the top five languages).

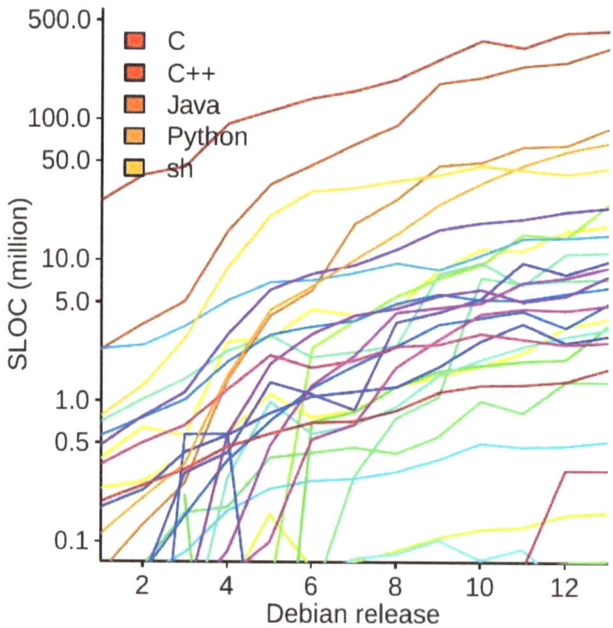

Figure 4.51: Lines of code written in the 32 programming languages appearing in the source code of the 13 major Debian releases between 1998 and 2019. Data from the Debsources developers. Github-Local

Sources of information on language use include:

- Job adverts: The number of organizations that appear to be willing to pay money to someone to use a language, is both a measure of actual usage and perceived popularity. Languages listed in job adverts are chosen for a variety of reasons including: appearing trendy in order to attract young developers to an interview, generating a smokescreen to confuse competitors, and knowledge of the language is required for the job advertised.
- A study by Davis and de la Parra [445] investigated the monthly flow of jobs on an online job market-place owned by DHI (approximately 221 thousand vancies posted, and 1.1 million applications). Figure 4.52 shows the labour market slack (calculated, for each month and keyword, as applications for all applicable vacancies divided by the sum of the number of days each vacancy was listed) for jobs postings whose description included a particular keyword.

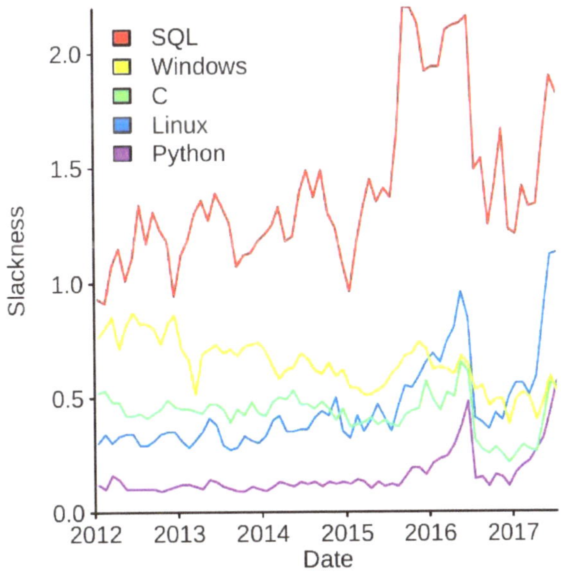

Figure 4.52: Monthly labor market slack (i.e., applications per days vacancy listed) for jobs whose description included a particular keyword (see legend). Data from Davis et al. Github-Local

- Social media includes postings to employment websites and adverts for jobs. Figure 4.53 shows the number of monthly developer job related tweets that included a language name,

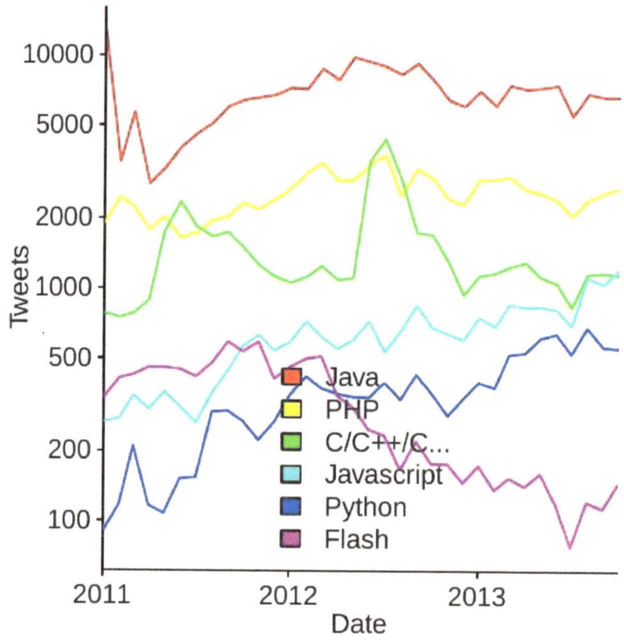

Figure 4.53: Number of monthly developer job related tweets specifying a given language. Data kindly provided by Destefanis. Github-Local

- quantity of existing code: the total quantity of existing code might be used as a proxy for the number of developers who have worked with a language in the past (see fig 11.10); recent changes in the quantity of existing code is likely to provide a more up to date picture,
- number of books sold: [804] spending money on a book is an expression of intent to learn the language. The intent may be a proxy for existing code (i.e., learning the language to get a job, or work on a particular project), existing course curriculum decisions, or because the language has become fashionable. Sales data from individual publishers is likely to be affected by the popularity of their published books, and those of competing publishers; see Github-ecosystems/LangBooksSold.R,
- miscellaneous: prior to the growth of open source, the number of commercially available compilers was an indicator of size of the professional developer market for the language.

- Question & answer websites are unreliable indicators because languages vary in complexity, and questions tail off as answers on common issues become available. Figure 4.54 shows the normalised percentage of language related tags associated with questions appearing on Stack Overflow each month.

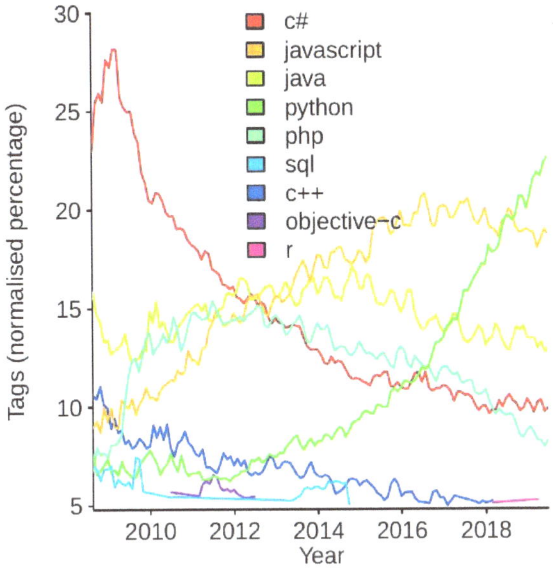

Figure 4.54: Normalised percentage of 34 language tags associated with questions appearing on Stack Overflow in each month. Data extracted from Stack Overflow website. Github-Local

- Application domain specific usage, such as mobile phone development, [1562] embedded systems in general, [1838,1861] and Docker containers. [364] US Federal government surveys of its own usage: a 1981 survey [390] found most programs were written in Cobol, Fortran, Assembler, Algol and PL/1, a 1995 survey [850] of 148 million LOC in DOD weapon systems Ada represented 33%, the largest percentage of any language (C usage was 22%).

- Books are a source of programming language related discussion going back many decades Language names such as Fortran and Cobol are unlikely to be used in nonprogramming contexts, while names such as Java and Python are more likely to be used in a non-programming context. Single letter names, such as C , or names followed by non-alphabetic characters have a variety of possible interpretations, e.g., the phrase in *C* appears in music books as a key signature, also the OCR process sometimes inserts spaces that were probably not in the original. The lack of context means that any analysis based on the English unigrams and bigrams from the Google books project [1276] is likely to be very noisey.

Applications can only be ported to a platform when compilers for the languages used are available. The availability of operating systems and device drivers written in C, means that a C compiler is one of the first developer tools created for a new processor.

Will today's widely used languages continue to be reasonably as popular over the next decade (say)? Some of the factors involved include:

- implementing a software system is expensive; it is often cheaper to continue working with what exists. The quantity of existing source contained in commercially supported applications is likely to be a good indicator of continuing demand for developers capable of using the implementation language(s),
- in a rapidly changing environment developers want to remain attractive to employers, there is a desire to have a CV that lists experience in employable languages. Perception (i.e., not reality) within developer ecosystems about which languages are considered worthwhile knowing, becoming popular or declining in usage/popularity, [1272]
- Open source developers may choose to use a language because it is the one they were first taught. Reid [1572] investigated the first language used in teaching computer science majors; between 1992 and 1999 over 20 lists of languages taught were published, with an average of 400 + universities per list. More recent surveys [1702] have been sporadic. Figure 4.55 shows the percentage of languages taught by at least 3% of the responding universities. The main language taught in universities during the 1990s (i.e., Pascal) ceased being widely used in industry during the late 1980s.

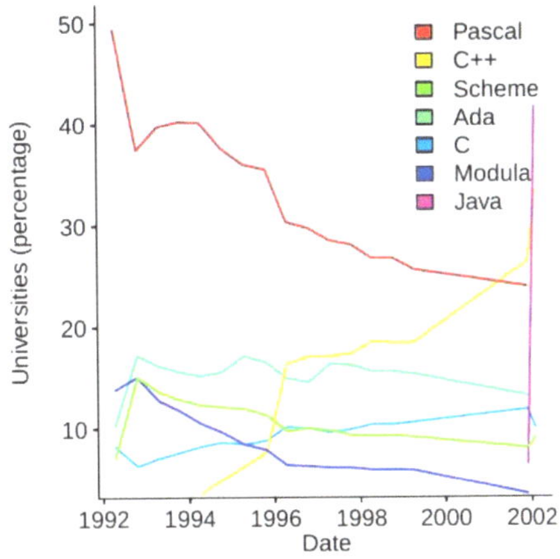

Figure 4.55: Percentage of universities reporting the first language used to teach computer science majors. Data from Reid, via the Wayback Machine,. Github-Local

Compiler vendors enhance their products by supporting features not specified in the language standard (if one exists). The purpose of adding these features is to attract customers (by responding to demand), and over time to make it more difficult for customers to switch to a different vendor. Some language implementations become influential because of the widespread use of the source code they compile (or interpret). The language extensions supported by an influential implementation have to be implemented by any implementation looking to be competitive for non-trivial use.

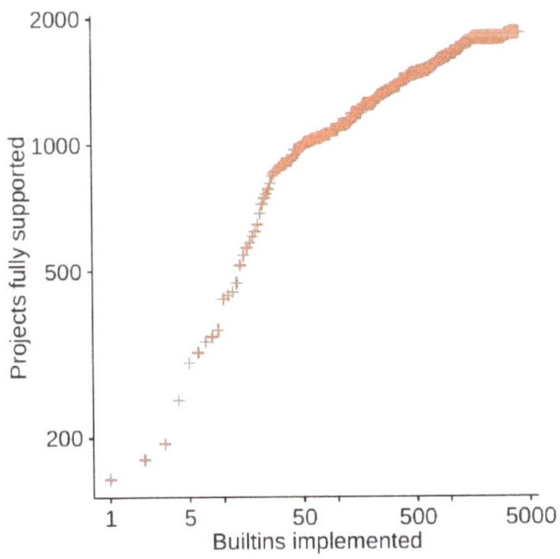

Figure 4.56: Cumulative number of Github projects that can be built as more gcc built-ins are implemented. Data from Rigger et al. Github-Local

A study by Rigger, Marr, Adams and Mössenböck [1585] investigated the use of compiler specific built-in functions supported by gcc, in 1,842 Github projects. In C and C++ source code, use of built-ins appear as function calls, but are subject to special processing by the compiler. Analysis of the C compiler source found 12,339 distinct built-ins (some were internal implementations of other built-ins), and 4,142 unique built-ins were encountered in the C projects analysed. Figure 4.56 shows the cumulative growth in the number of Github projects supported, as support is added for more built-ins (the growth algorithm assumes an implementation order based on the frequency of unique built-in usage across projects).

4.6.2 Libraries and packages

Program implementation often involves functionality that is found in many other programs, e.g., opening a file and reading from it, and writing to a display device. Developers working on the first computers had access to a library of commonly used functions, [1961] and over time a variety of motivations have driven the creation and supply of libraries.

Some programming languages were designed with specific uses in mind, and include support for application domain library functions, e.g., Fortran targeted engineering/scientific users and required implementations to provide support for trigonometric functions, Cobol targeted business users, and required support for sorting. [xviii]

Manufacturers discovered that the libraries they had bundled with the operating system [204] to attract new customers, could also be used to increase customer lock-in (by tempting developers with extensive library functionality having characteristics specific to the manufacturer, that could not be easily mapped to the libraries supplied by other vendors).

The decreasing cost of hardware, and the availability of an operating system, in the form of Unix source code, enabled many manufacturers to enter the minicomputer/workstation market. [303] Vendors' attempts to differentiate their product lines led to the Unix wars [1631,1632] of the 1980s (in the mid-1990s, platforms running a Unix-derived OS typically shipped with over a thousand C/C++ header files [930]).

The POSIX standard [899] was intended provide the core functionality needed to write portable programs; this functionality was derived from existing implementation practice of widely used Unix systems. [2032] POSIX became widely supported (in part because large organizations, such as the US Government, required vendors to supply products that included POSIX support, although some implementations felt as-if they were only intended to tick a box during a tender process, rather than be used).

A study by Atlidakis, Andrus, Geambasu, Mitropoulos and Nieh [85] investigated POSIX usage (which defines 1,177 functions) across Android 4.3 (1.1 million apps measured, 790 functions tracked, out of 821 implemented) and Ubuntu 12.04 (71,199 packages measured, 1,085 functions tracked, out of 1,115 implemented). Figure 4.57 shows the use of POSIX functions by Apps/packages available for the respective OS (these numbers do not include calls to ioctl, whose action is to effectively perform an implementation defined call).

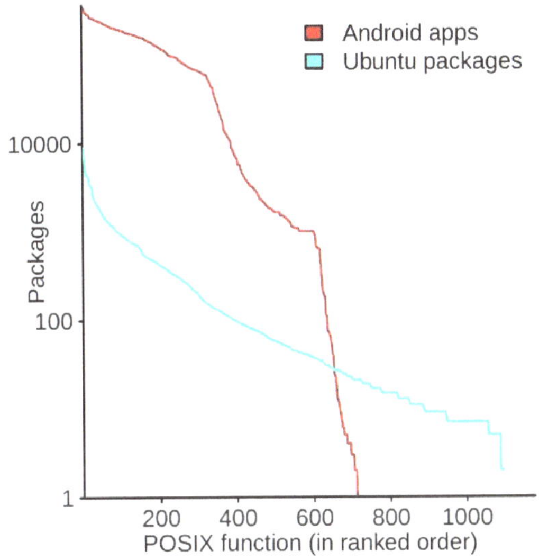

Figure 4.57: Number of Android/Ubuntu (1.1 million apps)/(71,199 packages) linking to a given POSIX function (sorted into rank order). Data from Atlidakis et al. Github-Local

Linux came late to the Unix wars, and emerged as the primary base Unix kernel. The Linux Standard Base [xix] is intended to support a binary compatibility interface for application executables; this interface includes pseudo-file systems (e.g., /proc) that provide various kinds of system information.

A study by Tsai, Jain, Abdul and Porter [1848] investigated use of the Linux API by the 30,976 packages in the Ubuntu 15.04 repository, including system calls, calls to function in libc, ioctl argument value, and pseudo-file system usage (the measurements were obtained via static analysis of program binaries). Figure 4.58 shows each API use (e.g., call to a particular function or reference to a particular system file) provided by the respective service, as a percentage of the possible 30,976 packages that could reference them, in API rank order.

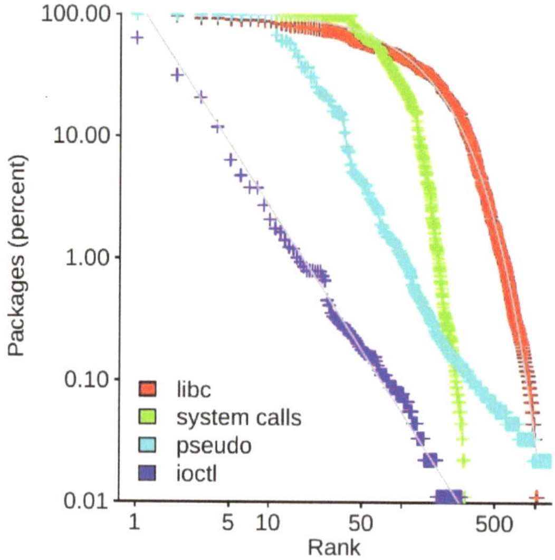

Figure 4.58: Percentage of packages referencing a particular API provided by a given service (sorted in rank order); grey lines are a fitted power law and exponential, to ioctl and libc respectively. Data from Tsai et al. Github-Local

The internet created a new method of software distribution: a website. People and organizations have built websites to support the distribution of packages available for a particular language (rather than a particular OS), and some have become the primary source of third-party packages for their target language, e.g., npm for Javascript, and CRAN for R.

Publicly available package repositories are a relatively new phenomena; a few were started in the mid-1990s (e.g., CRAN and CPAN), and major new repositories are still appearing 15years later, e.g., Github in 2008 and npm in 2010. The age of a repository can have a large impact on the results of an analysis of the characteristics measured, e.g., rate of change is likely to be high in the years immediately after a repository is created.

Package repositories are subject to strong network effects. Developers want to minimise the effort invested in searching for packages, and the repository containing the most packages is likely to attract the most searches; also, the number of active users of a repository is a signal for authors of new packages, seeking to attract developers, who need to choose a distribution channel.

A study by Caneill and Zacchiroli [299] investigated package usage in the official Debian releases and updates. Figure 4.59 shows the survival curve of the latest version of a package included in 10 official Debian releases, along with the survival of the same version of a package over successive releases.

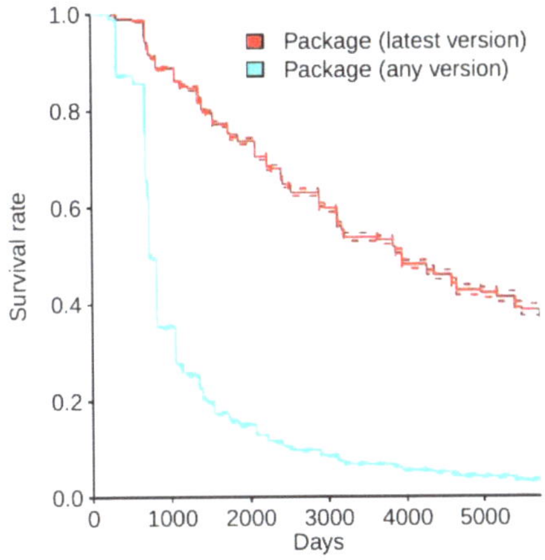

Figure 4.59: Survival curve of packages included in 10 official Debian releases, and inclusion of the same release of a package; dashed lines are 95% confidence intervals. Data from Caneill et al. Github-Local

A niche market may be large enough, and have sufficiently specialist needs, for a repository catering to its requirements to become popular within the niche, e.g., the Bioconductor website aims to support the statistical analysis of biological assays and contains a unique collection of R packages targeting this market. Figure 4.60 shows the number of *R* packages in three large repositories (a fourth, *R*-forge is not displayed), along with the number of packages present in multiple repositories (colored areas not scaled by number of packages). Each website benefits from its own distinct network effects, e.g., Github provides repositories, and gives users direct control of their files.

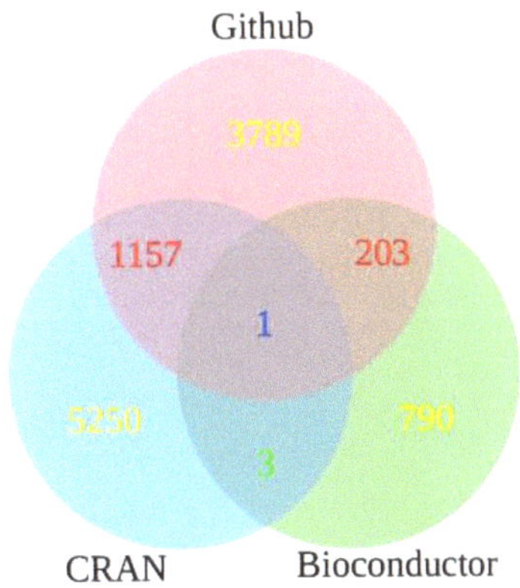

Figure 4.60: Number of packages in three widely used *R* repositories (during 2015), overlapping regions show packages appearing in multiple repositories (areas not to scale). Data from Decan et al. Github-Local

The requirements, imposed by the owners of a repository, for a package to be included, may add friction to the workflow of a package under active development, e.g., package authors may want the latest release to be rapidly available to potential users. For instance, some R packages under active development are available on GitHub, with updates being submitted to CRAN once they are stable (some package have dependencies on packages in the other repositories, and dependency conflicts exist [469]).

In some cases a strong symbiotic relationship between a language and package ecosystem has formed, which has influenced the uptake of new language revisions, e.g., one reason for the slowed uptake of Python 3 has been existing codes' use of packages that require the use of Python 2.

Many packages evolve, and versioning schemes have been created to provide information about the relative order of releases and the compatibility of a release with previous releases. The semver [1530] semantic versioning specification has become widely used; the version string contains three components denoting a major release number (not guaranteed to be compatible with previous releases), minor release number (when new functionality is added), and patch number (correction of mistake(s)).

Package managers often provide a means of specifying version dependency constraints, e.g., ^ 1.2.3 specifies a constraint that can be satisfied by any version between 1.2.3 and 2.0.0. Studies [466] have found that package developers' use of constraints does not always fully comply with the semver specification.

The installation of a package may fail because of dependency conflicts between the packages already installed and this new package, e.g., installed package P_1 may depend on package P_2 having a version less than 2.0, while package P_3 depends on package P_2 having a version of at least 2.0. A study by Drobisz, Mens and Di Cosmo [511] investigated Debian package dependency conflicts. Figure 4.61 shows the survival curve of package lifetime, and the interval to a package's first conflict.

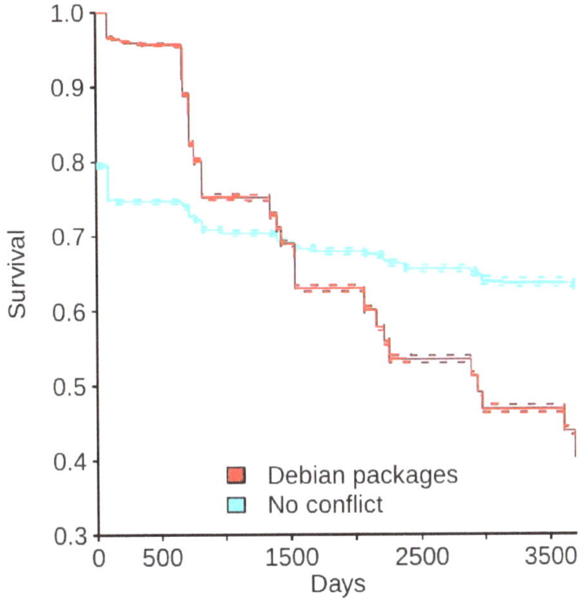

Figure 4.61: Survival curves for Debian package lifetime and interval before a package contains its first dependency conflict; dashed lines are 95% confidence intervals. Data from Drobisz et al. Github-Local

A study by Decan, Mens and Claes [467] investigated how the package dependencies of three ecosystems changed over time (npm over 6 -years, CRAN 18 -years, and RubyGems over 7-years). The dependencies in roughly two-thirds of CRAN and RubyGems packages specified greater-than or equal to some version, with the other third not specifying any specific version; npm package dependencies specified greater-than in just under two-thirds of cases, with a variety of version strings making up the other uses (particular version numbers were common); see Github-ecosystems/SANER-2017.R

Third-party libraries may contain undocumented functionality that is accessible to developers. This functionality may be intended for internal library use, and is only accessible because it is not possible to prevent developers accessing it; or, the vendor intent is to provide privileged access to internal functionality for their own applications, e.g., Microsoft Word using undocumented functionality in the libraries available in Microsoft Windows. [658]

There may be a short term benefit for developers making use of internal functionality, that makes it worth the risk of paying an unknown cost later if the internal functionality is removed or modified; see fig 11.76. Information on undocumented functionality in

Microsoft Windows was widely available, [1655] with major Windows updates occurring every three years, or so.

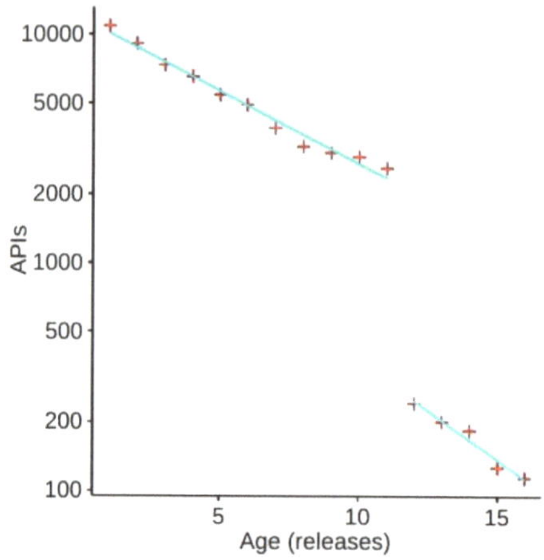

Figure 4.62: Number of Android APIs surviving a given number of releases (measured over 17 releases), with fitted regression lines. Data from Li et al. Github-Local

Major updates to Android have occurred once or twice a year (see fig 8.37), and figure 4.62 shows how the lifetime of internal functionality has been declining exponentially.

When creating an application that is very similar to another application, if the source code is available it can be treated as a library from which to pick and choose functionality to reuse in the new application (assuming license compatibility).

A study by Reibel, Yousaf and Meiklejohn [1570] investigated the sharing of source code files across 1,663 cryptocurrency platforms. Figure 4.63 shows a phylogenetic tree based on the similarity of implementations across 1,663 cryptocurrency platforms (based on the fraction of identical source code files shared between implementations).

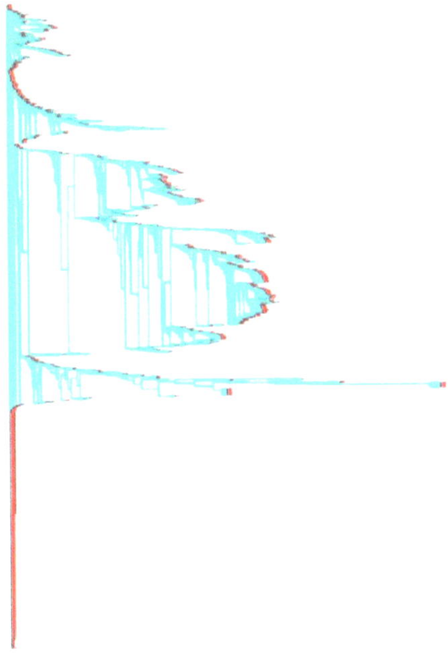

Figure 4.63: Phylogenetic tree of 1,663 cryptocurrency implementations, based on the fraction of shared source code files. Data kindly provided by Yousaf. [1570] Github-Local

4.6.3 Tools

Computer manufacturers were the primary suppliers of software development tools until suppliers of third-party tools gained cost-effective access to the necessary hardware, and the potential customer base became large enough to make it commercially attractive for third-parties to create and sell tools.

When developer tools are sold for profit, the vendor has an incentive to keep both customer and the tool users happy. [xx] Open source has significantly reduced the number of customers for some tools (e.g., compilers), without decreasing the number of users. A company creating their own cpu needs to support at least a C compiler. Funding the implementation of a code generator, based on an Open source compiler allows them to make available a free compiler tool chain for their cpu; the users of this tool chain are the actual product.

The development environment in which tools are used can have a big impact on the functionality provided, with sophisticated functionality being dropped in new products only to reappear again many years later. For instance, during the early years of computing, interaction with computers was usually via batch processing, rather than one-line access; [694] users submitted a job for the computer to perform (i.e., a sequence of commands to execute), and it joined the queue of jobs waiting to be run. Developers might only complete one or two edit/compile/execute cycles per day. In this environment, high quality compiler error recovery can significantly boost developer productivity; having an executable for an error corrected version of the submitted source (along with a list of errors found), gives developers a binary that may be patched to do something useful. [xxi] Borland's Turbo-Pascal stopped compiling at the first error it encountered, dropping the user into an editor with the cursor located at the point the error was detected. Compilation was so fast, within its interactive environment on a personal computer, developers loved using it. Error recovery in modern compilers, at the time of writing, has yet to return to the level of sophistication available in some early mainframe compilers.

Adding support for new language features, new processors and environments is a source of income for compiler vendors; the performance of code generated by compilers are often benchmarked, to find which generates the faster and/or more compact code.

Compile time options provide a means for users to tailor compiler behavior to their needs. Figure 4.64 shows the number of options supported by gcc for specific C and C^{++}options, and various compiler phases, for 96 releases between 1999 and 2019; during this time the total number of supported options grew from 632 to 2,477 .

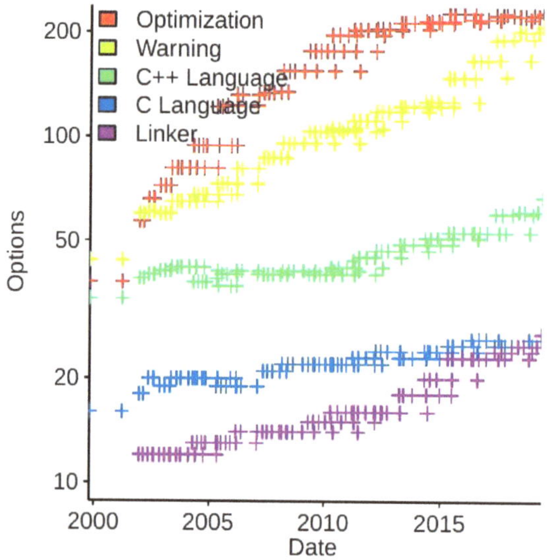

Figure 4.64: Number of gcc compiler options, for all supported versions, relating to languages and the process of building an executable program. Data extracted from gcc website. Github-Local

Support for an option is sometimes removed; of the 1,091 non-processor specific options supported, 214 were removed before release 9.1. Since 1999, the official release of GCC has included support for 80 cpus, with support for 20 of these removed before release 9.1; see fig 4.13.

4.6.4 Information sources

Readily available sources of reliable information can help reduce the friction of working within an ecosystem, and can significantly reduce the investment that has to be made by outsiders to join an ecosystem.

Vendors that support an API have to document the available interfaces and provide examples, if they want developers, third-party or otherwise, to make use of the services they provide. APIs evolve, and the documentation has to be kept up todate. [1694] The growth of popular APIs, over time, can result in an enormous collection of documentation, e.g., the 130 + documents for the Microsoft Server protocol specifications [1277] contain over 16 thousand pages; see fig 8.24. Figure 4.65 shows how the number of words in Intel's x86 architecture manual has grown over time.

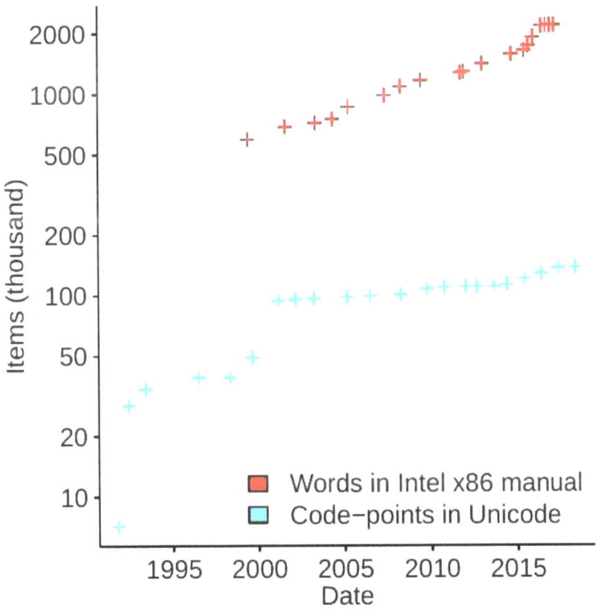

Figure 4.65: Words in Intel ×86 architecture manuals, and code-points in Unicode Standard over time. Data for Intel x86 manual kindly provided by Baumann. Github-Local

Books are a source of organized and collated material. Technical books are rarely profitable for their authors, but can act as an advert for the author's expertise, who may offer consultancy or training services. A high quality book, or manual, may reduce the size of the pool of potential clients, but is a signal to those remaining of a potential knowledgeable supplier of consultancy/training.

While executable source code is definitive, comments contained in code may be incorrect or out of date; in particular links in source code may cease to work. [783]

Chapter 5

Projects

5.1 Introduction

The hardest part of any project is, generally, obtaining the funding to implement it. [1658] Clients [i] are paying for a solution to a problem, and have decided that a software system is likely to provide a cost effective solution. The client might be a large organization contracting a third party to develop a new system, or update an existing system, a company writing software for internal use, or an individual spending their own time scratching an itch (who might then attract other developers [809]).

Successfully implementing a software system involves creating a financially viable implementation that solves the client's problem. Financial viability means not so expensive the client is unable to pay for it, and not so cheap that the software vendor fails to make a reasonable profit.

Commercial software projects aim to implement the clients' understanding of the world (in which they operate, or want to operate), in a computer executable model that can be integrated into the business, and be economically operated.

It can be unwise to ask clients why they want the software. Be thankful that somebody is willing to pay to have bespoke software written, [754] creating employment for software developers. For instance:

"The first go-around at it was about $750 million, so you figure that's not a bad cost overrun for an IT project. Then I said, "Well, now, tell me. Did you do an NPV? Did you do a ROI? What did you do on a $750 million IT investment?" And she sort of looked a little chagrined and she said, "Well, actually, there was no analysis done on that." I said, "Excuse me . . . can you explain that to me please. That's not what the textbook says." She said, "Well, it was a sales organization, the brokers worked for the sales organization." The sales organization - this was a few years ago when the brokerage business was extremely good - said, "you know, the last two years we've made more than enough money to pay for this. We want it, and we're going to pay for it." And the board of directors looked at how much money they were making and they said, "You go pay for it". So that was the investment analysis for a $750 million IT investment that turned into a billion dollars." [1808]

The difference between projects in evidence-based engineering disciplines (e.g., bridge building in civil engineering), and projects in disciplines where evidence-based practices have not been established (e.g., software development), is that in the former implementation involves making the optimum use of known alternatives, while the latter involves discovering what the workable alternatives might be, e.g., learning, by trying ideas until something that works well enough is discovered.

Building a software system is a creative endeavour; however, it differs from artistic creative endeavours in that the externally visible narrative has to interface with customer reality. Factory production builds duplicates based on an exemplar product, and can be a costly process; software duplication is a trivial process that has virtually zero cost.

Useful programs vary in size from a few lines of code, to millions of lines, and might be written by an individual in under an hour, or by thousands of developers over many years.

Much of the existing software engineering research has focused on large projects, reasons for this include: the bureaucracy needed to support large projects creates paperwork from which data can be extracted for analysis, and the large organizations providing the large sums needed to finance large projects are able to sway research agendas. This book is driven by the availability of data, and much of this data comes from large projects and open source; small commercial projects are important; they are much more common than large projects, and it is possible they are economically more important.

What are the characteristics of the majority of software projects? Figure 5.1, using data from a multi-year data collection process [27] by the Software Engineering Center, of Japan's Information-Technology Promotion Agency, shows that most are completed in under a year, contain less than 40 KSLOC and that much of the effort is performed by external contractors

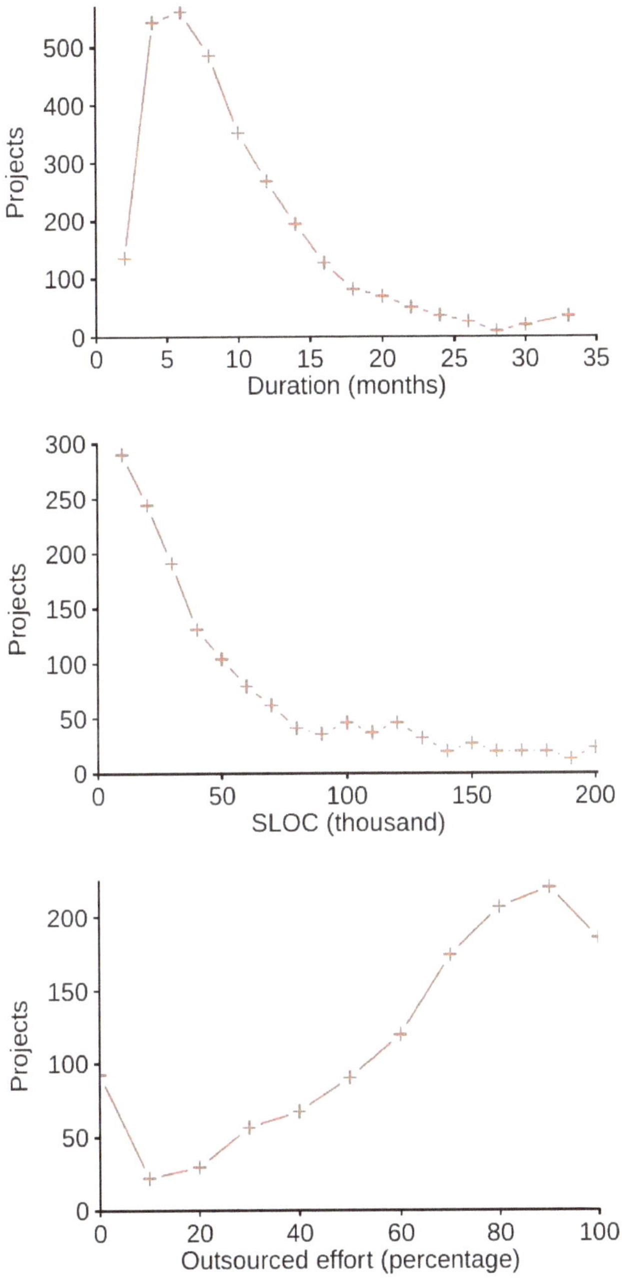

Figure 5.1: Number of projects having a given duration (upper; 2,992 projects), delivered containing a given number of SLOC (middle; 1,859 projects), and using a given percentage of out-sourced effort (lower; 1,267 projects). Data extracted from Akita et al. Github-Local

When approached by a potential client, about creating a bespoke software system, the first question a vendor tries to answer is: does the client have the resources needed to pay for implementing such a software system? If the client appears to be willing to commit the money (and internal resources), the vendor may consider it worth investing to obtain a good-enough view on the extent to which the client desires can be implemented well enough for them to pay for a bespoke software system to be built.

The head of NASA told President Kennedy that \$20 billion was the price tag for landing on the Moon (NASA engineers had previously estimated a cost of $\$10 - 12$ billion [1666]); the final cost was \$24 billion.

A study by Anda, Sjøberg and Mockus [54] sent a request to tender to 81 software consultancy companies in Norway, 46 did not respond with bids. Figure 5.2 shows the estimated schedule days, and bid price received, from 14 companies (21 companies provided a bid price without a schedule estimate). Fitting a regression model that includes information on an assessment of the analysis, and design performed by each company, along with estimated planned effort, explains almost 90% of the variation in the schedule estimates; see Github-projects/effort-bidprice.R.

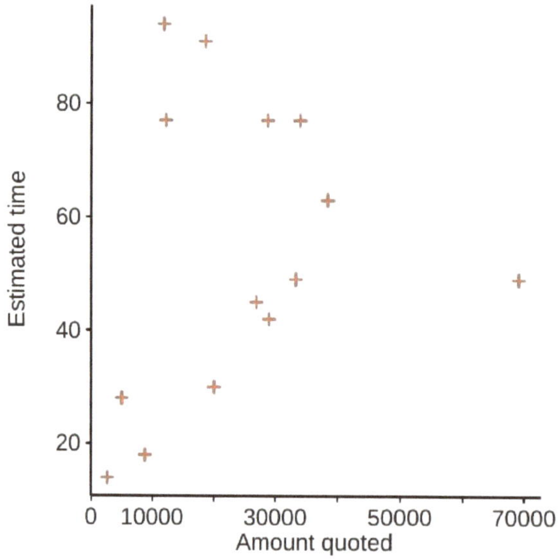

Figure 5.2: Firm bid price (in euros) against schedule estimate (in days), received from 14 companies, for the same tender specification. Data from Anda et al. Github-Local

Both the client and the vendor want their project to be a success. What makes a project a success?

From the vendor perspective (this book's point of view), a successful project is one that produces an acceptable profit [ii]. A project may be a success from the vendor's perspective, and be regarded as a failure by the client (because the client paid, but did not use the completed system, [22] or because users under-utilised the delivered system, or avoided using it [1096]), or by the developers who worked on the project (because they created a workable system despite scheduling and costing underestimates by management [1150]). These different points of view mean that the answers given to project success surveys [51] are open to multiple interpretations.

A study by Milis [1281] investigated views of project success by professionals in the roles of management, team member (either no subsequent project involvement after handover, or likely to receive project benefits after returning to their department), and end-user. Fitting regression models to the data from 25 projects, for each role, finds one explanatory variable of project success common to all roles: user happiness with the system. Management considered being within budget as an indicator of success, while other roles were more interested in meeting the specification; see Github-projects/Milis-PhD.R.

A project may fail because the users of a system resist its introduction into their workflow, [1085] e.g., they perceive its use as a threat to their authority. Failure to deliver a system can result in the vendor having to refund any money paid by the client, and make a payment for work performed by the client. [86]

The Queensland Health Payroll System Commission of inquiry report [348] provides a detailed analysis of a large failed project.

A study by Zwikael and Globerson [2035] investigated project cost and schedule overruns, and success in various industries, including software. The results suggest that except for the construction industry, overrun rates are broadly similar.

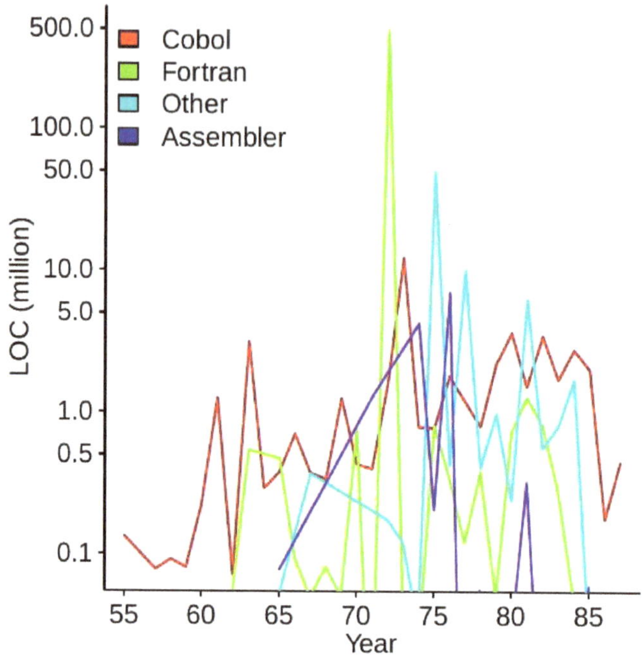

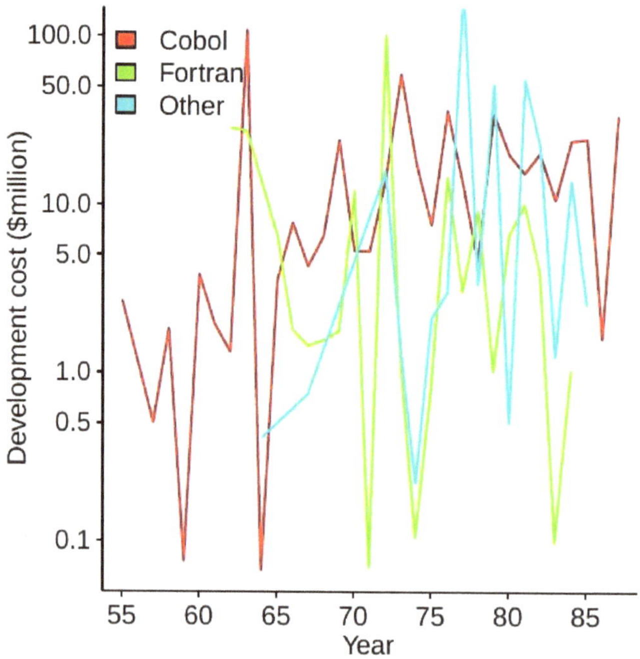

Figure 5.3: Annual development cost and lines of code delivered to the US Air Force between 1960 and 1986. Data extracted from NeSmith. Github-Local

Almost as soon as computers became available million line programs were being written to order. Figure 5.3 shows lines of code and development costs for US Air Force software projects, by year, excluding classified projects and embedded systems; the spiky nature of the data suggests that LOC and development costs are counted in the year a project is delivered.

5.1.1 Project culture

Software projects are often implemented within existing business cultural frameworks, which provides the structure for the power and authority to those involved. A project's assigned or perceived power and authority controls the extent to which either: outsiders have to adapt to the needs of the project, or the project has to be adapted to the ecosystems in which it is being created and is intended to be used. The following are some common development culture frameworks:

- one-off projects within an organization, which treats software as a necessary investment that has to be made to keep some aspect of the business functioning. Employees involved in the development might treat working on the project as a temporary secondment that is part of what they perceive to be their main job, or perhaps a stepping stone to a promotion, or a chance to get hands-on experience developing software (maybe with a view to doing this kind of job full time). External contractors may be hired to work on the project,
- projects within an organization, which derives most of its income from software products, e.g., software developed to be sold as a product; see fig 5.56. In the case of startups, the projects implemented early in the company's life may be produced in an organizational vacuum, and thus have the opportunity to mold the company culture experienced by future projects,
- projects within an organization, where software is the enabler of the products and services that form the basis of its business model, e.g., embedded systems.

A study by Powell [1517] investigated software projects for engine control systems at Rolls-Royce. Figure 5.4 shows effort distribution (in person hours) over four projects (various colors), plus non-project work (blue) and holidays (purple'ish, at the top), over 20 months. Staff turnover and use of overtime during critical periods means that total effort changes over time; also see fig 11.73.

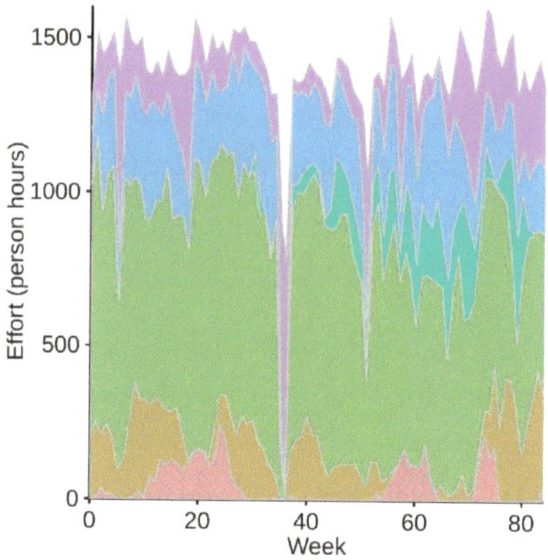

Figure 5.4: Distribution of effort (person hours) during the development of four engine control system projects (various colors), plus non-project work (blue) and holidays (purple'ish, at top), at Rolls-Royce. Data extracted from Powell. Github-Local

In its 2015 financial year Mozilla, a non-profit company that develops and supports the Firefox browser, had income of $421,275 million and spent $214,187 million on software development. [849] Almost all of this income came from Google, who paid to be Firefox's default search engine,

- contract software development, where one-off projects are paid for by other organization for their own use. Companies in the contract software development business need to keep their employees busy with fee earning work, and assigning them to work on multiple projects is one way of reducing the likelihood of an employee not producing income, i.e., while a single project may be put on hold until some event occurs, multiple projects are less likely to be on hold at the same time.

Companies in the business of bespoke software development have to make a profit on average, over all projects undertaken within some period, i.e., they have some flexibility in over- and underestimating the cost of individual projects. Figure 5.5 shows the percentage loss/profit made by a software house on 146 fixed-price projects.

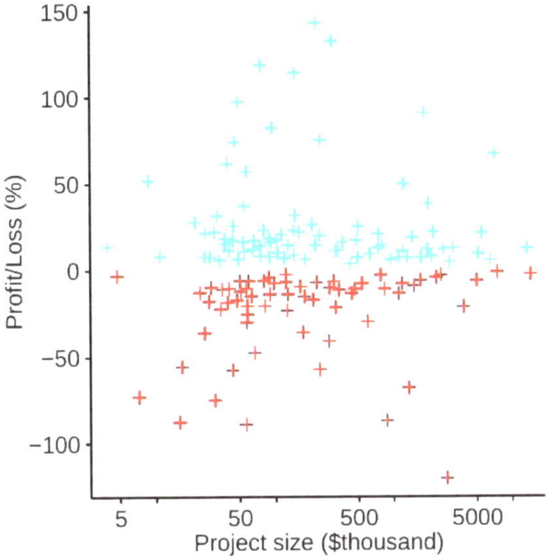

Figure 5.5: Percentage profit/loss on 145 fixed-price software development contracts. Data extracted from Coombs. Github-Local

- projects where the participants receive income in the form of enjoyment derived from the work involved; the implementation is part of the developers' lifestyle.

The characteristics of single person projects are likely to experience greater variation than larger projects, not because the creator is driven by hedonism, but because a fixed release criteria may not exist, and other activities may cause work to be interrupted for indefinite periods of time, i.e., measurements of an individual is likely to have greater variance than a collection of people.

A few single developer projects grow to include hundreds of paid and volunteer developers. The development work for projects such as Linux [401] and GCC is spread over multiple organizations, making it difficult to estimate the level of commercial funding.

Code commits made by volunteer developers are less likely to occur during the working week than commits made by paid developers. Figure 5.6 shows the hourly commits during a week (summed over all commits) for Linux and FreeBSD. The significant difference in number of commits during the week, compared to the weekend, suggests that Linux has a higher percentage of work performed by paid developers than FreeBSD.

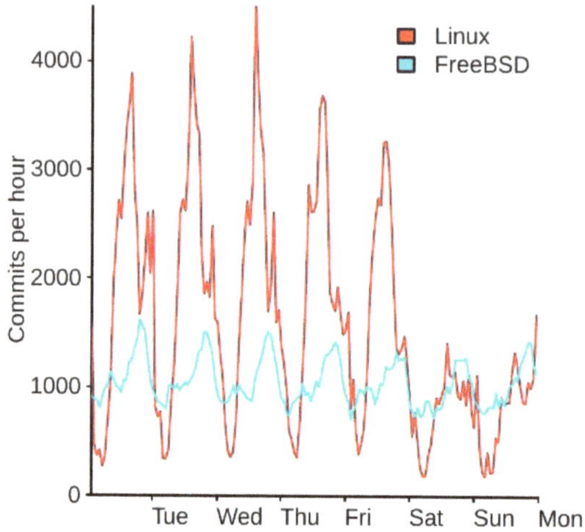

Figure 5.6: Commits within a particular hour and day of week for Linux and FreeBSD. Data from Eyolfson et al. Github-Local

Academic software projects can appear within any of these categories (with personal reputation being the income sought [1330]).

Those involved in software projects, like all other human activities, sometimes engage in subversion and lying, [1608] activities range from departmental infighting to individual rivalry, and motivations include: egotism, defending one's position, revenge, or a disgruntled employee.

5.1.2 Project lifespan

Projects continue to live for as long as they are funded, and can only exceed their original budget when the client is willing to pay (because they have an expectation of delivery). Having a solution to some problems is sufficiently important that clients have no choice but to pay what it takes, and wait for delivery. [1250] For instance, when not having a working software system is likely to result in the client ceasing to be competitive, resulting in ruin or a loss significantly greater than the cost of paying for the software.

The funding of some projects is driven by company politics, [181] and/or senior management ego, and a project might be cancelled for reasons associated with how it came to be funded, independently of any issues associated with project performance.

A non-trivial percentage of projects, software and non-software, [1249] are cancelled without ever being used, e.g., VMware cancelled the project [276] to enhance their x86 emulator to support the x86 architecture functionality needed to support OS/2. Open source and personal projects are not cancelled as-such, those involved simply stop working on them. [377] The cost-effectiveness of any investment decision (e.g., investing to create software that is cheaper to maintain) has to include the risk that the project is cancelled.

- a study by El Emam and Koru [538] surveyed 84 midlevel and senior project managers, between 2005 and 2007; they found the majority reporting IT project cancellation rates in the range 11 – 40%. A study by Whitfield [1949] investigated 105 outsourced UK government related ICT (Information and Communication Technology) projects between 1997 and 2007 having a total value of £29.6 billion; 57% of contracts experienced cost overruns (totalling £9.0 billion, with an average cost overrun of 30.5%), of which 30% were terminated,
- the 1994 CHAOS report [1758] is a commonly cited survey of project cost overruns and cancellations. This survey is not representative because it explicitly focuses on failures, subjects were asked: ". . . to share failure stories.", i.e., the report lists many failures and high failure rates because subjects were asked to provide this very information. The accuracy of the analysis used to calculate the summary statistics listed in the report has been questioned. [565,956]

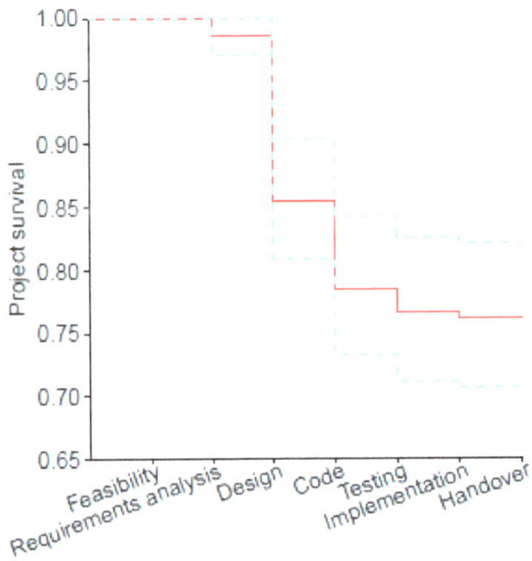

Figure 5.7: Survival rate of 214 projects, by development stage, with 95% confidence intervals. Data from Mc-Manus et al.

A study by McManus and Wood-Harper [1245] investigated the sources of failure of information systems projects. Figure 5.7 shows the survival curve for 214 projects, by development stage.

Software systems are sometimes used for many years after development on them has stopped.

5.2 Pitching for projects

Bidding on a request for tender, convincing senior management to fund a project, selling the benefits of a bespoke solution to potential a client: all involve making commitments that can directly impact project implementation. An appreciation of some of the choices made when pitching for a project is useful for understanding why things are the way they are.

What motivates anyone to invest the resources needed to form a good enough estimate to implement some software?

The motivation for bidding on a tender comes from the profit derived from winning the implementation contract, while for internal projects, developers are performing one of the jobs they are employed to perform.

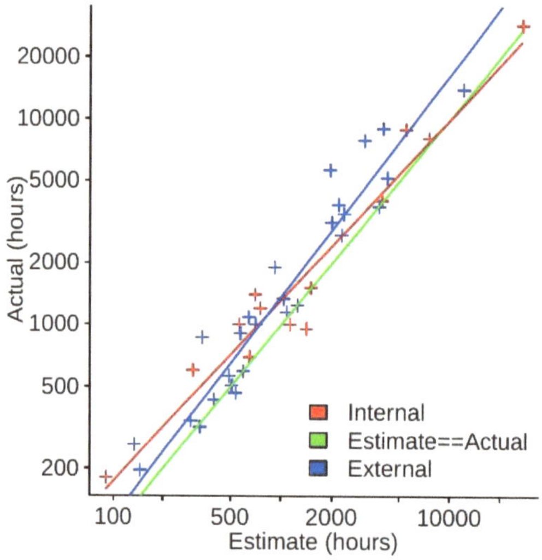

Figure 5.8: Estimated and Actual effort for internal and external projects, lines are fitted regression models; both lines are fitted regression models of the form: Actual $\propto$ Estimate ^{a}, where a takes the value 0.9 or 1.1. Data from Moløkken-Østvold et al. Github-

A study by Moløkken-Østvold, Jørgensen, Tanilkan, Gallis, Lien and Hove [1307] investigated 44 software project estimates made by 18 companies; the estimates were either for external client projects, or internal projects. A fitted regression model finds that estimated project duration was longer for internal projects, compared to external client projects; see Github-projects/RK31-surveycostestim.R.

Figure 5.8 shows the estimated and actual effort for internal (red) and external (blue) projects, along with fitted regression models. Most estimates are underestimates (i.e., above the green line); for smaller projects external projects are more accurately estimated than internal estimates, but for larger projects internal projects are more accurately estimated.

A client interested in funding the development of bespoke software may change their mind, if they hear a price that is much higher than expected, or a delivery date much later than desired. Optimal frog boiling entails starting low, and increasing at a rate that does not disturb. However, estimates have to be believable (e.g., what do clients consider to be the minimum credible cost, and what is their maximum willing to spend limit), and excessive accuracy can cause people to question the expertise of those providing the estimate. [1161]

Companies in the business of developing bespoke software need to maintain a pipeline of projects, opening with client qualification and closing with contract signature. [1733] Acquiring paying project work is the responsibility of the sales department, and is outside the scope of this book.

Many of the factors involved in project bidding are likely to be common to engineering projects in general, e.g., highway procurement. [119] Bidding decisions can be driven by factors that have little or no connection with the technical aspects of software implementation, or its costs; some of these factors include:

- likelihood of being successful on bids for other projects. If work is currently scarce, it may be worthwhile accepting a small profit margin, or even none at all, simply to have work that keeps the business ticking over. A software development organization, whether it employs one person or thousands, needs to schedule its activities to keep everyone busy, and the money flowing in.
- Some of the schedule estimates in figure 5.2 might be explained by companies assigning developers to more than one project at the same time; maintaining staff workload by having something else for them to do, if they are blocked from working on their primary project,

- bid the maximum price the client is currently willing to pay; a profitable strategy when the client estimate is significantly greater than the actual. If the client perceives a project to be important enough, they are likely to be willing to pay more once existing monies have been spent. From the client perspective, it is better to pay £2 million for a system that provides a good return on investment, than the £1 million actually budgeted, if the lower price system is not worth having,
- the likely value of estimates submitted by other bidders; competition is a hard taskmaster,
- bidding low to win, and ensuring that wording in the contract allows for increases due to unanticipated work. Prior experience shows that clients often want to change the requirements, and estimates for these new requirements are made after the competitive bidding process; see fig 3.23. The report by the Queensland health payroll system commission of inquiry [348] offers some insight into this approach. Clients often prefer to continue to work with a supplier who has run into difficulties, [231] even substantial ones,
- bidding low to win, with the expectation of recouping any losses and making profit during the maintenance phase. This strategy is based on having a reasonable expectation that the client will use the software for many years, that the software will need substantial maintenance, and that the complexity of the system and quality of internal documentation will deter competitive maintenance bids,
- bidding on projects that are small, relative to the size of the development company, as a means of getting a foot in the door to gain access to work involving larger projects, e.g., becoming an approved supplier.

The bidding process for projects usually evolves over time.A study by Jørgensen and Carelius investigated the impact of changes to the project specification on the amount bid. Estimators in group A made an estimate based on a one-page specification, and sometime later a second estimate based on an eleven-page specification; estimators in group B made an estimate based on the eleven-page specification only. Figure 5.9 shows bids made by two groups of estimators from the same company; for additional analysis, see Github-projects/proj-bidding.R.

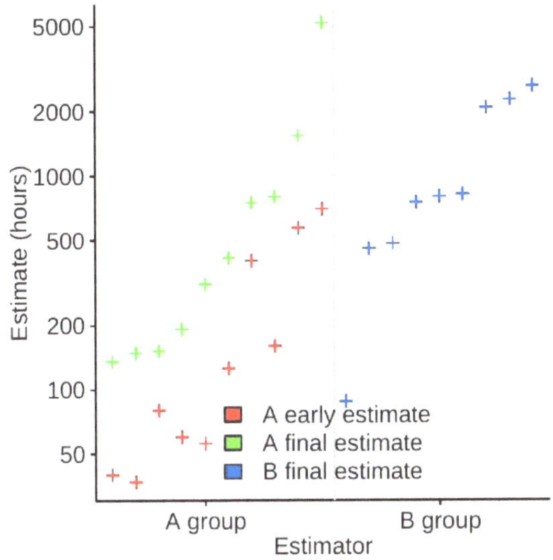

Figure 5.9: Bids made by 19 estimators from the same company (divided by grey line into the two experimental groups). Data from Jørgensen et al. Github-Local

The signing of a contract signals the start of development work, not the end of client cost negotiation.

The bidding on a project for a new IT system for Magistrates' Courts (the Libra project), [231] started with ICL submitting a bid of £146 million, when it became public there was only one bidder this was increased to £184 million over 10.5 years, a contract was signed, then a revised contract was renegotiated for £319 million, then ICL threatened to repudiate the renegotiated contract and proposed a new price of £400 million, then reduced its proposed price to £384 million, and after agreement could not be reached signed a revised contract for £232 million over 8.5 years.

5.2.1 Contracts

Contract signing is the starting point for investing resources in project implementation (although some projects never involve a contract, and some work may start before a contract is signed). Having to read a contract after it has been signed is an indication that one of the parties involved is not happy; nobody wants to involve lawyers in sorting out a signed contract. [1233]

A practical contract includes provisions for foreseeable items such as client changes to the requirements and schedule slippage. Developers and clients can have very different views about the risks involved in a project. [1061]

What is the payment schedule for the project? The two primary contract payment schedules are fixed price and time and materials (also known as cost plus; where the client pays the vendors costs plus an agreed percentage profit, e.g., a margin of $10 - 15\%$[1534]).

On projects of any size, agreed payments are made at specified milestones. Milestones are a way for the client to monitor progress, and the vendor to receive income for the work they have done. The use of milestones favours a sequential development viewpoint, and one study [84] found that the waterfall model is effectively written into contracts.

From the client's perspective a fixed price contract appears attractive, but from the vendor's perspective this type of contract may be unacceptably risky. One study [709] found that vendors preferred a fixed price contract when they could increase their profit margin by leveraging particular staff expertise; another study [1135] found that fixed-price was only used by clients for trusted vendors. Writing a sufficiently exact specification of what a software system is expected to do, along with tightly defined acceptance criteria is timeconsuming and costly, which means the contract has to contain mechanisms to handle changes to the requirements; such mechanisms are open to exploitation by both clients and vendors.

A time and materials contract has the advantage that vendors are willing to accept openended requirements, but has the disadvantage (to the client) that the vendor has no incentive to keep costs down.

Contracts sometimes include penalty clauses and incentive fees (which are meaningless unless linked to performance targets [547]).

A study by Webster [1938] analysed legal disputes involving system failures in the period 1976-2000 (120 were found). The cases could be broadly divided into seven categories: client claims the installed system is defective in some way and vendor fails to repair it, installed system does not live up to the claims made by the vendor, a project starts and the date of final delivery continues to slip and remain in the future, unplanned obsolescence (client discovers that the system either no longer meets its needs or that the vendor will no longer support it), the vendor changes the functionality or configuration of the system resulting in unpleasant or unintended consequences for one or more clients, a three-way tangle between vendor, leasing company and client, and miscellaneous.

Many commercial transactions are governed by standard form contracts. A study by Marotta-Wurgler [1208] analysed 647 software license agreements from various markets; almost all had a net bias, relative to relevant default rules, in favor of the software company (who wrote the agreement).

A contract involving the licensing of source code, or other material, may require the licensor to assert that they have the rights needed to enter into the licensing agreement; intellectual property licensing is discussed in section 3.3.1. Project management has to be vigilant that developers working on a project do not include material licensed under an agreement that is not compatible with the license used by the project, e.g., material that has been downloaded from the Internet. [1734]

It is possible for both the client and vendor to be in an asymmetric information situation, in terms of knowledge of the problem being solved, the general application domain, and what software systems are capable of doing; the issue of moral hazard is discussed in section 3.4.7.

A study by Ahonen, Savolainen, Merikoski and Nevalainen [23] investigated the impact of contract type on reported project management effort for 117 projects; 61 projects had fixed-price contracts, and 56 time-and-materials contracts.

Figure 5.10 shows project effort (in thousands of hours) against percentage of reported management time, broken down by fixed-priced and time-and-material contracts; lines are fitted regression models. Fitting a regression model that includes team size (see Github-projects/ahonen2015.R), finds that time-and-materials contracts involve 25% less management time (it is not possible to estimate the impact of contract choice on project effort).

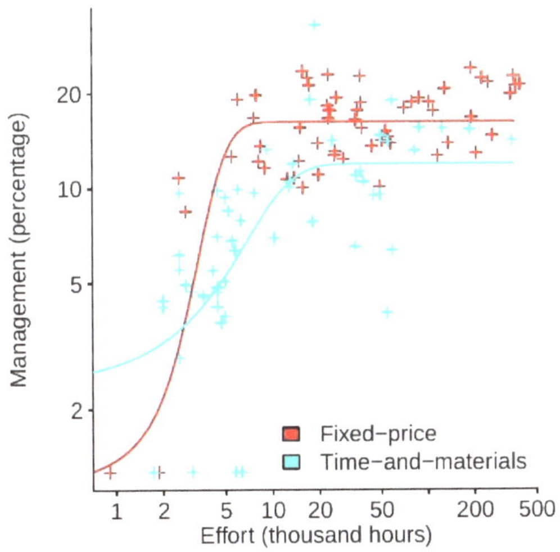

Figure 5.10: Project effort, in thousands of hours, against percentage of management time, broken down by contract type; both lines are fitted logistic equations with maximums of 12% and 16%. Data extracted from Ahonen. Github-Local

Tools intended to aid developers in checking compliance with the contractual rights and obligations specified in a wide range of licenses are starting to become available. [1197]

5.3 Resource estimation

Resource estimation is the process of calculating a good enough estimate [iii] of the resources needed to create software whose behavior is partially specified, when the work is to be done by people who have not previously written software having the same behavior. Retrospective analysis of previous projects [1501] can provide insight into common mistakes.

This section discusses the initial resource estimation process; ongoing resource estimation, performed once a project is underway, is discussed in section 5.4.4. The techniques used to produce estimate values are based on previous work that is believed to have similarities with the current project; the more well known of these techniques are discussed in section 5.3.1.

Client uncertainty about exactly what they want can have a major impact on the reliability of any estimate of the resources required. Discovering the functionality needed for acceptance is discussed in section 5.4.5.

When making an everyday purchase decision, potential customers have an expectation that the seller can, and will, provide information on cost and delivery date; an expectation of being freely given an accurate answer is not considered unreasonable. People cling to the illusion that it's reasonable to ask for accurate estimates to be made about the future (even when they have not measured the effort involved in previous projects).

Unless the client is willing to pay for a detailed analysis of the proposed project, there is no incentive for vendors to invest in a detailed analysis until a contract is signed.

While the reasons of wanting a cost estimate cannot be disputed, an analysis of the number of unknowns involved in a project, and the experience of those involved can lead to the conclusion that it is unreasonable to expect accurate resource estimates.

The largest item cost for many projects is the cost of the time of people involved. These people need to have a minimum set of required skills, and a degree of dedication; this issue is discussed in section 5.5.

Cost overruns are often blamed on poor project management, [1102] however, the estimates may be the product of rational thinking during the bidding process, e.g., a low bid swayed the choice of vendor.

People tend to be overconfident, and a cost/benefit analysis shows that within a population, individual overconfidence is an evolutionary stable cognitive bias; see section 2.8.5.

It should not be surprising that inaccurate resource estimates are endemic in many industries [1267] (and perhaps all human activities), software projects are just one instance. A study by Flyvbjerg, Holm and Buhl [619] of 258 transportation projects (worth $90 billion) found costs are underestimating in around 90% of projects, with an average cost overrun of 28% (sd 39); a study of 35 major US DOD acquisitions [218] found a 60% average growth in total costs; an analysis of 12 studies, [848] covering over 1,000 projects, found a

Those working on a project may have experience from personal involvement in the implementation of other projects (organizational forgetting is discussed in section 3.4.5). The extent to which experience gained on the implementation of other projects can be used to help formulate a reliable estimate for a new project depends on shared similarities, such as: performance of the individuals involved (e.g., knowledge, skill and cognitive capacity; figure 2.36 shows that a developer can sometimes spend more time reimplementing the same specification), interactions between team members, interactions with real-world events that occur during the projects, e.g., interruptions, uncontrolled delays, client involvement.

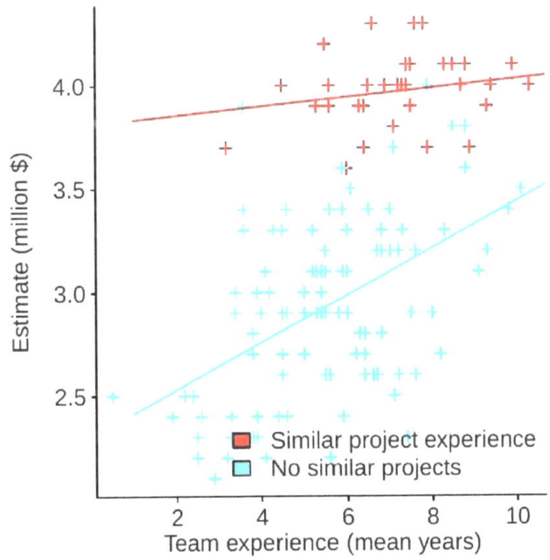

Figure 5.11: Mean number of years experience of each team against estimated project code, with fitted regression models; broken down by teams containing one or more members who have had similar project experience, or not. Data from Mcdonald. Github-Local

A study by Mcdonald [1238] investigated the impact of team experience on the estimated cost of one project (which teams of professional managers had each planned for approximately 20 hours). Figure 5.11 shows the mean number of years experience of each of the 135 teams, and their estimate; teams are broken down into those having at least one member who had previous experience on a similar project, and those that did not (straight lines are fitted regression models).

Unknown and changeable factors introduce random noise into the estimation process; on average, accuracy may be good. Figure 5.12 shows regression models fitted to two estimation datasets, the green line shows where actual equals estimate. The trend for the 49 blue projects [946] is to (slightly) overestimate, while the 145 red project [1014] trend is to (slightly) underestimate.

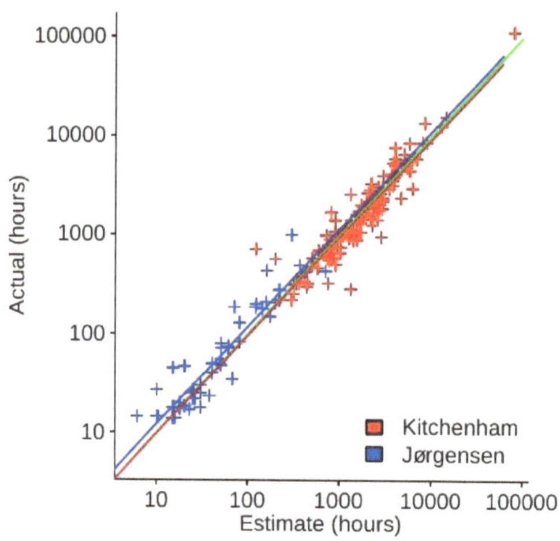

Figure 5.12: Estimated and actual project implementation effort; 49 web implementation tasks (blue), and 145 tasks performed by an outsourcing company (red). Data from Jørgensen and Kitchenham et al. Github-Local

Resource estimation is a knowledge based skill, acquired through practical experience and learning from others (expertise is discussed in section 2.5.2); an individual's attitude to risk has also been found to have an impact. [941]

A study by Grimstad and Jørgensen investigated the consistency of estimates made by the same person. Seven developers were asked to estimate sixty tasks (in work hours), over a period of three months; unknown to them, everybody estimated six tasks twice. Figure 5.13 shows the first/second estimates for the same task made by the same subject; identical first/second estimates appear on the grey line, with estimates for identical tasks having the same color (the extent of color clustering shows agreement between developers).

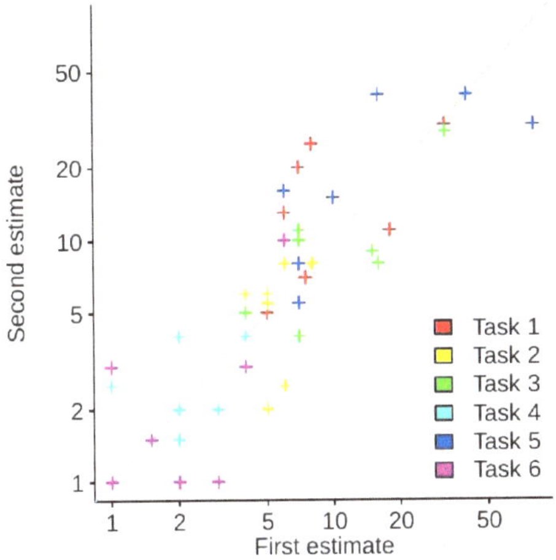

Figure 5.13: Two estimates (in work hours), made by seven subjects, for each of six tasks. Data from Grimstad et al. Github-Local

A study by Jørgensen [947] selected six vendors, from 16 proposals received from a tender request, to each implement the same database-based system. The estimated price per work-hour ranged from $9.1 to $28.8 (mean $13.85).

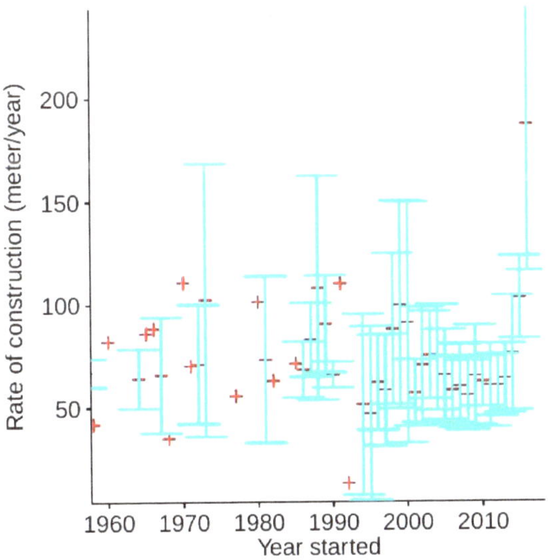

Figure 5.14: Mean rate of construction, in meters per year, of skyscrapers taller than 150 m (error bars show standard deviation). Data kindly provided by Recon. Github-Local mean estimation error of 21%; Butts and Linton give a detailed discussion of overruns on the development of over 150 NASA spacecraft.

Skyscraper construction is like software projects, in that each is a one-off, sharing many implementation details with other skyscrapers, but also having significant unique implementation features. Figure 5.14 shows that the rate of construction of skyscrapers (in meters per year), has remaining roughly unchanged.

Some of the factors influencing the client and/or vendor resource estimation process include:

- the incentives of those making the estimate.

When estimating in a competitive situation (e.g., bidding on a request to tender), the incentive is to bid as low as possible; once a project is underway, the client has little alternative but to pay more (project overruns receive the media attention, and so this is the more well-known case).

When estimating is not part of a bidding process (e.g., internal projects, where those making the estimate may know the work needs to be done, and are not concerned with being undercut by competitors), one strategy is to play safe and overestimate, delivering under budget is often seen by management in a positive light, [iv]

- the cost of making the estimate.

Is it cost effective to invest as much time estimating as it is likely to take doing the job? It depends on who is paying for the estimate, and the probability of recouping the investment in making the estimate. Unless the client is paying, time spent estimating is likely to be a small fraction of an initial crude estimate of the time needed to do the job.

- estimating is a social process (see fig 2.64), people often want to get along with others, which means prior estimation information can have an impact. Client expectations can have an anchoring effect on cost estimates [957] (one study [1693] found that it was possible to reduce this effect; see Github-projects/DeBiasExptData.R).

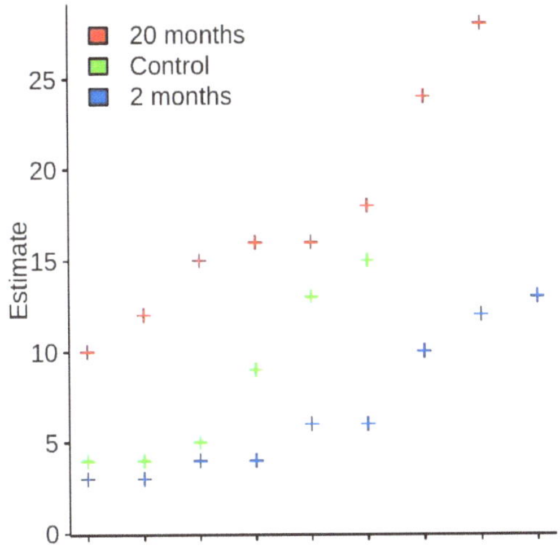

Figure 5.15: Estimates given by three groups of subjects after seeing a statement by a middle manager containing an estimate (2 months or 20 months) or no estimate (control); sorted to highlight distribution. Data from Aranda. Github-Local

- A study by Aranda [68] investigated the impact of anchoring on estimated task effort. Subjects (13 professionals, 10 academics) were asked to estimate how long it would take to deliver a software system specified in a document they were given. The document contained a statement from a middle manager, either expressing no opinion, or guessing that the project would take 2 -months, or 20 -months. Figure 5.15 shows the estimates made by subjects who saw a particular middle manager opinion (sorted to show estimate variability),
- pressure is applied to planners [1912] to ensure their analysis presents a positive case for project funding. A former president of the American Planning Association said: [618] "I believe planners and consultants in general deliberately underestimate project costs because their political bosses or clients want the projects. Sometimes, to tell the truth is to risk your job or your contracts or the next contract . . ."
- cognitive processing of numeric values can lead to different answers being given, e.g., the measurement units used (such monthly or yearly); [1863] see section 2.7.2.

Projects are often divided into separate phases of development, e.g., requirements analysis, design, implementation, and testing. What is the breakdown of effort between these phases?

A study by Wang and Zhang [1924] investigated the distribution of effort, in man-hours, used during the five major phases of 2,570 projects (the types of project were: 20% new development, 68% enhancement, 7% maintenance, 5% other projects). Figure 5.16 shows a density plot of the effort invested in each phase, as a fraction of each project's total effort; the terminology in the legend follows that used by the authors (a mapping of those terms that differ from Western usage might be: Produce is implementation, Optimize is testing, and Implement is deployment). The distribution of means and medians does not vary much with project duration.

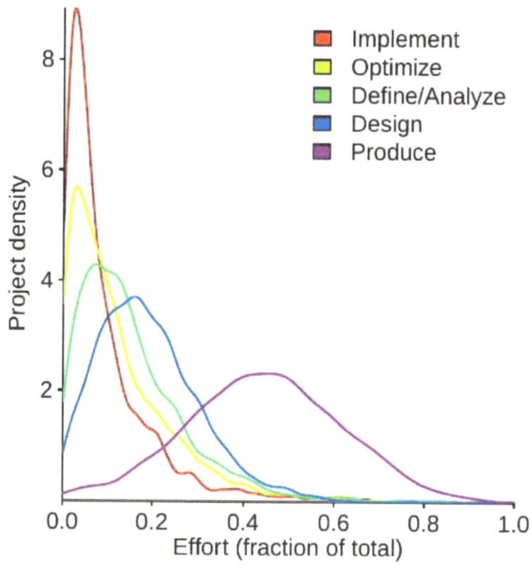

Figure 5.16: Density plot of the investment, by 2,570 projects, of a given fraction of total effort in a given project phase. Data kindly provided by Wang. Github-Local

A study by Jones and Cullum [941] investigated 8,252 agile tasks estimated and actual implementation time. Figure 5.17 shows the number of tasks having a given estimated effort and the number requiring a given actual effort. Some time estimates stand out as occurring a lot more or less frequently than nearby values, e.g., peaks at multiples of seven (there were seven hours in a work day), and very few estimates of six, eight and nine hours; the preference for certain numeric values is discussed in section 2.7.1.

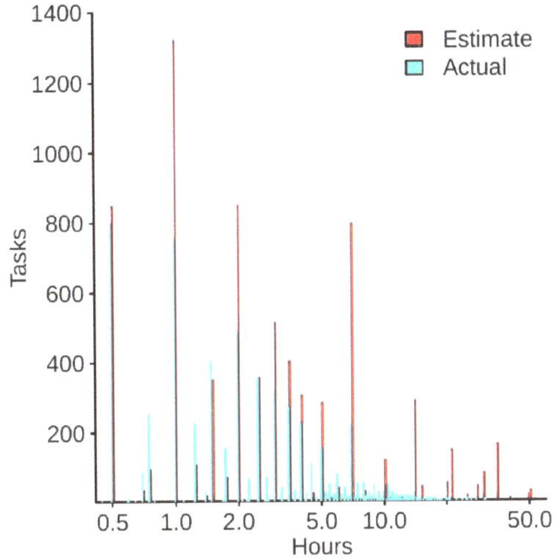

Figure 5.17: Number of tasks having a given estimate, and a given actual implementation time. Data from Jones et al. Github-Local

A preference for round numbers has also been seen in estimates made on other projects; see Github-projects/hemmati2018.R.

In an attempt to reduce costs some companies have offshored the development of some projects, i.e., awarded the development contract to companies in other countries. A study by Šmite, Britto and van Solingen [1730] of outsourced project costs, found additional costs outside the quoted hourly rates; these were attributable to working at distance, cost of transferring the work and characteristics of the offshore site. For the projects studied, the time to likely break-even, compared to on-shore development, was thought to be several years later than planned. One study [487] attempted to calculate the offshoring costs generated by what they labeled psychic distance (a combination of differences including cultural, language, political, geographic, and economic development).

5.3.1 Estimation models

Estimation of software development costs has proved to be a complex process, with early studies [575,576] identifying over fifty factors; a 1966 management cost estimation handbook [1364] contained a checklist of 94 questions (based on an analysis of 169 projects). Many of the existing approaches used to build estimation models were developed in the 1960s and 1970s, with refinements added over time; these approaches include: finding equations that best fit data from earlier projects, deriving and solving theoretical models, and building project development simulators.

Fitting data: Early cost estimation models fitted equations to data on past projects. [1943] The problem with fitting equations to data, is that the resulting models are only likely to perform well when estimating projects having the same characteristics as the projects from which the data was obtained. A study by Mohanty compared the estimates produced by 12 models. Figure 5.18 shows how widely the estimates varied.

A 1991 study by Ourada evaluated four effort estimation models used for military software (two COCOMO derivatives REVIC and COSTMODL, plus SASET and SEER; all fitted to data); he reached the conclusion: "I found the models to be highly inaccurate and very much dependent upon the interpretation of the input parameters." Similar conclusions were reached by Kemerer [985] who evaluated four popular cost estimation models (SLIM, COCOMO, Function Points and ESTIMACS) on data from 15 large business data processing projects; Ferens [594] compared 10 models against DOD data and came to the same conclusion, as did another study in 2003 using data from ground based systems. [778]

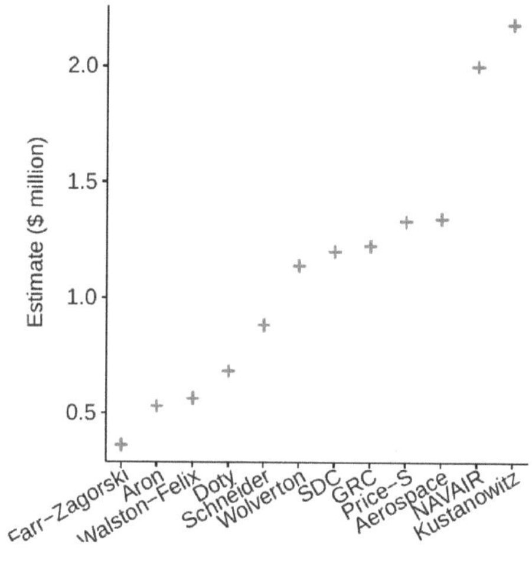

Figure 5.18: Estimated project cost from 12 estimating models. Data from Mohanty. Github-Local

Current machine learning models perform estimate adjustment; they require an estimate to be given as one of the input variables, and return an adjusted value (existing public estimation data sets don't contain enough information to allow viable models to be built unless the known estimated values are used during training).

Deriving equations: In the early 1960s, Norden [1387] studied projects, which he defined as ". . . a finite sequence of purposeful, temporarily ordered activities, operating on a homogeneous set of problem elements, to meet a specified set of objectives . . .". Completing a project involves solving a set of problems (let $W(t)$ be the proportion of problems solved at time), and these problems are solved by the people resources ($p(t)$ encodes information on the number of people, and their skill); the rate of problems solving depends on the number of people available, and the number of problems remaining to be solved; this is modeled by the differential equation:

$$\frac{dW}{dt} = p(t)[1 - W(t)], \text{ whose solution is: } W(t) = 1 - e^{-\int^{t} p(\tau)d\tau}$$

If the skill of the people resource grows linearly, as the project progresses, i.e., team members learn at the rate $p(t) = at$, the work rate is:

$$\frac{dW}{dt} = ate^{-\frac{at^2}{2}}$$

This equation is known, from physics, as the Rayleigh curve. Putnam [1537] evangelised the use of Norden's model for large software development projects. Criticism of the Norden/Putnam model has centered around the linear growth assumption (i.e., $(t) = at$) being unrealistic.

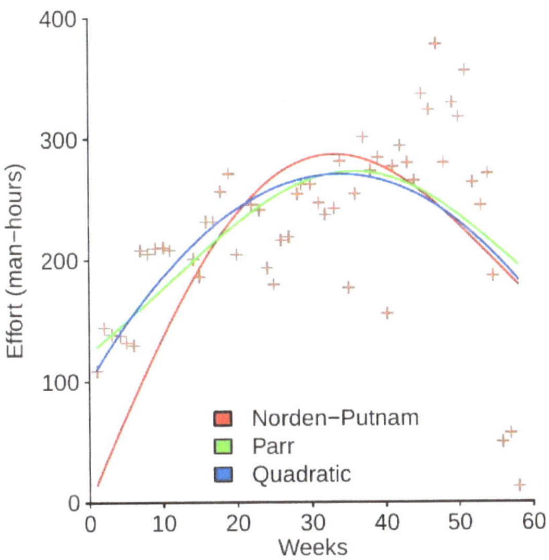

Figure 5.19: Elapsed weeks (x -axis) against effort in manhours per week (y -axis) for a project, plus three fitted curves. Data extracted from Basili et al. Github-Local

An analysis by Parr [1448] modeled the emergence of problems during a project as a binary tree, and assumed that enough resources are available to complete the project in the shortest possible time. Under these assumptions the derived work rate is:

$$\frac{dW}{dt} = \frac{1}{4}\text{sech}^2\frac{\alpha t + c}{2},$$

where sech is the hyperbolic secant: $\text{sech}(x) = \frac{2}{e^x + e^{-x}}$.

While these two equations look very different, their fitted curves are similar; one difference is that the Rayleigh curve starts at zero, while the Parr curve starts at some positive value.

A study by Basili and Beane [139] investigated the quality of fit of various models to six projects requiring around 100 man-months of effort. Figure 5.19 shows Norden-Putnam, Parr and quadratic curves fitted to effort data for project 4.

The derivation of these, or any other equation, is based on a set of assumptions, e.g., a model of problem discovery (the Norden/Putnam and Parr models assume there are no significant changes to the requirements), and the necessary manpower can be added or removed at will. The extent to which the derived equation apply to a project depends on how closely the characteristics of the project meet the assumptions used to build the model. Both the Norden-Putnam and Parr equations can be derived using hazard analysis, [1891] with the lifetime of problems to be discovered having a linear and logistic hazard rate respectively.

Simulation models: A simulation model that handles all the major processes involved in a project could be used to estimate the resources likely to be needed. There have been several attempts to build such models using Systems Dynamics. [3,275,1188] Building a simulation model requires understanding the behavior of all the important factors involved, and as the analysis in this book shows, we are a long way from having this understanding.

Subcomponent based: Breaking a problem down into its constituent parts may enable a good enough estimate to be made (based on the idea that smaller tasks are easier to understand, compared to larger, more complicated tasks), assuming there are no major interactions between components that might affect an estimate. Examples of subcomponent based estimation methods include: function-points (various function-point counting algorithms are in use), use case points and story points.

Uses case points is an estimation method that makes use of weighting factors derived from the end-user, environmental and technical complexity of a project; the appropriate weighting for over 20 factors has to be selected. A study by Ochodek, Nawrocki and Kwarciak [1402] investigated the performance of use case points for 27 projects; see Github-projects/simplifying-ucp.R.

The function point analysis methods are based on a unit of measurement, known as a function point, and take as input a requirements' specification or functional requirements. A formula or algorithm (they vary between the methods) is used to derive the size of each requirement in function points. The implementation cost of a function point is obtained from the analysis of previous projects, where the number of function points and costs is known.

The accuracy of function point analysis methods depends on the accuracy with which requirements are measured (in function points), and the accuracy of function point to cost mapping. Figure 11.18 suggests that the requirements measuring processing process produces consistent values.

A study by Kampstra and Verhoef [970] investigated the reliability of function point counts. Figure 5.20 shows the normalised cost for 149 projects, from one large institution, having an estimated number of function points; also see Github-projects/82507128-kitchenham and Github-projects/HuijgensPhD.R.

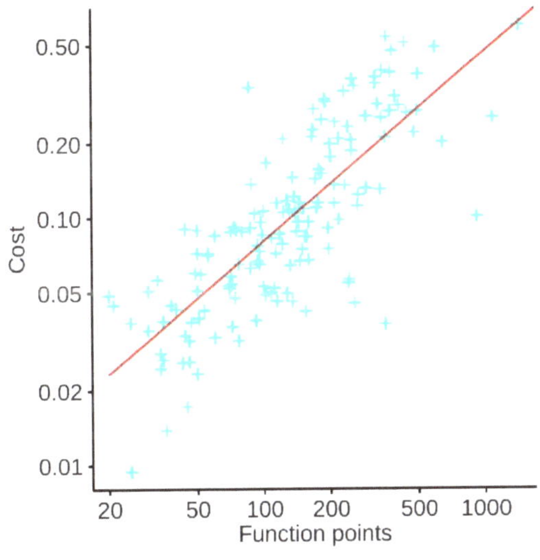

Figure 5.20: Function points and corresponding normalised costs for 149 projects from one large institution; line is a fitted regression model of the form: Cost ∝ Function_Points $^{0.75}$. Data extracted from Kampstra el al. Github-Local

A study by Huijgens and van Solingen investigated two projects considered to be best-in-class, out of 345 projects, from three large organizations. Figure 5.21 shows the cost per requirement, function point, and story point for these two projects over 13 releases.

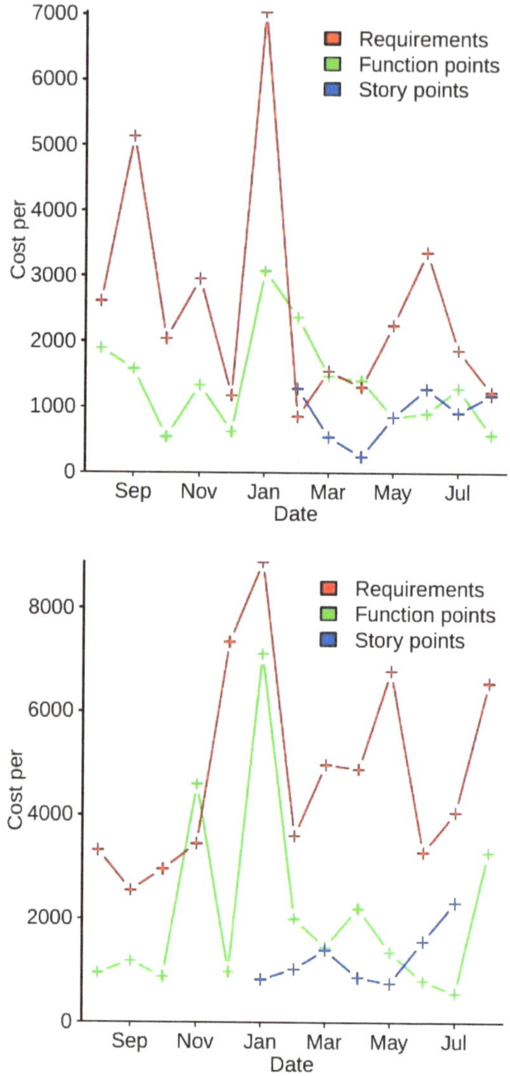

Figure 5.21: Cost per requirement, function point and story point for two projects, over 13 monthly releases. Data from Huijgens. Github-Local

A study by Commeyne, Abran and Djouab investigated effort estimates made using COSMIC function-points and story-points. Figure 5.22 shows the estimated number of hours needed to implement 24 story-points, against the corresponding estimated functionpoints.

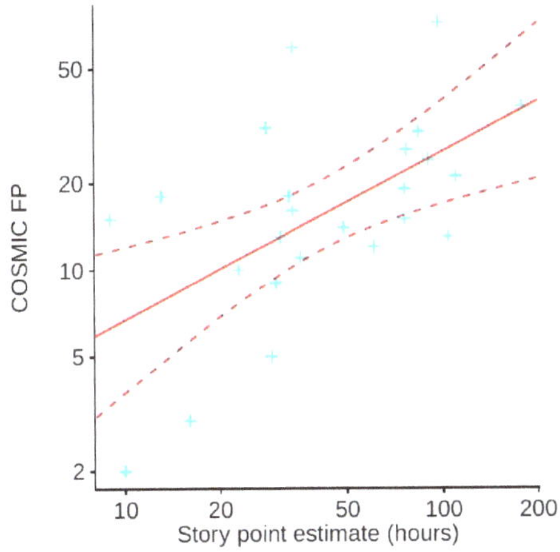

Figure 5.22: Estimated effort to implement 24 story-points and corresponding COSMIC function point; line is a fitted regression model of the form: CosmicFP ∝ storyPoint $^{0.6}$, with 95% confidence intervals. Data from Commeyne et al. Github-Local

Some estimation models include, as input, an estimate of the number of lines of code likely to be contained in the completed program; see fig 3.34. How much variation is to be expected in the lines of code contained in programs implementing the same functionality, using the same language?

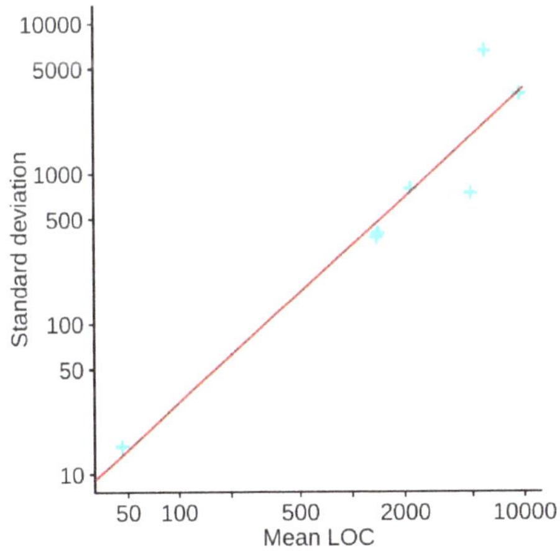

Figure 5.23: Mean LOC against standard deviation of LOC, for multiple implementations of seven distinct problems; line is a fitted regression model of the form: Standard_deviation ∝ $SLOC$. Data from: Anda et al, Jørgensen, Lauterbach, McAllister et al, Selby et al, Shimasaki et al, van der Meulen. Github-Local

Figure 5.23 shows data from seven studies, where multiple implementations of the same specification were written in the same language. The fitted regression model finds that the standard deviation is approximately one quarter of the mean. With so much variation, in LOC, between different implementations of the same specification, a wide margin of error must be assumed for any estimation technique where lines of code is a significant component of the calculation; also see fig 7.34.

Figure 9.14 shows the number of lines contained in over 6,300C programs implementing the $3n + 1$ problem. A more substantial example is provided by the five Pascal compilers targeting the same mainframe. [1697]

5.3.2 Time

When will the system be ready for use? This is the questions clients often ask immediately after the cost question (coming before the cost question can be a good sign, i.e., time is more important than cost). Many factors have been found to have a noticeable impact on the accuracy of predictions for the time needed to perform some activity. [767]

In some cases time and money are interchangeable project resources, [1122] but there may be dependencies that prevent time (or money being spent) until some item becomes available. A cost plus contract provides an incentive to spend money, with time only being a consideration if the contract specifies penalty clauses.

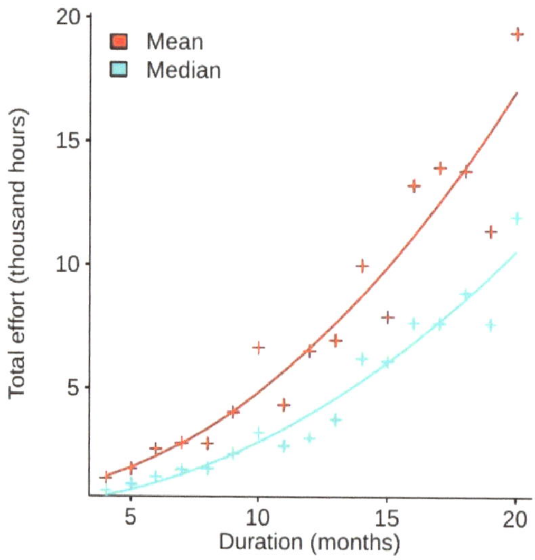

Figure 5.24: Mean and median effort (thousand hours) for projects having a given elapsed time; both lines are a fitted regression model of the form: Effort ∝ Duration. Data from Wang et al. Github-Local

Figure 5.24 shows the mean and median effort spent on 2,103 projects taking a given number of elapsed months to complete; regression lines are fitted quadratic equations. Assuming 150 man-hours per month, project team size appears increase from one to perhaps six or seven, as project duration increases.

Studies have investigated the explanations given by estimators, for their inaccurate estimates; see Github-projects/Regression-models.R.

5.3.3 Size

Program size is an important consideration when computer memory capacity is measured in kilobytes. During the 1960s, mainframe computer memory was often measured in kilobytes, as was minicomputer memory during the 1970s, and microcomputer memory during the 1980s. Today, low cost embedded controllers might contain a kilobyte of memory, or less, e.g., electronic control units (ECU) used in car engines contain a few kilobytes of flash memory.

Pricing computers based on their memory capacity is a common sales technique. Figure 5.25 shows IBM's profit margin on sales of all System 360s sold in 1966 (average monthly rental cost, for 1967, in parentheses). Low-end systems, with minimal memory, were sold below cost to attract customers (and make it difficult for competitors to gain a foothold in the market [482]).

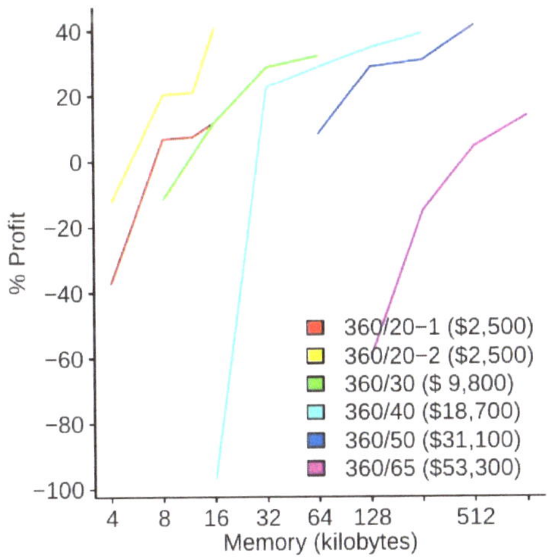

Figure 5.25: IBM's profit margin on all System 360s sold in 1966, by system memory capacity in kilobytes; monthly rental cost during 1967 in parentheses. Data from DeLamarter. Github-Local

The practices adopted to handle these memory size constraints continue to echo in software engineering folklore.

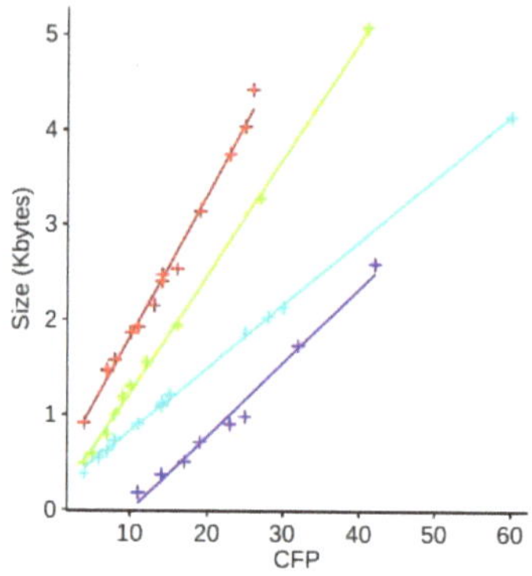

Figure 5.26: COSMIC function-points and compiled size (in kilobytes) of components in four different ECU modules; lines show fitted regression model. Data from Lind et al. Github-Local

A study by Lind and Heldal investigated the possibility of using COSMIC function points to estimate the compiled size of software components used in ECUs. Function points were counted for existing software components in the ECUs used by Saab and General Motors. Figure 5.26 shows COSMIC function points against compiled size of components from four ECU modules; lines are fitted regression models for each module. While a consistent mapping exists for components within each module, the function point counting technique used did not capture enough information to produce consistent results across modules.

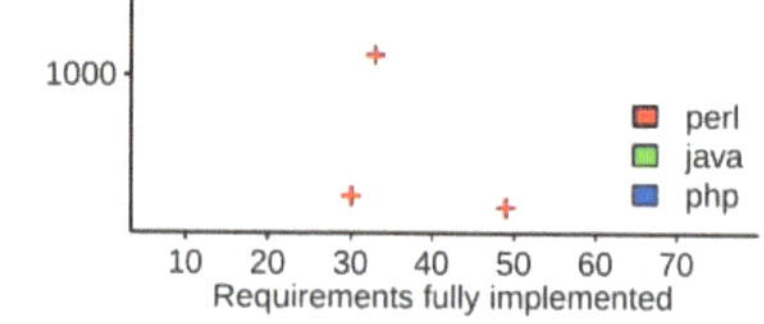

Figure 5.27: Number of requirements and corresponding lines of manually created source code, for each team (colors denote language used). Data from Prechelt Github-Local

A study by Prechelt [1523] investigated a competition in which nine teams, each consisting of three professional developers, were given 30 hours to implement 132 functional and 19 non-functional requirements, for a web-based system; three teams used Java, three used Perl, and three used PHP (two teams used Zend, and every other team chose a different framework).

Figure 5.27 shows how the number of lines of manually written code, and the number of requirements implemented, varied between teams; many more significant differences between team implementations are discussed in the report. [1523]

5.4 Paths to delivery

There are many ways of implementing a software system, and those involved have to find one that can be implemented using the available resources.

The path to delivery may include one or more pivots, where a significant change occurs. [120] Pivots can vary from fundamental changes (e.g., involving the target market, or the client's requirements), to technical issues over which database to use.

Creating a usable software system involves discovering a huge number of interconnected details; [1327] these details are discovered during: requirements gathering to find out what the client wants (and ongoing client usability issues during subsequent phases [1200]), formulating a design [423] for a system having the desired behavior, implementing the details and their interconnected relationships in code, and testing the emergent behavior to ensure an acceptable level of confidence in its behavior; testing is covered in chapter 6.

Managing the implementation of a software system is an exercise in juggling the available resources, managing the risks (e.g., understanding what is most likely to go wrong, [103] and having some idea about what to do about it), along with keeping the client convinced [v] that a working system will be delivered within budget and schedule; these are all standard project management issues. [1020] Managements interest in technical issues focuses on the amount of resource they are likely to consume, and the developer skill-sets needed to implement them.

Figure 5.28 shows an implementation schedule for one of the projects studied by Ge and Xu. [663] This plot gives the impression of a project under control, in practice schedules evolve, sometimes beyond all recognition. As work progresses, discovered information can result in schedule changes, e.g., slippage on another project can prevent scheduled staff being available, and a requirement change creates a new dependency that prevents some subcomponents being implemented concurrently;

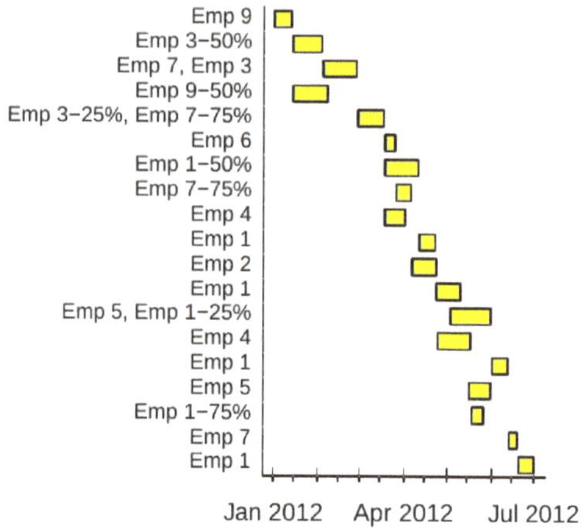

Figure 5.28: Initial implementation schedule, with employee number(s) given for each task (percentage given when not 100%) for a project. Data from Ge et al. Github-Local

Large projects sometimes involve multiple companies, and the initial division of work between them may evolve over time.

A study by Yu[1995] investigated the development of three multi-million pound projects. The chronology of events documented provides some insight into how responsibility for the implementation of functionality, and associated costs, can shift between project contractors as new issues are uncovered, and contracted budgets are spent. Figure 5.29 shows the changes in contractors' project cost estimates, for their own work, over the duration of the project.

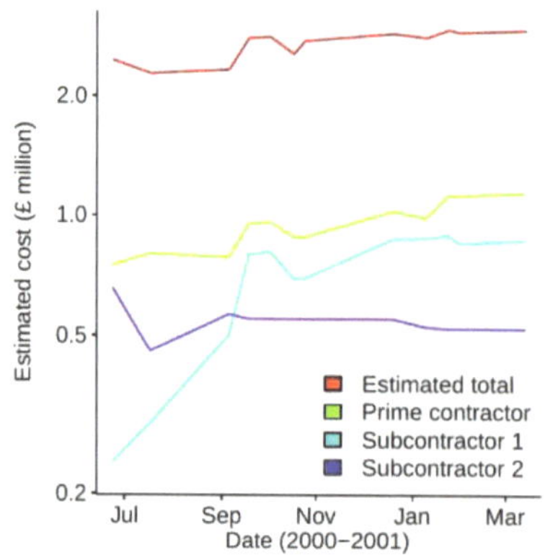

Figure 5.29: Evolution of the estimated cost of developing a bespoke software system, as implementation progressed; over time the estimated costs shift between the Prime contractor and its two subcontractors. Data from Yu. Github-Local

Vendors want to keep their clients happy, but not if it means loosing lots of money. A good client relationship manager knows when to tell the client that extra funding is needed to support the requested change, and when to accept it without charging (any connection with implementation effort is only guaranteed to occur for change requests having significant cost impact).

Daily client contact has been found to have an impact on final project effort; see fig 11.44. The study did not collect data on the extent to which the planned project goals were achieved, and it is possible that daily contact enabled the contractor to convince the client to be willing to accept a deliverable that did not support all the functionality originally agreed.

5.4.1 Development methodologies

Software development is a punctuated information arrival process. [vi] It took several decades before a development methodology designed to handle this kind of process started to be widely used.

The first development methodology, [699] written in 1947, specified a six-step development process, starting with the people who performed the high-level conceptual activities (i.e., the scientists and engineers), and ending with the people who performed what was considered to be the straightforward coding activity (performed by the coders). Over time, the complexity of development has resulted in a significant shift of implementation authority, and power, to those connected with writing the code. [548]

A study by Rico, [1582] going back over 50 -years from 2004, identified 32 major techniques (broken down by hardware era and market conditions) that it was claimed would produce savings in development or maintenance. There have been a few field studies of the methodologies actually used by developers (rather than what managers claim to be using); system development methodologies have been found to provide management support for necessary fictions, [1351] e.g., a means to creating an image of control to the client, or others outside the development group.

The Waterfall model [1270] continues to haunt software project management, despite repeated exorcisms over several decades. [1087] The paper [1614] that gave birth to this demon meme contained a diagram, with accompanying text claiming this approach was risky and invited failure, with diagrams and text on subsequent pages showing the recommended approach to producing the desired outcome. The how not to do it approach, illustrated in the first diagram, was taken up, becoming known as the waterfall model, and included in the first version of an influential standard, DoD-Std-2167, [473] as the recommended project management technique. [vii] Projects have been implemented using a Waterfall approach. [1975] Iterative development has been independently discovered many times. [1087]

The U.S. National Defense Authorization Act, for fiscal year 2010, specified that an iterative acquisition process be used for information technology systems; Section 804:[1177] contains the headline requirements "(B) multiple, rapidly executed increments or releases of capability; (C) early, successive prototyping to support an evolutionary approach; . . . ". However, the wording used for the implementation of the new process specifies: "... well-scoped and well-defined requirements.", i.e., bureaucratic inertia holds sway.

The battle fought over the communication protocols used to implement the Internet is perhaps the largest example of a waterfall (the OSI seven-layer model, ISO 7498 or ITU-T X. 200 , documented the requirements first, which vendors could then implement, but few ever did) vs. an iterative approach (the IETF process was/is based on rough consensus and running code, [1621] and won the battle).

The economic incentives and organizational structure in which a project is developed can be a decisive factor in the choice of development methodology. For instance, the documentation and cost/schedule oversight involved in large government contracts requires a methodology capable of generating the necessary cost and schedule documents; in winner take-all markets, there is a strong incentive to be actively engaging with customers as soon as possible, and a methodology capable of regularly releasing updated systems provides a means of rapidly responding to customer demand, as well as reducing the delay between writing code and generating revenue from it.

The choice of project implementation strategy is strongly influenced by the risk profile of changes to requirements and company cash flow.

The benefits of using iterative development include: not requiring a large upfront investment in requirements gathering, cost reduction from not implementing unwanted requirements (based on feedback from users of the current system), working software makes it possible to start building a customer base (a crucial requirement in winner take-all markets), and reducing the lag between writing code and earning income from it.

The additional cost incurred from using iterative development, compared to an upfront design approach, come from having to continually rearchitect programs to enable them to support functionality that they were not originally designed to support.

If the cost of modifying the design is very high, it can be cost effective to do most of the design before implementing it. The cost of design changes may be high when: hardware that cannot be changed is involved, or when many organizations are involved and all need to work to the same design.

When customer requirements are rapidly changing, or contain many unknowns, the proposed design may quickly become out-of-date, and it may be more cost effective to actively drive the design by shipping something working, e.g., evolving a series of languages, and their corresponding compilers; [142] see Github-projects/J04.R. User feedback is the input to each iteration, and without appropriate feedback iterative projects can fail. [723]

The growth of the Internet provided an ideal ecosystem for the use of iterative techniques. With everything being new, and nobody knowing what was going to happen next: requirements were uncertain and subject to rapid change, many market niches had winner-takeall characteristics. Also, the Internet provided a distribution channel for frequent software updates.

Project lifespan by be sufficiently uncertain that it dictates the approach to system development. For instance, building the minimum viable product, and making it available to potential customers to find out if enough of them are willing to pay enough for it to be worthwhile investing in further development.

In an environment where projects are regularly cancelled before delivery, or delivered systems have a short lifespan, it may be a cost effective to make short term cost savings that have a larger long term cost.

A study by Özbek [1433] investigated attempts to introduce software engineering innovations into 13 open source projects within one-year. Of the 83 innovations identified in the respective project email discussions 30(36.1%) were successful, 37(44.6%) failed, and 16(19.3%) classified as unknown.

5.4.2 The Waterfall/iterative approach

The major activities involved in the waterfall/iterative approach to building a software system include: requirements, design, implementation (or coding), testing and deployment. These activities have a natural ordering in the sense that it is unwise to deploy without some degree of testing, which requires code to test, which ideally has been designed and implements a known requirement. The extent to which documentation is a major activity, or an after-thought, depends on the client.

The term phase is sometimes used to denote project activities, implying both an ordering, and a distinct period during which one activity is performed.

A study by Zelkowitz investigated when work from a particular activity was performed, relative to other activities (for thirteen projects, average total effort 13,522 hours). Figure 5.30 shows considerable overlap between all activity, e.g., 31.3% of the time spent on design occurred during the coding and testing activity; also see Github-projects/zelkowitzeffect.R.

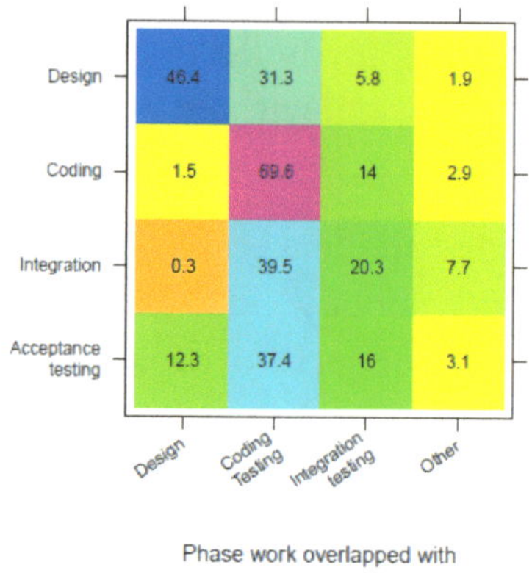

Figure 5.30: Phase during which work on a given activity of development was actually performed, average percentages over 13 projects. Data from Zelkowitz. Github-Local

How are the available resources distributed across the major project activities?

A study by Condon, Regardie, Stark and Waligora [392] investigated 39 applications developed by the NASA Flight Dynamics Division between 1976 and 1992. Figure 5.31 shows ternary plots of the percentage effort, in time (red), and percentage schedule, in elapsed time (blue), for design, coding and testing (mean percentages for the three activities were: effort time: 24%, 43 and 33 respectively and schedule elapsed time: 33%, 34 and 33).

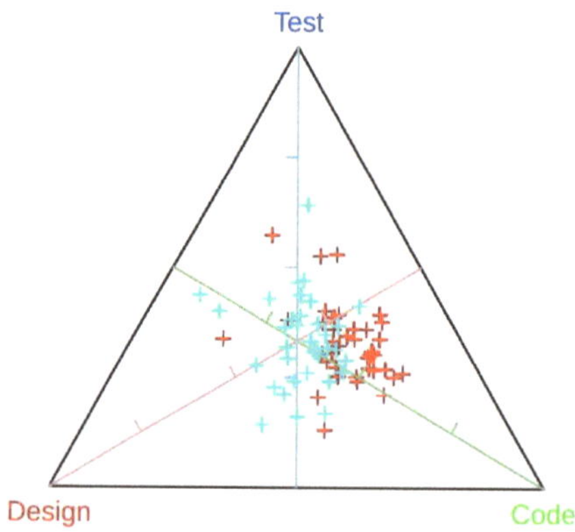

Figure 5.31: Percentage distribution of effort time (red) and schedule time (blue) across design/coding/testing for 38 NASA projects. Data from Condon et al. [392] Github-Local

To what extent does resources distribution across major project activities vary between organizations?

Figure 5.32 shows a ternary plot for the design/coding/test effort for projects developed by various organizations: a study by Kitchenham and Taylor [1015] investigated a computer manufacturer (red) and a telecoms company (green), a study by Graver, Carriere, Balkovich and Thibodeau [729] investigated space projects (blue) and major defense systems (purple).

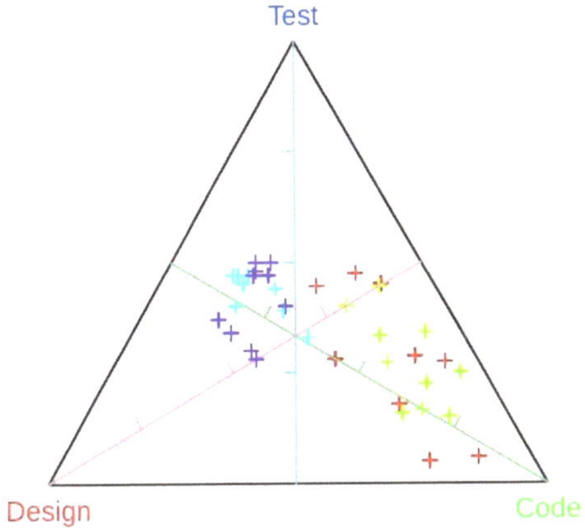

Figure 5.32: Percentage distribution of effort across design/coding/testing for 10 ICL projects (red), 11 BT projects (green), 11 space projects (blue) and 12 defense projects (purple). Data from Kitchenham et al [1015] and Graver et al. [729] Github-Local

There is a clustering of effort breakdowns for different application areas; the mean percentage design, coding and testing effort were: computer/telecoms (17%, 57,26) and Space/Defence (36%, 20,43). There is less scope to recover from the failures of software systems operating in some space/defense environments; this operational reality makes it worthwhile investing more in design and testing.

5.4.3 The Agile approach

The Agile manifesto specified "Individuals and interactions over processes and tools", but this has not stopped the creation and marketing of a wide variety of processes claiming to be the agile way of doing things. The rarity of measurement data for any of the agile processes means this evidence-based book has little to say about them.

5.4.4 Managing progress

How is the project progressing, in implemented functionality, cost and elapsed time, towards the target of a project deliverable that is accepted by the client?

A project involves work being done and people doing it. Work and staff have to be meshed together within a schedule; project managers will have a view on what has to be optimized. A company employing a relatively fixed number of developers may seek to schedule work so that employees always have something productive to do, while a company with a contract to deliver a system by a given date may seek to schedule staff to optimise for delivery dates (subject to the constraints of any other projects).

Scheduling a software project involves solving many of the kinds of problems encountered in non-software projects, e.g., staff availability (in time and skills), dependencies between work items [237] and other projects, and lead time on the client making requirements' decisions. [1973] Common to engineering projects in general, [209] issues include the difficulty of finding people with the necessary skills, and high turnover rate of current staff; staffing is discussed in section 5.5.

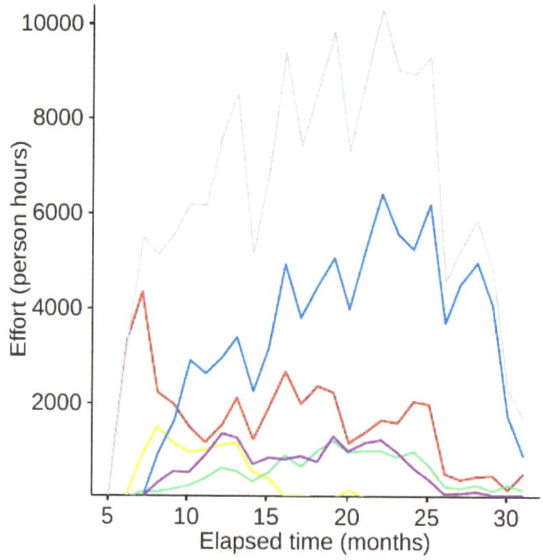

Figure 5.33: Effort, in person hours per month, used in the implementation of the five components making up the PAVE PAWS project (grey line shows total effort). Data extracted from Curtis et al. Github-Local

Analyzing project progress data in isolation can be misleading. A study by Curtis, Sheppard and Kruesi [424] investigated the characteristics (e.g., effort and mistakes found) of the implementation of five relatively independent subcomponents of one system. Figure 5.33 shows how effort, in person hours, changes as the subcomponent projects progressed. While the five subcomponents were implemented by different teams, it is not known whether teams members worked on other projects within the company. Across multiple ongoing projects, total available effort may not change significantly, but large changes can occur on single projects (because senior management are optimizing staffing across all projects); see fig 5.4.

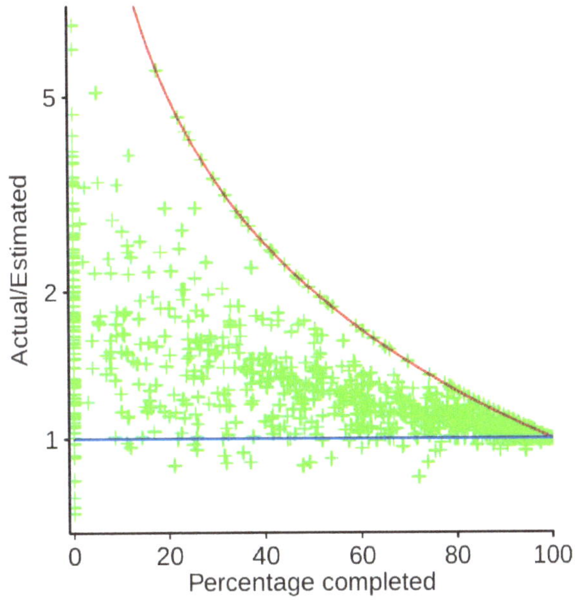

Figure 5.34: Percentage of actual project duration elapsed at the time 882 schedule estimates were made, during 121 projects, against estimated/actual time ratio (y -axis has a log scale; boundary maximum in red). Data kindly provided by Little. Github-Local

While it may be obvious to those working on a project that the schedule will not be met, nobody wants to be the bearer of bad news, and management rarely have anything to gain by reporting bad news earlier than they have to. Progress reports detailing poor progress, and increased costs, may be ignored, [983] or trigger an escalation of commitment. [205]

Once the client believes the estimated completion date and/or cost is not going to be met, either: the project objectives are scaled back, the project cancelled, or a new completion estimate is accepted. Scheduling when to tell clients about project delivery slippage, and/or a potential cost overrun, is an essential project management skill.

The scheduling uncertainty around a successful project is likely to decrease as it progresses towards completion. The metaphor of a cone of uncertainty is sometimes used when discussing project uncertainty; this metaphor is at best useless. The cone-shaped curve(s) that are sometimes visible in plots where the *y*-axis is the ratio of actual and estimated, and the x -axis is percentage completed (a quantity that is unknown until project completion, i.e., the duration of the project), are a mathematical artefact. Figure

5.34 shows a plot of percentage actually completed against the ratio $\frac{\text{Actual}}{\text{Estimated}}$, for each corresponding project (4.6% of estimate completion dates are less than the actual date), for 882 estimates made during the implementation of 121 projects; the curved boundary is a mathematical artefact created by the choice of axis, i.e., the following holds: $\frac{\text{Actual}}{\text{Estimated}} \leq x_{\text{percentage}}$ Actual, cancelling Actual gives: $\frac{1}{\text{Estimated}} \leq x_{\text{percentage}}$, i.e., whatever the value of Estimated, the plotted point always appears below, or on, the $\frac{1}{x}$ curve.

A study by Little [1153] investigated schedule estimation for 121 projects at Landmark Graphics between 1999 and 2002. An estimated release date was made at the start, and whenever the core team reached consensus on a new date (averaging 7.2 estimates per project; Figure 5.35 shows the number of release date estimates made for 121 projects, for a corresponding initial estimated project duration, on the x -axis). The extent to which the schedule estimation characteristics found in Landmark projects are applicable to other companies will depend on issues such as corporate culture and requirements volatility. The Landmark Graphics corporate culture viewed estimates as targets, i.e., "what's the earliest date by which you can't prove you won't be finished?", [1153] different schedule characteristics are likely to be found in a corporate culture that punishes the bearer of bad news.

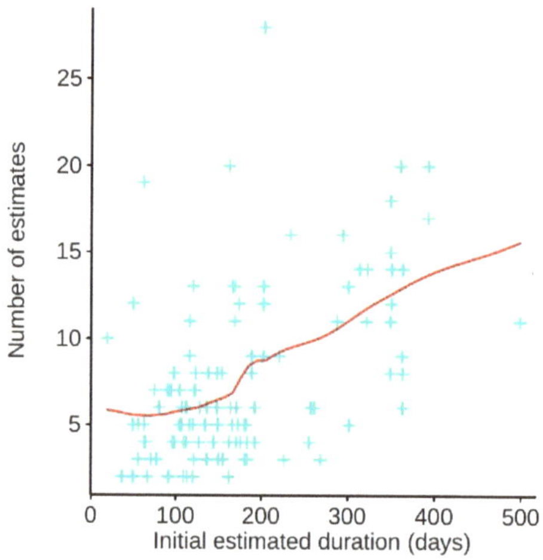

Figure 5.35: Initial estimated project duration against number of schedule estimates made before completion, for 121 projects; line is a loess fit. Data kindly provided by Little. Github-Local

Reasons for failing to meet a project deadline include (starting points for lawyers looking for strategies to use, to argue their client's case after a project fails [1598]): an unrealistic schedule, a failure of project management, changes in the requirements, encountering unexpected problems, staffing problems (i.e., recruiting or retaining people with the required skills), and being blocked because a dependency is not available. [237] Missed deadlines are common, and a common response is to produce an updated schedule.

If a project is unlikely to meet its scheduled release date, those paying for the work have to be given sufficient notice about the expected need for more resources, so the resources can be made available (or not).

Figure 5.36 shows 882 changed delivery date announcements, with percentage elapsed time when the estimate was announced along the x -axis (based on the current estimated duration of the project), and percentage change in project duration (for the corresponding project) along the y -axis; red line is a loess fit. On average larger changes in duration occur near the start of projects, with smaller changes made towards the estimated end date. The blue line is a density plot of the percentage elapsed time of when schedule change announcements are made (density values not shown). There is a flurry of new estimates after a project starts, but over 50% of all estimates are made in the last 71% of estimated remaining time, and 25% in the last 6.4% of remaining time.

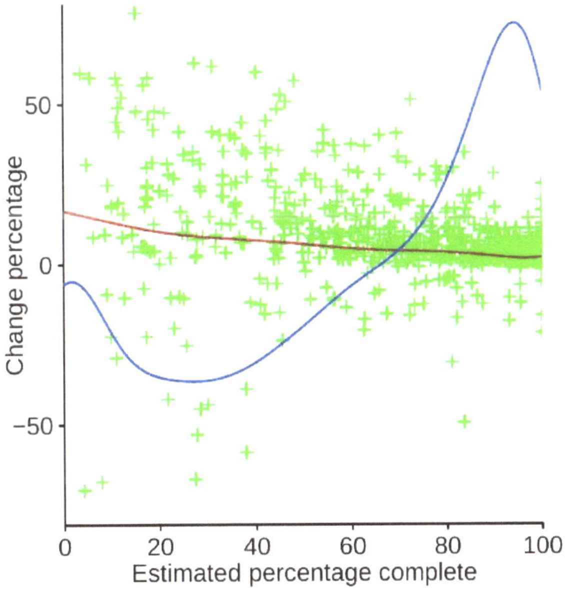

Figure 5.36: Percentage change in 882 estimated delivery dates, announced at a given percentage of the estimated elapsed time of the corresponding project, for 121 projects (red is a loess fit); blue line is a density plot of percentage estimated duration when the estimate was made. Data kindly provided by Little. Github-Local

Parkinson's law says that work expands to fill the time available. When management announces an estimated duration for a project, it is possible that those involved choose to work in a way that meets the estimate (assuming it would have been possible to complete the project in less time).

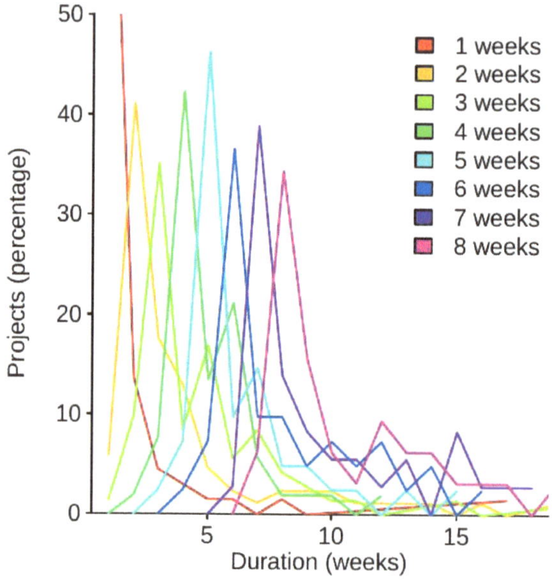

Figure 5.37: Percentage of work packages having a given lead time that are completed within a given duration; colored lines are work packages having the same estimated lead time. Data extracted from van Oorschot et al. Github-Local

A study by van Oorschot, Bertrand and Rutte [1879] investigated the completion time of 424 work packages involving advanced micro-lithography systems, each having an estimated lead time. Figure 5.37 shows the percentage of work packages having a given management estimated lead time that are actually completed within a given amount of time, with colored lines showing stratification by management estimate.

People sometimes strive to meet a prominent deadline.

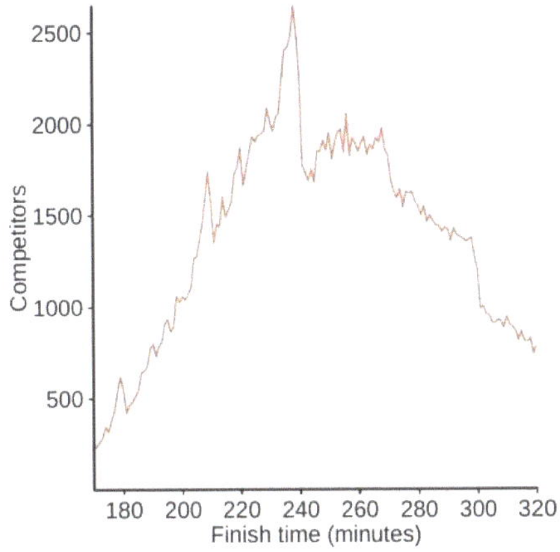

Figure 5.38: Number of Marathon competitors finishing in a given number of minutes (250,000 runner sample size). Data from Allen et al. Github-Local

A study by Allen, Dechow, Pope and Wu [33] investigated Marathon finishing times for nine million competitors. Figure 5.38 shows the number of runners completing a Marathon in a given number of minutes, for a sample of 250,000 competitors. Step changes in completion times are visible at 3,3.5,4,4.5, and 5 hour finish times.

5.4.5 Discovering functionality needed for acceptance

What functionality does a software system need to support for a project delivery to be accepted [viii] by the client?

Requirements gathering is the starting point of the supply chain of developing bespoke software, and is an iterative process. [340]

Bespoke software development is not a service that many clients regularly fund, and they are likely to have an expectation of agreeing costs and delivery dates for agreed functionality, before signing a contract.

The higher the cost of failing to obtain good enough information on the important requirements, the greater the benefit from investing to obtain more confidence that all the important requirements are known in good enough detail. Building a prototype [1731] can be a cost-effective approach to helping decide and refine requirements, as well as evaluating technologies. Another approach to handling requirement uncertainty is to build a minimum viable prototype, and then add features in response to feedback from the customer, e.g., using an agile process.

The requirements gathering process (other terms used include: requirements elicitation, requirements capture and systems analysis) is influenced by the environment in which the project is being developed:

- when an existing manual way of working, or computer system, is being replaced (over half the projects in one recent survey [948]), the stakeholders of the existing system are an important source of requirements information,
- when the software is to be sold to multiple customers, as a product, those in charge of the project select the requirements. In this entrepreneurial role, the trade-off involves minimising investment in implementing functionality against maximising expected sales income,
- when starting an open source project the clients are those willing to do the work, or contribute funding.

The client who signs the cheques is the final authority on which requirements have to be implemented, and their relative priority. Clients who fail to manage the requirements process end up spending their money on a bespoke system meeting somebody else's needs. [1518]

It is not always obvious whether a requirement has been met; [1523] ambiguity in requirement specifications is discussed in chapter 6. Sometimes existing requirements are modified on the basis of what the code does, rather than what the specification said it should do. [275] Gause and Weinberg [659] provide a readable tour through requirements handling in industry.

What is a cost effective way of discovering requirements, and their relative priority?

A stakeholder is someone who gains or loses something (e.g., status, money, change of job description) as a result of a project going live. Stakeholders are a source of political support, resistance to change, [1911] and active subversion [1608] (i.e., doing what they can to obstruct progress on the project), they may provide essential requirements' information, or may be an explicit target for exclusion, e.g., criminals with an interest in security card access systems.

Failure to identify the important stakeholders can result in missing or poorly prioritized requirements, which can have a significant impact on project success. What impact might different stakeholder selection strategies have?

A study by Lim [1143] investigated the University College London project to combine different access control mechanisms into one, e.g., access to the library and fitness centre. The Replacement Access, Library and ID Card (RALIC) project had been deployed two years before the study started, and had more than 60 stakeholder groups. The project documentation, along with interviews of those involved (gathering data after project completion means some degree of hindsight bias will be present), was used to create the Ground truth of project stakeholder identification (85 people), their rank within a role, requirements and relative priorities.

The following two algorithms were used to create a final list of stakeholders:

- starting from an initial list of 22 names and 28 stakeholder roles, four iterations of Snowball sampling resulted in a total of 61 responses containing 127 stakeholder names and priorities, and 70 stakeholder roles (known as the Open list),
- a list of 50 possible stakeholders was created from the project documentation. The people on this list were asked to indicate which of those names on the list they considered to be stakeholders, and to assign them a salience [ix] between 1 and 10 , they were also given the option to suggest other names as possible stakeholders. This process generated a list containing 76 stakeholders names and priorities, and 39 stakeholder roles (known as the Closed list).

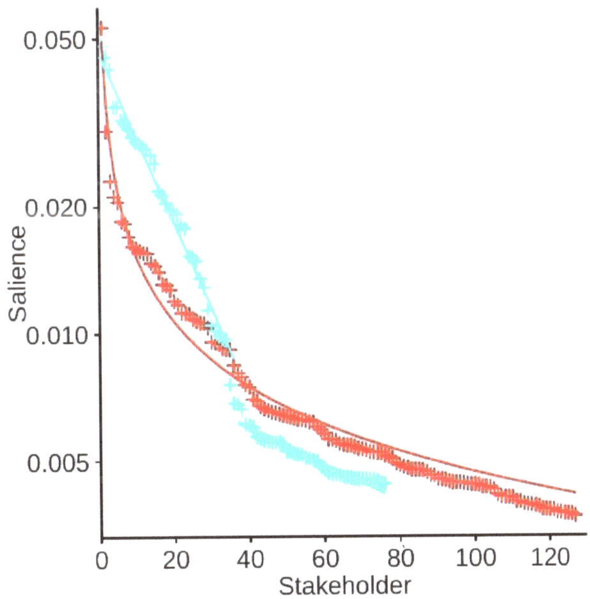

Figure 5.39: Aggregated salience of each stakeholder, calculated using the pagerank of the stakeholders in the network created from the Open (red) and Closed (blue) stakeholder responses (values for each have been sorted). Data from Lim. Github-Local

How might a list of people, and the salience each of them assigns to others, be combined to give a single salience value for each person?

Existing stakeholders are in a relationship network. Lim assumed that the rank of stakeholder roles, calculated using social network metrics, would be strongly correlated with the rank ordering of stakeholder roles in the Grounded truth list. Figure 5.39 shows the Open and Closed stakeholder aggregated salience values, calculated using Pagerank (treating each stakeholder as a node in the network created using the respective lists; Pagerank was chosen for this example because it had one of the strongest correlations with the Ground truth ranking); also, see Github-projects/requirements/stake-ground-cor.R.

Identifying stakeholders and future users is just the beginning. Once found, they have to be convinced to commit some of their time to a project they may have no immediate interest in; stakeholders will have their own motivations for specifying requirements. When the desired information is contained in the heads of a few key players, these need to be kept interested, and involved throughout the project. Few people are practiced in requirements' specification, and obtaining the desired information is likely to be an iterative process, e.g., they describe solutions rather than requirements.

Prioritization: Clients will consider some requirement to be more important than others; concentrating resources on the high priority requirements is a cost-effective way of keeping the client happy, and potentially creating a more effective system (for the resources invested). Techniques for prioritising requirements include:

- aggregating the priority list: this involves averaging stakeholders' list of priority values, possibly weighting by stakeholder.

To what extent are the final requirements' priorities dependent on one stakeholder? Calculating an average, with each stakeholder excluded in turn, is one method of estimating the variance of priority assignments.

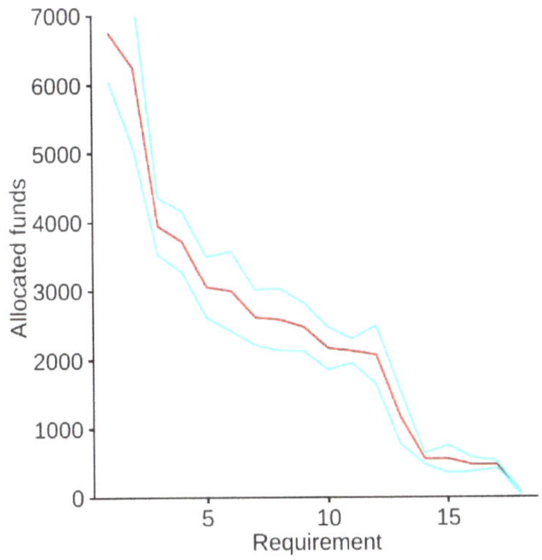

Figure 5.40: Average value assigned to requirements (red) and one standard deviation bounds (blue) based on omitting one stakeholder's priority value list. Data from Regnell et al. Github-Local

A study by Regnell, Höst, Dag, Beremark and Hjel [1569] asked each stakeholder/subject to assign a value to every item on a list of requirements, without exceeding a specified maximum amount, i.e., to act as-if they had a fixed amount of money to spend on the listed requirements. Figure 5.40 shows the average value assigned to each requirement, and the standard deviation in this value when stakeholders were excluded, one at a time.

- performing a cost/benefit analysis on each requirement, and prioritizing based on the benefits provided for a given cost; [977] see Github-projects/requirements/cost-value.R.

How much effort might need to be invested to produce a detailed requirements' specification? One effort estimate [930] for the writing of the 1990 edition of the C Standard is 50 person years, a 219-page A4 document; the effort for the next version of the standard, C99 (a 538-page document), was estimated to be 12 person years.

The development of a new product will involve the writing of a User manual. There are benefits to writing this manual first, and treating it as a requirements' specification. [188]

When a project makes use of a lot of existing source code, it may be necessary to retrofit requirements, i.e., establish traceability between existing code that is believed to implement another set of requirements. It is sometimes possible to reverse engineer links from existing code to a list of requirements. [1025]

5.4.6 Implementation

The traditional measures of implementation activity are staffing (see section 5.5), and lines of code produced; management activities don't seem to have attracted any evidencebased research. Implementation activities include: meetings, design, coding, waiting for other work to be ready to use, and administration related activities; see Github-projects/E100.D_2016-TaskLog.R.

Figure 5.10 shows that as the size of a project increases, the percentage of project effort consumed by management time rapidly increases to a plateau, with fixed-price contracts involving a greater percentage of management time.

Issues around the source code created during implementation are discussed in chapter 7, and issues involving the reliability of the implementation are discussed in chapter 6.

The assorted agile methodologies include various implementation activities that can be measured, e.g., number and duration of sprints, user stories and features.

How might patterns in agile implementation activities be used to gain some understanding of the behavior of processes that are active during implementation? 7digital [1] is a digital media delivery company using an agile process to develop an open API platform providing business to business digital media services; between April 2009 and July 2012, 3,238 features were implemented by the development team (this data was kindly made available).

Figure 5.41 shows the number of features requiring a given number of elapsed working days for their implementation (red first 650 -days, blue post 650 -days); a zero-truncated negative binomial distribution is a good fit to both sets of data (green lines). One interpretation for the fitted probability distribution is that there are many distinct processes involved in the implementation of a feature, with the duration of each process being a distinct Poisson process; a sum of independent Poisson processes can produce a Negative Binomial distribution. In other words, there is no single process dominating implementation time; improving feature delivery time requires improving many different processes (the average elapsed duration to implement a feature has decreased over time).

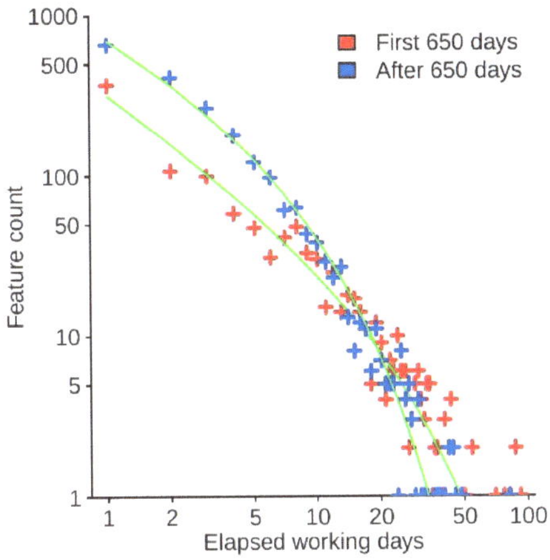

Figure 5.41: Number of features whose implementation took a given number of elapsed workdays; red first 650days, blue post 650 -days, green lines are fitted zerotruncated negative binomial distributions. Data kindly supplied by 7Digital. Github-Local

The same distribution being a good fit for both the pre and post 650 -day implementation time suggests that changes in behavior were not a fundamental, but akin to turning a dial on the distribution parameters, one-way or the other (the first 650-days has a greater mean and variance than post 650 -days). If the two sets of data were better fitted by different distributions, the processes generating the two patterns of behavior are likely to have been different.

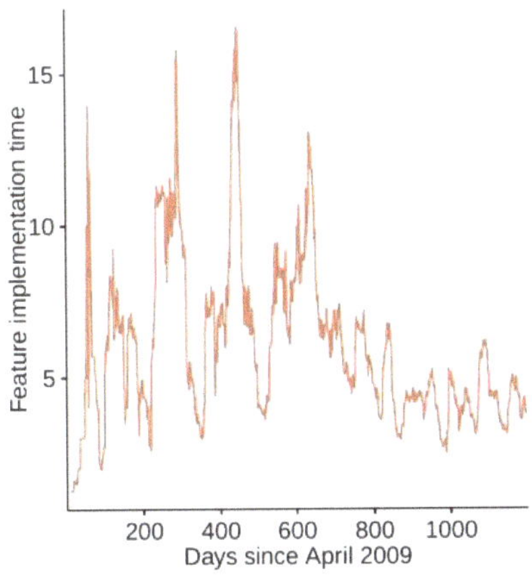

Figure 5.42: Average number of days taken to implement a feature, over time; smoothed using a 25-day rolling mean. Data kindly supplied by 7 Digital. Github-Local

Why was a 650-days boundary chosen? Figure 5.42 shows a time series of the feature implementation time (smoothed using a 25-day rolling average). The variance in average implementation time has a change-point around 650 days (a change-point in the mean occurs around 780 days).

Figure 5.43 shows the number of new features and number of bug fixes started per day (smoothed using a 25 -day rolling mean).

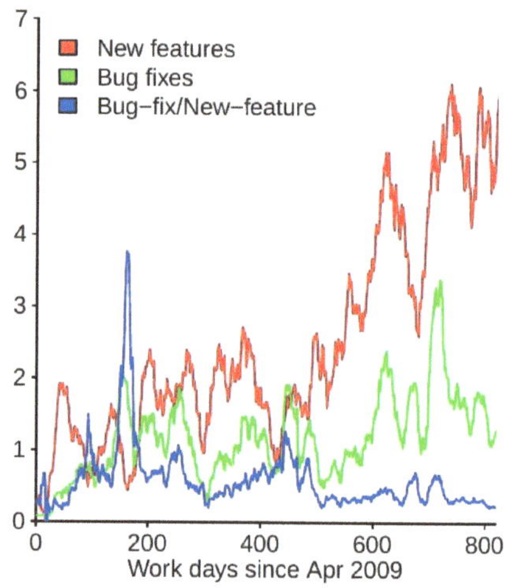

Figure 5.43: Number of feature developments started on a given work day (red new features, green bugs fixes, blue ratio of two values; 25-day rolling mean). Data kindly supplied by 7Digital. Github-Local

During the measurement period the number of developers grew from 14 to 35 (the size of its code base and number of customers is not available). The number of developers who worked on each feature was not recorded, and while developers write the software, it is clients who often report most of the bugs (client information is not present in the dataset).

Possible causes for the increase in new feature starts include: an increase in the number of developers, and/or existing developers becoming more skilled at breaking work down into smaller features (i.e., feature implementation time stays about the same because fewer developers are working on each feature, leaving more developers available to start on new features), or having implemented the basic core of the products less effort is now needed to create new features.

A study by Jones and Cullum [941] analysed 8,252 agile tasks whose duration was estimated in hours, with many taking a few hours to complete. Figure 5.44 shows the number of tasks having a given interval between being estimated and starting, and work starting and completing; the lines are fitted regression models (both power laws).

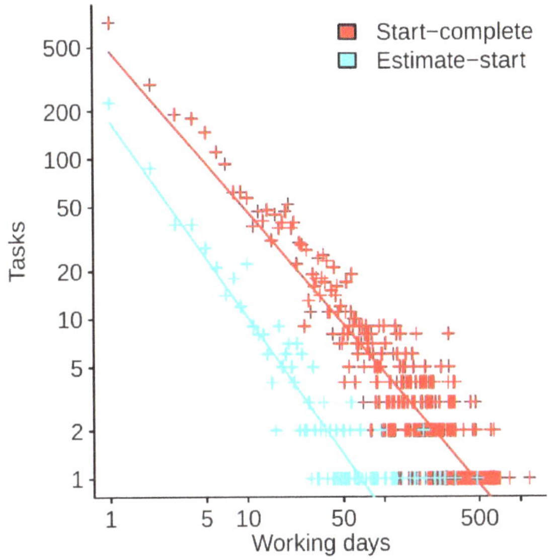

Figure 5.44: Number of tasks having a given duration, in elapsed working days, between estimating/starting (blue), and starting/completing (red). Data from Jones et al. Github-Local

For the 7digital and SiP agile data, knowing that a particular distribution is a good fit is a step towards understanding the processes that generated the measurements (not an end in itself); see section 9.2. More projects need to be analysed to evaluate whether the fitted distribution (e.g., Negative Binomial or Power law) is an inconsequential fact, particular to the kind of client interaction, an indicator of inefficient organizational processes, or some other factor.

The Scrum Agile process organizes implementation around a basic unit of time, known as a sprint. During a sprint, which has a fixed elapsed time (two weeks is a common choice), the functionality agreed at the start is created; the functionality may be specified using story points and estimated using values from a Fibonacci sequence.

A study by Vetrò, Dürre, Conoscenti, Fernández and Jørgensen investigated techniques for improving the estimation process for the story points planned for a sprint. Figure 5.45 shows the total number of story points and hours worked during each sprint for project P1 (sprint duration was 2-weeks, up to sprint 26, and then changed to 1-week; 3 to 7 developers worked on the project).

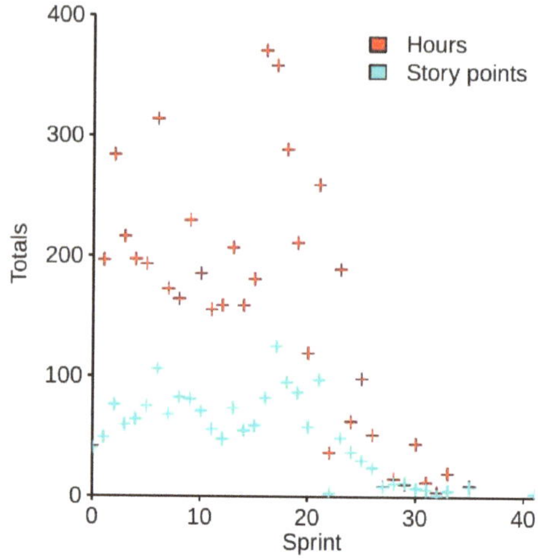

Figure 5.45: Total number of story points and hours worked during each sprint of project P1. Data kindly provided by Vetrò. Github-Local

Changes to software sometimes noticeably change its performance characteristics; performance regression testing can be used to check that runtime performance remains acceptable, after source updates. A study by Horký [856] investigated the performance of SAX builder (an XML parser) after various commits to the source tree. Figure 5.46 shows the range of times taken to execute a particular benchmark after a sample of 33 commits (average number of performance measurements per commit was 7,357 ; red dot is the mean value).

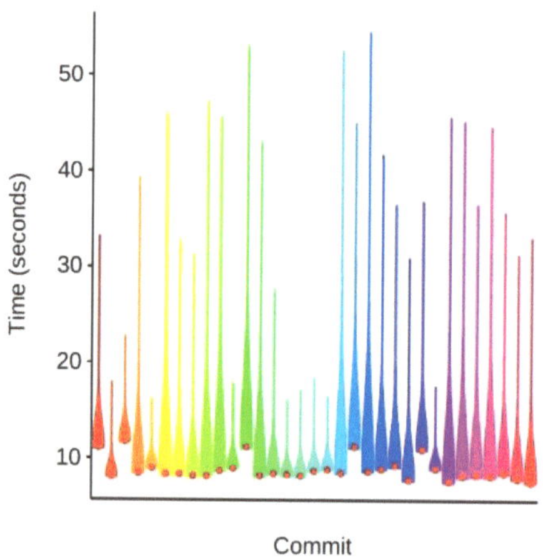

Figure 5.46: Violin plots of benchmark times for a sample of 33 commits to SAX builder (average of 7,357 measurements per commit). Data from Horký. Github-Local

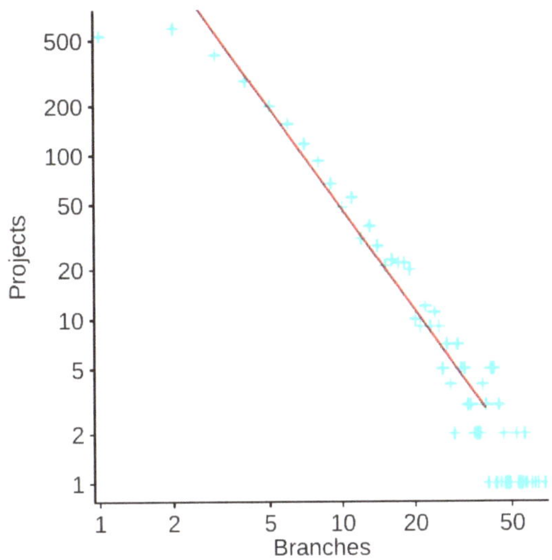

Figure 5.47: Number of projects on Github (out of 2,923) having a given number of branches; the line is a fitted regression model of the form: projects $\propto$ branches $^{-2}$. Data from Zou et al. Github-Local

A study by Zou, Zhang, Xia, Holmes and Chen [2033] investigated the use of version control branches during the development of 2,923 projects (which had existed for at least 5 -years, had at least 100 commits and three contributors). Figure 5.47 shows the number of projects that have had a given number of branches, with fitted regression line (which excluded the case of a single branch).

5.4.7 Supporting multiple markets

As the amount of functionality supported by a program grows, it may become more profitable to sell targeted configurations (i.e., programs supporting a subset of the available features), rather than one program supporting all features. Reasons for supporting multiple configurations include targeting particular market segments and reducing program resource usage, e.g., the likely cpu time and memory consumed when running the program with the options enabled/disabled. [1703]

Rather than maintaining multiple copies of the source, conditional compilation may be used to select the code included in a particular program build (e.g., using macro names); this topic is discussed in section 7.2.10.

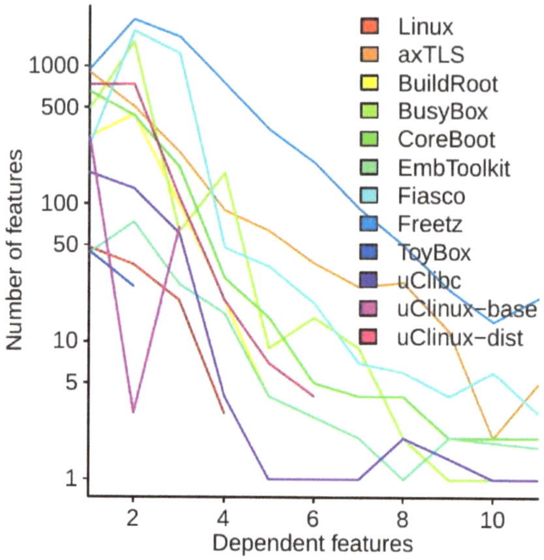

Figure 5.48: Number of optional features selected by a given number of flags. Data kindly provided by Berger. Github-Local

A study by Berger, She, Lotufo, Wąsowski and Czarnecki investigated the interaction between build flags and optional program features in 13 open source projects. Figure 5.48 shows the number of optional features that are enabled when a given number of build flags are set.

5.4.8 Refactoring

Refactoring is an investment that assumes there will be a need to modify the code again in the future, and it is more cost effective to restructure the code now, rather than at some future date. Possible reasons for time shifting an investment in reworking code include: developers not having alternative work to do, or an expectation that the unknown future modifications will need to be made quickly, and it is worth investing time now to reduce future development schedules; also, developers sometimes feel peer pressure to produce source that follows accepted ecosystem norms, e.g., open source that is about to be released.

A justification sometimes given for refactoring is to reduce technical debt. Section 3.2.5 explains why the concept of debt is incorrect in this context, and discusses how to analyse potential investments (such as refactoring).

While models of the evolution of software systems developed with a given cash flow have been proposed, [1589] finding values for the model parameters requires reliable data, which is rarely available.

A study by Kawrykow and Robillard [980] investigated 24,000 change sets from seven longlived Java programs. They found that between 3% and 16% of all method updates consisted entirely of non-essential modifications, e.g., renaming of local variables, and trivial keyword modifications.

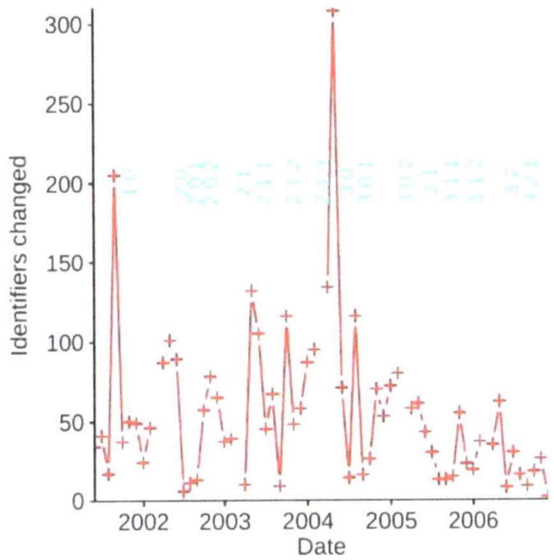

Figure 5.49: Number of identifiers renamed, each month, in the source of Eclipse-JDT; version released on given date shown. Data from Eshkevari et al. Github-Local

A study by Eshkevari, Arnaoudova, Di Penta, Oliveto, Guéhéuc and Antoniol [559] of identifier renamings in Eclipse-JDT and Tomcat, found that almost half were applied to method names, a quarter to field names, and most of the rest to local variables and parameter names. No common patterns of grammatical form, of the renaming, were found, e.g., changing from a noun to a verb occurred in under 1% of cases. Figure 5.49 shows the number of identifiers renamed in each month, along with release dates; no correlation appears to exist between the number of identifiers renamed and releases. Other studies [1333,1885] have found that moving fields and methods, and renaming methods are very common changes.

5.4.9 Documentation

The term documentation might be applied to any text: requirements, specifications, code documentation, comments in code, testing procedures, bug reports and user manuals; source code is sometimes referred to as its own documentation or as self-documenting. Section 4.6.4 discusses information sources.

Motivations for creating documentation include:

- a signal of commitment, e.g., management wants people to believe that the project will be around for the long term, or is important,
- fulfil a contract requirement. This requirement may have appeared in other contracts used by the customer, and nobody is willing to remove it; perhaps customer management believes that while they do not understand code, they will understand prose,
- an investment intended to provide a worthwhile return by reducing the time/cost of learning for future project members.

Development projects that derive income from consultancy and training have an incentive to minimise the publicly available documentation. Detailed knowledge of the workings of a software system may be the basis for a saleable service, and availability of documentation reduces this commercial potential.

Issues around interpreting the contents of documentation are covered in chapter 6. The existence of documentation can be a liability, in that courts have considered vendors liable for breach of warranty when differences exist between product behavior and the behavior specified in the associated documentation. [972]

5.4.10 Acceptance

Is the behavior of the software, as currently implemented, good enough for the client to agree to pay for it?

A study by Garman [653] surveyed 70 program and project managers of US Air Force projects about their priorities. Meeting expectations (according to technical specifications) was consistently prioritized higher than being on budget or on time; your author could not model priority decisions by fitting the available explanatory variables using regression; see Github-projects/ADA415138.R.

Benchmarking of system performance is discussed in section 13.3.

A study by Hofman [840] investigated user and management perceptions of software product quality, based on 15 commercial development projects. Quality assessment did not appear to be objective, suffering from issues such as: incomplete information, the effort needed to perform a complete evaluation, and anchoring of opinions based on quality evaluations of earlier releases; see Github-developers/Hofman-exp1.R.

5.4.11 Deployment

New software systems often go through a series of staged releases (e.g., alpha, followed by beta releases and then release candidates); the intent is to uncover any unexpected customer problems.

Traditionally releases have been either time-based (i.e., specified as occurring on a given date), or feature based, i.e., when a specific set of features has been implemented. Iterative development can enable faster, even continuous, releases (in a rapidly changing market the ability to respond quickly to customer feedback is a competitive advantage issues). Decreasing the friction experienced by a customer, in updating to a new release, increases the likelihood that the release is adopted.

One approach to working towards a release at a future date, is to pause work on new features sometime prior to the release, switching development effort to creating a system that is usable by customers; the term code freeze is sometimes used to describe this second phase of development.

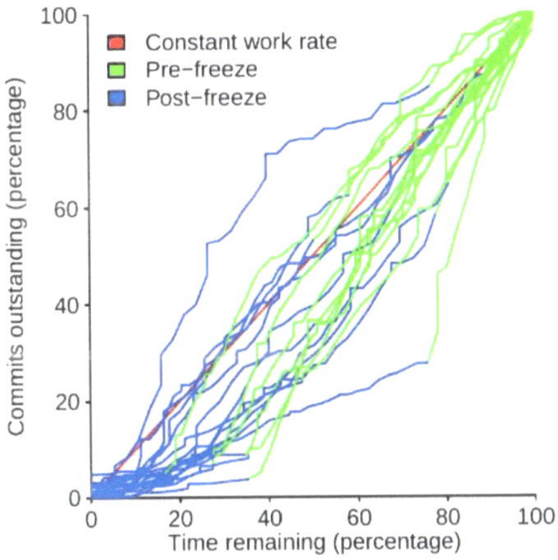

Figure 5.50: Percentage of commits outstanding against percentage the time remaining before deployment, for 18 releases; blue/green transition is the feature freeze date, red line shows a constant commit rate. Data kindly provided by Laukkanen. Github-Local

A study by Laukkanen, Paasivaara, Itkonen, Lassenius and Arvonen [1095] investigated the number of commits prior to 19 releases of four components of a software system at Ericsson; the length of the code freeze phase varied between releases. Figure 5.50 shows the percentage of commits not yet completed against percentage of time remaining before deployment, for 18 releases; red line shows a constant commit rate, green lines are prefreeze date, blue lines post-freeze. See Githubrojects/laukkanen2017/laukkanen2017.R for component break-down, and regression models.

A basic prerequisite for making a new release is being able to build the software, e.g., being able to compile and link the source to create an executable. Modifications to the source may have introduced mistakes that prevent an executable being built. One study [1852] of 219,395 snapshots (after each commit) of 100 Java systems on Github found that 38% of snapshots could be compiled. Being able to build a snapshot is of interest to researchers investigating the evolution of a system, but may not be of interest to others.

Continuous integration is the name given to the development process where checks are made after every commit to ensure that the system is buildable (regression tests may also be run).

A study by Zhao, Serebrenik, Zhou, Filkov and Vasilescu [2016] investigated the impact of switching project development to use continuous integration, e.g., Travis CI. The regression models built showed that, after the switch, the measured quantity that changed was the rate of increase of monthly merged commits (these slowed considerably, but there was little change in the rate of non-merged commits); see Github-projects/ASE2017.R.

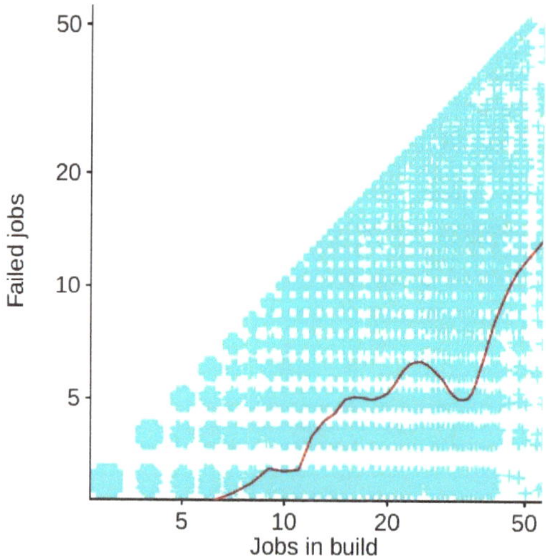

Figure 5.51: Number of failed jobs in Travis CI builds involving a given number of jobs (points have been jittered); line is a loess fit. Data from Gallaba et al. Github-Local

A study by Gallaba, Macho, Pinzger and McIntosh [644] investigated Travis CI logs from 123,149 builds, from 1,276 open source projects; 12% of passing builds contained an actively ignored failure. Figure 5.51 shows the number of failed jobs in each build involving a given number of jobs; line is a loess regression fit.

Building software on platforms other than the one on which it is currently being developed can require a lot of work. One approach, intended to do away with platform specific issues, is virtualization, e.g., Docker containers. One study, [364] from late 2016, was not able to build 34% of a sample of 560 Docker containers available on Github.

While some bespoke software is targeted at particular computing hardware, long-lasting software may be deployed to a variety of different platforms. The cost/benefit analysis of investing in reducing the cost of porting to a different platform (i.e., reducing the switching cost) requires an estimate of the likelihood that this event will occur.

For systems supporting many build-time configurations options, it may be more cost effective [766] to concentrate on the popular option combinations, and wait until problems with other configurations are reported (rather than invest resources checking many options that will never be used; various configuration sampling algorithms are available [1254]).

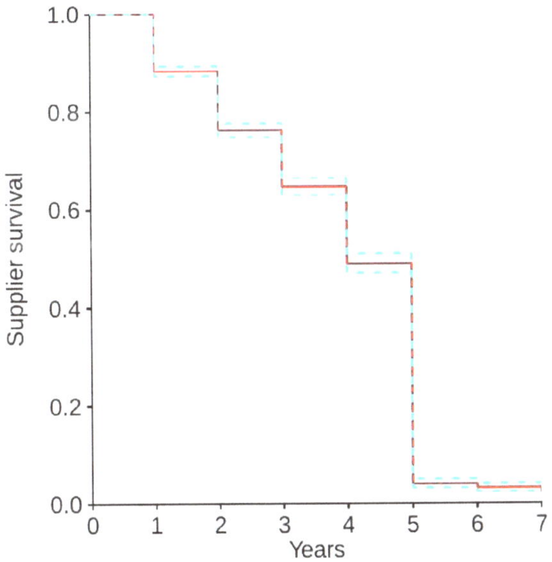

Figure 5.52: Survival curve of IT outsourcing suppliers continuing to work for 2,382 Credit Unions. Data kindly provided by Peukert. Github-Local

A study by Peukert [1476] investigated the switching costs of outsourced IT systems, as experienced by U.S. Credit Unions. Figure 5.52 shows the survival curve of IT outsourcing suppliers employed by 2,382 Credit Unions, over the period 2000 to 2010.

5.5 Development teams

A project needs people in possession of a minimum set of skills (i.e., they need to be capable of doing the technical work), and for individuals to be able to effectively work together as a team. Team members may have to manage a portfolio of project activities.

People working together need to maintain a shared mental model. Manned space exploration is one source for evidence-based studies of team cognition. [471]

Team members might be drawn from existing in-house staff, developers hired for the duration of the project (e.g., contractors), and casual contributors (common for open source projects [95]). Some geographical locations are home to a concentration of expertise in particular application domains, e.g., Cambridge, MA for drug discovery. The O-ring theory [1043] offers an analysis of the benefits, to employers and employees in the same business, of clustering together in a specific location. [625]

If a group of potential team members is available for selection, along with their respective scores in a performance test, it may be possible to select an optimal team based on selecting individuals, but selection of an optimal team is not always guaranteed. [1022] Personnel economics [1099] (i.e., how much people are paid) can also be an important factor in who might be available as a team member.

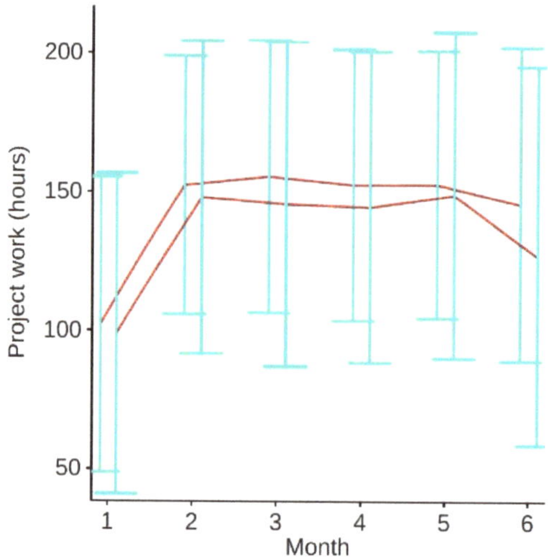

Figure 5.53: Average number of hours worked per month (by an individual), with standard deviation, for two projects staffed by 1,657 and 834 people; two red lines and corresponding error bars offset either side of month value. Data kindly provided by Bao. Github-Local

Developers can choose what company to work for, have some say in what part of a company they work in, and may have control over whether to work with people on the implementation of particular product features.

A study by Bao, Xing, Xia, Lo and Li [131] investigated software development staff turnover within two large companies. Figure 5.53 shows the mean number of hours worked per month, plus standard deviation, by staff on two projects (of 1,657 and 834 people). A regression model containing the monthly hours worked by individuals fits around 10% of the variance present in the data.

When a project uses multiple programming languages, a team either needs to include developers familiar with multiple languages, or include additional developers to handle specific languages. Figure 5.54 shows the number of different languages used in a sample of 100,000 GitHub projects (make was not counted as a language).

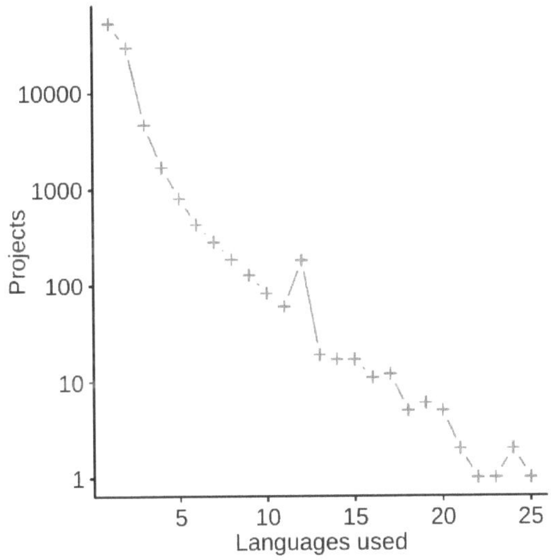

Figure 5.54: Number of projects making use of a given number of different languages in a sample of 100,000 GitHub project. Data kindly provided by Bissyande. Github-Local

What is the distribution of team size for common tasks undertaken on a development project?

Figure 5.55 shows the number of tasks that involved a given number of developers, for tasks usually requiring roughly an hour or two of an individual's time. The SiP tasks are from one company's long-running commercial projects, while the other tasks are aggregated from three companies following the Team Software Process.

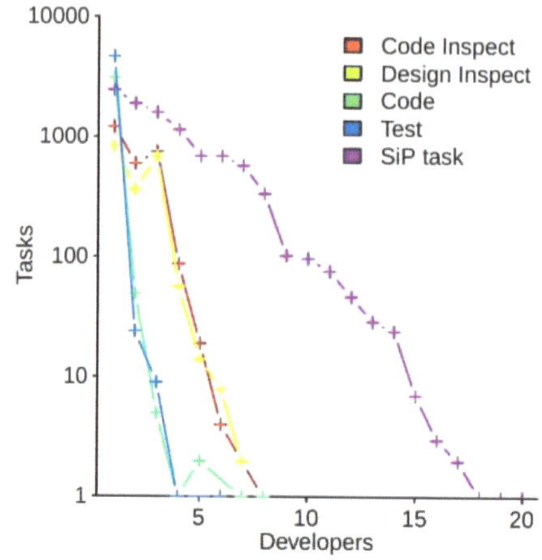

Figure 5.55: Number of tasks worked on by a given number of developers. Data from Nichols et al and Jones et al. Github-Local

Microsoft's postmortem analysis [907] of the development of what was intended to be Windows office, but became a Windows word processor, illustrates the fits and starts of project development. Figure 5.56 shows the number of days remaining before the planned ship date, for each of the 63 months since the start of the project, against number of full time engineers. The first 12 months were consumed by discussion, with no engineers developing software. See figure 3.17 for a more consistent approach to project staffing.

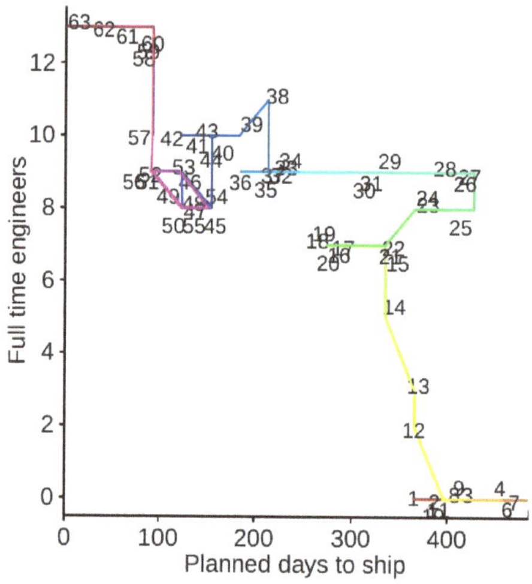

Figure 5.56: Number of days before planned product ship date, against number of full time engineers, for each of the 63 months since the project started (numbers show months since project started). Data from Jackson. Github-Local

What is a cost effective way of organizing and staffing a software project team?

There have been few experimental comparisons [1965] of the many project development techniques proposed over the years.

The early software developers were irregulars, in that through trial and error each found a development technique that worked for them. Once software development became a recurring activity within the corporate environment, corporate management techniques were created to try to control the process. [1042]

Drawing a parallel with the methods of production used in manufacturing, the factory concept has been adapted for software projects [425] by several large companies. [x] The claimed advantages of this approach are the same as those it provides to traditional manufacturers, e.g., control of the production process and reduction in the need for highly skilled employees.

The chief programmer team [122] approach to system development was originally intended for environments where many of the available programmers are inexperienced (a common situation in a rapidly growing field); an experienced developer is appointed as the chief programmer, who is responsible for doing detailed development, and allocating the tasks requiring less skill to others. This form of team organization dates from the late 1960s, when programming involved a lot of clerical activity, and in its original formulation emphasis is placed on delegating this clerical activity. Had it been successful, this approach could also be applied to reduce costs in environments where experienced programmers are available (by hiring cheaper, inexperienced programmers).

Once a system has been delivered and continues to be maintained, developers are needed to fix reported problems, and to provide support. [1803] Once initial development is complete, management need to motivate some of those involved to continue to be available to work on the software they are familiar with; adding new features provides a hedonic incentive for existing developers to maintain a connection with the project, and potential new development work is an enticement for potential new team members. A study by Buettner [275] investigated large software intensive systems, and included an analysis of various staffing related issues, such as: staffing level over time (fig 14.4) and staff work patterns (fig 11.61).

If team member activities are divided into communicating and non-communication (e.g., producing code), how large can a team become before communication activities cause total team output to decline when another person is added?

Assuming that communications overhead, [xi] for each team member, is: $t_0(D^\alpha - 1)$, where t_0 is the percentage of one person's time spent communicating in a two-person team, D

the number of people in the team and α a constant greater than zero. The peak team size, before adding people starts reducing total output, is given by: [1815]

$$D_{\text{peak}} = \left[\frac{1+t_0}{(1+\alpha)t_0}\right]^{\frac{1}{\alpha}}$$

If $\alpha = 1$ (i.e., everybody on the project incurs the same communications overhead), then $D_{\text{peak}} = \frac{1+t_0}{2t_0}$, which for small t_0 is: $D_{\text{peak}} \approx \frac{1}{2t_0}$. For example, if team members spend 10% of their time communicating with every other team member: $D_{\text{peak}} = \frac{1+0.1}{2\times 0.1} \approx 5$.

In this team of five, 50% of each person's time is spent communicating.

If $\alpha = 0.8$, then: $D_{\text{peak}} = \left[\frac{1+0.1}{(1+0.8)\times 0.1}\right]^{\frac{1}{0.8}} \approx 10$.

Figure 5.57 shows the effective rate of production (i.e., sum of the non-communications work of all team members) of a team of a given size, whose culture has a particular form of communication overhead.

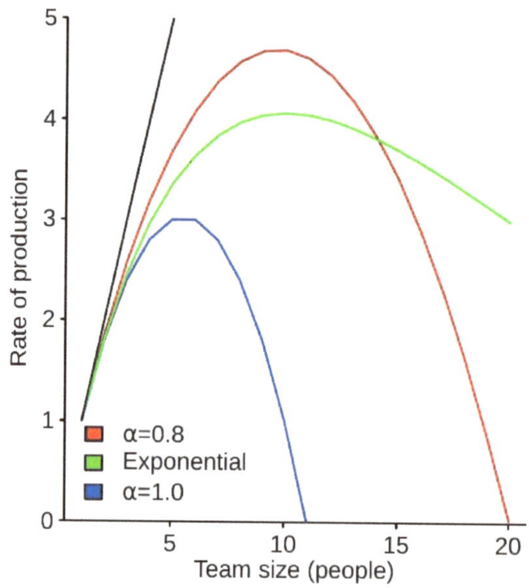

Figure 5.57: Effective rate of production of a team containing a given number of people, with communication overhead $t_0 = t_1 = 0.1$, and various distributions of percentage communication time; black line is zero communications overhead. Github-Local

If people spend most of their time communicating with a few people and very little with the other team members, the distribution of communication time may have an exponential distribution; the (normalised) communications overhead is: $1 - e^{-(D-1)t_1}$, where t_1 is a constant found by fitting data from the two-person team (before any more people are added to the team).

Peak team size is now:

$$D_{\text{peak}} = \frac{1}{t_1}, \text{ and, if } t_1 = 0.1, \text{ then: } D_{\text{peak}} = \frac{1}{0.1} = 10.$$

In this team of ten, 63% of each person's time is spent communicating (team size can be bigger, but each member will spend more time communicating compared to the linear overhead case).

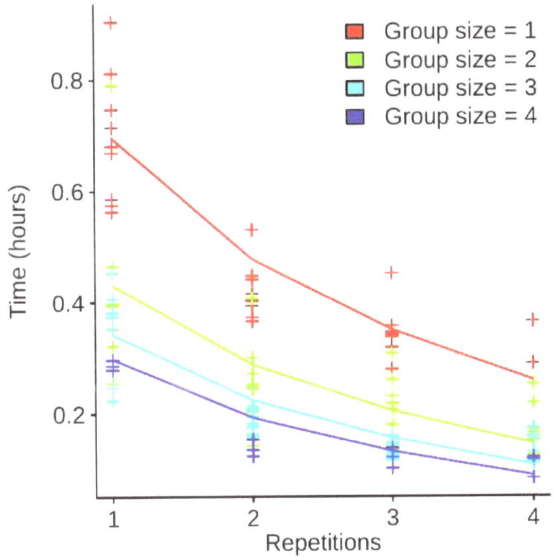

Figure 5.58: Time taken by groups of different sizes to manually assembly a product, over multiple trials; lines are fitted regression models of the form: Time $\propto \frac{0.5-0.2\log(\text{Repetitions})}{\text{Group\_size}} - 0.1\log(\text{Repetitions})$. Data kindly provided by Peltokorpi et al. Github-Local

A study by Peltokorpi and Niemi [1464] investigated the impact of learning and team size on the manual construction of a customised product. Figure 5.58 shows how the time taken to manually assemble the product, for groups containing various numbers of members, decreases with practice. Group learning is discussed in section 3.4.5.

5.5.1 New staff

New people may join a project as part of planned growth, the need to handle new work, existing people leaving, management wanting to reduce the dependency on a few critical people, and many other reasons.

Training people (e.g., developers, documentation writers) who are new to a project reduces the amount of effort available for building the system in the short term. Training is an investment in people, whose benefit is the post-training productivity these people bring to a project.

Brooks' Law [266] says: "Adding manpower to a late software project makes it later", but does not say anything about the impact of not adding manpower to a late project. Under what conditions does adding a person to a project cause it to be delayed?

If we assume a new person diverts, from the project they join, a total effort, T_e, in training and that after D_t units of time the trained person contributes E_n effort per unit time until the project deadline; unless the following inequality holds, training a new person results in the project being delayed (in practice a new person's effort contribution ramps up from zero, starting during the training period):

$E_{a1}D_r < (E_{a1}D_t - T_e) + (E_{a2} + E_n)(D_r - D_t)$, where E_{a1} is the total daily effort produced by the team before the addition of a new person, E_{a2} the total daily effort produced by the original team after the addition, and D_r is the number of units of time between the start of training, and the delivery date/time.

Adding a person to a team can both reduce the productivity of the original team (e.g., by increasing the inter-person communication overhead) and increase their productivity (e.g., by providing a skill that enables the whole to be greater than the sum of its parts). Assuming that $E_{a2} = cE_{a1}$, the equation simplifies to: $T_e < (D_r - D_t)(E_n - (1 - c)E_{a1})$. If a potential new project member requires an initial investment greater than this value, having them join the team will cause the project deadline to slip.

The effort, T_e, that has to be invested in training a new project member will depend on their existing level of expertise with the application domain, tools being used, coding skills, etc (pretty much everything was new, back in the day, for the project analysed by Brooks, so T_e was probably very high). There is also the important ability, or lack of, to pick things up quickly, i.e., their learning rate.

How often do new staff encounter tasks they have not previously performed?

A study by Jones and Borgatti [940] analysed the tags (having the form @word) used to classify each task in the Renzo Pomodoro dataset; all @ words were selected by one person, for the tasks they planned to do each day. Figure 5.59 shows the time-line of the use of @words, with the y-axis ordered by date of first usage. The white lines are three fitted regression models, each over a range of days; the first and last lines have the form: at_num $= a + b(1 - e^{c\times \text{days}})$, and the middle line has the form: at_num $= a \times$ days; with a, b, and c constants fitted by the regression modeling process.

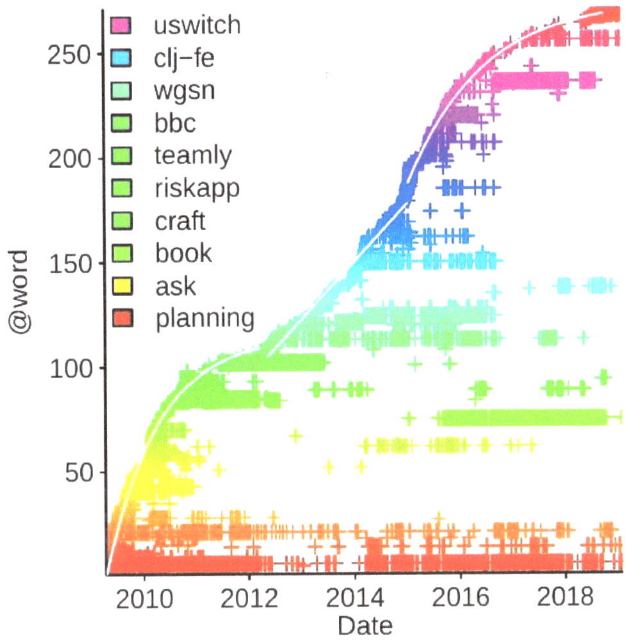

Figure 5.59: Time-line of first @word usage, ordered on y -axis by date of first appearance; legend shows @words with more than 500 occurrences. Data from Jones et al. Github-Local

The decreasing rate of new @words, over two periods (of several years), shows how a worker within a company experienced a declining rate of new tasks, the longer the time spent within a particular role.

5.5.2 Ongoing staffing

Software systems that continue to be used may continue to be supported by software developers, e.g., reported faults addressed and/or new features added.

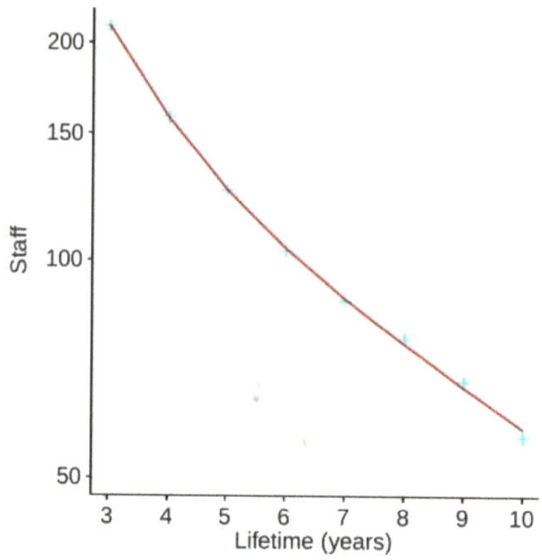

Figure 5.60: Average number of staff required to support renewal of code having a given average lifetime (green); blue/red lines show fitted biexponential regression model. Data extracted from Elliott. Github-Local

A study by Elliott [540] investigated the staffing levels for large commercial systems (2 MLOC) over the lifetime of the code (defined as the time between a system containing the code first going live and the same system being replaced; renewal was the terminology used by the author); the study did not look at staffing for the writing of new systems or maintenance of existing systems. Figure 5.60 shows the average number of staff needed for renewal of code having a given average lifetime, along with a biexponential regression fit.

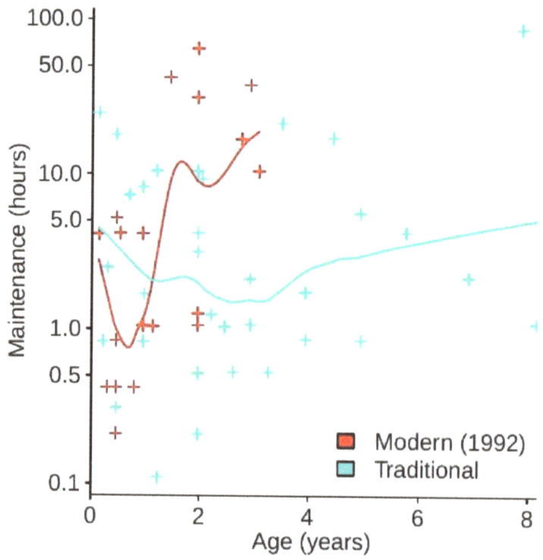

Figure 5.61: Age of systems, developed using one of two methodologies, and corresponding monthly maintenance effort, lines are loess regression fits. Data extracted from Dekleva. Github-Local

A study by Dekleva [481] investigated the average monthly maintenance effort (in hours) spent on products developed using traditional and modern methods (from a 1992 perspective). Figure 5.61 shows the age of systems, and the corresponding time spent on monthly maintenance.

5.6 Post-delivery updates

Once operational, software systems are subject to the economics of do nothing, update or replace. The, so-called, maintenance of a software system is a (potentially long term) project in its own right.

Software is maintained in response to customer demand, and changes are motivated by this demand, e.g., very large systems in a relatively stable market are likely to have a different change profile than smaller systems sold into a rapidly changing market. Reasons motivating vendors to continue to invest in developing commercial products are discussed in chapter 4; also see Github-ecosystems/maint-dev-ratio.R.

Work on software written for academic research projects often stops once project funding drys up. A study [867] of 214 packages associated with papers published between 20012015, in the journal Molecular Ecology Resources, found that 73% had not been updated since publication.

Updating software used in safety-critical systems is a non-trivial process; [451] a change impact analysis needs to be made during maintenance, and formal update processes followed.

Buildings are sometimes held up as exemplars of creative items that experience long periods of productive use with little change. In practice buildings that are used, like software, often undergo many changes, [244] and the rearchitecting can be as ugly as that of some software systems. Brand [244] introduced the concept of shearing layers to refer to the way buildings contain multiple layers of change (Lim [1143] categorised the RALIC requirements into five layers).

A new release contains code not included in previous releases, and some of the code contained in earlier releases may not be included.

A study by Ozment and Schechter investigated security vulnerabilities in 15 successive versions of OpenBSD, starting in May 1998. The source added and removed in each release was traced. Figure 5.62 shows the number of lines in each release (x -axis) that were originally added in a given release (colored lines).

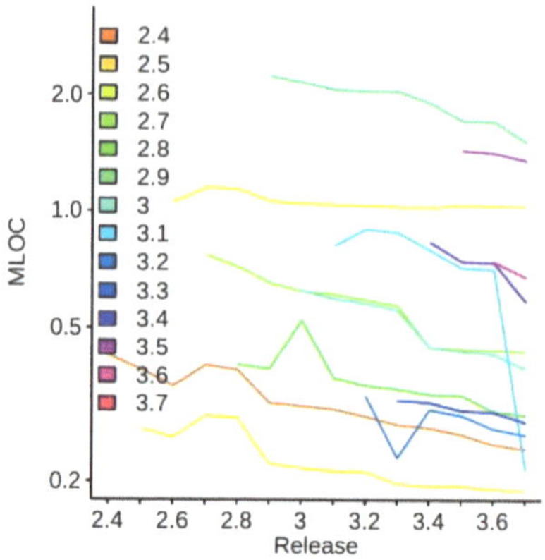

Figure 5.62: Number of lines of code in a release (x -axis) originally added in a given release (colored lines). Data kindly provided by Ozment. Github-Local

Existing customers are the target market for product updates, and vendors try to keep them happy (to increase the likelihood they will pay for upgrades). Removing, or significantly altering, the behavior of a widely used product feature has the potential to upset many customers (who might choose to stay with the current version that has the behavior they desire). The difficulty of obtaining accurate information on customer interaction with a product incentivizes vendors to play safe, e.g., existing features are rarely removed or significantly changed. If features are added, but rarely removed, a product will grow over time.

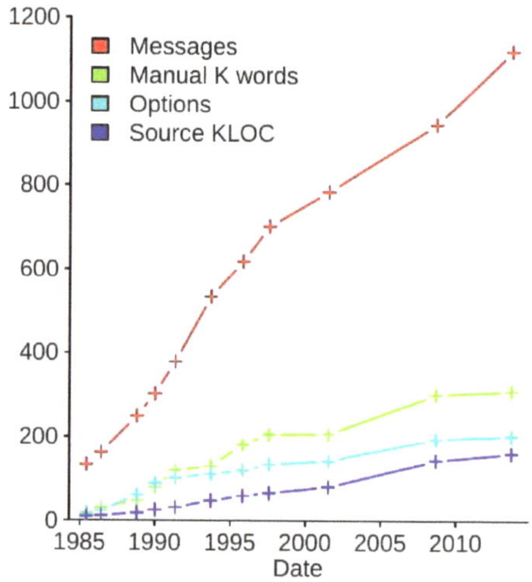

Figure 5.63: Growth of PC-Lint, over 11 major releases in 28 years, of messages supported, command line options, kilo-words in product manual, and thousands of lines of code in the product. Data kindly provided by Gimpel. Github-Local

Figure 5.63 shows the growth of lines of code, command line options, words in the manual and messages supported by PC-Lint (a C/C+ +static analysis tool), in the 11 major releases over 28 years.

Companies in the business of providing software systems may be able to charge a monthly fee for support (e.g., fixing problems), or be willing to be paid on an ad-hoc basis. [1784]

An organization using in-house bespoke software may want the software to be adapted, as the world in which it is used changes. The company that has been maintaining software for a customer is in the best position to estimate actual costs, and the price the client is likely to be willing to continue paying for maintenance; see fig 3.23. Without detailed maintenance cost information, another company bidding to take over maintenance of an existing system [198] has to factor in an unknown risk; in some cases the client may be willing to underwrite their risk.

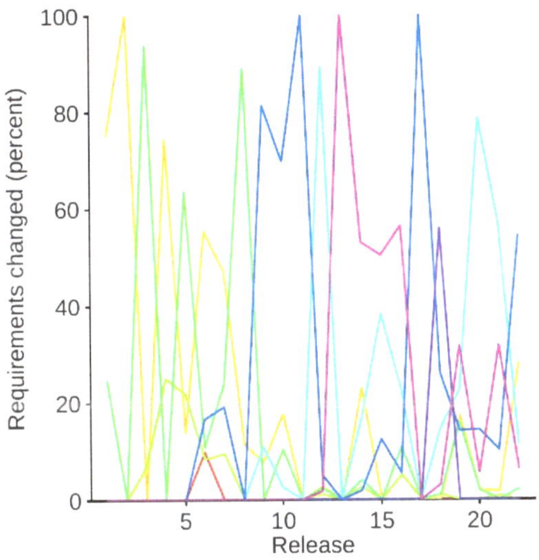

Figure 5.64: Percentage of requirements added/deleted/modified for eight features (colored lines) of a product over 22 releases. Data extracted from Felici. Github-Local

A study by Felici [591] analysed the evolution of requirements, over 22 releases, for eight features contained in the software of a safety-critical avionics system. Figure 5.64 shows the requirements for some features completely changing between releases, while the requirements for other features were unchanged over many releases.

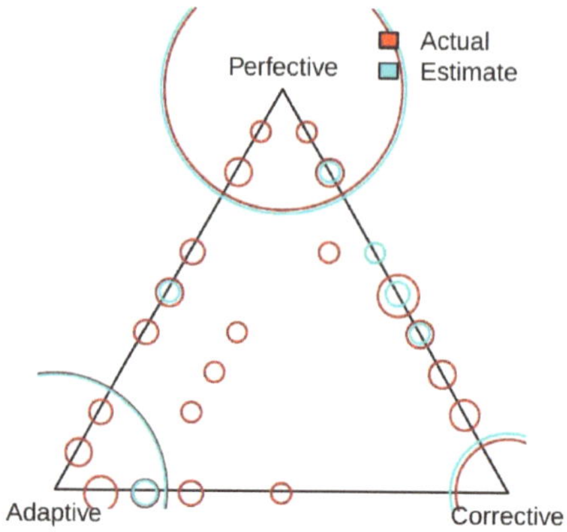

Figure 5.65: Ternary plot showing developers' estimated and actual percentage time breakdown performing adaptive, corrective and perfective work accumulated over 1,294 maintenance tasks; size of accumulation denoted by circle size. Data from Hatton. Github-Local

A study by Hatton [786] investigated 1,294 distinct maintenance tasks. For each task, developers estimated the percentage time expected to be spent on adaptive, corrective and perfective activities, this was recorded, along with the actual percentage. Figure 5.65 shows a ternary plot of accumulated (indicated by circle size) estimated and actual percentage time breakdown for all tasks.

With open source projects, changes may be submitted by non-core developers, who do not have access rights to change the source tree.

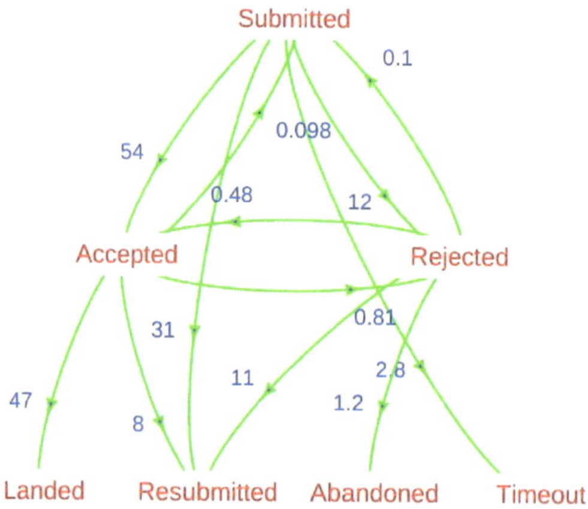

Figure 5.66: Percentage of patches submitted to WebKit (34,535 in total) transitioning between various stages of code review. Data from Baysal et al. Github-Local

A study by Baysal, Kononenko, Holmes and Godfrey [154] tracked the progress of 34,535 patches submitted through the WebKit and Mozilla Firefox code review process, between April 2011 and December 2012. Figure 5.66 shows the percentage of patches (as a percentage of submitted patches) being moved between various code review states in WebKit.

Source code is changed via patches to existing code. In the case of the Linux kernel submitted patches first have to pass a review process; patches that pass review then have to be accepted by the maintainer of the appropriate subsystem, these maintainers submit patches they consider worth including in the official kernel to Linus Torvalds (who maintains the official version).

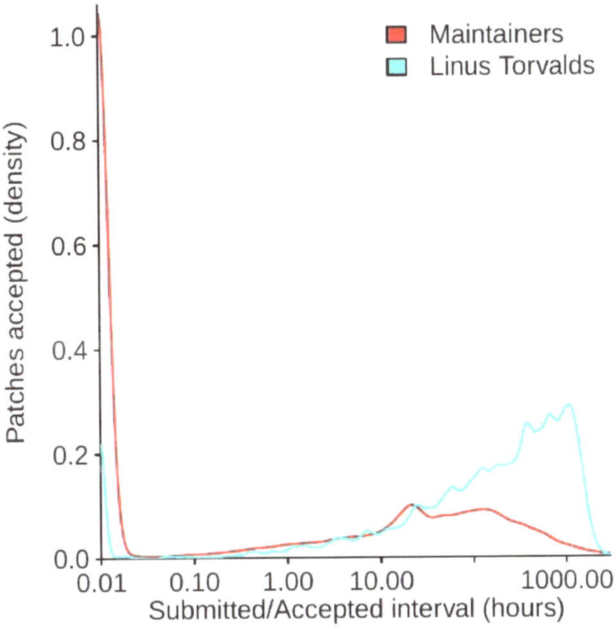

Figure 5.67: Density plot of interval between a patch passing review and being accepted by a maintainer, and interval between a maintainer pushing the patch to Linus Torvalds, and it being accepted into the blessed mainline (only patches accepted by Torvalds included). Data from Jiang et al. Github-Local

A study by Jiang, Adams and German [918] investigated attributes of the patch submission process, such as the time between submission and acceptance (around 30% of the patches that make it through review are accepted into the kernel); the data includes the 81,000 + patches to the kernel source, between 2005 and 2012. Figure 5.67 shows a kernel density plot of the interval between a patch passing review and being accepted by the appropriate subsystem maintainer, and the interval between a maintainer pushing a patch and it being accepted by Torvalds. Maintainers immediately accept half of patches that pass review (Torvalds 6%). The kernel is on roughly an 80 day (sd 12 days) release cycle; the rate at which Torvalds accepts patches steadily increases, before plummeting at the end of the cycle.

Open source projects may be forked, that is a group of developers may decide to take a copy of the code, to work on it as an independent project; see section 4.2.1. Features added to a fork or fixed coding mistakes may be of use to the original project. A study by Zhou, Vasilescu and Kästner [2024] investigated factors that influence whether a pull request submitted to the parent project, by a forked project, are accepted. The 10 variables in the fitted model explained around 25% of the variance [xii]; see Github-economics/fse19ForkEfficency.R.

A variety of packages implementing commonly occurring application functionality are freely available e.g., database and testing [2006] frameworks.

The need to interoperate with other applications can cause a project to switch the database framework used by an application, or to support multiple database frameworks. The likelihood of an increase/decrease in the number of database frameworks used, and the time spent using different frameworks, is analysed in table 11.6.

5.6.1 Database evolution

Many applications make use of database functionality, with access requests often having the form of SQL queries embedded in strings within the source code. The structure of a database, its schema, may evolve, e.g., columns are added/removed from tables, and tables are added/removed; changes may be needed to support new functionality, or involve a reorganization, e.g., to save space or improve performance.

The kinds of changes made to a schema will be influenced by the need to support existing users (who may not want to upgrade immediately), and the cost of modifying existing code.

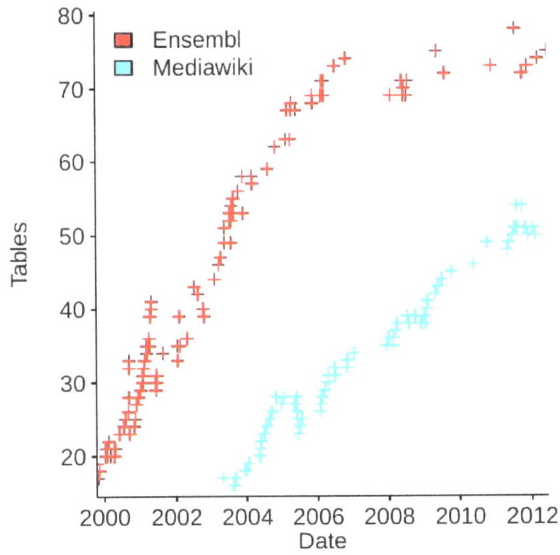

Figure 5.68: Evolution of the number of tables in the Mediawiki and Ensembl project database schema. Data from Skoulis. Github-Local

A study by Skoulis [1720] investigated changes to the database schema of several projects over time, including: Mediawiki (the software behind Wikipedia and other wikis), and Ensembl (a scientific project). Figure 5.68 shows one database schema in a linear growth phase (like the source code growth seen in some systems, e.g., fig 11.2), while the other has currently stopped growing, e.g., source code example fig 11.52. Systems change in response to customer requirements, and there is no reason to believe that the growth patterns of these two databases won't change.

Figure 5.69 shows the table survival curve for the Mediawiki and Ensembl database schema. Why is the table survival rate for Wikimedia much higher than Ensembl? Perhaps there are more applications making use of the contents of the Wikimedia schema, and the maintainers of the schema don't want to generate discontent in their user-base, or the maintainers are just being overly conservative. Alternatively, uncertainty over what data might be of interest in the Ensembl scientific project may result in the creation of tables that eventually turn out to be unnecessary, and with only two institutions involved, table removal may be an easier decision. The only way of finding out what customer demands are driving the changes is to talk to those involved.

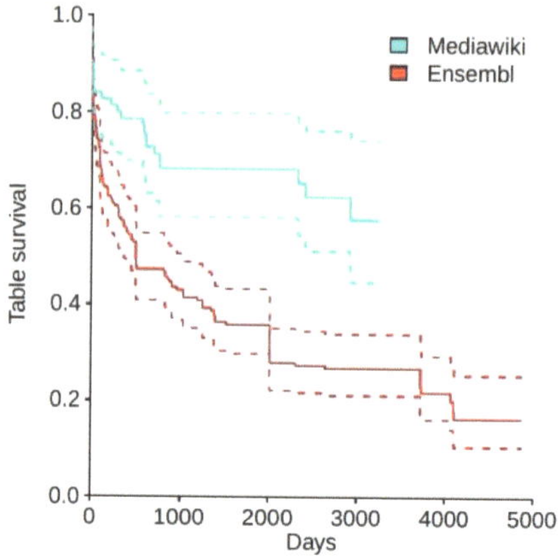

Figure 5.69: Survival curve for tables in Wikimedia and Ensembl database schema, with 95% confidence intervals. Data from Skoulis. Github-Local

The presence of tables and columns in a schema does not mean the data they denote is used by applications; application developers and the database administrator may be unaware they are unused, or they may have been inserted for use by yet to be written code.

A database may contain multiple tables, with columns in different tables linked using foreign keys. One study [1886] of database evolution found wide variation in the use of foreign keys, e.g., foreign keys being an integral part of the database, or eventually being completely removed (sometimes driven to a change of database framework).

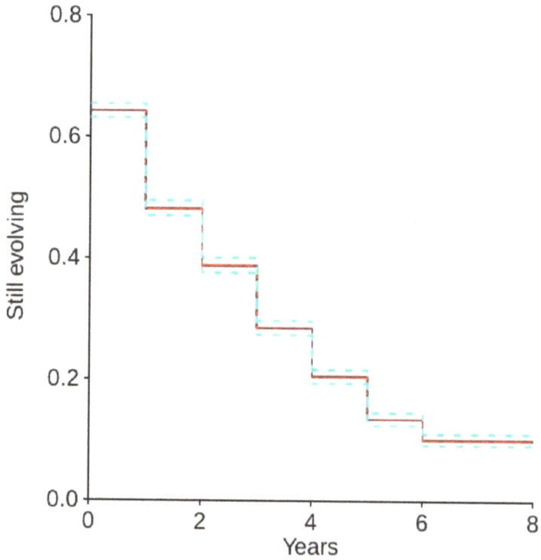

Figure 5.70: Survival curve for year of last modification of database programs, i.e., years before they stopped being changed, with 95% confidence intervals. Data from Blum. Github-Local

A study by Blum [213] investigated the evolution of databases and associated programs in the Johns Hopkins Oncology Clinical Information System (OCIS), a system that had been in operational use since the mid-1970s. Many small programs (a total of 6,605 between 1980 and 1988, average length 15 lines) were used to obtain information from the database. Figure 5.70 shows the survival curve for the year of last modification of a program, i.e., the probability that they stopped evolving after a given number of years.

Chapter 6
Reliability

6.1 Introduction

People are willing to continue using software containing faults, which they sometimes experience, [1] provided it delivers a worthwhile benefit. The random walk of life can often be nudged to avoid unpleasantness, or the operational usage time can be limited to keep within acceptable safety limits. Regions of acceptability may exist in programs containing many apparently major mistakes, but supporting useful functionality.

Software systems containing likely fault experiences are shipped because it is not economically worthwhile fixing all the mistakes made during their implementation; also, finding and fixing mistakes, prior to release, is often constrained by available resources and marketing deadlines. [334]

Software release decisions involve weighing whether the supported functionality provides enough benefit to be attractive to customers (i.e., they will spend money to use it), after factoring in likely costs arising from faults experienced by customers (e.g., from lost sales, dealing with customer complaints and possible fixing reported problems, and making available an updated version).

How many fault experiences will customers tolerate, before they are unwilling to use software, and are some kinds of fault experiences more likely to be tolerated than others (i.e., what is the customer utility function)? Willingness-to-pay is a commonly used measure of risk acceptability, and for safety-critical applications terms such as As Low As Reasonably Practicable (ALARP) [764] and So Far As Is Reasonably Practicable (SFAIRP) are used.

Some hardware devices have a relatively short lifetime, e.g., mobile phones and graphics cards. Comparing the survival rate of reported faults in Linux device drivers, and other faults in Linux, [1438] finds that for the first 18 months, or so (i.e., 500 days), the expected lifetime of reported fault experiences in device drivers is much shorter than fault experiences in other systems (see figure 6.1); thereafter, the two reported fault lifetimes are roughly the same.

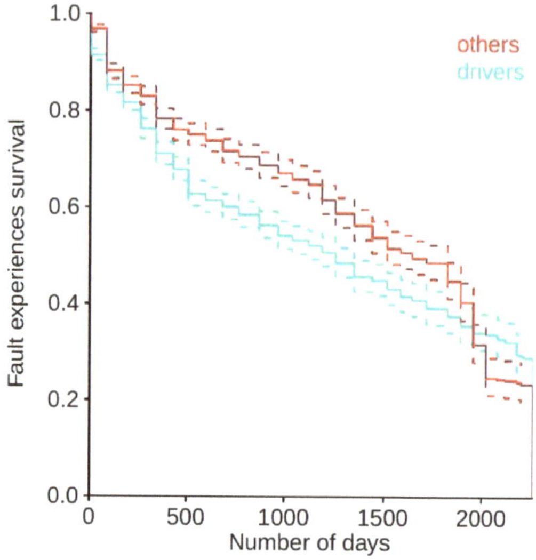

Figure 6.1: Survival rate of reported fault experiences in Linux device drivers and the other Linux subsystems. Data from Palix et al. Github-Local

People make mistakes; [1533,1566] economic considerations dictate how much is invested in reducing the probability that mistakes leading to costly fault experiences remain (either contained in delivered software systems, or as a component of a larger system). The fact that programs often contained many mistakes was a surprise to the early computer developers, [1960] as it is for people new to programming. [ii]

Developers make the coding mistakes that create potential fault experiences, and the environment in which the code executes provides the input that results in faults occurring (which may be experienced by the user). This chapter discusses the kinds of mistakes made, where they occur in the development process, methods used to locate them and techniques for estimating how many fault experiences can potentially occur. Issues around the selection of algorithms is outside the scope of this chapter; algorithmic reliability issues include accuracy [484] and stability of numerical algorithms, [826] and solutions include minimising the error in a dot product by normalizing the values being multiplied. [541]

Operating as an engineering discipline does not in itself ensure that a constructed system has the desired level of reliability. There has been, roughly, a 30 -year cycle for bridge failures; [1475] new design techniques and materials are introduced, and growing confidence in their use leads to overstepping the limits of what can safely be constructed.

What constitutes reliability, in a given context, is driven by customer requirements, e.g., in some situations it may be more desirable to produce an inaccurate answer than no answer at all, while in other situations no answer is more desirable than an inaccurate one.

Program inputs that cause excessive resource usage can also be a reliability issue. Examples of so-called denial of service attacks include regular expressions that are susceptible to nonlinear, or exponential, matching times for certain inputs. [442]

The early computers were very expensive to buy and operate, and much of the software written in the 1960s and 1970s was funded by large corporations or government bodies; the US Department of Defence took an active role in researching software reliability, and much of the early published research is based on the kinds of software development projects undertaken on behalf of the DOD and NASA projects during this period.

The approach to software system reliability promoted by these early research sponsors set the agenda for much of what has followed, i.e., a focus on large projects that are expected to be maintained over many years, or systems operating in situations where the cost of failure is extremely high and there is very limited time, if any, to fix issues, e.g., Space shuttle missions. [706]

This chapter discusses reliability from a cost/benefit perspective; the reason that much of the discussion involves large software systems is that a data driven discussion has to follow the data, and the prexisting research focus has resulted in more data being available for large systems. Mistakes have a cost, but these may be outweighed by the benefits of releasing the software containing them. As with the other chapters, the target audience is software developers and vendors, not users; it is possible for vendors to consider a software system to be reliable because it has the intended behavior, but for many users to consider it unreliable because it does not meet their needs.

The relative low cost of modifying existing software, compared to hardware, provides greater flexibility for trading-off upfront costs against the cost of making changes later (e.g., by reducing the amount of testing before release), knowing that it is often practical to provide updates later. For some vendors, the Internet provides an almost zero cost update distribution channel.

In some ecosystems it is impractical or impossible to update software once it has been released, e.g., executable code associated with the Ethereum cryptocurrency is stored on a blockchain (coding mistakes can have permanent crippling consequences [1827]).

Mistakes in software can have a practical benefit for some people, for instance, authors of computer malware have used mistakes in cpu emulators to detect that their activity may be monitored [1436] (and therefore the malware should remain inactive).

Mistakes are not unique to software systems; a study [1268] of citations in research papers found an average error rate of 20%.

Proposals [835] that programming should strive to be more like mathematics are based on the misconception that the process of creating proofs in mathematics is less error prone than creating software. [453]

The creation of mathematics shares many similarities with the creation of software, and many mistakes are made in mathematics; [1511] mathematical notation is a language with rules specifying syntax and permissible transformations. The size, complexity and technicality of modern mathematical proofs has raised questions about the ability of anybody to check whether they are correct, e.g., Mochizuki's proof of the *abc* conjecture, [306] and the Hales-Ferguson proof of the Kepler Conjecture. [1068] Many important theorems don't have proofs, only sketches of proofs and outline arguments that are believed to be correct; [1354] the sketches provide evidence used by other mathematicians to decide whether they believe a theorem is true (a theorem may be true, even though mistakes are made in the claimed proofs).

Mathematical proof differs from software in that the proof of a theorem may contain mistakes, and the theorem may still be true. For instance, in 1899 Hilbert found mistakes [1927] in Euclid's Elements (published around 300 BC); the theorems were true, and Hilbert was able to add the material needed to correct the proofs. Once a theorem is believed to be true, mathematicians have no reason to check its proof.

The social processes involved in the mathematics community coming to believe that a theorem is true, is evolving, to come to terms with believing machine-checked proofs. [1502] The nature and role of proof in mathematics continues to be debated. [819]

Mistakes are much less likely to be found in mathematical proofs than software, because a lot of specialist knowledge is needed to check new theorems in specialised areas, but a clueless button pusher can experience a fault in software simply by running it; also, there are few people checking proofs, while software is being checked every time it is executed. One study [313] found that 7% of small random modifications to existing proofs, written in Coq, did not cause the proof to be flagged as invalid.

Fixing a reported fault experience is one step in a chain of events that may result in users of the software receiving an update.

For instance, operating system vendors have different approaches to the control they exercise over the updates made available to customers. Apple maintains a tight grip over use of iOS, and directly supplies updates to customers cryptographically signed for a particular device, i.e., the software can only be installed on the device that downloaded it.

Google supplies the latest version of Android to OEMs and has no control over what, if any, updates these OEMs supply to customers (who may chose to install versions from third-party suppliers). Microsoft sells Windows 10 through OEMs, but makes available security fixes and updates for direct download by customers.

Figure 6.2 shows some of the connections between participants in the Android ecosystem (number of each kind in brackets), and some edges are labeled with the number of known updates flowing between particular participants (from July 2011 to March 2016).

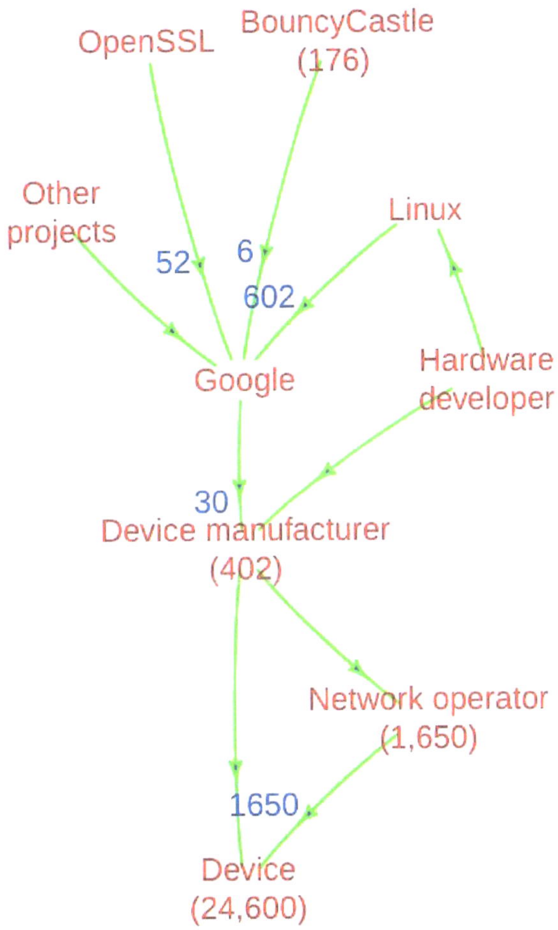

Figure 6.2: Flow of updates between participants in one Android ecosystem; number of each kind of member given in brackets, number of updates shipped on edges (in blue). Data from Thomas. Github-Local

Experiments designed to uncover unreliability issues may fail to find any. This does not mean that they are rare, the reason for failing to find a mistake may be lack of statistical power (i.e., the likelihood of finding an effect if one exists); this topic is discussed in section 10.2.3.

The software used for some applications is required to meet minimum levels of reliability, and government regulators (e.g., Federal Aviation Administration) may be involved in some form of certification (these regulators may not always have the necessary expertise, and delegate the work to the vendor building the system [508]).

In the U.S., federal agencies are required to adhere to an Executive Order [iii] that specifies: "Regulatory action shall not be undertaken unless the potential benefits to society for the regulation outweigh the potential costs to society." In some cases the courts have required that environmental, social and moral factors be included in the cost equation. [311]

Quality control: Manufacturing hardware involves making a good enough copy of a reference product. Over time [383] manufacturers have developed quality control techniques that support the consistent repetition of a production process, to deliver a low defect finished product. Software manufacturing involves copying patterns of bits, and perfect copies are easily made. The quality assurance techniques designed for the manufacture hardware are solving a problem relevant to software production.

The adoption of a quality certification process by an organization, such as ISO 9000, may be primarily symbolic. [813]

6.1.1 It's not a fault, it's a feature

The classification of program behavior as a fault, or a feature, can depend on the person doing the classification, e.g., user or developer. For instance, software written to manage a parts inventory may not be able to add a new item once the number of items it contains equals 65,536; a feature/fault that users will not encounter until an attempt is made to add an item that would take the number of parts in the inventory past this value.

Studies [493,820] of fault reports have found that many of the issues are actually requests for enhancement.

The choice of representation for numeric values places maximum/minimum bounds on the values that can be represented, and in the case of floating-point a percentage granularity on representable values. Business users need calculations on decimal values to be exact, something that is not possible using binary floating-point representations (unless emulated in software), and business oriented computers sometimes include hardware support for decimal floating-point operations; in other markets, implementation costs [414] resulted in binary becoming the dominant hardware representation for floating-point. While implementation costs eventually decreased to a point where it became commercially viable for processors to support both binary and decimal, much existing software has been written for processors that use a binary floating-point representation.

Intel's Pentium processor was introduced in 1993, as the latest member of the x86 family of processors. Internally the processor contains a 66-bit hardwired value for π. [iv] A double precision floating-point value is represented using a 53-bit mantissa, which means internal operations involving values close to π (e.g., using one of the instructions that calculate a trigonometric function) may have only 13 -bits of accuracy, i.e., $66 - 53$. To ensure that the behavior of new x86 family processors are consistent with existing processors, subsequent processors have continued to represented π internally using 66-bits (rather than the 128 -bits needed to achieve an accuracy of better than 1.5 ULP).

Figure 6.3 shows the error in the values returned by the cos instruction in Intel's Core i7-2600 processor, for 52,521 argument values close to $\frac{\pi}{2}$, expressed in units in the last place (ULP); from a study by Duplichan. [519]

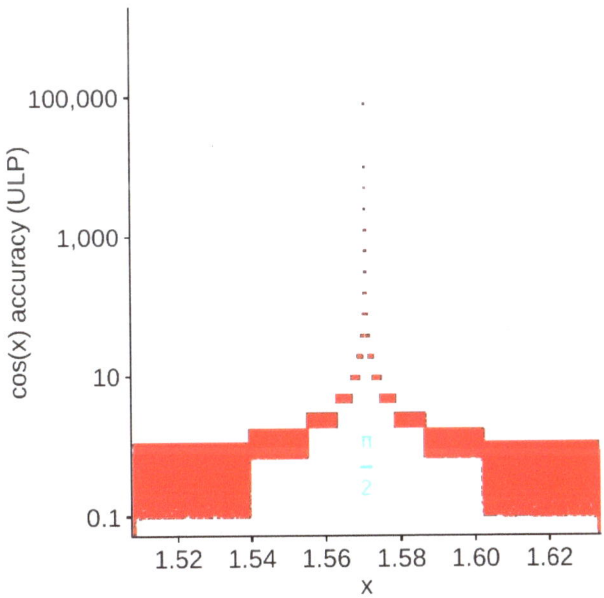

Figure 6.3: Accuracy of the value returned by the cos instruction on an Intel Core i7, for 52,521 argument values close to $\frac{\pi}{2}$. Data kindly provided by Duplichan. Github-Local

The variation in the behavior of software between different releases, or running the same code on different hardware can be as large as the behavior affect the user is looking for, potentially a serious issue when medical diagnosis is involved. [746]

The accuracy of calculated results may be specified in the requirements, or the developer writing the code may be the only person to give any thought to the issue. Calculations involving floating-point values may not be exact, and the algorithms used may be sensitive to rounding errors. [1962] Developers may believe they are playing safe by using variables declared to have types capable of representing greater accuracy than is required [1619] (leading to higher than necessary resource usage, [726] e.g., memory, time and battery power). Small changes to numerical code can produce a large difference in the output produced, [1813] and simple calculations may require complex code to correctly implement, e.g., calculating $\sqrt{a^2 + b^2}$.[222]

6.1.2 Why do fault experiences occur?

Two events are required for a running program to experience a software related fault:

- a mistake exists in the software,
- the program processes input values that cause it to execute the code containing the mistake in a way that results in a fault being experienced [411] (software that is never used has no reported faults).

Some coding mistakes are more likely to be encountered than others, because the input values needed for them to trigger a fault experience are more likely to occur during the use of the software. Any analysis of software reliability has to consider the interplay between the probabilistic nature of the input distribution, and coding mistakes present in the source code (or configuration information).

An increase in the number of people using a program is likely to lead to an increase in fault reports, because of both an increase in possible reporters and an increase in the diversity of input values.

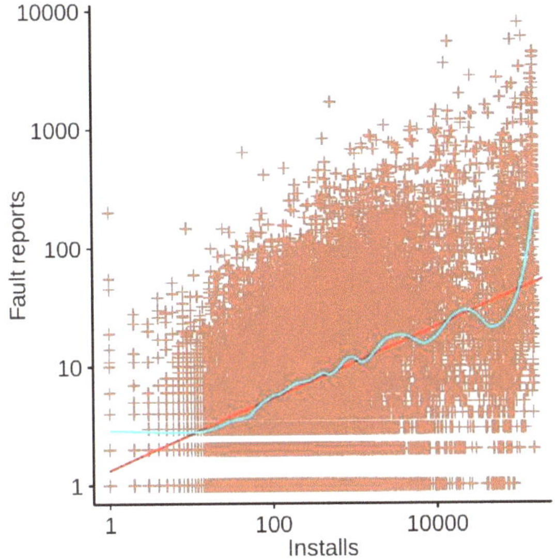

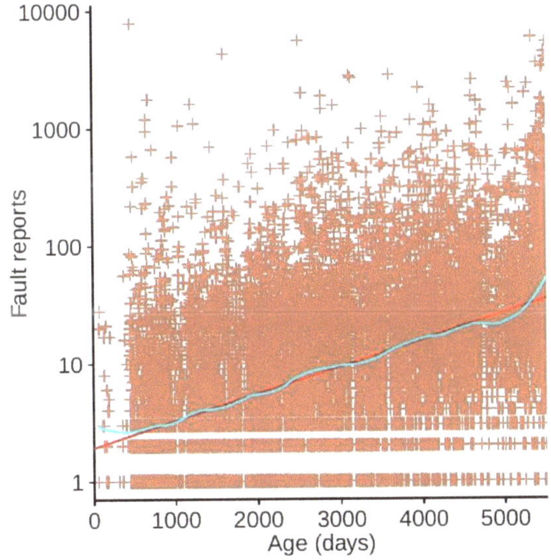

Figure 6.4: Reported faults against number of installations (upper) and age (lower). Data from the "wheezy" Debian release. Github-Local

The Ultimate Debian Database project collects information about packages included in the Debian Linux distribution, from users who have opted-in to the Debian Popularity Contest. Figure 6.4 shows the numbers of installs (for the "wheezy" release) of each packaged application against faults reported in that package, and also age of the package against faults reported (data from the Debian Bug Tracking System, which is not the primary fault reporting system for some packages); also, see fig 11.23. A fitted regression model is:

$$reported\_bugs = e^{-0.15+0.17\log(insts)+(30+2.3\log(insts))\times age\times 10^{-5}}$$

For an age between 1,000-6,000 and installs between 10-20,000 (log (insts) is between 2-10), the number of installations (a proxy for number of users) appears to play a larger role in the number of reported faults, compared to age (i.e., the amount of time the package has been included in the Debian distribution). The huge amount of variance in the data points to other factors having a major impact on number of reported faults.

A study [1787] of TCP checksum performance found that far fewer corrupt network packets were detected in practice, than expected (by a factor of between 10 and 100). The difference between practice and expectation was found to be caused by the non-uniform distribution of input values (the proof that checksum values are uniformly distributed assumes a uniform distribution of input values).

A hardware fault may cause the behavior of otherwise correctly behaving software to appear to be wrong; hardware is more likely to fail as the workload increases. [903]

6.1.3 Fault report data

While fault reports have been studied almost since the start of software development, until open source bug repositories became available there was little publicly available fault report data. The possibility of adverse publicity, and the fear of legal consequences, from publishing information on mistakes found in software products was not lost on commercial organizations, with nearly all of them treating such information as commercially confidential. While some companies maintained software fault report databases, [724] these were rarely publicly available.

During the 1970s, the Rome Air Defence Center published many detailed studies of software development, [424] and some included data on faults experienced by military software projects. [1967] However, these reports were not widely known about, or easy to obtain, until they became available via the Internet; a few studies were published as books. [1826]

The few pre-Open source datasets analysed in research papers contained relatively small numbers of fault reports, and if submitted for publication today would probably be rejected as not worthy of consideration. These studies [1471,1473] usually investigated particular systems, listing percentages of faults found by development phase, and the kinds of faults found; one study [1918] listed fault information relating to one application domain: medical device software. An early comprehensive list of all known mistakes in a widely used program was for LATEX. [1030]

The economic impact of loss of data, due to poor computer security, has resulted in some coding mistakes in some programs (e.g., those occurring in widely used applications that have the potential to allow third parties to gain control of a computer) being recorded in security threat databases. Several databases of security related issues are actively maintained, including: the NVD (National Vulnerability Database [890]), the VERIS Community Database (VCDB); [1887] an Open source vulnerability database, the Exploit database (EDB) [529] lists proof of concept vulnerabilities; mistakes in code that may be exploited to gain unauthorised access to a computer (vulnerabilities discovered by security researchers who have a motivation to show off their skills), and the Wooyun program. [2014]

While many coding mistakes exist in widely used applications, only a tiny fraction are ever exploited to effectively mount a malicious attack on a system. [1470]

In some application domains the data needed to check the accuracy of a program's output may not be available, or collected for many years, e.g., long range weather forecasts. The developers of the Community Earth System Model compare the results from previous climate calculations to determine whether modified code produces statistically different results. [121]

A study by Sadat, Bener and Miranskyy [1625] investigated issues involving connecting duplicate fault reports, i.e., reports involving the same mistake. Figure 6.5 shows the connection graph for Eclipse report 6325 (report 4671 was the earliest report covering this issue).

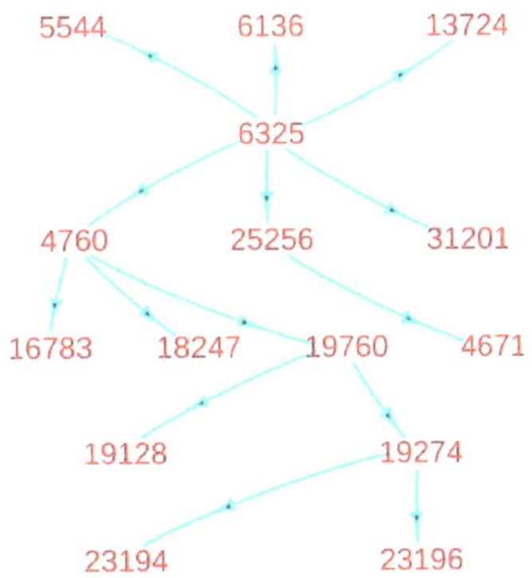

Figure 6.5: Duplicates of Eclipse fault report 4671 (report 6325 was finally chosen as the master report); arrows point to report marked as duplicate of an earlier report. Data from Sadat et al. Github-Local

Fixing a mistake may introduce a new mistake, or may only be a partial fix, i.e., fixing commits may be a continuation of a fix for an earlier fault report.

A study by Xiao, Zheng, Jiang and Sui [1985] investigated regression faults in Linux (the name given to fault experiences involving features that worked correctly, up until a code change). Figure 6.6 shows a graph of six fault reports for Linux (in red), the commits believed to fix the coding mistake (in blue), and subsequent commits needed to fix mistake(s) introduced by an earlier commit (in blue, follow arrows).

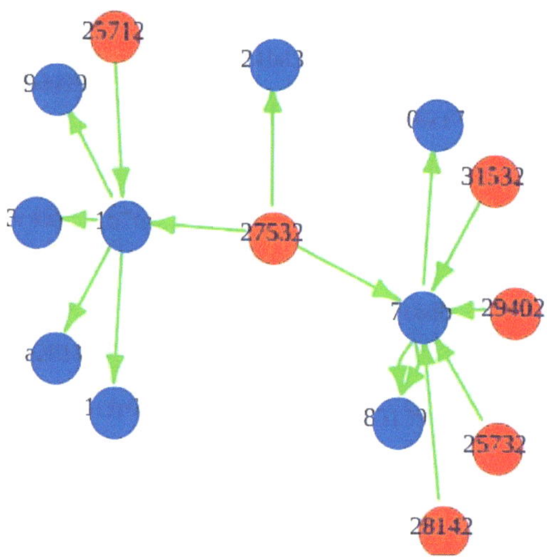

Figure 6.6: Six fault reports (red), their associated bug fixing commits (blue), and subsequent commits to fix mistakes introduced by the earlier commit (blue). Data from Xiao et al. Github-Local

How similar are the characteristics of Open source project fault report data, compared to commercial fault report data?

Various problems have been found with Open source fault report data, which is not to say that fault report data on closed source projects is not without its own issues; known problems include:

- reported faults do not always appear in the fault report databases; e.g., serious bugs tend to be under-reported in commit logs. One study of fault reports for Apache, over a 6-week period, found that only 48% of bug fixes were recorded as faults in the Bugzilla database; the working practice of the core developers was to discuss serious problems on the mailing list, and many fault experiences were never formally logged with Bugzilla,

- fault reports are misclassified. One study of fault reports (also see section 14.1.1) found that 42.6% of fault reports had been misclassified, with 39% of files marked as defective not actually containing any reported fault (e.g., were requests for enhancement),
- reporting bias: fault experiences discovered through actively searching for them, [574] rather than normal program usage (e.g., Linux is a popular target for researchers using fuzzing tools, and csmith generated source code designed to test compilers). The reporting of vulnerabilities contained, or not, in the NVD has been found to be driven by a wide variety social, technical and economic pressures. [359,1374] Data on fault reports discovered through an active search process may have different characteristics compared to faults experienced through normal program usage,
- the coding mistake is not contained within the source of the program cited, but is contained within a third-party library. One study [1178] surveyed developers about this issue,
- fault experience could not be reproduced or was intermittent: a study [1628] of six servers found that on average 81% of the 266 fault reports analysed could be reproduced deterministically, 8% non-deterministically, 9% were timing dependent, plus various other cases,

Fault report data does not always contain enough information to answer the questions being asked of it, e.g., using incidence data to distinguish between different exponential order fault growth models [1283] (information is required on the number of times the same fault experience has occurred; see section 4.3.2).

6.1.4 Cultural outlook

Cultures vary in their members' attitude to the risk of personal injury and death; different languages associate different concepts with the word reliability (e.g., Japanese), and the English use of the term at risk has changed over time. A study by Viscusi and Aldy investigated the value of a statistical life in 11 countries, and found a range of estimates from $0.7 million to $20 million (adjusted to the dollar rate in 2000). Individuals in turn have their own perception of risk, and sensitivity to the value of life. [1728] Some risks may be sufficiently outside a persons' experience that they are unable to accurately estimate their relative likelihood, or be willing to discount an occurrence affecting them, e.g., destruction of a city, country, or all human life, by a meteor impact. [1737]

Public perception of events influences, and is influenced by, media coverage (e.g., in a volcano vs. drought disaster, the drought needs to kill 40,000 times as many people as the volcano to achieve the same probability of media coverage). A study of disasters and media coverage found that when a disaster occurs at a time when other stories are deemed more newsworthy, aid from U.S. disaster relief is less likely to occur.

Table 6.1, from a 2011 analysis by the UK Department for Transport, lists the average value that would have been saved, per casualty, had an accident not occurred. A report [354] from the UK's Department for Environment, Food and Rural Affairs provides an example of the kind of detailed analysis involved in calculating a monetary valuation for reducing risk.

Table 6.1: Average value of prevention per casualty, by severity and element of cost (human cost based on willingness-to-pay values); last line is average over all casualties. Data from UK Department for Transport. [1842]

Injury severity	Lost output	Human costs	Medical and ambulance	Total
Fatal	£545,040	£1,039,530	£940	£1,585,510
Serious	£21,000	£144,450	£12,720	£178,160
Slight	£2,220	£10,570	£940	£13,740
Average	£9,740	£35,740	£2,250	£47,470

A study by Costa and Kahn [408] investigated changes in the value of life in the USA, between 1940 and 1980. The range of estimates, adjusted to 1990 dollars, was $713,000 to $996,000 in 1940, and $4.144 million to $5.347 million in 1980.

Some government related organizations, and industrial consortia, have published guidelines covering the use of software in various applications, e.g., in medical devices, [581] cybersecurity, [1558] and automotive. [92,1291,1292] Estimates of the number of deaths associated with computer related accidents contain a wide margin of error. [1186] Governments are aware of the dangers of society becoming overly risk-averse, and some have published risk management policies. [1916]

People often express uncertainty using particular phrases, rather than numeric values. Studies [1317] have found that when asked to quantify a probabilistic expression, the range of values given can be quite wide.

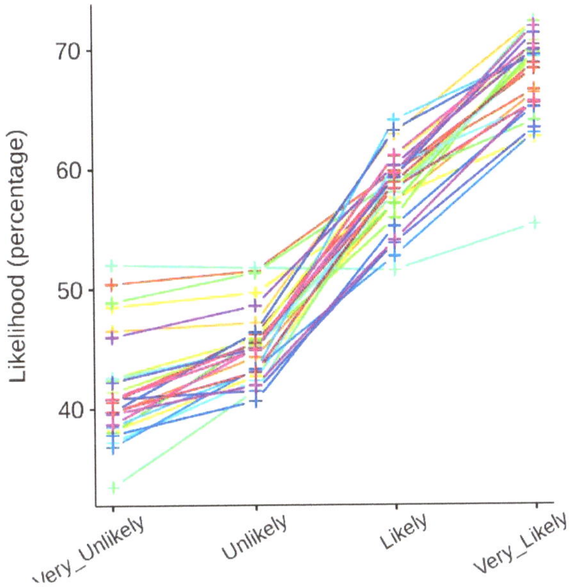

Figure 6.7: Mean percentage likelihood of (translated) statements containing a probabilistic term; one colored line per country. Data from Budescu et al. [274] Github-Local

A study by Budescu, Por, Broomell and Smithson investigated how people in 24 countries, speaking 17 languages, interpreted uncertainty statements containing four probability terms, i.e., very unlikely, unlikely, likely and very likely, translated to the subjects' language. Figure 6.7 shows the mean percentage likelihood estimated by people in each country to statements containing each term.

The U.S. Department of Defense Standard MIL-STD-882E [474] defines numeric ranges for some words that can be used to express uncertainty, when applied to an individual item; these words include:

- Probable: "Will occur several times in the life of an item"; probability of occurrence less than 10^{-1} but greater than 10^{-2}.
- Remote: "Unlikely, but possible to occur in the life of an item"; probability of occurrence less than 10^{-3} but greater than 10^{-6}.

- Improbable: "So unlikely, it can be assumed occurrence may not be experienced in the life of an item"; probability of occurrence less than 10^{-6}. Some phrases are used to express relative position on a scale, e.g., hot/warm/cold water describe position on a temperature scale. A study by Sharp, Paul, Nagesh, Bell and Surdeanu [1679] investigated, so-called gradable adjectives, e.g., huge, small. Subjects saw statements such as: "Most groups contain 1470 to 2770 mards. A particular group has 2120 mards. There is a moderate increase in this group."; subjects were then asked: "How many mards are there?". Figure 6.8 shows violin plots for the responses given to statements/questions involving various gradable quantity adjectives (see y -axis); the x -axis is in units of standard deviation from the mean response, i.e., a normalised scale.

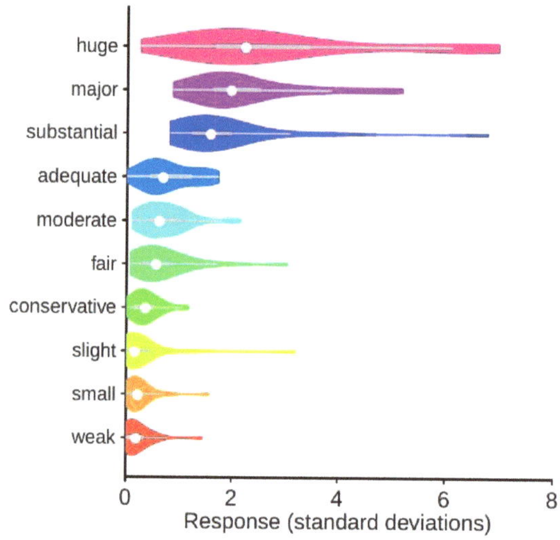

Figure 6.8: Subjects' perceived change in the magnitude of a quantity, when the given gradable size adjective is present. Data from Sharp et al. Github-Local

The interpretation of a quantifier (i.e., a word indicating quantity) may be context dependent. For instance, "few of the juniors were accepted" may be interpreted as: a small number were accepted; or, as: less than the expected number were accepted. [1866]

6.2 Maximizing ROI

A vendor's approach to product reliability is driven by the desire to maximize return on investment. The reliability tradeoff involves deciding how much to invest in finding and fixing implementation mistakes prior to release, against fixing fault experiences reported after release. Factors that may be part of the tradeoff calculation include:

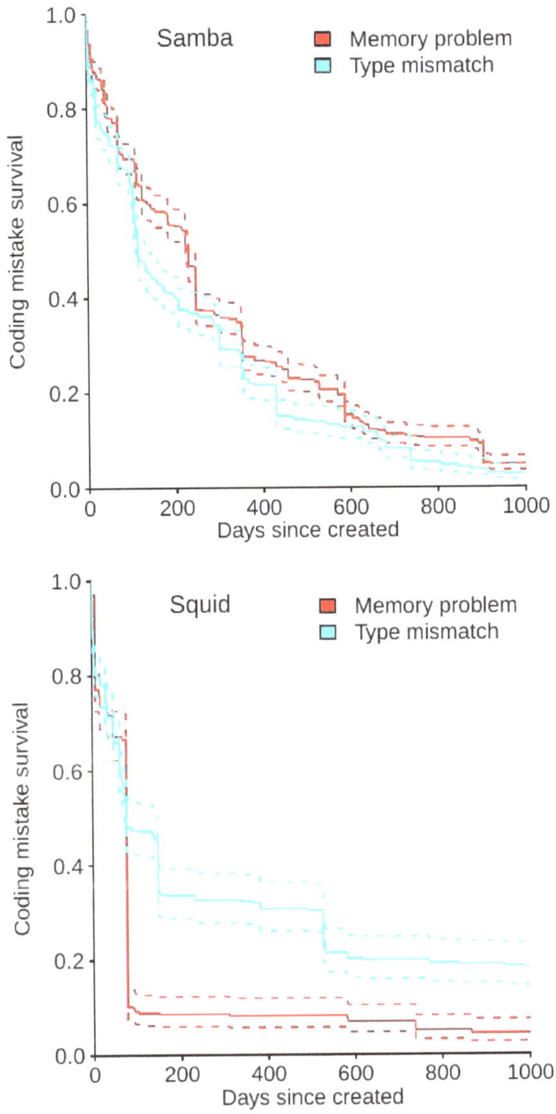

Figure 6.9: Survival curves of the two most common warnings reported by Splint in Samba and Squid, where survival was driven by code changes and not fixing a reported fault; with 95% confidence intervals. Data from De Penta et al. [492] Github-Local

- some mistakes will not generate fault experiences, and it is a waste of resources finding and fixing them. The lack of fault experiences, for a particular coding mistake, may be a consequence of software having a finite lifetime (see fig 3.7), or the source code containing the mistake being rewritten before it causes a fault to be experienced.

- A study by Di Penta, Cerulo and Aversano [492] investigated the issues reported by three static analysis tools (Rats, Splint and Pixy), when run on each release of several large software systems, e.g., Samba, Squid and Horde. The reported issues were processed, to find the first/last release where each issue was reported for a particular line of code (in some cases the issue was reported in the latest release). Figure 6.9 shows the survival curve for the two most common warnings reported by Splint (memory problem and type mismatch, make up over 85% of all generated warnings), where the warnings ceased because of code modifications that were not the result of a reported fault being fixed; also see fig 11.80.

The average lifetime of coding mistakes varies between programs and kind of mistake. [1437]

- there may be a competitive advantage to being first to market with a new or updated product; the largest potential costs may be lost sales, rather than the cost of later correction of reported faults, i.e., it may be worth taking the risk that customers are not deterred by the greater number of fault experiences; so-called frontier risk thinking,
- too much investment in finding and fixing mistakes can be counterproductive, e.g., customers who do not encounter many fault experiences may be less motivated to renew a maintenance agreement,
- whether the vendor cost of a fault experience includes the user costs associated with the user fault experience, e.g., when software is developed for in-house use. In extreme cases the cost of a fault experience can be hundreds of millions of dollars. [1332]

With COTS the cost of fault experiences is asymmetric, i.e., the customer bears the cost of the fault experience itself, while the vendor can choose whether to fix the mistake and ship an update. Existing consumer laws provide some legal redress [973] (at least until the existing legal landscape changes [1662]).

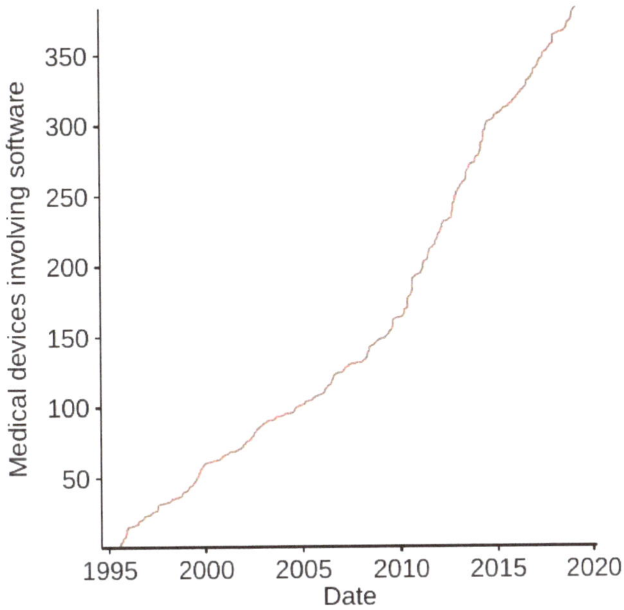

Figure 6.10: Cumulative number of class III (high-risk) medical devices, containing software in their product summary, achieving premarket approval from the FDA. Data from FDA. Github-Local

While coding mistakes are exploited by computer viruses, causing business disruption, the greatest percentage of computer related loses come from financial fraud by insiders, and traditional sources of loss such as theft of laptops and mobiles. [1581]

All mistakes have the potential to have costly consequences, but in practice most appear to be an annoyance. One study [39] found that only 2.6% of the vulnerabilities listed in the NVD have been used, or rather their use has been detected, in viruses and network threat attacks on computers.

Figure 6.10 shows the growth in the number of high-risk medical devices, containing the word software in their product summary, achieving premarket approval from the Federal Food and Drug Administration.

The willingness-to-pay (WTP) approach to reliability aims to determine the maximum amount that those at risk would individually be willing to pay for improvements to their, or other people's safety. Each individual may only be willing to pay a small amount, but as a group the amounts accumulate to produce an estimated value for the group "worth" of a safety improvement. For instance, assuming that in a group of 1.5 million people, each person is willing to pay £1 for safety improvements that achieve a 1 in 1 million reduction in the probability of death; the summed WTP Value of Preventing a Statistical Fatality

(VPF) is £1.5 million (the same approach can be used to calculate Value of Preventing non-fatal Injuries).

A market has developed for coding mistakes that can be exploited to enable third parties to gain control of other peoples' computers [38] (e.g., spying agencies and spammers), and some vendors have responded by creating vulnerability reward programs. The list of published rewards are both a measure of the value vendors place on the seriousness of particular kinds exploitable mistakes, and the minimum amount the vendor considers sufficient to dissuade discoverers spending time finding someone willing to pay more.

Bountysource is a website where people can pledge a monetary bounty, payable when a specified task is performed. A study by Zhou, Wang, Bezemer, Zou and Hassan [2021] investigated bounties offered to fix specified open issues, of some Github project (the 2,816 tasks had a total pledge value of $365,059). Figure 6.11 shows the total dollar amount pledged for each task; data broken down by issue reporting status of person specifying the task.

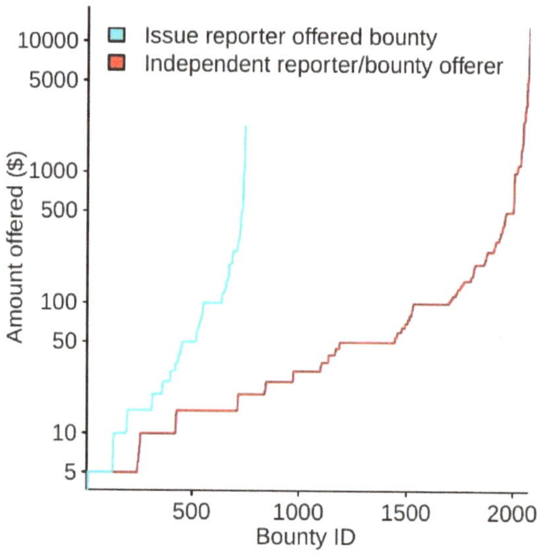

Figure 6.11: Value of bounties offered for 2,816 tasks addressing specified open issues of a Github project; pledges stratified by status of person reporting the pledge issue. Data from Zhou et al. Github-Local

The viability of making a living from bug bounty programs is discussed in connection with figure 4.43.

If a customer reports a fault experience, in software they have purchased, what incentive does the vendor have to correct the problem and provide an update (they have the customers' money; assuming the software is not so fault ridden that it is returned for a refund)? Possible reasons include:

- a customer support agreement requires certain kinds of reported faults to be fixed,
- public perception and wanting to maintain customer good will, in the hope of making further sales. One study [78] found that the time taken to fix publicly disclosed vulnerabilities was shorter than for vulnerabilities privately disclosed to the vendor; see section 11.11.3.1,
- a fill-in activity for developers, when no other work is available,
- it would be more expensive not to fix the coding mistake, e.g., the change in behavior produced by the fault experience could cause an accident, or negative publicity, that has an economic impact greater than the cost of fixing the mistake. Not wanting to lose money because a mistake has consequences that could result in a costly legal action (the publicity around a decision driven by a vendors' cost/benefit analysis may be seen as callous, e.g., the Ford Motor Company had to defend itself in court [1110] over its decision not to fix a known passenger safety issue, because they calculated the cost of loss of human life and injury did not exceed the benefit of fixing the issue).

Which implementation mistakes are corrected? While there is no benefit in correcting mistakes that customers are unlikely to experience, it may not be possible to reliably predict whether a mistake will produce a customer fault experience (leading to every mistake having to treated as causing a fault experience). Once a product has been released and known to be acceptable to many customers, there may not be any incentive to actively search for potential fault experiences, i.e., the only mistakes corrected may be those associated with a customer fault reports.

In some cases applications are dependent on the libraries supplied by the vendor of the host platform. One study [1149] of Apps running under Android found that those Apps using libraries that contained more reported faults had a slightly smaller average user rating in the Google Play Store.

What motivates developers to fix faults reported in Open source projects? Possible reasons include:

- they work for a company that provides software support services for a fee. Having a reputation as the go-to company for a certain bundle of packages is a marketing technique for attracting the attention of organizations looking to outsource support services, or pay for custom modifications to a package, or training.

Correcting reported faults is a costly signal that provides evidence a company employs people who know what they are doing, i.e., status advertising,

- developers dislike the thought of being wrong or making a mistake; a reported fault may be fixed to make them feel better (or to stop it preying on their mind), also not responding to known problems in code is not considered socially acceptable behavior in some software development circles. Feelings about what constitutes appropriate behavior may cause developers to want to redirect their time to fixing mistakes in code they have written or feel responsible for, provided they have the time; problems may be fixed by developers when management thinks they are working on something else.

6.3 Experiencing a fault

Unintended software behavior is the result of an interaction between a mistake in the code (or more rarely an incorrect translation by a compiler [1136]), and particular input values.

A program's source code may be riddled with mistakes, but if typical user input does not cause the statements containing these mistakes to be executed, the program may gain a reputation for reliability. Similarly, there may only be a few mistakes in the source code, but if they are frequently experienced the program may gain a reputation for being fault-ridden.

Almost all existing research on software reliability has focused on the existence of the mistakes in source code. This is convenience sampling, large amounts of Open source is readily available, while information on the characteristics of program input is very difficult to obtain.

The greater the number of people using a software system, the greater the volume and variety of inputs it is likely to process: consequently there are likely to be more reported fault experiences.

A study by Shatnawi [1681] investigated the impact of the number of sites using a release of telecommunication switch software, on the number of software failures reported. A regression model fitted to the data shows that reported fault experiences decreased over time, and increases with the number of installed sites; see Github-reliability/2014-04-13.R.

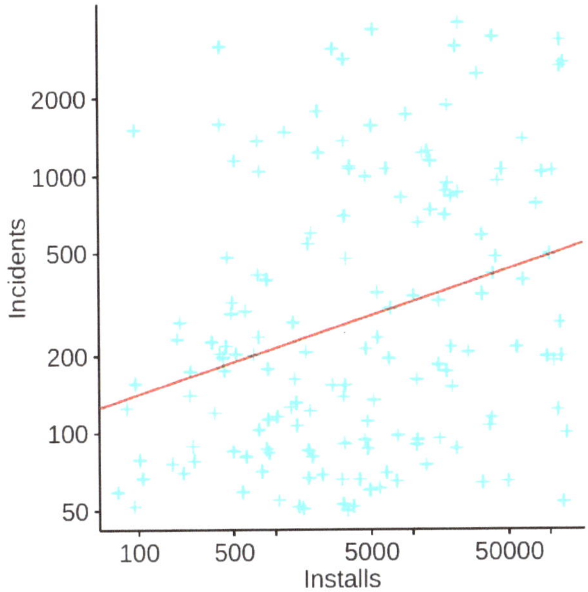

Figure 6.12: Number of incidents reported for each of 800 applications installed on over 120,000 desktop machines; line is fitted regression model. Data from Lucente. Github-Local

A study by Lucente [1165] investigated help desk incident reports, from 800 applications used by a 100,000 employee company with over 120,000 desktop machines. Figure 6.12 shows the number of incidents reported increasing with the number of installs (as is apparent from the plot, the number of installs only explains a small percentage of the variance).

A comparison of the number of fault experiences reported in different software systems [1489] might be used to estimate the number of people using the different systems; any estimate of system reliability has to take into account the volume of usage, and the likely distribution of input values.

The same user input can produce different fault experiences in different implementations of the same functionality, e.g., the POSIX library on 15 different operating systems. [488]

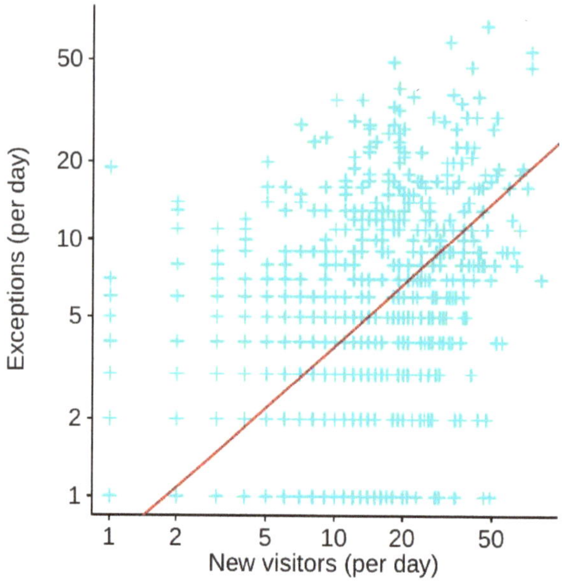

Figure 6.13: Number of exceptions experienced per day against number of new users of the application, for one application prior to its general release; line is a fitted regression model of the form: Exceptions $\propto$ newUserUses $^{0.8}$. Data from Dey et al. [489] Github-Local

A study by Dey and Mockus [489] investigated the impact of number of users, and time spent using a commercial mobile application, on the number of exceptions the App experienced. The App used Google analytics to log events, which provides daily totals. On many days no exceptions were logged, and when exceptions did occur it is likely that the same set of faults were repeatedly experienced. The fitted regression models (with exceptions as the response variable) contain both user-uses and new-user-uses as power laws, with the exponent for new-user-uses being the largest, and the impact of the version of Android installed on the users' device varied over several orders of magnitude; see Github-reliability/2002-09989.R.

Figure 6.13 shows, for one application on prerelease, the number of exceptions per day for a given number of new users.

6.3.1 Input profile

The environments in which we live, and software systems operate, often experience regular cycles of activity; events are repeated with small variations at a variety of scales (e.g., months of the year, days of the week, and frequent use of the same words; [1106] also see section 2.4.4).

The input profile that results in faults being experienced is an essential aspect of any analysis of program reliability. For instance, when repeatedly adding pairs of floatingpoint values, with each value drawn from a logarithmic distribution, the likelihood of experiencing an overflow [590] may not be low enough to be ignored (the probability for a single addition overflowing is 5.3×10^{-5} for single precision IEEE and 8.2×10^{-7} for double [v]).

Undetected coding mistakes [vi] exist in shipped systems because the input values needed to cause them to generate a fault experience were not used during the testing process.

Address traces illustrate how the execution characteristics of a program can be dramatically changed by its input. Figure 6.14 shows the number of memory accesses made while executing gzip on two different input files. The small colored boxes representing 100,000 executed instruction on the x-axis, and successive 4,096 bytes of stack on the y-axis, the colors denote number of accesses within the given block (using a logarithmic scale).

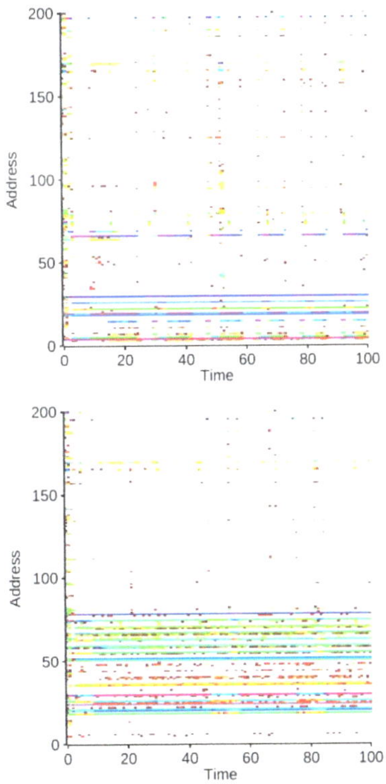

Figure 6.14: Number of accesses to memory address blocks, per 100,000 instructions, when executing gzip on two different input files. Data from Brigham Young via Feitelson. Github-Local

Mistakes in code that interact with input values that are likely to be selected by developers, during testing, are likely to be fixed during development; beta testing is one method for discovering customer oriented input values that developers have not been testing against. Ideally the input profiles of the test and actual usage are the same, otherwise resources are wasted fixing mistakes that the customer is less likely to experience.

The test process may include automated generation of input values; see section 6.6.2.1.

Does the interaction between mistakes in the source code, and an input profile, generate any recurring patterns in the frequency of fault experiences?

One way of answering this question is to count the number of inputs successfully processed by a program between successive fault experiences.

A study by Nagel and Skrivan [1347] investigated the timing characteristics of fault experiences in three programs, each written independently by two developers. During execution, each program processed inputs selected from the set of permissible values, when a fault was experienced its identity, execution time up to that point and number of input cases processed were recorded; the coding mistake was corrected and program execution continued until the next fault experience, until five or six faults had been experienced, or the mistake was extremely time-consuming to correct (the maximum number of input cases on any run was 32,808). This cycle was repeated 50 times, always starting with the original, uncorrected, program; the term repetitive run modeling was used to denote this form of testing. A later study by Nagel, Scholz and Skrivan [1346] partially replicated and extended this study.

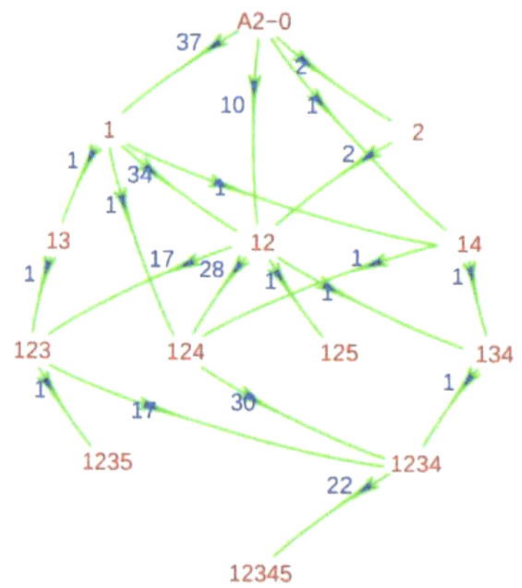

Figure 6.15: Transition counts of five distinct fault experiences in 50 runs of program A2; nodes labeled with each fault experienced up to that point. Data from Nagel et al. Github-Local

Figure 6.15 shows the order in which distinct faults were experienced by implementation. A2, over 50 replications; edge values show the number of times the nth fault experience was followed by a particular fault experience. For example, starting in state A2-0 fault experience 1 was the first encountered during 37 runs, and this was followed by fault experience 3 during one run.

Figure 6.16, upper plot, shows the number of input cases processed before a given number of fault experiences, during the 50 runs of implementation A2; the lower plot shows the number of inputs processed before each of five distinct fault experiences.

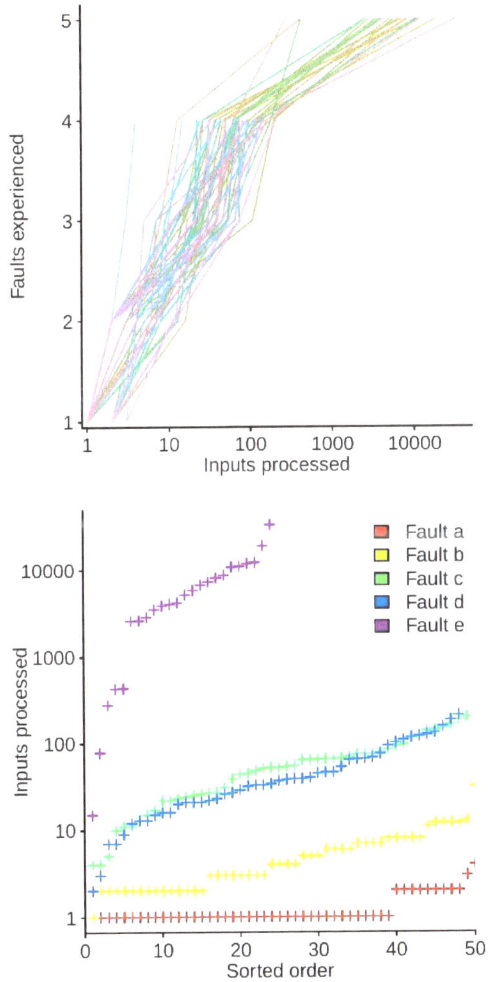

Figure 6.16: Number of input cases processed before a particular fault was experienced by program A2; the list is sorted for each distinct fault. Data from Nagel et al. Github-Local

What is the likely number of inputs that have to be processed by implementation A2 for the sixth distinct fault to be experienced? A regression model could be fitted to the data seen in the upper plot of figure 6.16, but a model fitted to this sample of five distinct fault experiences will have a wide confidence interval. There is no reason to expect that the sixth fault will be experienced after processing any number of inputs, there appears to be a change point after the fourth fault, but this may be random noise that has been magnified by the small sample size.

The time and cost of establishing, to a reasonable degree of accuracy, that users of a program have a very low probability of experiencing a fault [286] may not be economically viable.

A study by Dunham and Pierce [516] replicated and extended the work of Nagel and Skriva; problem 1 was independently reimplemented by three developers. The three implementations were each tested with 500,000 input cases, when a fault was experienced the number of inputs processed was recorded, the coding mistake corrected, and program execution restarted. This cycle was repeated four times, always starting with the original implementation, fixing and recording as faults were experienced.

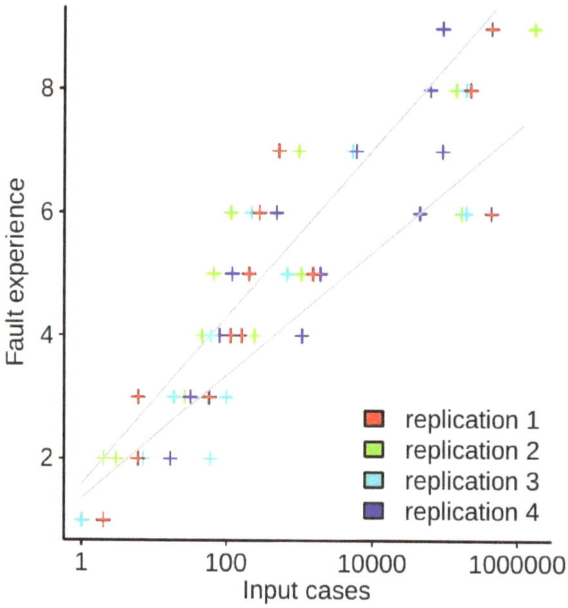

Figure 6.17: Number of input cases processed by two implementations before a fault was experienced, with four replications (each a different color); grey lines are a regression fit for one implementation. Data from Dunham et al. Github-Local

Figure 6.17 shows the number of input cases processed, by two of the implementations (only one fault was ever experienced during the execution of the third implementation), before a given number of fault experiences, during each of the four runs. The grey lines are an exponential regression model fitted to each implementation; these two lines show that as the number of faults experienced grows, more input cases are required to experience another fault, and that code written by different developers has different fault experience rates per input.

A second study by Dunham and Lauterbach [515] used 100 replications for each of the three programs, and found the same pattern of results seen in the first study.

Some published fault experience experiments have used time (computer or user), as a proxy for the quantity of input data. It is not always possible to measure the quantity of input processed, and time may be more readily available.

A study by Wood [1977] analysed fault experiences encountered by a product Q/A group in four releases of a subset of products. Figure 6.18 shows that the fault experience rate is similar for the first three releases (the collection of test effort data for release 4 is known to have been different from the previous releases).

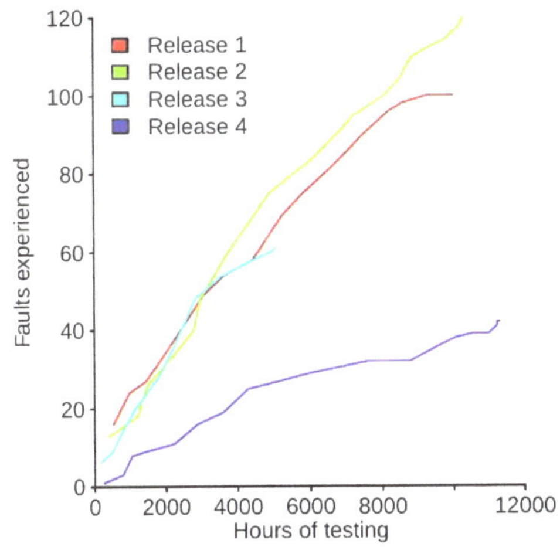

Figure 6.18: Faults experienced against hours of testing, for four releases of a product. Data from Wood. Github-Local

A study by Pradel [1519] searched for thread safety violations in 15 classes in the Java standard library and JFreeChart, that were declared to be thread safe, and 8 classes in JodaTime not declared to be thread safe; automatically generated test cases were used. Thread safety violations were found in 22 out of the 23 classes; for each case the testing process was run 10 times, and the elapsed time to discover the violation recorded. Figure 6.19 illustrates the variability in the timing of the violations experienced.

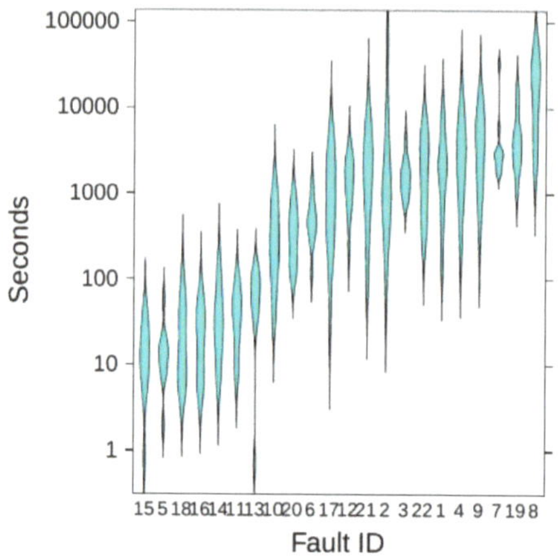

Figure 6.19: Time taken to encounter a thread safety violation in 22 Java classes, violin plots for 10 runs of each class. Data kindly supplied by Pradel. Github-Local

A study by Adams [7] investigated reported faults in applications running on IBM mainframes between 1975 and 1980. Figure 6.20 shows that approximately one third of fault experiences first occurred on average every 5,000 months of execution time (over all uses of the product). Only around 2% of fault experiences first occurred after five months of execution time.

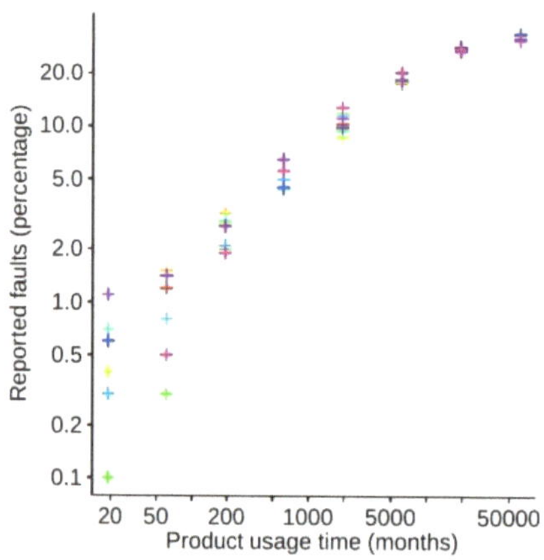

Figure 6.20: Percentage of fault experiences having a given mean time to first experience (in months, over all installations of a product), for nine products. Data from Adams. Github-Local

Multiple fault experiences produced by the same coding mistake provide information about the likelihood of encountering input that can trigger that fault experience. Regression models fitted using a biexponential equation (i.e., $a \times e^{b \times x} + c \times e^{d \times x}$, where x is the rank order of occurrences of each fault experience) have been fitted to a variety of program crash data; see fig 11.53.

A study by Zhao and Liu [2015] investigated the crash faults found by fuzzing the files processed by six Open source programs. Figure 6.21 shows the number of unique crash faults experienced by convert and autotrace (estimated by tracing back to a program location), along with lines fitted using biexponential regression models.

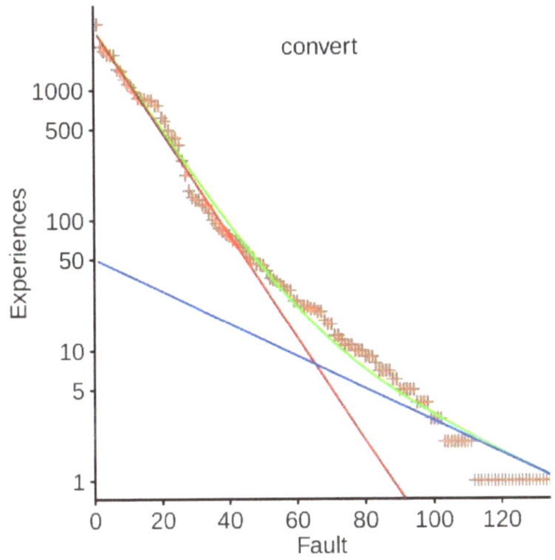

Figure 6.21: Number of times the same fault was experienced in one program, crashes traced to the same program location; with fitted biexponential equation (green line; red/blue lines the two components). Data kindly provided by Zhao. Github-Local

Why is a biexponential model such a good fit? A speculative idea is that the two exponentials are driven by the two independent processes that need to interact to produce a fault experience: the distribution of input values, and the mistakes contained in the source code. [vii]

6.3.2 Propagation of mistakes

The location in the code that triggers a fault experience may appear many executable instructions after the code containing the mistake (that is eventually modified to prevent further the fault experiences).

In some input values a coding mistake may not propagate from the mistake location, to a code location where it can trigger a fault experience. For instance, if variable x is mistakenly assigned the value 3 , rather than 2 , the mistake will not propagate past the condition: if $(x < 8)$ (because the behavior is the same for both the correct and mistake value); for this case, an opportunity to propagate only occurs when the mistaken value of x changes the value of the conditional test.

How robust is code to small changes to the correct value of a variable?

A study by Danglot, Preux, Baudry and Monperrus [435] investigated the propagation of one-off perturbations in 10 short Java programs (42 to 568 LOC). The perturbations were created by modifying the value of an expression once during the execution of a program, e.g., by adding, or subtracting, one. The effect of a perturbation on program behavior could be to cause it to raise an exception, output an incorrect result, or have no observed effect, i.e., the output is unchanged. Each of a program's selected perturbation points were executed multiple times (e.g., the 41 perturbation points selected for the program quicksort were executed between 840 and 9,495 times, per input), with one modification per program execution (requiring quicksort to be executed 151,444 times, so that each possible perturbation could occur, for the set of 20 inputs used).

Figure 6.22 shows violin plots for the likelihood that an add-one perturbation has no impact on the output of a program; not all expressions contained in the programs were perturbed, so a violin plot is a visual artefact.

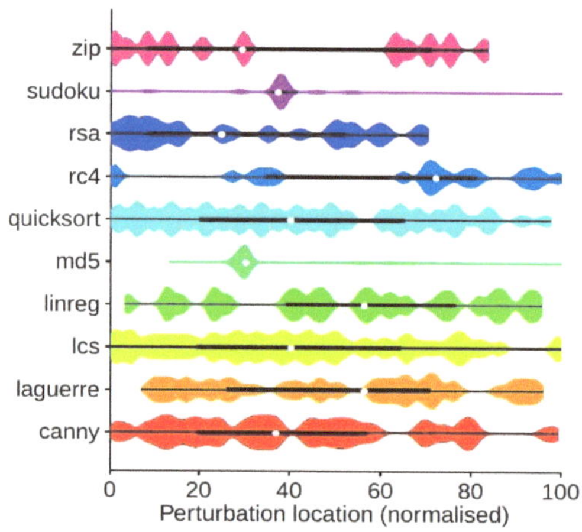

Figure 6.22: Violin plots of likelihood (local y-axis) that an add-one perturbation at a (normalised) program location will not change the output behavior. Data from Danglot et al. Github-Local

Studies [356] of the impact of soft errors (i.e., radiation induced bit-flips) have found that over 80% of bit-flips have no detectable impact on program behavior.

6.3.3 Remaining faults: closed populations

In a closed population no coding mistakes are added (e.g., no new code is added) or removed (i.e., reported faults are not fixed), and the characteristics of the input distribution remain unchanged.

After *N* distinct faults have been experienced, what is the probability that there exists new, previously unexperienced, faults?

Data on reported faults commonly takes two forms: incidence data (i.e., a record of the date of first report, with no information on subsequent reports involving the same fault experience), and abundance data, i.e., a record of every fault experience.

Software reliability growth has often been modeled as a nonhomogeneous Poisson process, with researchers fitting various formulae to small amounts of incidence data. [1127] Unfortunately, it is not possible to use one sample of incidence data to distinguish between different exponential order growth models, [1283] i.e., this data does not contain enough information to do the job asked of it. It is often possible to fit a variety of equations to fault report data, using regression modeling: however, predictions about future fault experiences made using these models is likely to be very unreliable; see fig 11.50.

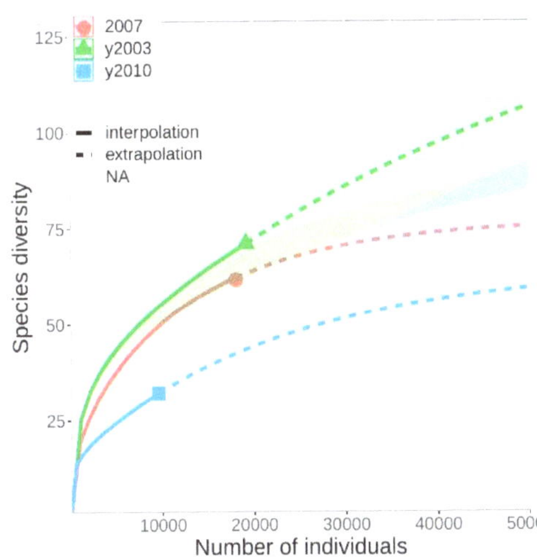

Figure 6.23: Predicted growth, with 95% confidence intervals, in the number of new crash fault experiences in the 2003, 2007 and 2010 releases of Microsoft Office. Data from Kaminsky et al. Github-Local

When abundance data is available, the modeling approach discussed in section 4.3.2 can be used to estimate the number of unique items within a population, and the number of new unique items likely to be encountered with additional sampling.

A study by Kaminsky, Eddington and Cecchetti [966] investigated crash faults in three releases of Microsoft Office and OpenOffice (plus other common document processors), produced using fuzzing. Figure 6.23 shows actual and predicted growth in crash fault experiences in the 2003, 2007 and 2010 releases of Microsoft Office, along with 95% confidence intervals. Later versions are estimated to contain fewer crash faults, although the confidence interval for the 2010 release is wide enough to encompass the 2007 rate.

Figure 6.24 shows the number of duplicate crashes experienced when the same fuzzed files were processed by the 2003, 2007 and 2010 releases of Microsoft Office. The blue/purple lines are the two components of fitted biexponential models for the three curves.

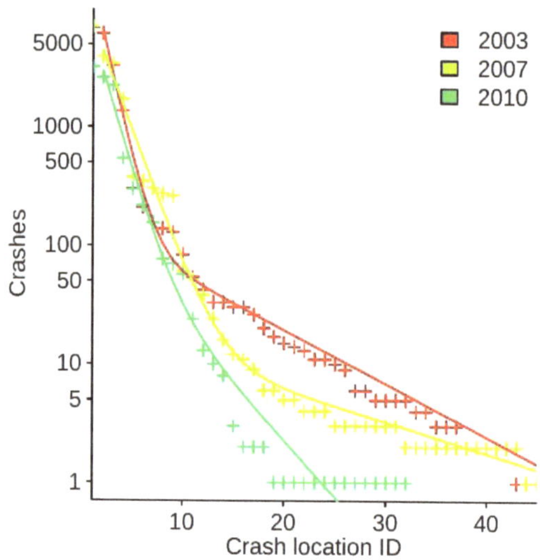

Figure 6.24: Number of crashes traced to the same executable location (sorted by number of crashes), in the 2003, 2007 and 2010 releases of Microsoft Office; lines are fitted biexponential regression models. Data from Kaminsky et al. Github-Local

The previous analysis is based on information about faults that have been experienced. What is the likelihood of a fault experience, given that no faults have been experienced in the immediately previous time, ?

An analysis by Bishop and Bloomfield [202] derived a lower bound for the reliability function, R, for a program executing without experiencing a fault for time t, after it has executed for time T without failure; it is assumed that the input profile does not change during time $T + t$. The reliability function is:

$$R(t \mid T) \geq 1 - \frac{t}{T+t} e^{-\frac{T}{t}\log\left(1+\frac{t}{T}\right)}$$

If t is much smaller than T, this equation can be simplified to: $R(t \mid T) \geq 1 - \frac{t}{(T+t)\times e}$ For instance, if a program is required to execute for 10 hours with reliability 0.9999 , the initial failure free period, in hours, is:

$$0.9999 \geq 1 - \frac{10}{(T+10)\times e}$$

$$T \geq \frac{10}{(1-0.9999)\times e} - 10 \approx 36{,}778$$

If T is much smaller than t, the general solution can be simplified to: $R(\, t \mid T\,) \geq \frac{T}{t}$

How can this worst case analysis be improved on?

Assuming a system executes N times without a failure, and has a fixed probability of failing, p, the probability of one or more failures occurring in N executions is given by:

$$C = \textstyle\sum_{n=1}^{N} p(1-p)^{n-1} = p\dfrac{1-(1-p)^N}{1-(1-p)} = 1-(1-p)^N$$

How many executions, without failure, need to occur to have a given confidence that the actual failure rate is below a specified level? Rearranging, gives: $N = \left\lceil \frac{\log\,(1-C)}{\log\,(1-p)} \right\rceil$

Plugging in values for confidence, $C = 0.99$, and failure probability, $p < 10^{-4}$, then the system has to execute without failure for 46,050 consecutive runs.

This analysis is not realistic because it assumes that the probability of failure, p, remains constant for all input cases; studies show that p can vary by several orders of magnitude.

6.3.4 Remaining faults: open populations

In an evolving system, existing coding mistakes are corrected and new ones are made; new features may be added that interact with existing functionality (i.e., there may be a change of behavior in the code executed for the same input), and the user base is changing (e.g., new users arrive, existing users leave, and the number of users running a particular version changes as people migrate to a newer release); the population of mistakes is open.

Studies of fault reports in an open population that fail to take into account the impact of the time varying population [816] will not produce reliable results.

Section 4.3.2.2 discusses estimation in open populations.

What form of regression models can be fitted to data on fault reports from an open population?

A study by Sun, Le, Zhang and Su [1793] investigated the fault reports for GCC and LLVM. Figure 6.25 shows the number of times a distinct mistake has been responsible for a fault report in GCC (from 1999 to 2015), with a fitted biexponential, and its component exponentials.

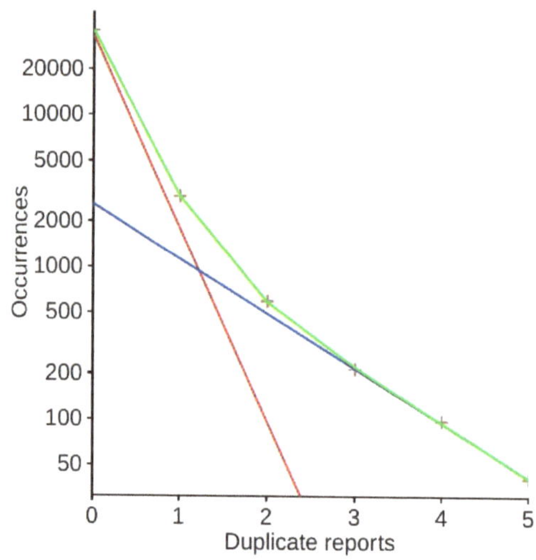

Figure 6.25: Number of occurrences of the same mistake responsible for a reported fault in GCC, with fitted biexponential regression model, and component exponentials. Data from Sun et al. Github-Local

A study by Sadat, Bener and Miranskyy [1625] investigated duplicate fault reports in Apache, Eclipse and KDE over 18-years. Figure 6.26 shows the number of times distinct faults reported in KDE, with a fitted triexponential (green) and the three component exponentials.

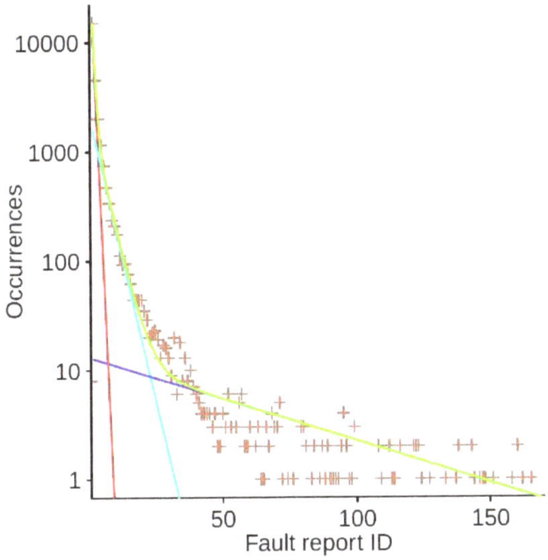

Figure 6.26: Number of instances of the same reported fault in KDE, with fitted triexponential regression model. Data from Sadat et al. Github-Local

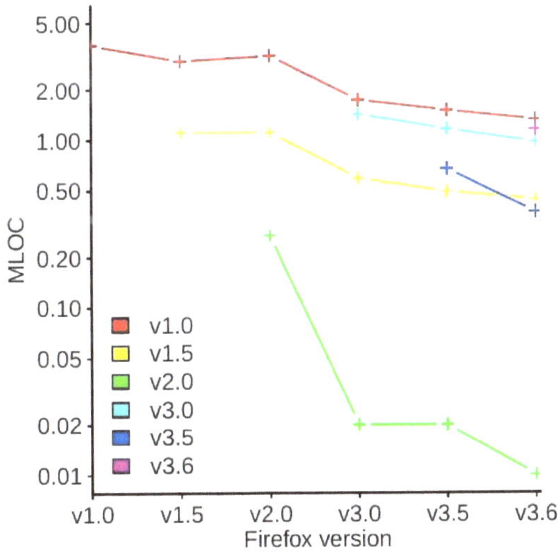

Figure 6.27: Lines of source in early versions of Firefox, broken down by the version in which it first appears. Data extracted from Massacci et al. Github-Local

Being able to fit this form of model suggests a pattern that may occur in other collections of reported faults, but there is no underlying theory offering an explanation for the pattern seen.

Successive releases of a software system often include a large percentage of code from earlier releases. The collection of source code that is new in each release can be treated as a distinct population containing a fixed number of mistakes; these populations do not grow but can shrink (when code is deleted). The code contained in the first release is the foundation population.

If the only changes made to code are fixes of mistakes, the number of faults experiences caused by that code should decrease (assuming the input profile and number of users does not change).

A study by Massacci, Neuhaus and Nguyen [1217] investigated 899 security advisories in Firefox, reported against six major releases. Their raw data is only available under an agreement that does not permit your author to directly distribute it to readers; the data used in the following analysis was reverse engineered from the paper, or extracted by your author from other sources.

Table 6.2 shows the earliest version (columns) of Firefox containing a known mistake in the source code, and the latest version (rows) to which a corresponding fault report exists. For instance, 42 faults were discovered in version 2.0 corresponding to mistakes made in the source code written for version 1.0. Only corrected coding mistakes have been counted, unfixed mistakes are not included in the analysis. Each version of Firefox has a release, and retirement date, after which the version is no longer supported, i.e., coding mistakes are not corrected in retired versions.

Table 6.2: Number of reported security advisories in versions of Firefox; coding mistake made in version columns, advisory reported in version row. Data from Massacci et al. [1217]

	1.0	1.5	2.0	3.0	3.5	3.6
1.0	79					
1.5	71	108				
2.0	42	104	126			
3.0	97	15	22	67		
3.5	32			30	32	
3.6	13		1	5	41	14

The 1.0 column in table 6.2 shows that 97 security advisories reported in Firefox release 3.0 were fixed by changing code written for release 1.0, while 42 were reported in release 2.0. Is this increase in version 3.0 due to an increase in end-user usage, a change of input profile, or some other reason?

The Massacci study includes a break-down of the amount of source code contained in each released version of Firefox by the version in which it was first released.

The number of Firefox users can be estimated from the claimed internet usage over time (see Github-faults/internet-population.R), and Firefox market share. Figure 6.28 shows the market share of the six versions of Firefox between their official release and end-ofsupport dates. Estimated values appear to the left of the vertical grey line, values from measurements to the right; note: at their end-of-support dates, post 1.5 versions had a significant market share.

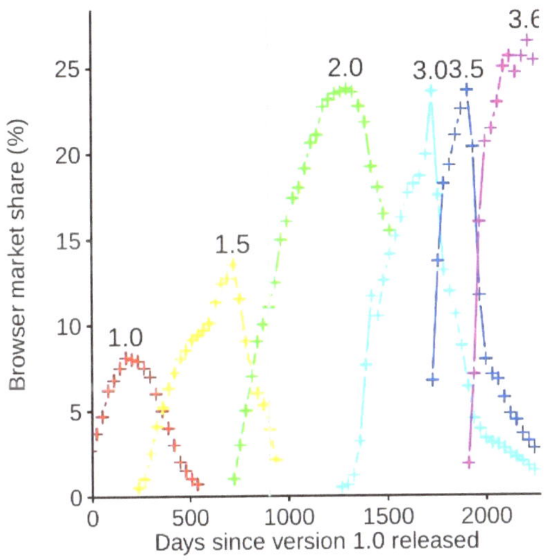

Figure 6.28: Market share of Firefox versions between official release and end-of-support (left of grey line are estimates, right are measurements). Data from Jones. Github-Local

The end-user usage of source code originally written for a particular version of Firefox, over time, is calculated as follows (data is been binned by week): number of lines of code originally written for a particular version contained within the code used to build a later version, or that particular version (call this the build version) multiplied by the market share of the build version multiplied by the number of Internet users (based on the developed world user count); the units are LOC × Users.

Figure 6.29 shows the amount of end-user usage of the source code originally written for Firefox version 1.0. The yellow line is the code usage for version 1.0 code executing in Firefox build version 1.0, the green line the code usage for version 1.0 code executing in build version 1.5 and so on. The red points show version 1.0 code usage summed over all build versions.

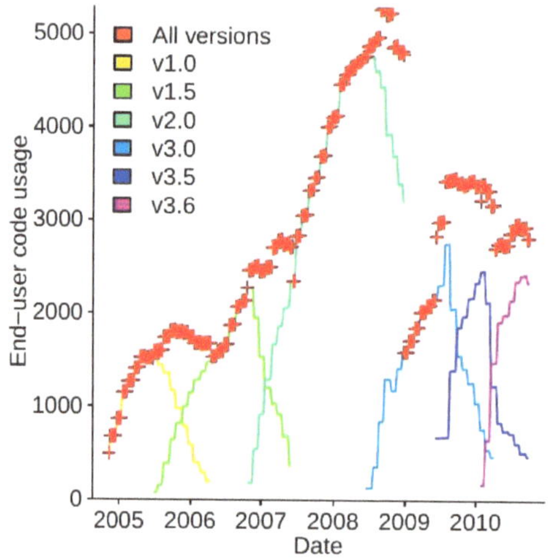

Figure 6.29: End-user usage of code originally written for Firefox version 1.0, by major released versions (in units of LOC*Users); red points show sum over all versions. Based on data from Jones and extracted from Massacci et al. Github-Local

Comparing end-user usage of version 1.0 source code in Firefox versions 2.0 and 3.0 (see figure 6.29) shows significantly greater usage in version 2.0, i.e., quantity of enduser usage is not the factor responsible for the increase in version 1.0 sourced security vulnerabilities seen in the 1.0 column of table 6.2.

Other possible reasons for the increase include a significant change in the input profile caused by changes in webpage content, starting around mid-2008, or an increase in researchers actively searching for vulnerabilities in browsers.

6.4 Where is the mistake?

Information about where mistakes are likely to be made can be used to focus problemsolving resources in those areas likely to produce the greatest returns. A few studies [424] have measured across top-level entities such as project phase (e.g., requirements, coding, testing, documentation), while others have investigated specific components (e.g., source code, configuration file), or low level constructs, e.g., floating-point. [490]

The root cause of a mistake, made by a person, may be knowledge based (e.g., lack of knowledge about the semantics of the programming language used), rule based (e.g., failure to correctly apply known coding rules), or skill based (e.g., fail to copy the correct value of a numeric constant in an assignment). [1566]

Mistakes in hardware [342,505,892] tend to occur much less frequently than mistakes in software, and mistakes in hardware are not considered here [viii]

The user interface, the interaction between people and an application, can be a source of fault experiences in the sense that a user misinterprets correct output, or selects a parameter option that produces unintended program behavior. User interface issues are not considered here.

Accidents where a large loss occurs (e.g., fatalities) are often followed by an accident investigation. The final report produced by the investigation may involve language biases that affect what has been written, and how it may be interpreted. [1892]

A study by Brown and Altadmri [268] investigated coding mistakes made by students, and the beliefs their professors had about common student mistakes; the data came from 100 million compilations across 10 million programming sessions using Blackbox (a Java programming environment). There was very poor agreement between professor beliefs and the actual ranked frequency of student mistakes; see Github-reliability/educators.R.

One study [1378] found that 36% of mistakes logged during development were made in phases that came before coding (Team Software Process was used, and many of the mistakes may have been minor); see Github-reliability/2018_005_defects.R.

Software supply chains are a target for criminals seeking to infect computers with malicious software; [1409] an infected software update may be downloaded and executed by millions of users

6.4.1 Requirements

The same situation can be approached from multiple viewpoints, depending on the role of the viewer; see fig 2.49. Those implementing a system may fail to fully appreciate all the requirements implied by the specification; context is important, see fig 2.48.

A requirements mistake is made when one or more requirements are incorrect, inconsistent or incomplete; an ambiguous specification [189] contains potential mistakes. The number of mistakes contained in requirements may be of the same order of magnitude, [424] or exceed, the number of mistakes found in the code; [1551] different people bring different perspectives to requirements analysis, which can result in them discovering different problems. [1097]

Software systems are implemented by generating and interpreting language (human and programming). Reliability is affected by human variability in the use of language, [192] what individuals consider to be correct English syntax, [1752] and the interpretation of numeric phrases. Language issues are discussed in section 6.1.4 and section 6.4.2.

During the lifetime of a project, existing requirements are misinterpreted or changed, and new requirements are added.

Non-requirement mistakes may be corrected by modifying the requirements; see fig 8.28. In cases where a variety of behaviors are considered acceptable, modifying the requirements documents may be the most cost effective path to resolving a mistake.

A study by van der Meulen, Bishop and Revilla [1877] investigated the coding mistakes made in 29,000 implementations of the $3n + 1$ problem (the programs had been submitted to a programming contest). All submitted implementations were tested, and programs producing identical outputs were assigned to the same equivalence class (competitors could make multiple submissions, if the first failed to pass all the tests). In many cases the incorrect output, for an equivalence class, could be explained by a failure of the competitor to implement a requirement implied by the problem being solved, e.g., failing to swap input number pairs, when the first was larger than the second.

Figure 6.30 shows the 36 equivalence classes containing the most members; the most common is the correct output, followed by always returning 0 (zero).

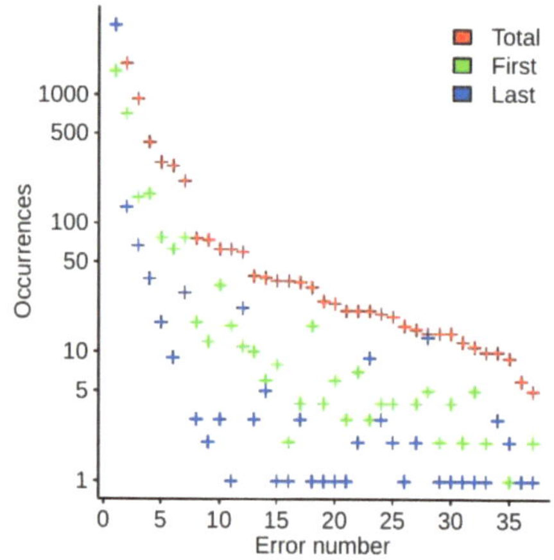

Figure 6.30: Total number of implementations in each of 36 equivalence classes, plus both first and last competitor submissions. Data from van der Meulen et al. Github-Local

Studies [358] have found that people take longer to answer question involving a negation, and are less likely to give a correct answer.

A study by Winter, Femmer and Vogelsang [1971] investigated subject performance on requirements expressed using affirmative and negative quantifiers. Subjects saw affirmative (e.g., "All registered machines must be provided in the database.") and negative (e.g., "No deficit of a machine is not provided in the database.") requirements, and had to decide which of three situations matched the sentence. Affirmative wording had a greater percentage of correct answers in four of the nine quantifier combinations (negative wording had a higher percentage of correct answers for the quantifiers: All but and More than). Figure 6.31 shows the response time for each quantifier, broken down by affirmative/negative. Average response time for negative requirements was faster for two, of the nine, quantifiers: All but and None (there was no statistical difference for At most).

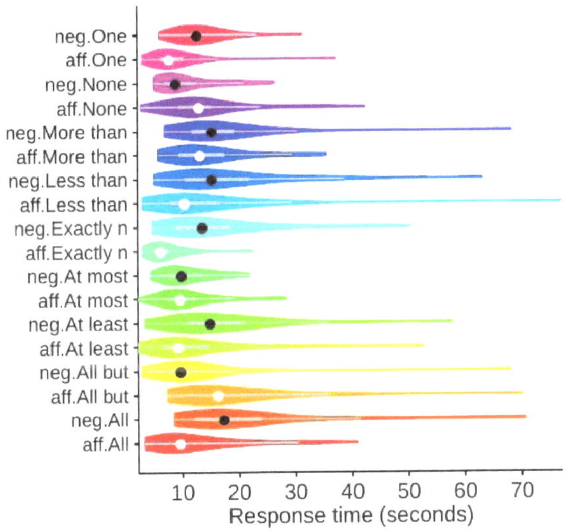

Figure 6.31: Violin plot of the time taken to response to a question about a requirement, for nine quantifiers paired by affirmative/negative. Data from Winter et al. Github-Local

The minimum requirements for some software (e.g., C and C+ compilers) is specified in an ISO Standard. The ISO process requires that the committee responsible for a standard maintain a log of potential defect submissions received, along with the committee's response. Figure 6.32 shows the growth of various kinds of defects reported against the POSIX standard. [899]

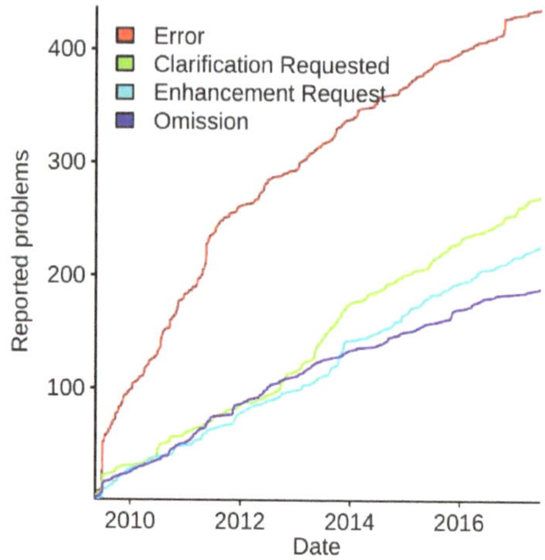

Figure 6.32: Cumulative number of potential defects logged against the POSIX standard, by defect classification. Data kindly provided by Josey. Github-Local

There have been very few studies [1692] of the impact of the form of specification on its implementation.

Two studies [363,926] have investigated the requirements' coverage achieved by two compiler validation suites.

Source code is written to implement a requirement, or to provide support for code that implements requirements. An if-statement represents a decision and each of these decisions should be traceable to a requirement or an internal housekeeping requirement. A project by Jones and Corfield [927] cross-referenced the if-statements in the source of a C compiler to every line in the 1990 version of the C Standard. [1637] Of the 53 files containing references to either the C Standard or internal documentation, 13 did not contain any references to the C Standard (for the 53 files the average number of references to the C Standard was 46.6). The average number of references per page of the language chapter of the Standard was approximately 14. For more details see Github-projects/Model-C/.

6.4.2 Source code

Source code is the focus of much software engineering research: it is the original form of an executable program that contains the mistakes that can lead to fault experiences, and is usually what is modified by developers to correct a reported fault. From the research perspective it is now available in bulk, and techniques for analysing it are known, and practical to implement.

There are recurring patterns in the changes made to source code to correct mistakes, [1443] one reason for this is that some language constructs are used much more often than others. [930] The idea that there is an association between fault reports and particular usage patterns in source code, or program behavior, is popular; over 40 association measures have been proposed. [1167]

Errors of omission can cause faults to be experienced. One study [756] of error handling by Linux file systems found that possible returned error codes were not checked for 13% of function calls, i.e., the occurrence of an error was not handled. Cut-and-paste is a code editing technique that is susceptible to errors of omission, that is, failing to make all the necessary modifications to the pasted version; [169] significant numbers of cut-and-paste errors have been found in JavaDoc documentation. [1428]

Common patterns of mistakes are also seen in the use of programming language syntax and semantics. Figure 6.33 shows ranked occurrences of each kind of compiler message generated by Java and Python programs, submitted by students.

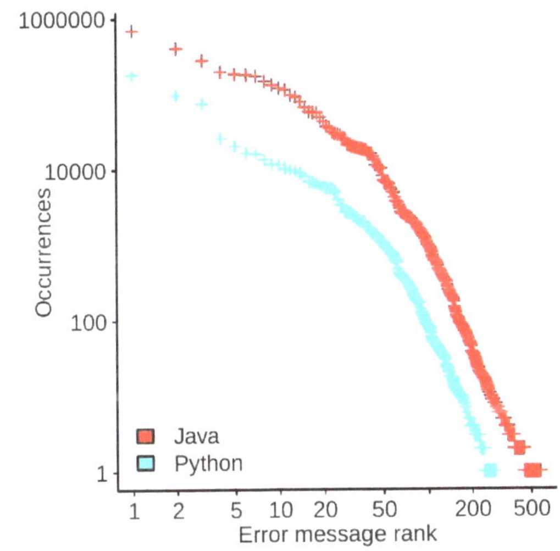

Figure 6.33: Ranked occurrences of compiler messages generated by student submitted Java and Python programs. Data from Pritchard. Github-Local

Proponents of particular languages sometimes claim that programs written in the language are more reliable (other desirable characteristics may also be claimed), than if written in other languages. Most experimental studies comparing the reliability of programs written in different languages have either used students, [691] or had low statistical power. A language may lack a feature that, if available and used, would help to reduce the number of mistakes made by developers, e.g., support for function prototypes in C, [1672] which were added to the language in the first ANSI Standard.

To what extent might programs written in some languages be more likely to appear to behave as expected, despite containing mistakes?

A study by Spinellis, Karakoidas and Lourida [1749] made various kinds of small random changes to 14 different small programs, each implemented in 10 different languages (400 random changes per program/language pair). The ability of these modified programs to compile, execute and produce the same output as the unmodified program was recorded.

Figure 6.34 shows the fraction of programs that compiled, executed and produced correct output, for the various languages. There appear to be two distinct language groupings, each having similar successful compilation rates; one commonality of languages in each group is requiring, or not, variables to be declared before use. One fitted regression model (see Github-reliability/fuzzer/fuzzer-mod.R) contains an interaction between language and program (the problems implemented did not require many lines of code, and in some cases could be solved in a single line in some languages), and a logarithmic dependency on program length, i.e., number of lines.

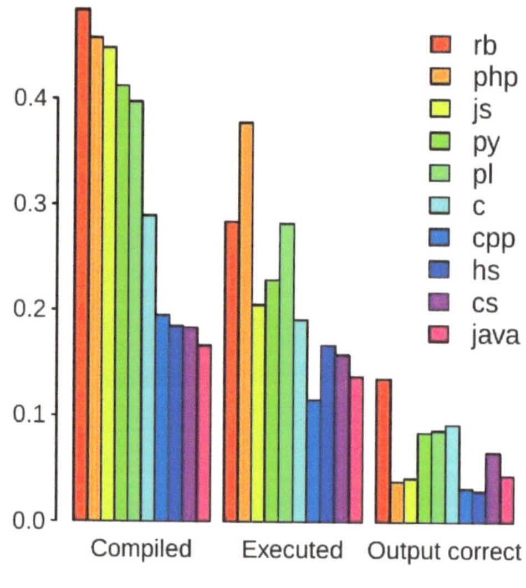

Figure 6.34: Fraction of mutated programs, in various languages, that successfully compiled/executed/produced the same output. Data from Spinellis et al. Github-Local

Other studies [146] have investigated transformations that modify a program without modifying its behavior.

A study by Aman, Amasaki, Yokogawa and Kawahara [49] investigated time-to-bug-fix events, in the source files of 50 projects implemented in Java and 50 in C++ . The survival time of files (i.e., time to fault report causing the source to be modified) was the same for both languages, and number of developers, and number of project files; they had almost zero impact on a Cox model fitted to the data; see Github-survival/Profes2017-aman.R.

Various metrics have been proposed as measures of some desirable, or undesirable, characteristic of a unit of code, e.g., a function. Halstead's and McCabe's cyclomatic complexity are perhaps the most well-known such metrics (see section 7.1.4), both count the source contained within a single function. Irrespective of whether these metrics strongly correlate with anything other than lines of code, [1077] they can be easily manipulated by splitting functions with high values into two or more functions, each having lower metric values (just as it is possible to reduce the number of lines of code in a function, by putting all the code on one line).

The value of McCabe's complexity (number of decisions, plus one) for the following function is 5 , and there are 16 possible paths through the function:

```
int main(void)
{
if (W) a(); else b();
if (X) c(); else d();
if (Y) e(); else f();
if (Z) g(); else h();
}
```

each if...else contains two paths and there are four in series, giving $2 \times 2 \times 2 \times 2$ paths. Restructuring the code, as below, removes the multiplication of paths caused by the sequences of if...else:

```
void a_b(void)
    {if (W) a(); else b();}
void c_d(void)
    {if (X) c(); else d();}
void e_f(void)
    {if (Y) e(); else f();}
void g_h(void)
    {if (Z) g(); else h();}
int main(void)
{
a_b();
```

```
c_d();
e_f();
g_h();
}
```

reducing the McCabe complexity of main to 1 , with the four new functions each having a McCabe complexity of two. Where has the complexity that main once had, gone? It now exists in the relationship between the functions, a relationship that is not included in the McCabe complexity calculation; the number of paths that can be traversed, by a call to main at runtime, has not changed, but a function based count now reports one path.

A metric that assigns a value to individual functions (i.e., its value is calculated from the contents of single functions) cannot be used as a control mechanism (i.e., require that values not exceed some limit), because its value can be easily manipulated by moving contents into newly created functions. The software equivalent of what is known as accounting fraud in accounting.

Predictions are sometimes attempted [1696,2029] at the file level of granularity, e.g., predicting which files are more likely to be the root cause of fault experiences; the idea being that the contents of highly ranked files be rewritten. Any reimplementation will include mistakes, and the cost of rewriting the code may be larger than handling the fault reports in the original code, as they are discovered.

The idea that there is an optimal value for the number of lines of code in a function body has been an enduring meme (when object-oriented programming became popular, the meme mutated to cover optimal class size). See fig 8.39 for a discussion of the Ushaped defect density paper chase; other studies [1037] investigating the relationship between reported fault experiences and number of lines of code, have failed to include program usage information (i.e., number of people using the software) in the model.

The fixes for most user fault reports involve changing a few lines in a single function, and these changes occur within a single file. A study [713] of over 1,000 projects for each of C , Java, Python and Haskell found that correcting most coding mistakes involved adding and deleting a few tokens.

A study by Lucia [1166] investigated fault localization techniques. Figure 6.35 shows the percentage of fault reports whose correction involved a given number of files, modules or lines; lines are power laws fitted using regression.

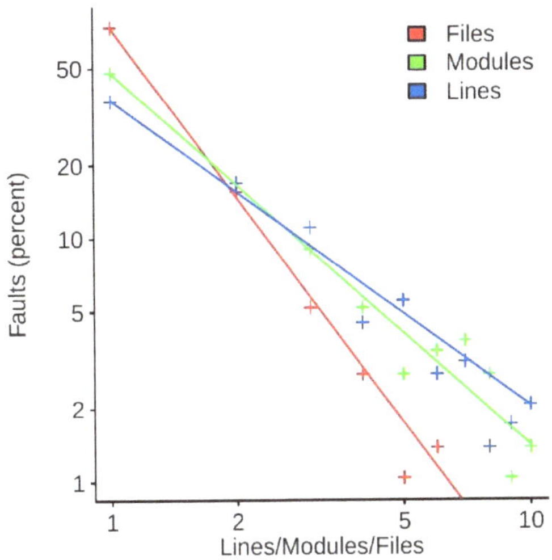

Figure 6.35: Number of fault reports whose fixes involved a given number of files, modules or lines in a sample of 290 faults in AspectJ; lines are fitted power laws. Data from Lucia. Github-Local

A study by Zhong and Su[2019] investigated commits associated with fault reports in five large Open source projects. Figure 6.36 shows the number of files modified while fixing reported faults, against normalized (i.e., each maximum is 100) number of commits made while making these changes.

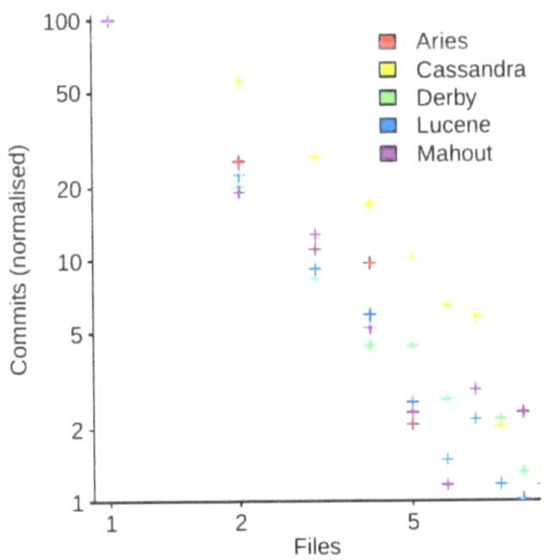

Figure 6.36: Normalized number of commits (i.e., each maximum is 100), made to address fault reports, involving a given number of files in five software systems; grey line is representative of regression models fitted to each project, and has the form: Commits ∝ Files $^{-2.1}$. Data from Zhong et al via M. Monperrus. Github-Local

When existing code is changed, there is a non-zero probability of a mistake being made.

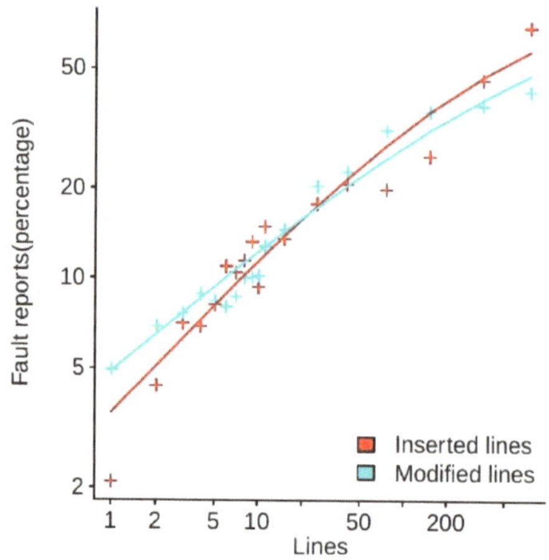

Figure 6.37: Percentage of insertions/modifications of a given number of lines resulting in a reported fault; lines are fitted beta regression models of the form: percent_faultReports ∝ log (Lines). Data from Purushothaman et al. Github-Local

A study by Purushothaman and Perry [1536] investigated small source code changes made to one subsystem of the 5ESS telephone switch software (4,550 files containing almost 2MLOC, with 31,884 modification requests after the first release changing 4,293 of these files). Figure 6.37 is based on an analysis of fault reports traced to updates, that involved modifying/inserting a given number of lines, and shows the percentage of each kind of modification that eventually led to a fault report.

Using configuration files to hold literal values that would otherwise need to be present in the source code can greatly increase runtime flexibility. Mistakes in the use of configuration options can lead to fault experiences; see Github-reliability/fse15.R.

6.4.3 Libraries and tools

Libraries provide functionality believed to be of use to many programs, or that is difficult to correctly implement without specialist knowledge, e.g., mathematical functions. Many language specifications include a list of functions that conforming implementations are required to support.

The implementation of some libraries requires domain specific expertise, e.g., the handling of branch cuts in some maths functions. [1700] Some library implementations may contain subtle, hard to detect mistakes: for instance, random number generators may generate sequences containing patterns [1101] that create spurious correlations in the results; even widely used applications can suffer from this problem, e.g., Microsoft Excel. [1236]

The availability of many open source libraries can make it more cost effective to use third-party code, rather than implementing a bespoke solution.

A study by Decan, Mens and Constantinou [470] investigated the time taken for security vulnerabilities in packages hosted in the npm repository to be fixed, along with the time taken to update packages that depended on a version of a package having a reported vulnerability. Figure 6.38 shows survival curves (with 95% confidence bounds), for high and medium severity vulnerabilities, of time to fix a reported vulnerability (Base), and time to update a dependency (Depend) to a corrected version of a package.

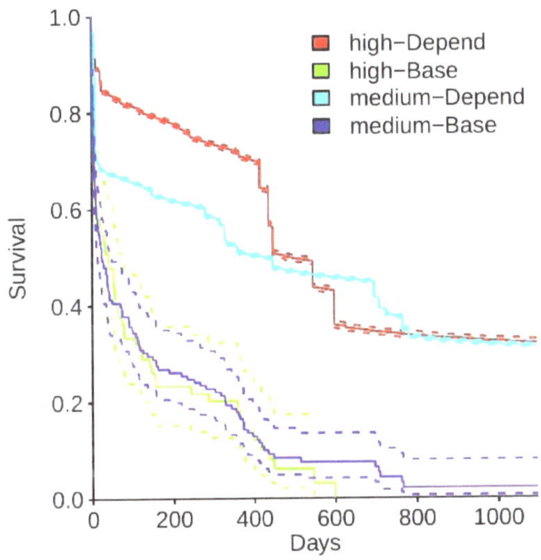

Figure 6.38: Survival curve (with 95% confidence bounds) of time to fix vulnerabilities reported in npm packages (Base) and time to update a package dependency (Depend) to a corrected version (i.e., not containing the reported vulnerability); for vulnerabilities with severity high and medium. Data from Decan et al. Github-Local

The mistake that leads to a fault experience may be in the environment in which a program is built and executed. Many library package managers support the installation of new packages via a command line tool. One study [1849] made use of typos in the information given to command line package managers to cause a package other than the one intended to be installed.

Compilers, interpreters and linkers are programs, and contain mistakes (e.g., see fig 6.25), and the language specification may also be inconsistent or under specified, e.g., ML. [961]

Different support tools may produce different results, e.g., statement coverage, [1990] and call graph construction; see fig 13.1.

6.4.4 Documentation

Documentation is a cost paid today, that is intended to provide a benefit later for somebody else, or the author.

If user documentation specifies functionality that is not supported by the software, the vendor may be liable to pay damages to customers expecting to be able to perform the documented functionality. [972] Non-existent documentation is not unreliable, but documentation that has not been updated to match changes to the software is.

There have been relatively few studies of the reliability of documentation (teachers of English as a foreign language study the language usage mistakes of learners [257]). A study by Rubio-Gonzalez and Libit [1618] investigated the source code of 52 Linux file systems, which invoked 42 different system calls and returned 30 different system error codes. The 871 KLOC contained 1,784 instances of undocumented error return codes; see Github-projects/err-code_mismatch.R. A study by Ma, Liu and Forin [1179] tested an Intel x86 cpu emulator and found a wide variety of errors in the documentation specifying the behavior of the processor.

The Microsoft Server protocol documents [1277] sometimes specify that the possible error values returned by an API function are listed in the Windows error codes document, which lists over 2,500 error codes.

6.5 Non-software causes of unreliability

Hardware contains moving parts that wear out. Electronic components operate by influencing the direction of movement of electrons; when the movement is primarily in one direction atoms migrate in that direction, and over time this migration degrades device operating characteristics. [1755] Fabricating devices with smaller transistors decreases mean time to failure; expected chip lifetimes have dropped from 10 years to 7 , and continue to decrease. [1947]

As the size of components shrinks, and the number of components on a device increases, the probability that thermal noise will cause a bit to change state increases. [1011]

Faulty hardware does not always noticeably change the behavior of an executing program; apparently correct program execution can occur in the presence of incorrect hardware operation, e.g., image processing. [1392] Section 6.3.2 discusses studies showing that many mistakes have no observable impact on program behavior.

For a discussion of system failure traced to either cpu or DRAM failures see table 10.7, and for a study investigating the correlation between hardware performance and likelihood of experiencing intermittent faults see section 10.2.3.

A software reliability problem rarely encountered outside of science fiction, a few decades ago, now regularly occurs in modern computers: cosmic rays (plus more local sources of radiation, such as the materials used to fabricate devices) flipping the value of one or more bits in memory, or a running processor. Techniques for mitigating the effects of radiation induced events have been proposed. [1339]

The two main sources of radiation are alpha-particles generated within the material used to fabricate and package devices, and Neutrons generated by Cosmic-rays interacting with the upper atmosphere. The data in figure 6.39, from a study by Autran, Semikh, Munteanu, Serre, Gasiot and Roche, [94] comes from monitoring equipment located in the French Alps; either, 1,700 m under the Fréjus mountain (i.e., all radiation is generated by the device), or on top of the Plateau de Bure at an altitude of 2,552 m (i.e., radiation sources are local and Cosmic). [93] For confidentiality reasons, the data has been scaled by a small constant.

Figure 6.39 shows how the number of bit-flips increased over time (measured in Megabits per hour), for SRAM fabricated using 130 nm, 65 nm and 40 nm processes. The 130 nm and 65 nm measurements were made underground, and the lower rate of bit-flips for the 65 nm process is the result of improved materials selection, that reduced alpha-particle emissions; the 40 nm measurements were made on top of the Plateau de Bure, and show the impact of external radiation sources.

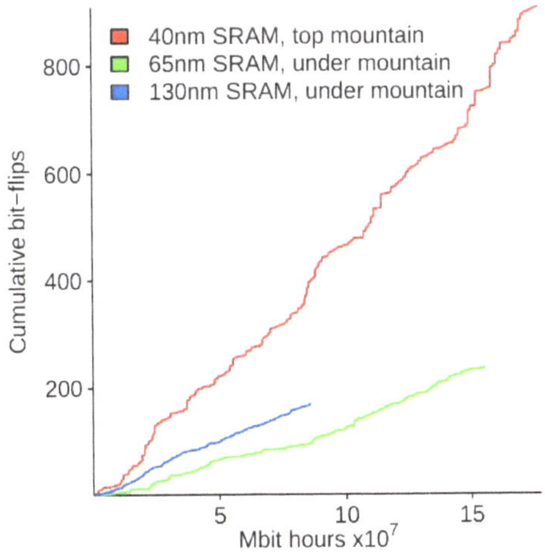

Figure 6.39: Number of bit-flips in SRAM fabricated using various processes, with devices on top of, or under a mountain in the French Alps. Data kindly provided by Autran. Github-Local

The soft error rate is usually quoted in FITs (Failure in Time), with 1 FIT corresponding to 1 error per 10^9 hours per megabit, or 10^{-15} errors per bit-hour. Consider a system with 4 GB of DRAM (1000 FIT/Mb is a reasonable approximation for commodity memory, [1825] which increases with altitude, being 10 times greater in Denver, Colorado), the system has an MTBF of $1000 \times 10^{-15} \times 4.096 \times 10^9 \times 8 = 3.2 \times 10^{-2}$ hours (around once every 33 hours). Soft errors are a regular occurrence for installations containing hundreds of terabytes of memory. [880]

The Cassini spacecraft experienced an average of 280 single bit memory errors per day [1804] (in two identical flight recorders containing 2.5 G of DRAM); also see fig 8.31. The rate of double-bit errors was higher than expected (between 1.5 and 4.5%) because the incoming radiation had enough energy to flip more than one bit.

Uncorrected soft errors place a limit on the maximum number of computing nodes that can be usefully used by one application; at around 50,000 nodes, a system would spend half its time saving checkpoints, and restarting from previous checkpoints after an error occurred. [1584]

Error correcting memory reduces the probability of an uncorrected error by several orders of magnitude, but with modern systems containing terabytes the probability of an error adversely affecting the result remains high. [880] The Cray Blue Waters system at the National Center for Supercomputing Applications experienced 28 uncorrected memory errors (ECC and Chipkill parity hardware checks corrected 722,526 single bit errors, and 309,359 two-bit errors, a 99.995% success rate). [491] Studies [1258] have investigated assigning variables deemed to be critical to a subset of memory that is protected with error correcting hardware, along with various other techniques. [1173]

Calculating the FIT for processors is complicated. [1128]

Redundancy can be used to continue operating after experiencing a hardware fault, e.g., three processors performing the same calculation, and a majority vote used to decide which outputs to accept. [1993] Software only redundancy techniques include having the compiler generate, for each source code sequence, two or more independent machine code sequences [1574] whose computed values are compared at various check points, and replicating computations across multiple cores [2013] (and comparing outputs). The overhead of duplicated execution can be reduced by not replicating those code sequences that are less affected by register bit flips [592] (e.g., the value returned from a bitwise AND that extracts 8 bits from a 32 -bit register is 75% less likely to deliver an incorrect result than an operation that depends on all 32 bits). Optimizing for reliability can be traded off against performance, [1295] e.g., ordering register usage such that the average interval between load and last usage is reduced. [1986]

Developers don't have to rely purely on compiler or hardware support, reliability can be improved by using algorithms that are robust in the presence of faulty hardware. For instance, the traditional algorithms for two-process mutual exclusion are not fault tolerant; a fault tolerant mutual exclusion algorithm using $2f + 1$ variables, where a single fault may occur in up to f variables is available. [1316] Researchers are starting to investigate how best to prevent soft errors corrupting the correct behavior of various algorithms. [262]

Bombarding a system with radiation increases the likelihood of radiation induced bitflips, [1275] and can be used for testing system robustness.

The impact of level of compiler optimization on a program's susceptibility to bitflips is discussed in section 11.2.2.

Vendor profitability is driving commodity cpu and memory chips towards cheaper and less reliable products, just like household appliances are priced low and have a short expected lifetime. [1721]

A study by Dinaburg [501] found occurrences of bit-flips in domain names appearing within HTTP requests, e.g., a page from the domain ikamai.net being requested rather than from akamai.net (the 2.10^{-9} bit error rate was thought to occur inside routers and switches). Undetected random hardware errors can be used to redirect a download to another site, [501] e.g., to cause a maliciously modified third-party library to be loaded.

If all the checksums involved in TCP/IP transmission are enabled, the theoretical error rate is 1 in 10^{17} bits; which for 1 billion users visiting Facebook on average once per day and downloading 2 M bytes of Javascript per visit, gives an expected bit flip rate of once every 5 days for a single Facebook user.

6.5.1 System availability

A system is only as reliable as its least reliable critical subsystem, and the hardware on which software runs is a critical subsystem that needs to be included in any application reliability analysis; some applications also require a working internet connection, e.g., for database access.

Before cloud computing became a widely available commercial service, companies built their own clustered computer facilities (low usage rates of such systems [895] is what can make cloud providers more cost effective).

The reliability of Internet access to the services provided by other computers is currently not high enough for people to overlook the possibility that failures can occur; [185] see the example in section 10.5.4.

Long-running applications need to be able to recover from hardware failures, if they are to stand a reasonable chance of completing. A process known as checkpointing periodically stores the current state of every compute unit, so that when any unit fails, it is possible to restart from the last saved state, rather than restarting from the beginning. A tradeoff has to be made [1989] between frequency of checkpointing, which takes resources away from completing execution of the application but reduces the total amount of lost calculation, and infrequent checkpointing, which diverts less resources but incurs greater losses when a fault is experienced. Calculating the optimum checkpoint interval [430] requires knowing the distribution of node uptimes; see figure 6.40.

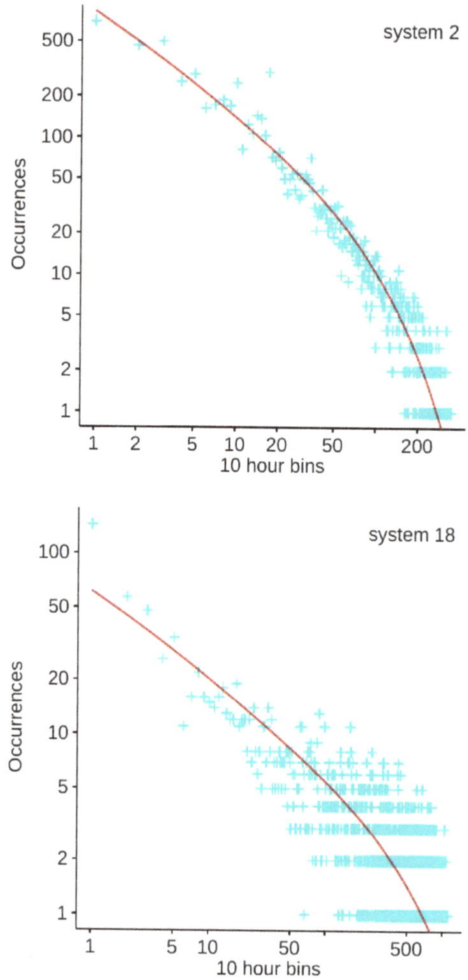

Figure 6.40: For systems 2 and 18, number of uptime intervals, binned into 10 hour intervals, red lines are both fitted negative binomial distributions. Data from Los Alamos National Lab (LANL). Github-Local

The Los Alamos National Laboratory (LANL) has made public, data from 23 different systems installed between 1996 and 2005. [1084] These systems run applications that "... perform long periods (often months) of CPU computation, interrupted every few hours by a few minutes of I/O for check-pointing." Figure 6.40 shows the 10 -hour binned data fitted to a zero-truncated negative binomial distribution for systems 2 and 18 .

Operating systems and many long-running programs sometimes write information about a variety of events to one or more log files. One study [1997] found that around 1 in 30 lines of code in Apache, Postgresql and Squid was logging code; this information was estimated to reduce median diagnosis time by a factor of 1.4 to 3 . The information diversity of system event logs tends to increase, with new kinds of information being added, with the writing of older information not being switched off (because it might be useful); log files have been found to contain [1413] large amounts of low value information, more than one entry for the same event, changes caused by software updates, poor or no documentation, and inconsistent information structure within entries.

6.6 Checking for intended behavior

The two main methods for checking that code behaves as intended, are: analyzing the source code to work out what it does, and reviewing the behavior of the code during execution, e.g., testing. Almost no data is available on the kinds of mistakes found, and the relative cost-effectiveness of the various techniques used to find them.

So-called formal proofs of correctness are essentially a form on N-version programming, with $N = 2$. Two programs are written, with one nominated to be called the specification; one or more tools are used to analyse both programs, checking that their behavior is consistent, and sometimes other properties. Mistakes may exist in the specification program or the non-specification program. [622,668] One study [1320] of a software system that had been formally proved to be correct, found at least two mistakes per thousand lines, remained.

The further along in the development process a mistake is found, the more costly it is likely to be to correct it; possible additional costs include having to modify something created between the introduction of the mistake and its detection, and having to recheck work. This additional cost does not necessarily make it more cost effective to detect problems as early as possible. The relative cost of correcting problems vs. detecting problems, plus practical implementation issues, decide where it is most cost effective to check for mistakes during the development process.

A study by Hribar, Bogovac and Marinčić [864] investigated Fault Slip Through by analyzing the development phase where a fault was found compared to where it could have been found. Figure 6.41 shows the number of faults found in various test phases (deskcheck is a form of code review performed by the authors of the code), and where the fault could have been found (as specified on the fault report); also see Antolić. [66]

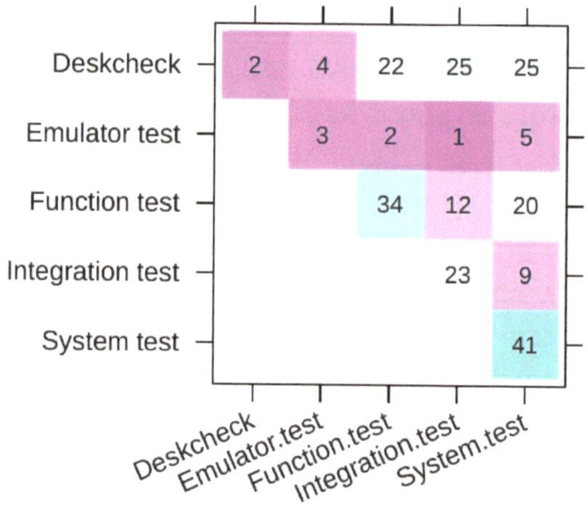

Figure 6.41: Fault slip throughs for a development project at Ericsson; y-axis lists phase when fault could have been detected, x -axis phase when fault was found. Data from Hribar et al. Github-Local

The cost of correcting problems will depend on the cost characteristics of the system containing the software; developing software for a coffee vending machine is likely to be a lot cheaper than for a jet fighter, because of, for instance, the cost of the hardware needed for testing. Data from NASA and the US Department of Defense, on the relative costs of fixing problems discovered during various phases of development are large, because of the very high cost of the hardware running the software systems developed for these organizations.

To reduce time and costs, the checking process may be organized by level of abstraction, starting with basic units of code (or functionality), and progressively encompassing more of the same, e.g., unit testing is performed by individual developers, integration testing checks that multiple components or subsystems work together, and systems testing is performed on the system as a whole.

A study by Nichols, McHale, Sweeney, Snavely and Volkman [1378] investigated the economics of detecting mistakes in system development (the organizations studies all used Team Software Process). One of the organizations studied developed avionics software, which required performing manual reviews and inspections of the high-level design, design and coding phases, followed by testing.

Figure 6.42 shows the reported time taken to correct 7,095 mistakes (for one avionics project), broken down by phase introduced/corrected, against the number of major phases between its introduction and correction (x -axis). Lines are fitted exponentials, with fix times less than 1,5 and 10 -minutes excluded (72% of fixes are recorded as taking less than 10 -minutes); also see fig 3.33 .

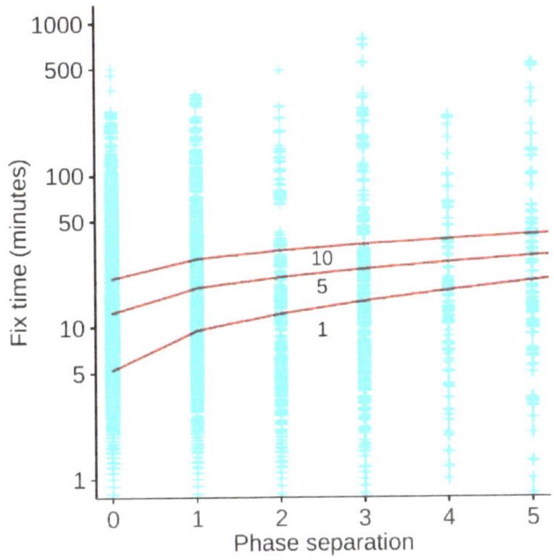

Figure 6.42: Reported time taken to correct 7,095 mistakes (in one project), broken down by phase the mistake was introduced/corrected (y-axis), against number of phases between introduction/correction (x -axis); lines are fitted regression models of the form: Fix_time $\propto e^{\sqrt{\text{phase\_sep}}}$, with fix times less than 1,5 and 10 -minutes excluded. Data from Nichols et al. Github-Local

Many software systems support a range of optional constructs, and support for these may be selected by build time configuration options. When checking for intended behavior, a decision has to be made on the versions of the system being checked; some systems support so many options, that checking whether all possible configurations can be built requires an unrealistic investment of resources [766] (algorithms for sampling configurations are used [1254]).

6.6.1 Code review

Traditionally a code review (other terms include code inspection and walkthroughs [631]) has involved one or more people reading another developer's code, and then meeting with the developer to discuss what they have found. These days the term is also applied to reviewing code that has been pushed to a project's version control system, to check whether it is ok to merge the changes into the main branch; with geographically disperse teams, online reviews and commenting have become a necessity.

Review meetings support a variety of functions, including: highlighting of important information between project members (i.e., ensuring that people are kept up to date with what others are doing), and uncovering potential problems before changes becomes more expensive. Detecting issues may not even be the main reason for performing code reviews, [104] keeping teams members abreast of developments and creating an environment of shared ownership of code may be considered more important.

A variety of different code review techniques have been proposed, including: Ad-hoc (no explicit support for reviewers), Checklist (reviewers work from a list of specific questions that are intended to focus attention towards common problems), Scenarios-based (each reviewer takes on a role intended to target a particular class of problems), and Perspective-based reading (reviewers are given more detailed instructions, than they are given in Scenario-based reviews, about how to read the document; see section 13.2 for an analysis). The few experimental comparisons of review techniques have found that the relative performance of the techniques is small compared to individual differences in performance.

The range of knowledge and skills needed to review requirements and design documents may mean that those involved focus on topics that are within their domain of expertise. [534] Many of the techniques used for estimating population size assume that capture sites (i.e., reviews) have equal probabilities of flagging an item; estimates based on data from meetings where reviewers have selectively read documents will be biased; see Github-reliability/eickt1992.R.

Most published results from code review studies have been based on small sample sizes. For instance, Myers, [1340] investigated the coding mistakes detected by 59 professionals, using program testing and code walkthroughs/inspections, for one PL/1 program containing 63 statements and 15 known mistakes; see Github-reliability/myers1978.R. Also, researcher often use issues-found as the metric for evaluating review meetings, in particular potential fault experiences found during code reviews. Issues found is something that is easy to measure, code is readily available, and developers to review it are likely to be more numerous than people with the skills needed to review requirements and design documents (which do not always exist, as such).

Studies where the data is available include:

- Hirao, Ihara, Ueda, Phannachitta and Matsumoto [833] investigated the impact of positive and negative code reviews on patches being merged or abandoned (for Qt and OpenStack). A logistic regression model found that for Qt positive votes were more than twice as influential, on the outcome, as negative votes, while for, OpenStack negative votes were slightly more influential; see Github-reliability/OSS2016.R.
- Porter, Siy, Mockus and Votta [1507] recorded code inspection related data from a commercial project over 18 months (staffed by six dedicated developers, and five developers who also worked on other projects). The best fitting regression model had the number of mistakes found proportional to the log of the number of lines reviewed, and the log of meeting duration; this study is discussed in section 13.2, also see fig 11.33.

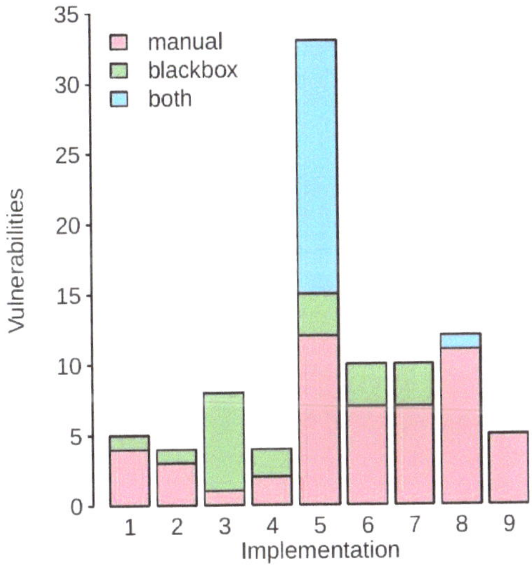

Figure 6.43: Number of vulnerabilities found using blackbox testing, and manual code review of nine implementations of the same specification. Data from Finifter. Github-Local

- Finifter investigated mistakes found and fault experiences, using manual code review and black box testing, in nine implementations of the same specification. Figure 6.43 shows the number of vulnerabilities found by the two techniques in the nine implementations; some of the difference is due to the variation in the abilities and kinds of mistakes made by different implementers, plus skill differences in using the programming languages.

While there has been a lot of activity applying machine learning to fault prediction, the models have not proved effective outside the data used to build them, or even between different versions of the same project; [2028] see Github-faults/eclipse/eclipse-pred.R. Noisy data is one problem, along with a lack of data on program usage; see section 6.1.3.

During a review, there is an element of chance associated with the issues noticed by individual reviewers, and some issues may only be noticed by reviewers with a particular skill or knowledge. If all reviewers have the same probability, p, of finding a problem, and there are N issues available to be found, by S reviewers, then the expected number of issues found is: $N[1-(1-p)^S]$.

A study by Nielsen and Landauer [1380] investigated the number of different usability problems discovered, as the number of subjects increased, based on data from 12 studies. Figure 6.44 shows how the number of perceived usability problems increased as the number of subjects increased; lines show the regression model fitted by the above equation (both N and p are constants returned by the fitting process).

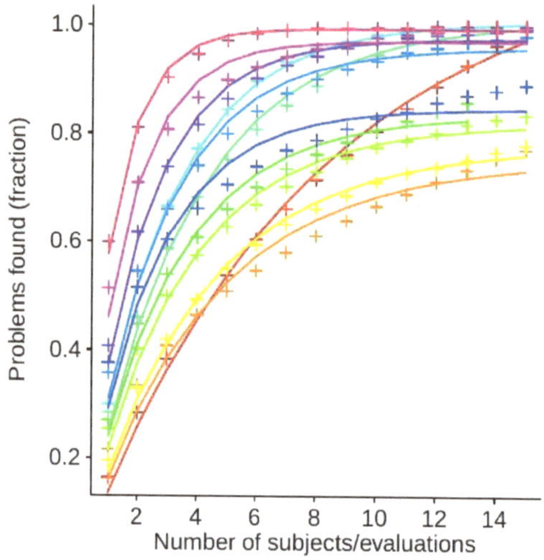

Figure 6.44: Fraction of usability problems found by a given number of subjects/evaluations in 12 system evaluations; lines are fitted regression model for each system. Data extracted from Nielsen et al. Github-Local

When the probability of finding a problem varies between reviewers, there can be a wide variation in the number of problems reported by different groupings of individuals.

A study by Lewis [1123] investigated usability problem-discovery rates; the results included a list of the 145 usability problems found by 15 reviewers. How many problems are two of these reviewers likely to find, how many are three likely to find? Figure 6.45 is based on the issues found by every pair, triple (etc, up to five) of reviewers. The mean of the number of issues found increases with review group size, as does the variability of the number found. Half of all issues were only found by one reviewer, and 15% found by two reviewers.

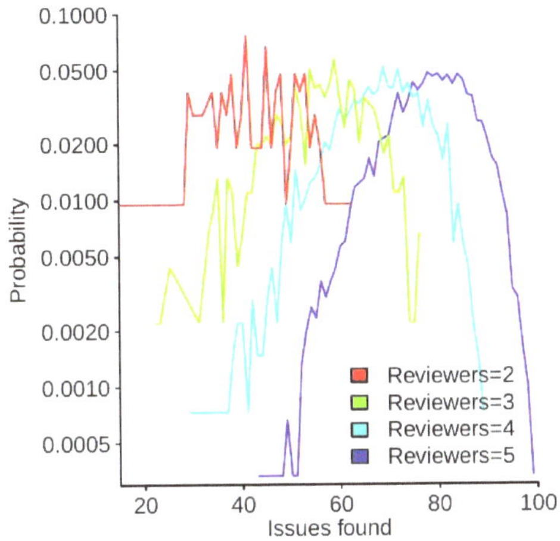

Figure 6.45: Probability (*y*-axis) of a given number of issues being found (x -axis), by a review group containing a given number of people (colored lines). Data from Lewis. Github-Local

Some coding mistakes occur sufficiently often that it can be worthwhile searching for known patterns. Ideally coding mistakes flagged by a tool are a potential cause of a fault experience (e.g., reading from an uninitialized variable), however the automated analysis performed may not be sophisticated enough to handle all possibilities [1639] (e.g., there may be some uncertainty about whether the variable being read from has been written to), or the usage may simply be suspicious (e.g., use of assignment in the conditional expression of an if-statement, when an equality comparison was intended, i.e., the single character = had been typed, instead of the two characters ==). The issue of how developers might respond to false positive warnings is discussed in section 9.1.

A study of one tool [2017] found a strong correlation between mistakes flagged, and faults experienced during testing, and faults reported by customers (after the output of the tool had been cleaned by a company specializing in removing false positive warnings from static analysis tool output).

6.6.2 Testing

The purpose of testing is to gain some level of confidence that software behaves in a way that is likely to be acceptable to customers. For the first release, the behavior may be specified by the implementation team (e.g., when developing a product to be sold to multiple customers), or the customer, e.g., the vendor is interested in meeting the criteria for acceptance, so they get paid. Subsequent releases usually include checks that the behavior is consistent with previous releases.

During testing, a decrease in the number of previously unseen fault experiences, per unit of test effort, is sometimes taken as an indication that the software is becoming more reliable; other reasons for a decrease in new fault experiences is replacement of existing testers by less skilled staff, or repetition of previously used input values. The extent to which reliability improves, as experienced by the customer, depends on the overlap between the input distribution used during testing, and the input distribution provided in real world use.

A study by Stikkel [1782] investigated three industrial development projects. Figure 6.46 shows the number of faults discovered per man-hour of testing, averaged over a week, for these projects (each normalised to sum to 100). The sharp decline in new fault experiences may be due to there being few mistakes remaining, a winding down of investment in the closing weeks of testing (i.e., rerunning the same tests with the same input), or some other behavior.

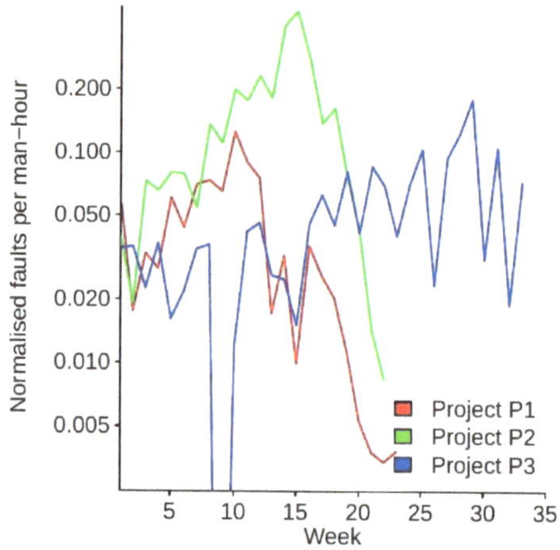

Figure 6.46: Number of faults experienced per unit of testing effort, over a given number of weeks (each normalised to sum to 100). Data from Stikkel. Github-Local

An example of how the input used for random testing can be unrepresentative of customer input is provided by a study [367] that performed random testing of the Eiffel base library. The functions in this library contain extensive pre/post condition checks, and random testing found twice as many mistakes in these checks as the implementation of the functionality; the opposite of the pattern seen in user fault reports.

To what extent are fault experiences generated by fuzzers representative of faults experienced by users of the software?

A study by Marcozzi, Tang, Donaldson and Cadar [1204] investigated the extent to which fault experiences obtained using automated techniques are representative of the fault experiences encountered by code written by developers. The source code involved in the fixes of 45 reported faults in the LLVM compiler were instrumented to log when the code was executed, and when the condition needed to trigger the fault experience occurred; the following is an example of instrumented code:

```
warn ("Fixing patch reached");
if (Not.isPowerOf2()) {
    if (!(C-> getValue().isPowerOf2() // Check needed to fix fault
            && Not != C->getValue()))
        {
        warn("Fault possibly triggered");
        }
    else { /* CODE TRANSFORMATION */ } } // Original, unfixed code
```

The instrumented compiler was used to build 309 Debian packages (around 10 million lines of C/C++), producing possibly miscompiled versions of the packages; the build process included running each package's test suite. A package built from miscompiled code may successfully pass its test suite.

A bitwise compare of the program executables generated by the unfixed and fixed compilers was used to detect when different code was generated.

Table 6.3 shows a count, for each fault detector (Human, fuzzing tools, and one formal verifier), of fix locations reached, fix condition triggered, bitwise difference of generated code and failed tests (build tests are not expected to fail). One way of measuring whether there is a difference between faults detected (column 1) in human and automatically generated code is to compare number of fault triggers encountered (column 4).

Table 6.3: Fault detector, number of source locations fixed, number of fix locations reached, number of fix condition triggered, number of programs having a bitwise difference of generated code and number of failed tests. Data from Marcozzi et al. [1204]

Detector	Faults	Reached	Triggered	Bitwise-diff	Tests failed
Human	10	1,990	593	56	1
Csmith	10	2,482	1,043	318	0
EMI	10	2,424	948	151	1
Orange	5	293	35	8	0
yarpgen	2	608	257	0	0
Alive	8	1,059	327	172	0

Comparing the counts for the number of trigger occurrences experienced for each of the 10 fixes in each of the Human, Csmith and EMI detected source mistakes, finds that the differences between the counts is not statistically different across method of detection; see Github-reliability/OOPSLA-compiler.R.

The behavior of some software systems is sufficiently important to some organizations that they are willing to fund the development of a test suite intended to check behavior: cases include:

- the economic benefits of being able to select from multiple hardware vendors is dependent on being able to port existing software to the selected hardware; at a minimum, different compilers must be capable of processing the same source code to produce the same behavior. The US Government funded the development of validation suites for Cobol and Fortran, [1414] and later SQL, POSIX and Ada; [5] a compiler testing service was also established, [10]
- there were a sufficient number of C compiler vendors that several companies were able to build a business supplying test suites for this language, expanding to support C^{++}

when this language started to become popular, [ix]

- the "Write once, run anywhere" design goal for Java required Sun Microsystems to fund the development of a conformance test suite, and to litigate when licensees shipped products that did not conform. [1319,1950]

While manual tests can be very effective, creating them is very time-consuming [1414] and expensive. Various kinds of automatic test generation are available, including exhaustive testing of short sequences of input [2009] and fuzzing. [2004]

Testing that a program behaves as intended requires knowledge of the intended behavior, for a given input. While some form of automatic input generation is possible, in only a few cases [61] is it possible to automatically predict the expected output from the input, independently of the software being tested. One form of program behavior is easily detected: abnormal termination, and some forms of fuzz testing use this case as their test criteria; see fig 6.23.

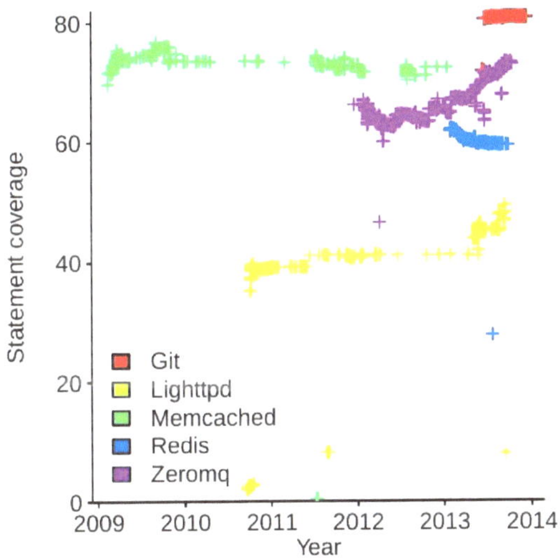

Figure 6.47: Statement coverage achieved by the respective program's test suite (data on the sixth program was not usable). Data from Marinescu et al. Github-Local

When multiple programs supporting the same functionality are available, it may be possible to use differential testing to compare the outputs produced from a given input (a difference being a strong indicator that one of the systems is behaving incorrectly). [345]

There are ISO Standards that specify methods for measuring conformance to particular standards [900,901] and requirements for test laboratories. [898] However, very few standards become sufficiently widely used for it to be commercially viable to offer conformance testing services.

Like source code, tests can contain mistakes. [1868]

To what extent do test suites change over time? A study by Marinescu, Hosek and Cadar [1207] measured the statement and branch coverage of six open source programs over time, using the test suite distributed with the program's source. Figure 6.47 shows that for some widely used programs the statement coverage of the test suite did not vary much over five years.

One study [1999] found no correlation between the growth of a project and its test code; see Github-time-series/argouml_complete.R.

The application build process may require the selection of a consistent set of configuration options. The Linux 2.6.33.3 kernel supports 6,918 configuration options, giving over $10^{23,563}$ option combinations. One study [1139] using a random sample of 1,000,000 different option combinations failed to find any that were valid according to the variability model; a random sampling of the more than $10^{1,377}$ possible option combinations supported by OpenSSL found that 3% were considered valid. Various techniques have been proposed for obtaining a sample of valid configuration options, [965] which might then be used for testing different builds of an application, or analyzing the source code. [1910]

Regular expressions are included within the syntax of some languages (e.g., awk and SNOBOL 4[743]), while in others they are supported by the standard library. [333] A given regular expression may match (or fail to match) different character sequences in different languages [443] (e.g., support different escape sequences, and different disambiguation policies; PCRE based libraries use a leftmost-greedy disambiguation, while POSIX based libraries use the leftmost-longest match [182]).

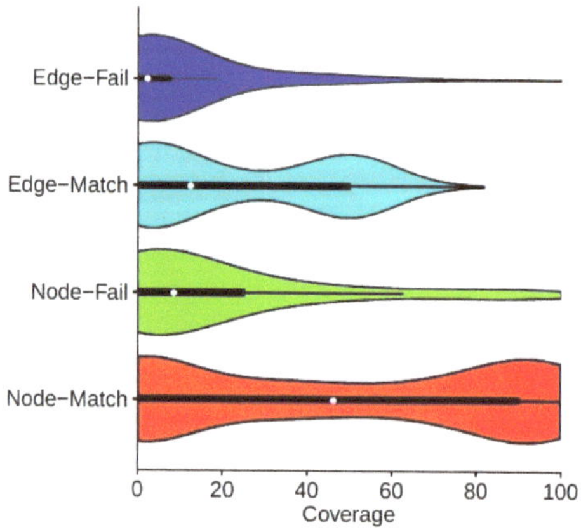

Figure 6.48: Violin plots of percentage of regular expression components having a given coverage, (measured using the nodes and edges of the DFA representation of

the regular expression, broken down by the match failing/succeeding) for 15,096 regular expressions, when passed the corresponding project test input strings. Data kindly provided by Wang. Github-Local

A study by Wang and Stolee [1921] investigated how well 1,225 Java projects tested the regular expressions appearing in calls to system libraries (such as java.lang.String. matches); there were 18,426 call sites. The regular expression methods were instrumented to obtain the regular expression and the input strings passed as arguments. When running the associated project test suite 3,096(16.8%) of call sites were evaluated; method argument logging during test execution obtained 15,096 regular expressions and 899,804 test input strings (at some call sites, regular expressions were created at runtime).

A regular expression can be represented as a deterministic finite state automata (DFA), with nodes denoting states and each edge denoting a basic subcomponent of the regular expression. Coverage testing of a regular expression involves counting the number of nodes and edges visited by the test input.

Figure 6.48 shows a violin plot of the percentage of regular expression components having a given coverage. The nodes and edges of the DFA representation of each of the 15,096 regular expressions are the components measured, using the corresponding test input strings for each regex; coverage if measured for both matching and failing inputs.

6.6.2.1 Creating tests

Traditionally tests were written by people employed to test software; some companies have Q/A (quality assurance) departments. The tests developers write to check their code may become part of the systems formal test suite; there are development methodologies in which include testing is a major component of implementation, e.g., test driven development.

Automated test generation can reduce the time and costs associated with testing software. A metric often used by researchers for evaluating test generation tools is the number of fault experiences produced by the generated tests, i.e., one of the factors involved in gaining confidence that program behavior is likely to be acceptable.

Automated test generation techniques include (there is insufficient evidence to evaluate the extent to which an automatic technique is the most cost effective to use in a particular development):

- random modification of existing tests: so-called fuzzing makes random changes to existing test inputs, and little user input is required to test for one particular kind of fault experience, abnormal termination; see fig 6.23. Some tools use a fuzzing selection strategy intended to maximise the likelihood of generating a file that causes a crash fault, e.g., CERT's BFF uses a search strategy that gives greater weight to files that have previously produced faults [861] (i.e., it is a biased random process),

- source code directed random generation: this involves a fitness function, such as number of statements covered or branches executed.

A study by Salahirad, Almulla and Gay [1630] investigated the ability of eight fitness functions, implemented in the EvoSuite tool, to generate tests that produced fault experiences for 516 known coding mistakes; a test generation budget of two and ten-minutes per mistake was allocated on the system used. The branch coverage fitness function was found to generate tests that produced the most fault experiences,

- input distribution directed random generation: the generation process uses information about the characteristics of the expected input (e.g., the probability of an item appearing, or appearing in sequence with other items) to generate tests having the same input characteristics.

A study by Pavese, Soremekun, Havrikov, Grunske and Zeller [1455] used the measured characteristics of input tests to create a probabilistic grammar that generated tests having either the same distribution or were uncommon inputs (created by inverting the measured input item probabilities).

Automated test generation techniques are used to find vulnerabilities by those seeking to hijack computer systems for their own purposes. To counter this threat, tools and techniques have been created to make automatic test generation less cost effective. [960]

A program's input may be include measurements of a set of different items (e.g., the time of day, the temperature and humidity), and within the code there may be an interaction between these different items (these items are sometimes called factors). A coding mistake may only be a source of a fault experience when two different items each take a particular range of values, and not when just one of the items is in this range.

Combinatorial testing involves selecting patterns of input that are intended to detect situations where a fault experience is dependent on a combination of different item input values. The generation of the change patterns used in combinatorial testing can be very similar to those used in the design of experiments, and the same techniques can be used to help minimise the number of test cases; see section 13.2.5.

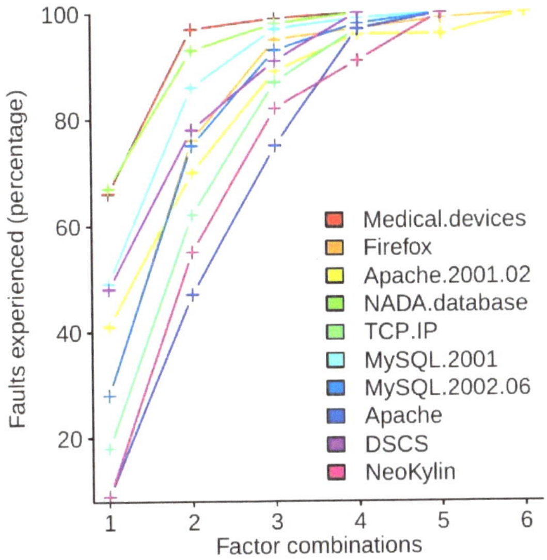

Figure 6.49: Percentage of known faults experienced for tests involving a given number of combinations of factors (x -axis), for ten programs. Data from Kuhn et al. Github-Local

A study by Kuhn, Kacker and Lei [1053] investigated the percentage of fault experiences likely to require a given number of factors, in some combination. Figure 6.49 shows the cumulative growth in the percentage of known faults experienced, for tests involving combinations of a given number of factors (x -axis).

A study by Czerwonka [429] investigated the statement and branch coverage achieved, in four Microsoft Windows utilities, by combinatorial tests. The tests involved values for a single factor, and interaction between factors (from two to five factors). The results found that most of the variance in the measurements of branch and statement coverage could be explained by models fitted using the log of the number of combination of factors and the log of the number of tests; see Github-reliability/Coverage-Combin.R.

6.6.2.2 Beta testing

The input profiles generated by the users of a software system may be very different from those envisaged by the developers who tested the software. Beta testing is a way of discovering problems with software (e.g., coding mistakes and incomplete requirements), when processing the input profiles of the intended users. The number of problems found during beta testing, compared to internal testing provides feedback on the relevance of the usage profile that drives the test process. [1201]

Beta testing is also a form of customer engagement.

6.6.2.3 Estimating test effectiveness

Does the project test process provide a reliable estimate, to the desired level of confidence, that the software is likely to be acceptable to the customer?

A necessary requirement for checking the behavior of code is executing it, every statement not executed is untested. Various so called coverage criteria are used, for instance percentage of program methods or statements executed by the test process (the coverage achieved by a test suite is likely to vary between platforms, different application configurations, [1544] and even the compiler used [651]).

The conditional expression in if-statements controls whether a block of statements is executed, or not. Branch coverage simply counts the number of branches executed, e.g., one branch for each of the true and false arms of an if-statement. More thorough coverage criteria measure the coverage of the decisions involved in the conditional expression, which can be an involved process; an expression may involve decisions conditions (e.g., $\&\&(y| \mid z)$), with each subcondition derived from a different requirement. Modified Condition and Decision Coverage (MC/DC) [352] is one measure of coverage of the combination of possible decisions that may be involved in the evaluation of a conditional expression. For this example, the MC/DC requirements are met by x, y and z (assumed to take the values T or F) taking the values: TFF , TTF , TFT , and FTF , respective.

The probability of tests written to the MC/DC requirements detecting an incorrect condition is always at least 93.75%; [353] see Github-reliability/MCDC_FP.R.

One weakness of MC/DC is its dependence on the way conditions are expressed in the code. In the previous example, assigning a subexpression to a variable: a = (y||z);, simplifies the original expression to: x&&a, and reduces the number of combinations of distinct values that need to be tested to achieve 100% MC/DC coverage. [x] One study [660] was able to restructure code to achieve 100%MC/DC coverage using 50% fewer tests than the non-restructured code (in some cases even fewer tests were needed). Achieving MC/DC coverage is often a requirement for software used within safety critical applications.

A study by Inozemtseva and Holmes [891] investigated test coverage of five very large Java programs. The results showed a consistent relationship between percentage statement coverage, sc, and percentage branch coverage, bc (i.e., $bc \propto sc^{1.2}$), and percentage modified condition coverage, mc (i.e., $mc \propto sc^{1.7}$); see Github-reliability/coverage_icse-2014.R.

The most common use of branches is as a component of the conditional expression in an if-statement, which decides whether to execute the statements in the enclosed compound statement. Most compound statements contain a few statements, [930] so a close connection between branch and statement coverage is to be expected.

A study by Gopinath, Jensen and Groce [712] investigated the characteristics of coverage metrics for the test suites of 1,023 Java projects. Figure 6.50 shows the fraction of statement coverage against branch coverage; each circle is data from one project. The various lines are fitted regression models, which contain a non-simple interaction between coverage and log $(KLOC)$.

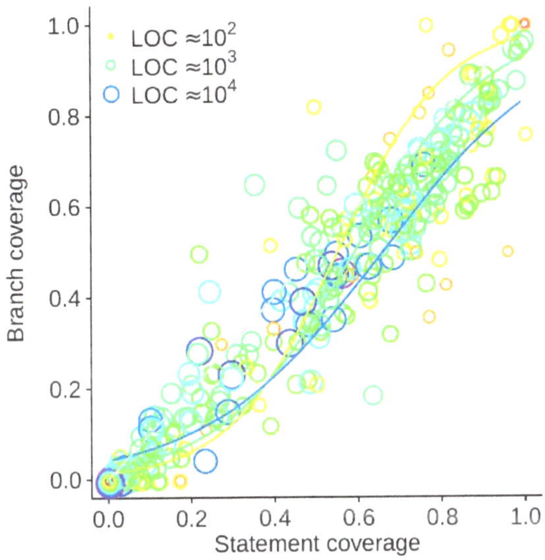

Figure 6.50: Statement coverage against branch coverage for 300 or so Java projects; colored lines are fitted regression models for three program sizes (see legend), equal value line in grey. Data from Gopinath et al. Github-Local

In figure 6.50, why does branch coverage tend to grow more slowly than statement coverage? Combining the findings from the following two studies suggest a reason:

- A study by Kang, Ray and Jana [974] investigated the number of statements encountered along the execution paths, within a function, executed after a call to a function that could return an error, i.e., the error and non-error paths. Figure 6.51, lower plot, shows that non-error paths often contain more statements than the error paths; in the upper plot most of the points are below the line of equal statement-path length, i.e., there are a greater number of longer non-error paths.

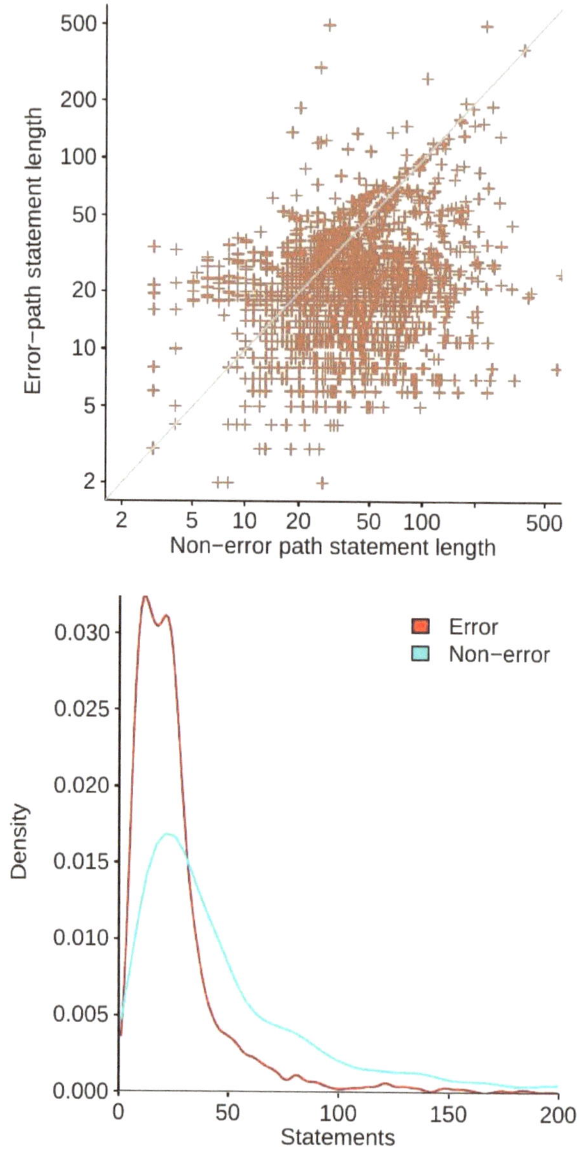

Figure 6.51: Number of statements executed along error and non-error paths within a function (top), and density plots of the number of statements along error and non-error paths. Data kindly provided by Kang. Github-Local

- A study by Čaušević, Shukla, Punnekkat and Sundmark [308] found that developers wrote almost twice as many positive tests as negative tests, [xi] for the problem studied; see Github-reliability/3276-TDD.R. This behavior may be confirmation bias; see section 2.2.1.

If a test suite contains more positive than negative tests, and positive tests involve more statements than negative tests, then statement coverage would be expected to grow faster than branch coverage.

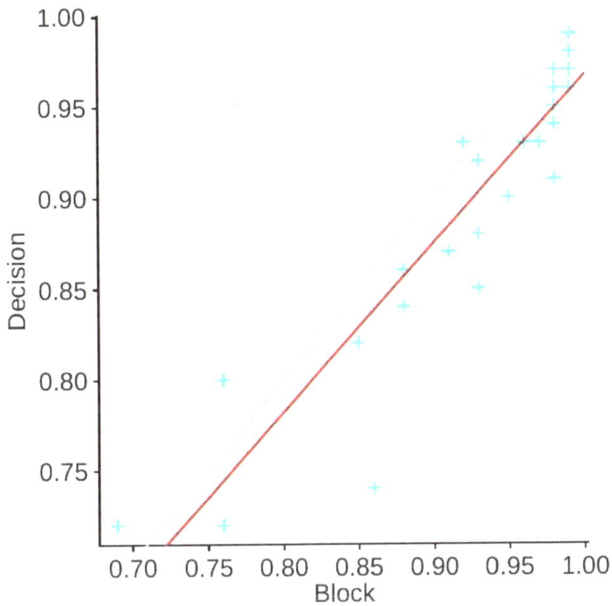

Figure 6.52: Basic-block coverage against branch coverage for a 35 KLOC program; lines are a regression fit (red) and Decision = Block (grey). Data from Gokhale et al. Github-Local

A basic-block is a sequence of code that has one entry point and one exit point (a function call would be an exit point, as would any form of goto statement). In figure 6.52, the fitted regression line shows a linear relationship between basic-block coverage and decision coverage, i.e., the expected relationship (grey line shows Decision = Block).

A study by McAllister and Vouk [1228] investigated the coverage of 20 implementations of the same specification. Two sets of random tests were generated using different selection criteria, along with 796 tests designed to provide full functional coverage of the specification. Figure 6.53 shows the fraction of basic-blocks covered as the number of tests increases, for the 20 implementations (sharing the same color), and three sets of tests (the different colors); the lines are fitted regression models of the form: $coverage_{BB} = a \times (1 - b \times \log(tests)^c)$, where: a, b and c are constants (c is between -0.35 and -1.7 , for this specification).

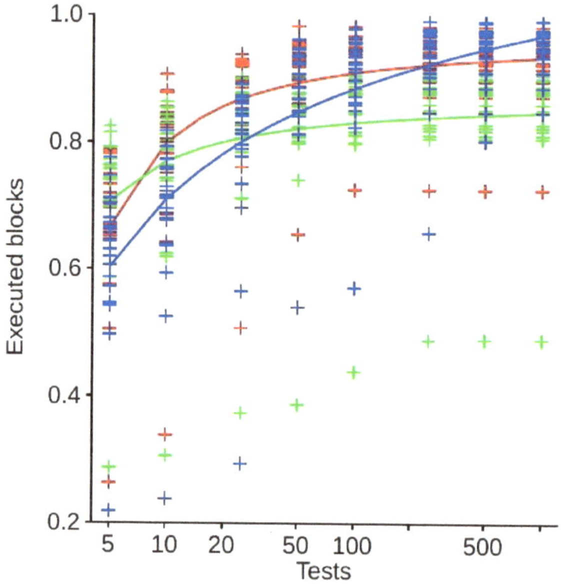

Figure 6.53: Fraction of basic-blocks executed by a given number of tests, for 20 implementations using three test suites. . Data from McAllister et al. Github-Local

Another technique for estimating the effectiveness of a test suite, in detecting coding mistakes, is to introduce known mistakes into the source and measure the percentage detected by the test suite, i.e., the mistake produces a change of behavior that is detected by the test process; the modified source is known as a mutant. For this technique to be effective, the characteristics of the mutations have to match the characteristics of the mistakes made by developers; existing mutant generating techniques don't appear to produce coding mistakes that mimic the characteristics of developer coding mistakes. [710,713] A test suite that kills a high percentage of mutants (what self-respecting developer would ever be happy just detecting mutants?) is considered to be more effective than one killing a lesser percentage.

Figure 6.54 shows statement coverage against percentage of mutants killed. The various lines are fitted regression models, which contain a non-simple interaction between coverage and log $(KLOC)$.

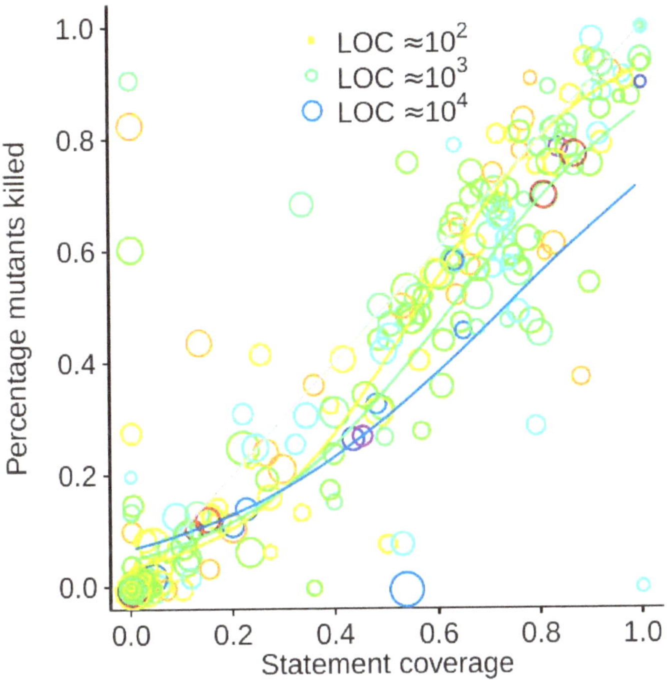

Figure 6.54: Statement coverage against mutants killed for 300 or so Java projects; colored lines are fitted regression models for three program sizes, equal value line in grey. Data from Gopinath et al. Github-Local

A test suite's mutation score converges to a maximum value, as the number of mutants used increases. For programs containing fewer than 16 K executable statements, E, the number of mutants needed has been found to grow no faster than $O(E^{0.25})$, [2008] a worst case confidence interval for the error in the mutation score can be calculated. [711]

6.6.3 Cost of testing

Testing costs include the cost of creating the tests, subsequent maintenance costs (e.g., updating them to reflect changes in program behavior), and the cost of running the tests.

For some kinds of test creation, automatic test generation tools may be more cost effective than human written tests; [336] see Github-reliability/1706-01636a.R.

The higher the cost of performing system testing, the fewer opportunities there are likely to be to check software at the system level. Figure 6.55 shows the relationship between the unit cost of a missile (being developed for the US military), and the number of development test flights made.

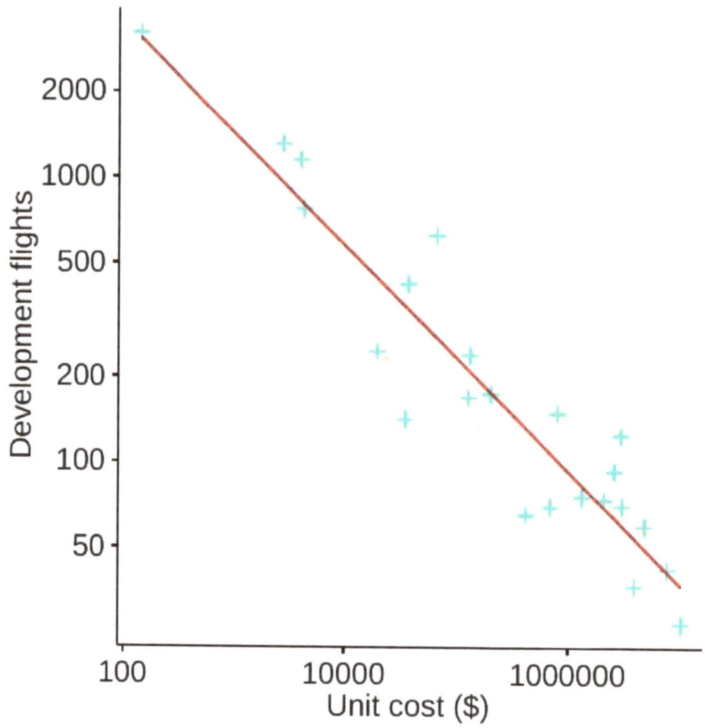

Figure 6.55: Unit cost of a missile, developed for the US military, against the number of development test flights carried out, with fitted power law. Data extracted from Augustine. Github-Local

When does it become cost effective to stop testing software? Some of the factors involved in stopping conditions are discussed in section 13.2.4. Studies [331,1988] have analysed stopping rules for testing after a given amount of time, based on number of faults experienced.

A study by Do, Mirarab, Tahvildari and Rothermel investigated test case prioritization, and attempted to model the costs involved; multiple versions of five programs (from 3 to 15 versions) and their respective regression suites were used as the benchmark. The performance of six test prioritization algorithms were compared, based on the number of seeded coding mistakes detected when test resource usage was limited (reductions of 25 , 50 and 75% were used). The one consistent finding was that the number of faults experienced decreased as the amount of test resource used decreased, there were interactions between program version and test prioritization algorithm; see Github-reliability/fse-08.R.

Index

W

www.ingramcontent.com/pod-product-compliance
Lightning Source LLC
LaVergne TN
LVHW071247210926
848486LV00008B/360